T0305351

EMPIRICAL ASSET PRICING

EMPIRICAL ASSET PRICING

The Cross Section of Stock Returns

TURAN G. BALI

ROBERT F. ENGLE

SCOTT MURRAY

Copyright © 2016 by John Wiley & Sons, Inc. All rights reserved

Published by John Wiley & Sons, Inc., Hoboken, New Jersey
Published simultaneously in Canada

No part of this publication may be reproduced, stored in a retrieval system, or transmitted in any form or
by any means, electronic, mechanical, photocopying, recording, scanning, or otherwise, except as
permitted under Section 107 or 108 of the 1976 United States Copyright Act, without either the prior
written permission of the Publisher, or authorization through payment of the appropriate per-copy fee to
the Copyright Clearance Center, Inc., 222 Rosewood Drive, Danvers, MA 01923, (978) 750-8400, fax
(978) 750-4470, or on the web at www.copyright.com. Requests to the Publisher for permission should
be addressed to the Permissions Department, John Wiley & Sons, Inc., 111 River Street, Hoboken, NJ
07030, (201) 748-6011, fax (201) 748-6008, or online at http://www.wiley.com/go/permission.

Limit of Liability/Disclaimer of Warranty: While the publisher and author have used their best efforts in
preparing this book, they make no representations or warranties with respect to the accuracy or
completeness of the contents of this book and specifically disclaim any implied warranties of
merchantability or fitness for a particular purpose. No warranty may be created or extended by sales
representatives or written sales materials. The advice and strategies contained herein may not be suitable
for your situation. You should consult with a professional where appropriate. Neither the publisher nor
author shall be liable for any loss of profit or any other commercial damages, including but not limited to
special, incidental, consequential, or other damages.

For general information on our other products and services or for technical support, please contact our
Customer Care Department within the United States at (800) 762-2974, outside the United States at
(317) 572-3993 or fax (317) 572-4002.

Wiley also publishes its books in a variety of electronic formats. Some content that appears in print may
not be available in electronic formats. For more information about Wiley products, visit our web site at
www.wiley.com.

Library of Congress Cataloging-in-Publication Data

Names: Bali, Turan G., author. | Engle, R. F. (Robert F.) author. | Murray,
    Scott, 1979- author.
Title: Empirical asset pricing : the cross section of stock returns / Turan
    G. Bali, Robert F. Engle, Scott Murray.
Description: Hoboken : Wiley, 2016. | Includes bibliographical references and
    index.
Identifiers: LCCN 2015036767 (print) | LCCN 2016003455 (ebook) | ISBN
    9781118095041 (hardback) | ISBN 9781118589663 (ePub) | ISBN 9781118589472
    (Adobe PDF)
Subjects: LCSH: Stocks–Prices. | Rate of return. | Stock exchanges. | BISAC:
    BUSINESS & ECONOMICS / Finance.
Classification: LCC HG4636 .B35 2016 (print) | LCC HG4636 (ebook) | DDC
    332.63/221–dc23
LC record available at http://lccn.loc.gov/2015036767

Typeset in 10/12pt TimesLTStd by SPi Global, Chennai, India

Printed in the United States of America

10 9 8 7 6 5 4 3 2 1

"The empirical analysis of the cross section of stock returns is a monumental achievement of half a century of finance research. Both the established facts and the methods used to discover them have subtle complexities that can mislead casual observers and novice researchers. Bali, Engle, and Murray's clear and careful guide to these issues provides a firm foundation for future discoveries."

John Campbell, Morton L. and Carole S. Olshan Professor of Economics, Harvard University

"Bali, Engle, and Murray have produced a highly accessible introduction to the techniques and evidence of modern empirical asset pricing. This book should be read and absorbed by every serious student of the field, academic and professional."

Eugene Fama, Robert R. McCormick Distinguished Service Professor of Finance, University of Chicago

"Bali, Engle, and Murray provide clear and accessible descriptions of many of the most important empirical techniques and results in asset pricing."

Kenneth R. French, Roth Family Distinguished Professor of Finance, Tuck School of Business, Dartmouth College

"This exciting new book presents a thorough review of what we know about the cross section of stock returns. Given its comprehensive nature, systematic approach, and easy-to-understand language, the book is a valuable resource for any introductory PhD class in empirical asset pricing."

Lubos Pastor, Charles P. McQuaid Professor of Finance, University of Chicago

CONTENTS

PREFACE

The objective of this book is to provide an overview of the empirical research on the cross-section of expected stock returns. The book is intended for use in doctoral-level empirical asset pricing classes and by investors who are looking for a review of the most important predictors of future stock returns. A doctoral student reader should come away with a solid understanding of the most fundamental results in the field and a strong base upon which to pursue future research in empirical asset pricing. For the reader whose intention is to apply the results presented in this book to practice, our hope is that the book provides a basis upon which investment strategies can be constructed as well as a strong understanding of the most prevalent patterns of risk and returns in the cross-section of stocks.

It is assumed that the reader of this book has at least an MBA level understanding of theoretical asset pricing and a solid grasp of basic econometric techniques. Fantastic books on these topics have been written by Cochrane (2005), Campbell, Lo, and MacKinlay (1996), and Elton, Gruber, Brown, and Goetzmann (2014).[1] More in-depth knowledge in either of these areas is obviously a benefit. While all of the analyses in this book are statistical in nature, the book is not designed to be an econometrics or statistics reference. Our discussions of statistical concepts, therefore, will

---

[1] Several other books have been written on related topics. Ang (2014) gives an in-depth insight into factor investing. Factor analysis plays a large role in the empirical asset pricing literature and is used heavily throughout this book. Karolyi (2015) gives a comprehensive exposition of risks associated with investing in emerging markets. Pedersen (2015) provides a strong introduction into the trading strategies used by hedge funds, many of which have their roots in the phenomena documented throughout this book. Campbell (2015) provides a theoretical and empirical overview of empirical asset pricing research.

be primarily conceptual. For a more detailed discussion of the statistical theory under-lying our methodologies, we suggest that the reader find an econometrics or statistics text appropriate for the reader's level of knowledge in this area.

This book is divided into two main parts. Part I is devoted to a discussion of the most widely used statistical methodologies in empirical asset pricing research. The objective of this section is to give readers a detailed understanding of how to conduct such analyses and how to interpret the results. In addition, we discuss how the results are summarized and presented in academic research articles. The techniques can, very generally, be separated into two groups. Techniques in the first group are designed to summarize the data upon which the research is based. Techniques in the second group are designed to assess relations between the variables used in a study. These are the tools used to investigate the cross-sectional relations between a set of variables and future stock returns. Analysis of such relations is the primary objective of this book and, more generally, the majority of empirical asset pricing research. That being said, these techniques can be used for other purposes as well.

The second, and by far most important, part of this book discusses the major find-ings in empirical asset pricing research. In presenting each of the findings, we begin by discussing in detail the calculation of the main variables used to capture the charac-teristic of the stock that is under investigation. We then apply the techniques discussed in Part I, with the main objective being to understand the relation between the charac-teristic being examined and expected stock returns. While there are literally hundreds of different variables that have been shown to be related to future stock returns, we focus on the most widely recognized and cited phenomena in the literature.

We would like to acknowledge substantial support from our colleagues at George-town University, Georgia State University, and New York University. We would like to specifically thank Viral Acharya, Vikas Agarwal, Yakov Amihud, Andrew Ang, Gurdip Bakshi, Hank Bessembinder, Jacob Boudoukh, Brian Boyer, Stephen Brown, Nusret Cakici, Fousseni Chabi-Yo, Peter Christoffersen, Martijn Cremers, Ozgur Demirtas, Elroy Dimson, Rory Ernst, Wayne Ferson, Fangjian Fu, Thomas Gilbert, Hui Guo, Umit Gurun, Cam Harvey, Bing Han, David Hirshleifer, Armen Hovakimian, Kris Jacobs, Andrew Karolyi, Haim Kassa, Haim Levy, Jonathan Lewellen, Lasse Pedersen, Lin Peng, Jeff Pontiff, Anna Scherbina, Rob Schoen, Robert Stambaugh, Avanidhar Subrahmanyam, Yi Tang, Raman Uppal, Grigory Vilkov, David Weinbaum, Robert Whitelaw, Liuren Wu, Yuhang Xing, Jianfeng Yu, Lu Zhang, Xiaoyan Zhang, Guofu Zhou, and Hao Zhou for their valuable feedback on both this book and on our previous research that has informed its writing. Your input has substantially improved the quality of this book. We are especially grateful to John Campbell, Gene Fama, Kenneth French, and Lubos Pastor for their meticulous reading and detailed feedback, as well as for writing valuable reviews of our book. The creation of this book would not have been possible without the help of Sari Friedman, Jon Gurstelle, Saleem Hameed, and Steve Quigley at Wiley and Sons, Inc. The efficiency and skill with which they executed all facets of the production of this book far surpassed any reasonable expectations. Finally, we would like to thank our wives and children, Marianne, Jordan, Lindsay, Mehtap, Kaan, and Dara, for their unwavering support. Your love, encouragement, and tolerance played an integral role in our ability to produce Empirical Asset Pricing: The Cross Section of Stock Returns.

Turan G. Bali, Robert F. Engle, and Scott Murray New York, 2016.

REFERENCES

Ang, A. *Asset Management A Systematic Approach to Factor Investing*. Oxford University Press, Oxford, 2014.

Campbell, J. Y. *Financial Decisions and Markets*. Princeton University Press, Princeton, NJ, 2015, manuscript in preparation.

Campbell, J. Y., Lo, A. W., and MacKinlay, A. C. *The Econometrics of Financial Markets*. Princeton University Press, Princeton, NJ, 1996.

Cochrane, J. H. *Asset Pricing*. Princeton University Press, Princeton, NJ, 2005.

Elton, E. J., Gruber, M. J., Brown, S. J., and Goetzmann, W. N. *Modern Portfolio Theory and Investment Analysis*. John Wiley & Sons, Hoboken, NJ, 9th Edition, 2014.

Karolyi, G. A. *Cracking the Emerging Markets Enigma*. Oxford University Press, Oxford, 2015.

Pedersen, L. H. *Effficiently Inefficient: How Smart Money Invests & Market Prices Are Determined*. Princeton University Press, Princeton, NJ, 2015.

PART I

STATISTICAL METHODOLOGIES

1

PRELIMINARIES

In this chapter, we present a number of items that are essential components of the methodologies presented in (Part I) of this book. We present these elements here for several reasons. First, they are common to many of the different analyses that will be discussed. Second, being that they are common to many of the methodologies, there is no one logical alternative as to where to present this material. Thus, to avoid repetition, we present these items here and will assume them to be understood for the remainder of the book.

Specifically, in this chapter, we first introduce the type of sample, or data, required for each of the analyses presented in this part. We then discuss winsorization, a technique that is used to adjust data, in order to minimize the effect of outliers on statistical analyses. Finally, we explain Newey and West (1987)-adjusted standard errors, t-statistics, and p-values, which are commonly used to avoid problems with statistical inference associated with heteroscedasticity and autocorrelation in time-series data.

1.1 SAMPLE

Each of the statistical methodologies presented and used in this book is performed on a panel of data. Each entry in the panel corresponds to a particular combination of entity and time period. The entities are referred to using i and the time periods are referenced using t. In most asset pricing studies, the entities correspond to stocks,

Empirical Asset Pricing: The Cross Section of Stock Returns, First Edition.
Turan G. Bali, Robert F. Engle, and Scott Murray.
© 2016 John Wiley & Sons, Inc. Published 2016 by John Wiley & Sons, Inc.

bonds, options, or firms. The time periods used in most studies are months, weeks, quarters, years, and in some cases days. Frequently, the data corresponding to any given time period are referred to as a cross section. Thus, for a fixed value of t, the set of entities i for which data are available in the given time period t is the cross section of entities in time t. In almost all cases, the sample is not a full panel, meaning that the set of entities included in the sample varies from time period to time period. For each entity and time period combination (i, t), the data include several variables. In general, the variable X for entity i during period t will be referred to as $X_{i,t}$. It is frequently the case that when the data contain more than one variable, for example, X and Y, for a given observation i, t, the value of $X_{i,t}$ is available but the value of $Y_{i,t}$ is not available. When this is the case, analyses that require values of both X and Y will not make use of the data point i, t. Most studies create their sample such that the main sample includes all data points for which values of the focal variables of the study are available. Analyses that use nonfocal or control variables will then use only the subset of observations for which the necessary data exist. This approach allows each analysis to be applied to the largest data set for which the required variables are available. However, in some cases, researchers prefer to restrict the sample used for all analyses to only those observations where valid values of each variable used in the entire study are available. The downside of this approach is that frequently a large number of observations are lost. The upside is that all analyses are performed on an identical sample, thus negating concerns related to the use of different data sets for each of the analyses.

In the remaining chapters of Part I, we will use a sample where each entity i corresponds to a stock and each time period t corresponds to a year. The sample covers a period of 25 years from 1988 through 2012 inclusive. For each year t, the sample includes all stocks i in the Center for Research in Security Prices (CRSP) database that are listed as U.S.-based common stocks on December 31 of the year t. Exactly how to determine which stocks are U.S.-based common stocks will be discussed later in the book. At this point, it suffices to say that the sample for each year t consists of U.S. common stocks that were traded on exchanges as of the end of the given year. We will use this sample to exemplify each of the methodologies that are discussed in the remainder of Part I. We use a short sample period and annual periodicity because having a small number of periods in the sample will facilitate presentation of the methodologies. We refer to this sample as the methodologies sample. In Part II of this book, which is devoted to the presentation of the main results in the empirical asset pricing literature, we use monthly data covering a much longer sample period.

For each observation in the methodologies sample, we calculate five variables. We should remind the reader that in many cases, one or more of the variables may be unavailable or missing for certain observations. This is one of the realities under which empirical asset pricing research is conducted. Here, we briefly describe these variables. Detailed discussions of exactly how these variables are calculated will be presented in later chapters.

We calculate the beta (β) of stock i in year t as the slope coefficient from a regression of the excess returns of the stock on the excess returns of the market portfolio using daily stock return data from all days during year t. We require a minimum of 200 days worth of valid daily return data to calculate β. Values of β for which this criterion is not met are considered missing.[1] We define the market capitalization (*MktCap*) for stock i in year t as the number of shares outstanding times the price of the stock at the end of year t divided by one million. Thus, *MktCap* is measured in millions of dollars. We take *Size* to be the natural log of *MktCap*. As will be discussed in Chapter 2, the distribution of *MktCap* is highly skewed; thus, most researchers use *Size* instead of *MktCap* to measure the size of a firm.[2] The book-to-market ratio (*BM*) of a stock is calculated as the book value of the firm's equity divided by the market value of the firm's equity (*MktCap*).[3] Finally, the excess return of stock i in year t is calculated as the return of stock i in year t minus the return of the risk-free security in year t. All returns are recorded as percentages; thus, a value of 1.00 corresponds to a 1% return. Stock return, price, and shares outstanding data come from CRSP. The data used to calculate the book value of equity come from the Compustat database. Risk-free security return data come from Kenneth French's data library.[4]

1.2 WINSORIZATION AND TRUNCATION

Financial data are notoriously subject to outliers (extreme data points). In many statistical analyses, such data points may exert an undue influence on the results, making the results unreliable. Thus, if these outliers are not adjusted or accounted for, it is possible that they may lead to a failure to detect a phenomenon that does exist (a type II error), or even worse, results that indicate a phenomenon where no such phenomenon is actually present (a type I error). While there are several statistical methods that are designed to assess the effect of outliers or ameliorate their effect on results, empirical asset pricing researchers usually take a more ad hoc approach to dealing with the effect of outliers.

There are two techniques that are commonly used in empirical asset pricing research to deal with the effect of outliers. The first technique, known as winsorization, simply sets the values of a given variable that are above or below a certain cutoff to that cutoff. The second technique, known as truncation, simply takes values of a given variable that are deemed extreme to be missing. We discuss each technique in detail. In doing so, we assume that we are dealing with a variable X for which there are n different observations, which we denote $X_1, X_2, \ldots, X_n$.

Winsorization is performed by setting the values of X that are in the top h percent of all values of X to the 100-hth percentile of X. Similarly, values of X in the bottom l percent of X values are set to the lth percentile of X. For example, assume that we want to winsorize X on the high end at the 0.5% level ($h = 0.5$). We begin by calculating the 99.5th percentile of the values of X. We denote this value $Pctl_{99.5}(X)$. Then, we set all values of X that are higher than $Pctl_{99.5}(X)$ to $Pctl_{99.5}(X)$. Now, assume that we want to winsorize X on the low end at the 1.0% level ($l = 1.0$). This is done by

---

[1] The details of the calculation of β are discussed in Chapter 8.
[2] The details of the calculation of *MktCap* and *Size* are discussed in Chapter 9.
[3] The details of the calculation of *BM* are discussed in Chapter 10.
[4] Kenneth French's data library is found at http://mba.tuck.dartmouth.edu/pages/faculty/ken.french/data_library.html.

calculating the first percentile value of X, $Pctl_1(X)$, and setting all values of X that are lower than $Pctl_{1\%}(X)$ to $Pctl_1(X)$. In most cases, the values of h and l are the same, and common values at which researchers winsorize are 0.5% and 1.0%. Throughout this book, we frequently say that we winsorize the data at the 0.5% level. What this means is that both h and l are 0.5, and that winsorization takes place at both the high and low ends of the variable. The level at which winsorization should be performed depends largely on the noise in the variable being winsorized, with more noisy variables being winsorized at higher levels.

Truncation is very similar to winsorization, except instead of setting the values of X above $Pctl_h(X)$ to $Pctl_h(X)$, we set them to missing or unavailable. Similarly, values of X that are less than $Pctl_l(X)$ are taken to be missing. Thus, the main difference between truncation and winsorization is that in truncation, observations with extreme values of a certain variable are effectively removed from the sample for analyses that use the variable X, whereas with winsorization, the extreme values of X are set to more moderate levels.

There are a few ways that winsorization or truncation can be implemented. The first is to winsorize or truncate using all values of the given variable X over all entities i and time periods t. The second is to winsorize or truncate X separately for each time period t. Which approach to winsorization is taken depends on the type of statistical analysis that will be conducted. If a single analysis will be performed on the entire panel of data, the first method of winsorization or truncation is most appropriate. However, most of the methodologies used throughout this book are performed in two stages. The first stage involves performing some analysis on each cross section (time period) in the sample. The second stage analyzes the results of each of these cross-sectional analyses. In this case, the second approach to winsorization or truncation is usually preferable. Throughout this book, when we perform winsorization, it is on a period-by-period basis (the second approach).

When to use winsorization or truncation is a difficult question to answer because some outliers are legitimate while others are data errors. In addition, researchers sometimes use simple functional forms that are not well suited for capturing outliers. In a statistical sense, one might argue that truncation should be used when the data points to be truncated are believed to be generated by a different distribution than the data points that are not to be truncated. Winsorization is perhaps preferable when the extreme data points are believed to indicate that the true values of the given variable for the entities whose values are to be winsorized are very high or very low, but perhaps not quite as extreme as is indicated by the calculated values. Most empirical asset pricing researchers choose to use winsorization instead of truncation. However, if the results of an analysis are substantially impacted by this choice, they should be viewed with skepticism.

1.3   NEWEY AND WEST (1987) ADJUSTMENT

As eluded to in Section 1.2, the methodologies presented in the remainder of Part I and used throughout this book are executed in two steps: a cross-sectional step and a time-series step. In many cases, the values used during the time-series step may exhibit autocorrelation and/or heteroscedasticity. If this is the case, the standard errors and thus p-values and t-statistics used to test a null hypothesis may be inaccurate. To account for these issues in a time-series analysis, empirical asset pricing researchers frequently employ a methodology, developed by Newey and West (1987), that adjusts the standard errors of estimated values to account for the impact of autocorrelation and heteroscedasticity. In this section, we briefly describe implementation of this technique. The details can be found by reading Newey and West (1987).

In most empirical asset pricing research, the Newey and West (1987) adjustment is used when examining the time-series mean of a single variable. We refer to this variable measured at time t as A_t. Notice here that there is no entity dimension to A, as A represents a single time series. The basic idea is that if values of A_t are autocorrelated or heteroscedastic, then using a simple t-test to examine whether the mean of A is equal to some value specified by the null hypothesis (usually zero) may result in incorrect inference, as the autocorrelation and heteroscedasticity may deflate (or inflate) the standard error of the estimated mean. To adjust for this, instead of using a simple t-test, the time-series values of A_t are regressed on a unit constant. The result is that the estimated intercept coefficient is equal to the time-series mean of A and the regression residuals capture the time-series variation in A and thus A's autocorrelation and heteroscedasticity. The standard error of the estimated mean value of A is a function of these residuals. So far, this is not different from a standard t-test. Applying the Newey and West (1987) adjustment to the results of the regression, however, produces a new standard error for the estimated mean that is adjusted for autocorrelation and heteroscedasticity. The only input required for the Newey and West (1987) adjustment is the number of lags to use when performing the adjustment. As discussed in Newey and West (1994), the choice of lags is arbitrary. Frequently, econometrics software sets the number of lags to $4(T/100)^a$, where T is the number of periods in the time series, $a = 2/9$ when using the Bartlett kernel, and $a = 4/25$ when using the quadratic spectral kernel to calculate the autocorrelation and heteroscedasticity-adjusted standard errors.[5] A large proportion of empirical asset pricing studies use monthly samples covering the period from 1963 through the present (2012, or $T = 600$ months for the data used in this book). Plugging in the value $T = 600$ and taking a to be either $2/9$ or $4/25$ results in a value between five and six. Most studies, therefore, choose six as the number of lags. Once the Newey and West (1987)-adjusted standard error has been calculated, t-statistics and p-values can be adjusted to perform inference on the time-series mean of A. As is standard, the new t-statistic is the difference between the coefficient on the constant (same as the sample mean) and the null hypothesis mean divided by the adjusted standard error. The p-value can then be calculated using the adjusted t-statistic and the same number of degrees of freedom as would be used to calculate the unadjusted p-value.

The astute reader may have noticed that in the previous paragraph it was completely unnecessary to present the Newey and West (1987) adjustment within the

---

[5]See Newey and West (1987, 1994) and references therein for further discussion of the Bartlett and quadratic spectral kernels.

context of a regression, because regression on a unit constant simply produces an estimated coefficient equal to the mean value and residuals that represent variation in the time series of A. We present the Newey and West (1987) adjustment in this manner for two reasons. First, in most statistical software, the Newey and West (1987) adjustment is executed by appropriately setting a certain parameter or argument to the regression function. The second is that the Newey and West (1987) adjustment is actually much more general than described in the previous paragraph. In the general case, the Newey and West (1987) adjustment can be applied to any time-series regression. It is for this reason that statistical software implements the Newey and West (1987) adjustment within the context of regression analysis.

In its general form, the Newey and West (1987) adjustment can be used to adjust the standard errors on all estimated coefficients from a time-series regression for autocorrelation and heteroscedasticity in the regression residuals. The procedure to do so is exactly as described earlier, except that the time-series A is regressed on one or more additional time series and, in most cases, a constant as well. The Newey and West (1987) adjustment will then generate an adjusted variance–covariance matrix of the estimated regression coefficients that accounts for autocorrelation and heteroscedasticity in the residuals. The square roots of the diagonal entries of this adjusted variance–covariance matrix then serve as the standard errors of the estimated regression coefficients. These adjusted standard errors are used to calculate adjusted t-statistics and p-values. As in the univariate case, the researcher must determine the appropriate number of lags to use in the adjustment. While the Newey and West (1987) adjustment may seem a bit abstract at this point, its use will become much more clear in subsequent chapters. This nontrivial case of the Newey and West (1987) adjustment is commonly employed in factor regressions of portfolio excess returns on a set of common risk factors. This will be discussed in more detail in Section 5.1.7.

1.4 SUMMARY

In this chapter, we have presented three elements that are common to most of the empirical methodologies that will be discussed in the remainder of Part I and heavily employed in the analyses of Part II. We have also described the sample that will be used to exemplify the methodologies throughout the remainder of Part I, which we refer to as the methodologies sample. The reason for presenting these items here is to avoid repetition in the remaining chapters of Part I.

REFERENCES

Newey, W. K. and West, K. D. 1987. A simple, positive semi-definite, heteroskedasticity and autocorrelation consistent covariance matrix. Econometrica, 55(3), 703–708.
Newey, W. K. and West, K. D. 1994. Automatic lag selection in covariance matrix estimation. Review of Economic Studies, 61(4), 631–653.

2

SUMMARY STATISTICS

Perhaps one of the most important elements of conducting high-quality empirical research is to have a strong understanding of the data that are being used in the study. Similarly, for a reader of empirical research, to fully comprehend the results of the study and assess the applicability of these results beyond the scope of the study, it is important to have at least a cursory understanding of the data upon which the analyses presented in the article were performed. For these reasons, most empirical research papers present summaries of the data prior to discussing the main results. Frequently, the first table of a research paper presents such a summary.

In this chapter, we present the most commonly used approach in the empirical asset pricing literature to calculating and presenting summary statistics. Effective presentation of summary statistics represents a trade-off between showing enough results to give the reader a good sense of the important characteristics of the data and not presenting so much that the reader is overwhelmed. The optimal approach to presenting summary statistics depends greatly on the type of study being conducted. The approach presented in this chapter is most appropriate when the objective of the study is to understand a cross-sectional phenomenon of the entities (stocks, bonds, firms, etc.) being studied. The procedure, therefore, is geared toward understanding the cross-sectional distribution of the variables used in the study.

Empirical Asset Pricing: The Cross Section of Stock Returns, First Edition.
Turan G. Bali, Robert F. Engle, and Scott Murray.
© 2016 John Wiley & Sons, Inc. Published 2016 by John Wiley & Sons, Inc.

2.1   IMPLEMENTATION

The summary statistics procedure consists of two steps. In the first step, for each time period t, certain characteristics of the cross-sectional distribution of the given variable, X, are calculated. In the second step, the time-series properties of the periodic cross-sectional characteristics are calculated. In most cases, the time-series property of interest is the mean, in which case the final results that are presented represent the average cross section, where the average is taken over all periods t during the sample period.

2.1.1   Periodic Cross-Sectional Summary Statistics

The details of the first step are as follows. For each time period t, we calculate the cross-sectional mean, standard deviation, skewness, excess kurtosis, minimum value, median value, maximum value, and selected additional percentiles of the distribution of the values of X, where each of these statistics is calculated over all available values of X in period t. We let $Mean_t$ be the mean, SD_t denote the sample standard deviation, $Skew_t$ represent the sample skewness, $Kurt_t$ be the sample excess kurtosis, Min_t be the minimum value, $Median_t$ denote the median value, and Max_t represent the maximum value of X in period t. In addition, we will record the fifth, 25th, 75th, and 95th percentiles of X in month t, which we denote $P5_t$, $P25_t$, $P75_t$, and $P95_t$, respectively. Depending on the data and the objective of the study, it may be desirable to include additional percentiles of the distribution. For example, if the study focuses on extreme values of X, then it may be valuable to record the first, second, third, fourth, 96th, 97th, 98th, and 99th percentiles of the distribution as well. Alternatively, calculating the minimum, maximum, fifth percentile, and 95th percentile of the data may not be necessary if the data are reasonably well behaved. Exactly which statistics to record and present is a decision made by the researcher, who, presumably, has a much deeper understanding of the data than could possibly be presented in a research article. In addition to these statistics describing the time t cross-sectional distribution of X, we also record the number of entities for which a valid value of X is available in period t and denote this number n_t.

In Table 2.1, we present the annual summary statistics for market beta (β) from our methodologies sample. The results show that, for example, in 1988, the average β of the stocks in the sample is 0.46; the cross-sectional standard deviation of the values of β is 0.48; the sample skewness of β is 0.17; and the sample excess kurtosis of β is 2.80. Furthermore, the minimum, fifth percentile, 25th percentile, median, 75th percentile, 95th percentile, and maximum values of β in 1988 are -4.29, -0.20, 0.13, 0.40, 0.75, 1.31, and 3.28, respectively. Finally, there are 5690 stocks with a valid value of β in 1988.

Table 2.1 presents a detailed account of the cross-sectional distribution of β on a period-by-period basis. In this case, presenting the periodic summary statistics in detail is possible because our sample consists of only 25 periods, and we only present summary statistics for one variable, β. While it is certainly valuable to present all of these statistics, in most empirical asset pricing studies, the sample has many more

TABLE 2.1   Annual Summary Statistics for β

This table presents summary statistics for β for each year during the sample period. For each year t, we calculate the mean ($Mean_t$), standard deviation (SD_t), skewness ($Skew_t$), excess kurtosis ($Kurt_t$), minimum (Min_t), fifth percentile ($P5_t$), 25th percentile ($P25_t$), median ($Median_t$), 75th percentile ($P75_t$), 95th percentile ($P95_t$), and maximum (Max_t) values of the distribution of β across all stocks in the sample. The sample consists of all U.S.-based common stocks in the Center for Research in Security Prices (CRSP) database as of the end of the given year t and covers the years from 1988 through 2012. The column labeled n_t indicates the number of observations for which a value of β is available in the given year.

t	$Mean_t$	SD_t	$Skew_t$	$Kurt_t$	Min_t	$P5_t$	$P25_t$	$Median_t$	$P75_t$	$P95_t$	Max_t	n_t
1988	0.46	0.48	0.17	2.80	−4.29	−0.20	0.13	0.40	0.75	1.31	3.28	5690
1989	0.46	0.53	0.15	1.88	−3.51	−0.27	0.11	0.40	0.79	1.38	3.63	5519
1990	0.58	0.59	0.23	1.14	−3.15	−0.24	0.16	0.51	0.96	1.61	3.66	5409
1991	0.57	0.61	0.23	1.96	−3.28	−0.29	0.17	0.52	0.95	1.62	5.29	5303
1992	0.65	0.83	0.34	6.10	−5.21	−0.50	0.17	0.59	1.09	2.05	9.90	5389
1993	0.62	0.77	−0.10	4.29	−4.70	−0.56	0.20	0.57	1.04	1.90	7.59	5670
1994	0.70	0.71	−0.17	6.59	−6.92	−0.32	0.27	0.67	1.07	1.89	6.50	6148
1995	0.64	0.84	0.30	5.17	−6.32	−0.49	0.19	0.56	1.02	2.15	8.77	6288
1996	0.67	0.64	0.46	1.97	−4.32	−0.20	0.26	0.59	1.01	1.89	3.98	6586
1997	0.53	0.48	0.39	1.46	−2.36	−0.13	0.21	0.48	0.80	1.38	3.20	6867
1998	0.71	0.51	0.49	0.95	−1.80	0.01	0.34	0.67	1.03	1.62	3.75	6608
1999	0.41	0.50	1.39	4.81	−2.21	−0.18	0.11	0.32	0.61	1.33	3.77	6097
2000	0.70	0.72	1.27	1.33	−1.10	−0.06	0.19	0.49	1.01	2.23	3.76	5901
2001	0.76	0.73	1.29	2.13	−1.48	−0.05	0.25	0.60	1.07	2.25	4.21	5508
2002	0.67	0.55	0.70	0.69	−1.19	−0.04	0.25	0.62	0.97	1.73	2.99	5099
2003	0.72	0.56	0.40	0.49	−2.17	−0.04	0.29	0.68	1.06	1.72	3.04	4737
2004	1.03	0.70	0.43	0.24	−1.75	0.01	0.53	0.99	1.46	2.30	4.02	4574
2005	0.95	0.64	0.00	−0.17	−1.60	−0.06	0.46	0.99	1.39	1.96	3.69	4495
2006	1.02	0.70	0.08	0.17	−3.71	−0.02	0.48	1.00	1.51	2.18	3.75	4453
2007	0.87	0.54	−0.04	−0.20	−1.50	0.01	0.45	0.91	1.26	1.72	3.06	4332
2008	0.87	0.53	0.17	0.06	−1.49	0.03	0.48	0.87	1.22	1.74	3.45	4264
2009	1.10	0.72	0.51	0.62	−1.74	0.09	0.55	1.03	1.57	2.36	5.31	3977
2010	1.04	0.54	−0.06	−0.15	−0.85	0.10	0.68	1.05	1.41	1.90	2.95	3805
2011	1.07	0.54	−0.14	−0.37	−0.62	0.14	0.70	1.13	1.45	1.93	3.03	3682
2012	1.04	0.57	0.04	0.48	−2.33	0.11	0.66	1.05	1.40	1.99	3.43	3545

periods than the 25 periods in the methodology sample. Presenting results such as those in Table 2.1 when there are a large number of periods will not only make it difficult to display the periodic summary statistics but will also make it difficult for the reader to get a general understanding of the characteristics of the data. These issues are magnified when, as in most studies, showing summary statistics for several variables is desirable. Thus, while there are certainly interesting patterns to be observed by presenting such a detailed account of each variable, doing so is usually not necessary to inform a reader about the most salient characteristics of the data, and thus most articles present statistics that are substantially more summarized than the results in Table 2.1. We proceed now to describe how to further summarize the periodic cross-sectional summary statistics.

2.1.2 Average Cross-Sectional Summary Statistics

The second step in the summary statistics procedure is to calculate the time-series averages of the periodic cross-sectional values. For example, the average cross-sectional mean of the variable X, which we denote *Mean* (no subscript), is found by taking the time-series average of the values of $Mean_t$ over all periods t in the sample. Similarly, we calculate the times-series means of the other cross-sectional summary statistics.

For most studies, it is these time-series average values that are presented in the research article. These values describe the average cross section in the sample. This is appropriate when the objective of the study is to examine a cross-sectional phenomenon, as is the case for the analyses in this book. Table 2.2 presents the time-series averages of the annual cross-sectional summary statistics for β. The numbers in the table, therefore, represent the cross-sectional distribution of β for the average year in the methodologies sample. As can be seen, in the average year, the mean value of β is 0.75 and the median value of β is 0.71. Consistent with the mean being slightly greater than the median, in the average year, the skewness of the distribution of β of 0.34 is slightly positive. The cross-sectional distribution of β, in the average year, is leptokurtic because the average excess kurtosis of 1.78 is positive. The average cross-sectional standard deviation of β is 0.62. Finally, in the average year, there are 5198 stocks for which there is a valid value of β.

TABLE 2.2   Average Cross-Sectional Summary Statistics for β
This table presents the time-series averages of the annual cross-sectional summary statistics for β. The table presents the average mean (*Mean*), standard deviation (*SD*), skewness (*Skew*), excess kurtosis (*Kurt*), minimum (*Min*), fifth percentile (*P5*), 25th percentile (*P25*), median (*Median*), 75th percentile (*P75*), 95th percentile (*P95*), and maximum (*Max*) values of the distribution of β, where the average is taken across all years in the sample. The column labeled n indicates the average number of observations for which a value of β is available.

Mean	SD	Skew	Kurt	Min	P5	P25	Median	P75	P95	Max	n
0.75	0.62	0.34	1.78	−2.78	−0.13	0.33	0.71	1.12	1.85	4.40	5198

2.2   PRESENTATION AND INTERPRETATION

In most studies, there are many variables for which summary statistics should be presented. It is usually optimal to present the summary statistics for all variables in a single table. While each paper will present summary statistics in a slightly different manner, the approach we take in this book is to compile a table in which each row (with the exception of the header row) presents summary statistics for one of the variables.

Table 2.3 gives an example of how we present summary statistics throughout this text. The first column indicates the variable whose summary statistics are presented in the given row. The subsequent columns present the time-series averages of the cross-sectional summary statistics.

The objectives in analyzing the summary statistics are twofold. First, the summary statistics are intended to give a basic overview of the cross-sectional properties of the variables that will be used in the study. This is useful for understanding the types of entities that comprise the sample. Second, the summary statistics can be used to identify any potential issues that may arise when using these variables in statistical analyses. We exemplify how the summary statistics can be used for each of these objectives in the following two paragraphs using the methodology sample and the results in Table 2.3.

The mean column in Table 2.3 can roughly be interpreted as indicating that the average stock in our sample has a β of 0.75, a market capitalization of just over $2 billion, and a book-to-market ratio of 0.71. More precisely, the table indicates that in the average month, the cross-sectional means of the given variables are as indicated in the table, but we frequently adopt the simpler language used in the previous sentence. The average value of *Size*, which is the natural log of *MktCap*, is 5.04, and the average one-year-ahead excess return is 12.40%.

Table 2.3 shows that for β, the mean and the median are quite similar and, consistent with this, the skewness is quite small in magnitude and values of β are reasonably symmetric about the mean. The distribution of β is also slightly leptokurtic as the excess kurtosis of its cross-sectional distribution in the average year is 1.78.

The results for *MktCap* show that the distribution of market capitalization is highly positively skewed. This is driven by a small number of observations that have very large values of *MktCap*. The summary statistics therefore indicate that the sample is comprised predominantly of low-market capitalization stocks along with a few stocks that have very high market capitalizations. The median stock in the sample has a market capitalization of $188 million, which is much smaller than the mean of more than $2 billion. It is also worth noting that the smallest value of *MktCap* of 0, which means that the stock has market capitalization of less than $0.5 million, is less than 0.02 standard deviations from the median and less than 0.1 standard deviations from the mean. This indicates that a very large portion of the variability of *MktCap* comes from extremely large values, consistent with the high positive skewness. The distribution of *MktCap* presents potential issues for statistical analyses, such as regression, that rely on the magnitude of the variables used, as the data points corresponding to the very large values may exert undesirably strong influence on the results of such analyses. Therefore, most empirical studies use *Size*, defined as the natural log of *MktCap*, in such analyses. Table 2.3 shows that the distribution of *Size* is much more symmetric than that of *MktCap*, as the average skewness is only 0.32. Furthermore, the excess kurtosis of −0.07 indicates that tails of the distribution of *Size* are, in the average year, very similar to those of a normal distribution. *Size*, therefore, appears much better suited for use in statistical analyses than *MktCap*.

TABLE 2.3 Summary Statistics for β, MktCap, and BM

This table presents summary statistics for our sample. The sample covers the years t from 1988 through 2012, inclusive, and includes all U.S.-based common stocks in the CRSP database. Each year, the mean (*Mean*), standard deviation (*SD*), skewness (*Skew*), excess kurtosis (*Kurt*), minimum (*Min*), fifth percentile (*5%*), 25th percentile (*25%*), median (*Median*), 75th percentile (*75%*), 95th percentile (*95%*), and maximum (*Max*) values of the cross-sectional distribution of each variable are calculated. The table presents the time-series means for each cross-sectional value. The column labeled n indicates the average number of stocks for which the given variable is available. β is the beta of a stock calculated from a regression of the excess stock returns on the excess market returns using all available daily data during year t. *MktCap* is the market capitalization of the stock calculated on the last trading day of year t and recorded in $millions. *Size* is the natural log of *MktCap*. *BM* is the ratio of the book value of equity to the market value of equity. r_{t+1} is the one-year-ahead excess stock return.

	Mean	SD	Skew	Kurt	Min	5%	25%	Median	75%	95%	Max	n
β	0.75	0.62	0.34	1.78	−2.78	−0.13	0.33	0.71	1.12	1.85	4.40	5198
MktCap	2030	10,230	14.20	282.85	0	9	48	188	802	7524	287,033	5550
Size	5.04	2.07	0.32	−0.07	−1.19	1.89	3.56	4.91	6.39	8.70	12.33	5550
BM	0.71	2.90	−9.49	1,226.68	−124.31	0.05	0.29	0.57	0.97	2.11	44.87	4273
r_{t+1}	12.40	80.83	5.94	125.33	−97.86	−67.46	−26.87	0.90	31.84	124.54	1,841.43	5381

As for the book-to-market ratio (BM), Table 2.3 shows that while the vast majority of the BM values fall between 0.05 (the fifth percentile) and 2.11 (the 95th percentile), the tails of the distribution are extremely long, as the kurtosis of BM is greater than 1226. Interestingly, despite the fact that the mean is greater than the median, in the average month, the distribution of BM is negatively skewed, as the average cross-sectional skewness of BM is −9.49.

Finally, the table indicates that the average one-year-ahead excess return (r_{t+1}) of the stocks in the methodology sample is 12.40% per year. The cross-sectional distribution of r_{t+1} is highly skewed and leptokurtic, with an average skewness of 5.94 and excess kurtosis of more than 125. This is driven by the fact that the minimum possible return is −100%, whereas there is no upper bound on the value that r_{t+1} can take. Table 2.3 shows that, in the average year, the maximum r_{t+1} is more than 1841%, with more than 5% of stock realizing excess returns greater than 100%.

There is one more aspect of the return data that is worth mentioning because it is not apparent in the presentation of the summary statistics. The latest data in the version of the CRSP database used to construct the methodology sample are from 2012. However, when t corresponds to year 2012, then r_{t+1} corresponds to excess returns from 2013. Unfortunately, return data for 2013 are not available. Thus, the summary statistics for r_{t+1} reported in Table 2.3 actually cover returns for the 24 years from 1989 through 2012, whereas the summary statistics for the other variables cover the 25 years from 1988 through 2012. While this detail of the summary statistics is not usually discussed in a research article because it rarely has a meaningful impact on the interpretation of the results, it is something that should be clearly understood by the researcher.

Although Table 2.3 is certainly expository, there are many characteristics of the data that are not captured in the highly summarized results. The most important drawback of summarizing the data in such a manner is that it does not indicate any time-series variation in the variables used in the study. For example, referring back to Table 2.1, it is evident that the mean and median values of β increase quite substantially over time. This feature of the data is not in any way captured in the summary presented in Table 2.3. Additionally, given that the values of market capitalization ($MktCap$) have not been adjusted for inflation, it is reasonable to assume that value of $MktCap$ will exhibit generally increasing pattern over time as well. This is confirmed in unreported results. Furthermore, values of $MktCap$ are likely to drop when the stock market experiences a large loss and increase as the stock market realizes gains. The opposite would be true for the book-to-market ratio (BM) as the market capitalization is the denominator of this variable, although in this case the increase in values of BM may be delayed due to the timing of the calculation of BM, which is discussed in detail in Chapter 10.

None of these characteristics of the data are captured in the summary statistics as presented in Table 2.3. In most cases, these details are not very important when interpreting and drawing conclusions from the results of subsequent analyses in the article. However, as a researcher, it is important to be aware of such patterns and to assess whether these patterns may have a significant impact on the main conclusions of the study. In many cases, this is done by subsample analyses aimed at examining whether the main conclusions hold in both early periods of the study as well as in late periods. Frequently, it is also worthwhile to investigate whether the main results hold in periods of normal economic conditions as well as periods of deteriorating or poor economic conditions. This is especially the case if the summary statistics for the focal variables of the study are substantially different for these subperiods.

2.3 SUMMARY

In summary, the main objective of presenting summary statistics is to give the reader a sufficient but succinct understanding of the data being used and the characteristics of the entities that comprise the sample. In addition, the summary statistics can be used to identify and remedy any potential issues with using statistical analysis on the data. The approach that we have discussed presents the distribution of the given variables in the average cross section. While the results presented in the summary statistics table may be sufficient for a reader, they are likely not sufficient for the researcher. It is difficult to conduct high-quality research without having an in-depth understanding of the data. A good researcher will understand any potential issues with the data that are not evident in the summary statistics and address these issues in the statistical analyses presented in the research article.

3

CORRELATION

Summary statistics, discussed in Chapter 2, provide an overview of the univariate distributions of the variables used in a study. They do not, however, give any indication as to the relations between the variables. Understanding how the variables relate to each other is usually more important than understanding the variables' univariate characteristics, as in almost all cases, it is the relations that are the focus of the research. Therefore, in addition to presenting univariate summary statistics, researchers frequently present correlations between the main variables. Correlations provide a preliminary look at the bivariate relations between pairs of variables used in the study.

This chapter introduces a widely used methodology for calculating and presenting correlations. As with the summary statistics procedure presented in Chapter 2, the objective of the methodology discussed in this chapter is to understand the cross-sectional properties of the variables. This technique is therefore most appropriate when the economic phenomenon under investigation is cross-sectional in nature. While most studies present only Pearson product–moment correlations, here and in the remainder of this book, we will present both the Pearson product–moment correlations and the Spearman rank correlation.

The Pearson product–moment correlation is most applicable when the relation between the two variables, which we denote X and Y, is thought to be linear. If this is the case, the Pearson correlation can be roughly interpreted as the signed percentage of variation in X that is related to variation in Y, with the sign being positive if X

Empirical Asset Pricing: The Cross Section of Stock Returns, First Edition.
Turan G. Bali, Robert F. Engle, and Scott Murray.
© 2016 John Wiley & Sons, Inc. Published 2016 by John Wiley & Sons, Inc.

tends to be high when Y is high, and the sign being negative when high values of X tend to correspond to low values of Y. The Pearson correlation can take values between -1 and 1, with -1 indicating a perfectly negative linear relation, 0 indicating no linear relation between the variables, and 1 indicating a perfectly positive linear relation.

The Spearman rank correlation is most applicable when the relation between the variables is thought to be monotonic, but not necessarily linear. The rank correlation, as the name implies, measures how closely related the ordering of X is to the ordering of Y, with no regard to the actual values of the variables. As with the product–moment correlation, the rank correlation can take on values between -1 and 1, with a Spearman correlation of 1 indicating that X and Y are perfectly monotonically increasing functions of each other and a value of -1 indicating that X and Y are perfectly monotonically decreasing functions of each other.

3.1 IMPLEMENTATION

Similar to the summary statistics procedure, the correlation procedure is executed in two steps. The first step is to calculate the cross-sectional correlation between the two variables in question, X and Y, for each period t. The second step is to take the time-series average of these cross-sectional correlations.

3.1.1 Periodic Cross-Sectional Correlations

In step one, for each time period t, we calculate the Pearson product–moment correlation and the Spearman rank correlation between X and Y. The Pearson product–moment correlation between X and Y for period t is defined as

$$\rho_t(X, Y) = \frac{\sum_{i=1}^{n_t} (X_{i,t} - \overline{X}_t)(Y_{i,t} - \overline{Y}_t)}{\sqrt{\sum_{i=1}^{n_t} (X_{i,t} - \overline{X}_t)^2} \sqrt{\sum_{i=1}^{n_t} (Y_{i,t} - \overline{Y}_t)^2}} \tag{3.1}$$

where each of the summations is taken over all entities i in the sample for which there are valid values of both X and Y in period t, and $\overline{X}_t$ and $\overline{Y}_t$ are the sample means of $X_{i,t}$ and $Y_{i,t}$, respectively, taken over the same set of entities. Here, n_t is the number of entities for which there are valid values of both X and Y in the given period t. In many cases, the values of X and Y are winsorized prior to calculating the Pearson product–moment correlation to minimize the effect of a small number of extreme observations. Winsorization is performed on a period-by-period basis using only entities for which valid values of both X and Y are available.

To calculate the Spearman rank correlation, one must first calculate the ranking for each entity i on each of X and Y. We let $x_{i,t}$ be the rank of $X_{i,t}$ calculated over all entities that have valid values of both X and Y during period t. Thus, if entity i has the lowest value of X, $x_{i,t}$ is 1. If entity i has the highest value of X, then $x_{i,t}$ is n_t. If there are multiple entities for which the value of X is the same, then each of these entities is assigned a ranking equal to the average position of these entities in the ordered list of the entities when sorted on the variable X. The rankings for Y are calculated analogously and are denoted $y_{i,t}$. It should be noted that when calculating the Spearman rank correlation, the data should not be winsorized. For each entity i, the difference between the entity's ranking on X and it's ranking on Y is defined as $d_{i,t} = x_{i,t} - y_{i,t}$. Finally, the Spearman rank correlation between X and Y for period t is calculated as

$$\rho_t^S(X, Y) = 1 - \frac{6 \sum_{i=1}^{n_t} d_{i,t}^2}{n_t(n_t^2 - 1)}. \tag{3.2}$$

We exemplify the cross-sectional step of the correlation procedure by calculating both the Pearson product–moment correlation ($\rho_t(X, Y)$) and the Spearman rank correlation ($\rho_t^S(X, Y)$) between each pair of the variables β (beta), $Size$ (log of market capitalization in \$millions), BM (book-to-market ratio), and r_{t+1} (one-year-ahead excess return), for each year t during our sample period. Pearson product–moment correlations are calculated after winsorizing both of the variables at the 0.5% level using only data point for which both variables in the given calculation have valid values.

In Table 3.1, we present the Pearson product–moment and Spearman rank cross-sectional correlations between each pair of variables during each year t of our sample. The table shows that, in all years, β and $Size$ are positively correlated, regardless of which measure of correlation is used. β and BM exhibit negative correlation in all years except for 2009, when this correlation is positive but small in magnitude. The relation between β and r_{t+1} varies substantially over time. $Size$ and BM have a negative correlation in all time periods. This is not surprising given that market capitalization is the denominator of the calculation of BM and $Size$ is the log of market capitalization. Thus, this effect is likely mechanical. The signs of the correlation between $Size$ and r_{t+1}, as well as between BM and r_{t+1}, vary over time. Finally, it is worth noting that for year 2012 there are no correlations for pairs of variables that include r_{t+1}. This is because for $t = 2012$, r_{t+1} is the excess return in 2013, which is not available in the version of the Center for Research in Security Prices (CRSP) database used to generate the methodologies sample.

3.1.2 Average Cross-Sectional Correlations

Step two in the correlation procedure is to calculate the time-series averages of the periodic cross-sectional correlations between each pair of variables. These values represent the correlations in the average period. The time-series average correlations for each pair of variables used in the example are presented in Table 3.2. We denote these time-series averages as $\rho(X, Y)$ for the Pearson product–moment correlation and $\rho^S(X, Y)$ for the Spearman rank correlation. We therefore have

$$\rho(X, Y) = \frac{\sum_{t=1}^N \rho_t(X, Y)}{N} \tag{3.3}$$

TABLE 3.1 Annual Correlations for β, *Size*, *BM*, and r_{t+1}

This table presents the cross-sectional Pearson product–moment (ρ_t) and Spearman rank (ρ_t^S) correlations between pairs of β, *Size*, *BM*, and r_{t+1}. Each column presents either the Pearson or Spearman correlation for one pair of variables, indicated in the column header. Each row represents results from a different year, indicated in the column labeled t.

t	$\rho_t(\beta,Size)$	$\rho_t^S(\beta,Size)$	$\rho_t(\beta,BM)$	$\rho_t^S(\beta,BM)$	$\rho_t(\beta,r_{t+1})$	$\rho_t^S(\beta,r_{t+1})$	$\rho_t(Size,BM)$	$\rho_t^S(Size,BM)$	$\rho_t(Size,r_{t+1})$	$\rho_t^S(Size,r_{t+1})$	$\rho_t(BM,r_{t+1})$	$\rho_t^S(BM,r_{t+1})$
1988	0.47	0.45	−0.10	−0.12	0.04	0.06	−0.15	−0.11	0.13	0.24	0.04	0.04
1989	0.44	0.45	−0.15	−0.16	0.02	0.02	−0.14	−0.11	0.07	0.17	0.01	0.05
1990	0.43	0.45	−0.17	−0.23	0.07	0.15	−0.19	−0.16	−0.07	0.10	−0.04	−0.05
1991	0.45	0.49	−0.09	−0.16	−0.09	−0.09	−0.23	−0.22	−0.15	−0.03	0.13	0.19
1992	0.34	0.37	−0.20	−0.29	−0.10	−0.10	−0.20	−0.17	−0.14	−0.04	0.10	0.20
1993	0.36	0.38	−0.18	−0.25	−0.01	−0.03	−0.19	−0.17	−0.00	0.07	0.11	0.16
1994	0.31	0.35	−0.18	−0.22	0.03	0.02	−0.17	−0.11	−0.00	0.11	0.01	0.06
1995	0.30	0.32	−0.16	−0.21	−0.06	−0.08	−0.21	−0.19	−0.01	0.09	0.10	0.14
1996	0.30	0.32	−0.26	−0.36	−0.17	−0.19	−0.21	−0.17	0.04	0.10	0.12	0.21
1997	0.42	0.43	−0.23	−0.29	0.03	−0.00	−0.20	−0.18	0.08	0.18	0.03	0.07
1998	0.38	0.40	−0.25	−0.33	0.15	0.11	−0.24	−0.25	−0.09	−0.04	−0.04	−0.03
1999	0.48	0.47	−0.24	−0.32	−0.11	−0.10	−0.34	−0.38	0.04	0.07	0.03	0.08
2000	0.23	0.27	−0.39	−0.54	−0.20	−0.27	−0.27	−0.26	−0.19	−0.14	0.08	0.17
2001	0.32	0.38	−0.20	−0.34	−0.38	−0.44	−0.32	−0.40	−0.13	−0.09	0.17	0.25
2002	0.46	0.55	−0.23	−0.30	0.01	0.04	−0.27	−0.29	−0.23	−0.15	0.05	0.04
2003	0.51	0.59	−0.13	−0.17	−0.14	−0.13	−0.24	−0.31	−0.08	0.03	0.11	0.10
2004	0.32	0.40	−0.26	−0.28	−0.09	−0.08	−0.17	−0.13	0.06	0.14	0.08	0.13
2005	0.45	0.50	−0.16	−0.15	−0.01	0.03	−0.13	−0.11	−0.01	0.08	0.07	0.12
2006	0.41	0.47	−0.20	−0.22	0.07	0.06	−0.17	−0.15	0.12	0.19	−0.02	−0.04
2007	0.47	0.52	−0.12	−0.14	−0.01	−0.01	−0.17	−0.17	0.09	0.16	−0.01	0.00
2008	0.44	0.48	−0.09	−0.13	0.03	0.09	−0.24	−0.23	−0.18	−0.04	0.08	−0.06
2009	0.31	0.37	0.02	0.01	0.11	0.13	−0.28	−0.34	−0.00	0.09	0.03	0.04
2010	0.39	0.39	−0.18	−0.15	−0.10	−0.12	−0.31	−0.28	0.14	0.18	−0.01	0.00
2011	0.37	0.36	−0.26	−0.22	−0.05	−0.02	−0.29	−0.27	−0.04	0.04	0.12	0.12
2012	0.35	0.35	−0.17	−0.17			−0.32	−0.32				

and

$$\rho^S(X, Y) = \frac{\sum_{t=1}^{N} \rho_t^S(X, Y)}{N} \tag{3.4}$$

where N is the number of periods in the sample.

3.2 INTERPRETING CORRELATIONS

The correlations give preliminary indications of the nature of the cross-sectional relations between each pair of variables. If two variables that are measured

TABLE 3.2　Average Correlations for β, *Size*, *BM*, and r_{t+1}

This table presents the time-series averages of the annual cross-sectional Pearson product–moment (ρ) and Spearman rank (ρ^S) correlations between pairs of β, *Size*, *BM*, and r_{t+1}. Each column presents either the Pearson or Spearman correlation for one pair of variables, indicated in the column header.

$\rho(\beta, Size)$	$\rho^S(\beta, Size)$	$\rho(\beta, BM)$	$\rho^S(\beta, BM)$	$\rho(\beta, r_{t+1})$	$\rho^S(\beta, r_{t+1})$	$\rho(Size, BM)$	$\rho^S(Size, BM)$	$\rho(Size, r_{t+1})$	$\rho^S(Size, r_{t+1})$	$\rho(BM, r_{t+1})$	$\rho^S(BM, r_{t+1})$
0.39	0.42	−0.18	−0.23	−0.04	−0.04	−0.23	−0.22	−0.02	0.06	0.06	0.08

contemporaneously exhibit correlations that are very high in magnitude, this indicates that the information content of both variables is very similar and that the two variables are likely capturing the same characteristic of the entity. If variables that are not measured contemporaneously exhibit strong correlation, this is an indication that one variable (the variable measured chronologically earlier) may be a predictor of future values of the other variable. In making such a determination, it is important to ensure that such predictive power is not mechanical. To do so usually requires an in-depth understanding of exactly how the variables are calculated. If the correlation between a pair of variables is close to zero, this indicates that the variables contain completely different information regarding the underlying entities.

In addition to providing preliminary indications on the relations between the variables, correlation analysis can indicate potential issues associated with multivariate statistical analyses. For example, if two variables are very highly correlated, either positively or negatively, regression analyses that include both variables as independent variables in a regression specification may have difficulty distinguishing between the effect of one variable and the other on the dependent variable. This results in high standard errors on the regression coefficients. If the Spearman rank correlation is substantially larger in magnitude than the Pearson product–moment correlation, this likely indicates that there is a monotonic, but not linear, relation between the variables. This type of relation signals that linear regression analysis is a potentially problematic statistical technique to apply to the given variables if one of the variables is used as the dependent variable. If the Pearson product–moment correlation is substantially larger in magnitude than the Spearman rank correlation, this may indicate that there are a few extreme data points in one of the variables that are exerting a strong influence on the calculation of the Pearson product–moment correlation. In this case, it is possible that winsorizing one or both of the variables at a higher level will alleviate this issue. Finally, it is worth noting here that, because of the assumption of linearity in the calculation of the Pearson product–moment correlation, this measure is usually more indicative of results that will be realized using regression techniques such as Fama and MacBeth (1973) regression analysis (presented in Chapter 6). Because the Spearman rank correlation is based on the ordering of the variables, Spearman rank correlations are more likely indicative of the results of analyses that rely on the ranking, or ordering, of the variables, such as portfolio analysis (presented in Chapter 5).

The average Pearson product–moment correlation of 0.39 between β and *Size* indicates that larger stocks tend to have higher betas. Stated alternatively, this correlation indicates that stocks with high betas tend to be larger. That being said, the correlation is not so high as to indicate that the two variables are capturing essentially the same information. There is certainly a substantial component of β that is orthogonal to *Size* and a substantial component of *Size* that is orthogonal to β. Thus, while there is an economically important relation between beta and size, they certainly cannot be seen as the same. The average Spearman rank correlation between β and *Size* of 0.42 is quite similar to the Pearson product–moment correlation. The results also indicate an economically important negative relation between β and *BM*, since the Pearson product–moment (Spearman rank) correlation between these variables is -0.18 (-0.23). The magnitude of these correlations indicates once again that while there is a substantial common component to these variables, there is also a very substantial component of each of these variables that is orthogonal to the other. The same conclusions hold when examining the correlations between *Size* and *BM*. Once again, the Pearson product–moment correlation of -0.23 and Spearman rank correlation of -0.22 are very similar in magnitude and indicate a moderate negative cross-sectional relation between *Size* and *BM*. Thus, while each of these pairs of variables exhibit some cross-sectional correlation, the correlations are low enough to alleviate concerns about potential statistical issues when several of these variables are included in multivariate statistical analyses. Furthermore, the Pearson product–moment and Spearman rank measures are similar enough to alleviate any serious concerns about potential data issues or severe lack of linearity in the relations between these variables. It is important to realize that β, *Size*, and *BM* are all measured contemporaneously; thus, in the analysis of these correlations, the primary objective is to assess the information content of each of these variables. It is also important to realize that just because the magnitudes of the pairwise correlations are not high enough to raise concern about subsequent statistical analysis, it remains possible that some combination of two of these variables is highly correlated with a third variable (multicollinearity). Correlation analysis cannot detect such issues.

The one-year-ahead excess return (r_{t+1}) is measured in the year subsequent to the time at which each of the other variables (β, *Size*, and *BM*) are calculated. Thus, correlation between r_{t+1} and any of these variables is likely indicative of a predictive relation. Furthermore, because each of β, *BM*, and *Size* are calculated using information that is readily available in year t, and r_{t+1} is calculated using only information that is generated during year $t + 1$, we are not concerned about a potential mechanical effect between r_{t+1} and any of the other variables. The results in Table 3.2 indicate a slightly negative average Pearson and Spearman correlations of -0.04 between β and r_{t+1}, indicating that, in the average year, high β stocks may generate lower excess returns than low β stocks. While this result is inconsistent with the predictions of the Capital Asset Pricing Model of Sharpe (1964), Lintner (1965), and Mossin (1966), we will postpone in-depth economic analysis of this result until the chapter that studies the relation between β and future stock returns in depth (Chapter 8). The Pearson product–moment correlation between *Size* and r_{t+1} of -0.02 indicates almost no relation between *Size* and future excess stock returns, whereas the positive Spearman rank correlation of 0.06 indicates a slightly positive relation. While it is a little bit concerning that the two measures of correlation have, on average, the opposite sign, the magnitudes of these correlations are small enough so that we are not overly worried about this result. Finally, the results indicate a positive relation between *BM* and future stock returns, as the Pearson product–moment correlation of 0.06 and Spearman rank correlation of 0.08 are larger than any other correlation that includes r_{t+1}. It should be noted that, while the correlations between r_{t+1} and the other variables are all quite small in magnitude, as will be seen throughout the remainder of this text, what seems here to be only a minimal ability to predict future stock returns may be indicative of a very strong and important economic phenomenon.

3.3 PRESENTING CORRELATIONS

The standard way to present correlations is in a correlation matrix. Each row corresponds to one variable, indicated in the first column of the table. Similarly, each column corresponds to a variable, indicated in the first row of the table. The remaining entries in the table present the average cross-sectional correlations between the row and column variables. Diagonal entries, which represent the correlation between a variable and itself (equal to 1.00 by definition), are either left blank or the number 1.00 is displayed. In this book, we will leave these entries blank, as we feel that doing so makes for a cleaner presentation. If only the Pearson product–moment correlation is used, frequently only the entries below the diagonal or the entries above the diagonal entry are presented to avoid repetition. Here, and in the remainder of this book, we present both the average Pearson product–moment correlations and average Spearman rank correlations. The below-diagonal entries show the average Pearson product–moment correlations and the above-diagonal entries present the Spearman rank correlations. For the reasons discussed in the previous section, we feel it is valuable to present both types of correlations. Table 3.3 presents the average pairwise correlations between β, *Size*, *BM*, and r_{t+1} for our sample of stocks.

TABLE 3.3 Correlations Between β, *Size*, *BM*, and r_{t+1}
This table presents the time-series averages of the annual cross-sectional Pearson product–moment and Spearman rank correlations between pairs of β, *Size*, *BM*, and r_{t+1}. Below-diagonal entries present the average Pearson product–moment correlations. Above-diagonal entries present the average Spearman rank correlation.

	β	*Size*	*BM*	r_{t+1}
β		0.42	-0.23	-0.04
Size	0.39		-0.22	0.06
BM	-0.18	-0.23		0.08
r_{t+1}	-0.04	-0.02	0.06	

3.4 SUMMARY

In summary, correlation analysis gives us a first look at the relations between the variables used in a study. The procedure discussed in this chapter is designed to examine the cross-sectional correlation between pairs of variables, and the results presented are indicative of the relation between each pair of variables during the average period in the sample. We use two different measures of correlation. The first is the Pearson product–moment correlation, which is designed to indicate the strength of a linear relation between the two variables. The second is the Spearman rank correlation, which detects monotonicity in the relation between the two variables. Large differences between the two measures of correlation should be taken as indications that the data need to be examined in more depth to assess the cause of this difference.

REFERENCES

Fama, E. F. and MacBeth, J. D. 1973. Risk, return, and equilibrium: empirical tests. Journal of Political Economy, 81(3), 607.

Lintner, J. 1965. Security prices, risk, and maximal gains from diversification. Journal of Finance, 20(4), 687–615.

Mossin, J. 1966. Equilibrium in a capital asset market. Econometrica, 34(4), 768–783.

Sharpe, W. F. 1964. Capital asset prices: a theory of market equilibrium under conditions of risk. Journal of Finance, 19(3), 425–442.

4

PERSISTENCE ANALYSIS

Many of the variables in empirical asset pricing research are intended to capture persistent characteristics of the entities in the sample. This means that the characteristic of the entity that is captured by the given variable is assumed to remain reasonably stable over time. Such variables are frequently estimated using historical data, and the value calculated from the historical data is assumed to be a good estimate of the given characteristic for the entity going forward. For example, the value of a stock's beta from the Capital Asset Pricing Model (Sharpe (1964), Lintner (1965), Mossin (1966)) is generally assumed to be a persistent characteristic of the stock, and it is frequently estimated from regressions of the stock's returns on the returns of the market portfolio using historical data. This is exactly how our variable β is calculated.

In this chapter, we discuss a technique that we call persistence analysis. We use persistence analysis to examine whether a given characteristic of the entities in our sample is in fact persistent. Persistence analysis can also be used to examine the ability of the variable in question to capture the desired characteristic of the entity. The basic approach is to examine the cross-sectional correlation between the given variable measured at two different points in time. If this correlation is high, this indicates that the variable is persistent, whereas low correlations indicate little or no persistence. This technique is not as widely used in the empirical asset pricing literature as the other techniques presented in Part I. We discuss it here and use it throughout this text because one of the objectives of this book is to provide a thorough understanding of the variables most commonly used throughout the empirical asset pricing literature.

Empirical Asset Pricing: The Cross Section of Stock Returns, First Edition.
Turan G. Bali, Robert F. Engle, and Scott Murray.
© 2016 John Wiley & Sons, Inc. Published 2016 by John Wiley & Sons, Inc.

4.1 IMPLEMENTATION

As with the other methodologies presented in this text, implementation of persistence analysis is done in two steps. The first step involves calculating cross-sectional correlations between the given variable X measured a certain number of periods apart. The second step involves calculating the time-series average of each of these cross-sectional correlations.

4.1.1 Periodic Cross-Sectional Persistence

The first step in persistence analysis is to calculate the cross-sectional correlation between the variable under consideration, X, measured τ periods apart. This will be done for each time period t where both the time period t and the time period $t + \tau$ fall during the sample period. The entities used to calculate the cross-sectional correlation will be all entities i for which a valid value of the variable X is available for both period t and period $t + \tau$. For each time period t, we therefore define $\rho_{t,t+\tau}(X)$ as the cross-sectional Pearson product–moment correlation between X measured at time t and X measured at time $t + \tau$. Specifically, we have

$$\rho_{t,t+\tau}(X) = \frac{\sum_{i=1}^{n_t} [(X_{i,t} - \overline{X}_t)(X_{i,t+\tau} - \overline{X}_{t+\tau})]}{\sqrt{\sum_{i=1}^{n_t} (X_{i,t} - \overline{X}_t)^2} \sqrt{\sum_{i=1}^{n_t} (X_{i,t+\tau} - \overline{X}_{t+\tau})^2}} \tag{4.1}$$

where $\overline{X}_t$ is the mean value of $X_{i,t}$ and the summations and means are taken over all entities i for which a valid value of X is available in both periods t and $t + \tau$. n_t represents the number of such entities. Frequently, before the correlations are calculated, the values of X from month t are winsorized to remove the effect of outliers. The values of X from month $t + \tau$ are separately winsorized at the same level.

   We illustrate this using β and values of τ between 1 and 5 inclusive. Our analysis will therefore examine the persistence of β measured one, two, three, four, and five years apart. Prior to calculating the cross-sectional correlations for each period t, the data are winsorized at the 0.5% level. To be perfectly clear, for each month t, we first find all entities that have valid values of β in both periods t and $t + \tau$. We then winsorize the corresponding values of β in each of the months t and $t + \tau$ separately. The annual values for these cross-sectional correlations are presented in Table 4.1. The year t is presented in the first column and the subsequent columns present the values of $\rho_{t,t+\tau}(\beta)$ for $\tau \in \{1, 2, 3, 4, 5\}$.

   The results in Table 4.1 indicate that values of β measured one year apart $(\rho_{t,t+1}(\beta))$ exhibit cross-sectional correlations between 0.39 $(t = 1992)$ and 0.80 $(t = 2008)$. As might be expected, the correlations between β measured at longer lags τ tend to be lower than the correlations measured at shorter lags, although this is not always the case. When measured five years apart $(\rho_{t,t+5}(\beta))$, the table indicates that the correlation between β and its lagged counterpart is between 0.25 $(t = 2000)$ and 0.56 $(t = 2006)$. We withhold further interpretation of the results until later in the chapter.

TABLE 4.1   Annual Persistence of β

This table presents the cross-sectional Pearson product–moment correlations between β measured in year t and β measured in year $t + \tau$ for $\tau \in \{1, 2, 3, 4, 5\}$. The first column presents the year t. The subsequent columns present the cross-sectional correlations between β measured at time t and β measured at time $t + 1$, $t + 2$, $t + 3$, $t + 4$, and $t + 5$.

t	$\rho_{t,t+1}(\beta)$	$\rho_{t,t+2}(\beta)$	$\rho_{t,t+3}(\beta)$	$\rho_{t,t+4}(\beta)$	$\rho_{t,t+5}(\beta)$
1988	0.50	0.48	0.47	0.39	0.34
1989	0.52	0.45	0.38	0.35	0.36
1990	0.55	0.45	0.42	0.40	0.37
1991	0.46	0.43	0.41	0.37	0.40
1992	0.39	0.37	0.36	0.41	0.38
1993	0.40	0.33	0.38	0.39	0.39
1994	0.38	0.39	0.38	0.37	0.33
1995	0.46	0.44	0.38	0.40	0.48
1996	0.53	0.48	0.43	0.52	0.53
1997	0.55	0.46	0.48	0.51	0.53
1998	0.51	0.50	0.53	0.53	0.50
1999	0.57	0.59	0.53	0.52	0.40
2000	0.79	0.58	0.56	0.58	0.25
2001	0.70	0.66	0.62	0.35	0.41
2002	0.79	0.64	0.50	0.49	0.38
2003	0.70	0.54	0.51	0.42	0.39
2004	0.62	0.60	0.45	0.38	0.34
2005	0.73	0.60	0.55	0.48	0.53
2006	0.67	0.56	0.50	0.56	0.56
2007	0.69	0.60	0.60	0.59	0.51
2008	0.80	0.69	0.64	0.60	
2009	0.73	0.65	0.59		
2010	0.76	0.70			
2011	0.79				

However, it is worth noting that for years t toward the end of the sample, in some cases the persistence values are missing. The reason for this is that, for example, in year 2009, to calculate the correlation between β measured in 2009 and β measured four years in the future ($\tau = 4$), we would need data from year 2013. As these data are not available in the version of the Center for Research in Security Prices (CRSP) database used to construct the methodology sample, we are unable to calculate this value. The reasons for the other missing entries are analogous.

4.1.2 Average Cross-Sectional Persistence

Although periodic cross-sectional persistence values such as those presented in Table 4.1 are quite informative, they are quite difficult to read and draw conclusions from. We therefore want to summarize these periodic values more succinctly. As with the other analyses we discuss, the main objective is to understand the persistence of the variable X in the average cross section. We therefore summarize the results by simply taking the time-series average of the periodic cross-sectional correlations. We denote these average persistence values using $\rho_\tau(X)$ where the subscript indicates the number of lags. Specifically, we have

$$\rho_\tau(X) = \frac{\sum_{t=1}^{N-\tau} \rho_{t,t+\tau}(X)}{N - \tau} \qquad (4.2)$$

where N is the number of periods in the sample. Throughout the remainder of this book, we will refer to these values as the persistence of X at lag τ.

In Table 4.2, we present the persistence of β at lags of one, two, three, four, and five years. The results indicate that, consistent with what was observed in the annual persistence values presented in Table 4.1, the persistence of values of β measured one year apart, 0.62, is quite strong. The level of persistence drops off substantially as the amount of time between the measurement periods increases. When measured at a lag of 5 years, the average persistence of β has decreased to 0.42.

4.2 INTERPRETING PERSISTENCE

Interpreting the results of the persistence analyses is fairly straightforward. In general, a higher degree of time-lagged cross-sectional correlation in the given variable is indicative of higher persistence, although there are several caveats to this that must be understood to properly make use of this technique.

We begin our discussion of the interpretation of persistence analysis results by discussing potential causes of low persistence. Exactly what qualifies as low persistence is not perfectly well defined and depends on how long the lag is between the times of measurement (τ), how persistent the actual characteristic being captured by the variable is thought to be, and how accurately the variable is expected to capture the actual characteristic. There are generally two reasons that a variable may exhibit low or zero persistence. The first is that the characteristic being measured is in fact

TABLE 4.2 Average Persistence of β
This table presents the time-series averages of the cross-sectional Pearson product–moment correlations between β measured in year t and β measured in year $t + \tau$ for $\tau \in \{1, 2, 3, 4, 5\}$.

$\rho_1(\beta)$	$\rho_2(\beta)$	$\rho_3(\beta)$	$\rho_4(\beta)$	$\rho_5(\beta)$
0.61	0.53	0.48	0.46	0.42

not persistent. The second is that the variable used to proxy for the given characteristic does a poor job at measuring the characteristic under examination. In this case, even if the given characteristic of the entities in the sample is highly cross-sectionally persistent, the failure of the variable X to capture cross-sectional variation in this characteristic will cause the persistence analysis to generate a low value of $\rho_\tau(X)$. In this sense, the persistence analysis suffers from a dual hypothesis problem, as failure to find persistence does not necessarily indicate a lack of persistence in the characteristic under investigation. Low values of $\rho_\tau(X)$ may also indicate a failure of X to capture that characteristic. Thus, we must be careful when concluding that a certain characteristic of the entities in the sample is not cross-sectionally persistent based on the results of the persistence analysis. To reach such a conclusion, we must be highly confident that the variable X does in fact capture the characteristic under examination. On the other hand, if one is extremely confident, for reasons beyond the scope of the persistence analysis, that the characteristic in question is in fact highly cross-sectionally persistent, low values of $\rho_{t,t+\tau}(X)$ likely indicate that the variable X does a poor job at capturing cross-sectional variation in the characteristic. In the end, however, regardless of the reason for the lack of persistence in X, if X is intended to capture a persistent characteristic of a firm, but X does not exhibit persistence, then X is not a good measure of the characteristic of interest.

When the persistence analysis produces high values of $\rho_\tau(X)$, this very likely indicates both that the characteristic in question is in fact persistent and that the variable X does a good job at measuring the characteristic. There are two caveats with this statement that must be addressed. The first is that it is possible that the variable X is unintentionally capturing some persistent characteristic of the entities in the sample that is different from the characteristic that X is designed to capture. Thus, perhaps a more correct statement is that high values of $\rho_\tau(X)$ indicate that whatever characteristic is being captured by X is in fact persistent. If X does in fact capture the intended characteristic, then we can conclude that the characteristic is in fact persistent. Therefore, assuming sufficient effort has been devoted to designing the calculation of X such that it can reasonably be expected to capture the intended characteristic, high values of $\rho_\tau(X)$ are interpreted as indicating that the given characteristic is in fact persistent.

The second, and much more important, caveat associated with concluding that a characteristic is persistent is that in many cases there is a mechanical reason related to the calculation of X that would result in strong cross-sectional correlation between X_t and $X_{t+\tau}$ even if the characteristic in question is not persistent. In most cases, the reason for such a mechanical effect is that some subset of the data used to calculate X at times t and $t + \tau$ are the same. This is frequently the case when a variable is calculated from historical data covering more than τ periods. For example, if X_t is calculated using k periods of historical data up to and including period t, where $k > \tau$, then X_t and $X_{t+\tau}$ are calculated using some of the same data and are therefore likely to be correlated in the cross section as a result. For this reason, when X is calculated using k periods of historical data, persistence analysis is only effective when $\tau \geq k$.

In addition to examining whether a given characteristic of the entities in the sample is cross-sectionally persistent, persistence analysis can also be helpful in determining the optimal measurement period that should be used to calculate a given variable. Many of the variables used throughout the empirical asset pricing literature are calculated based on historical data. When calculating these variables, researchers are faced with the decision of how long a calculation period to use. Increasing the length of the calculation period means that more data are used in the calculation of the variable, which can increase the accuracy of the measurement. However, using longer calculation periods also means that when calculating the variable for time period t, data from many periods prior to t are used, and this data may no longer be reflective of the given characteristic of the entity at time t. For this reason, extending the calculation period too long may result in decreasing accuracy of measurement. How to optimally make this trade-off depends on the persistence of the characteristic being measured. While certainly none of the variables studied in asset pricing research are perfectly persistent, different variables exhibit different degrees of persistence.

To help determine the optimal calculation period for a variable calculated from historical data, we can examine the patterns in the persistence of the variable measured using different calculation periods. The main concept behind this application of persistence analysis is that the cross-sectional persistence of even the most persistent characteristic is likely to decay over time. Therefore, let us assume we have two variables X_1 and X_2 that measure the same characteristic using the same formula but applied to different calculation periods of length τ_1 and τ_2, respectively, and without loss of generality, let $\tau_1 > \tau_2$. Let us also make the assumption that X^1 and X^2 are equally accurate measures of the given characteristic.

If X^1 and X^2 are equally accurate measures of the characteristic, then based on the assumed decay in persistence as the value of τ increases, we would expect the persistence of X^1 measured at a lag of $\tau = \tau_1$ to be greater than the persistence of X^2 measured at lag $\tau = \tau_2$. Notice here that the lag at which the comparison of the persistence is done is such that neither analysis has the overlapping data issue discussed earlier. If the persistence of X_2 at lag $\tau = \tau_2$ is actually greater than that of X_1 at lag $\tau = \tau_1$, this is a contradiction of what would be expected if X_1 and X_2 were equally accurate measures. This therefore indicates that using τ_2 periods of data to calculate X provides a more accurate measure of the underlying characteristic than using τ_1 periods, as the additional amount of data used in the calculation apparently overcomes the decay in the persistence at longer lags τ.

If the persistence of X^2 at lag $\tau = \tau_2$ is less than that of X^1 at lag $\tau = \tau_1$, the results are a bit more challenging to interpret, but it can generally be taken to mean that the decay in the persistence over a period of $\tau_2 - \tau_1$ periods is substantial enough to overcome any additional benefit of using τ_2 periods of data, compared to τ_1, to calculate X. If this is the case, it may also be an indication that using a full τ_2 periods of data is too long a measurement period because the given characteristic of the firm does in fact change substantially over periods of length τ_2.

There is a practical consideration that may have an effect on using persistence to determine the optimal measurement period for the given variable X. This consideration is that the sample changes over time. The calculation of the value of $\rho_{t,t+\tau}(X)$ is done using only those entities that are in the sample at both times t and $t + \tau$. In most cases, the set of entities in the sample at both time t and time $t + \tau_1$ is likely to be a superset of the set of entities in the sample at both time t and time $t + \tau_2$ ($\tau_2 > \tau_1$). Furthermore, in many cases, the set of entities that remain in the sample until time $t + \tau_2$ is likely to be more "well-behaved" than those that do not remain in the sample, where well-behaved can be taken to mean that the calculation of the variable X is a more accurate measure of the characteristic being examined for such entities than for entities that are not well-behaved. If these not well-behaved entities are more likely to enter and then drop out of the sample over a small number of periods, it is possible that using persistence analysis to examine the quality of a variable as described in this section may be misleading. That being said, for the analyses performed in this text this is unlikely to be a substantial issue, as the number of entities (stocks in this case) in each cross section is quite large relative to the number of stocks that drop out of the sample each period.

4.3 PRESENTING PERSISTENCE

Throughout this book, we will present the results of persistence analyses by displaying the values of $\rho_\tau(X)$. Each column in the tables that present the persistence analysis results will correspond to a given variable, indicated in the first row of the column. Each row will correspond to a given value of τ.

The results of persistence analyses for each of β, Size, and BM using lags of one, two, three, four, and five years are presented in Table 4.3. The results indicate that all three variables are highly persistent. The persistence of β measured at lag of one year ($\tau = 1$) is 0.61 and that of Size is 0.96, and for BM the persistence at lag of one year is 0.74. The results for each of these variables indicate fairly strong persistence at lags of up to five years. Size is very highly persistent, as the average cross-sectional

TABLE 4.3 Persistence of β, Size, and BM

This table presents the results of persistence analyses of β, Size, and BM. For each year t, the cross-sectional correlation between the given variable measured at time t and the same variable measured at time $t + \tau$ is calculated. The table presents the time-series averages of the annual cross-sectional correlations. The column labeled τ indicates the lag at which the persistence is measured.

τ	β	Size	BM
1	0.61	0.96	0.74
2	0.53	0.92	0.59
3	0.48	0.90	0.50
4	0.46	0.89	0.46
5	0.42	0.88	0.43

correlation between *Size* measured five years apart is 0.88, only slightly lower than when the persistence is measured at a lag of one year. The decay in the persistence of β and *BM* is substantially more pronounced, but even after five years, β and *BM* continue to exhibit substantial persistence.

4.4 SUMMARY

In this chapter, we have presented a methodology for examining the persistence of a given variable. The methodology has two primary applications. If we assume that the variable accurately measures the characteristic that it is intended to capture, then persistence analysis can be used to examine how persistent the given characteristic is in the cross section of the entities in the sample. If we assume the characteristic that the variable is intended to measure is in fact persistent, then we can use persistence analysis to examine the accuracy with which the variable captures the given characteristic and the optimal measurement period to use when calculating the variable. Of course, no characteristic is perfectly persistent and no variable perfectly captures the characteristic it is designed to measure. Despite these caveats, persistence analysis is a useful tool that we will employ throughout this text.

REFERENCES

Lintner, J. 1965. Security prices, risk, and maximal gains from diversification. Journal of Finance, 20(4), 687–615.

Mossin, J. 1966. Equilibrium in a capital asset market. Econometrica, 34(4), 768–783.

Sharpe, W. F. 1964. Capital asset prices: a theory of market equilibrium under conditions of risk. Journal of Finance, 19(3), 425–442.

5

PORTFOLIO ANALYSIS

Portfolio analysis is one of the most commonly used statistical methodologies in empirical asset pricing. Its objective is to examine the cross-sectional relation between two or more variables. The most frequent application of portfolio analysis is to examine the ability of one or more variables to predict future stock returns. The general approach is to form portfolios of stocks, where the stocks in each portfolio have different levels of the variable or variables posited to predict cross-sectional variation in future returns and to examine the returns of these portfolios.

While the most common application of portfolio analysis is to examine future return predictability, the portfolio methodology can also be employed to understand cross-sectional relations between any set of variables. This is useful for understanding variation in the characteristics of the entities (stocks) across the different portfolios. Thus, in the very general sense, portfolio analysis is useful for understanding the cross-sectional relation between one variable and combinations of other variables.

Perhaps the most important benefit of portfolio analysis is that it is a nonparametric technique. This means that it does not make any assumptions about the nature of the cross-sectional relations between the variables under investigation. Many other methodologies rely on some assumptions regarding the functional form of the relation between the variables being examined. For example, linear regression analysis assumes that the relation between the dependent and independent variables is linear. Portfolio analysis does not require this assumption. In fact, portfolio analysis can be helpful in uncovering nonlinear relations between variables that are quite difficult to detect using parametric techniques. Perhaps the

Empirical Asset Pricing: The Cross Section of Stock Returns, First Edition.
Turan G. Bali, Robert F. Engle, and Scott Murray.
© 2016 John Wiley & Sons, Inc. Published 2016 by John Wiley & Sons, Inc.

main drawback of the technique is that it is difficult to control for a large number of variables when examining the cross-sectional relation of interest. This compares to regression analysis in which it is easy to control for a large number of independent variables in the analysis.

In this chapter, we present and exemplify the details of implementing a portfolio analysis and interpreting the results. There are several different variations of portfolio analysis. While some researchers have implemented variations that are not covered in this chapter, the vast majority of portfolio analyses in empirical asset pricing research follow one of the approaches discussed herein.

Throughout this chapter, we use Y to denote the outcome variable of the portfolio analysis. Y can be thought of as the variable of interest, similar to the dependent variable in a regression analysis. We use X to denote the sort variable or variables. X is analogous to the independent variable or variables in a regression. We refer to Y and X the outcome and sort variables, respectively, to avoid confusion in our presentation of independent and dependent sorts, discussed in Sections 5.2 and 5.3, respectively. We demonstrate the portfolio methodology using the methodology sample described in Section 1.1.

5.1 UNIVARIATE PORTFOLIO ANALYSIS

We begin with the most basic type of portfolio analysis: univariate portfolio analysis. A univariate portfolio analysis has only one sort variable X. The objective of the analysis is to assess the cross-sectional relation between X and the outcome variable Y. A univariate portfolio analysis does not allow us to control for any other effects when examining this relation.

The univariate portfolio analysis procedure has four steps. The first step is to calculate the breakpoints that will be used to divide the sample into portfolios. The second step is to use these breakpoints to form the portfolios. The third step is to calculate the average value of the outcome variable Y within each portfolio for each period t. The fourth step is to examine variation in these average values of Y across the different portfolios.

5.1.1 Breakpoints

The first step in univariate portfolio analysis is to calculate the periodic breakpoints that will be used to group the entities in the sample into portfolios based on values of the sort variable X. Entities with values of X that are less than the first breakpoint will be placed into the first portfolio. Entities with values of X that are between the first and second breakpoints will comprise the second portfolio, etc. Finally, entities with X values higher than the highest breakpoint will be placed in the last portfolio. We denote the number of portfolios to be formed each time period as n_P. The number of breakpoints that need to be calculated each period is therefore $n_P - 1$. The number of portfolios to be formed and, thus, the number of breakpoints to be calculated is the same for all time periods. The value of the kth breakpoint, however, will almost certainly vary from time period to time period. We denote the kth breakpoint for period t as $B_{k,t}$ for $k \in \{1, 2, \ldots, n_P - 1\}$.

The breakpoints for period t are determined by percentiles of the time t cross-sectional distribution of the sort variable X. Specifically, letting p_k be the percentile that determines the kth breakpoint, the kth breakpoint for period t is calculated as the p_kth percentile of the values of X across all entities in the sample for which X is available in period t. We therefore define the breakpoints as

$$B_{k,t} = Pctl_{p_k}(\{X_t\}) \tag{5.1}$$

where $Pctl_p(Z)$ is the pth percentile of the set Z and $\{X_t\}$ represents the set of valid values of the sort variable X across all entities i in the sample in time period t. The percentiles, and thus the breakpoints, increase as k increases, giving $0 < p_1 < p_2 < \cdots < p_{np-1}$ and $B_{1,t} \leq B_{2,t} \leq \cdots \leq B_{np-1,t}$ for all periods t. While the chosen percentiles $(p_1, p_2, \ldots, p_{np-1})$ are required to be strictly increasing, this does not necessarily mean that the actual breakpoints, calculated as the chosen percentile values of X, are strictly increasing. In some cases, there may be a large number of entities for which the values of X are the same, causing two or more of the breakpoints to be the same. If the variable X is truly continuous, the probability of this happening should be zero. However, there are examples of variables used in asset pricing research that at first glance would appear to be continuous but actually have many entities for which the value of the variable is the same.

It is worth mentioning here that, in some cases, breakpoints are calculated using only a subset of the entities that are in the sample for the given period t. For example, in research where the entities are stocks, sometimes researchers form breakpoints using only stocks that trade on the New York Stock Exchange, and then use those breakpoints to sort all stocks in the sample (including stocks that trade on other exchanges) into portfolios. Thus, in the previous paragraph as well as for the remainder of Section 5.1.1, when we refer to the sample, what we actually mean is the subset of the full sample that is being used to calculate the breakpoints. In most cases, this subset is the entire sample, but there are many examples where a strict subset is used. It is for this reason that we consider the calculation of breakpoints and the formation of portfolios, two separate steps in the portfolio analysis procedure.

Choosing an appropriate number of portfolios and choosing appropriate percentiles for the breakpoints are important decisions in portfolio analysis. As the entities in the sample will eventually be grouped into portfolios based on the breakpoints, the decision is largely based on trading off the number of entities in each portfolio against the dispersion of the sort variable among the portfolios. As the number of portfolios increases, the number of entities in each portfolio decreases, and vice versa. When the average value of the outcome variable Y for each portfolio is eventually calculated (the average value of Y is the focal point of the portfolio analysis and will be discussed in Section 5.1.3), a small number of entities in each portfolio results in increased noise when using the sample mean value of Y as an estimate of the true mean. Thus, having a large number of entities in each portfolio increases the accuracy of our estimate of the true mean value for each portfolio and is thus desirable. On the other hand, the more entities we group into each portfolio, the smaller the number of portfolios and the smaller the dispersion in the sort variable

X among the portfolios. Decreased dispersion in X across the portfolios can make it more difficult to detect cross-sectional relations between X and Y, as the values of X in the portfolios may not differ substantially if we have too few portfolios.

Most commonly, portfolios are formed using breakpoints that represent evenly spaced percentiles of the cross-sectional distribution of the sort variable. This means that the $n_P - 1$ breakpoints are defined to be the $k \times (1/n_P)$ percentiles of X, where $k \in \{1, \ldots, n_P - 1\}$. For example, if we want to split the sample into five portfolios, we may use the 20th, 40th, 60th, and 80th percentiles of the sort variable as the portfolio breakpoints. While the evenly spaced percentile approach to calculating breakpoints is most common, other approaches have been used. For example, when splitting the sample into only three portfolios, it is common to use the 30th and 70th percentiles of the sort variable as the breakpoints.

In choosing the number of portfolios and breakpoint percentiles, it is important to remember that new portfolios are formed for each time period t. Thus, when assessing the number of entities that fall into each portfolio, it is important to look not only at the average number of entities in the sample during the different time periods t but also at the minimum number of entities in any time period. The number of entities that will put into each portfolio is easily determined by the number of entities in the sample and the percentiles used to calculate the breakpoints. When the breakpoints are determined by equally spaced percentiles, the number of entities in each portfolio for any given time period t will be the number of entities in the sample for that time period divided by the number of portfolios. In the general sense, the minimum number of entities in any portfolio in a given time period t will be the number of entities in the sample during time period t, which we denote n_t, multiplied by the minimum of the lowest percentile, the differences between successive percentiles, and one minus the highest percentile. The exception to these cases is when the sample used to calculate the breakpoints is a strict subset of the set of entities that will be placed in the portfolios. In this case, the minimum number of entities in a portfolio will be higher. Finally, almost all studies use between three and 20 portfolios, with most researchers choosing either five or 10.

To exemplify the calculation of breakpoints in univariate portfolio analysis, we use the methodology sample discussed in Section 1.1 and take β to be the sort variable. Our analysis uses seven portfolios ($n_P = 7$) and thus six breakpoints will be calculated each year. The breakpoints will be the 10th, 20th, 40th, 60th, 80th, and 90th percentiles of β. We choose uneven breakpoints simply to exemplify the flexibility of the portfolio procedure. In some cases, researchers choose to make the distance between the percentiles that determine the breakpoints smaller for the lowest and highest portfolios because doing so can help us understand whether the relation under investigation is stronger for entities with extreme (low or high) values of the sort variables X. It is not uncommon in the empirical finance literature for a cross-sectional phenomenon to be driven by a small number of stocks with extreme values of one of the variables under investigation.

The results of the calculation of the breakpoints are presented in Table 5.1. The table shows that, for example, breakpoints one, two, three, four, five, and six for year

37

TABLE 5.1 Univariate Breakpoints for β-Sorted Portfolios
This table presents breakpoints for β-sorted portfolios. Each year t, the first $(B_{1,t})$, second $(B_{2,t})$, third $(B_{3,t})$, fourth $(B_{4,t})$, fifth $(B_{5,t})$, and sixth $(B_{6,t})$ breakpoints for portfolios sorted on β are calculated as the 10th, 20th, 40th, 60th, 80th, and 90th percentiles, respectively, of the cross-sectional distribution of β. Each row in the table presents the breakpoints for the year indicated in the first column. The subsequent columns present the values of the breakpoints indicated in the first row.

t	$B_{1,t}$	$B_{2,t}$	$B_{3,t}$	$B_{4,t}$	$B_{5,t}$	$B_{6,t}$
1988	−0.05	0.07	0.29	0.51	0.86	1.11
1989	−0.11	0.05	0.29	0.54	0.89	1.17
1990	−0.06	0.10	0.37	0.68	1.07	1.37
1991	−0.09	0.09	0.38	0.67	1.05	1.33
1992	−0.22	0.08	0.42	0.77	1.23	1.66
1993	−0.21	0.10	0.44	0.73	1.18	1.55
1994	−0.05	0.19	0.52	0.81	1.19	1.56
1995	−0.17	0.10	0.42	0.71	1.16	1.65
1996	0.00	0.19	0.46	0.73	1.14	1.52
1997	−0.00	0.15	0.36	0.59	0.89	1.15
1998	0.13	0.28	0.54	0.79	1.13	1.38
1999	−0.06	0.06	0.24	0.42	0.70	0.99
2000	0.03	0.14	0.37	0.63	1.22	1.79
2001	0.05	0.18	0.46	0.76	1.23	1.75
2002	0.04	0.17	0.48	0.75	1.06	1.37
2003	0.05	0.22	0.54	0.83	1.16	1.46
2004	0.14	0.40	0.81	1.16	1.56	1.96
2005	0.09	0.33	0.80	1.14	1.49	1.74
2006	0.10	0.35	0.82	1.21	1.64	1.94
2007	0.13	0.33	0.75	1.04	1.33	1.54
2008	0.16	0.38	0.74	1.02	1.31	1.54
2009	0.24	0.45	0.84	1.23	1.70	2.06
2010	0.29	0.56	0.92	1.19	1.49	1.72
2011	0.26	0.56	0.99	1.25	1.52	1.73
2012	0.28	0.55	0.91	1.18	1.48	1.75

1988 are −0.05, 0.07, 0.29, 0.51, 0.86, and 1.11, respectively. These are the break-points that will be used to sort stocks into portfolios at the end of year 1988. As necessitated by the calculation, the breakpoints are increasing across the columns for each year t.

5.1.2 Portfolio Formation

Having calculated the breakpoints, the next step in univariate portfolio analysis is to group the entities in the sample into portfolios. Each time period t, all entities in the sample with values of the sort variable X that are less than or equal to the first breakpoint, $B_{1,t}$, are put in portfolio one. Portfolio two holds entities with values of X that are greater than or equal to the first breakpoint and less than or equal to the second breakpoint. Portfolio three holds entities with values of X greater than or equal to the second breakpoint and less than or equal to the third breakpoint, and so on. Finally, portfolio n_P holds entities with values of X that are greater than or equal to $B_{n_p-1,t}$. In general, portfolio k holds entities i with period t values of the sort variable, $X_{i,t}$, that are greater than or equal to the $k-1$st breakpoint $B_{k-1,t}$ and less than or equal to the jth breakpoint $B_{k,t}$ for $k \in \{1, \ldots, n_P\}$, where we define $B_{0,t} = -\infty$ and $B_{n_P,t} = \infty$. Thus, letting $P_{k,t}$ be the set of entities in the kth portfolio formed at the end of period t, we have

$$P_{k,t} = \{i | B_{k-1,t} \leq X_{i,t} \leq B_{k,t}\} \qquad (5.2)$$

for $k \in \{1, 2, \ldots, n_P\}$. We refer to $P_{k,t}$ as the kth portfolio or portfolio k for period t.

Forming portfolios as such puts all entities with the lowest values of the sort variable $X_{i,t}$ in portfolio one and all entities with the highest values of the $X_{i,t}$ in the last (n_Pth) portfolio, with values of $X_{i,t}$ increasing as the portfolio number increases. As discussed earlier, it is not necessary that the set of entities that is grouped into the portfolios is the same as the set of entities that is used to calculate the breakpoints. Once the breakpoints are calculated, they can be applied to any set of entities, whether it is a superset, subset, or the same set as was used to calculate the breakpoints. We should also point out that when forming the portfolios, if a given entity has a value of X during time period t that is exactly equal to the kth breakpoint, $B_{k,t}$, then this entity is included in both portfolio k and portfolio $k + 1$. We define the portfolios in this manner for a good reason. The reason is that, as discussed previously, it is possible that two (or more) consecutive breakpoints have exactly the same value. This occurs when there are a large number of entities with the same value of X in period t. In such situations, if we had defined the portfolios using a strict inequality for either the lower or upper values of X, then one or more of the portfolios would contain no entities. For example, imagine that we are sorting stocks into decile portfolios (the breakpoints are the 10th, 20th, 30th, ... , 90th percentiles) based on past returns, but the 30th and 40th percentile of past returns are both zero in the given period t, meaning that breakpoints 3 and 4 would both be zero. If the stocks in the fourth portfolio are those that have returns that are greater than the third breakpoint, which is zero, and less than or equal to the fourth breakpoints, which is also zero, then there would be no stocks in the fourth portfolio. To alleviate this issue, we define the portfolios to be inclusive of entities with values of X that are equal to either the low breakpoint or the high breakpoint that define the portfolio. The ramification of this is that, in this situation, there will be some entities that are included in more than one portfolio. We consider this issue to be minor compared to the issues that arise when a portfolio has no entities. That being said, as a researcher, if such a situation arises in your analysis, special attention should be paid to ensuring that this does not have an important impact on any of the conclusions drawn from the portfolio analysis.

When the set of entities used to calculate the breakpoints is the same as the set of entities that are grouped into portfolios, the number of entities in each of the portfolios should be approximately dictated by the percentiles used to calculate the breakpoints and the number of stocks in the sample during the given period t. We say "approximately" because, as mentioned earlier, if the value of X for a given entity i is exactly

TABLE 5.2   Number of Stocks per Portfolio
This table presents the number of stocks in each of the portfolios formed in each year during the sample period. The column labeled t indicates the year. The subsequent columns, labeled $n_{k,t}$ for $k \in \{1, 2, \ldots, 7\}$ present the number of stocks in the kth portfolio.

t	$n_{1,t}$	$n_{2,t}$	$n_{3,t}$	$n_{4,t}$	$n_{5,t}$	$n_{6,t}$	$n_{7,t}$
1988	569	569	1138	1138	1138	569	569
1989	552	552	1104	1103	1104	552	552
1990	541	541	1082	1081	1082	541	541
1991	531	530	1060	1061	1061	529	531
1992	539	539	1078	1077	1078	539	539
1993	567	567	1134	1134	1134	567	567
1994	615	615	1229	1230	1229	615	615
1995	629	629	1257	1258	1257	629	629
1996	659	658	1317	1318	1316	659	659
1997	687	687	1373	1373	1373	687	687
1998	661	661	1321	1322	1321	661	661
1999	610	610	1219	1219	1219	610	610
2000	591	590	1180	1180	1180	589	591
2001	551	551	1101	1102	1101	551	551
2002	510	510	1020	1019	1020	510	510
2003	474	474	947	947	947	474	474
2004	458	457	915	914	915	457	458
2005	450	449	899	899	898	450	450
2006	446	445	890	891	890	445	446
2007	434	433	866	866	866	433	434
2008	427	426	853	853	852	426	427
2009	398	398	795	795	795	398	398
2010	381	380	761	761	761	380	381
2011	369	368	736	736	736	368	369
2012	355	354	709	709	709	354	355

equal to one of the breakpoints, then because the portfolios are constructed to be inclusive of the breakpoints at both the low and high ends of X, the entity i will be held in more than one portfolio.

Table 5.2 presents the number of stocks in each of the portfolios for each year t in our example sample. As expected, as the 10th percentile is used to calculate the first breakpoint, approximately 10% of the stocks. Similarly, the second, sixth, and seventh portfolios each hold approximately 10% of the stocks in each cross section. Portfolios three, four, and five each hold approximately 20% of the stocks in the sample.

5.1.3   Average Portfolio Values

The third step in univariate portfolio analysis is to calculate the average value of the outcome variable Y for each of the n_P portfolios in each time period t. In many cases, instead of taking the simple average of the outcome variable values, it is desirable to weight the entities within each portfolio according to some other variable $W_{i,t}$. The most commonly used weight variable is market capitalization. In cases where market capitalization is used as the weight variable, the average is referred to as the value-weighted average.[1] When a simple average is desired, the values of the $W_{i,t}$ are set to one ($W_{i,t} = 1 \; \forall i, t$). In this case, we refer to the portfolios as equal-weighted portfolios. This is equivalent to giving a weight of $1/n_t$ to each entity. Thus, in its general form, the average value of the outcome variable for portfolio k in period t is defined as

$$\overline{Y}_{k,t} = \frac{\sum_{i \in P_{k,t}} W_{i,t} Y_{i,t}}{\sum_{i \in P_{k,t}} W_{i,t}} \tag{5.3}$$

for $k \in \{1, \ldots, n_P\}$. The summations in equation (5.3) are taken over all entities i in the kth portfolio for time period t ($P_{k,t}$).

A few details are worthy of discussion. Given that the grouping of entities into portfolios was performed without any consideration for whether a value of Y is available for each of the entities in the portfolio, it is possible, and in practice quite common, that there will be some entities i in any given portfolio $P_{k,t}$ for which the value of Y is not available. In this case, the set over which the average is taken should be the set of entities i in $P_{k,t}$ for which a value of Y is available. A similar consideration arises when the portfolio weights are not equal but are determined by some other variable W. In this case, the summation is taken over all entities i for which values of both W and Y are available.

In addition to calculating the average value of the outcome variable ($\overline{Y}$) for each portfolio, we also calculate the difference in average values between portfolio n_P and portfolio one. For each period t, we define the difference in the average outcome variable between the highest and lowest portfolios to be

$$\overline{Y}_{Diff,t} = \overline{Y}_{n_P,t} - \overline{Y}_{1,t}. \tag{5.4}$$

This value represents the difference in the average value of the outcome variable Y for entities with high values of the sort variable compared to those with low values of the sort variable. This difference in averages is the primary value used to detect a cross-sectional relation between the sort variable and the outcome variable,

---

[1] Value-weighting is most appropriate when the entities in the analysis are stocks. In such cases, the results of equal-weighted analyses are indicative of phenomena for the average stock. The results of value-weighted analyses account for the importance, from the point of view of the stock market as a whole, of each individual stock relative to the other stocks in the given portfolio. When the outcome variables (Y) is the future stock return, the results of value-weighted analyses are generally considered to be more indicative of return that an investor would have realized by implementing the portfolio in question. The reason for this is that value-weighted portfolios have large weights on stocks with large market capitalizations, which tend to be highly liquid. The returns of equal-weighted portfolios are potentially driven by the low-market capitalization stocks in the portfolio, which are more expensive to trade. The result is often that the average return indicated by the portfolio analysis cannot be realized by an actual investor because of transaction costs.

which is the main objective of portfolio analysis. We frequently refer to the difference between the average value of the n_pth portfolio and the average value of the first portfolio as the average value of the difference portfolio.

Turning to our example, we use the one-year-ahead excess stock return (r_{t+1}) as our outcome variable. Because r_{t+1} represents the excess return of the stock in the year after the calculation of β (the sort variable), the average excess stock returns represent the excess returns that would have been realized by an investor who, at the end of year t, created the portfolios as described previously and held the portfolios without further trading for the entirety of year $t + 1$. To be specific, the timing of the portfolio formation is as follows. At the end of each year t, we calculate β for each stock and form seven different portfolios as described earlier. We then enter into positions as indicated by these portfolios. The prices paid for each of the stocks are the prices as of the close of the last trading day during year t. We hold the portfolios unchanged until the end of year $t + 1$, at which point all portfolios are liquidated at the closing prices on the last trading day of year $t + 1$. We repeat the procedure for each year t. We refer to the year t as the portfolio formation period and the year $t + 1$ as the portfolio holding period. Because r_{t+1} is the excess stock return, we assume that all positions are financed by borrowing at the risk-free rate.

Table 5.3 presents the average equal-weighted portfolio excess returns for each of the seven portfolios as well as for the difference between portfolio seven and portfolio one. To make the timing clear, in the table, we present both the portfolio formation year (column labeled t) and the portfolio holding year (column labeled $t + 1$). As can be seen from the table, the portfolio that holds stocks in the lowest decile of β (portfolio 1) as of the end of 1988 generated an excess return of -0.97% during 1989. Similarly, portfolios two through seven generated excess returns of 1.12%, 2.12%, 6.77%, 3.18%, 9.04%, and 8.96%. The difference in excess return between portfolios seven and one is 9.93% (8.96% $-$ [-0.97%]). The corresponding values for portfolios formed at the end of (held during) year 1989 through 2011 (1990 through 2012) are also presented. As the return data for year 2013 are not available in the version of the Center for Research in Security Prices (CRSP) database used to construct the methodology sample, we cannot determine the 2013 excess returns of the portfolios that are formed at the end of year 2012.

We now repeat the analysis using value-weighted portfolios. Thus, the weights in each of the portfolios are determined by the market capitalization (*MktCap*) measured as of the end of the portfolio formation year t. Table 5.4 presents the average portfolio excess returns for the value-weighted portfolios. As can be seen from the results, the weighting scheme can have a substantial impact of the average portfolio returns. This will become much more apparent in the analyses presented throughout Part II.

5.1.4 Summarizing the Results

The main objective of portfolio analysis is to determine whether there is a cross-sectional relation between the sort variable X and the outcome variable Y. To do so, we begin by calculating the time-series means of the period average values of the outcome variable, $\overline{Y}_{k,t}$, for each of the n_p portfolios as well as for the difference

TABLE 5.3   Univariate Portfolio Equal-Weighted Excess Returns
This table presents the one-year-ahead excess returns of the equal-weighted portfolios formed
by sorting on β. The column labeled t indicates the portfolio formation year. The column
labeled $t + 1$ indicates the portfolio holding year. The columns labeled 1 through 7 show the
excess returns of the seven β-sorted portfolios. The column labeled 7-1 presents the difference
between the return of portfolio seven and that of portfolio one.

t	$t+1$	1	2	3	4	5	6	7	7-1
1988	1989	−0.97	1.12	2.12	6.77	3.18	9.04	8.96	9.93
1989	1990	−30.21	−29.09	−28.72	−29.81	−27.85	−26.85	−25.75	4.45
1990	1991	56.81	28.99	36.22	40.42	54.51	64.44	66.49	9.68
1991	1992	55.37	30.93	29.45	21.99	19.16	15.95	20.12	−35.26
1992	1993	36.07	27.60	22.98	24.03	19.78	15.39	7.86	−28.21
1993	1994	−4.51	−4.47	−5.55	−4.16	−5.88	−10.42	−4.74	−0.23
1994	1995	28.38	21.81	24.95	29.62	26.82	23.90	37.46	9.08
1995	1996	21.04	16.14	18.46	14.16	12.32	11.73	9.07	−11.97
1996	1997	22.72	39.12	28.28	20.44	18.00	6.13	−7.58	−30.30
1997	1998	−6.68	−9.02	−7.01	−10.42	−6.52	−6.60	0.13	6.81
1998	1999	14.69	10.32	19.71	23.15	38.11	61.77	93.44	78.74
1999	2000	−11.18	−4.54	−0.96	−1.23	−3.50	−10.26	−31.33	−20.16
2000	2001	37.64	28.96	27.08	28.23	22.53	−1.75	−22.09	−59.73
2001	2002	11.60	11.08	−0.27	−8.09	−22.56	−36.19	−53.83	−65.43
2002	2003	76.69	68.50	85.65	64.78	63.70	76.56	86.90	10.22
2003	2004	27.56	21.07	25.82	21.34	15.75	12.89	−0.10	−27.65
2004	2005	6.06	5.52	2.97	3.40	3.11	−3.15	−10.24	−16.31
2005	2006	8.85	17.13	13.32	10.62	6.87	12.98	12.26	3.41
2006	2007	−13.52	−13.06	−6.97	−7.65	−6.57	−2.60	−4.19	9.33
2007	2008	−42.54	−42.30	−41.36	−39.18	−40.75	−45.34	−44.46	−1.92
2008	2009	57.06	65.73	64.76	59.46	55.19	60.47	73.60	16.55
2009	2010	20.31	20.19	23.14	22.98	33.39	30.27	36.77	16.46
2010	2011	−3.87	−5.50	−1.04	−4.24	−7.11	−14.11	−16.48	−12.61
2011	2012	27.95	27.11	16.22	20.33	16.10	17.83	18.05	−9.89

portfolio. We define these average values as

$$\overline{Y}_k = \frac{\sum_{t=1}^{T} \overline{Y}_{k,t}}{T} \tag{5.5}$$

and

$$\overline{Y}_{Diff} = \frac{\sum_{t=1}^{T} \overline{Y}_{Diff,t}}{T} \tag{5.6}$$

where $t = 1$ indicates the first period in the sample and T is the number of periods in
the sample.

The time-series means serve as estimates of the true average values of the outcome
variable for entities in each of the portfolios in the average time period. Similarly, the

TABLE 5.4   Univariate Portfolio Value-Weighted Excess Returns
This table presents the one-year-ahead excess returns of the value-weighted portfolios formed by sorting on β. The column labeled t indicates the portfolio formation year. The column labeled $t + 1$ indicates the portfolio holding year. The columns labeled 1 through 7 show the excess returns of the seven β-sorted portfolios. The column labeled 7-1 presents the difference between the return of portfolio seven and that of portfolio one.

t	$t+1$	1	2	3	4	5	6	7	7-1
1988	1989	−2.98	11.14	9.04	16.29	20.25	29.16	18.21	21.19
1989	1990	−28.42	−33.78	−18.81	−19.12	−16.14	−11.51	−11.88	16.53
1990	1991	−0.45	18.50	12.28	17.79	22.08	31.14	51.51	51.96
1991	1992	−1.18	22.64	14.17	8.47	5.44	0.43	12.45	13.62
1992	1993	21.22	18.77	14.44	9.45	7.33	5.64	3.35	−17.87
1993	1994	−14.71	−7.26	−3.17	−4.07	−2.86	−9.35	1.52	16.23
1994	1995	17.44	21.81	25.41	32.54	31.73	28.45	29.02	11.57
1995	1996	5.38	17.64	18.34	14.51	13.71	18.02	29.65	24.27
1996	1997	3.37	34.35	26.16	21.17	27.71	27.54	22.22	18.85
1997	1998	−7.37	−6.09	−0.99	−0.63	12.21	16.51	31.82	39.20
1998	1999	−17.35	−17.55	−9.51	1.20	0.22	31.34	57.98	75.33
1999	2000	−23.95	−1.23	8.74	14.82	5.78	0.02	−26.46	−2.50
2000	2001	−11.02	3.53	−14.41	−9.48	−5.48	−2.79	−52.09	−41.08
2001	2002	−3.26	−14.06	−14.71	−13.39	−18.92	−31.44	−46.53	−43.27
2002	2003	61.15	41.66	22.03	23.18	23.98	28.01	55.03	−6.12
2003	2004	10.16	26.60	18.88	16.89	9.60	8.39	−4.06	−14.22
2004	2005	6.56	0.85	2.75	2.57	3.44	3.26	1.44	−5.12
2005	2006	4.83	15.65	13.43	9.53	7.75	11.26	11.11	6.28
2006	2007	−13.27	12.99	−1.88	−1.57	7.57	7.66	1.51	14.78
2007	2008	−36.55	−22.48	−24.84	−35.30	−40.15	−52.41	−60.52	−23.97
2008	2009	11.32	29.50	12.89	35.12	26.63	40.36	35.67	24.35
2009	2010	8.67	9.59	12.54	17.22	24.11	25.04	19.59	10.92
2010	2011	3.48	14.68	7.41	4.64	−8.02	−20.42	−20.61	−24.09
2011	2012	26.83	8.12	15.10	18.62	19.19	16.04	35.77	8.94

time-series mean of the difference portfolio estimates the difference, in the average time period, of the average value of the outcome variable for entities in the n_Pth portfolio compared to those in the first portfolio.

5.1.5   Interpreting the Results

In addition to calculating the time-series means for each of the portfolios, we frequently want to test whether the time-series mean for each of the portfolios differs from some null hypothesis mean value. That value is often zero. Most importantly, we want to examine whether the time-series mean of the difference portfolio is statistically distinguishable from zero. A statistically nonzero mean for the difference portfolio is evidence that, in the average time period, a cross-sectional relation exists between the sort variable and the outcome variable. To make such an assessment, for each of the n_P portfolios, as well as the difference portfolio, we calculate standard errors, t-statistics, and p-values for the test with null hypothesis that the time-series mean of the average portfolio outcome variable value is equal to zero. Because for each portfolio the portfolio average values ($\overline{Y}_{k,t}$) represent a time series, the standard errors are frequently adjusted following Newey and West (1987). The details of the Newey and West (1987) adjustment are discussed in Section 1.3. Most researchers use a 5% level of significance to determine whether a test rejects or fails to reject the null hypothesis.[2] Thus, t-statistics greater than 2.00 (approximately) in magnitude, or p-values less than 0.05, result in rejection of the null hypothesis that the time-series mean is equal to zero. In addition to examining whether the time-series mean for the difference portfolio is statistically distinguishable from zero, researchers frequently examine the average values of Y across the n_P portfolios ($\overline{Y}_k, k \in \{1, 2, \ldots, n_P\}$) for monotonicity. If a monotonic or near monotonic pattern arises, it is a strong indication that the results of the difference portfolio are not spurious.[3]

The results for our example are presented in Table 5.5. The row labeled Average shows the time-series average of the annual portfolio excess returns for portfolios 1 through 7 as well as for the difference portfolio (column labeled 7-1). The rows labeled Standard error, t-statistic, and p-value present the standard error of the estimated mean portfolio excess return, adjusted following Newey and West (1987) using six lags, and the corresponding t-statistics and p-values, respectively.

The results indicate that the average excess returns for portfolios 1 through 7 are 16.47%, 13.89%, 14.55%, 12.79%, 11.99%, 10.92%, and 10.43%, respectively. Each of these average returns is found to be highly statistically significant, as the corresponding t-statistics range from 3.43 for portfolio 7 to 6.73 for portfolio 4, and all p-values are very close to zero. This indicates that in the average year, each of these seven portfolios produces positive excess returns. This is not surprising because stocks are known to generate average returns that are higher than the return on the risk-free security. The average return of the difference portfolio, presented in the column labeled 7-1, is −6.04%. This difference is not statistically distinguishable from zero as the t-statistic is −1.31 and the p-value is 0.20. Thus, our portfolio analysis fails to detect a cross-sectional relation between β and one-year-ahead excess stock returns (r_{t+1}).

We do not examine the results for the value-weighted portfolio analysis here because the procedure for generating the results is identical to that for the equal-weighted portfolios. However, for many of the analyses in Part II of this text, both equal-weighted and value-weighted portfolio results will be investigated.

---

[2]Harvey, Liu, and Zhu (2015) argue that due to data mining and the large amount of research examining the cross section of expected returns, a 5% level of significance is too low a threshold and argue in favor of using much more stringent requirements for accepting empirical results as evident of true economic phenomena.
[3]Patton and Timmermann (2010) develop a statistical test of monotonicity.

TABLE 5.5   Univariate Portfolio Equal-Weighted Excess Returns Summary
This table presents the results of a univariate portfolio analysis of the relation between beta (β) and future stock returns (r_{t+1}). The row labeled Average presents the equal-weighted average annual return for each of the portfolios. The row labeled Standard error presents the standard error of the estimated mean portfolio return. Standard errors are adjusted following Newey and West (1987) using six lags. The row labeled t-statistic presents the t-statistic (in parentheses) for the test with null hypothesis that the average portfolio excess return is equal to zero. The row labeled p-value presents the two-sided p-value for the test with null hypothesis that the average portfolio excess return is equal to zero. The columns labeled 1 through 7 show the excess returns of the seven β-sorted portfolios. The column labeled 7-1 presents the results for the difference between the return of portfolio seven and that of portfolio one.

	1	2	3	4	5	6	7	7-1
Average	16.47	13.89	14.55	12.79	11.99	10.92	10.43	−6.04
Standard error	3.62	2.42	2.50	1.90	1.83	1.80	3.04	4.61
t-statistic	4.55	5.74	5.83	6.73	6.57	6.06	3.43	−1.31
p-value	0.00	0.00	0.00	0.00	0.00	0.00	0.00	0.20

5.1.6   Presenting the Results

There are many different approaches to presenting the results of one or more portfolio analyses. Exactly which approach is chosen depends on the objective of the analysis. Here, we discuss some of the most common approaches to presenting portfolio analysis results.

Single Portfolio Analysis
We begin with a presentation of the results analyzing the relation between β and r_{t+1} discussed throughout this chapter. While the results of this analysis are well summarized by Table 5.5, several of the results in Table 5.5 are redundant, as the standard error, t-statistic, and p-value all contain essentially the same information. Thus, only one of these values, most commonly the t-statistic, is presented. Furthermore, t-statistics are frequently presented in parentheses to enhance the appearance of the presentation. Thus, the results of the portfolio analysis may be presented as in Table 5.6. Only the average excess return and the corresponding Newey and West (1987) adjusted (six lags) t-statistics are displayed.

Multiple Analyses, Same Sort Variable, Different Outcome Variables
Frequently, we want to examine the cross-sectional relation between the sort variable X and many different outcome variables Y. To do this, we repeat the univariate portfolio analysis for each outcome variable Y. Notice that the breakpoints step does not need to be repeated as the sort variable has not changed. We can then present the results of all of these portfolio analyses in one table. Often, it is not of particular interest to examine whether the average value of the outcome variable in any of the n_P portfolios is equal to zero. For example, we know that all stocks have a positive

TABLE 5.6 β-Sorted Portfolio Excess Returns
This table presents the results of a univariate portfolio analysis of the relation between beta (β) and future stock returns (r_{t+1}). The table shows that average excess return for each of the seven portfolios as well as for the long–short zero-cost portfolio, that is, long stocks in the seventh portfolio and short stocks in the first portfolio. Newey and West (1987) t-statistics, adjusted using six lags, testing the null hypothesis that the average portfolio excess return is equal to zero, are shown in parentheses.

1	2	3	4	5	6	7	7-1
16.47	13.89	14.55	12.79	11.99	10.92	10.43	−6.04
(4.55)	(5.74)	(5.83)	(6.73)	(6.57)	(6.06)	(3.43)	(−1.31)

market capitalization. Thus, testing whether the average market capitalization of a certain set of stocks is not of interest. We may only be interested in whether the average value of the difference portfolio is equal to zero, as nonzero differences indicate a cross-sectional relation between the sort variable X and the outcome variable Y. Therefore, sometimes the only t-statistic presented is that of the difference portfolio. The objective of such analyses is often to understand the complexion of each of the portfolios formed by sorting on the variable X.

To exemplify this, Table 5.7 presents the results of a portfolio analysis using the same β-sorted portfolios but taking each of β, $MktCap$, and BM to be the outcome variable. In this analysis, it is worth noting that the values of the outcome variables β, $MktCap$, and BM are measured contemporaneously with β. Thus, for each portfolio, we have the full 25 years of average values of these variables instead of the 24 years that we had when using future excess returns. Here, t-statistics for the difference portfolio are reported in a separate column at the end of the table instead of in parentheses under the average value.

Because the portfolios are formed by sorting on β, the average value of β is monotonically increasing across the seven portfolios and the time-series mean of the differences in average β between portfolios seven and one of 2.16 is highly statistically

TABLE 5.7   Univariate Portfolio Average Values of β, $MktCap$, and BM
This table presents the average values of β, $MktCap$, and BM for each of the β-sorted portfolios. The first column of the table indicates the variable for which the average value is being calculated. The columns labeled 1 through 7 present the time-series average of annual portfolio mean values of the given variable. The column labeled 7-1 presents the average difference between portfolios 7 and 1. The column labeled 7-1 t presents the t-statistic, adjusted following Newey and West (1987) using six lags, testing the null hypothesis that the average of the difference portfolio is equal to zero.

Outcome Variable	1	2	3	4	5	6	7	7-1	7-1 t-statistic
β	−0.22	0.14	0.41	0.71	1.03	1.37	1.94	2.16	21.08
$MktCap$	153	1065	2307	2572	2529	2519	2523	2369	3.98
BM	0.94	0.96	0.77	0.71	0.64	0.53	0.51	−0.42	−3.69

significant with a t-statistic of 21.08. The table indicates that stocks with low β tend to be small market capitalization stocks, as the average $MktCap$ of stocks in the first portfolio is only \$153 million. The average market capitalization increases monotonically through portfolio four, and the average market capitalization of portfolios four through seven are very similar, each being a little higher than \$2.5 billion. The average difference in market capitalization between the stocks in portfolio seven and those in portfolio one of more than \$2.3 billion is highly statistically significant with a t-statistic of 3.98. Finally, the portfolios exhibit a nearly monotonically decreasing (the exception is portfolio one) pattern in average book-to-market ratio (BM). The average difference between portfolio seven and portfolio one of -0.42 is highly statistically significant (t-statistic $= -3.69$). In summary, the portfolio analysis detects a positive relation between β and $MktCap$ and a negative relation between β and BM. It is worth noting that the direction of the relations uncovered by the portfolio analyses is consistent with the results of the correlation analysis presented in Table 3.2.

Multiple Analyses, Different Sort Variables, Same Outcome Variable

Sometimes, we want to present the results of portfolio analyses with different sort variables X but with the same outcome variable Y. This is often the case when we are examining the ability of many different variables to predict future stock returns.

Table 5.8 presents an example of how the results of such portfolio analyses can be presented. The table shows the average excess returns and the associated t-statistics for portfolios sorted on each of β, $MktCap$, and BM. The results for the portfolios formed by sorting on β are identical to those presented in Table 5.5. The results for the portfolios sorted on $MktCap$ indicate a strong negative relation between market capitalization and future stock returns as the average return of the difference portfolio is -20.89% per year with a t-statistic of -4.80. The results also indicate a strong positive relation between book-to-market ratio (BM) and future stock returns as the average return of the difference portfolio is 17.59% per year (t-statistic $= 8.28$). In both the $MktCap$ and BM cases, the average excess returns are nearly monotonic across the seven portfolios. These results, known as the size and value effects, respectively, will be discussed in detail in Chapters 9 and 10, respectively.

In general, there is no one correct way to present the results of portfolio analyses. The exact format of the presentation should be chosen to highlight the focal results of the analysis. The above examples are indicative of some of the most common presentation formats.

5.1.7   Analyzing Returns

When the entities in the sample are securities and the outcome variable Y measures the returns of the securities, the average values $\overline{Y}_{k,t}$ represent the returns of the portfolios that hold long positions in each of the portfolio's securities.[4] In such cases, it is usually desirable to perform some additional analyses that are intended to examine

---

[4]It is worth noting here that Asparouhova, Bessembinder, and Kalcheva (2013) find that deviations from fundamental values can produce biases in the estimates of expected returns generated by portfolio analyses.

TABLE 5.8   Average Returns of Portfolios Sorted on β, *MktCap*, and *BM*

This table presents the average excess returns of equal-weighted portfolios formed by sorting on each of β, *MktCap*, and *BM*. The first column of the table indicates the sort variable. The columns labeled 1 through 7 present the time-series average of annual one-year-ahead excess portfolio returns. The column labeled 7-1 presents the average difference in return between portfolios 7 and 1. *t*-statistics testing the null hypothesis that the average portfolio return is equal to zero, adjusted following Newey and West (1987) using six lags, are presented in parentheses.

Sort Variable	1	2	3	4	5	6	7	7-1
β	16.47	13.89	14.55	12.79	11.99	10.92	10.43	−6.04
	(4.55)	(5.74)	(5.83)	(6.73)	(6.57)	(6.06)	(3.43)	(−1.31)
MktCap	29.08	16.85	12.16	10.12	8.47	9.25	8.19	−20.89
	(7.00)	(5.48)	(4.55)	(5.23)	(5.97)	(5.93)	(4.32)	(−4.80)
BM	7.61	6.65	11.06	13.55	13.74	17.50	25.21	17.59
	(3.47)	(4.21)	(6.67)	(7.43)	(6.51)	(6.37)	(8.77)	(8.28)

whether patterns in the average portfolio returns are driven by cross-sectional variation in portfolio sensitivities to systematic risk factors. Stated alternatively, we want to examine whether after controlling for sensitivity of the portfolios to systematic risk factors, the patterns in the average portfolio returns persist.[5]

There are three very common models of risk-adjustment that are used throughout the finance literature. While the objective of this chapter is not to discuss these models in detail, we will provide a brief overview. The risk models will be discussed in detail in Part II. The first model, based on the Capital Asset Pricing Model (CAPM) of Sharpe (1964), Lintner (1965), and Mossin (1966) and known as the one-factor market model, is designed to adjust the portfolio returns for the effect of the overall stock market return. The specification of the one-factor market model is

$$r_{p,t} = \alpha + \beta_{MKT}MKT_t + \epsilon_t \qquad (5.7)$$

where $r_{p,t}$ is the excess return of the portfolio and MKT_t is the excess return on the market factor mimicking portfolio during the period t.

The second risk model, originally proposed by Fama and French (1993) and known as the Fama and French (FF) three-factor model, uses two additional risk factors that proxy for the returns associated with the size (see Chapter 9) and value (see Chapter 10) effects.[6] The size effect refers to the fact that stocks with small market capitalizations have, on average and in the long run, outperformed stocks with large market capitalizations. The time series of returns associated with taking one unit of size factor risk are proxied by the returns of a zero-cost portfolio that is long small capitalization stocks and short large capitalization stocks. This zero-cost portfolio and its returns are referred to as *SMB* for "small minus big." The value effect refers to the

---

[5] Ang (2014) provides a comprehensive overview of factor investing.
[6] A recent paper by Fama and French (2015) proposes a five-factor model that includes the FFC factors along with factors based on profitability and investment. Another article, Hou, Xue, and Zhang (2015), proposes a similar model that excludes the value (*SMB*) factor.

fact that stocks with high book-to-market ratios (value stocks) have historically out-performed stocks with low book-to-market ratios (growth stocks). The time series of returns associated with taking one unit of value factor risk are proxied by the returns of a zero-cost portfolio, that is, long high book-to-market ratio stocks and short low book-to-market ratio stocks. The value portfolio and its returns are denoted *HML* for "high minus low." Therefore, the FF model is

$$r_{p,t} = \alpha + \beta_{MKT}MKT_t + \beta_{SMB}SMB_t + \beta_{HML}HML_t + \epsilon_t. \tag{5.8}$$

where SMB_t and HML_t are the returns of the size and value factor mimicking portfo-lios, respectively, during time period t.

The third commonly used risk model augments the FF model with an additional factor that accounts for the momentum phenomenon documented by Jegadeesh and Titman (1993) and Carhart (1997). This model is known as the Fama, French, and Carhart (FFC) four-factor model. The momentum factor, denoted *MOM* for "momen-tum" (sometimes researchers refer to this factor using *UMD* for "up minus down"), represents the returns of a portfolio that is long stocks with the highest recent per-formance and short stocks with the lowest recent performance, where recent perfor-mance is defined as the return of the stock over the 11-month period beginning 12 months ago and ending one month ago. The FFC model can be written as

$$r_{p,t} = \alpha + \beta_{MKT}MKT_t + \beta_{SMB}SMB_t$$
$$+ \beta_{HML}HML_t + \beta_{MOM}MOM_t + \epsilon_t. \tag{5.9}$$

As each of the regressions used to risk-adjust the portfolio returns is a time-series regression, the Newey and West (1987) adjustment is usually applied. The result of the regression is a set of coefficients (intercept and slopes), as well as the corresponding standard errors, t-statistics, and p-values. The intercept coefficient (α) is interpreted as the average excess return of the portfolio that is not due to sensitivity to any of the factors included in the chosen factor model. This value is frequently referred to as the portfolio's alpha, Jensen (1968)'s alpha, or average abnormal return. To examine whether the portfolio generates statistically significant average abnormal returns, we use the t-statistic and/or p-value associated with the intercept coefficient.

Each slope coefficient is an estimate of the portfolio's sensitivity to the corre-sponding factor. The coefficients, as well as the associated inferential statistics, can be used to determine which factor or factors are related to the returns of the portfolio in question.

To exemplify the use of risk-adjustment in portfolio analysis, we adjust the returns of the β-sorted portfolios used previously in this chapter. Table 5.9 presents the esti-mated alphas (α) and factor sensitivities (β_{MKT}, β_{SMB}, β_{HML}, and β_{MOM}) for each of the seven portfolios as well as for the difference portfolio.

The section of Table 5.9 corresponding to the excess return (Model = Excess Return) replicates the results in Table 5.3. Notice that each of the seven portfolios generates large and highly statistically significant average excess returns, as the

TABLE 5.9 β-Sorted Portfolio Risk-Adjusted Results

This table presents the risk-adjusted alphas and factor sensitivities for the β-sorted portfolios. Each year t, all stocks in the sample are sorted into seven portfolios based on an ascending sort of β with breakpoints set to the 10th, 20th, 40th, 60th, 80th, and 90th percentiles of β in the given year. The equal-weighted average one-year-ahead excess portfolio returns are then calculated. The table presents the average excess returns (Model = Excess return) for each of the seven portfolios as well as for the zero-cost portfolio that is long the seventh portfolio and short the first portfolio. Also presented are the alphas (Coefficient = α) and factor sensitivities (Coefficient = β_{MKT}, β_{SMB}, β_{HML}, and β_{UMD}) for each of the portfolios using the CAPM (Model = CAPM), Fama and French (1993) three-factor model (Model = FF), and Fama and French (1993) and Carhart (1997) four-factor model (Model = FFC). t-statistics, adjusted following Newey and West (1987) using six lags, are presented in parentheses.

Model	Coefficient	1	2	3	4	5	6	7	7-1
Excess	Excess	16.47	13.89	14.55	12.79	11.99	10.92	10.43	−6.04
return	return	(4.55)	(5.74)	(5.83)	(6.73)	(6.57)	(6.06)	(3.43)	(−1.31)
CAPM	α	8.89	6.78	6.75	5.32	3.58	0.45	−2.49	−11.38
		(1.41)	(1.32)	(1.33)	(1.31)	(1.13)	(0.19)	(−1.11)	(−1.72)
	β_{MKT}	1.02	0.96	1.05	1.01	1.13	1.41	1.74	0.72
		(3.30)	(3.05)	(3.80)	(3.75)	(5.20)	(7.63)	(8.70)	(1.89)
FF	α	3.44	1.57	2.20	1.44	0.86	−0.77	−1.32	−4.76
		(1.36)	(1.01)	(1.79)	(1.39)	(0.69)	(−0.53)	(−0.69)	(−1.82)
	β_{MKT}	1.12	1.08	1.13	1.06	1.12	1.31	1.50	0.38
		(7.55)	(6.11)	(7.64)	(7.72)	(12.01)	(11.55)	(11.20)	(1.83)
	β_{SMB}	1.53	1.17	1.35	1.25	1.37	1.47	1.64	0.12
		(8.98)	(6.99)	(7.55)	(10.29)	(29.78)	(11.01)	(9.86)	(0.41)
	β_{HML}	0.71	0.76	0.57	0.46	0.18	−0.16	−0.72	−1.43
		(7.36)	(13.40)	(6.39)	(5.19)	(1.66)	(−1.45)	(−6.25)	(−11.97)
FFC	α	5.54	6.21	6.49	4.54	2.37	−0.01	−0.12	−5.66
		(2.43)	(4.91)	(5.16)	(5.53)	(2.35)	(−0.01)	(−0.04)	(−1.14)
	β_{MKT}	1.06	0.95	1.00	0.97	1.07	1.29	1.47	0.41
		(8.59)	(9.30)	(18.20)	(13.77)	(16.98)	(15.76)	(11.21)	(1.62)
	β_{SMB}	1.42	0.92	1.12	1.08	1.29	1.43	1.58	0.16
		(6.57)	(3.94)	(5.47)	(6.29)	(13.85)	(8.25)	(7.61)	(0.69)
	β_{HML}	0.66	0.65	0.47	0.38	0.14	−0.18	−0.75	−1.41
		(5.27)	(9.15)	(7.96)	(7.38)	(1.53)	(−1.79)	(−6.96)	(−11.95)
	β_{MOM}	−0.16	−0.36	−0.33	−0.24	−0.12	−0.06	−0.09	0.07
		(−1.91)	(−3.38)	(−5.83)	(−2.90)	(−2.05)	(−0.51)	(−0.44)	(0.29)

t-statistics for each portfolio are positive and substantially greater than 2.00. This indicates that on average, each of the portfolios generates positive excess returns. This is not surprising because each of these portfolios is a portfolio of stocks. It is well known that, on average, stocks generate returns that are higher than the return of the risk-free security. Therefore, it is not surprising that portfolios comprised a large number of stocks exhibit similar behavior. The average return of the difference portfolio of −6.04% per year is statistically indistinguishable from zero.

When the returns are adjusted for exposure to the market factor using the CAPM risk model (Model = CAPM), the results indicate that none of the seven portfolios generates abnormal returns that are statistically distinguishable from zero as all t-statistics are substantially less than 2.00 in magnitude. This indicates that the excess returns generated by the portfolios are a manifestation of the portfolios' exposures to the market factor. After controlling for this, the average abnormal return of each of the portfolios is statistically insignificant. The table also presents the sensitivities of each of the portfolios to the market factor. The results indicate that all portfolios have a positive and statistically significant sensitivity to the market portfolio. Furthermore, the sensitivities are nearly monotonically increasing from portfolios 1 to 7. This is not surprising given that the portfolios were formed by sorting on β, which measures stock-level sensitivity to the market portfolio. The abnormal return of the difference portfolio remains statistically insignificant when using the CAPM risk model, and the sensitivity of the difference portfolio to the market portfolio of 0.72 is marginally statistically significant.

The remainder of Table 5.9 presents the results for the FF and FFC models. While some of these results are interesting, the objective here is to discuss the implementation and interpretation of portfolio analysis, not to examine the economic implications of these results. This will be done in Part II of this text.

In almost all cases, only a subset of the results in Table 5.9 are presented in a research article. Unless the factor sensitivities are of particular interest, they are usually not reported. Furthermore, frequently only results from one of the risk models are shown. The FFC model is the most common choice.

At this point, the reader may be wondering why, throughout this chapter, we have used the excess stock return, which is equal to the return on the stock minus the return on the risk-free security, instead of simply the stock return itself (without subtracting the risk-free security return). The reason for this is that the excess return represents the additional return that was realized by forgoing the certain return associated with the risk-free security in favor of a risky return. Asset pricing theory dictates that to be willing to take the risk associated with a given security, investors demand that, on average, the return of that security is greater than the risk-free rate. A major objective of empirical asset pricing research is to understand exactly which risks investors care about and how much of an average return, in excess of the return on the risk-free security, investors require to entice them to take such risk. It is for this reason that the CAPM, FF, and FFC (as well as all other) risk factor models are based on excess returns and not raw returns. Thus, when analyzing the time series of the returns of the n_P portfolios, it is important to make sure that the excess portfolio returns, not the raw portfolio returns, are used as the dependent variable in the factor regression. For this reason, it is advisable to use the excess stock return, not the raw stock return, as the outcome variable Y. Regardless of whether the excess return or the raw return is used as the outcome variable Y, the difference between the (excess or raw) return of the n_Pth portfolio and the first portfolio should be interpreted as an excess return. In fact, this difference will be the same regardless of whether the excess or raw return is used. Despite the fact that this difference in returns is interpreted as an excess return, it is commonly referred to as the return of the difference portfolio, the difference portfolio return, or the high minus low portfolio return. We frequently adopt this terminology throughout this book.

5.2 BIVARIATE INDEPENDENT-SORT ANALYSIS

The previous section presented the simplest form of portfolio analysis, designed to assess the cross-sectional relation between two variables without accounting for the effects of any other variables. In this section, we present bivariate portfolio analysis. Bivariate portfolio analysis is very similar to univariate portfolio analysis, except in bivariate portfolio analysis there are two sort variables.

There are two types of sorting procedures, independent and dependent, that are commonly employed in bivariate portfolio analysis. In the present section, we discuss independent-sort analysis. In Section 5.3, we discuss dependent-sort analysis.

Bivariate independent-sort portfolio analysis is designed to assess the cross-sectional relations between two sort variables, which we refer to as $X1$ and $X2$, and an outcome variable Y.

5.2.1 Breakpoints

As the name implies, in bivariate independent-sort portfolio analysis, portfolios are formed by sorting on two variables independently. Thus, in each period, two sets of breakpoints will be calculated. The first set of breakpoints corresponds to values of the first sort variable $X1$. The second set of breakpoints corresponds to values of the second sort variable $X2$ and is calculated completely independently of the breakpoints for $X1$. Thus, the name *independent* sort. The fact that the sorts are independent means it makes no difference which sort variable is considered the first sort variable, and which is considered the second. Switching the order will have no effect on the results of the analysis.

The first step in a bivariate independent-sort portfolio analysis is to sort all entities in the sample into groups according to each of the sort variables. We use the term "groups" here to differentiate the groups that are formed by independent univariate sorts of the entities from the eventual portfolios that are formed. The portfolios will represent intersections of groups from sorts based on the first and second sort variables. Letting n_{P1} represent the number of groups that will be created based on the first sort variable and n_{P2} be the number of groups that will be created based on the second sort variable, the number of portfolios that will be formed is $n_{P1} \times n_{P2}$. There are therefore n_{P1} and n_{P2} breakpoints for the first and second sort variables, respectively.

The breakpoints for each of the two sort variables are calculated in exactly the same way as for a univariate portfolio analysis. The breakpoints (percentiles used to calculate the breakpoints) used to form the groups for the first sort variable are denoted $B1_{j,t}$ $(p1_j)$ for $j \in \{1, 2, \ldots, n_{P1} - 1\}$, and the breakpoints (percentiles) for the second sort variable are $B2_{k,t}$ $(p2_k)$ for $k \in \{1, 2, \ldots, n_{P2} - 1\}$. The actual breakpoints are calculated as

$$B1_{j,t} = Pctl_{p1_j}(\{X1_t\}) \tag{5.10}$$

and

$$B2_{k,t} = Pctl_{p2_k}(\{X2_t\}) \tag{5.11}$$

where $Pctl_p(Z)$ is the pth percentile of the set Z and $\{X1_t\}$ and $\{X2_t\}$ are the set of available values of $X1$ and $X2$, respectively, in period t. It should be noted that frequently the set of entities in the sample for which values of $X1$ are available may differ from those for which $X2$ is available. In this case, the researcher must decide whether the breakpoints are formed using only entities for which valid values of both variables are available or whether the breakpoints are formed using all available data for each variable. In some cases, the set of entities used to calculate the breakpoints for $X1$ may be different than the set of entities used to calculate the $X2$ breakpoints. Furthermore, neither of these sets of entities is necessarily the same as the set of entities that will eventually be grouped into the portfolios. As in the univariate analysis, breakpoints are calculated for each time period t. Throughout this text, in our bivariate portfolio analyses, we use only entities for which valid values of both $X1$ and $X2$ are available when calculating breakpoints for bivariate (both independent-sort and dependent-sort) portfolio analyses.

We exemplify the calculation of breakpoints for the bivariate independent-sort portfolio analysis using beta $(X1 = \beta)$ and market capitalization $(X2 = MktCap)$ as our sort variables. We divide the sample into three groups based on β ($n_{P1} = 3$) and four groups based on $MktCap$ ($n_{P2} = 4$). We use the 30th and 70th percentiles to calculate the β breakpoints, and the 25th, 50th, and 75th percentiles to calculate the $MktCap$ breakpoints.

The annual breakpoints for this analysis are shown in Table 5.10. The table shows that, in year 1988, the first β breakpoint is 0.18 and the second β breakpoint is 0.66. The first, second, and third $MktCap$ breakpoints are 9.65, 34.83, and 159.85, respectively. The breakpoints for other years are presented in the subsequent rows of the table.

As discussed in Section 5.1.1, the decision of how many groups to form based on each of the sort variables, and therefore how many total portfolios to use, is based on trade-offs between the number of stocks in each portfolio and dispersion among the portfolios of the sort variables. In bivariate independent-sort portfolio analysis, there is one additional criterion that may factor into the decision of how many breakpoints to use, as well as what percentiles of each sort variable to use as breakpoints. If the sort variables are highly positively correlated, then this may result in a large number of entities being put into the portfolio that holds entities with high values of both sort variables as well as the portfolio holding entities with low values of both sort variables. Portfolios that hold entities with low values of one sort variable and high values of the other will contain relatively fewer entities. The situation is reversed when the sort variables are negatively correlated. The more extreme the correlation between the two sort variables, the more exacerbated this effect will be. The number of groups to form based on each sort variable, therefore, should take this correlation into account and ensure that for each time period during the sample, each of the $n_{P1} \times n_{P2}$ portfolios contains a sufficient number of entities. This will become more clear shortly when we discuss portfolio formation. Apart

TABLE 5.10   Bivariate Independent-Sort Breakpoints
This table presents the breakpoints for a bivariate independent-sort portfolio analysis The first sort variable is β and the second sort variable is *MktCap*. The sample is split into three groups (and thus two breakpoints) based on the 30th and 70th percentiles of β, and four groups (and thus three breakpoints) based on the 25th, 50th, and 75th percentiles of *MktCap*. The column labeled t indicates the year for which the breakpoints are calculated. The columns labeled $B1_{1,t}$ and $B1_{2,t}$ present the first and second β breakpoints, respectively. The columns labeled $B2_{1,t}$, $B2_{2,t}$, and $B3_{3,t}$ present the first, second, and third *MktCap* breakpoints, respectively.

t	$B1_{1,t}$	$B1_{2,t}$	$B2_{1,t}$	$B2_{2,t}$	$B2_{3,t}$
1988	0.18	0.66	9.65	34.83	159.85
1989	0.17	0.70	9.77	37.04	184.14
1990	0.23	0.86	6.53	25.90	149.54
1991	0.24	0.85	9.70	41.56	223.70
1992	0.26	0.97	16.21	62.88	284.60
1993	0.29	0.92	22.48	78.32	345.67
1994	0.36	0.97	20.72	72.17	304.26
1995	0.27	0.90	26.03	91.38	382.85
1996	0.32	0.90	28.54	102.21	438.55
1997	0.26	0.72	32.62	119.62	521.35
1998	0.41	0.94	28.78	106.66	509.71
1999	0.15	0.53	33.79	128.21	623.06
2000	0.25	0.85	24.36	102.25	610.68
2001	0.31	0.95	34.09	142.62	717.07
2002	0.33	0.89	33.28	130.81	635.43
2003	0.38	0.97	70.06	270.53	1054.81
2004	0.63	1.36	90.64	334.90	1308.59
2005	0.60	1.30	96.99	349.11	1410.58
2006	0.61	1.40	108.61	406.64	1592.96
2007	0.56	1.18	92.95	352.91	1513.62
2008	0.57	1.14	38.11	197.13	879.62
2009	0.65	1.45	68.54	307.83	1352.40
2010	0.76	1.33	95.47	420.44	1850.99
2011	0.82	1.38	80.78	393.16	1771.85
2012	0.76	1.31	105.41	485.94	2034.15

from the additional consideration relating to correlation among the sort variables, the factors impacting the decision of how many groups to use for each variable (and thus the number of portfolios), and the choice of breakpoint percentiles, are similar in bivariate independent-sort portfolio analysis to those discussed in the univariate analysis (Section 5.1.1). We do not repeat the discussion here.

5.2.2   Portfolio Formation

As with the univariate portfolio analysis, the next step in bivariate portfolio analysis is to form the periodic portfolios. As mentioned earlier, if there are n_{P1} groups based on the first sort variable $X1$ and n_{P2} groups based on the second sort variable $X2$, then there will be $n_{P1} \times n_{P2}$ portfolios each time period. The portfolios for period t are denoted $P_{j,k,t}$, where the first subscript indicates the group of the first sort variable and the second subscript indicates that of the second sort variable. In general, the portfolios are defined as

$$P_{j,k,t} = \{i | B1_{j-1,t} \leq X1_{i,t} \leq B1_{j,t}\} \cap \{i | B2_{k-1,t} \leq X2_{i,t} \leq B2_{k,t}\} \qquad (5.12)$$

for $j \in \{1, 2, \ldots, n_{P1}\}$, $k \in \{1, 2, \ldots, n_{P2}\}$, where $B1_{0,t} = B2_{0,t} = -\infty$, $B1_{n_{P1},t} = B2_{n_{P2},t} = \infty$, and $\cap$ is the intersection operator. Thus, for a given entity i to be held in portfolio $P_{j,k,t}$, the entity must have a value of $X1$ in period t that is between the $j - 1$st and jth (inclusive) period t breakpoints for the first sort variable, and also have a period t value of $X2$ between the $k - 1$st and kth (inclusive) period t breakpoints for the second sort variable.

In a bivariate independent-sort portfolio analysis, the percentage of entities held by each of the portfolios will likely not reflect the percentiles used to calculate the break-points. The reason is that the sort variables are likely to have nonzero correlation. As each portfolio represents the intersection of sets formed based on the independent sorts, positive correlation between $X1$ and $X2$ results in portfolios that contain enti-ties with high (or low) values of both sort variables having a disproportionately large number of entities, while those portfolios comprised entities with low values of one sort variable and high values of the other contains fewer entities. The opposite is the case when the sort variables are negatively correlated. As discussed in Section 5.1.2, when the breakpoint sample and the full sample are not the same, in addition to the correlation effect, the number of entities in each portfolio will also depend on how the sort variables are distributed in the different samples. However, when the break-point sample and the sample grouped into portfolios are the same, the total number of entities in all portfolios (across all n_{P2} groups of $X2$) that correspond to the jth group of $X1$ will reflect the percentiles used to calculate the breakpoints based on the first sort variable $X1$. The same can be said for the total number of entities in the set of portfolios corresponding to a particular group of the second sort variable $X2$.

The number of stocks in each annual portfolio for our example is presented in Table 5.11. At this point, it is worth reminding ourselves that the correlation anal-ysis presented in Table 3.3 as well as the portfolio analysis presented in Table 5.7 indicate a positive cross-sectional relation between β and $MktCap$. This manifests in portfolios that hold entities with high values of β and high values of $MktCap$ having a large number of stocks. Similarly, portfolios comprised entities with low values of both sort variables have a large number of stocks. On the other hand, portfolios that hold entities with low values of one of the sort variables and high values of the other contain relatively few stocks. For example, in 1988, the table shows that the portfo-lio holding low β (β 1) and low $MktCap$ ($MktCap$ 1) stocks has 736 stocks and the portfolio holding high β (β 3) and high $MktCap$ ($MktCap$ 4) stocks has 788 stocks. On the other hand, the portfolio comprised high β (β 3) and low $MktCap$ ($MktCap$ 1) stocks has only 217 such stocks, and the portfolio containing low β (β 1) and high

TABLE 5.11   Bivariate Independent-Sort Number of Stocks per Portfolio
This table presents the number of stocks in each of the 12 portfolios formed by sorting independently into three β groups and four *MktCap* groups. The columns labeled *t* indicate the year
of portfolio formation. The columns labeled β 1, β 2, and β 3 indicate the β group. The rows
labeled *MktCap* 1, *MktCap* 2, *MktCap* 3, and *MktCap* 4 indicate the *MktCap* groups.

t		β 1	β 2	β 3	t		β 1	β 2	β 3
1988	MktCap 1	736	468	217	1998	MktCap 1	842	557	252
	MktCap 2	539	585	297		MktCap 2	622	667	361
	MktCap 3	335	683	403		MktCap 3	368	709	574
	MktCap 4	95	538	788		MktCap 4	149	708	794
1989	MktCap 1	736	419	224	1999	MktCap 1	785	484	253
	MktCap 2	537	574	268		MktCap 2	635	608	279
	MktCap 3	298	663	418		MktCap 3	338	729	455
	MktCap 4	84	549	746		MktCap 4	69	613	840
1990	MktCap 1	725	439	187	2000	MktCap 1	609	522	342
	MktCap 2	507	574	269		MktCap 2	663	455	354
	MktCap 3	287	604	459		MktCap 3	290	640	542
	MktCap 4	102	543	706		MktCap 4	205	738	530
1991	MktCap 1	763	393	169	2001	MktCap 1	686	465	225
	MktCap 2	508	570	247		MktCap 2	612	459	305
	MktCap 3	254	606	465		MktCap 3	190	647	539
	MktCap 4	65	551	709		MktCap 4	163	631	582
1992	MktCap 1	681	428	237	2002	MktCap 1	759	387	126
	MktCap 2	507	530	309		MktCap 2	649	397	225
	MktCap 3	306	562	478		MktCap 3	93	641	537
	MktCap 4	121	634	591		MktCap 4	25	609	638
1993	MktCap 1	738	409	270	2003	MktCap 1	835	275	73
	MktCap 2	531	579	307		MktCap 2	488	454	241
	MktCap 3	330	611	475		MktCap 3	51	587	545
	MktCap 4	102	667	648		MktCap 4	46	577	560
1994	MktCap 1	767	437	333	2004	MktCap 1	772	265	106
	MktCap 2	596	593	348		MktCap 2	405	390	348
	MktCap 3	352	684	501		MktCap 3	55	485	603
	MktCap 4	130	744	663		MktCap 4	140	688	315
1995	MktCap 1	784	430	358	2005	MktCap 1	834	231	58
	MktCap 2	584	595	392		MktCap 2	400	434	289
	MktCap 3	373	698	500		MktCap 3	33	429	662
	MktCap 4	145	791	636		MktCap 4	81	704	339
1996	MktCap 1	792	518	336	2006	MktCap 1	816	251	46
	MktCap 2	623	581	441		MktCap 2	357	427	329
	MktCap 3	421	676	548		MktCap 3	19	467	626
	MktCap 4	139	857	650		MktCap 4	144	635	334
1997	MktCap 1	865	571	280	2007	MktCap 1	808	236	39
	MktCap 2	688	654	374		MktCap 2	390	351	341
	MktCap 3	415	779	520		MktCap 3	28	451	604
	MktCap 4	91	740	885		MktCap 4	74	693	316

TABLE 5.11   (*Continued*)

t		β 1	β 2	β 3	t		β 1	β 2	β 3
2008	*MktCap* 1	742	247	77	2011	*MktCap* 1	721	152	48
	MktCap 2	429	289	347		*MktCap* 2	155	337	428
	MktCap 3	43	548	474		*MktCap* 3	49	460	411
	MktCap 4	65	620	381		*MktCap* 4	180	523	218
2009	*MktCap* 1	690	219	85	2012	*MktCap* 1	662	151	74
	MktCap 2	264	322	408		*MktCap* 2	135	396	355
	MktCap 3	75	509	409		*MktCap* 3	85	444	356
	MktCap 4	164	539	291		*MktCap* 4	182	426	279
2010	*MktCap* 1	715	184	52					
	MktCap 2	158	398	395					
	MktCap 3	69	472	410					
	MktCap 4	199	468	284					

MktCap (*MktCap* 3) stocks contains only 95 stocks. Similar patterns are observed in most years, although the patterns are not always as perfect as they are in 1988.

5.2.3   Average Portfolio Values

Having created the portfolios, the next step is to calculate, for each time period t, the average value of the outcome variable Y for each of the $n_{P1} \times n_{P2}$ portfolios. As was discussed in Section 5.1.3, the average values can be either equal-weighted or weighted according to some weight field W, which is quite often market capitalization (value-weighted). Thus, the average value of the outcome variable for portfolio $P_{j,k,t}$ is

$$\overline{Y}_{j,k,t} = \frac{\sum_{i \in P_{j,k,t}} W_{i,t} Y_{i,t}}{\sum_{i \in P_{j,k,t}} W_{i,t}} \tag{5.13}$$

for $j \in \{1, 2, \ldots, n_{P1}\}$ and $k \in \{1, 2, \ldots, n_{P2}\}$, where the summations in both the numerator and denominator are taken over all entities in portfolio $P_{j,k,t}$. If no weighting field is used, then $W_{i,t} = 1$ for all i and t. This is exactly the same as in the univariate case.

In addition to calculating the average values of Y for each of the portfolios, for each of the n_{P1} groups of the first sort variable $X1$, we calculate the difference in average Y value of the portfolio that holds the entities with the highest and lowest values of the second sort variable $X2$. Thus, for each time period t, we have

$$\overline{Y}_{j, \text{Diff}, t} = \overline{Y}_{j,n_{P2},t} - \overline{Y}_{j,1,t} \tag{5.14}$$

for $j \in \{1, \ldots, n_{P1}\}$. Similarly, for each group of the second sort variable $X2$, we calculate the difference in average Y value between the portfolio with the highest and lowest values of the first sort variable $X1$, giving

$$\overline{Y}_{Diff,k,t} = \overline{Y}_{n_{P1},k,t} - \overline{Y}_{1,k,t} \tag{5.15}$$

for $k \in \{1, \dots, n_{P2}\}$.

In addition to calculating differences, in bivariate independent-sort portfolio analysis, we can also calculate the average value of the outcome variables, across all groups of one of the sort variables and within a given group of the other sort variable. Thus, the average value of $\overline{Y}$ across all groups of sort variable $X1$ and within the kth group of sort variable $X2$ is defined as

$$\overline{Y}_{Avg,k,t} = \frac{\sum_{j=1}^{n_{P1}} \overline{Y}_{j,k,t}}{n_{P1}} \tag{5.16}$$

This calculation can be performed not only for $k \in \{1, 2, \dots, n_{P2}\}$ but also for the difference between the high and low sort variable two portfolios ($k = Diff$). Similarly, we calculate the average value of $\overline{Y}$ across all groups of the second sort variable $X2$ and within the jth group of the first sort variable $X1$, giving

$$\overline{Y}_{j,Avg,t} = \frac{\sum_{k=1}^{n_{P2}} \overline{Y}_{j,k,t}}{n_{P2}}. \tag{5.17}$$

for $j \in \{1, 2, \dots, n_{P1}, Diff\}$.

There are two more values that may be calculated each month. The first is the average of the averages. There are many ways that this can be calculated. The first is to take the average across the n_{P1} averages for groups formed on the first sort variable ($\overline{Y}_{j,Avg,t}, j \in \{1, 2, \dots, n_{P1}\}$). The second is to take the average across the n_{P2} averages for groups formed on the second sort variable ($\overline{Y}_{Avg,k,t}, k \in \{1, 2, \dots, n_{P2}\}$). The third is to take the average of all $n_{P1} \times n_{P2}$ portfolio average values ($\overline{Y}_{j,k,t}, j \in \{1, 2, \dots, n_{P1}\}$ and $k \in \{1, 2, \dots, n_{P2}\}$). Each of these approaches yields the same result. We therefore have

$$\overline{Y}_{Avg,Avg,t} = \frac{\sum_{j=1}^{n_{P1}} \overline{Y}_{j,Avg,t}}{n_{P1}} = \frac{\sum_{k=1}^{n_{P2}} \overline{Y}_{Avg,k,t}}{n_{P2}} = \frac{\sum_{j=1}^{n_{P1}} \sum_{k=1}^{n_{P2}} \overline{Y}_{j,k,t}}{n_{P1} \times n_{P2}}. \tag{5.18}$$

Finally, we come to the difference in the differences. The difference in differences can be used to examine how the average value of Y relates to $X1$ for high values of $X2$ compared to how the average value of Y relates to $X1$ for low values of $X2$. Alternatively, the difference in differences portfolio can be interpreted as indicating how the average value of Y relates to $X2$ for high values of $X1$ compared to how the average values of Y relates to $X2$ for low values of $X1$. This is most easily seen graphically.

In Table 5.12, we illustrate the calculation of the difference in the differences between the average values of Y. To simplify notation, we let $A = Y_{1,1,t}, B = Y_{n_{P1},1,t}$,

TABLE 5.12 Average Value for the Difference in Difference Portfolio
This diagram describes how the difference in difference portfolio for a bivariate-sort portfolio analysis is constructed.

	$X1\ 1$	$\cdots$	$X1\ n_{P1}$	$X1\ Diff$
$X2\ 1$	$\overline{Y}_{1,1,t}$ A	$\cdots$	$\overline{Y}_{n_{P1},1,t}$ B	$\overline{Y}_{Diff,1,t}$ $B-A$
$\vdots$	$\vdots$	$\ddots$	$\vdots$	$\vdots$
$X2\ n_{P2}$	$\overline{Y}_{1,n_{P2},t}$ C	$\cdots$	$\overline{Y}_{n_{P1},n_{P2},t}$ D	$\overline{Y}_{Diff,n_{P2},t}$ $D-C$
$X2\ Diff$	$\overline{Y}_{1,Diff,t}$ $C-A$	$\cdots$	$\overline{Y}_{n_{P1},Diff,t}$ $D-B$	$(D-C)-(B-A)$ $=$ $(D-B)-(C-A)$ $=$ $D-C-B+A$

$C = \overline{Y}_{1,n_{P2},t}$, and $D = \overline{Y}_{n_{P1},n_{P2},t}$. These values correspond to the interior values (within the square) of Table 5.12. The difference in average Y values between entities with the highest values of $X1$ ($X1\ n_{P1}$) and the lowest values of $X1$ ($X1\ 1$), in the group that corresponds to the lowest values of $X2$ ($X2\ 1$), is therefore $B - A = \overline{Y}_{Diff,1,t}$. Similarly, the corresponding value for the group with the highest values of $X2$ is $D - C = \overline{Y}_{Diff,n_{P2},t}$. These values are indicated in the right-center portion of Table 5.12. Going in the other direction, the difference in average Y between entities with high $X2$ and low $X2$ values among entities with low $X1$ values is $C - A = \overline{Y}_{1,Diff,t}$, and the corresponding value for entities with high values of $X1$ is $D - B = \overline{Y}_{n_{P1},Diff,t}$. These differences are shown in the center-bottom part of the table. Thus, if we take the difference along the $X2$ dimension in $X1$ differences, we get $\overline{Y}_{Diff,n_{P2},t} - \overline{Y}_{Diff,1,t} = (D - C) - (B - A) = D - C - B + A$. If we take the difference along the $X1$ dimension in $X2$ differences, we get the same result. $\overline{Y}_{n_{P1},Diff,t} - \overline{Y}_{1,Diff,t} = (D - B) - (C - A) = D - C - B + A$.

Putting all of this together, we get

$$\overline{Y}_{Diff,Diff,t} = \overline{Y}_{n_{P1},n_{P2},t} - \overline{Y}_{n_{P1},1,t} - \overline{Y}_{1,n_{P2},t} + \overline{Y}_{1,1,t}$$

$$= \overline{Y}_{Diff,n_{P2},t} - \overline{Y}_{Diff,1,t}$$

$$= \overline{Y}_{n_{P1},Diff,t} - \overline{Y}_{1,Diff,t}. \tag{5.19}$$

To help understand this difference in differences portfolio, consider the case when $\overline{Y}_{j,k,t}$ represents the return of the j,kth portfolio in time period t. Then, the difference in difference portfolio can be thought of as the return associated with going long portfolios D and A in equal dollar amounts and short portfolios C and D in the same dollar amounts. In a more general sense, this value indicates how the relation between $X1$ and Y changes across different levels of $X2$. Similarly, it indicates how the relation between $X2$ and Y changes across different levels of $X1$.

We exemplify calculation of the mean dependent variable using the one-year-ahead stock excess return (r_{t+1}) as the outcome variable. We use equal-weighted portfolios in this analysis, thus $W_{i,t}$ is one for all i and t. Table 5.13 presents the average one-year-ahead stock excess returns for each of the $n_{P1} \times n_{P2}$ portfolios, as well as for the difference and average portfolios. The table indicates the portfolio formation year (t) as well as the portfolio holding year ($t + 1$). Taking the year $t = 1988$ and $t + 1 = 1989$ as an example, the table shows that the portfolio comprised low-β (β 1) and low-MktCap (MktCap 1) stocks generated an excess return of 1.13%. The portfolios comprised high-β and low-MktCap stocks generated an excess return of 1.69%. The difference between the high-β and low-β portfolio returns for low-MktCap stocks was therefore 0.56% (1.69% − 1.13%). The average of the low-MktCap portfolios generated a return equal to 0.62%. This process can be repeated for all four MktCap groups and performed analogously for the three β groups. For the average market capitalization group (MktCap Avg), the difference in excess return between the high-β and low-β (β Diff) portfolio is 0.05% ((0.56% + (−8.47%) + 0.97% + 7.15%)/4). For the average β group (β Avg), the difference in excess return between the high-MktCap and low-MktCap (MktCap Diff) portfolio is 13.20% ((8.80%+15.40%+15.39%)/3). Moving to the difference of the differences portfolio (β Diff, MktCap Diff), the excess return of this portfolio is 6.59% (17.08% − 1.69% − 9.92% + 1.13% = 7.15% − 0.56% = 15.39% − 8.80%). Finally, the average of the average (β Avg, MktCap Avg) portfolio generates an excess return of 3.57%.

5.2.4 Summarizing the Results

Having calculated, for each period t, the average values of Y for each of the portfolios as well as for the difference and average portfolios, the final calculation required to complete the bivariate dependent-sort portfolio analysis is the time-series means of the periodic average values along with the corresponding standard errors, t-statistics, and p-values for each of the portfolios. This is done in exactly the same manner as for the univariate portfolio analysis. Usually, the standard errors, and therefore t-statistics and p-values, are Newey and West (1987) adjusted.

Table 5.14 presents the time-series averages of the annual portfolio excess returns for the β- and MktCap-sorted portfolios used in our example. As the periodic values represent portfolio excess returns, we adjust the excess returns for risk using the FF and FFC models. We choose to use only one risk model here to save space. We also present only the average excess returns, alphas, and corresponding Newey and West (1987) adjusted (six lags) t-statistics. We omit the standard errors, p-values, as well as all of the sensitivity coefficients. The table shows that the average annual excess return for the portfolio that holds low-MktCap (MktCap 1) and low-β (β 1) stocks is 20.96%, with a t-statistic of 6.12. The FFC alpha of this portfolio is 11.96% per year (t-statistic = 5.05). Within the low-β group (β 1), the difference in average excess return between the high-MktCap and low-MktCap portfolios is −14.51% per year (t-statistic = −4.81) and the corresponding FFC alpha is −12.87% per year (t-statistic = −3.83). The average excess return of the difference of the differences portfolio (β Diff, MktCap Diff) is 1.95% per year (t-statistic = 0.60) and the alpha of this portfolio is 1.56% per year (t-statistic = 0.43).

TABLE 5.13   Bivariate Independent-Sort Portfolio Excess Returns
This table presents the equal-weighted excess returns for each of the 12 portfolios formed by sorting independently into three β groups and four $MktCap$ groups, as well as for the difference and average portfolios. The columns labeled $t/t + 1$ indicate the year of portfolio formation (t) and the portfolio holding period ($t + 1$). The columns labeled β 1, β 2, β 3, β Diff, and β Avg indicate the β groups. The rows labeled $MktCap$ 1, $MktCap$ 2, $MktCap$ 3, $MktCap$ 4, $MktCap$ Diff, and $MktCap$ Avg indicate the $MktCap$ groups.

$t/t + 1$		β 1	β 2	β 3	β Diff	β Avg
1988/1989	$MktCap$ 1	1.13	−0.96	1.69	0.56	0.62
	$MktCap$ 2	−2.02	−1.49	−10.49	−8.47	−4.67
	$MktCap$ 3	4.48	3.62	5.45	0.97	4.52
	$MktCap$ 4	9.92	14.45	17.08	7.15	13.82
	$MktCap$ Diff	8.80	15.40	15.39	6.59	13.20
	$MktCap$ Avg	3.38	3.90	3.43	0.05	3.57
1989/1990	$MktCap$ 1	−27.14	−31.81	−15.01	12.14	−24.65
	$MktCap$ 2	−32.32	−37.25	−39.78	−7.46	−36.45
	$MktCap$ 3	−27.72	−31.88	−32.50	−4.78	−30.70
	$MktCap$ 4	−24.15	−20.04	−19.69	4.46	−21.29
	$MktCap$ Diff	2.99	11.77	−4.69	−7.68	3.36
	$MktCap$ Avg	−27.83	−30.25	−26.75	1.09	−28.28
1990/1991	$MktCap$ 1	54.21	64.97	106.14	51.92	75.11
	$MktCap$ 2	38.00	44.27	73.81	35.80	52.03
	$MktCap$ 3	22.96	41.38	53.57	30.60	39.30
	$MktCap$ 4	15.71	28.61	47.77	32.06	30.69
	$MktCap$ Diff	−38.50	−36.37	−58.37	−19.86	−44.41
	$MktCap$ Avg	32.72	44.81	70.32	37.60	49.28
1991/1992	$MktCap$ 1	56.71	41.73	64.00	7.30	54.15
	$MktCap$ 2	24.66	25.09	18.36	−6.30	22.71
	$MktCap$ 3	24.28	18.93	10.83	−13.45	18.01
	$MktCap$ 4	16.09	14.16	9.64	−6.45	13.29
	$MktCap$ Diff	−40.62	−27.57	−54.37	−13.75	−40.85
	$MktCap$ Avg	30.43	24.98	25.71	−4.73	27.04
1992/1993	$MktCap$ 1	42.33	46.82	35.10	−7.23	41.42
	$MktCap$ 2	21.13	25.05	13.77	−7.37	19.98
	$MktCap$ 3	18.02	15.32	5.55	−12.47	12.96
	$MktCap$ 4	15.89	11.82	11.96	−3.93	13.22
	$MktCap$ Diff	−26.44	−35.00	−23.14	3.30	−28.19
	$MktCap$ Avg	24.34	24.75	16.59	−7.75	21.90
1993/1994	$MktCap$ 1	−1.88	0.31	−7.36	−5.48	−2.98
	$MktCap$ 2	−8.69	−4.96	−8.41	0.28	−7.35
	$MktCap$ 3	−5.71	−4.23	−10.38	−4.68	−6.77
	$MktCap$ 4	−4.93	−6.19	−6.00	−1.07	−5.71
	$MktCap$ Diff	−3.05	−6.50	1.36	4.41	−2.73
	$MktCap$ Avg	−5.30	−3.77	−8.04	−2.74	−5.70
1994/1995	$MktCap$ 1	28.18	29.95	26.75	−1.43	28.29
	$MktCap$ 2	25.19	34.46	35.39	10.20	31.68
	$MktCap$ 3	22.53	26.73	29.23	6.71	26.17
	$MktCap$ 4	19.72	23.67	24.42	4.70	22.60
	$MktCap$ Diff	−8.46	−6.28	−2.33	6.13	−5.69
	$MktCap$ Avg	23.90	28.71	28.95	5.04	27.19

(continued)

TABLE 5.13   *(Continued)*

$t/t+1$		$\beta 1$	$\beta 2$	$\beta 3$	β Diff	β Avg
1995/1996	MktCap 1	24.86	15.18	15.79	−9.07	18.61
	MktCap 2	13.64	12.10	8.62	−5.01	11.45
	MktCap 3	19.98	16.12	7.56	−12.42	14.56
	MktCap 4	15.87	15.41	9.42	−6.45	13.57
	MktCap Diff	−8.98	0.23	−6.36	2.62	−5.04
	MktCap Avg	18.59	14.70	10.35	−8.24	14.55
1996/1997	MktCap 1	27.39	15.21	0.38	−27.01	14.33
	MktCap 2	34.26	21.36	0.33	−33.93	18.65
	MktCap 3	33.10	24.20	−0.22	−33.32	19.02
	MktCap 4	24.78	24.34	14.43	−10.35	21.18
	MktCap Diff	−2.62	9.14	14.05	16.66	6.86
	MktCap Avg	29.88	21.28	3.73	−26.15	18.30
1997/1998	MktCap 1	−6.19	−7.08	−9.26	−3.07	−7.51
	MktCap 2	−12.35	−13.48	−18.68	−6.32	−14.84
	MktCap 3	−5.25	−9.09	−10.07	−4.82	−8.13
	MktCap 4	−2.88	−2.48	5.52	8.40	0.05
	MktCap Diff	3.31	4.59	14.79	11.47	7.56
	MktCap Avg	−6.67	−8.03	−8.12	−1.45	−7.61
1998/1999	MktCap 1	32.76	66.89	114.46	81.70	71.37
	MktCap 2	9.58	38.21	79.21	69.63	42.33
	MktCap 3	−8.57	17.84	56.12	64.69	21.80
	MktCap 4	−14.56	−4.59	46.49	61.05	9.11
	MktCap Diff	−47.32	−71.48	−67.97	−20.65	−62.26
	MktCap Avg	4.80	29.59	74.07	69.27	36.15
1999/2000	MktCap 1	−6.74	−14.10	−33.47	−26.74	−18.10
	MktCap 2	−8.91	−10.52	−26.62	−17.71	−15.35
	MktCap 3	−0.22	4.16	−13.24	−13.01	−3.10
	MktCap 4	7.68	13.11	−8.71	−16.39	4.03
	MktCap Diff	14.42	27.20	24.76	10.34	22.13
	MktCap Avg	−2.05	−1.84	−20.51	−18.46	−8.13
2000/2001	MktCap 1	44.30	53.06	20.51	−23.79	39.29
	MktCap 2	29.88	43.64	0.82	−29.06	24.78
	MktCap 3	31.84	22.49	0.29	−31.55	18.21
	MktCap 4	−2.73	4.54	−20.47	−17.74	−6.22
	MktCap Diff	−47.03	−48.52	−40.98	6.05	−45.51
	MktCap Avg	25.82	30.93	0.29	−25.53	19.01
2001/2002	MktCap 1	7.03	−6.41	−31.57	−38.60	−10.32
	MktCap 2	14.58	−8.38	−41.64	−56.22	−11.82
	MktCap 3	3.14	−10.19	−42.42	−45.56	−16.49
	MktCap 4	−7.97	−8.65	−38.66	−30.69	−18.43
	MktCap Diff	−15.01	−2.24	−7.09	7.91	−8.11
	MktCap Avg	4.19	−8.41	−38.57	−42.77	−14.26
2002/2003	MktCap 1	104.77	132.30	184.10	79.34	140.39
	MktCap 2	56.30	100.00	108.86	52.56	88.39
	MktCap 3	36.95	45.07	71.55	34.61	51.19
	MktCap 4	23.00	30.87	49.36	26.36	34.41
	MktCap Diff	−81.76	−101.43	−134.74	−52.98	−105.98
	MktCap Avg	55.25	77.06	103.47	48.22	78.59

TABLE 5.13 (*Continued*)

$t/t+1$		$\beta 1$	$\beta 2$	$\beta 3$	β Diff	β Avg
2003/2004	*MktCap* 1	28.52	24.02	23.09	−5.44	25.21
	MktCap 2	20.52	17.48	7.45	−13.07	15.15
	MktCap 3	23.70	22.21	6.76	−16.94	17.56
	MktCap 4	27.28	19.84	10.89	−16.39	19.34
	MktCap Diff	−1.24	−4.18	−12.19	−10.96	−5.87
	MktCap Avg	25.01	20.89	12.05	−12.96	19.31
2004/2005	*MktCap* 1	2.77	3.03	−28.68	−31.45	−7.63
	MktCap 2	4.73	−2.27	−7.45	−12.19	−1.66
	MktCap 3	14.58	4.23	−0.63	−15.21	6.06
	MktCap 4	3.06	7.56	4.59	1.53	5.07
	MktCap Diff	0.29	4.53	33.27	32.98	12.70
	MktCap Avg	6.28	3.14	−8.04	−14.33	0.46
2005/2006	*MktCap* 1	13.00	13.66	−5.47	−18.47	7.06
	MktCap 2	14.45	13.71	11.06	−3.39	13.08
	MktCap 3	11.97	9.42	11.62	−0.35	11.00
	MktCap 4	9.24	9.24	8.07	−1.17	8.85
	MktCap Diff	−3.76	−4.41	13.54	17.30	1.79
	MktCap Avg	12.17	11.51	6.32	−5.85	10.00
2006/2007	*MktCap* 1	−12.82	−10.28	−28.89	−16.07	−17.33
	MktCap 2	−11.36	−12.18	−11.42	−0.06	−11.65
	MktCap 3	−12.44	−9.85	−5.79	6.65	−9.36
	MktCap 4	−0.45	−0.98	8.37	8.82	2.32
	MktCap Diff	12.37	9.30	37.26	24.89	19.64
	MktCap Avg	−9.27	−8.32	−9.43	−0.16	−9.01
2007/2008	*MktCap* 1	−46.58	−49.30	−56.63	−10.05	−50.84
	MktCap 2	−38.65	−48.25	−45.66	−7.01	−44.19
	MktCap 3	−37.78	−34.51	−37.15	0.63	−36.48
	MktCap 4	−32.35	−34.83	−50.83	−18.48	−39.34
	MktCap Diff	14.22	14.47	5.79	−8.43	11.50
	MktCap Avg	−38.84	−41.72	−47.57	−8.73	−42.71
2008/2009	*MktCap* 1	94.97	156.50	150.77	55.80	134.08
	MktCap 2	29.40	49.10	87.00	57.60	55.17
	MktCap 3	15.41	37.43	51.26	35.85	34.70
	MktCap 4	16.16	32.86	48.35	32.19	32.46
	MktCap Diff	−78.81	−123.64	−102.42	−23.61	−101.62
	MktCap Avg	38.99	68.97	84.35	45.36	64.10
2009/2010	*MktCap* 1	22.10	34.09	30.45	8.36	28.88
	MktCap 2	20.57	25.63	37.38	16.81	27.86
	MktCap 3	13.03	24.95	34.39	21.36	24.12
	MktCap 4	17.52	23.59	29.29	11.77	23.46
	MktCap Diff	−4.58	−10.50	−1.17	3.41	−5.41
	MktCap Avg	18.30	27.07	32.88	14.57	26.08
2010/2011	*MktCap* 1	−8.37	−19.22	−39.11	−30.73	−22.23
	MktCap 2	−5.42	−8.15	−15.23	−9.82	−9.60
	MktCap 3	4.75	−0.11	−7.95	−12.70	−1.11
	MktCap 4	10.67	1.62	−10.53	−21.20	0.59
	MktCap Diff	19.04	20.84	28.58	9.54	22.82
	MktCap Avg	0.41	−6.47	−18.21	−18.61	−8.09

(*continued*)

TABLE 5.13   *(Continued)*

$t/t+1$		$\beta\,1$	$\beta\,2$	$\beta\,3$	β Diff	β Avg
2011/2012	*MktCap* 1	27.77	9.70	−9.06	−36.83	9.47
	MktCap 2	28.61	19.69	19.03	−9.59	22.44
	MktCap 3	9.71	17.22	20.34	10.64	15.76
	MktCap 4	12.35	17.85	16.67	4.32	15.62
	MktCap Diff	−15.42	8.16	25.73	41.15	6.15
	MktCap Avg	19.61	16.11	11.74	−7.87	15.82

TABLE 5.14   Bivariate Independent-Sort Portfolio Excess and Abnormal Returns

This table presents the average excess returns (rows labeled Excess Return) and FFC alphas (rows labeled FFC α) for portfolios formed by grouping all stocks into three β groups and four *MktCap* groups. The numbers in parentheses are t-statistics, adjusted following Newey and West (1987) using six lags, testing the null hypothesis that the time-series average of the portfolio's excess return or FFC alpha is equal to zero.

	Coefficient	$\beta\,1$	$\beta\,2$	$\beta\,3$	β Diff	β Avg
MktCap 1	Excess return	20.96	23.68	21.20	0.24	21.95
		(6.12)	(6.81)	(3.62)	(0.06)	(5.66)
	FFC α	11.96	18.63	9.90	−2.06	13.50
		(5.05)	(5.46)	(1.31)	(−0.38)	(3.44)
MktCap 2	Excess return	11.07	13.45	11.49	0.41	12.00
		(4.13)	(4.03)	(4.98)	(0.13)	(5.20)
	FFC α	0.18	1.42	0.92	0.74	0.84
		(0.08)	(0.45)	(0.43)	(0.16)	(0.65)
MktCap 3	Excess return	8.86	10.48	8.51	−0.36	9.28
		(3.01)	(5.50)	(5.18)	(−0.11)	(5.52)
	FFC α	−0.27	1.33	−1.14	−0.87	−0.02
		(−0.09)	(1.21)	(−0.88)	(−0.20)	(−0.03)
MktCap 4	Excess return	6.45	8.99	8.64	2.19	8.03
		(3.85)	(6.74)	(4.00)	(1.17)	(5.37)
	FFC α	−0.91	1.78	−1.41	−0.50	−0.18
		(−0.81)	(3.23)	(−0.94)	(−0.24)	(−0.25)
MktCap Diff	Excess return	−14.51	−14.69	−12.55	1.95	−13.92
		(−4.81)	(−4.37)	(−2.16)	(0.60)	(−3.67)
	FFC α	−12.87	−16.85	−11.31	1.56	−13.68
		(−3.83)	(−5.23)	(−1.57)	(0.43)	(−3.29)
MktCap Avg	Excess return	11.84	14.15	12.46	0.62	12.82
		(4.90)	(6.59)	(5.14)	(0.25)	(6.29)
	FFC α	2.74	5.79	2.07	−0.67	3.53
		(1.72)	(5.12)	(0.84)	(−0.19)	(3.00)

5.2.5   Interpreting the Results

In most cases, the focal results of the portfolio analysis are the differences between the portfolios that contain high and low values of a given variable. The differences in average Y values between portfolios with high values of $X1$ and low values of $X1$ ($X1$ Diff portfolios) indicate whether a cross-sectional relation between $X1$ and Y exists after controlling for the effect of $X2$. The logic is reversed to examine the cross-sectional relation between $X2$ and Y after controlling for $X1$ ($X2$ Diff portfolios).

Turning to our example in Table 5.14, the results indicate that among low-β (β 1) stocks, high-$MktCap$ stocks have significantly lower average returns than low-$MktCap$ stocks, since the $MktCap$ difference portfolio ($MktCap$ Diff) generates an average excess return of -14.51% (t-statistic $= -4.81$) and an FFC alpha of -12.87% (t-statistic $= -3.83$) per year. Similar results are obtained for stocks with moderate levels of β (β 2), as the $MktCap$ Diff portfolio generates an average annual excess return of -14.69% and FFC alpha of -16.85%, both of which are highly statistically significant. For high-β stocks (β 3), the average excess return of the $MktCap$ Diff portfolio of -12.55% (t-statistic $= -2.16$) is statistically significant, but after adjusting for factor sensitivities using the FFC model, the abnormal return of -11.31% is no longer statistically significant. Examination of the relation between β and future stock returns presents no evidence of such a relation after controlling for the effect of $MktCap$ as, within each of the four $MktCap$ groups, the average return differences and FFC alphas between the portfolios comprised high-β stocks and low-β stocks (β Diff) are economically small and statistically insignificant, as all associated t-statistics are well below 2.00 in magnitude.

In some cases, looking at the $X1$ difference portfolio within the different groups of $X2$ may give differing indications for different $X2$ groups. For example, in some cases, there may be a statistically significant relation between $X1$ and Y among entities with low values of $X2$, but this relation may not exist, or may even take the opposite sign, for entities with high $X2$ values. For this reason, it is instructive to examine the $X1$ difference portfolio for the average $X2$ group. The results for this portfolio indicate whether, for the average group of $X2$, there is a relation between $X1$ and Y. Furthermore, it is frequently of interest to examine whether any detected relation between $X1$ and Y is driven by entities with low values of $X1$ or by entities with high values of $X1$. To do this, we can examine the average $X1$ portfolio in the low $X2$ group and the average $X1$ portfolio in the high $X2$ group. If the average $X1$ portfolio in the low (high) $X2$ group generates statistically significant results but the average $X1$ portfolio in the high (low) $X2$ group does not, this may indicate that the relation is being driven by entities with low (high) values of $X2$. If the average $X1$ portfolio for both high and low $X2$ groups are statistically significant but with opposite signs, it indicates that the difference is driven by entities with both high and low values of $X2$. Obviously, the roles of $X1$ and $X2$ can be reversed to examine the relation between $X2$ and Y.

Table 5.14 shows that, in our example, for the average β group (β Avg), the difference in annual returns between the high-$MktCap$ portfolio and the low-$MktCap$ portfolio ($MktCap$ Diff) is -13.92% with a corresponding t-statistic of -3.67. The FFC alpha of this portfolio is -13.68% per year with a t-statistic of -3.29. However, if we examine the alphas of portfolios with different levels of $MktCap$ for the average β (β Avg) portfolio, we see that only entities with low-$MktCap$ ($MktCap$ 1) generate statistically significant abnormal returns relative to the FFC model. The FFC alpha of this portfolio is 13.50% per year with a corresponding t-statistic of

3.44. The abnormal returns for the average β group for stocks in *MktCap* groups two through four of 0.84% (*t*-statistic = 0.65), −0.02% (*t*-statistic = −0.03), and −0.18% (*t*-statistic = −0.25) per year, respectively, are all statistically indistinguishable from zero. Similar patterns are also observed within each of the three β groups. The results therefore indicate that the negative abnormal returns of the portfolios that take long positions in high-*MktCap* stocks and short positions in low-*MktCap* stocks are driven by the low-*MktCap* stocks. A similar analysis examining the relation between β and portfolio excess returns and alphas shows that for the average *MktCap* (*MktCap* Avg) group, the difference in excess return and FFC alpha between the high-β (β 3) and low-β (β 1) portfolios are 0.62% and −0.67%, respectively, per year, both of which are statistically insignificant. This is not surprising given that we failed to detect a relation between β and future returns in any of the *MktCap* groups.

In some cases, it may be of interest to researchers to examine the difference of the differences portfolio. This portfolio indicates whether the relation between $X1$ and Y changes for the high and low $X2$ groups. It also indicates whether the relation between $X2$ and Y changes for different groups of $X1$. A positive (negative) and statistically significant result for the difference of the differences portfolio indicates that the relation between $X1$ and Y is more positive (negative) for entities with high levels of $X2$ than for entities with low levels of $X2$. The same can be said reversing the roles of $X1$ and $X2$.

Examining our example results, we find no evidence that the relation between *MktCap* and future returns is different for stocks with different levels of β, because the β Diff, *MktCap* Diff portfolio does not generate statistically significant excess or abnormal returns. Similarly, the same result provides no evidence that the relation between β and future stock returns is different for stocks with high *MktCap* compared to stocks with low *MktCap*.

Analysis of the results for the average of the averages portfolio is rarely, if ever, undertaken in the empirical asset pricing literature. However, it can roughly be interpreted as indicative of the average Y value if all categories of entities are given equal weight, where a category corresponds to an intersection of the $X1$ and $X2$ groups. When the Y variable is the excess return, this portfolio indicates the returns associated with a long-only portfolio that gives higher weights to entities in categories that have fewer entities. Thus, it may have application in assessing the effects of different weighting schemes on portfolio returns.

5.2.6 Presenting the Results

There are many ways that the results of bivariate independent-sort portfolio analyses can be presented. Here, we describe a few of these. As always, the optimal approach depends largely on which elements of the analysis are to be emphasized.

Single Analysis

One common approach is to present only the average values ($\overline{Y}$) for each of the $n_{P1} \times n_{P2}$ portfolios, and to present both values of $\overline{Y}$ and the associated *t*-statistics for the difference and average portfolios. Sometimes, results for the average portfolios are not shown. When the outcome variable Y is a return variable, frequently the alphas relative to a factor model are shown instead of the average returns or excess returns.

TABLE 5.15   Bivariate Independent-Sort Portfolio Results
This table presents the average abnormal returns relative to the FFC model for portfolios sorted independently into three β groups and four *MktCap*. The breakpoints for the β portfolios are the 30th and 70th percentiles. The breakpoints for the *MktCap* portfolios are the 25th, 50th, and 75th percentiles. Table values indicate the alpha relative to the FFC model with corresponding t-statistics in parentheses.

	β 1	β 2	β 3	β 3-1	β Avg
MktCap 1	11.96	18.63	9.90	−2.06	13.50
				(−0.38)	(3.44)
MktCap 2	0.18	1.42	0.92	0.74	0.84
				(0.16)	(0.65)
MktCap 3	−0.27	1.33	−1.14	−0.87	−0.02
				(−0.20)	(−0.03)
MktCap 4	−0.91	1.78	−1.41	−0.50	−0.18
				(−0.24)	(−0.25)
MktCap 4-1	−12.87	−16.85	−11.31	1.56	−13.68
	(−3.83)	(−5.23)	(−1.57)	(0.43)	(−3.29)
MktCap Avg	2.74	5.79	2.07	−0.67	
	(1.72)	(5.12)	(0.84)	(−0.19)	

In Table 5.15, we present the results of our example bivariate independent-sort portfolio analysis. We show only the FFC alpha for the 12 portfolios formed by sorting on β and *MktCap*. We also show the FFC alpha and the associated t-statistics for the difference and average portfolios, although frequently researchers present the average returns or excess returns and only present alphas for the difference portfolios. As it is rarely if ever used by researchers, we will not show any results for the average of the averages portfolio.

Multiple Analyses, Same Relation of Interest

Another common approach is to present only the results for the difference or average portfolios. This is frequently the case when the objective of the analysis is to examine the relation between one of the sort variables (say $X2$) and Y while controlling for the other sort variable ($X1$), but we are not interested in the relation between $X1$ and Y when controlling for $X2$. This presentation style also allows the researcher to present results for more than one bivariate portfolio analysis while minimizing the amount of space required to do so. In exemplifying each of these approaches to presenting the results of bivariate portfolio analyses, we present not only the results for our analysis using β and *MktCap* as the sort variables, but also the results of a similar analysis using *BM* and *MktCap* as the sort variables. In this second analysis, we once again use the 30th and 70th percentiles of *BM* to calculate the *BM* breakpoints and the 25th, 50th, and 75th percentiles of *MktCap* for the *MktCap* breakpoints.

Table 5.16 gives an example of how the results of only the difference portfolios may be presented. The column labeled Control indicates the first sort variable ($X1$) used in the sorting procedure. Thus, the results for the analysis sorting on β and

TABLE 5.16   Bivariate Independent-Sort Portfolio Results—Differences
This table presents the average abnormal returns relative to the FFC model for long–short zero-cost portfolios that are long stocks in the highest quartile of *MktCap* and short stocks in the lowest quartile of *MktCap*. The portfolios are formed by sorting all stocks independently into groups based on β and *MktCap*. The breakpoints used to form the β groups are the 30th and 70th percentiles of β. Table values indicate the alpha relative to the FFC model with the corresponding *t*-statistics in parentheses.

Control	Coefficient	1	2	3	Avg	3-1
β	Excess return	−14.51	−14.69	−12.55	−13.92	1.95
		(−4.81)	(−4.37)	(−2.16)	(−3.67)	(0.60)
	FFC α	−12.87	−16.85	−11.31	−13.68	1.56
		(−3.83)	(−5.23)	(−1.57)	(−3.29)	(0.43)
BM	Excess return	−7.74	−13.31	−18.18	−13.08	−10.44
		(−2.17)	(−3.41)	(−6.57)	(−3.97)	(−6.53)
	FFC α	−6.19	−11.24	−22.04	−13.15	−15.85
		(−2.23)	(−3.00)	(−8.32)	(−4.73)	(−7.75)

MktCap are presented in the rows where the control variable is β, and the results for the analysis sorting on *BM* and *MktCap* are shown in the portion of the table where the control variable is *BM*. The columns labeled 1, 2, 3, Avg, and 3-1 indicate the control variable portfolio. Thus, for example, the column labeled 2 indicates the results for portfolios in the middle group of the given control variable (β or *BM*). The table presents the average excess returns and FFC alphas for the long–short zero-cost portfolio that is long stocks in the fourth quartile of *MktCap* and short stocks in the first *MktCap* quartile (*MktCap* Diff portfolio). The FFC alpha results when the control variable is β are therefore identical to those in the row labeled *MktCap* 4-1 in Table 5.15. In some cases, it is not necessary or important to present both the average excess returns and FFC alphas. In fact, when the outcome variable is not a return, the FFC alpha does not exist and therefore cannot be presented. We present both the average excess returns and the FFC alphas here for completeness.

The results in Table 5.16 indicate that the negative relation between *MktCap* and future stock returns persists after controlling for β and after controlling for *BM*. Furthermore, as mentioned previously, presenting the results for the *MktCap* difference portfolio within each control variable group allows us to see that this result is robust across all levels of both β and *BM* because, within each group of each control variable, this relation is detected. We should stress here that neither of these analyses controls simultaneously for both β and *BM*. Each analysis includes only one control variable. The column labeled Avg shows that for the average β group, the negative relation between *MktCap* and future excess returns persists. This is not surprising given that this relation exists within each of the individual β groups. A similar result holds when controlling for *BM*. Finally, the column labeled 3-1 presents the results for the difference in differences portfolio. The results fail to detect any difference in the relation between *MktCap* and future excess returns among stocks with low values of β compared to stocks with high values of β. However, the results indicate a strong difference in the relation between *MktCap* and future stock returns among stocks with differing levels of *BM*, because the average excess return of -10.44% per year for the difference in differences portfolio is highly statistically significant with a t-statistic of -6.53. Adjusting the returns of this portfolio for risk only strengthens this result, as the FFC alpha for this portfolio is -15.85% per year (t-statistic $= -7.75$). These results indicate that the negative relation between *MktCap* and future stock returns is much stronger for stocks with high values of *BM* than for low-*BM* stocks.

While Table 5.16 allows us to examine the relation between *MktCap* and future excess returns among stocks with differing levels of β or *BM*, it does not give us an idea of whether it is the low-*MktCap* or high-*MktCap* stocks that are generating the results. Another way of presenting the results is to show only the results that correspond to the average $X1$ (β or *BM* in this example) portfolio for each level of $X2$ (*MktCap* in this example). This allows the reader to get an understanding of how the average value of Y varies with $X2$ after controlling for $X1$. This presentation style is frequently desirable when a univariate sort portfolio analysis indicates a relation between $X2$ and Y but the bivariate independent-sort portfolio analysis indicates that after controlling for $X1$, this relation disappears. This is because by showing results for each $X2$ group, it emphasizes the fact that there is no difference in average Y values for high and low values of $X2$ (after controlling for $X1$). Alternatively, this approach is useful when there is no univariate relation between $X2$ and Y but a relation appears after controlling for $X1$. In our example, we find a negative univariate relation between *MktCap* and future stock returns, but we do not find that controlling for β or *BM* explains this relation. Nonetheless, we exemplify this presentation style in Table 5.17.

Multiple Analyses, Different Relations of Interest

The results in Tables 5.16 and 5.17 examine the relation between *MktCap* and future stock returns after controlling for each of β and *BM*. Sometimes, however, we may

TABLE 5.17   Bivariate Independent-Sort Portfolio Results—Averages
This table presents the average abnormal returns relative to the FFC model for portfolios formed by sorting independently on β and *MktCap*. The table shows the portfolio FFC alphas and the associated Newey and West (1987) adjusted t-statistics calculated using six lags (in parentheses) for the average β group within each group of *MktCap*.

Control	Coefficient	MktCap 1	MktCap 2	MktCap 3	MktCap 4	MktCap 4-1
β	Excess return	21.95	12.00	9.28	8.03	−13.92
		(5.66)	(5.20)	(5.52)	(5.37)	(−3.67)
	FFC α	13.50	0.84	−0.02	−0.18	−13.68
		(3.44)	(0.65)	(−0.03)	(−0.25)	(−3.29)
BM	Excess return	22.04	11.78	9.27	8.97	−13.08
		(6.48)	(5.59)	(6.70)	(6.76)	(−3.97)
	FFC α	13.98	1.76	0.56	0.82	−13.15
		(5.00)	(1.31)	(1.33)	(1.21)	(−4.73)

TABLE 5.18   Bivariate Independent-Sort Portfolio Results—Differences
This table presents the average excess returns and FFC alphas for portfolios formed by sorting independently on β and a second sort variable, which is either $MktCap$ or BM. The table shows the average excess returns and FFC alphas, along with the associated Newey and West (1987) adjusted t-statistics calculated using six lags (in parentheses), for the difference between the portfolios with high and low values of the second sort variable ($MktCap$ or BM). The first column indicates the second sort variable. The remaining columns correspond to different β groups, as indicated in the header.

Sort Variable	Coefficient	β 1	β 2	β 3	β Avg	β 3-1
$MktCap$	Excess return	−14.51	−14.69	−12.55	−13.92	1.95
		(−4.81)	(−4.37)	(−2.16)	(−3.67)	(0.60)
	FFC α	−12.87	−16.85	−11.31	−13.68	1.56
		(−3.83)	(−5.23)	(−1.57)	(−3.29)	(0.43)
BM	Excess return	10.21	10.52	11.79	10.84	1.58
		(3.74)	(3.90)	(4.34)	(5.46)	(0.55)
	FFC α	8.93	8.97	7.72	8.54	−1.21
		(3.91)	(2.74)	(2.71)	(3.68)	(−0.35)

want to examine the relation between several different variables, perhaps $MktCap$ and BM, after controlling for another variable, say β. In this case, we can generate tables that look similar to Tables 5.16 and 5.17, except instead of the first column of the table indicating the control variable, it will indicate the variable whose relation with the outcome variable Y is of interest.

In Table 5.18, we present the results of two bivariate portfolio analyses. The first is the same analysis that we have been using throughout this section that takes β and $MktCap$ to be the sort variables. The second takes β and BM to be the sort variables. The relations of interest are those between future stock returns and each of $MktCap$ and BM. Table 5.18 presents the average excess returns and FFC alphas for the difference portfolios for each of the sort variables of interest ($MktCap$ and BM) within each of the β groups.

The results indicate a negative relation between $MktCap$ and future stock returns after controlling for β. This is the same result as was presented in Tables 5.15 and 5.16. The table also detects a strong positive relation between BM and future stock returns after controlling for β. These results indicate that after controlling for β, the positive relation between BM and future stock returns detected in the univariate analysis (see Table 5.8) persists. The last column in the table indicates that this relation appears to be quite similar among stocks with low and high values of β.

Finally, in Table 5.19, we present the results of the same two portfolio analyses as were presented in Table 5.18. The only difference here is that, instead of presenting the results for the difference portfolios, we present the results for the average portfolios across each group of the control variable, $X1$ (β in this example), and within each group of the sort variables of interest, $X2$ ($MktCap$ and BM in this example). Thus, the columns labeled 1 through 4 show results for the average (across the β groups) portfolio within the given group of the indicated sort variable ($MktCap$ or BM). The

TABLE 5.19 Bivariate Independent-Sort Portfolio Results—Averages
This table presents the average excess returns and FFC alphas for portfolios formed by sorting independently on β and a second sort variable, which is either *MktCap* or *BM*. The table shows the average excess returns and FFC alphas, along with the associated Newey and West (1987) adjusted t-statistics calculated using six lags (in parentheses), for the difference between the portfolios with high and low values of the second sort variable (*MktCap* or *BM*). The first column indicates the second sort variable. The remaining columns correspond to different β groups, as indicated in the header.

Sort Variable	Coefficient	1	2	3	4	4-1
MktCap	Excess return	21.95	12.00	9.28	8.03	−13.92
		(5.66)	(5.20)	(5.52)	(5.37)	(−3.67)
	FFC α	13.50	0.84	−0.02	−0.18	−13.68
		(3.44)	(0.65)	(−0.03)	(−0.25)	(−3.29)
BM	Excess return	8.92	12.63	12.98	19.76	10.84
		(4.92)	(7.75)	(6.35)	(7.88)	(5.46)
	FFC α	1.41	4.37	4.28	9.95	8.54
		(0.88)	(3.90)	(2.32)	(5.41)	(3.68)

column labeled 4-1 presents results for the difference in these averages (which is the same as the average difference) between portfolios in the fourth and first groups of the indicated sort variable.

5.3 BIVARIATE DEPENDENT-SORT ANALYSIS

Bivariate dependent-sort portfolio analysis is similar to its independent-sort counterpart in that the portfolios are formed by sorting entities based on values of two sort variables $X1$ and $X2$. The only difference between the dependent-sort and independent-sort analyses is that in the dependent-sort analysis, breakpoints for the second sort variable are formed within each group of the first sort variable. For this reason, dependent-sort analysis is used when the objective is to understand the relation between $X2$ and Y conditional on $X1$. The relation between $X1$ and Y is not examined in dependent-sort analysis. $X1$ is used only as a control variable.

5.3.1 Breakpoints

Calculation of the breakpoints for the bivariate dependent-sort portfolio analysis begins exactly the same way as in the independent-sort analysis. In the dependent-sort analysis, however, it is extremely important to distinguish which independent variable is the control variable, $X1$, and which variable is part of the relation of interest, $X2$, as unlike independent-sort analysis, in the dependent-sort analysis, the order of sorting is critically important.

The dependent-sort portfolio procedure begins by calculating breakpoints for the first sort variable ($X1$, the control variable). Letting n_{P1} be the number of groups based on $X1$, and $p1_j, j \in \{1, \dots, n_{P1} - 1\}$ be the percentiles used to calculate the breakpoints, the breakpoints for $X1$ are calculated exactly as described in Section 5.2 and equation (5.10). As always, breakpoints may be calculated using a different set of entities than the set that will eventually be sorted into portfolios.

Having calculated the breakpoints for the first sort variable $X1$ for each time period t, the entities are divided into n_{P1} groups based on the breakpoints $B1_{j,t}$. The next step is what differentiates dependent-sort portfolio analysis from independent-sort portfolio analysis. In dependent-sort analysis, the second sort, based on values of $X2$, is done separately for each of the n_{P1} groups of entities created by the breakpoints for the first sort variable. Thus, the breakpoints that determine how the sample is divided into portfolios based on the second independent variable $X2$ will be different for each of the n_{P1} groups formed by sorting on the first sort variable. We therefore define the breakpoints for the second sort variable as

$$B2_{j,k,t} = Pctl_{p2_k}(\{X2_t|B1_{j-1,t} \leq X1_t \leq B1_{j,t}\}) \tag{5.20}$$

where $j \in \{1, \dots, n_{P1}\}$, $k \in \{1, \dots, n_{P2} - 1\}$, $p2_k$ is the percentile for the kth breakpoint based on the second sort variable, n_{P2} is the number of groups to be formed based on the second sort variable $X2$, $B1_{0,t} = -\infty$, $B1_{n_{P1},t} = \infty$, and $\{X2_t|B1_{j-1,t} \leq X1_t \leq B1_{j,t}\}$ is the set of values of $X2$ across all entities in the sample with values of $X1$ that are between $B1_{j-1,t}$ and $B1_{j,t}$ inclusive. Thus, for each of the n_{P1} groups of entities formed on $X1$, there will be $n_{P2} - 1$ breakpoints for the second sort variable $X2$.

Before proceeding to an example, a brief discussion of the choice of the number of groups to use for each of the sort variables is warranted. As always, the objective is to find a reasonable balance between the number of entities in each portfolio and the number of portfolios. In dependent-sort portfolio analysis, there is one major difference in choosing the number of groups compared to independent-sort portfolio analysis. In dependent-sort analysis, because sorting based on the second sort variable $X2$ is done within each group of entities formed by the first sort, correlation between the sort variables does not play a role in determining an appropriate number of breakpoints. As long as there are sufficient entities in each group formed by sorting on the first sort variable $X1$ to form n_{P2} groups of entities when sorting based on the chosen percentiles of $X2$, the dependent-sort analysis should provide an accurate assessment of the relation between $X2$ and Y.

We exemplify the bivariate dependent-sort procedure by calculating breakpoints for portfolios formed using β as the control variable, $X1$, and $MktCap$ as the sort variable of interest, $X2$. As in previous analyses, the β breakpoints are the 30th and 70th percentiles and the $MktCap$ breakpoints are the 25th, 50th, and 75th percentiles. Table 5.20 shows the breakpoints for each year during our sample period. The table shows that in 1988, the β breakpoints are 0.18 (column $B1_{1,t}$) and 0.66 (column $B1_{2,t}$). These breakpoints are identical to the β breakpoints used in the independent-sort portfolio analysis (see Table 5.10). As β is the first sort variable, these are the breakpoints that are used to group the stocks according to β, regardless of the level of $MktCap$. Within the set of stocks with the lowest values of β ($\beta \leq 0.18$), we see that the first, second, and third $MktCap$ breakpoints are 4.57, 12.36, and 35.38, respectively. Thus, the portfolio $P_{1,1}$, which holds low-β and low-$MktCap$ stocks, comprised

TABLE 5.20 Bivariate Dependent-Sort Breakpoints

This table presents the breakpoints for portfolios formed by sorting all stocks in the sample into three groups based on the 30th and 70th percentiles of β, and then, within each β group, into four groups based on the 25th, 50th, and 75th percentiles of $MktCap$ among only stocks in the given β groups. The columns labeled t indicates the year of the breakpoints. The columns labeled $B1_{1,t}$ and $B1_{2,t}$ present the β breakpoints. The columns labeled $B2_{1,k,t}$, $B2_{2,k,t}$, and $B2_{3,k,t}$ indicate the kth $MktCap$ breakpoint for stocks in the first, second, and third β group, respectively, where k is indicated in the columns labeled k.

t	k	$B2_{1,k,t}$	$B1_{1,t}$	$B2_{2,k,t}$	$B1_{2,t}$	$B2_{3,k,t}$	t	k	$B2_{1,k,t}$	$B1_{1,t}$	$B2_{2,k,t}$	$B1_{2,t}$	$B2_{3,k,t}$
1988	1	4.57	0.18	12.49	0.66	25.31	2001	1	16.71	0.31	45.87	0.95	91.00
	2	12.36		39.76		126.79		2	44.75		231.86		350.97
	3	35.38		142.60		796.57		3	113.32		886.00		1162.14
1989	1	4.29	0.17	14.05	0.70	26.72	2002	1	12.80	0.33	56.33	0.89	140.84
	2	12.05		46.16		135.74		2	33.43		234.04		415.02
	3	33.94		183.14		929.26		3	69.34		851.28		1455.45
1990	1	2.74	0.23	8.62	0.86	21.50	2003	1	26.39	0.38	151.58	0.97	302.73
	2	8.40		30.99		98.69		2	57.59		415.27		714.81
	3	24.50		151.58		583.68		3	110.03		1480.06		2090.83
1991	1	3.76	0.24	14.27	0.85	38.90	2004	1	34.44	0.63	203.14	1.36	250.79
	2	10.60		55.37		169.80		2	75.35		702.06		562.28
	3	31.59		242.53		909.57		3	151.62		2530.95		1211.46
1992	1	8.16	0.26	23.08	0.97	38.17	2005	1	34.51	0.60	211.76	1.30	344.26
	2	22.05		79.97		140.75		2	72.25		748.77		680.42
	3	67.79		384.71		681.30		3	135.07		3277.05		1414.81
1993	1	11.03	0.29	34.12	0.92	43.02	2006	1	37.80	0.61	226.34	1.40	382.07
	2	28.81		101.77		180.90		2	82.29		778.31		734.76
	3	79.28		480.49		789.78		3	161.21		2900.79		1588.50
1994	1	11.60	0.36	30.21	0.97	35.30	2007	1	33.25	0.56	208.68	1.18	316.60
	2	26.86		105.28		144.17		2	67.62		848.39		607.85
	3	76.27		439.81		694.79		3	127.17		3253.81		1474.95
1995	1	13.60	0.27	41.60	0.90	38.33	2008	1	12.40	0.57	136.70	1.14	137.59
	2	34.46		145.19		152.81		2	31.09		475.72		356.81
	3	105.74		611.37		739.47		3	63.84		1611.62		1122.37
1996	1	14.99	0.32	40.72	0.90	49.92	2009	1	22.53	0.65	180.11	1.45	185.19
	2	41.62		163.43		177.91		2	54.22		632.27		427.60
	3	120.22		692.85		769.25		3	149.12		2220.07		1311.04
1997	1	15.50	0.26	42.75	0.72	80.59	2010	1	26.98	0.76	219.47	1.33	263.99
	2	44.11		155.84		346.42		2	61.05		721.38		609.64
	3	116.47		603.98		1524.24		3	259.80		2455.43		1828.61
1998	1	14.04	0.41	37.38	0.94	74.16	2011	1	22.28	0.82	246.05	1.38	215.12
	2	38.47		126.92		323.19		2	49.47		891.90		514.69
	3	109.89		568.93		1175.07		3	123.80		3048.15		1281.89
1999	1	17.39	0.15	48.04	0.53	95.04	2012	1	28.27	0.76	254.37	1.31	245.38
	2	43.43		165.40		477.36		2	64.96		797.94		680.17
	3	109.53		626.78		2278.61		3	498.84		2779.50		2144.59
2000	1	15.66	0.25	29.98	0.85	39.78							
	2	42.57		203.66		192.66							
	3	117.48		915.58		908.20							

stocks with $\beta \leq 0.18$ and $MktCap \leq 4.57$. The portfolio $P_{1,2}$ contains stocks with $\beta \leq 0.18$ and $4.57 \leq MktCap \leq 12.36$. Portfolio $P_{1,3}$ holds stocks with $\beta \leq 0.18$ and $12.36 \leq MktCap \leq 35.38$. Finally, the low-$\beta$ and high-$MktCap$ portfolio ($P_{1,4}$) holds stocks with $\beta \leq 0.18$ and $MktCap \geq 35.38$.

Turning to the second β-based group of stocks, we see that this group contains stocks with $0.18 \leq \beta \leq 0.66$. Within this group, the $MktCap$ breakpoints are 12.49, 39.76, and 142.60. Thus, for example, the portfolio $P_{2,3}$, which corresponds to stocks with βs between the 30th and 70th β percentiles and $MktCap$s between the 50th and 75th $MktCap$ percentiles, holds stocks with $0.18 \leq \beta \leq 0.66$ and $39.76 \leq MktCap \leq 142.60$. Notice that the $MktCap$ breakpoints are very different in the second β group than in the first β group. This is the ramification of performing a dependent sort. Finally, in the third β group, the $MktCap$ breakpoints are 25.31, 126.79, and 796.57. The increasing $MktCap$ breakpoints across the different groups of β are a manifestation of the positive correlation between β and $MktCap$.

5.3.2 Portfolio Formation

Portfolio formation for the dependent-sort analysis proceeds as one would expect given the procedure for calculating the breakpoints. Each time period t, all entities in the sample are first sorted into groups based on the breakpoints calculated using the first sort variable $X1$. Each of those groups is then sorted into portfolios based on the conditional breakpoints of the second sort variable, $X2$. In general, we can describe the portfolio holding stocks in group j of the first sort variable $X1$ and group k of the second sort variable $X2$ as

$$P_{j,k,t} = \{i | B1_{j-1,t} \leq X1_{i,t} < B1_{j,t}\} \cap \{i | B2_{j,k-1,t} \leq X2_{i,t} < B2_{j,k,t}\} \qquad (5.21)$$

for $j \in \{1, 2, \ldots, n_{P1}\}$, $k \in \{1, 2, \ldots, n_{P2}\}$. As with the independent-sort analysis, the result is that all entities in the sample for each period t are placed into one of $n_{P1} \times n_{P2}$ portfolios. When the sample used to calculate the breakpoints is the same as the sample that is sorted into portfolios, the percentage of entities in any given portfolio is easily calculated from the percentiles used to calculate the breakpoints. This does not hold when the breakpoints sample is not identical to the sample that is used to form the portfolios.

Table 5.21 presents the number of stocks in each of the portfolio for each year t during our sample period. Notice that for each year t and within each β group, each of the $MktCap$ portfolios has approximately 25% of the stocks. This is because we chose to use quartile breakpoints. There are two reasons that the number of stocks in each portfolio is not exactly 25% of the number of stocks in the given β group. The first is that the number of stocks in the given β group may not be divisible by four. The second is that when a stock has a value of a certain variable that is exactly equal to one of the breakpoints, it gets put in more than one portfolio. These issues are very minor, however. If these issues have a substantial impact on the conclusions drawn from the portfolio analysis, it means that the number of stocks (or entities in the general sense) in each portfolio is too small and that either the breakpoints must be adjusted or there are simply too few stocks (or entities) in the sample to effectively conduct a bivariate portfolio analysis.

TABLE 5.21 Bivariate Dependent-Sort Number of Stocks per Portfolio
This table presents the number of stocks in each of the 12 portfolios formed by sorting dependently into three β groups and then into four MktCap groups. The columns labeled t indicate
the year of portfolio formation. The columns labeled β 1, β 2, and β 3 indicate the β group.
The rows labeled MktCap 1, MktCap 2, MktCap 3, and MktCap 4 indicate the MktCap groups.

t		β 1	β 2	β 3	t		β 1	β 2	β 3
1988	MktCap 1	426	568	426	1998	MktCap 1	496	661	495
	MktCap 2	426	569	426		MktCap 2	496	660	496
	MktCap 3	427	568	426		MktCap 3	496	660	495
	MktCap 4	426	569	427		MktCap 4	496	661	495
1989	MktCap 1	414	551	414	1999	MktCap 1	457	609	457
	MktCap 2	413	551	413		MktCap 2	457	608	456
	MktCap 3	413	551	413		MktCap 3	456	608	457
	MktCap 4	414	552	414		MktCap 4	457	609	457
1990	MktCap 1	406	540	406	2000	MktCap 1	442	589	442
	MktCap 2	405	540	406		MktCap 2	441	589	442
	MktCap 3	406	540	405		MktCap 3	442	589	441
	MktCap 4	406	540	405		MktCap 4	442	589	442
1991	MktCap 1	398	530	398	2001	MktCap 1	413	551	413
	MktCap 2	397	530	397		MktCap 2	413	550	412
	MktCap 3	397	530	397		MktCap 3	413	550	413
	MktCap 4	398	530	398		MktCap 4	413	551	413
1992	MktCap 1	404	538	404	2002	MktCap 1	382	509	382
	MktCap 2	404	538	404		MktCap 2	381	508	381
	MktCap 3	404	538	403		MktCap 3	381	508	381
	MktCap 4	404	539	404		MktCap 4	382	509	382
1993	MktCap 1	425	567	425	2003	MktCap 1	355	473	355
	MktCap 2	425	567	425		MktCap 2	355	472	355
	MktCap 3	425	565	425		MktCap 3	355	473	355
	MktCap 4	425	567	425		MktCap 4	355	474	354
1994	MktCap 1	461	615	462	2004	MktCap 1	343	457	343
	MktCap 2	462	614	462		MktCap 2	343	457	343
	MktCap 3	462	614	460		MktCap 3	343	457	343
	MktCap 4	462	615	462		MktCap 4	343	457	343
1995	MktCap 1	472	629	472	2005	MktCap 1	337	450	337
	MktCap 2	471	628	471		MktCap 2	337	449	337
	MktCap 3	471	628	471		MktCap 3	337	448	337
	MktCap 4	472	629	472		MktCap 4	337	450	337
1996	MktCap 1	494	658	494	2006	MktCap 1	334	444	334
	MktCap 2	494	658	493		MktCap 2	334	445	333
	MktCap 3	494	658	494		MktCap 3	334	446	334
	MktCap 4	494	658	494		MktCap 4	334	446	334
1997	MktCap 1	514	686	515	2007	MktCap 1	325	432	325
	MktCap 2	515	687	515		MktCap 2	325	434	325
	MktCap 3	515	686	514		MktCap 3	325	432	325
	MktCap 4	515	685	515		MktCap 4	325	434	325

(*continued*)

TABLE 5.21   *(Continued)*

t		β 1	β 2	β 3	t		β 1	β 2	β 3
2008	MktCap 1	320	426	320	2011	MktCap 1	276	368	277
	MktCap 2	320	426	319		MktCap 2	277	368	276
	MktCap 3	319	426	320		MktCap 3	277	368	275
	MktCap 4	320	426	320		MktCap 4	276	368	277
2009	MktCap 1	298	398	298	2012	MktCap 1	266	354	266
	MktCap 2	299	396	298		MktCap 2	266	355	266
	MktCap 3	298	398	298		MktCap 3	266	355	266
	MktCap 4	299	397	299		MktCap 4	266	354	266
2010	MktCap 1	285	381	286					
	MktCap 2	285	380	285					
	MktCap 3	286	380	284					
	MktCap 4	286	381	286					

5.3.3   Average Portfolio Values

After the portfolios have been created, the next step is to calculate, for each time period t, the average value of the dependent variable Y for each of the portfolios. For each of the $n_{P1} \times n_{P2}$ portfolios, the procedure for calculating the average dependent variable value is identical to the procedure in the independent-sort analysis (see equation (5.13)). Similarly, calculation of the difference in averages between group n_{P2} and group one of the second sort variable, for each of the groups of the first sort variable ($\overline{Y}_{j, Diff, t}$, equation (5.14)), as well as the calculation of the average portfolio value for each $X2$ group across all $X1$ groups ($\overline{Y}_{Avg,k,t}$, equation (5.17)), for $k \in \{1, 2, \ldots, n_{P2}, Diff\}$, remain unchanged.

The only difference between the dependent-sort analysis and the independent-sort analysis is that, in dependent-sort analysis, we do not calculate the differences in mean values between groups n_{P1} and group one of the first sort variable $X1$ (equation (5.15)). The reason for this is that the dependent-sort analysis is only designed to assess the relation between the second sort variable $X2$ and the outcome variable Y. The conditional nature of the portfolio formation procedure leads to uncertain interpretation of the difference in average Y values between portfolio n_{P1} and portfolio one of the first sort variable $X1$ for a given group of $X2$. The one exception to this rule is the difference in differences portfolio, which can be used to detect differences in the relation between $X2$ and Y for entities with different levels of $X1$. We are also not interested in the average portfolio within each of the groups of the first sort variable (equation (5.16)).

The average one-year-ahead future excess returns for each of the portfolios in our example bivariate dependent-sort analysis are presented in Table 5.22. While the numbers are different from those of the independent-sort analysis, the discussion of these results would be similar to the previous discussion in Section 5.2.3. Further discussion is not necessary. We present these results so that the reader attempting to replicate the analysis has a reference point.

TABLE 5.22   Bivariate Dependent-Sort Mean Values
This table presents the equal-weighted excess returns for each of the 12 portfolios formed by sorting all stocks in the sample into three β groups and then, within each of the β groups, into four *MktCap* groups. The columns labeled $t/t + 1$ indicate the year of portfolio formation (t) and the portfolio holding period ($t + 1$). The columns labeled β 1, β 2, β 3, and β Avg indicate the β groups. The rows labeled *MktCap* 1, *MktCap* 2, *MktCap* 3, *MktCap* 4, and *MktCap* Diff indicate the *MktCap* groups.

$t/t + 1$		β 1	β 2	β 3	β Avg
1988/1989	*MktCap* 1	−3.02	−0.24	−3.63	−2.29
	MktCap 2	3.22	−1.67	1.44	1.00
	MktCap 3	−0.91	3.96	12.38	5.14
	MktCap 4	5.75	13.61	19.98	13.11
	MktCap Diff	8.77	13.84	23.61	15.41
1989/1990	*MktCap* 1	−20.67	−32.48	−27.18	−26.78
	MktCap 2	−34.95	−38.05	−33.72	−35.58
	MktCap 3	−31.57	−30.87	−25.74	−29.39
	MktCap 4	−27.67	−19.88	−15.97	−21.17
	MktCap Diff	−7.00	12.60	11.21	5.60
1990/1991	*MktCap* 1	75.86	57.12	86.67	73.22
	MktCap 2	32.31	47.48	63.18	47.66
	MktCap 3	35.88	41.68	51.85	43.14
	MktCap 4	20.89	28.56	39.91	29.79
	MktCap Diff	−54.97	−28.57	−46.75	−43.43
1991/1992	*MktCap* 1	78.25	38.34	37.76	51.45
	MktCap 2	31.13	23.22	10.40	21.58
	MktCap 3	24.36	18.48	11.07	17.97
	MktCap 4	24.93	14.20	8.67	15.94
	MktCap Diff	−53.31	−24.14	−29.09	−35.51
1992/1993	*MktCap* 1	45.88	42.00	25.77	37.89
	MktCap 2	31.54	23.36	7.28	20.73
	MktCap 3	21.03	15.09	9.93	15.35
	MktCap 4	17.84	11.34	12.12	13.77
	MktCap Diff	−28.04	−30.67	−13.65	−24.12
1993/1994	*MktCap* 1	1.63	−1.48	−8.00	−2.62
	MktCap 2	−6.68	−4.60	−10.08	−7.12
	MktCap 3	−9.21	−4.70	−7.91	−7.28
	MktCap 4	−5.38	−6.10	−5.52	−5.66
	MktCap Diff	−7.00	−4.62	2.49	−3.05
1994/1995	*MktCap* 1	28.15	27.40	30.11	28.55
	MktCap 2	27.43	36.11	33.51	32.35
	MktCap 3	24.75	24.16	22.22	23.71
	MktCap 4	21.69	25.31	27.22	24.74
	MktCap Diff	−6.46	−2.09	−2.89	−3.82
1995/1996	*MktCap* 1	34.29	13.58	13.95	20.61
	MktCap 2	13.10	12.84	10.80	12.25
	MktCap 3	11.36	18.16	2.11	10.54
	MktCap 4	20.16	14.54	12.97	15.89
	MktCap Diff	−14.13	0.96	−0.98	−4.72

(continued)

TABLE 5.22   *(Continued)*

$t/t+1$		$\beta\,1$	$\beta\,2$	$\beta\,3$	β Avg
1996/1997	*MktCap* 1	26.75	16.86	2.99	15.53
	MktCap 2	31.27	21.71	−2.49	16.83
	MktCap 3	33.86	25.86	1.50	20.40
	MktCap 4	30.37	22.93	17.32	23.54
	MktCap Diff	3.63	6.08	14.33	8.01
1997/1998	*MktCap* 1	−2.22	−8.19	−16.45	−8.95
	MktCap 2	−12.88	−13.97	−6.83	−11.23
	MktCap 3	−11.64	−6.85	−10.62	−9.71
	MktCap 4	−4.84	−2.75	14.63	2.34
	MktCap Diff	−2.63	5.44	31.08	11.30
1998/1999	*MktCap* 1	43.73	59.50	93.85	65.69
	MktCap 2	18.83	42.90	70.65	44.13
	MktCap 3	4.90	11.46	53.39	23.25
	MktCap 4	−10.56	−4.72	37.46	7.39
	MktCap Diff	−54.29	−64.21	−56.39	−58.30
1999/2000	*MktCap* 1	−4.05	−13.45	−31.33	−16.28
	MktCap 2	−7.70	−8.89	−13.70	−10.10
	MktCap 3	−11.01	5.20	−10.31	−5.37
	MktCap 4	−0.19	13.59	−8.62	1.59
	MktCap Diff	3.86	27.04	22.71	17.87
2000/2001	*MktCap* 1	42.66	49.62	16.59	36.29
	MktCap 2	35.91	45.46	−3.51	25.95
	MktCap 3	31.95	12.97	3.05	15.99
	MktCap 4	14.93	2.80	−23.98	−2.08
	MktCap Diff	−27.73	−46.82	−40.57	−38.37
2001/2002	*MktCap* 1	7.86	−6.53	−34.32	−10.99
	MktCap 2	7.17	−9.37	−44.22	−15.47
	MktCap 3	16.93	−9.66	−42.12	−11.62
	MktCap 4	−0.45	−8.74	−37.27	−15.49
	MktCap Diff	−8.31	−2.21	−2.95	−4.49
2002/2003	*MktCap* 1	126.16	126.13	130.07	127.45
	MktCap 2	83.70	77.30	76.57	79.19
	MktCap 3	60.81	38.73	56.68	52.08
	MktCap 4	44.81	30.37	44.05	39.74
	MktCap Diff	−81.35	−95.76	−86.01	−87.71
2003/2004	*MktCap* 1	35.21	21.61	10.52	22.45
	MktCap 2	25.11	17.13	7.53	16.59
	MktCap 3	22.03	24.40	8.80	18.41
	MktCap 4	20.05	19.33	10.48	16.62
	MktCap Diff	−15.15	−2.28	−0.05	−5.83

TABLE 5.22 *(Continued)*

$t/t+1$		β 1	β 2	β 3	β Avg
2004/2005	MktCap 1	3.31	0.26	−15.96	−4.13
	MktCap 2	1.76	1.13	−0.99	0.64
	MktCap 3	5.06	5.89	0.06	3.67
	MktCap 4	5.28	8.37	3.59	5.75
	MktCap Diff	1.97	8.12	19.55	9.88
2005/2006	MktCap 1	16.66	14.56	8.44	13.22
	MktCap 2	11.25	8.20	12.91	10.79
	MktCap 3	7.71	12.13	9.98	9.94
	MktCap 4	17.20	8.79	8.22	11.40
	MktCap Diff	0.53	−5.77	−0.22	−1.82
2006/2007	MktCap 1	−11.31	−11.33	−13.36	−12.00
	MktCap 2	−12.62	−13.25	−9.96	−11.94
	MktCap 3	−15.20	−4.46	−2.81	−7.49
	MktCap 4	−5.24	−0.24	8.37	0.96
	MktCap Diff	6.07	11.09	21.74	12.97
2007/2008	MktCap 1	−45.41	−51.23	−47.10	−47.91
	MktCap 2	−46.82	−37.86	−37.19	−40.62
	MktCap 3	−45.96	−33.62	−38.36	−39.31
	MktCap 4	−34.59	−35.08	−50.46	−40.05
	MktCap Diff	10.82	16.15	−3.36	7.87
2008/2009	MktCap 1	144.10	115.09	112.15	123.78
	MktCap 2	66.00	39.84	52.92	52.92
	MktCap 3	37.20	33.54	49.62	40.12
	MktCap 4	18.80	31.57	48.88	33.09
	MktCap Diff	−125.30	−83.52	−63.27	−90.69
2009/2010	MktCap 1	21.77	31.15	38.62	30.51
	MktCap 2	22.93	24.74	32.02	26.56
	MktCap 3	20.63	25.66	36.43	27.58
	MktCap 4	16.79	21.93	28.51	22.41
	MktCap Diff	−4.97	−9.22	−10.11	−8.10
2010/2011	MktCap 1	−10.16	−14.32	−19.46	−14.64
	MktCap 2	−7.71	−4.01	−12.26	−7.99
	MktCap 3	−5.92	0.35	−7.94	−4.50
	MktCap 4	8.45	2.10	−10.49	0.02
	MktCap Diff	18.61	16.42	8.97	14.67
2011/2012	MktCap 1	32.28	18.52	14.59	21.80
	MktCap 2	23.86	13.74	18.93	18.85
	MktCap 3	29.16	17.57	19.85	22.19
	MktCap 4	13.06	19.13	18.04	16.74
	MktCap Diff	−19.22	0.62	3.44	−5.05

5.3.4 Summarizing the Results

The procedure for summarizing the results for each of the time series of portfolio average values in a bivariate dependent-sort portfolio analysis is identical to that for univariate portfolio analysis and bivariate independent-sort portfolio analysis, described in Sections 5.1.4 and 5.2.4, respectively. For each portfolio, the time-series mean and inferential statistics are calculated. If the outcome variable Y is a return variable, then risk-adjustment may be performed. The Newey and West (1987) adjustment is usually employed.

The summarized results for our example are presented in Table 5.23. As with the bivariate independent-sort analysis, we present results for only the average one-year-ahead excess portfolio returns, risk-adjusted alphas using the FFC model, and the corresponding t-statistics, which are adjusted following Newey and West (1987) using six lags. For reasons discussed earlier, in a dependent-sort portfolio analysis, results for the average $MktCap$ portfolio, as well as the β difference portfolios, are not calculated.

5.3.5 Interpreting the Results

The main difference in the interpretation of the bivariate dependent-sort portfolio analysis is that the only relation we are interested in understanding is the relation

TABLE 5.23 Bivariate Dependent-Sort Portfolio Results Risk-Adjusted Summary
This table presents the results of a bivariate dependent-sort portfolio analysis of the relation between $MktCap$ and future stock returns after controlling for β.

	Coefficient	β 1	β 2	β 3	β Avg
$MktCap$ 1	Excess return	27.82	20.52	16.89	21.74
		(7.29)	(6.18)	(5.56)	(6.95)
	FFC α	21.91	12.30	6.83	13.68
		(7.49)	(5.44)	(2.09)	(5.08)
$MktCap$ 2	Excess return	14.05	12.65	9.30	12.00
		(4.82)	(4.05)	(5.06)	(5.34)
	FFC α	4.39	0.73	−1.84	1.09
		(2.45)	(0.29)	(−1.35)	(0.91)
$MktCap$ 3	Excess return	10.67	10.21	8.46	9.78
		(3.62)	(6.21)	(4.87)	(6.20)
	FFC α	0.24	1.10	−0.54	0.27
		(0.09)	(1.75)	(−0.37)	(0.42)
$MktCap$ 4	Excess return	8.84	8.79	8.67	8.77
		(4.17)	(6.55)	(3.46)	(5.62)
	FFC α	0.31	1.51	−0.45	0.46
		(0.17)	(2.35)	(−0.33)	(1.33)
$MktCap$ Diff	Excess return	−18.98	−11.73	−8.22	−12.98
		(−6.08)	(−3.74)	(−2.66)	(−4.50)
	FFC α	−21.60	−10.79	−7.27	−13.22
		(−5.74)	(−4.26)	(−3.00)	(−4.87)

between $X2$ and Y after controlling for $X1$. Interpretation of the results therefore will focus on the difference portfolios for the second sort variable. Statistically significant differences indicate a cross-sectional relation between $X2$ and Y after controlling for $X1$. Otherwise, interpretation of the results of the bivariate dependent-sort portfolio analysis is similar to that for the bivariate independent-sort portfolio analysis.

Examination of the results in Table 5.23 indicates that there is a strong negative cross-sectional relation between $MktCap$ and future portfolio returns, as within each β group, the difference in returns between the portfolio comprised high-$MktCap$ stocks and that of low-$MktCap$ stocks is negative, economically large, and highly statistically significant. These results persist after adjusting for risk using the FFC risk model. The abnormal returns relative to the FFC model are driven by the low-$MktCap$ portfolios, as the alphas of low-$MktCap$ portfolio ($MktCap$ 1) are statistically significant, but this is not the case for the second, third, and fourth $MktCap$ portfolios (with two exceptions). Thus, it can be seen that, in this case, the results of the bivariate dependent-sort portfolio analysis are qualitatively the same as those of the independent-sort analysis discussed in Section 5.2.4. While it is usually the case that both types of bivariate-sort analyses produce similar results, this is not necessarily the case. Thus, it is standard to check the robustness of any results using both sorting methodologies.

5.3.6   Presenting the Results

The presentation of the results of bivariate dependent-sort portfolio analysis is basically identical to that of the independent-sort analysis, except that results for the $X1$ difference portfolios and $X2$ average portfolios are not presented. The reason for this is that, as discussed earlier, the objective of the dependent-sort analysis is to examine the relation between $X2$ and Y after controlling for $X1$. The excluded portfolios are of no use in assessing this relation. Due to the similarities between the presentation of the results for bivariate independent-sort portfolio analyses and bivariate dependent-sort analyses, we describe only briefly the different presentation styles for dependent-sort results. For completeness, however, we present the results of analyses analogous to all results presented in Section 5.2.6. Of course, in this section, the results are different because they are generated by dependent-sort, not independent-sort, analyses.

In Table 5.24, we present the average return for each of the 12 portfolios formed by sorting on β and then $MktCap$, as well as for the average β portfolio within each $MktCap$ group. At the bottom of the table, we present average excess returns and FFC alphas for the $MktCap$ difference portfolios, along with the associated Newey and West (1987) adjusted t-statistics. The results indicate that the negative relation between $MktCap$ and future stock returns persists after controlling for β. The relation is strong within each of the β groups.

Notice that in Table 5.24, for $MktCap$ groups one through four, we presented only the average excess returns, not the FFC alphas, as was done in Table 5.15. Presenting the excess returns for all portfolios and FFC alphas for only the difference portfolios is a common approach. The reason for this is that, if the excess returns do not exhibit a pattern across the different groups of $X2$ ($MktCap$ in this case), then there is usually

TABLE 5.24   Bivariate Dependent-Sort Portfolio Results
This table presents the average abnormal returns relative to the FFC model for portfolios sorted dependently into three β groups and then, within each of the β groups, into four *MktCap* groups. The breakpoints for the β portfolios are the 30th and 70th percentiles. The breakpoints for the *MktCap* portfolios are the 25th, 50th, and 75th percentiles. Table values indicate the alpha relative to the FFC model with the corresponding t-statistics in parentheses.

	β 1	β 2	β 3	β Avg
MktCap 1	27.82	20.52	16.89	21.74
MktCap 2	14.05	12.65	9.30	12.00
MktCap 3	10.67	10.21	8.46	9.78
MktCap 4	8.84	8.79	8.67	8.77
MktCap 4-1	−18.98	−11.73	−8.22	−12.98
	(−6.08)	(−3.74)	(−2.66)	(−4.50)
FFC α	−21.60	−10.79	−7.27	−13.22
	(−5.74)	(−4.26)	(−3.00)	(−4.87)

little need to risk-adjust the returns. While it is possible that there is no significant pattern in returns but a significant pattern emerges after adjusting for risk, this sort of result is rare.

The results in Table 5.25 show the results of bivariate dependent-sort analyses of the relation between *MktCap* and future stock returns after controlling for each of β and *BM*. The table presents the average excess returns and FFC alphas for the *MktCap* difference portfolio within each group of the control variable, which is indicated in the first column of the table. The results indicate that the relation between *MktCap* and future stock returns is strong after controlling for each of β and *BM*. The results of the dependent-sort analyses are therefore similar, and lead to the same conclusions, as the results of the corresponding independent-sort analyses (see Table 5.16). The only exception to this is for the difference in differences portfolios (column 3-1). The results indicate that the negative relation between *MktCap* and future stock excess returns is much stronger for low-β stocks than for high-β stocks as the average excess return of the difference in differences portfolio is 10.77% per year with a corresponding t-statistic of 6.60. The FFC alpha for this portfolio of 14.32% per year (t-statistic = 5.99) is even larger. On the other hand, the negative relation between *MktCap* and future stock excess returns is stronger in high-*BM* stocks than in low-*BM* stocks because the difference in differences portfolio generates an average return of −15.18% per year (t-statistic = −8.17) and alpha of −23.76% per year (t-statistic = −6.86).

In Table 5.26, we present the excess return and FFC alpha for average portfolio across all groups of the control variable within each group of *MktCap*. These results help show that the strong negative relation between *MktCap* and future stock returns is driven mostly by stocks with low values of *MktCap*. The results are qualitatively similar to those from the independent-sort analyses (Table 5.17).

TABLE 5.25 Bivariate Dependent-Sort Portfolio Results—Differences
This table presents the average abnormal returns relative to the FFC model for long–short zero-cost portfolios that are long stocks in the highest quartile of *MktCap* and short stocks in the lowest quartile of *MktCap*. The portfolios are formed by sorting all stocks independently into groups based on β and *MktCap*. The breakpoints used to form the β groups are the 30th and 70th percentiles of β. Table values indicate the alpha relative to the FFC model with the corresponding *t*-statistics in parentheses.

Control	Coefficient	1	2	3	Avg	3-1
β	Excess return	−18.98	−11.73	−8.22	−12.98	10.77
		(−6.08)	(−3.74)	(−2.66)	(−4.50)	(6.60)
	FFC α	−21.60	−10.79	−7.27	−13.22	14.32
		(−5.74)	(−4.26)	(−3.00)	(−4.87)	(5.99)
BM	Excess return	−6.79	−10.31	−21.98	−13.03	−15.18
		(−2.01)	(−3.10)	(−7.04)	(−4.19)	(−8.17)
	FFC α	−4.26	−9.05	−28.02	−13.77	−23.76
		(−1.64)	(−2.81)	(−8.06)	(−5.59)	(−6.86)

TABLE 5.26 Bivariate Dependent-Sort Portfolio Results—Averages
This table presents the average abnormal returns relative to the FFC model for portfolios formed by sorting independently on β and *MktCap*. The table shows the portfolio FFC alphas and the associated Newey and West (1987)-adjusted *t*-statistics calculated using six lags (in parentheses) for the average β group within each group of *MktCap*.

Control	Coefficient	*MktCap* 1	*MktCap* 2	*MktCap* 3	*MktCap* 4	*MktCap* 4-1
β	Excess return	21.74	12.00	9.78	8.77	−12.98
		(6.95)	(5.34)	(6.20)	(5.62)	(−4.50)
	FFC α	13.68	1.09	0.27	0.46	−13.22
		(5.08)	(0.91)	(0.42)	(1.33)	(−4.87)
BM	Excess return	22.01	12.78	10.06	8.99	−13.03
		(6.84)	(6.27)	(6.66)	(6.62)	(−4.19)
	FFC α	14.64	3.48	0.54	0.87	−13.77
		(5.45)	(2.47)	(1.29)	(2.00)	(−5.59)

In Table 5.27, we present results of bivariate dependent-sort portfolio analyses of the relation between future stock returns and each of *MktCap* and *BM* after controlling for β. The table shows the average excess returns and FFC alphas for the *MktCap* and *BM* difference portfolios within each β group. Consistent with the independent-sort analyses (Table 5.18), the negative relation between *MktCap* and future stock returns and the positive relation between *BM* and future stock returns are both strong when using dependent-sort analyses. The strength of the positive relation between *BM* and future stock returns appears to be quite similar for stocks with high and low βs because the difference in differences portfolio (β 3-1 column) generates statistically insignificant average excess returns and alpha.

TABLE 5.27 Bivariate Dependent-Sort Portfolio Results—Differences
This table presents the average excess returns and FFC alphas for portfolios formed by sorting independently on β and a second sort variable, which is either *MktCap* or *BM*. The table shows the average excess returns and FFC alphas, along with the associated Newey and West (1987)-adjusted t-statistics calculated using six lags (in parentheses), for the difference between the portfolios with high and low values of the second sort variable (*MktCap* or *BM*). The first column indicates the second sort variable. The remaining columns correspond to different β groups, as indicated in the header.

Sort Variable	Coefficient	β 1	β 2	β 3	β Avg	β 3-1
MktCap	Excess return	−18.98	−11.73	−8.22	−12.98	10.77
		(−6.08)	(−3.74)	(−2.66)	(−4.50)	(6.60)
	FFC α	−21.60	−10.79	−7.27	−13.22	14.32
		(−5.74)	(−4.26)	(−3.00)	(−4.87)	(5.99)
BM	Excess return	12.33	9.29	9.84	10.48	−2.49
		(4.72)	(3.21)	(3.77)	(5.27)	(−1.09)
	FFC α	12.38	6.82	7.38	8.86	−5.00
		(5.54)	(2.07)	(2.25)	(3.45)	(−1.46)

TABLE 5.28 Bivariate Dependent-Sort Portfolio Results—Averages
This table presents the average excess returns and FFC alphas for portfolios formed by sorting independently on β and a second sort variable, which is either *MktCap* or *BM*. The table shows the average excess returns and FFC alphas, along with the associated Newey and West (1987)-adjusted t-statistics calculated using six lags (in parentheses), for the difference between the portfolios with high and low values of the second sort variable (*MktCap* or *BM*). The first column indicates the second sort variable. The remaining columns correspond to different β groups, as indicated in the header.

Sort Variable	Coefficient	1	2	3	4	4-1
MktCap	Excess return	21.74	12.00	9.78	8.77	−12.98
		(6.95)	(5.34)	(6.20)	(5.62)	(−4.50)
	FFC α	13.68	1.09	0.27	0.46	−13.22
		(5.08)	(0.91)	(0.42)	(1.33)	(−4.87)
BM	Excess return	8.63	11.93	13.89	19.11	10.48
		(4.98)	(7.38)	(8.09)	(7.68)	(5.27)
	FFC α	0.97	3.80	4.85	9.83	8.86
		(0.59)	(3.23)	(4.47)	(5.34)	(3.45)

Finally, in Table 5.28, we present the results of the same bivariate dependent-sort portfolio analyses whose results were presented in Table 5.27. In Table 5.28, however, we show the results for the average β portfolio within each of the different groups of *MktCap* and *BM*. The columns labeled 1, 2, 3, 4, and 4-1 indicate the *MktCap* or *BM* group for which the average β portfolio results are shown. The results in the column labeled 4-1 demonstrate that the negative relation between *MktCap* and future stock returns as well as the positive relation between *BM* and future stock returns, both persist after controlling for β. These results are qualitatively similar to those of the independent-sort analyses (Table 5.19).

In summary, our examples show that the results of bivariate independent-sort and dependent-sort portfolio analyses produce similar results. While this will usually be the case, it is not necessarily so. It is therefore a good idea to perform both sets of analyses. If the results of the independent-sort and dependent-sort analyses lead to substantially different conclusions, then further investigation is warranted.

5.4 INDEPENDENT VERSUS DEPENDENT SORT

Having separately presented the bivariate independent-sort and dependent-sort portfolio methodologies, we proceed to a comparison of the two sorting procedures. While in most cases both sorting procedures produce qualitatively similar results, this is not always the case, and when it is not the case, it is important to understand what may be driving the difference. As mentioned previously, the most salient difference between the two types of bivariate portfolio analyses is that dependent-sort analysis can only be used to examine the relation between the second sort variable, $X2$, and the outcome variable, Y, after controlling for $X1$. Independent-sort analysis permits examination of this relation, as well as the relation between $X1$ and Y, controlling for $X2$. Our discussion therefore focuses on differences in the examination of the relation between $X2$ and Y after controlling for $X1$, as investigation of this relation is common to both types of sorts. We exemplify the differences between the sorting procedures using the analyses that take β to be the first sort variable and $MktCap$ to be the second sort variable.

When using the independent-sort procedure, each of the sorts is an unconditional sort, meaning that the sort on $X2$ ($MktCap$ in our example) is performed on all entities regardless of the value of $X1$ (β in our example). As a result, any given portfolio $P_{j,k,t}$ contains the set of entities that fall into the jth group based on sort variable $X1$ and the kth *unconditional* group based on sort variable $X2$. For example, stocks in the low-β and low-$MktCap$ portfolio represent stocks that have both unconditionally low values of β and, more importantly, unconditionally low values of $MktCap$. Similarly, stocks in the low-β and high-$MktCap$ portfolio have unconditionally low values of β and, more importantly, unconditionally high values of $MktCap$. Thus, when taking the difference in returns between the high-$MktCap$ portfolio and the low-$MktCap$ portfolio, we are comparing average returns for stocks with unconditionally high values of $MktCap$ and stocks with unconditionally low values of $MktCap$, among only stocks with low values of β. Similarly, when taking the difference in returns between the high-$MktCap$ and low-$MktCap$ portfolios in the high-β group, the comparison is once again between stocks with unconditionally high and low values of $MktCap$, this time among only stocks with high values of β.

To see this, in Table 5.29 we present the average values of $MktCap$ for each of the 12 portfolios generated by the bivariate independent-sort analysis. The results show that, regardless of the level of β, the average values of $MktCap$ within each $MktCap$ quartile are similar (a small exception may be found in the high-$MktCap$ group).

TABLE 5.29 Bivariate Independent-Sort Portfolio Average *MktCap*

This table presents the average *MktCap* for portfolios formed by sorting independently on β and *MktCap*.

	β 1	β 2	β 3
MktCap 1	21	22	25
MktCap 2	85	110	117
MktCap 3	421	432	421
MktCap 4	8767	7427	6983

Thus, regardless of which β group we are examining, the difference in average excess returns between the high-*MktCap* and low-*MktCap* portfolios represents a difference in average excess returns between stocks with unconditionally high values of *MktCap* and unconditionally low values of *MktCap*. Despite the fact that we are, in some way, controlling for the effect of β ($X1$) when examining the relation between *MktCap* ($X2$) and future stock returns (Y), the results of an independent-sort analysis must, therefore, be interpreted as indicative of the unconditional relation between *MktCap* ($X2$) and future excess stock returns (Y).

When using the dependent-sort methodology, the groupings on the second sort variable are conditional on the values of the first sort variable. Thus, any given portfolio $P_{j,k,t}$ contains entities that fall into the jth group based on sort variable $X1$ and the kth group based on sort variable $X2$ *conditional* on the entity having a value of $X1$ that places it in the jth $X1$ group. To exemplify this, we begin by recalling that the correlations presented in Table 3.3 and the portfolio analysis shown in Table 5.7 indicate a strong positive cross-sectional relation between β and *MktCap*. Thus, stocks in the low-β group are likely to have low values of *MktCap* relative to the entire sample. When performing the second sort within the low-β group, therefore, we are effectively stratifying a group of stocks that are mostly low-*MktCap* stocks into conditional levels of *MktCap*. Thus, the low-β and low-*MktCap* portfolio is likely to contain stocks with very low values of *MktCap*. The low-β and high-*MktCap* portfolio contains stocks with the highest values of *MktCap* among (conditional on) low-β stocks, but these values of *MktCap* may actually be quite low relative to the entire sample because the low-β group contains predominantly low *MktCap* stocks. Thus, when we calculate the difference in average excess returns between the high-*MktCap* and low-*MktCap* portfolios within the low-β group, we are effectively comparing stocks with conditionally high values of *MktCap* to stocks with conditionally low values of *MktCap*, with β being the conditioning variable. The same can be said for any of the groups of β ($X1$).

In Table 5.30, we present the average values of *MktCap* for each of the portfolios formed using the dependent-sort methodology. The results are exactly as would be expected. Stocks in the low-β and high-*MktCap* portfolio have high values of *MktCap* relative to other stocks with low values of β, but unconditionally, the average *MktCap* of these stocks is not as high as the average *MktCap* of stocks in the high-*MktCap* portfolios within groups two and three of β are much higher. Similarly,

TABLE 5.30   Bivariate Dependent-Sort Portfolio Average *MktCap*

This table presents the average *MktCap* for portfolios formed by sorting dependently on β and then on *MktCap*.

	$\beta\,1$	$\beta\,2$	$\beta\,3$
MktCap 1	10	44	76
MktCap 2	29	202	237
MktCap 3	69	726	689
MktCap 4	3974	9523	9008

the high-β and low-*MktCap* portfolio contains stocks with conditionally low values of *MktCap*, but unconditionally, these stocks do not have low *MktCap*, especially compared to the low-*MktCap* portfolios for the first and second β groups. The results of a dependent-sort analysis are therefore indicative of the relation between *MktCap* ($X2$) and future stock excess returns (Y), conditional on β ($X1$).

In summary, while both independent-sort and dependent-sort analyses control for the effect of one sort variable ($X1$) while examining the relation between the other sort variable ($X2$) and the outcome variable (Y), the method of controlling for the effect of the first variable is different. Independent-sort analyses examine the unconditional relation between $X2$ and Y, while dependent sorts examine the relation between $X2$ and Y conditional on $X1$.

5.5   TRIVARIATE-SORT ANALYSIS

While univariate-sort and bivariate-sort portfolio analyses are most common, some researchers employ trivariate-sort portfolio analysis to assess the relations between three sort variables and an outcome variable. As with the bivariate-sort analysis, trivariate sorts can be independent or dependent in nature. In fact, it is possible to make the second sort dependent on the first sort, but the third sort independent of the second sort, or vice versa. The procedure for implementing a trivariate-sort portfolio analysis can easily be inferred from the above discussions of bivariate independent-sort and dependent-sort analyses, and thus will not be discussed in detail here. Perhaps the main drawback of trivariate portfolio analyses is that, unless the sample being used is very large or the number of breakpoints used in each sort is low, the number of entities in each portfolio is likely to be quite small. This is especially true when using independently sorted portfolios with sort variables that exhibit substantial cross-sectional correlation.

5.6   SUMMARY

In summary, in this section, we have discussed the procedure for implementing univariate-sort, bivariate dependent-sort, and bivariate independent-sort portfolio analyses. Univariate-sort analysis, as the name implies, examines the cross-sectional relation between two variables. Bivariate-sort analyses examine the relation between a given sort variable and the outcome variable after controlling for the effect of the other sort variable. While the interpretation of the results of the different types of bivariate-sort analyses differs slightly, in most cases, they lead to similar conclusions. When the outcome variable represents a security return, then the average portfolio values represent portfolio returns. In this case, it is usually appropriate to risk-adjust the excess returns using a factor model.

REFERENCES

Ang, A. Asset Management: A Systematic Approach to Factor Investing. Oxford University Press, Oxford, 2014.

Asparouhova, E., Bessembinder, H., and Kalcheva, I. 2013. Noisy prices and inference regarding returns. Journal of Finance, 68(2), 665–714.

Carhart, M. M. 1997. On persistence in mutual fund performance. Journal of Finance, 52(1), 57–82.

Fama, E. F. and French, K. R. 1993. Common risk factors in the returns on stocks and bonds. Journal of Financial Economics, 33(1), 3–56.

Fama, E. F. and French, K. R. 2015. A five-factor asset pricing model. Journal of Financial Economics, 116(1), 1–22.

Harvey, C. R., Liu, Y., and Zhu, H. 2015. … and the cross-section of expected returns. Review of Financial Studies, forthcoming.

Hou, K., Xue, C., and Zhang, L. 2015. Digesting anomalies: an investment approach. Review of Financial Studies, 28(3), 650–705.

Jegadeesh, N. and Titman, S. 1993. Returns to buying winners and selling losers: implications for stock market efficiency. Journal of Finance, 48(1), 65–91.

Jensen, M. C. 1968. The performance of mutual funds in the period 1945–1964. Journal of Finance, 23(2), 389–416.

Lintner, J. 1965. Security prices, risk, and maximal gains from diversification. Journal of Finance, 20(4), 687–615.

Mossin, J. 1966. Equilibrium in a capital asset market. Econometrica, 34(4), 768–783.

Newey, W. K. and West, K. D. 1987. A simple, positive semi-definite, heteroskedasticity and autocorrelation consistent covariance matrix. Econometrica, 55(3), 703–708.

Patton, A. J. and Timmermann, A. 2010. Monotonicity in asset returns: new tests with applications to the term structure, the CAPM, and portfolio sorts. Journal of Financial Economics, 98(3), 605–625.

Sharpe, W. F. 1964. Capital asset prices: a theory of market equilibrium under conditions of risk. Journal of Finance, 19(3), 425–442.

6

FAMA AND MACBETH REGRESSION ANALYSIS

In Chapter 5, we presented a technique, portfolio analysis, for examining the cross-sectional relation between two variables. The major benefit of portfolio analysis is that it is a nonparametric technique, meaning that it does not make any assumptions about the nature of the relation between the variables under investigation. The drawback of portfolio analyses is that it is difficult to include a large set of controls when examining the relation. (Fama and MacBeth 1973, FM hereafter) regression analysis is an alternative statistical methodology designed to examine the relation between pairs of variables. Unlike portfolio analysis, FM regression analysis allows us to control for a large set of other variables when examining the relation of interest. However, doing so comes at a cost. The cost is that we must make assumptions about the nature of the relation between the variables. In most cases, the assumption is that the relation of interest, as well as the relation between each control variable and the outcome variable of interest, is linear.

In the remainder of this chapter, we present the FM regression technique and exemplify its implementation using the data from our methodology sample. Specifically, we illustrate the FM regression technique using future excess stock returns (r_{t+1}) as the dependent variable, with the stock's beta (β), size (*Size*), and book-to-market ratio (*BM*) as the independent variables. We use *Size*, which is the natural log of *MktCap* (market capitalization in \$millions), instead of *MktCap*, because the cross-sectional distribution of *MktCap* makes it potentially problematic for use in regression analysis (see Table 2.3 and the corresponding discussion in Section 2.2 for more details).

Empirical Asset Pricing: The Cross Section of Stock Returns, First Edition.
Turan G. Bali, Robert F. Engle, and Scott Murray.
© 2016 John Wiley & Sons, Inc. Published 2016 by John Wiley & Sons, Inc.

6.1 IMPLEMENTATION

FM regression analysis is implemented using a two-step procedure. The first step is to run periodic cross-sectional regressions of the dependent variable of interest, which we denote Y, on one or more independent variables $X1$, $X2$, etc., using data from each time period t. Doing so produces slope coefficients, as well as an intercept coefficient (assuming that a constant term was included in the regression specification), on each independent variable for each period. The second step is to analyze the time series of each of the regression coefficients to determine whether the average coefficient differs from zero.[1]

6.1.1 Periodic Cross-Sectional Regressions

The first step in the FM regression technique is to run a cross-sectional regression of the dependent variable Y on the independent variables $X1$, $X2$, etc. In most cases, the cross-sectional regressions will include an intercept term. Thus, our cross-sectional regression specification is

$$Y_{i,t} = \delta_{0,t} + \delta_{1,t} X1_{i,t} + \delta_{2,t} X2_{i,t} + \cdots + \epsilon_{i,t}. \qquad (6.1)$$

The independent variables are usually winsorized to ensure that a small number of extreme independent variable values do not have a large effect on the results of the regression. In some cases, the dependent variable is also winsorized. When the dependent variable is a security return or excess return, this variable is usually not winsorized. In most other cases, it is common to winsorize the dependent variable.

The result is a time series of intercept and slope coefficients $\delta_{0,t}$, $\delta_{1,t}$, $\delta_{2,t}$, etc. Each time period will also produce regression statistics such as the R-squared, adjusted R-squared, and number of observations used in the regression. We denote these values from the cross-sectional regression for period t as R_t^2, Adj. R_t^2, and n_t, respectively.

Before proceeding to an example, it is worth mentioning that the type of cross-sectional regression used when implementing the FM regression procedure need not be a standard ordinary-least-squares (OLS) regression. It is straightforward to replace the OLS regression with a weighted-least-squares regression or even a logistic regression or probit model if the dependent variable is binary.[2] Multinomial models are also possible. The procedure is therefore quite flexible and can be applied to examine a wide array of economic phenomena.

---

[1] Pastor, Stambaugh, and Taylor (2015) show that for a univariate regression specification (one independent variable), when the data being used form a balanced panel (same entities in each cross-section) and the cross-sectional variance of the independent variable is constant across all time periods, the average slope coefficient generated by FM regression analysis is identical to the slope coefficient generated by a panel regression with time fixed effects.

[2] Asparouhova, Bessembinder, and Kalcheva (2010), Asparouhova, Bessembinder, and Kalcheva (2013) demonstrate that microstructure issues can introduce bias into the results of OLS regression analyses when the independent variables are cross-sectionally correlated with the amount of measurement noise and propose using weighted-least-squares to mollify this issue.

We exemplify the FM regression technique using the methodology sample discussed in Section 1.1. We execute the methodology using four different regression specifications. In all specifications, the dependent variable Y is the one-year-ahead excess return of the given stock (r_{t+1}). The first specification includes only beta (β) as an independent variable. The only independent variable in the second specification is $Size$. The third specification takes BM as the lone independent variable. The fourth specification includes all three variables, β, $Size$, and BM, as independent variables. Therefore, the full specification (the fourth specification) of our cross-sectional regressions is

$$r_{i,t+1} = \delta_{0,t} + \delta_{1,t}\beta_{i,t} + \delta_{2,t}Size_{i,t} + \delta_{3,t}BM_{i,t} + \epsilon_{i,t+1}. \tag{6.2}$$

Table 6.1 presents the results of the annual cross-sectional regressions. Panel A shows that for the specification using only β as the independent variable, for year $t = 1988$ (the year during which the independent variables are measured) and $t + 1 = 1989$ (the year from which the excess return is calculated), the estimated intercept coefficient ($\delta_{0,t}$) is 1.68 and the estimated slope on β is 5.53 ($\delta_{1,t}$). The R-squared from this regression is 0.17% (R_t^2) and the adjusted R-squared is 0.16% (Adj. R_t^2). Finally, the number of observations used in this regression is 5646 (n_t). Results of the regressions using the first specification for each time period are presented in Panel A. Results for specifications 2, 3, and 4 are shown in Panels B, C, and D, respectively.

6.1.2   Average Cross-Sectional Regression Results

The second step of the FM regression procedure is to compute the time-series averages of the periodic cross-sectional regression coefficients and other regression results (R-squared, adjusted R-squared, and number of observations). When calculating the time-series averages of the regression coefficients, we want to examine whether the average coefficient is statistically different than zero. Therefore, we also calculate the standard errors and the associated t-statistics and p-values to test the null hypothesis that the average coefficient is equal to zero. In most cases, the standard errors are adjusted following Newey and West (1987).

The summarized results for our example regression specifications are presented in Table 6.2. Standard errors, t-statistics, and p-values are calculated using the Newey and West (1987) adjustment with six lags. The table shows that, for example, using the specification that includes β, $Size$, and BM as independent variables (specification (4)), the average value of the intercept coefficient (δ_0) is 21.74 and its standard error is 4.58, giving a t-statistic of 4.75 and a p-value of very close to zero. The average coefficient on β (δ_1) is 0.96 with a standard error of 1.68, t-statistic of 0.57, and p-value of 0.57. For $Size$, the average coefficient (δ_2) is -2.49 with a standard error of 0.57, giving a t-statistic of -4.37 and a p-value close to zero. The average coefficient on BM is 3.08 with a standard error, t-statistic, and p-value of 0.79, 3.89, and close to zero, respectively. The average R-squared (R^2) and adjusted

TABLE 6.1   Periodic FM Regression Results
This table presents the estimated intercept ($\delta_{0,t}$) and slope ($\delta_{1,t}$, $\delta_{2,t}$, $\delta_{3,t}$) coefficients, as well as the values of R-squared (R_t^2), adjusted R-squared (Adj. R_t^2), and the number of observations (n_t) from annual cross-sectional regressions of one-year-ahead future stock excess return (r_{t+1}) on beta (β), size (*Size*), and book-to-market ratio (*BM*). Panels A, B, and C present results for univariate specifications using only β, *Size*, and *BM*, respectively, as the independent variable. Panel D presents results from the multivariate specification using all three variables as independent variables. All independent variables are winsorized at the 0.5% level on an annual basis prior to running the regressions. The column labeled $t/t + 1$ indicates the year during which the independent variables were calculated (t) and the year from which the excess return, the dependent variable, is taken ($t + 1$).

Panel A					
$r_{i,t+1} = \delta_{0,t} + \delta_{1,t}\beta_{i,t} + \epsilon_{i,t}$					
$t/t + 1$	$\delta_{0,t}$	$\delta_{1,t}$	R_t^2	Adj. R_t^2	n_t
1988/1989	1.68	5.53	0.002	0.002	5646
1989/1990	−29.52	2.28	0.001	0.000	5470
1990/1991	41.11	11.66	0.002	0.002	5360
1991/1992	36.36	−17.58	0.008	0.008	5265
1992/1993	28.09	−9.24	0.009	0.009	5353
1993/1994	−5.21	−0.52	0.000	−0.000	5634
1994/1995	25.42	2.87	0.001	0.000	6108
1995/1996	18.27	−5.41	0.004	0.004	6234
1996/1997	31.02	−17.29	0.024	0.024	6528
1997/1998	−9.34	4.41	0.001	0.001	6796
1998/1999	1.49	45.88	0.017	0.017	6520
1999/2000	−0.85	−14.61	0.010	0.010	6036
2000/2001	37.13	−24.58	0.028	0.028	5817
2001/2002	7.81	−27.26	0.114	0.114	5449
2002/2003	72.17	2.28	0.000	−0.000	5038
2003/2004	28.59	−13.70	0.018	0.018	4698
2004/2005	7.83	−5.93	0.008	0.008	4537
2005/2006	12.73	−1.54	0.000	0.000	4466
2006/2007	−12.06	4.39	0.004	0.004	4412
2007/2008	−41.07	−0.76	0.000	−0.000	4310
2008/2009	62.76	−1.42	0.000	−0.000	4229
2009/2010	18.21	7.70	0.008	0.008	3949
2010/2011	0.68	−6.91	0.009	0.009	3782
2011/2012	25.92	−5.87	0.003	0.003	3661

Panel B					
$r_{i,t+1} = \delta_{0,t} + \delta_{1,t}Size_{i,t} + \epsilon_{i,t}$					
$t/t + 1$	$\delta_{0,t}$	$\delta_{2,t}$	R_t^2	Adj. R_t^2	n_t
1988/1989	−7.72	3.17	0.011	0.011	5999
1989/1990	−32.77	1.10	0.002	0.002	5803
1990/1991	66.78	−5.40	0.007	0.007	5669

TABLE 6.1 *(Continued)*

Panel B

$$r_{i,t+1} = \delta_{0,t} + \delta_{1,t}Size_{i,t} + \epsilon_{i,t}$$

$t/t+1$	$\delta_{0,t}$	$\delta_{2,t}$	R_t^2	Adj. R_t^2	n_t
1991/1992	52.95	−7.16	0.020	0.019	5724
1992/1993	44.74	−5.43	0.021	0.020	5849
1993/1994	−3.69	−0.66	0.001	0.000	6387
1994/1995	30.69	−0.63	0.000	0.000	6682
1995/1996	18.45	−1.10	0.001	0.001	6902
1996/1997	14.79	0.57	0.000	0.000	7383
1997/1998	−17.49	2.12	0.004	0.004	7364
1998/1999	68.12	−6.88	0.007	0.007	6918
1999/2000	−16.07	1.07	0.001	0.001	6588
2000/2001	56.73	−8.08	0.030	0.030	6271
2001/2002	4.70	−3.48	0.017	0.017	5592
2002/2003	143.02	−13.83	0.047	0.047	5169
2003/2004	32.95	−2.45	0.007	0.007	4859
2004/2005	−3.72	1.00	0.001	0.001	4796
2005/2006	14.57	−0.57	0.001	0.000	4724
2006/2007	−24.23	2.76	0.011	0.011	4665
2007/2008	−51.14	1.50	0.006	0.005	4597
2008/2009	130.95	−13.13	0.020	0.019	4316
2009/2010	29.28	−0.56	0.000	0.000	4062
2010/2011	−21.58	2.36	0.015	0.014	3934
2011/2012	27.20	−1.33	0.003	0.002	3771

Panel C

$$r_{i,t+1} = \delta_{0,t} + \delta_{2,t}BM_{i,t} + \epsilon_{i,t}$$

$t/t+1$	$\delta_{0,t}$	$\delta_{3,t}$	R_t^2	Adj. R_t^2	n_t
1988/1989	2.94	3.52	0.002	0.002	4316
1989/1990	−24.94	−0.69	0.000	−0.000	4259
1990/1991	55.16	−6.58	0.001	0.001	4186
1991/1992	12.65	8.50	0.010	0.010	4180
1992/1993	16.30	5.82	0.006	0.006	4179
1993/1994	−11.08	7.61	0.011	0.011	4471
1994/1995	25.08	1.99	0.000	−0.000	4834
1995/1996	5.32	12.27	0.010	0.010	5023
1996/1997	6.09	13.13	0.013	0.012	5205
1997/1998	−9.61	5.11	0.002	0.002	5483
1998/1999	46.75	−10.65	0.001	0.001	5298
1999/2000	−10.46	2.97	0.001	0.001	4905
2000/2001	12.24	9.47	0.005	0.005	4630
2001/2002	−24.12	5.94	0.021	0.021	4454
2002/2003	74.51	7.04	0.002	0.002	4102
2003/2004	15.07	5.12	0.009	0.009	3843

TABLE 6.1 *(Continued)*

Panel C

$$r_{i,t+1} = \delta_{0,t} + \delta_{2,t}BM_{i,t} + \epsilon_{i,t}$$

$t/t+1$	$\delta_{0,t}$	$\delta_{3,t}$	R_t^2	Adj. R_t^2	n_t
2004/2005	−1.71	7.32	0.006	0.006	3702
2005/2006	7.68	7.23	0.004	0.004	3902
2006/2007	−5.03	−2.51	0.001	0.000	3852
2007/2008	−40.50	−1.50	0.000	−0.000	3743
2008/2009	51.47	23.12	0.004	0.003	3702
2009/2010	25.33	1.76	0.003	0.003	3526
2010/2011	−5.84	−0.54	0.000	−0.000	3375
2011/2012	12.70	9.01	0.011	0.011	3299

Panel D

$$r_{i,t+1} = \delta_{0,t} + \delta_{1,t}\beta_{i,t} + \delta_{2,t}Size_{i,t} + \delta_{3,t}BM_{i,t} + \epsilon_{i,t}$$

$t/t+1$	$\delta_{0,t}$	$\delta_{1,t}$	$\delta_{2,t}$	$\delta_{3,t}$	R_t^2	Adj. R_t^2	n_t
1988/1989	−11.10	−1.18	3.60	4.65	0.016	0.015	4301
1989/1990	−28.76	0.21	0.85	−0.34	0.002	0.001	4239
1990/1991	80.00	25.11	−10.50	−9.59	0.024	0.023	4176
1991/1992	42.12	−7.59	−5.53	6.15	0.025	0.025	4176
1992/1993	40.71	−3.83	−4.56	3.48	0.024	0.023	4166
1993/1994	−9.61	2.46	−0.70	7.93	0.013	0.012	4464
1994/1995	28.95	4.12	−1.53	1.92	0.002	0.001	4826
1995/1996	12.87	−4.09	−0.82	10.97	0.013	0.012	5009
1996/1997	6.39	−12.53	2.06	11.34	0.024	0.024	5203
1997/1998	−21.03	2.24	1.83	7.34	0.006	0.005	5475
1998/1999	69.93	61.01	−14.24	−9.63	0.036	0.035	5288
1999/2000	−31.70	−23.89	5.93	5.00	0.029	0.029	4885
2000/2001	70.83	−20.93	−6.95	−3.40	0.044	0.043	4617
2001/2002	−2.91	−22.14	−0.11	3.73	0.091	0.091	4444
2002/2003	152.96	30.13	−18.95	−0.46	0.062	0.061	4097
2003/2004	30.12	−15.71	−0.38	4.03	0.032	0.031	3831
2004/2005	−7.37	−7.93	2.52	6.35	0.022	0.022	3697
2005/2006	12.72	−0.50	−0.71	6.72	0.005	0.004	3893
2006/2007	−23.73	1.09	2.68	−0.24	0.013	0.013	3849
2007/2008	−49.72	−3.17	1.91	−0.42	0.007	0.007	3740
2008/2009	133.77	24.19	−17.69	8.21	0.029	0.029	3699
2009/2010	24.38	9.40	−1.49	1.17	0.014	0.013	3516
2010/2011	−15.02	−11.60	3.33	0.59	0.032	0.031	3372
2011/2012	16.92	−1.90	−0.28	8.33	0.012	0.011	3298

TABLE 6.2   Summarized FM Regression Results
This table presents summarized results of FM regressions of future stock excess returns (r_{t+1}) on beta (β), size (*Size*), and book-to-market ratio (*BM*). The columns labeled (1), (2), and (3) present results for univariate specifications using only β, *Size*, and *BM*, respectively, as the independent variable. The column labeled (4) presents results from the multivariate specification using all three variables as independent variables. δ_0 is the intercept coefficient. δ_1 is the coefficient on β. δ_2 is the coefficient on *Size*. δ_3 is the coefficient on *BM*. Standard errors, t-statistics, and p-values are calculated using the Newey and West (1987) adjustment with six lags.

Coefficient	Value	(1)	(2)	(3)	(4)
δ_0	Average	14.97	23.23	9.83	21.74
	Standard error	2.70	4.36	1.65	4.58
	t-statistic	5.55	5.32	5.94	4.75
	p-value	0.00	0.00	0.00	0.00
δ_1	Average	−2.73			0.96
	Standard error	1.86			1.68
	t-statistic	−1.47			0.57
	p-value	0.16			0.57
δ_2	Average		−2.29		−2.49
	Standard error		0.62		0.57
	t-statistic		−3.69		−4.37
	p-value		0.00		0.00
δ_3	Average			4.77	3.08
	Standard error			0.73	0.79
	t-statistic			6.51	3.89
	p-value			0.00	0.00
R^2		0.011	0.010	0.005	0.024
Adj. R^2		0.011	0.009	0.005	0.023
n		5221	5584	4270	4261

R-squared (AR^2) for the cross-sectional regressions are 0.024 and 0.023, respectively. Finally, the average number of observations used in the cross-sectional regressions is 4261. The summarized results for the regression using only β (specification (1)), only *Size* (specification (2)), and only *BM* (specification (3)) are also shown in the table.

6.2   INTERPRETING FM REGRESSIONS

Interpretation of the results of FM regressions is fairly straightforward. A statistically significant average slope coefficient indicates a cross-sectional relation between the given independent variable X and the dependent variable Y in the average time period. When the regression specification includes more than one independent variable, statistical significance indicates that a relation between X and Y exists after controlling for the effects of the other independent variables included in the regression specification.[3] Most researchers require statistical significance at the 5% level to reach such a conclusion.[4] This means that the p-value must be less than 0.05 or, equivalently, the t-statistic must be greater than approximately 1.96. Usually, for simplicity, researchers look for t-statistics greater than 2.00. Statistical significance at the 10% level, which corresponds to a t-statistic of greater than 1.645 in magnitude, is frequently referred to as marginal statistical significance. Researchers frequently examine the results using many different regression specifications to test whether the results of one analysis are robust to the inclusion of different sets of controls. If the coefficient of interest is statistically significant in one specification but insignificant when additional controls are added to the specification, then the relation between X and Y appears to be explained by some linear combination of the added control variables. Similarly, if a statistically significant relation appears after including additional controls, this indicates that it is necessary to control for other effects captured by the newly added control variables in order to detect the relation of interest.

In addition to investigating whether a statistically significant relation exists, it is usually important to understand the economic magnitude of the relation as well. In cases where the economic importance of a change of one unit in X is easily understood, the average magnitude of the coefficient itself is informative. In such situations, no additional calculation is necessary to assess the economic importance of the relation. In the general case, however, the magnitudes of X may not be easily understood. When this is the case, there are a few ways to assess the economic importance of the relation between X and Y. The first is to assess the effect of a one standard deviation change in X on the expected value of Y. To do this, we can simply multiply the average slope coefficient on X by the cross-sectional standard deviation of X in the average period, which is usually presented in the summary statistics (see Chapter 2). Alternatively, instead of the cross-sectional standard deviation, it may be reasonable to use the difference between two percentiles of the cross-sectional distribution of X. For example, one may use the interquartile range, defined as the difference between the third and first quartiles of X. One may also use the difference between the 95th and fifth percentiles to assess the difference in expected Y value between entities with high levels of X and low levels of X. Another similar approach is to refer to the results of a portfolio analysis to find the difference in average X values between portfolios comprised entities with high and low values of X (see Chapter 5). This difference can then be multiplied by the average slope coefficient to assess the difference in expected

---

[3]It should be noted that in some cases, the standard error of the estimated average slope coefficient has been shown to be biased downward, resulting in inflated statistical significance. Specifically, Shanken (1992) shows that an error-in-variables problem can result in overestimation of the statistical significance of risk-premia when standard statistical methodologies are used. Shanken and Zhou (2007) and Bai and Zhou (2015) examine empirical issues such as bias and precision associated with FM regression analysis.

[4]Harvey, Liu, and Zhu (2015) argue that due to data mining and the large amount of research examining the cross-section of expected returns, a 5% level of significance is too low a threshold and argue in favor of using much more stringent requirements for accepting empirical results as evident of true economic phenomena.

value of Y between entities with high and low X values. In most cases, the difference used is generated by a univariate portfolio analysis using X as the sort variable.

The average R-squared and adjusted R-squared can be used to determine the amount of total variation in the dependent variable that is explained by the independent variables in the average time period. Finally, the average number of observations is self-explanatory.

Examination of the results of our FM regression analysis, shown in Table 6.2, gives no indication of a relation between β and future stock returns, as the average coefficient on β (δ_1) is statistically indistinguishable from zero in all specifications that include β as an independent variable. In the specification that uses only β as an independent variable (specification (1)), the average coefficient is -2.73 with a corresponding t-statistic of -1.47. When *Size* and *BM* are also included as independent variables (specification (4)), the average coefficient on β is 0.96 with a t-statistic of 0.57.

Despite the fact that β is not statistically related to future stock returns, we go through the exercise of examining the economic importance of the relation between β and future stock returns to exemplify how this is usually done. Given that β measures the sensitivity of the given stock to the return of the market portfolio, the average coefficient on β should be an estimate of the premium associated with taking one unit of market risk. Using the full-specification results (specification (4)), the average coefficient of 0.96 indicates that one unit of market risk commands a premium of 0.96% per year. This estimate is obviously much lower than we would expect. Furthermore, when using the univariate specification (specification (1)), the result indicates a negative market risk premium. This is certainly contradictory to what we would expect. These results will be examined in more detail in Chapter 8. We can also assess the economic importance of the relation between β and future stock returns by multiplying the average coefficient with the standard deviation of β in the average year. Referring back to Table 2.3, we see that the cross-sectional standard deviation of β in the average year is 0.62. Multiplying this by the average slope from the full-specification regressions gives 0.59 (0.62×0.96). This indicates that a one standard deviation difference in β is associated with an increase in expected stock returns of 0.59% per year. Once again, this seems quite low. Finally, we can examine the economic importance of the relation between β and future stock returns by multiplying the average coefficient of 0.96 with the difference in average βs between a portfolio of high-β stocks and a portfolio of low-β stocks. This difference of 2.16 can be found in Table 5.7. Multiplying by 0.96 indicates that the difference in expected returns between stocks in the highest β decile and stocks in the lowest β decile is 2.07% (2.16×0.96) per year.

Our analysis indicates a strong negative relation between *Size* and future stock returns, as univariate regressions (specification (2)) produce an average slope on *Size* (δ_2) of -2.29 with a corresponding t-statistic of -3.69. This relation is robust to the inclusion of β and *BM* as independent variables (specification (4)), as the average coefficient in the full specification is -2.49 with corresponding t-statistic of -4.37. Multiplying this average coefficient by the standard deviation of *Size* in the average year of 2.07 (see Table 2.3) indicates that a one standard deviation difference in *Size* is associated with a difference of 5.15% (2.07×2.49) in expected annual returns.[5] This difference is quite economically important. To assess the difference in expected returns between stocks at the high and low ends of *Size*, we multiply average coefficient of -2.49 with the difference between the 95th and fifth percentile of the cross-sectional distribution of *Size*. This difference is 6.81 ($8.70 - 1.89$, see Table 2.3). Doing so indicates that very large stocks generate expected returns that are 16.96% lower, per year, than the expected returns of very small stocks.

Finally, we find a strong positive relation between *BM* and future stock returns. In the univariate specification (specification (3)), the average coefficient on *BM* is 4.77 with a *t*-statistic of 6.51. When β and *Size* are included in the regression model (specification (4)), the average coefficient of 3.08 remains highly statistically significant with a *t*-statistic of 3.89. Multiplying this coefficient by the standard deviation of *BM* in the average cross-section (0.71, see Table 2.3), we find that a one standard deviation difference in *BM* is associated with an expected return difference of 8.93% (2.90×3.08) per year, which is very economically important.

The average *R*-squared and adjusted *R*-squared values from the regressions that include all three variables are 0.024 and 0.023, respectively, indicating that only a little more than 2% of the total cross-sectional variation in future stock returns is explained by β, *Size*, and *BM*. Low levels of *R*-squared such as these are quite common in research that examines the ability to predict future stock returns.

In summary, our analysis finds statistically and economically important relations between expected returns and each of *Size* and *BM*, with *Size* being negatively related to expected returns and *BM* being positively related. The results indicate no relation between β and expected stock returns. These results are consistent with the results we found using portfolio analysis in Chapter 5.

6.3 PRESENTING FM REGRESSIONS

The results of FM regressions are usually presented in a manner very similar to Table 6.2, with a few modifications. In most cases, only one inferential statistic is presented. Thus, instead of presenting the standard errors, *t*-statistics, and *p*-values, only one of these is presented. In most cases, researchers choose to present *t*-statistics, and usually the *t*-statistics are presented in parentheses to alleviate the need for the column labeled Value in Table 6.2. To alleviate the need to refer back to the regression specification to figure out which coefficient refers to which independent variable, it is common to simply indicate the independent variable in the table instead of the character used to denote the slope (e.g., β instead of δ_1).

Table 6.3 illustrates how the results of FM regressions might be presented. This is the presentation style that we will use throughout this book. The table provides all information necessary to carry out each aspect of the interpretation of the results. As the results are exactly the same as those above, further discussion is not necessary.

---

[5] In most cases, the difference in expected outcome associated with a one standard deviation change in the independent variable is expressed as a positive value.

TABLE 6.3 FM Regression Results

This table presents the results of FM regressions of future stock excess returns (r_{t+1}) on beta (β), size (*Size*), and book-to-market ratio (*BM*). The columns labeled (1), (2), and (3) present results for univariate specifications using only β, *Size*, and *BM*, respectively, as the independent variable. The column labeled (4) presents results from the multivariate specification using all three variables as independent variables. *t*-statistics, adjusted following Newey and West (1987) using six lags, are presented in parentheses.

	(1)	(2)	(3)	(4)
Intercept	14.97	23.23	9.83	21.74
	(5.55)	(5.32)	(5.94)	(4.75)
β	−2.73			0.96
	(−1.47)			(0.57)
Size		−2.29		−2.49
		(−3.69)		(−4.37)
BM			4.77	3.08
			(6.51)	(3.89)
Adj. R^2	0.011	0.009	0.005	0.023
n	5221	5584	4270	4261

6.4 SUMMARY

In this chapter, we have presented the implementation, interpretation, and presentation of FM regression analysis. FM regression analysis is used to examine the cross-sectional relation between a dependent variable and one or more independent variables in the average time period. The main benefit of FM regression analysis is that it allows us to control for a large set of potential explanations for the phenomenon under investigation. The drawback is that it requires assumptions regarding the nature of the relation between the dependent and independent variables. In most cases, this relation is assumed to be linear, in which case OLS regression (or potentially weighted-least-squares regression) is used to perform the periodic cross-sectional analysis.

REFERENCES

Asparouhova, E., Bessembinder, H., and Kalcheva, I. 2010. Liquidity biases in asset pricing tests. Journal of Financial Economics, 96(2), 215–237.

Asparouhova, E., Bessembinder, H., and Kalcheva, I. 2013. Noisy prices and inference regarding returns. Journal of Finance, 68(2), 665–714.

Bai, J. and Zhou, G. 2015. Fama–MacBeth Two-Pass Regressions: Improving Risk-Premia Estimates. SSRN eLibrary.

Fama, E. F. and MacBeth, J. D. 1973. Risk, return, and equilibrium: empirical tests. Journal of Political Economy, 81(3), 607.

Harvey, C. R., Liu, Y., and Zhu, H. 2015. … and the cross-section of expected returns. Review of Financial Studies, forthcoming.

Newey, W. K. and West, K. D. 1987. A simple, positive semi-definite, heteroskedasticity and autocorrelation consistent covariance matrix. Econometrica, 55(3), 703–708.

Pastor, L., Stambaugh, R. F., and Taylor, L. A. 2015. Do Funds Make More When They Trade? SSRN eLibrary.

Shanken, J. 1992. On the estimation of beta-pricing models. Review of Financial Studies, 5(1), 1–33.

Shanken, J. and Zhou, G. 2007. Estimating and testing beta pricing models: alternative methods and their performance in simulations. Journal of Financial Economics, 84(1), 40–86.

PART II

THE CROSS SECTION OF STOCK RETURNS

7

THE CRSP SAMPLE AND MARKET FACTOR

The main objective of Part II of this text is to identify and understand cross-sectional patterns in expected stock returns. Before proceeding with this agenda in Chapter 8, we present an overview of the U.S. stock market and of the sample that will be used in the empirical analyses throughout the remainder of Part II. Our reasons for doing so are simple. First, to effectively execute empirical asset pricing research, it is important to have a deep understanding of the characteristics of the sample and data being used. Second, as we will be using the same sample for the majority of the analyses throughout this part of the book, we introduce this sample here and alleviate the need to discuss it in subsequent chapters.

7.1 THE U.S. STOCK MARKET

In this section, we provide an overview of the universe of stocks most commonly used in empirical asset pricing studies. This universe is comprised of U.S.-based common stocks that are listed on the New York Stock Exchange (NYSE), the American Stock Exchange (AMEX), or the National Association of Securities Dealers Automated Quotations (NASDAQ) system. The primary resource for data on this universe of stocks is the Center for Research in Security Prices (CRSP) database, which is maintained by the University of Chicago's Booth School of Business. CRSP provides data for NYSE-, AMEX-, and NASDAQ-listed securities for the period from December

Empirical Asset Pricing: The Cross Section of Stock Returns, First Edition.
Turan G. Bali, Robert F. Engle, and Scott Murray.
© 2016 John Wiley & Sons, Inc. Published 2016 by John Wiley & Sons, Inc.

31, 1925 through the present. In this book, as in almost all studies of the U.S. stock market, we use the data from CRSP as our primary source for U.S. stock market data.

There are several methods to access the CRSP database. Perhaps the most common method is through Wharton Research Data Services (WRDS), a system implemented by the University of Pennsylvania's Wharton School of Business that provides a web-based interface for accessing many of the databases frequently used for finance research. Another approach is to directly access the CRSP files stored by WRDS. This method, which is used to obtain the CRSP data used throughout this text, is accomplished by using an SSH client to log into the WRDS system (wrds.wharton.upenn.edu). Once logged into the WRDS system, one can access SAS files that contain the data. A third method to access the CRSP database is to obtain the data directly from CRSP. While each of these approaches gives access to the same data, the exact presentation of the data differs somewhat across these different interfaces. Thus, the files and fields indicated throughout this text assume that access to the data is gained by accessing the SAS files on wrds.wharton.upenn.edu. It is not difficult to identify the corresponding field names using other methods of access.

7.1.1   The CRSP U.S.-Based Common Stock Sample

The sample used in Part II of this book as well as in a large number of empirical asset pricing studies is a monthly sample that contains all U.S.-based common stocks in the CRSP database. Therefore, for each month t, the sample is constructed by taking all U.S.-based common stocks in the CRSP database as of the end of the given month. These securities can be identified using CRSP's monthly stock names (msenames) file. The set of all securities that are available as of the end of a month t includes all securities in the msenames file that have a start date (NAMEDT field) less than or equal to the last day of the given month and an end date (NAMEENDT field) that is greater than or equal to the last day of month t.[1] U.S.-based common stocks are identified as the subset of these securities that have a share code (SHRCD field in the msenames file) value of either 10 or 11.[2] We refer to this sample as the CRSP U.S.-based common stock sample, or simply the CRSP sample.

At this point, the reader may be wondering why we construct the sample to include only stocks that are in the CRSP database at the end of the given month t instead of stocks that are in the database at any point during the month t. The reason is purely notational. Most of the analyses in this text examine the ability of certain variables to predict cross-sectional variation in future stock returns. The notation we employ

---

[1] Most securities in the CRSP database have many entries in the msenames file. However, the date range for which a given entry applies, indicated by the NAMEDT and NAMEENDT fields, does not overlap the date range covered by any other entries for the same security.

[2] The first digit of the SHRCD field indicates the type of security, with 1 indicating an ordinary common share. The second digit further refines the security type. A second digit value of 0 corresponds to securities that have not been further defined, and a second digit value of 1 corresponds to securities that do not need to be further defined. Second digit values of 2 indicate companies incorporated outside of the United States and are therefore not considered to be U.S.-based. For a full description of the meanings of the different values of the SHRCD field, refer to the CRSP documentation.

is that the predictive variables are calculated using only data that are available as of the end of month t. These variables will then be used to predict stock returns in month $t + 1$. Thus, from the point of view of an investor looking to make investment decisions as of the end of month t, the set of common stocks available to such an investor is captured by the CRSP sample.

7.1.2   Composition of the CRSP Sample

We now turn our attention to examining the composition of the CRSP sample. We do so by decomposing the sample along two dimensions: stock exchange and sector. Along each of these dimensions, we examine the number of securities included in the sample as well as the total market capitalization of the stocks.

The month t market capitalization of stock i is calculated as the number of shares outstanding times the price of the stock as of the end of the last trading day of month t. The number of shares outstanding, in thousands, is given by the SHROUT field in CRSP's monthly stock (msf) file. The month-end price of the stock is taken from the ALTPRC field from the same file.[3] We therefore formally define our market capitalization variable, which we denote *MktCap*, as the absolute value of the product of the SHROUT and ALTPRC fields, divided by 1000. We divide by 1000 so that *MktCap* measures market capitalization in millions of dollars.[4] We take the absolute value because when there is no trading activity in a stock, CRSP reports the price as the negative of the average of the most recent bid and ask prices. There are some cases where either the SHROUT field or the ADJPRC field is missing in the CRSP database. In such cases, *MktCap* is taken to be missing.

Stock Exchange Composition of CRSP Sample

Figure 7.1 plots the number of stocks that are included in the CRSP sample for each month t from December 1925 through December 2012. The solid line presents the total number of stocks. The remaining lines indicate the number of stocks traded on a given exchange. The exchange on which a stock is traded is indicated in the exchange code (EXCHCD) field in the monthly stock names (msenames) CRSP file on WRDS. Stocks listed on the NYSE, AMEX, and NASDAQ are indicated with values of 1 or 31, 2 or 32, and 3 or 33, respectively, in the EXCHCD field. The short-dashed line shows the number of stocks listed on the NYSE. The number of stocks that are AMEX-listed is shown by the dotted line. The dash–dotted line indicates the number of stocks listed on the NASDAQ. The CRSP database also contains a small number of stocks traded on alternative exchanges such as the Arca Stock

---

[3]We use the ALTPRC field instead of the PRC field because the PRC field is either missing or set to 0 if there is no trading activity and no bid or ask prices available on the last trading day in the given month. The ALTPRC field is set to the last traded price, or the negative of the average of the bid and ask prices from the last trading day for which the necessary price or bid and ask data are available. When the PRC field is available (nonzero and not missing), the ALTPRC field holds the same value as the PRC field. There are many cases, however, where the PRC field is missing in the monthly stock file but the ALTPRC field is available.

[4]CRSP reports the number of shares outstanding in thousands of shares.

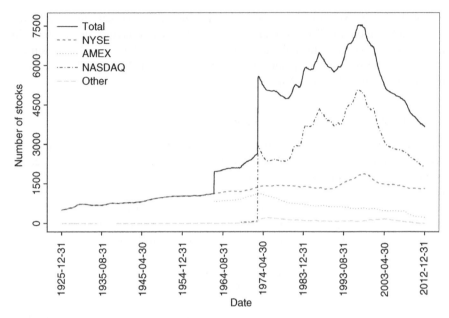

Figure 7.1   Number of Stocks in CRSP Sample by Exchange.
This figure shows the total number of stocks in the CRSP sample, as well as the number
of stocks listed on the New York Stock Exchange (NYSE), the American Stock Exchange
(AMEX), the NASDAQ, and other exchanges (Other) at the end of each month from December
1925 through December 2012

Market (EXCHCD = 4), the Boston Stock Exchange (EXCHCD = 10), the Chicago
Stock Exchange (EXCHCD = 13), the Pacific Stock Exchange (EXCHCD = 16),
the Philadelphia Stock Exchange (EXCHCD = 17), the Toronto Stock Exchange
(EXCHCD = 19), or in the over-the-counter market (EXCHCD = 20). Finally, an
exchange code of −2 indicates that trading in the stock has been halted by the NYSE
or AMEX, an exchange code of −1 indicates that the stock has been suspended by
the NYSE, AMEX, or NASDAQ, and an exchange code of 0 indicates that the stock
is not trading on the NYSE, NASDAQ, or AMEX, with no additional information
given. We put all non-NYSE, non-AMEX, and non-NASDAQ stocks into a group
that we call other. The number of stocks that are traded on these exchanges is shown
by the long-dashed line.

In December 1925 (the first month in the sample), the CRSP sample contains 499
stocks, all of which are listed on the NYSE. From then until June 1962, the total
number of stocks increases gradually, although not quite monotonically, to 1130, of
which 1121 are NYSE stocks with the remaining nine trading on Other (not AMEX
or NASDAQ) exchanges. In July 1962, 834 AMEX stocks are added to the sample,
causing the total number of stocks to jump from 1130 in June 1962 to 1963 (1125
NYSE, 834 AMEX, and 4 Other) in July 1962. The reason for this sudden increase is
that the CRSP database does not include AMEX stocks prior to July 1962. Because
of this, many studies restrict their sample to the period from 1963 through present. A
similar jump is observed in December 1972, when NASDAQ stocks are added to the

CRSP database. In November 1972, the sample is comprised of 2666 stocks (1378 NYSE, 1133 AMEX, 102 NASDAQ, and 53 Other). In December 1972, the total number of stocks in the market portfolio jumps to 5534 (1386 NYSE, 1135 AMEX, 2896 NASDAQ, and 117 Other). It is worth noting that while the vast majority of NASDAQ stocks are added to the CRSP database in December 1972, there are some NASDAQ stocks included in the sample for previous years. In fact, the first NASDAQ stock appears in January 1969. The number of stocks in the sample achieves its maximum in November 1997, at which point there are 7544 stocks (1862 NYSE, 572 AMEX, 5029 NASDAQ, 81 Other) in the CRSP sample. By the end of the sample period (December 2012), this number had been reduced by more than half. In December 2012, the CRSP sample is comprised of 3675 stocks, of which 1319 are listed on the NYSE, 226 are listed on the AMEX, and 2130 are listed on the NASDAQ, and two are listed on other exchanges.

We continue our analysis of the composition of the CRSP sample by plotting the total value of all stocks in the sample, measured in billions of U.S. dollars, as well its decomposition by exchange. We adjust the market capitalization values for inflation using the Consumer Price Index (CPI).[5] The chart is shown in Figure 7.2. The CPI-adjusted values represent market capitalizations in December 2012 dollars.

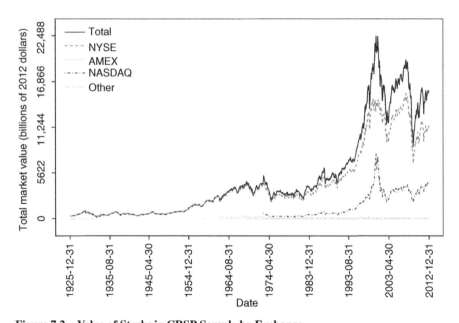

Figure 7.2   Value of Stocks in CRSP Sample by Exchange.
This figure shows the total value of all stocks in the CRSP sample, as well as the total value of stocks listed on the New York Stock Exchange (NYSE), the American Stock Exchange (AMEX), the NASDAQ, and other exchanges (Other) at the end of each month from December 1925 through December 2012

---

[5]CPI data are downloaded from the Bureau of Labor Statistics website. The data are available at www.bls .gov/cpi/data.htm. We use data for the All Urban Consumer series.

The total CPI-adjusted value of all stocks in the CRSP sample as of the end of December 1925 is $341 billion. For comparison sake, the total unadjusted market capitalization of these stocks is less than $27 billion. In June 1962, the month before the addition of AMEX stocks to the sample, the total CPI-adjusted market capitalization of all stocks in the sample is more than $2.15 trillion, all of which is from NYSE stocks. In July 1962, when AMEX stocks are added to the CRSP database, the total CPI-adjusted market capitalization increases only to $2.45 trillion, with approximately $2.3 billion of that being from NYSE stocks and the remaining $145 million from AMEX stocks. Thus, while the addition of AMEX stocks to the CRSP sample increased the number of stocks substantially, these stocks tended to have very small market capitalizations, resulting in only a small increase in the total market capitalization in all stocks in the sample. Similarly, when NASDAQ stocks enter the sample in December 1972, only $669 billion or 12.6% of the $5.3 trillion in total CPI-adjusted market capitalization comes from NASDAQ stocks. The sample achieves its maximum total CPI-adjusted market capitalization of nearly $22.5 trillion in March 2000. At this time, NASDAQ stocks make up nearly 36% of the total value of the stocks in the sample. As can be seen from the chart, at no point in time do AMEX stocks or stocks in the Other group comprise a substantial portion of the total market capitalization. Finally, in December 2012, the total value of the market portfolio is $15.7 trillion: $11.4 trillion of which comes from NYSE stocks with $4.3 trillion coming from NASDAQ stocks. The total market capitalization of all AMEX stocks at this time is less than $36 billion or 0.23% of the total market capitalization. In summary, the majority of the value of the stocks in the CRSP sample has always been derived from NYSE stocks. In months following their introduction into the sample in December 1972, NASDAQ stocks comprised a substantial portion of the total value of the sample, especially during the dot.com bubble of the late 1990s. The proportion of the total value of the CRSP sample coming from AMEX stocks is always very low.

Industry Composition of CRSP Sample

Having examined the composition of the CRSP sample along the stock exchange dimension, we proceed to examine the industry composition of the sample. We use the standard industrial classification (SIC) codes to group the stocks into industries.[6] SIC codes are numbers between one and 9999 that indicate the type of business activity conducted by a firm. The SIC code for each of the stocks in the CRSP sample is taken from the SICCD field in CRSP's monthly stock names (msenames) file. Table 7.1 presents the primary divisions of SIC codes. We group stocks according to these divisions for our analyses of the industry complexion of the CRSP sample.

The number of stocks in the CRSP sample in each of the SIC industries is plotted in Figure 7.3. The legend for the chart shows the first word from the industry, as listed in Table 7.1. The solid black line labeled "Missing" indicates the number

---

[6]SIC codes were created by the U.S. government in 1937. For more information on SIC codes, see the SIC manual on the United States Department of Labor's Occupational Safety and Health Administration website: https://www.osha.gov/pls/imis/sic_manual.html.

TABLE 7.1   SIC Industry Code Divisions

This table lists the industries corresponding to different SIC industry codes.

SIC Codes	Industries
1–999	Agriculture, forestry, and fishing
1000–1499	Mining
1500–1799	Construction
2000–3999	Manufacturing
4000–4999	Transportation, communications, electric, gas, and sanitary services
5000–5199	Wholesale trade
5200–5999	Retail trade
6000–6799	Finance, insurance, and real estate
7000–8999	Services
9000–9999	Public administration

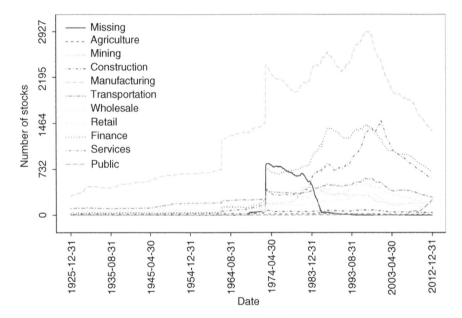

Figure 7.3   Number of Stocks in CRSP Sample by Industry.

This figure shows the total number of stocks in the CRSP sample in each SIC code industry at the end of each month from December 1925 through December 2012

of stocks with the value zero in the SICCD field.[7] The chart indicates that at all points in time, manufacturing firms make up the largest portion of the firms whose stocks are in the CRSP database. In December 1925, a total of 305 of the 499

[7]Zero is not a valid SIC industry code.

stocks in the CRSP sample are in the manufacturing industry. The proportion of manufacturing firms in the sample reaches its maximum of more than 67% (583 out of 864 stocks) in June 1946. During the later sample periods, financial firms and services firms make up a substantial portion of the firms in the sample, but even these two industries combined have fewer firms than manufacturing in all months except for the period from April 1999 through May 2006, during which these industries combined to have slightly fewer firms than manufacturing.[8] Finally, in December 1972, the number of agriculture stocks in the sample jumps to 810 from only 87 in November 1972. Similarly, the number of financial firms increases from 247 in November 1972 to 748 in December 1972. Both of these increases are caused by the introduction of NASDAQ stocks into the CRSP database in December 1972.

Finally, in Figure 7.4 we present the decomposition of total CRSP sample market capitalization by industry. All plotted values are in billions of CPI-adjusted December 2012 dollars. The chart of industry-level total market capitalization is quite consistent with that of the number of stocks. At all points in time, manufacturing firms comprise

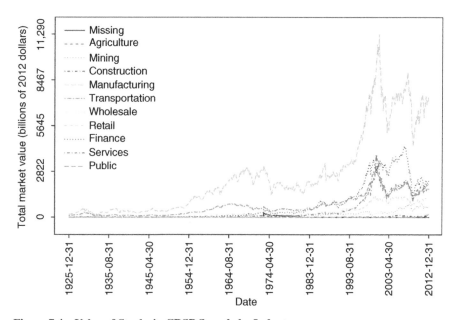

Figure 7.4   Value of Stocks in CRSP Sample by Industry.
This figure shows the total value of stocks in the CRSP sample in each SIC code industry at the end of each month from December 1925 through December 2012

---

[8]There are a few exceptions to this. During the months from November 2004 through April 2005 and August 2005, there were more manufacturing firms in the sample than financial and services firms combined. In May 2006, the number of manufacturing firms is exactly the same as the total number of financial and services firms.

the largest portion of the value of the CRSP sample. Toward the end of the sample period, financial firms begin to make up a substantial portion of the market portfolio value. As the dot.com bubble grew, the transportation (this division includes communications) and services industries grew substantially in value, but this phenomenon was reversed when the bubble burst.

7.2 STOCK RETURNS AND EXCESS RETURNS

We turn our attention now to calculation and examination of the returns of the stocks in the CRSP sample. Monthly stock returns are the focal variable in the majority of the analyses presented in this book and throughout the empirical asset pricing literature. In fact, the entire objective of this book is to identify and explain patterns in stock returns.

Monthly stock returns are found in the RET field in the monthly stock (msf) file in the CRSP database. CRSP calculates the RET field to be the return realized by holding the stock from its last trade in the previous month to its last trade in the current month. For the vast majority of the observations in the CRSP sample, the monthly return of a stock can simply be taken to be the value in the RET field in CRSP's msf file. The exceptions to this are the months when a stock delists from an exchange. In these cases, the last traded price in the given month is not necessarily indicative of the return an investor realizes by investing in a stock at the end of the previous month and holding until the end of the next month. The reason is that, when the stock delists, if the investor has not liquidated the position in the stock prior to the delisting, the investor will be stuck holding a stock that is no longer traded on an exchange. The value (or trade price) of that stock, therefore, may not be publicly observable, complicating the calculation of the monthly return. It is usually not reasonable to assume that an investor will liquidate the position prior to the delisting because, in many cases, delistings are unexpected and there is insufficient warning for an investor to trade out of the stock.

To deal with delistings, CRSP maintains a monthly delistings (msedelist) file. The file includes, among other things, the date of the stock delisting (DLSTDT field), a code indicating the reason for the delisting (DLSTCD field), and the return realized by an investor who bought the stock at the last traded price in the previous month and held the stock through the delisting (DLRET field). The DLRET field is known as the delisting return. When possible, CRSP determines the price of the stock after the delisting, calculates the return of the stock based on this price (adjusted for any distributions), and reports this value in the DLRET field. Unfortunately, in many cases, CRSP is not able to determine a post-delisting value of the stock. In such cases, the DLRET field is missing. To handle these situations, we adjust returns for delisting using an approach suggested by Shumway (1997). Specifically, if a delisting return is available in CRSP, we take the return of the stock to be the delisting return. If a delisting return is unavailable, we rely on the reason for the delisting, as indicated by the DLSTCD field, to determine the return. If the DLSTCD is 500, 520, between 551 and 573 inclusive, 574, 580, or 584, we take the stock's return during the delisting month to be -30%.[9] If the delisting return is not available and DLSTCD has any value other than those mentioned in the previous sentence, we take the return of the stock in the delisting month to be -100%.

To summarize, to calculate the return of a stock in any given month, we take either the return indicated in CRSP's monthly stock file or, if the stock is delisted during that month, we take the delisting return. If the delisting return is unavailable in a month during which as stock delists, we take the return to be either -30% or -100% depending on the reason for delisting as indicated by the delisting code.

In many cases, it is optimal to examine excess stock returns instead of simply the stock return. The excess return for a stock is defined as the difference between the stock return and the return on the risk-free security over the same period. The monthly risk-free security return data used throughout this book are taken from Ken French's data library.[10] The risk-free rate data are available beginning in July 1926, so excess returns for months prior to this are not available. Because the risk-free security return is the same for all stocks in any given month, the cross-sectional patterns in stock returns are identical to those in the excess returns. However, as discussed in Section 5.1.7, when evaluating a time series of returns using a factor model, it is important to use excess returns instead of returns in the analysis. The reason for this is that, in the time series, the risk-free rate is not constant. Thus, time-series variation in the risk-free rate may impact the results of time-series analyses, such as factor regressions. In addition, in factor regressions, the intercept coefficient is frequently an important part of the analysis. For these reasons, we use excess returns in the analyses presented throughout this text.

We denote the return of stock i in month t as $R_{i,t}$ and the excess return of stock i in month t as $r_{i,t}$, where both the return and excess return are calculated as discussed in the previous paragraphs. We record both return measures in percent, meaning that a value of 1.25 indicates a return of 1.25%, not 125%. At this point, a short word on the notation is required. The focus of the analyses in this book is to examine the ability of different variables to predict the cross section of future stock returns. The month of the return, therefore, is subsequent to the month during which the predictive variables are calculated. For the remainder of this text, we use t to denote the month during which the predictive variables are calculated. The returns being predicted, therefore, are from month $t + 1$. We refer to these returns as one-month-ahead returns or future returns. When the distinction between excess returns and returns is inconsequential,

---

[9]DLSTCD 500 indicates reason unavailable. DLSTCD 520 indicates trading over-the-counter. DLSTCD 551 indicates insufficient number of shareholders. DLSTCD 552 indicates price fell below acceptable level. DLSTCD 560 indicates insufficient capital, surplus, and/or equity. DLSTCD 561 indicates insufficient (or noncompliance with rules of) float or assets. DLSTCD 570 indicates company request (no reason given). DLSTCD 572 indicates company request, liquidation. DLSTCD 573 indicates company request, deregistration (gone private). DLSTCD 574 indicates bankruptcy, declared insolvent. DLSTCD 580 indicates delinquent in filing, nonpayment of fees. DLSTCD 584 indicates that the stock does not meet exchange's financial guidelines for continued listing. For more information on the meanings of different delisting codes, see the CRSP documentation.

[10]The URL for Ken French's data library is http://mba.tuck.dartmouth.edu/pages/faculty/ken.french/data& uscore;library.html.

we may simply use the term return when referring to excess return. However, all analyses throughout this text, unless otherwise stated, will use excess returns.

In Table 7.2, we present summary statistics for the one-month-ahead excess returns (r_{t+1}) and returns (R_{t+1}). To give an idea of how large of an effect the adjustment for delisting may have on statistical analyses, we also present the unadjusted excess returns and returns, defined as the value in the RET field minus the risk-free security return (denoted ret_{t+1}) and the value in the RET field (denoted RET_{t+1}), respectively. As the risk-free rate data are not available prior to July 1926, the first month t $(t + 1)$ used to calculate the summary statistics is June (July) 1926. Similarly, because the last month for which returns are available in the CRSP database is December 2012, the last month t $(t + 1)$ covered in the summary statistics is November (December) 2012. Thus, the summary statistics presented in the table are for sample months t from June 1926 through November 2012, which correspond to one-month-ahead returns for July 1926 through December 2012.

Table 7.2 shows that in the average month, the mean excess return (r_{t+1}) is 0.96% and the median excess return is -0.08%. Consistent with the mean being greater than the median, the average cross-sectional skewness of excess returns of 2.38 is strongly positive. This is in large part because stock returns are bounded below by -100%, making the excess return bounded below by -100% minus the risk-free security return, but there is no upper bound on the excess return a stock may realize. In the average month, the minimum excess return is -65.20%, the fifth percentile excess return is -16.44%, the 25th percentile excess return is -5.76%, the 75th percentile excess return is 6.17%, the 95th percentile excess return is 21.13%, and the maximum excess return is 208.10%. The cross-sectional standard deviation of monthly excess returns is 13.64%. Finally, the excess kurtosis of the cross-sectional distribution of monthly excess returns is 47.92, indicating that, in the average month, the distribution of excess returns has tails that are substantially larger than those of a normal distribution. The results for returns (R_{t+1}) are, by necessity, similar to those of the excess returns. The values of the returns (Mean, Min, 5%, 25%, Median, 75%, 95%, and Max) are all approximately 0.29% higher than the corresponding values for excess returns (the true differences are exactly the same, the reported values are rounded), indicating that in the average month, the risk-free security return is approximately 0.29%. The standard deviation, skewness, and excess kurtosis of returns are all necessarily identical to those of the excess returns. Finally, there are on average 3112 stocks per month that have valid values of excess returns (or returns) in the CRSP database.

Turning now to the summary statistics for the unadjusted excess returns (ret_{t+1}) and returns (RET_{t+1}), we see that the average values for these variables are slightly higher than their delisting-adjusted counterparts. The reason for this is that including delisting results in the inclusion of many returns that are either -30% or -100%. For the same reason, the minimum values of the unadjusted variables are, in the average month, not as negative as for the adjusted values. Interestingly, the maximum values of the unadjusted variables are a little bit lower than for the adjusted values. The reason for this is that, in some cases, delisting returns are extremely high. Finally, the standard deviation and excess kurtosis of the cross-sectional distribution of unadjusted returns are slightly lower than their counterparts from the adjusted returns.

TABLE 7.2 Summary Statistics for Returns (1926–2012)

This table presents summary statistics for return variables calculated using the CRSP sample for the months t from June 1926 through November 2012 or return months $t+1$ from July 1926 through December 2012. Each month, the mean (*Mean*), standard deviation (*SD*), skewness (*Skew*), excess kurtosis (*Kurt*), minimum (*Min*), fifth percentile (5%), 25th percentile (25%), median (*Median*), 75th percentile (75%), 95th percentile (95%), and maximum (*Max*) values of the cross-sectional distribution of each variable are calculated. The table presents the time-series means for each cross-sectional value. The column labeled n indicates that average number of stocks for which the given variable is available. r_{t+1} is the excess stock return, calculated as the stock's month $t+1$ return, adjusted following Shumway (1997) for delistings, minus the return on the risk-free security. R_{t+1} is the stock return in month $t+1$, adjusted following Shumway (1997) for delistings. ret_{t+1} is the unadjusted stock return in month $t+1$. RET_{t+1} is the unadjusted excess stock return in month $t+1$. All returns are calculated in percent.

	Mean	SD	Skew	Kurt	Min	5%	25%	Median	75%	95%	Max	n
r_{t+1}	0.96	13.64	2.38	47.92	−65.20	−16.44	−5.76	−0.08	6.17	21.13	208.10	3112
R_{t+1}	1.25	13.64	2.38	47.92	−64.90	−16.15	−5.47	0.21	6.46	21.42	208.40	3112
ret_{t+1}	1.00	13.28	2.38	39.32	−54.40	−16.34	−5.75	−0.09	6.18	21.13	186.80	3095
RET_{t+1}	1.28	13.27	2.38	39.34	−54.11	−16.04	−5.46	0.21	6.47	21.42	187.07	3095

For the most part, however, the cross-sectional distributions of unadjusted returns look very similar to the distributions of delisting-adjusted returns. It is not surprising, therefore, that the choice of whether to use the unadjusted or adjusted returns has very little impact on the results of most empirical analyses. That being said, to more accurately reflect the returns an investor would realize by making an investment at the end of month t and holding until the end of month $t + 1$, we use the delisting-adjusted future excess return (r_{t+1}) as the focal return variable throughout this text.

7.2.1 CRSP Sample (1963–2012)

In the previous sections of this chapter, we have presented analyses of the stock market covering the period from 1926 through 2012. Most empirical asset pricing studies, however, use only the latter portion of this sample. Specifically, most researchers use a sample that includes months t from June 1963 through November 2012, or whichever year is the last available year in the version of the CRSP database being used. This corresponds to months $t + 1$ (return months) from July 1963 through December 2012. The reason for starting the sample in June 1963 is that, as discussed previously, AMEX stocks are included in the CRSP database beginning in July 1962. Several of the variables studied in the empirical asset pricing literature are calculated using one year's worth of historical data. Thus, the first month that such variables are available for AMEX stocks is June 1963. Throughout this text, we follow this convention. The sample used for the majority of the analyses in the remainder of the book, therefore, will be for months t from June 1963 through November 2012.

To get a more exact understanding of the distribution of returns during the sample period that will be the focus of the analyses in this text, in Table 7.3, we present summary statistics for the returns during this sample period. We focus on the results for the delisting-adjusted excess return (r_{t+1}) because this is the primary measure of return that will be used throughout this text. Summary statistics for the other measures are presented for comparison.

Table 7.3 shows that in the average month, the average monthly excess return is 0.75% and the median excess return is −0.36%, consistent with a positive skewness of 3.18. The excess returns range from −82.42% to 302.74%, with the fifth, 25th, 75th, and 95th percentile excess returns being −19.52%, −6.70%, 6.49%, and 23.77%, respectively. In the average month, the standard deviation of the cross-sectional distribution of excess returns is 16.06%. Excess returns are highly leptokurtic because in the average cross section the excess kurtosis of the excess returns is 73.46. Finally, there are an average of 4782 stocks per month for which a valid excess return can be calculated.

7.3 THE MARKET FACTOR

Having examined the excess returns of individual stocks, we now examine the excess returns of the stock market as a whole. The market factor, defined as the excess return of the market portfolio, plays a very important role in asset pricing. According to the

TABLE 7.3 Summary Statistics for Returns (1963–2012)

This table presents summary statistics for return variables calculated using the CRSP sample for the months t from June 1963 through November 2012 or return months $t + 1$ from July 1963 through December 2012. Each month, the mean (*Mean*), standard deviation (*SD*), skewness (*Skew*), excess kurtosis (*Kurt*), minimum (*Min*), fifth percentile (5%), 25th percentile (25%), median (*Median*), 75th percentile (75%), 95th percentile (95%), and maximum (*Max*) values of the cross-sectional distribution of each variable are calculated. The table presents the time-series means for each cross-sectional value. The column labeled n indicates that average number of stocks for which the given variable is available. r_{t+1} is the excess stock return, calculated as the stock's month $t + 1$ return, adjusted following Shumway (1997) for delistings, minus the return on the risk-free security. R_{t+1} is the stock return in month $t + 1$, adjusted following Shumway (1997) for delistings. ret_{t+1} is the unadjusted excess stock return in month $t + 1$. RET_{t+1} is the unadjusted stock return in month $t + 1$. All returns are calculated in percent.

	Mean	SD	Skew	Kurt	Min	5%	25%	Median	75%	95%	Max	n
r_{t+1}	0.75	16.06	3.18	73.46	−82.42	−19.52	−6.70	−0.36	6.49	23.77	302.74	4782
R_{t+1}	1.17	16.06	3.18	73.46	−82.00	−19.10	−6.28	0.06	6.91	24.20	303.16	4782
ret_{t+1}	0.80	15.50	3.12	59.74	−67.88	−19.36	−6.69	−0.36	6.50	23.79	266.66	4754
RET_{t+1}	1.22	15.50	3.12	59.74	−67.45	−18.93	−6.26	0.06	6.93	24.21	267.08	4754

Capital Asset Pricing Model (CAPM, Sharpe (1964), Lintner (1965), Mossin (1966)), cross-sectional variation in expected asset returns is a function of the covariance between the return of the asset and the return on the market portfolio. Theoretically, the market portfolio contains the sum of all investments, including not just financial securities such as stocks and bonds but also other investments such as real estate and human capital. As the value of this portfolio is impossible to observe or calculate, applications requiring knowledge of the value or returns of the market portfolio have used more easily calculated proxies. The most conceptually appealing proxy is the portfolio of all financial securities, but even this seemingly straightforward concept is well beyond practicality, as this includes securities for which prices may be rarely, if ever, observable. Thus, in practice, most empirical research takes the market port-folio to be comprised of the set (or a subset) of securities traded on the U.S. stock exchanges. The value and returns of such portfolios are easily calculated from widely available security price data.

There are two main proxies for the market portfolio that are commonly used in empirical asset pricing research. The first is the value-weighted portfolio of all U.S.-based common stocks in the CRSP database. The daily and monthly excess returns for this portfolio are available from Ken French's website, as well as from the Fama–French database on WRDS. We follow common convention by referring to this portfolio and its excess returns as *MKT*, which stands for market minus risk-free. The second portfolio commonly used as a proxy for the market portfolio is the CRSP value-weighted portfolio, which contains all securities in the CRSP database, not just common stocks, but excluding American Depository Receipts (ADRs).[11] Following CRSP, we denote this portfolio *VWRETD*. The main difference between the *VWRETD* portfolio and the *MKT* portfolio is that the *VWRETD* portfolio contains shares of firms that are not based in the United States, closed-end funds, and other securities that are not common stocks. Daily and monthly returns for this portfolio are available from CRSP.

The excess returns of the *MKT* and *VWRETD* portfolios are nearly identical.[12] For the period from July 1926 through December 2012, the average monthly excess return of the *MKT* portfolio is 0.627% and that of the *VWRETD* portfolio is 0.624%. The standard deviations of the excess returns of these portfolios are 5.43% and 5.44%, respectively. Finally, the correlation between the excess returns of the two portfolios is 0.9995. The returns of these two portfolios are, therefore, nearly exactly the same, and which one to use in empirical analyses is purely a choice of the researcher. For the remainder of this book, we use the *MKT* portfolio as our proxy for the market portfolio. The excess returns of this portfolio will, therefore, proxy for the excess returns of the market factor.

For the period from July 1926 through December 2012, the average monthly excess return (log excess return) of the *MKT* portfolio is 0.627% (0.478%) per month, and the standard deviation of the monthly excess returns (log excess returns)

---

[11] ADRs are those securities in the CRSP database with a share code (SHRCD) between 30 and 39 inclusive.
[12] The excess return of the *VWRETD* portfolio is calculated by taking the return of the *VWRETD* portfolio from CRSP and subtracting the risk-free asset return.

is 5.43% (5.44%), respectively.[13] The annualized Sharpe ratio of the excess returns (log excess returns) of the *MKT* portfolio is therefore 0.400 (0.304).[14] The total compounded excess return of the *MKT* portfolio during this period is 14,209%, making the cumulative sum of log excess returns equal to 496%.

The cumulative excess returns realized by investing in the market portfolio from July 1926 through December 2012 are plotted in Figure 7.5. The solid line represents the compounded excess return. The scale for this line is shown on the left side of the plot. The dashed line represents the cumulative sum of the log excess returns. The scale for this series is displayed on the right side of the plot. The reason for presenting both the compounded excess return and cumulative log excess returns is

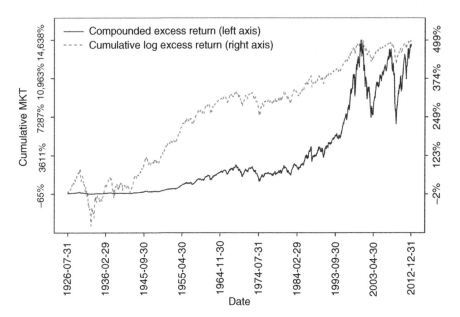

Figure 7.5   Cumulative Excess Returns of *MKT*.
This figure plots the cumulative returns of the *MKT* factor for the period from July 1926 through December 2012. The compounded excess return for month t is calculated as 100 times the cumulative product of one plus the monthly return up to and including the given month. The cumulative log excess return is calculated as the sum of the monthly log excess returns up to and including the given month

[13]The log excess return is defined as the natural log of one plus the excess return, where the excess return is represented in decimal form.

[14]The annualized Sharpe ratio is taken to be the mean of the monthly returns or log returns divided by the corresponding standard deviation, multiplied by $\sqrt{12}$. Multiplication by $\sqrt{12}$ is based on the assumption that the monthly returns are independent, making the annual mean equal to 12 times the monthly mean, and the annual standard deviation equal to $\sqrt{12}$ times the monthly standard deviation. Thus, the annualized Sharpe ratio is $\mu \times 12/(\sigma \times \sqrt{12}) = \mu\sqrt{12}/\sigma$, where μ and σ are the monthly mean and standard deviation, respectively.

that the compounded excess return gives an indication of how much money would have been made, in excess of the amount earned on the risk-free investment, by an investor who invested one dollar in the market portfolio at the end of June 1926. The line representing this value is in some ways misleading, as a quick glance at the solid line would seem to indicate that the returns of the market portfolio were much more volatile toward the end of the sample period than at the beginning. This result is simply due to the scale however, as the same percentage gain or loss is indicated by a larger vertical distance on the chart for the more recent periods, as the cumulative excess returns are larger toward the end of the sample period than at the beginning of the sample period. The cumulative sum of log returns does not suffer from this drawback, but the interpretation of the values on the sum of log excess returns scale is not as simple as those on the compounded excess returns scale. This is especially evident in the very early part of the sample where the dashed line representing the cumulative log excess return takes a substantial dip, but the solid line representing the compounded excess return does not seem to experience a substantial loss. This is the period of the crash of 1929, when the market experienced its largest percentage losses in history. Looking at the solid line representing the compounded excess return, however, is quite misleading, as it is nearly impossible to notice any loss in this line, when in fact, from high to low, the loss was nearly 85%.

Figure 7.5 illustrates both rewards and risks associated with investing in the market portfolio. As can be seen by the chart, the long-run average excess return is very strongly positive, but there are periods for which the portfolio realized substantial and prolonged losses. For example, from the beginning of September 1929 through the end of June 1932, the compounded excess return on the market portfolio was a loss of nearly 85%. This includes a loss of more than 23% between October 28, 1929, and October 29, 1929 inclusive. The compounded excess return did not obtain its previous maximum value again until the end of April 1945, more than 15 years and six months after the previous high water mark. This drawdown represents the largest and longest drawdown during our sample period. The second largest and longest drawdown begins in December 1968. From that point until the end of September 1974, the compounded excess return on market portfolio is −56%. The previous maximum compounded excess return, realized at the end of November 1968, was not reached again until the end of April 1983, 14 years and five months after the previous high. The third largest and most prolonged drawdown began in April 2000. From then until the end of February 2009, the market portfolio realized a compound excess return of −54%. As of the end of 2012, the previous high watermark is not yet attained. As can be seen in Figure 7.5, this drawdown covers two significant dips in the market. The decline that began in the middle of March 2000 is commonly referred to as the bursting of the dot.com bubble. Prior to this point, stocks of Internet-based companies had realized extremely large returns. Beginning in March 2000, prices of these stocks crashed, bringing with them the market portfolio. By May 2007, the subsequent rebound had nearly achieved the highs (in compound excess returns) realized prior to the bursting of the bubble. This rebound was cut short by the financial and subprime mortgage crises that began in 2007 and included the collapse of Bear Stearns investment bank on March 16, 2008, and the bankruptcy of another large investment bank, Lehman Brothers, on September 15, 2008. Finally, the fourth most pronounced and longest drawdown occurred beginning in September 1987. In October 1987, the excess return of the market was -23%. This month included the crash on October 19, 1987, known as Black Monday. On this one day, the market portfolio realized a loss of almost 17.5%. The low point of this drawdown came at the end of November 1987, at which point the compounded excess return of the market portfolio was 31% below its previous high, which was once again attained at the end of May 1991, less than four years after the drawdown began.

7.4   THE CAPM RISK MODEL

The last topic we discuss in this chapter is the CAPM risk model. The CAPM risk model is used to calculate the average abnormal return of a portfolio or a security after accounting for exposure of the portfolio or security to the risks associated with the market portfolio. The abnormal return, also known as the alpha, of any portfolio (or security) is estimated as the intercept coefficient from a time-series regression of the excess returns of the portfolio on the excess returns of the market portfolio. The regression specification is

$$r_{p,t} = \alpha_p + \beta_p MKT_t + \epsilon_{p,t} \tag{7.1}$$

where $r_{p,t}$ and MKT_t are the excess returns of the portfolio being evaluated and the market portfolio, respectively, during time period t. To determine whether the portfolio generates abnormal returns relative to the CAPM risk model, we evaluate whether the fitted intercept coefficient, which serves as the estimate of the average abnormal return per period, is statistically distinguishable from zero. If the intercept coefficient is shown to be non-zero, this is evidence that the portfolio generates non-zero average excess returns that are not due to the sensitivity of the portfolio's excess return to that of the market portfolio.

The most common application of the CAPM risk model is in portfolio analyses testing the ability of a given variable (any variable other than beta) to predict future stock returns. Typically, the abnormal return of the difference portfolio is the focal point of the analysis. Evidence that the difference portfolio generates abnormal returns that are statistically distinguishable from zero is interpreted as evidence that the variable in question has the ability to predict cross-sectional variation in future stock returns. Risk-adjusting the portfolio returns using the CAPM model is similar to controlling for cross-sectional differences in sensitivity to the market factor (beta). The assumption in doing so is that the beta of the portfolio (or security) under investigation remains constant throughout the sample period.

7.5   SUMMARY

We began this chapter by examining the composition of the U.S. stock market. The data for our analyses come from the CRSP database, the primary source for stock price and return data in empirical asset pricing research. From 1925 through June 1962, the CRSP database contains data for only NYSE-listed stocks. In July 1962, AMEX stocks are added to the CRSP database, and in January 1973 NASDAQ stocks are added. While in both cases the value of the newly added stocks is only a small percentage of the total value of the market portfolio, the number of stocks in the portfolio increases substantially with each of these additions. The majority of stocks in the CRSP database, both by count and by total market capitalization, are NYSE-listed. For the entire sample period from 1926 through 2012, the manufacturing sector has both the most stocks and highest total market capitalization of any sector.

We then discussed the calculation of returns and excess returns and examined the cross-sectional distribution of each. For the analyses presented in the remainder of this book, we use the sample of stocks covering the period from 1963 through 2012. During this period, the average (median) monthly excess return for stocks in the sample is 0.75% (−0.36%). The summary statistics indicate that the cross-sectional distribution of excess returns is highly positively skewed and leptokurtic.

Next, we examined the excess returns of the market portfolio, which we refer to as the market factor. While the average excess return of the market factor is positive in the long run, there are several periods during which the market realizes heavy losses. The most pronounced and prolonged losses correspond to the crash of 1929; the bursting of the dot.com bubble in 2001; the financial and subprime mortgage crises of 2007 and 2008; and the crash in October 1987.

Finally, we introduced that CAPM risk model used to adjust portfolio or individual security returns for sensitivity to the market factor. The CAPM risk model is frequently used to examine whether the difference portfolio in a portfolio analysis generates positive abnormal returns (alpha).

REFERENCES

Lintner, J. 1965. Security prices, risk, and maximal gains from diversification. Journal of Finance, 20(4), 687–615.

Mossin, J. 1966. Equilibrium in a capital asset market. Econometrica, 34(4), 768–783.

Sharpe, W. F. 1964. Capital asset prices: a theory of market equilibrium under conditions of risk. Journal of Finance, 19(3), 425–442.

Shumway, T. 1997. The delisting bias in CRSP data. Journal of Finance, 52(1), 327–340.

8

BETA

According to the Capital Asset Pricing Model (CAPM) of Sharpe (1964), Lintner (1965), and Mossin (1966), the expected return of any security is equal to the return on the riskless security plus the security's market beta multiplied by the market risk premium. Expressed mathematically, the CAPM is

$$E[R_{i,t}] = R_{f,t} + \beta_i(E[R_{m,t}] - R_{f,t}) \tag{8.1}$$

where the security's beta is given by

$$\beta_i = \frac{Cov(R_{i,t}, R_{m,t})}{Var(R_{m,t})}. \tag{8.2}$$

$R_{i,t}$, $R_{f,t}$, and $R_{m,t}$ are the return of security i, the riskless security, and the market portfolio, respectively, in period t; $E[\cdot]$ is the expectation operator; $E[R_{m,t}] - R_{f,t}$ is the market risk premium; $Cov(R_{i,t}, R_{m,t})$ is the covariance between the period t return of security i and the market return; and $Var(R_{m,t})$ is the variance of the period t market return.

The CAPM has several empirically testable predictions, two of which we examine in this chapter. First, the CAPM predicts that cross-sectional variation in the expected returns of different securities is driven only by cross-sectional variation in the betas of the securities. This hypothesis is perhaps the most researched, and one of the most strongly refuted, hypotheses in all of empirical asset pricing. Empirical tests

Empirical Asset Pricing: The Cross Section of Stock Returns, First Edition.
Turan G. Bali, Robert F. Engle, and Scott Murray.
© 2016 John Wiley & Sons, Inc. Published 2016 by John Wiley & Sons, Inc.

of this prediction can be broken into two groups. The first group of tests examines the cross-sectional ability of beta to predict the future excess returns. The results of these empirical analyses have been mixed. Early analyses by Blume and Friend (1973) and Fama and MacBeth (1973) find a positive relation between estimates of beta and future stock returns, but more recent analyses fail to detect the predicted relation (Reinganum (1981), Lakonishok and Shapiro (1986), Fama and French (1992, 1993)). A large portion of this chapter is devoted to examining this relation. The second group of tests examines the cross-sectional ability of other variables to predict future excess returns. The CAPM predicts that no variable other than market beta should exhibit such predictive ability. Much to the chagrin of CAPM enthusiasts, several variables such as market capitalization (Banz (1981), Fama and French (1992, 1993)), book-to-market ratio (Rosenberg, Reid, and Lanstein (1985), Fama and French (1992, 1993)), momentum (Jegadeesh and Titman (1993)), and liquidity (Amihud and Mendelson (1986), Amihud (2002)), to name a few, have been shown to be related to future stock returns. Much of the remainder of this book is devoted to investigations of these phenomena.

The second empirically testable prediction of the CAPM is that the average excess returns, after accounting for the effect of beta, should be zero. To test this hypothesis, researchers frequently examine the intercept term of cross-sectional regressions of security excess returns on estimates of beta. The CAPM predicts that the intercept of such regressions should be zero, but empirical analyses consistently find intercept terms that are significantly positive (Friend and Blume 1970, Stambaugh 1982). While the analyses in this chapter will focus on the cross-sectional relation between beta and stock returns, they will also provide insight into empirical viability of this prediction of the CAPM as well.

We proceed now to the two main objectives of this chapter. The first objective of this chapter is to present several different approaches that researchers use to estimate a stock's beta and empirically examine these measures. The second objective is to analyze the cross-sectional relation between market beta and stock returns.

8.1 ESTIMATING BETA

In this section, we introduce several different ways of estimating beta, all of which are based on regressions of a stock's excess returns on the excess returns of the market portfolio. The most commonly used approach to estimating a stock's market beta is to simply run a CAPM regression, also known as a one-factor market model regression. The regression specification is

$$r_{i,t} = \alpha_i + \beta_i MKT_t + \epsilon_{i,t} \qquad (8.3)$$

where $r_{i,t}$ is the excess return of stock i during period t, MKT_t is the excess return of the market portfolio (the market factor) during period t, and $\epsilon_{i,t}$ is the regression residual. If regression model (8.3) describes the returns of stock i and α_i is zero, then taking expectations on both sides yields the CAPM. The stock's market beta is then taken to be the estimated slope coefficient (β_i) generated by the regression.

Researchers differ in the periodicity of the data used to estimate market beta, as well as in length of the period used in the estimation. In most cases, market beta for any given period t is estimated using only data from periods prior to and including period t. A common approach is to estimate regression (8.3) using one year's worth of daily excess return data. Taking this approach, at the end of each month t, regression model (8.3) is estimated using daily return data from the 12-month period covering months $t - 11$ through t, inclusive. A minimum number of data points are usually required to ensure the quality of the values estimated by the regression. In the case of daily data over a one-year period, a reasonable requirement may be that the regression be fit using at least 200 data points. While using one year's worth of daily data to calculate beta is common, other estimation period lengths and data frequencies are also used. Another common approach is to use monthly excess return data from the past five years.

We examine nine different combinations of estimation periods and data frequencies, five using daily data and four using monthly data. For the daily data measures, we use period lengths of one, three, six, 12, and 24 months and require 15, 50, 100, 200, and 450 days of valid return data, respectively, to perform the calculation. We denote these estimates of market beta, calculated using daily excess return data, as β^{kM}, where $k \in \{1, 3, 6, 12, 24\}$. Thus, estimates of market beta calculated using daily data are identified by a superscript that indicates the number of months used in the calculation. The daily stock return data come from Center for Research in Security Prices (CRSP's) daily stock file (dsf). The daily MKT factor returns and daily risk-free security returns (needed to calculate excess returns from the raw return data from CRSP) come from Ken French's data library.

We also calculate market beta using monthly excess return observations over the past one, two, three, and five years, requiring 10, 20, 24, and 24 valid monthly excess return observations, respectively. Our choice to require a maximum of 24 monthly data points to calculate beta, even for the five-year measure, follows common practice when using monthly data to estimate beta. To denote the estimates of market beta calculated using monthly data, we use superscripts that indicate the number of years of data used in the calculation. Thus, β^{kY}, $k \in \{1, 2, 3, 5\}$, denote these measures of market beta. The monthly stock return data are from CRSP's monthly stock file (msf), and the monthly MKT factor and risk-free security return data are from Ken French's data library.

In addition to examining these measures of market beta calculated using simple CAPM regressions, we introduce two additional measures of beta. Scholes and Williams (1977) present evidence that nonsynchronous trading may affect empirical estimates of beta using the standard CAPM model. To account for this nonsynchronicity, they propose running the series of regressions

$$r_{i,t} = a_i + b_i^- MKT_{t-1} + e_{i,t}^- \tag{8.4}$$

$$r_{i,t} = a_i + b_i MKT_t + e_{i,t} \tag{8.5}$$

$$r_{i,t} = a_i + b_i^+ MKT_{t+1} + e_{i,t}^+ \tag{8.6}$$

and define beta as

$$\beta_i^{SW} = \frac{\hat{b}_i^- + \hat{b}_i + \hat{b}_i^+}{1 + 2\rho} \tag{8.7}$$

where ρ is the first-order serial correlation of the market portfolio's excess return, and $\hat{b}_i^-$, $\hat{b}_i$, and $\hat{b}_i^+$ are the estimated slope coefficients from regression models (8.4)–(8.6), respectively. The Scholes and Williams (1977) beta is best implemented using daily stock return data, as monthly return data are less likely to suffer from the issues caused by nonsynchronous trading. The length of the sample used to calculate the Scholes and Williams (1977) beta is once again a choice of the researcher. For our investigation, we calculate β^{SW} for stock i at the end month t using daily data covering the one-year period starting at the beginning of month $t - 11$ and ending at the end of month t. We require 200 valid excess return observations during the estimation period to calculate β^{SW}.

Our final measure of market beta comes from Dimson (1979), who shows that when a stock is infrequently traded, estimates of beta using the CAPM model (equation (8.3)) may be severely biased. To account for this, the Dimson (1979) beta is defined as[1]

$$\beta_i^D = \sum_{k=-5}^{k=5} \hat{b}_i^k \tag{8.8}$$

where the $\hat{b}_i^k$ are the estimated slope coefficients from the regression model

$$r_{i,t} = a_i + \sum_{k=-5}^{k=5} b_i^k MKT_{t+k} + e_{i,t}. \tag{8.9}$$

While the beta of Dimson (1979) is designed to improve measurement of market beta for stocks (or other securities) that are infrequently traded, implementing the calculation on frequently traded stocks does not introduce unwanted bias, thus the calculation is applicable to all stocks. As with our other measures of beta, we calculate β^D for stock i in month t using one year's worth of daily return data for the period covering months $t - 11$ through t, inclusive, and require a minimum of 200 data points to perform the calculation.

While other methods for estimating market beta have been proposed, the measures presented in the previous paragraphs are the most widely used. We proceed now to empirical examination of these measures using the CRSP U.S.-based common stock sample covering months t from June 1963 through November 2012.

---

[1] The superscripts on the b^k in equations (8.8) and (8.9) are not powers but are used to index the different regression coefficients.

8.2 SUMMARY STATISTICS

We begin our empirical analysis of beta by examining summary statistics for each of the measures of beta. Table 8.1 presents summary statistics for each of the estimates of beta described earlier. The summary statistics show that for the CAPM measures of beta calculated using daily stock returns (β^{1M}, β^{3M}, β^{6M}, β^{12M}, β^{24M}), the mean values of these measures of beta range from 0.74 to 0.79 and increase as the length of the measurement period increases from one to 24 months.[2] The median for each of these variables is somewhat lower than the mean, with values ranging from 0.64 for the one-month measure to 0.73 for the 24-month measure. The median, like the mean, exhibits an increasing pattern as the measurement period length increases. Similarly, each of the percentiles below the median (Min, 5%, 25%) exhibits an increasing pattern as the measure period increases, and percentiles above the median (75%, 95%, Max) exhibit decreasing patterns. These patterns are likely the result of two phenomena. First, as the measurement period gets longer, the standard error of the estimated beta gets smaller, meaning that the value generated by the regression is more likely to be close to the true value of beta. Along the same lines, as the regression is estimated using more and more data points, the effect of one outlier is diminished. Thus, it would be expected that, as the period used to fit the regression increases, the most extreme estimated values will get closer and closer to the median. For example, the minimum estimated value of beta using one month of daily data (β^{1M}) is -14.32. This value is likely the result of one or two outlier observations that have a large impact on the regression when there are only between 15 and 23 observations used to fit the regression and likely does not accurately reflect the actual beta of the stock. The effect of these data points is reduced as the sample period is extended.

The second likely reason for this phenomenon is more mechanical. Given the data requirements imposed in calculating our measures of beta, for a stock to have a valid value of 24-month beta (β^{24M}), the stock must have been publicly traded and part of the CRSP database for at least the past 450 business days, introducing a slight bias toward larger and more established stocks, which are more likely to behave in a manner similar to that of the median stock. As can be seen in the table, the average number of observations for which the minimum data requirements are satisfied decreases from 4742 for β^{1M} to 4019 for β^{24M}, indicating that the data screens have removed several stocks. The removed stocks are likely smaller stocks that have only recently become publicly traded, potentially creating a bias toward more established stocks in analyses that use the 24-month measure. The last observation worth noting is that the differences in the distributions of the daily return-based measures of beta get smaller as the length of the estimation period gets longer. Thus, the distribution of the β^{24M} is much more similar to that of the β^{12M} beta than the distribution of β^{3M} is to the distribution of β^{1M}. Thus, there appears to be more stability in the distribution of estimated values of beta as the estimation period is extended. This potentially

---

[2]We refer to β^{1M}, β^{3M}, β^{6M}, β^{12M}, β^{24M}, β^{1Y}, β^{2Y}, β^{3Y}, and β^{5Y} as CAPM measures of beta because they are calculated using a standard CAPM regression. We use the term CAPM to distinguish these measures from β^{SW} and β^{D}, for which the calculation is not purely based on a CAPM regression.

TABLE 8.1 Summary Statistics

This table presents summary statistics for variables measuring market beta calculated using the CRSP sample for the months t from June 1963 through November 2012. Each month, the mean *(Mean)*, standard deviation *(SD)*, skewness *(Skew)*, excess kurtosis *(Kurt)*, minimum *(Min)*, fifth percentile (5%), 25th percentile (25%), median *(Median)*, 75th percentile (75%), 95th percentile (95%), and maximum *(Max)* values of the cross-sectional distribution of each variable are calculated. The table presents the time-series means for each cross-sectional value. The column labeled n indicates that average number of stocks for which the given variable is available. β^{1M}, β^{3M}, β^{6M}, β^{12M}, and β^{24M} are calculated as the slope coefficient from a time-series regression of the stock's excess return on the excess return of the market portfolio using one, three, six, 12, and 24 months of daily return data, respectively. β^{1Y}, β^{2Y}, β^{3Y}, and β^{5Y} are calculated similarly using one, two, three, and five years of monthly return data. β^{SW} is calculated following Scholes and Williams (1977) using 12 months of daily return data. β^{D} is calculated following Dimson (1979) using 12 months of daily return data.

	Mean	SD	Skew	Kurt	Min	5%	25%	Median	75%	95%	Max	n
β^{1M}	0.74	1.39	0.18	23.63	−14.32	−1.14	0.05	0.64	1.38	2.90	15.44	4742
β^{3M}	0.76	0.87	0.30	9.12	−6.34	−0.42	0.23	0.68	1.23	2.23	7.88	4697
β^{6M}	0.77	0.71	0.41	3.87	−3.71	−0.19	0.30	0.70	1.18	2.02	5.46	4611
β^{12M}	0.78	0.61	0.49	1.46	−2.16	−0.05	0.35	0.71	1.15	1.89	3.90	4440
β^{24M}	0.79	0.54	0.55	0.57	−1.22	0.04	0.39	0.73	1.12	1.79	3.09	4019
β^{1Y}	1.13	1.34	0.93	21.15	−9.48	−0.66	0.37	1.01	1.78	3.33	16.17	4423
β^{2Y}	1.14	0.94	0.73	7.38	−4.74	−0.12	0.55	1.04	1.63	2.76	9.12	4072
β^{3Y}	1.14	0.80	0.64	4.26	−3.43	0.06	0.62	1.05	1.57	2.56	7.12	3958
β^{5Y}	1.14	0.72	0.50	6.68	−3.28	0.17	0.66	1.05	1.53	2.41	6.19	3992
β^{SW}	0.88	0.68	0.41	1.67	−2.68	−0.07	0.42	0.82	1.29	2.08	4.73	4440
β^{D}	1.06	1.01	0.52	10.64	−6.21	−0.34	0.44	0.97	1.60	2.76	9.22	4440

indicates that the longer measurement periods result in more accurately measured values of beta. We examine this in more detail when we perform persistence analyses of the measures of beta.

Turning our attention to the measures of beta calculated using monthly data (β^{1Y}, β^{2Y}, β^{3Y}, and β^{5Y}), Table 8.1 shows that the mean values of these measures are all between 1.13 and 1.14, substantially higher than the means of the daily return-based CAPM measures discussed in the previous paragraphs. This is true of the median as well, which has values that range from 1.01 to 1.05. Similar to the daily return-based CAPM measures, the minimum and maximum values for the monthly return-based measures are less extreme as the calculation period gets longer, with monthly average minima (maxima) of −9.48 (16.17), −4.74 (9.12), −3.43 (7.12), and −3.28 (6.19) for β^{1Y}, β^{2Y}, β^{3Y}, and β^{5Y}, respectively.

Examination of the Scholes and Williams (1977) and Dimson (1979) betas (β^{SW} and β^{D}, respectively) shows that β^{SW} has a distribution that is similar to those of the daily return-based CAPM measures of beta, while the distribution of β^{D} is more similar to those of the monthly return-based CAPM measures. The mean and median values of Scholes and Williams (1977) beta in the average month are 0.88 and 0.82

respectively, slightly higher than the corresponding values for the daily return-based CAPM measures, but substantially lower than the values for the monthly return-based CAPM measures. The mean and median values of β^D are 1.06 and 0.97, more similar to those of the monthly return-based measures than the daily return measures. The cross-sectional standard deviation of β^{SW} is 0.68, much smaller than that β^D, which is 1.01. Consistent with higher variation in values, the extreme values (Min and Max) for β^D are much larger in magnitude than those of β^{SW}. Thus, while both the Scholes and Williams (1977) and Dimson (1979) betas are calculated using daily return data, the calculation proposed by Scholes and Williams (1977) does not have a substantial effect on the distribution of estimated values of beta compared to those of the daily return-based CAPM measures. The same cannot be said about the distribution of Dimson (1979), which is substantially different than those of the daily return-based measures, especially that of the 12-month measure (β^{12M}), which serves as the best comparison because β^D is also calculated using 12 months of daily data. The fact that the distribution of β^D is substantially different than that of all of the other estimates of beta that use daily return data indicates that it potentially has some information that is not contained in the other daily measures.

8.3 CORRELATIONS

Table 8.2 presents the time-series averages of the monthly cross-sectional correlations between the different measures of market beta. Pearson product–moment correlations are presented in the below-diagonal entries of the matrix, and Spearman rank correlations are presented in the above-diagonal entries. Each of the measures of beta is winsorized at the 0.5% level on a monthly basis prior to calculating the Pearson product–moment correlations. We focus our conversation on the Pearson product–moment correlation, as both measures of correlation lead to the same general conclusions and are similar enough to not raise concerns about the data.

Looking first at the correlations among the CAPM measures of beta calculated using daily returns, the results in Table 8.2 show that average correlations for pairs of these measures range from 0.43 between β^{1M} and β^{24M} to a correlation of 0.89 between β^{12M} and β^{24M}. Correlations between the variables calculated using similar estimation periods tend to be higher than those for which the estimation periods differ substantially. A large part of this phenomenon, however, is likely to be mechanical. Furthermore, correlations between pairs of measures that both use longer estimation periods tend to be higher than the correlations between pairs of measures that both use shorter estimation periods, potentially indicating that the shorter calculation periods result in noisier measures. Similar patterns are present in the correlations among the monthly return-based CAPM measures of beta, which range from 0.58 for the correlation between β^{1Y} and β^{5Y} to 0.89 for the correlation between β^{3Y} and β^{5Y}. Correlations between pairs of CAPM measures of beta that both use daily return data, as well as pairs that both use monthly return data, tend to be higher than the correlations between pairs where one measure uses daily data and the other uses monthly data, as average correlations between the daily return-based

TABLE 8.2 Correlations
This table presents the time-series averages of the annual cross-sectional Pearson product–moment (below-diagonal entries) and Spearman rank (above-diagonal entries) correlations between pairs of variables measuring market beta.

	β^{1M}	β^{3M}	β^{6M}	β^{12M}	β^{24M}	β^{1Y}	β^{2Y}	β^{3Y}	β^{5Y}	β^{SW}	β^{D}
β^{1M}		0.67	0.57	0.51	0.47	0.22	0.25	0.26	0.26	0.43	0.29
β^{3M}	0.67		0.83	0.72	0.65	0.34	0.37	0.38	0.38	0.62	0.42
β^{6M}	0.56	0.83		0.87	0.77	0.40	0.44	0.45	0.45	0.73	0.51
β^{12M}	0.48	0.72	0.87		0.89	0.45	0.50	0.51	0.51	0.83	0.57
β^{24M}	0.43	0.64	0.77	0.89		0.43	0.55	0.57	0.57	0.77	0.54
β^{1Y}	0.19	0.31	0.38	0.43	0.40		0.74	0.65	0.58	0.52	0.64
β^{2Y}	0.22	0.35	0.42	0.48	0.53	0.75		0.87	0.77	0.54	0.58
β^{3Y}	0.23	0.35	0.43	0.50	0.55	0.66	0.87		0.89	0.55	0.55
β^{5Y}	0.23	0.35	0.43	0.49	0.56	0.58	0.78	0.89		0.54	0.52
β^{SW}	0.40	0.60	0.73	0.83	0.76	0.50	0.53	0.53	0.52		0.66
β^{D}	0.25	0.39	0.48	0.55	0.51	0.63	0.57	0.54	0.51	0.65	

and monthly return-based CAPM measures range from 0.19 between β^{1M} and β^{1Y} to 0.56 between β^{24M} and β^{5Y}. Once again, correlations seem to increase as the length of measurement period increases.

Consistent with observations from the summary statistics, β^{SW} has higher correlations with the daily return-based CAPM measures of beta (with the exception of β^{1M}) than with the monthly return-based measures, as the correlations between β^{SW} and CAPM measures of beta using between three and 24 months of daily data range from 0.60 to 0.76, while those of the monthly return-based measures range from 0.50 to 0.53. Also consistent with the summary statistics, correlations between β^{D} and the daily return-based CAPM measures, which range from 0.25 to 0.51, are lower than those for the monthly return-based measures, which range from 0.51 to 0.63. Finally, the correlation between β^{SW} and β^{D} is 0.65.

In short, there is a substantial common component between all of the measures of beta. The correlations between measures that use a longer measurement period are higher than those based on short measurement periods, potentially indicating that a longer measurement period provides stable and therefore more accurate measurement. The Scholes and Williams (1977) beta is quite similar to the daily return-based measure, while the Dimson (1979) beta is more like the monthly return-based measures.

8.4 PERSISTENCE

If a measure of beta calculated using historical data is to be used as an estimate of the stock's beta in the future, as is our intent here and in most empirical asset pricing research, it is important that beta be a persistent property of the stock. To examine whether this is the case, in Table 8.3, we present the results of persistence analyses for each of the different measures of beta. The table shows entries for measures of

TABLE 8.3 Persistence
This table presents the results of persistence analyses of variables measuring market beta. Each month t, the cross-sectional Pearson product–moment correlation between the month t and month $t + \tau$ values of the given variable is calculated. The table presents the time-series averages of the monthly cross-sectional correlations. The column labeled τ indicates the lag at which the persistence is measured.

τ	β^{1M}	β^{3M}	β^{6M}	β^{12M}	β^{24M}	β^{SW}	β^{D}	β^{1Y}	β^{2Y}	β^{3Y}	β^{5Y}
1	0.23										
3	0.20	0.41									
6	0.19	0.39	0.54								
12	0.18	0.36	0.49	0.63		0.53	0.30	0.20			
24	0.16	0.31	0.43	0.55	0.68	0.45	0.26	0.18	0.31		
36	0.15	0.29	0.40	0.50	0.61	0.41	0.24	0.16	0.29	0.37	
48	0.13	0.26	0.37	0.47	0.57	0.38	0.22	0.15	0.27	0.34	
60	0.12	0.25	0.34	0.44	0.53	0.36	0.21	0.14	0.25	0.32	0.41
120	0.10	0.20	0.28	0.35	0.43	0.30	0.17	0.11	0.20	0.26	0.33

persistence that are calculated using nonoverlapping data. Entries that correspond to lags for which the measurement periods overlap are left blank to avoid examining mechanical persistence. The table presents persistence for lags τ of one, three, six, 12, 24, 36, 48, 60, and 120 months. In calculating the persistence, each variable is winsorized at the 0.5% level on a monthly basis.

Looking first at the CAPM measures of beta calculated using daily data, the results are consistent with our conjecture from the summary statistics and correlations that calculation of beta using short measurement periods is very noisy. The persistence of β^{1M} calculated one month apart is only 0.23. Using three months of daily data seems to produce a better measure, as the persistence of β^{3M} calculated three months apart is 0.41. The table indicates that as the length of the measurement period increases, so does the persistence of beta calculated from daily return data using a standard CAPM regression, as the persistence of β^{6M}, β^{12M}, and β^{24M} measured six, 12, and 24 months apart is 0.54, 0.63, and 0.68, respectively. The persistence of β^{SW} calculated 12 and 24 months apart is 0.53 and 0.45, respectively. For β^{D}, the 12- and 24-month persistence values are 0.30 and 0.26, respectively. Interestingly, despite the claims by Scholes and Williams (1977) and Dimson (1979) that nonsynchronous or infrequent trading may result in poor empirical estimates of beta, the simple CAPM measure of beta calculated using 12 months of daily return data (β^{12M}) exhibits higher persistence at lags of 12 and 24 months than either of these more complicated measures (β^{SW} and β^{D}). The results provide no evidence that applying the Scholes and Williams (1977) or Dimson (1979) methodologies results in a more accurate measure of beta.

The measures of beta calculated using monthly data exhibit similar persistence patterns to the daily return-based measures of beta. Table 8.3 shows that the persistence of β^{1Y} measured one year apart is only 0.20. But, for β^{2Y} measured two years apart, the persistence increases to 0.31; for β^{3Y} measured three years apart, the persistence is 0.37; and finally for β^{5Y} measured five years apart, the persistence is 0.41.

As would be expected, the persistence of each of the beta measures decays as the time between estimation increases. However, regardless of the number of lags τ at which the persistence is calculated, for each data frequency (daily and monthly) the persistence of the measures calculated using longer measurement periods is higher than the persistence of measures that use shorter measurement periods. The only exception to this is β^D, which exhibits substantially lower persistence at all lags than any of the other daily return-based measures of beta except for β^{1M}.

The fact that measures of beta calculated using longer measurement periods, regardless of the data frequency, exhibit higher persistence is a strong indication that longer measurement periods result in a more accurate measurement. Additionally, the results indicate that beta is in fact highly persistent. If beta were not highly persistent, then we would expect that for some measurement period this lack of persistence would result in lower accuracy when measuring beta because long measurement periods use data from a long time ago, which may not reflect the current beta of the stock. Our analysis fails to detect this phenomenon even in the measure that uses five years of monthly return data (β^{5Y}). Thus, while a stock's beta is certainly not perfectly persistent, our results indicate that beta is highly persistent for periods of up to at least five years.

A comparison of the daily return-based measures to the monthly return-based measures indicates that for all lags, the daily return-based measures using 12 or 24 months of data (β^{12M} and β^{24M}) exhibit higher persistence than any of the monthly return-based measures. Even for lags of 10 years ($\tau = 120$), the persistence of both β^{12M} (persistence = 0.35) and β^{24M} (persistence = 0.43) is higher than the 10-year persistence of β^{5Y} (persistence = 0.33).

In summary, the results indicate that the use of longer measurement periods results in more accurate measures of beta. In addition, beta seems to be most accurately measured using daily return data.[3] The methodologies of Scholes and Williams (1977) and Dimson (1979) do not seem to improve the accuracy of the measurement of beta relative to using a simple CAPM regression model.

8.5 BETA AND STOCK RETURNS

Having analyzed the measures of market beta in isolation, we proceed to examine the relation between beta and future stock returns. The fundamental prediction of the CAPM of Sharpe (1964), Lintner (1965), and Mossin (1966) is that there is a positive relation between market beta and expected stock returns, and the slope defining this relation represents the market risk premium. Thus, we would expect to find a positive cross-sectional relation between beta future excess returns. As will be shown shortly, contrary to this prediction, portfolio and regression analyses fail to detect any strong relation between beta and future stock returns, and in some cases detect

---

[3]While our analyses provide evidence that beta is best estimated using daily return data, there are also arguments that can be made to support estimating beta from returns measured at monthly or longer frequency (see Gilbert, Hrdlicka, Kalodimos, and Siegel (2014)).

a negative relation. Thus, the most fundamental prediction of theoretical asset pricing has failed to gain substantial empirical support. This result is perhaps the most persistent empirical anomaly in all of empirical asset pricing.

8.5.1 Portfolio Analysis

We begin our analysis of the relation between beta and future stock returns by performing a univariate-sort portfolio analyses using each of the different measures of beta as the sort variable.

Equal-Weighted Portfolios

Table 8.4 presents the average value of the given measure of beta, as well as the average portfolio excess return and CAPM alpha for each of the equal-weighted decile portfolios as well as for the difference between the 10th and first decile portfolio.

We begin by examining the average values of beta in each of the decile portfolios for each of the different beta measures. The results show that, for each measure, the average values of beta are increasing monotonically across the decile portfolios. This result is by construction as the portfolios are formed by sorting on beta. Consistent with our finding from the summary statistics showing higher standard deviation for measures of beta calculated using shorter measurement periods, and persistence analyses indicating that measures of beta calculated using shorter measurement periods have more noise, the results indicate that for both the daily return-based and monthly return-based measures of beta, the difference in average beta between the 10th decile portfolio and the first decile portfolio is smaller for measures that use a longer measurement period.

The patterns in the average returns of the beta-sorted portfolios are very interesting. Contrary to the theoretical prediction of a positive relation between beta and expected stock returns, the results indicate that, regardless of the measure of beta used, the difference in average returns between the 10th decile portfolio and the first decile portfolio is negative for all measures of beta. For the measures of beta calculated with a simple CAPM regression model using six months (β^{6M}), 12 months (β^{12M}), and 24 months (β^{24M}) worth of daily return data, the average return of the difference portfolio is not only negative but statistically significant at the 5% level. For the one-month measure (β^{1M}) and the Scholes and Williams (1977) measure (β^{SW}), the average return of the difference portfolio is negative and significant at the 10% level. For all daily return-based measures of beta, the difference portfolio's average return is economically quite substantial, ranging from -0.33% per month for the β^{1M}-sorted portfolios to -0.54% per month for the β^{24M}-sorted portfolios.

The results for portfolios formed by sorting stocks on the monthly return-based measures of beta are a bit different. Regardless of the measure of beta, the average excess return of the difference portfolio is negative, but quite small in magnitude, ranging from -0.13 for portfolio formed by sorting on β^{3Y} to -0.08 for the β^{5Y}-sorted portfolios. In each case, the average return of the difference portfolio is statistically indistinguishable from zero.

TABLE 8.4 Univariate Portfolio Analysis—Equal-Weighted

This table presents the results of univariate portfolio analyses of the relation between each of measures of market beta and future stock returns. Monthly portfolios are formed by sorting all stocks in the CRSP sample into portfolios using decile breakpoints calculated based on the given sort variable using all stocks in the CRSP sample. The table shows the average sort variable value, equal-weighted one-month-ahead excess return (in percent per month), and the CAPM alpha (in percent per month) for each of the 10 decile portfolios as well as for the long-short zero-cost portfolio that is long the 10th decile portfolio and short the first decile portfolio. Newey and West (1987) t-statistics, adjusted using six lags, testing the null hypothesis that the average portfolio excess return or CAPM alpha is equal to zero, are shown in parentheses.

Sort Variable	Coefficient	1	2	3	4	5	6	7	8	9	10	10-1
β^{1M}		−1.55	−0.31	0.04	0.29	0.52	0.77	1.04	1.38	1.88	3.29	4.84
	Excess return	0.77	0.77	0.78	0.84	0.82	0.83	0.78	0.76	0.69	0.44	−0.33
		(2.16)	(2.76)	(3.05)	(3.28)	(3.13)	(3.05)	(2.72)	(2.49)	(2.00)	(1.05)	(−1.90)
	CAPM α	0.31	0.38	0.42	0.42	0.36	0.34	0.24	0.17	0.03	−0.32	−0.63
		(1.32)	(2.29)	(2.58)	(3.04)	(2.68)	(2.57)	(1.80)	(1.27)	(0.16)	(−1.39)	(−3.77)
β^{3M}		−0.62	0.01	0.23	0.42	0.59	0.78	0.98	1.23	1.58	2.41	3.04
	Excess return	0.74	0.76	0.85	0.79	0.83	0.80	0.80	0.76	0.68	0.43	−0.30
		(2.18)	(2.79)	(3.22)	(3.03)	(3.21)	(2.89)	(2.74)	(2.39)	(1.95)	(1.02)	(−1.37)
	CAPM α	0.34	0.41	0.47	0.37	0.38	0.30	0.25	0.15	−0.00	−0.34	−0.67
		(1.49)	(2.39)	(3.03)	(2.57)	(2.89)	(2.19)	(1.78)	(1.05)	(−0.00)	(−1.31)	(−2.85)
β^{6M}		−0.32	0.12	0.30	0.47	0.62	0.78	0.96	1.18	1.48	2.14	2.46
	Excess return	0.84	0.76	0.84	0.84	0.84	0.81	0.74	0.78	0.62	0.37	−0.47
		(2.69)	(2.94)	(3.12)	(3.23)	(3.15)	(2.86)	(2.50)	(2.45)	(1.74)	(0.87)	(−1.97)
	CAPM α	0.49	0.43	0.46	0.42	0.38	0.31	0.19	0.19	−0.07	−0.45	−0.94
		(2.25)	(2.60)	(2.84)	(2.94)	(2.76)	(2.12)	(1.32)	(1.12)	(−0.43)	(−1.93)	(−4.13)
β^{12M}		−0.13	0.18	0.35	0.50	0.64	0.79	0.95	1.15	1.42	1.98	2.11
	Excess return	0.92	0.87	0.91	0.85	0.86	0.87	0.77	0.65	0.60	0.38	−0.53
		(3.25)	(3.36)	(3.38)	(3.22)	(3.22)	(3.08)	(2.53)	(2.04)	(1.67)	(0.91)	(−2.04)
	CAPM α	0.61	0.55	0.53	0.43	0.40	0.40	0.21	0.04	−0.10	−0.45	−1.05
		(3.05)	(3.26)	(3.28)	(2.89)	(2.74)	(2.33)	(1.41)	(0.24)	(−0.61)	(−2.01)	(−4.45)

(continued)

TABLE 8.4 (Continued)

Sort Variable	Coefficient	1	2	3	4	5	6	7	8	9	10	10-1
β^{24M}	β^{24M}	-0.00	0.24	0.39	0.53	0.66	0.80	0.95	1.12	1.37	1.86	1.86
	Excess return	0.97	0.89	0.94	1.01	0.91	0.85	0.86	0.73	0.63	0.43	-0.54
		(3.84)	(3.47)	(3.51)	(3.86)	(3.31)	(2.96)	(2.82)	(2.30)	(1.79)	(1.05)	(-2.00)
	CAPM α	0.69	0.57	0.56	0.62	0.44	0.35	0.31	0.13	-0.06	-0.39	-1.08
		(3.87)	(3.45)	(3.35)	(3.52)	(2.97)	(2.24)	(2.01)	(0.80)	(-0.34)	(-1.85)	(-4.47)
β^{SW}	β^{SW}	-0.17	0.23	0.42	0.58	0.74	0.90	1.08	1.29	1.58	2.19	2.36
	Excess return	0.90	0.84	0.91	0.81	0.87	0.79	0.84	0.71	0.62	0.39	-0.50
		(3.15)	(3.46)	(3.79)	(3.15)	(3.18)	(2.81)	(2.78)	(2.16)	(1.68)	(0.89)	(-1.88)
	CAPM α	0.58	0.52	0.58	0.40	0.41	0.29	0.28	0.09	-0.08	-0.44	-1.02
		(2.88)	(3.35)	(3.49)	(2.69)	(2.80)	(1.99)	(1.89)	(0.60)	(-0.46)	(-1.88)	(-4.44)
β^{D}	β^{D}	-0.54	0.17	0.44	0.66	0.86	1.08	1.31	1.60	2.01	3.00	3.54
	Excess return	0.72	0.74	0.78	0.84	0.86	0.88	0.88	0.80	0.68	0.52	-0.20
		(2.40)	(3.06)	(3.19)	(3.34)	(3.31)	(3.15)	(2.89)	(2.47)	(1.85)	(1.16)	(-0.77)
	CAPM α	0.35	0.39	0.40	0.43	0.40	0.37	0.32	0.19	-0.01	-0.24	-0.58
		(1.67)	(2.63)	(2.87)	(3.09)	(3.04)	(2.75)	(2.24)	(1.26)	(-0.03)	(-0.85)	(-2.36)
β^{1Y}	β^{1Y}	-0.95	0.03	0.37	0.63	0.88	1.14	1.43	1.79	2.30	3.70	4.65
	Excess return	0.69	0.68	0.76	0.82	0.84	0.83	0.87	0.91	0.73	0.59	-0.10
		(2.12)	(2.60)	(3.03)	(3.31)	(3.24)	(3.00)	(2.93)	(2.86)	(2.05)	(1.40)	(-0.46)
	CAPM α	0.30	0.30	0.37	0.40	0.39	0.33	0.32	0.32	0.07	-0.16	-0.47
		(1.34)	(1.91)	(2.58)	(3.00)	(2.95)	(2.45)	(2.34)	(2.08)	(0.40)	(-0.65)	(-2.05)

β^{2Y}	-0.27	0.31	0.55	0.75	0.94	1.14	1.36	1.63	2.02	2.99	3.26
Excess return	0.73	0.71	0.87	0.86	0.91	0.92	0.90	0.84	0.80	0.64	-0.09
	(2.56)	(2.93)	(3.64)	(3.48)	(3.50)	(3.30)	(2.99)	(2.58)	(2.19)	(1.46)	(-0.36)
CAPM α	0.38	0.36	0.53	0.44	0.45	0.41	0.35	0.24	0.13	-0.14	-0.52
	(2.03)	(2.47)	(3.26)	(3.29)	(3.39)	(2.95)	(2.39)	(1.45)	(0.69)	(-0.56)	(-2.16)
β^{3Y}	-0.06	0.40	0.62	0.79	0.96	1.14	1.34	1.58	1.92	2.74	2.80
Excess return	0.82	0.78	0.86	0.90	0.85	0.87	0.88	0.88	0.84	0.69	-0.13
	(3.22)	(3.43)	(3.61)	(3.64)	(3.19)	(3.00)	(2.90)	(2.65)	(2.21)	(1.57)	(-0.45)
CAPM α	0.53	0.44	0.48	0.47	0.38	0.36	0.33	0.28	0.16	-0.09	-0.63
	(2.71)	(3.19)	(3.59)	(3.67)	(2.75)	(2.41)	(2.12)	(1.68)	(0.81)	(-0.36)	(-2.49)
β^{5Y}	0.07	0.47	0.66	0.82	0.98	1.14	1.31	1.53	1.84	2.56	2.49
Excess return	0.83	0.76	0.86	0.89	0.91	0.92	0.84	0.81	0.78	0.75	-0.08
	(3.53)	(3.45)	(3.72)	(3.58)	(3.31)	(3.24)	(2.68)	(2.40)	(2.04)	(1.69)	(-0.27)
CAPM α	0.57	0.43	0.48	0.47	0.43	0.40	0.28	0.20	0.11	-0.03	-0.60
	(3.05)	(3.18)	(3.76)	(3.63)	(3.02)	(2.83)	(1.74)	(1.18)	(0.52)	(-0.11)	(-2.35)

While none of the portfolio analyses produce average portfolio returns that are monotonic across the deciles of beta, the portfolio with the lowest average return is always the 10th decile portfolio. This result is quite strange given that theory predicts that the 10th decile portfolio should have the highest, not the lowest, average return. Furthermore, for portfolios sorted on the daily return-based measures of beta, the drop in average return between the ninth decile portfolio and the 10th decile portfolio is quite large. For example, when sorting on β^{12M}, the ninth decile portfolio generates an average monthly excess return of 0.60% while the average excess return of the 10th decile portfolio is only 0.38%. In fact, when sorting on β^{12M}, not only does the 10th decile portfolio generate the lowest average return but the first decile portfolio generates the highest excess return (0.92% per month). While this is not the case for all measures of beta, this fact is worth mentioning because β^{12M} is by far the most commonly used measure of beta in empirical asset pricing research.

Examination of the CAPM alphas of the portfolios indicates that the alphas of the difference portfolios are even more negative and much more statistically significant than the average returns. In fact, regardless of the measure of beta, the CAPM alpha of the difference portfolio is negative and highly statistically significant, with abnormal returns (alphas) ranging from −0.47% per month with a t-statistic of −2.05 for the β^{1Y}-sorted portfolios to −1.08% per month with a t-statistic of −4.47 for the β^{24M}-sorted portfolios. For each of the measures of beta, the 10th decile portfolio generates the lowest CAPM alpha although the abnormal return of this portfolio is only statistically significant at the 5% level for portfolios formed on β^{12M} (CAPM alpha = −0.45% per month, t-statistic = −0.45) and at the 10% level for β^{6M}-sorted (CAPM alpha = −0.45% per month, t-statistic = −1.93) and β^{24M}-sorted (CAPM alpha = −0.39% per month, t-statistic = −1.85) portfolios. When beta is calculated using more than six months of data (with the exception of β^{D} and β^{1Y}), the first decile portfolio generates positive and statistically significant average excess returns. Furthermore, with the exception of the second β^{1Y}-sorted portfolio, the second, third, fourth, fifth, and sixth decile portfolios for each of the measures of beta generate positive abnormal returns. These results seem to indicate that the CAPM risk model does not do a great job at explaining the returns of the beta-sorted portfolios.

Given the results of the analysis of excess returns, it is actually not surprising that adjusting the returns using the CAPM risk model results in negative alphas that are larger in magnitude than the returns of the difference portfolio. The reason for this is that risk-adjustment using the CAPM model adjusts the returns for sensitivity to the *MKT* factor, which is the same factor used to calculate beta. Thus, stocks in the 10th decile portfolio have high sensitivities, and stocks in the low decile portfolio have low sensitivities. As a result, the difference portfolio, which has long positions in stocks with high beta and short positions in stocks with low beta, has a high sensitivity to the market portfolio. Because the *MKT* factor generates positive average returns in the long run and the difference portfolio has a positive sensitivity to the market portfolio, the effect of adjusting for this sensitivity is that the risk-adjusted returns are lower than the unadjusted returns.

Value-Weighted Portfolios

We now repeat the portfolio analyses, this time using value-weighted portfolios. The results of the value-weighted portfolio analyses, presented in Table 8.5, show that the negative relation between beta and future stock returns detected using equal-weighted portfolios is much weaker when using value-weighted portfolios. For each measure of beta, the average return of the difference portfolio is economically small and statistically insignificant. These average returns range from -0.13% per month with a t-statistic of -0.50 for portfolios sorted on β^{1M} to 0.31% per month with a t-statistic of 0.97 for portfolios formed by sorting on β^{1Y}. In many cases, the 10th decile portfolio generates the lowest or second lowest average excess return. Specifically, for value-weighted portfolios sorted on β^{1M}, β^{12M}, β^{SW}, β^{D}, and β^{2Y}, the portfolio comprised stocks with the highest betas generates the lowest average return. For portfolios formed by sorting on β^{3M}, β^{6M}, and β^{24M}, the 10th decile portfolio generates the second lowest average excess returns. Interestingly, for portfolios sorted on β^{3M}, β^{6M}, β^{1Y}, β^{3Y}, and β^{5Y}, the lowest average return comes from the first decile portfolio, and for portfolios sorted on β^{1M}, β^{12M}, β^{SW}, β^{D}, and β^{2Y}, the first decile portfolio generates the second lowest average return. For seven (β^{1M}, β^{3M}, β^{6M}, β^{12M}, β^{SW}, β^{D}, and β^{2Y}) of the 11 measures of beta, the two portfolios that generate the lowest average excess returns are the first and 10th decile portfolios. None of the measures of beta generate a monotonic pattern in average returns across the decile portfolios.

The average abnormal returns of the difference portfolios relative to the CAPM risk model range from -0.64% per month (t-statistic $= -2.34$) for portfolios sorted on β^{D} to -0.10% per month (t-statistic $= -0.36$) for the β^{1Y}-sorted portfolios. The alpha of the difference portfolio is highly statistically significant for portfolios sorted on β^{12M}, β^{24M}, and β^{SW}, and marginally statistically significant for portfolios sorted on β^{1M}, β^{2Y}, and β^{5Y}. Thus, while the negative abnormal return of the difference portfolio exists when sorting on a few of the measures of beta, this result is not quite as strong in value-weighted portfolios as it is in equal-weighted portfolios. For all measures of beta, the portfolio of high-beta stocks generates the lowest abnormal return, and for each of the daily return-based measures as well as β^{2Y}, the CAPM alpha of the 10th decile portfolio is negative and statistically significant. These results are generally stronger than the results for the equal-weighted portfolios. None of the value-weighted decile one portfolios generate statistically significant abnormal returns.

In summary, the results of the portfolio analyses presented in this section provide evidence that strongly contradicts the predictions of the CAPM. According to the CAPM, the average returns of the decile portfolios should increase monotonically across the decile portfolios. Furthermore, the CAPM predicts that after risk-adjusting the returns of the portfolios using the CAPM risk model, the average abnormal return of each of the portfolios should be economically small and statistically indistinguishable from zero. As can be seen from Tables 8.4 and 8.5, not only do we fail to detect a positive relation between beta and expected returns, but in several cases we actually detect a negative relation.

TABLE 8.5 Univariate Portfolio Analysis—Value-Weighted

This table presents the results of univariate portfolio analyses of the relation between each of measures of market beta and future stock returns. Monthly portfolios are formed by sorting all stocks in the CRSP sample into portfolios using decile breakpoints calculated based on the given sort variable using all stocks in the CRSP sample. The table shows the value-weighted one-month-ahead excess return and CAPM alpha (in percent per month) for each of the 10 decile portfolios as well as for the long–short zero-cost portfolio that is long the 10th decile portfolio and short the first decile portfolio. Newey and West (1987) t-statistics, adjusted using six lags, testing the null hypothesis that the average portfolio excess return or CAPM alpha is equal to zero, are shown in parentheses.

Sort Variable	Coefficient	1	2	3	4	5	6	7	8	9	10	10-1
β^{1M}	Excess return	0.37	0.43	0.44	0.50	0.47	0.46	0.47	0.57	0.44	0.24	-0.13
		(1.44)	(2.13)	(2.43)	(2.78)	(2.69)	(2.43)	(2.37)	(2.54)	(1.69)	(0.62)	(-0.50)
	CAPM α	-0.04	0.09	0.10	0.14	0.09	0.06	0.03	0.06	-0.16	-0.51	-0.47
		(-0.25)	(0.91)	(1.15)	(1.83)	(1.46)	(0.81)	(0.47)	(0.91)	(-1.66)	(-2.58)	(-1.83)
β^{3M}	Excess return	0.16	0.45	0.48	0.45	0.54	0.45	0.55	0.50	0.44	0.35	0.19
		(0.64)	(2.37)	(2.59)	(2.50)	(2.99)	(2.39)	(2.75)	(2.25)	(1.63)	(0.93)	(0.64)
	CAPM α	-0.17	0.16	0.17	0.11	0.18	0.06	0.10	0.01	-0.15	-0.40	-0.24
		(-0.95)	(1.42)	(1.64)	(1.22)	(2.55)	(0.68)	(1.44)	(0.12)	(-1.45)	(-2.09)	(-0.83)
β^{6M}	Excess return	0.32	0.56	0.42	0.46	0.53	0.40	0.50	0.41	0.42	0.37	0.05
		(1.45)	(3.05)	(2.52)	(2.59)	(3.01)	(2.11)	(2.49)	(1.80)	(1.57)	(1.00)	(0.17)
	CAPM α	0.03	0.29	0.13	0.14	0.18	0.02	0.06	-0.08	-0.17	-0.38	-0.41
		(0.18)	(2.34)	(1.33)	(1.56)	(2.21)	(0.23)	(0.73)	(-1.07)	(-1.65)	(-2.12)	(-1.55)
β^{12M}	Excess return	0.39	0.53	0.54	0.43	0.56	0.48	0.51	0.43	0.39	0.34	-0.05
		(1.92)	(3.00)	(3.21)	(2.41)	(3.27)	(2.59)	(2.44)	(1.92)	(1.41)	(0.95)	(-0.18)
	CAPM α	0.14	0.26	0.27	0.11	0.21	0.10	0.07	-0.06	-0.20	-0.40	-0.54
		(0.95)	(2.26)	(2.66)	(1.10)	(2.65)	(1.23)	(0.78)	(-0.72)	(-1.93)	(-2.28)	(-2.13)
β^{24M}	Excess return	0.36	0.62	0.48	0.53	0.49	0.49	0.55	0.45	0.32	0.35	-0.01
		(1.81)	(3.34)	(2.82)	(3.15)	(2.79)	(2.66)	(2.68)	(1.92)	(1.19)	(1.01)	(-0.04)
	CAPM α	0.11	0.38	0.20	0.23	0.14	0.11	0.12	-0.02	-0.25	-0.37	-0.48
		(0.79)	(2.86)	(1.81)	(2.37)	(1.63)	(1.28)	(1.29)	(-0.23)	(-2.49)	(-2.46)	(-2.08)

β^{SW}	Excess return	0.31 (1.60)	0.44 (2.64)	0.52 (3.19)	0.44 (2.55)	0.47 (2.61)	0.59 (3.00)	0.38 (1.70)	0.50 (1.98)	0.47 (1.62)	0.26 (0.67)	−0.05 (−0.15)
	CAPM α	0.06 (0.39)	0.18 (1.71)	0.24 (2.41)	0.11 (1.34)	0.11 (1.46)	0.18 (1.93)	−0.09 (−1.22)	−0.05 (−0.60)	−0.16 (−1.38)	−0.54 (−2.87)	−0.60 (−2.22)
β^{D}	Excess return	0.29 (1.47)	0.43 (2.59)	0.54 (3.20)	0.49 (2.75)	0.54 (2.92)	0.54 (2.53)	0.53 (2.25)	0.47 (1.75)	0.42 (1.26)	0.17 (0.40)	−0.12 (−0.38)
	CAPM α	−0.02 (−0.12)	0.14 (1.38)	0.22 (2.43)	0.14 (1.63)	0.12 (1.86)	0.07 (1.29)	0.01 (0.10)	−0.13 (−1.47)	−0.28 (−2.03)	−0.66 (−3.10)	−0.64 (−2.34)
β^{1Y}	Excess return	0.21 (0.99)	0.40 (2.12)	0.44 (2.46)	0.56 (3.03)	0.69 (3.66)	0.51 (2.43)	0.48 (2.10)	0.47 (1.80)	0.47 (1.54)	0.52 (1.29)	0.31 (0.97)
	CAPM α	−0.16 (−1.24)	0.05 (0.47)	0.08 (0.81)	0.18 (2.37)	0.27 (3.95)	0.04 (0.65)	−0.04 (−0.56)	−0.11 (−1.21)	−0.19 (−1.40)	−0.27 (−1.21)	−0.10 (−0.36)
β^{2Y}	Excess return	0.39 (2.09)	0.39 (2.13)	0.54 (3.07)	0.65 (3.50)	0.54 (2.86)	0.52 (2.54)	0.52 (2.21)	0.43 (1.67)	0.54 (1.66)	0.38 (0.94)	−0.02 (−0.04)
	CAPM α	0.08 (0.63)	0.07 (0.64)	0.19 (2.17)	0.27 (3.28)	0.12 (1.65)	0.04 (0.56)	−0.02 (−0.20)	−0.15 (−1.71)	−0.13 (−0.94)	−0.42 (−2.04)	−0.50 (−1.75)
β^{3Y}	Excess return	0.33 (1.93)	0.42 (2.34)	0.50 (2.90)	0.60 (3.28)	0.46 (2.33)	0.47 (2.20)	0.53 (2.21)	0.41 (1.49)	0.54 (1.68)	0.50 (1.23)	0.17 (0.47)
	CAPM α	0.05 (0.43)	0.11 (0.96)	0.16 (1.86)	0.22 (2.51)	0.03 (0.35)	−0.02 (−0.27)	−0.01 (−0.10)	−0.19 (−2.11)	−0.13 (−0.98)	−0.31 (−1.59)	−0.37 (−1.34)
β^{5Y}	Excess return	0.43 (2.46)	0.43 (2.61)	0.59 (3.55)	0.44 (2.36)	0.47 (2.32)	0.54 (2.43)	0.49 (1.94)	0.45 (1.59)	0.51 (1.53)	0.50 (1.23)	0.08 (0.21)
	CAPM α	0.16 (1.22)	0.14 (1.36)	0.25 (2.83)	0.05 (0.65)	0.03 (0.43)	0.05 (0.61)	−0.06 (−0.77)	−0.16 (−1.73)	−0.17 (−1.10)	−0.31 (−1.64)	−0.47 (−1.73)

8.5.2 Fama–MacBeth Regression Analysis

We now investigate the relation between beta and stock returns using Fama and MacBeth (1973) regression analysis. Each month, for each of the measures of beta, we perform a cross-sectional regression of one-month-ahead future stock excess return (r_{t+1}) on the given measure. The independent variable in the regression (one of the measures of beta) is winsorized at the 0.5% level on a monthly basis prior to calculating the regression coefficients. Table 8.6 presents the time-series averages of the monthly cross-sectional regression coefficients for regressions using each of the measures of beta. The column names in the table indicate which measure of beta is used as the independent variable. The average slopes on the given measure of beta is presented in the row labeled β, and the average intercept coefficients are presented in the row labeled Intercept. t-statistics testing the null hypothesis that the average coefficient is equal to zero, adjusted following Newey and West (1987) using six lags, are presented in parentheses. The rows labeled Adj. R^2 and n present the average adjusted R-squared values and average number of observations used in the cross-sectional regressions, respectively.

The results in Table 8.6 indicate that for each of the daily return-based measures of beta, the average coefficient on beta is negative. For β^{12M}, the average coefficient of -0.26 is statistically significant at the 5% level with a t-statistic of -1.96. The regressions using β^{24M} give very similar results, with average coefficient of -0.30 and corresponding t-statistic of -1.97. The average slope on β^{SW} of -0.19 is not statistically significant (t-statistic $= -1.32$). The same conclusion holds for the average coefficient on β^D of -0.01 (t-statistic $= 0.19$). The results for the regressions using monthly return-based measures of beta detect no relation between beta and one-month-ahead excess stock returns, with average coefficients that are very small in magnitude, ranging from 0.01 to -0.04, and statistically indistinguishable from zero. One interpretation of the results in Table 8.6 is that the negative relation between beta and future stock returns detected when using β^{12M} and β^{24} is not very robust because this relation does not hold when using other measures of beta. An alternative interpretation of the results relies on the summary statistics, correlation analyses, and persistence analyses, from which the general conclusion was that β^{12M} and β^{24M} are the most accurate measures of beta. Therefore, the failure of the other measures to detect the negative relation found when using β^{12M} and β^{24M} may be due to the fact that the other measures are noisier proxies for a stock's true beta. Regardless of the interpretation, the results clearly give no evidence supporting a positive relation between beta and expected stock returns, the main prediction of the CAPM.

If we assume that the results from the regressions using β^{12M} and β^{24M} as the independent variable are in fact indicative of a negative relation between beta and expected stock returns, it is important to examine the economic magnitude of that relation. We take several approaches to doing so. We use the results from the regressions using β^{12M} in this analysis because β^{12M} is the most commonly used measure of beta in the asset pricing literature.

The most straightforward method to interpret the economic importance of the relation between beta and expected stock returns is to simply take the average slope

TABLE 8.6 Fama–MacBeth Regression Analysis

This table presents the results of Fama and MacBeth (1973) regression analyses of the relation between expected stock returns and market beta. Each column in the table presents results for a different cross-sectional regression specification. The dependent variable in all specifications is the one-month-ahead excess stock return. The independent variable in each specification is indicated in the column header. The independent variable is winsorized at the 0.5% level on a monthly basis. The table presents average slope and intercept coefficients along with t-statistics (in parentheses), adjusted following Newey and West (1987) using six lags, testing the null hypothesis that the average coefficient is equal to zero. The rows labeled Adj. R^2 and n present the average adjusted R-squared and number of data points, respectively, for the cross-sectional regressions.

	β^{1M}	β^{3M}	β^{6M}	β^{12M}	β^{24M}	β^{SW}	β^{D}	β^{1Y}	β^{2Y}	β^{3Y}	β^{5Y}
β	-0.06	-0.08	-0.17	-0.26	-0.30	-0.19	-0.01	0.02	0.01	-0.03	-0.04
	(-1.19)	(-0.90)	(-1.45)	(-1.96)	(-1.97)	(-1.46)	(-0.12)	(0.39)	(0.08)	(-0.22)	(-0.30)
Intercept	0.79	0.80	0.87	0.97	1.06	0.93	0.79	0.74	0.80	0.87	0.89
	(2.85)	(2.95)	(3.32)	(3.85)	(4.33)	(3.97)	(3.26)	(2.77)	(3.35)	(3.95)	(4.34)
Adj. R^2	0.01	0.01	0.02	0.02	0.02	0.02	0.01	0.01	0.01	0.02	0.02
n	4732	4686	4599	4426	4007	4426	4426	4410	4058	3935	3948

coefficient from the regressions of −0.26 as an indication of the additional expected return corresponding to a one-unit increase in beta. The results therefore indicate that a one-unit increase in beta results in a decrease in expected return of 0.26% per month or approximately 3.12% per year. A second method to examine the economic magnitude of the result is to calculate the change in expected return associated with a one-standard-deviation move in beta. Using this approach, we take the average regression coefficient of −0.26 and multiply it by 0.61, the standard deviation of the cross-sectional distribution of β^{12M} in the average month (see Table 8.1) to get −0.16. The regression analysis therefore indicates that a one-standard-deviation increase in beta corresponds to a decrease in expected return of 0.16% per month or approximately 1.92% per year. Finally, we can use the average slope coefficient to examine the difference in expected return between stocks with very high values of β^{12M} and stocks with very low values of β^{12M}. To do this, we multiply the regression coefficient of −0.26 by the difference in average β^{12M} between stocks in the highest and lowest deciles of β^{12M}. Table 8.4 shows that this difference in average beta for portfolios sorted on β^{12M} is 2.11. Multiplying by −0.26 gives −0.55. We therefore assess that the difference in expected return between stocks in the highest and lowest deciles of β^{12M} is approximately −0.55% per month (−6.6% per year). It is worth noting that the portfolio analysis found that the average monthly return of the difference portfolio is −0.53%, very close to the −0.55% found by multiplying the average regression coefficient by the difference in average betas.

The second prediction of the CAPM that can be investigated using the regression analyses in Table 8.6 is the prediction that after accounting for the effect of beta, the average excess stock return should be zero. We empirically assess this prediction by examining the average intercept coefficients from the regression analyses.

The results in Table 8.6 demonstrate that, regardless of the measure of beta used in the regression analysis, the average intercept coefficient is positive and highly statistically significant. The average coefficients range from 0.74 with a t-statistic of 2.77 when β^{1Y} is the independent variable to 1.06 with a t-statistic of 4.33 when β^{24M} is the independent variable. Thus, once again in stark contrast to the prediction of the CAPM, the results indicate that stocks earn very significant positive average excess returns after accounting for the effect of beta. The 0.74 coefficient from the β^{1Y} regressions indicates that the average stock earns 0.74% per month (8.88% per year) in excess return after accounting for the effect of beta. Taking the estimate from the β^{24M} regressions, we get an average excess return of 1.06% per month (12.72% per year) after accounting for the effects of beta.

Finally, it is worth noting that the average adjusted R-squared values presented in Table 8.6 are very low, ranging from 0.01 to 0.02 for the different measures of beta. Low R-squared values in cross-sectional regressions where the dependent variable is the future stock return are common in empirical asset pricing research. As will be seen throughout this book, regardless of the combination of independent variables used in the regression specification, R-squared values remain abysmally low. The main reason for this is that predicting future stock returns is a very difficult undertaking, and realized stock returns are a very noisy proxy for expected stock returns (see Elton (1999)).

In summary, our empirical investigations fail to provide much support for the predictions of the CAPM. There is no evidence of a positive relation between beta and future stock returns, while some analyses actually detect a negative relation. Estimates of the expected return of a stock with a beta of zero, taken to be the average intercept coefficient from Fama and MacBeth (1973) regressions, indicate that zero-beta stocks have an economically large and statistically significant average excess return.

8.6 SUMMARY

We began this chapter by discussing the estimation of the beta of a security. The most commonly used approach is to regress the historical excess returns of the stock on the market factor and to take the slope coefficient as an estimate of the stock's beta. This method is usually implemented using either daily or monthly excess returns. The most frequently used measure of a stock's beta in the empirical asset pricing literature is calculated by estimating this regression model using one year worth of daily return data. For the remainder of this book, we refer to this measure, denoted β^{12M} throughout this chapter, simply as β. Alternative approaches to estimating beta, designed to account for nonsynchronous and infrequent trading, have been proposed by Scholes and Williams (1977) and Dimson (1979).

Summary statistics, correlation analysis, and persistence analysis demonstrate that calculating beta using longer measurement periods results in more accurate measurement. Additionally, the results indicate that using daily returns instead of monthly returns in the regressions results in more accurate estimates of beta. The adjustments proposed by Scholes and Williams (1977) and Dimson (1979) do not appear to increase the accuracy of beta measurement.

Using several different estimates of stocks' betas, we empirically examine the cross-sectional relation between beta and expected stock returns. The CAPM predicts a positive relation between beta and expected returns. Specifically, the CAPM stipulates that the relation between beta and expected excess returns is described by a line with slope equal to the market risk premium and intercept of zero.

Empirical examination of these predictions fails to produce supporting evidence. Univariate portfolio and Fama and MacBeth (1973) regression analysis detect either a negative cross-sectional relation between beta and future excess returns or no relation. The exact results differ depending on which measure of beta is used in the analysis. For the most commonly used measure of beta, calculated using a regression of excess stock returns on the market factor using one year of daily data (β^{12M} or, for the rest of this book, β), the analyses generally indicate a negative relation. In addition to detecting a negative relation between beta and future stock returns, Fama and MacBeth (1973) regression analyses produce very large intercept coefficients, contradicting the second prediction of the CAPM that the expected excess return of a security with a beta of zero is zero.

These empirical results are perhaps the most persistent and investigated anomalies in all of empirical asset pricing research. The negative abnormal returns of a portfolio that is long high-beta stocks and short low-beta stocks was first documented by Black, Jensen, and Scholes (1972). Several subsequent papers such as Blume and Friend (1973), Fama and MacBeth (1973), Reinganum (1981), Lakonishok and Shapiro (1986), and Fama and French (1992, 1993) reach similar conclusions. Recently, several potential explanations for this puzzling result have been proposed. Baker, Bradley, and Wurgler (2011) show that the effect is potentially driven by benchmarking by institutional investors. Baker, Bradley, and Taliaferro (2014) demonstrate that this anomaly consists of both micro and macro components. Frazzini and Pedersen (2014) present theoretical and corroborating empirical evidence that the phenomenon is driven by leverage-constrained investors who buy high-beta stocks in an effort to increase the expected returns of their portfolios. In doing so, they push the price of high-beta stocks up and therefore depress future returns. Bali, Brown, Murray, and Tang (2014) find empirical evidence supporting their argument that the negative relation between beta and future stock returns is driven by investors' demand for lottery-like stocks, which also happen to be high-beta stocks. This lottery demand results in high prices, and thus low future returns, for high-beta stocks.

REFERENCES

Amihud, Y. 2002. Illiquidity and stock returns: cross-section and time-series effects. Journal of Financial Markets, 5(1), 31–56.

Amihud, Y. and Mendelson, H. 1986. Asset pricing and the bid-ask spread. Journal of Financial Economics, 17(2), 223–249.

Baker, M., Bradley, B., and Taliaferro, R. 2014. The low-risk anomaly: a decomposition into micro and macro effects. Financial Analysts Journal, 70(2), 43–58.

Baker, M., Bradley, B., and Wurgler, J. 2011. Benchmarks as limits to arbitrage: understanding the low-volatility anomaly. Financial Analysts Journal, 67(1), 40–54.

Bali, T. G., Brown, S. J., Murray, S., and Tang, Y. 2014. A Lottery Demand-Based Explanation of the Beta Anomaly. SSRN eLibrary.

Banz, R. W. 1981. The relationship between return and market value of common stocks. Journal of Financial Economics, 9(1), 3–18.

Black, F., Jensen, M. C., and Scholes, M. S. Studies in the Theory of Capital Markets, The capital asset pricing model: some empirical tests. Praeger, New York, 1972.

Blume, M. E. and Friend, I. 1973. A new look at the capital asset pricing model. Journal of Finance, 28(1), 19–33.

Dimson, E. 1979. Risk measurement when shares are subject to infrequent trading. Journal of Financial Economics, 7(2), 197–226.

Elton, E. J. 1999. Expected return, realized return, and asset pricing tests. Journal of Finance, 54, 1199–1220.

Fama, E. F. and French, K. R. 1992. The cross-section of expected stock returns. Journal of Finance, 47(2), 427–465.

Fama, E. F. and French, K. R. 1993. Common risk factors in the returns on stocks and bonds. Journal of Financial Economics, 33(1), 3–56.

Fama, E. F. and MacBeth, J. D. 1973. Risk, return, and equilibrium: empirical tests. Journal of Political Economy, 81(3), 607.

Frazzini, A. and Pedersen, L. H. 2014. Betting against beta. Journal of Financial Economics, 111(1), 1–25.

Friend, I. and Blume, M. 1970. Measurement of portfolio performance under uncertainty. American Economic Review, 60(4), 607–636.

Gilbert, T., Hrdlicka, C., Kalodimos, J., and Siegel, S. 2014. Daily data is bad for beta: opacity and frequency-dependent betas. Review of Asset Pricing Studies, 4(1), 78–117.

Jegadeesh, N. and Titman, S. 1993. Returns to buying winners and selling losers: implications for stock market efficiency. Journal of Finance, 48(1), 65–91.

Lakonishok, J. and Shapiro, A. 1986. Systematic risk, total risk and size as determinants of stock market returns. Journal of Banking & Finance, 10(1), 115–132.

Lintner, J. 1965. Security prices, risk, and maximal gains from diversification. Journal of Finance, 20(4), 587–615.

Mossin, J. 1966. Equilibrium in a capital asset market. Econometrica, 34(4), 768–783.

Newey, W. K. and West, K. D. 1987. A simple, positive semi-definite, heteroskedasticity and autocorrelation consistent covariance matrix. Econometrica, 55(3), 703–708.

Reinganum, M. R. 1981. A new empirical perspective of the CAPM. Journal of Quantitive and Empirical Finance, 16(4), 439–462.

Rosenberg, B., Reid, K., and Lanstein, R. 1985. Persuasive evidence of market inefficiency. Journal of Portfolio Management, 11(3), 9–16.

Scholes, M. and Williams, J. T. 1977. Estimating betas from nonsynchronous data. Journal of Financial Economics, 5(3), 309–327.

Sharpe, W. F. 1964. Capital asset prices: a theory of market equilibrium under conditions of risk. Journal of Finance, 19(3), 425–442.

Stambaugh, R. F. 1982. On the exclusion of assets from tests of the two-parameter model. Journal of Financial Economics, 10(3), 237–268.

9

THE SIZE EFFECT

The size effect refers to the observation that stocks with large market capitalizations (large stocks) tend to have lower returns than stocks with small market capitalizations (small stocks). This result has become one of the cornerstone findings in empirical examinations of stock return predictability. While Fama and French (1992, 1993) are the most commonly cited papers related to the size effect, the phenomenon was documented at least a decade earlier by Banz (1981) and then again by Lakonishok and Shapiro (1986). Fama and French (2012) find evidence of a size effect in international equity markets.

The main size-related result of Fama and French (1992) is that market capitalization has the ability to predict the cross section of future stock returns. Specifically, stocks with small market capitalizations have historically realized significantly higher average returns than large market capitalization stocks. Building upon this finding, Fama and French (1993) create a portfolio designed to have returns that mimic the returns associated with the size effect and propose using the returns of this portfolio as a risk factor, known as *SMB* for small minus big. They find that their risk model, known now as the Fama and French three-factor model, outperforms the Capital Asset Pricing Model (CAPM) of Sharpe (1964), Lintner (1965), and Mossin (1966) in terms of explaining portfolio returns.[1]

---

[1] The Fama and French three-factor model includes the market factor (*MKT*), the size factor (*SMB*), and the value factor (*HML*), which is based on the ratio of the book value of equity to the market value of equity, and will be discussed in Chapter 10.

Empirical Asset Pricing: The Cross Section of Stock Returns, First Edition.
Turan G. Bali, Robert F. Engle, and Scott Murray.
© 2016 John Wiley & Sons, Inc. Published 2016 by John Wiley & Sons, Inc.

The objectives of this chapter are to discuss the calculation of variables that measure market capitalization, demonstrate the empirical ability of these variables to predict future stock returns, and examine the properties of the *SMB* factor created by Fama and French (1993).

9.1   CALCULATING MARKET CAPITALIZATION

The market capitalization of a stock is defined as the total value of all of the outstanding shares of that stock. Market capitalization is therefore computed by taking the total number of equity shares outstanding times the price of one share.

While the calculation of market capitalization seems simple enough, there are a few implementation issues that are worthy of discussion. Most researchers take the data necessary to compute market capitalization from the Center for Research in Security Prices (CRSP) database. CRSP provides the number of shares outstanding in the SHROUT field in both the daily stock file (dsf) and the monthly stock file (msf). Values in the SHROUT field are recorded in thousands of shares. There are some cases in both the daily and monthly stock files where the value of the SHROUT field is zero. The interpretation of these values is unclear. We therefore take the number of shares outstanding to be missing if the SHROUT field has a value of zero. In the daily stock file, CRSP puts the price in the PRC field. The value in the PRC field indicates the closing price of the stock, taken to be the price of the last trade on the given day. If a closing price is unavailable, the most frequent reason for which is that there is no trading in the stock on the given date, CRSP reports the negative of the average of the last bid price and the last ask price for the stock. If neither a closing price nor the average of the bid and ask is available (because either the bid or ask is not available), then CRSP reports zero in the PRC field or leaves it blank.[2] If the daily stock file is used to calculate market capitalization, it is advisable to consider the price of the stock to be missing if the value in the PRC field is zero. CRSP also provides price data in the monthly stock file. In the monthly stock file, there are two price fields, PRC and ALTPRC (for alternate price). The PRC field in the monthly stock file is calculated in exactly the same manner as the PRC field in the daily stock file using data from the last trading day of the given month. The ALTPRC field contains the last non-missing price over all days during the given month. A non-missing price is taken to be an actual closing price or the negative of the average of the bid and ask prices. As with the PRC field, a negative value for the ALTPRC field indicates that the price is calculated as the average of the bid and ask prices. Finally, the ALTPRC field is set to zero or blank if no price is available for any trading day during the given month. As with PRC, we consider the price to be missing when the value of ALTPRC is set to zero.[3]

---

[2]The CRSP documentation on Wharton Research Data Services (WRDS) indicates that the PRC field will be set to zero when no price is available. However, our investigation fails to find any such entries. There are, however, many entries where the PRC field is not populated.

[3]As with the daily stock file, despite what is indicated in the CRSP documentation, we fail to find any entries in the monthly stock file where the PRC field or the ALTPRC field is set to zero. There are, however, many entries where these fields are not populated.

In addition to the data issues described in the previous paragraph, there are actually a few different ways that researchers commonly time the calculation of market capitalization. The simplest approach is to take the share price and number of shares outstanding as of the end of the period for which the market capitalization is being measured. For example, if the study uses a monthly sample, as is the case for the sample used in this book, market capitalization would be calculated using stock price and shares outstanding data from last trading day during the given month. Calculating market capitalization using this approach gives perhaps the most straightforward measure and has the benefit of using the most recent data available. Our primary market capitalization variable, $MktCap$, therefore, is calculated for stock i in month t as

$$MktCap_{i,t} = \frac{|SHROUT_{i,t} \times ALTPRC_{i,t}|}{1000} \tag{9.1}$$

where $SHROUT_{i,t}$ is the number of shares outstanding at the end of month t, taken from the SHROUT field in CRSP's monthly stock file, and $ALTPRC_{i,t}$ is the price of the stock, taken from the ALTPRC field in the same file on the same date. Because the SHROUT field in CRSP is recorded in thousands of shares, the division by 1000 indicated in equation (9.1) results in $MktCap$ measuring the market capitalization of the stock in millions of dollars. The absolute value is taken to account for the fact that CRSP reports a negative price when the reported value is calculated as the average of a bid and ask price. When either the SHROUT or ALTPRC fields are missing or set to zero, we take $MktCap$ to be missing.

An alternative approach to calculating market capitalization is taken by Fama and French (1992, 1993, FF hereafter), with several subsequent studies following their approach. FF calculate market capitalization as of the last trading day of June in each year y and hold the value constant for the months from June of that same year y until May of year $y + 1$. In June of year $y + 1$, market capitalization is recalculated. The benefit of this approach is that the market capitalization measure is not affected by short-term movements in the stock price, which may cause the market capitalization measure to exhibit unwanted time-series correlation with stock returns. To examine the ramifications of using the alternatively timed calculation of market capitalization proposed by Fama and French, we define this measure of market capitalization as

$$MktCap_{i,t}^{FF} = \frac{|SHROUT_{i, \text{June}} \times ALTPRC_{i, \text{June}}|}{1000} \tag{9.2}$$

where $SHROUT_{i, \text{June}}$ and $ALTPRC_{i, \text{June}}$ are taken from the SHROUT and ALTPRC fields, respectively, of CRSP's monthly stock file on the most recent June that falls prior to or contemporaneous with the month t. Using this approach, the market capitalization for each stock changes only once per calendar year, in June, and therefore remains constant from any given June through the following May. As with the calculation of $MktCap$, when either the SHROUT or ALTPRC field is set to zero, $MktCap^{FF}$ is taken to be missing.

Most empirical asset pricing research uses market capitalization variables calculated using one of these two approaches. In almost all cases, which approach is used has very little impact on the results of the empirical analysis, as the measures are very highly correlated and very similar in magnitude.

While the timing of the market capitalization calculation has a negligible effect, there is one issue with the measure that can have a substantial impact on empirical analyses. As will be seen shortly in Table 9.1, the cross-sectional distribution of market capitalization is very highly skewed. This phenomenon arises because there are a small number of stocks whose market capitalizations are very large. The presence of these large stocks can impair the ability of regression analyses or other analyses that rely on the magnitude of the measure (instead of just the ordering, as in portfolio analyses) to produce accurate parameter estimates. For this reason, researchers frequently use the natural log of market capitalization, which we denote *Size*, to measure market capitalization in regression analyses. We implement this for both *MktCap* and *MktCap^{FF}*, giving

$$Size_{i,t} = \ln\ (MktCap_{i,t}) \tag{9.3}$$

and

$$Size_{i,t}^{FF} = \ln\ (MktCap_{i,t}^{FF}). \tag{9.4}$$

TABLE 9.1 Summary Statistics
This table presents summary statistics for variables measuring firm size calculated using the CRSP sample for the months t from June 1963 through November 2012. Each month, the mean (*Mean*), standard deviation (*SD*), skewness (*Skew*), excess kurtosis (*Kurt*), minimum (*Min*), fifth percentile (5%), 25th percentile (25%), median (*Median*), 75th percentile (75%), 95th percentile (95%), and maximum (*Max*) values of the cross-sectional distribution of each variable are calculated. The table presents the time-series means for each cross-sectional value. The column labeled n indicates the average number of stocks for which the given variable is available. *MktCap* is calculated as the share price times the number of shares outstanding as of the end of month t, measured in millions of dollars. *Size* is the natural log of *MktCap*. *MktCap^{CPI}* is *MktCap* adjusted using the consumer price index to reflect 2012 dollars and *Size^{CPI}* is the natural log of *MktCap^{CPI}*. *MktCap^{FF}* is the share price times the number of shares outstanding calculated as of the end of the most recent June, measured in millions of dollars. *Size^{FF}* is the natural log of *MktCap^{FF}*. *MktCap^{FF,CPI}* is *MktCap^{FF}* adjusted using the consumer price index to reflect 2012 dollars, and *Size^{FF,CPI}* is the natural log of *MktCap^{FF,CPI}*.

	Mean	SD	Skew	Kurt	Min	5%	25%	Median	75%	95%	Max	n
MktCap	1101	5568	17.71	459.09	0	6	29	107	446	4108	161,217	4794
Size	4.33	1.92	0.38	−0.08	−1.18	1.46	2.93	4.16	5.57	7.74	11.48	4794
MktCap^{CPI}	1735	8834	17.71	459.09	2	13	55	188	751	6428	261,951	4794
Size^{CPI}	5.17	1.92	0.38	−0.08	−0.34	2.30	3.77	5.01	6.41	8.59	12.32	4794
MktCap^{FF}	1099	5509	17.44	442.14	1	7	30	108	449	4128	157,490	4601
Size^{FF}	4.35	1.90	0.41	−0.08	−0.85	1.54	2.96	4.18	5.58	7.75	11.46	4601
MktCap^{FF,CPI}	1733	8758	17.44	442.14	2	14	55	189	754	6446	256,799	4601
Size^{FF,CPI}	5.20	1.90	0.41	−0.08	−0.00	2.38	3.80	5.03	6.43	8.59	12.30	4601

The final issue that arises in the calculation of market capitalization is that inflation causes the interpretation of market capitalization to change over time. A market
capitalization of \$500 million in 1963 is very different from a market capitalization
of \$500 million in 2012. To make the results of statistical analyses for different time
periods comparable, it is therefore frequently desirable to adjust the measures of market capitalization for inflation. To do so, we use the Consumer Price Index (CPI). CPI
data are taken from the Bureau of Labor Statistics (BLS) website.[4] We then calculate
inflation-adjusted values of the market capitalization variables in 2012 dollars as

$$MktCap_{i,t}^{CPI} = MktCap_{i,t} \times \frac{CPI_{12/2012}}{CPI_t} \tag{9.5}$$

and

$$MktCap_{i,t}^{FF,CPI} = MktCap_{i,t}^{FF} \times \frac{CPI_{12/2012}}{CPI_t} \tag{9.6}$$

where $CPI_{12,2012}$ and CPI_t are the levels of the CPI index as of the end of December
2012 and the end of month t, respectively. We also calculate the corresponding size
(log-transformed) variables, which we define as

$$Size_{i,t}^{CPI} = \ln (MktCap_{i,t}^{CPI}) \tag{9.7}$$

and

$$Size_{i,t}^{FF,CPI} = \ln (MktCap_{i,t}^{FF,CPI}). \tag{9.8}$$

9.2 SUMMARY STATISTICS

We proceed now to present summary statistics for the different measures of stock
size for our sample of CRSP stocks covering the period from 1963 through 2012.
Table 9.1 presents summary statistics for all of the measures of market capitalization. The results show that in the average month, the mean market capitalization
(*MktCap*) is over \$1.1 billion while the median is only \$107 million, indicating that
the cross-sectional distribution of market capitalization is highly right-skewed. Even
the 75th percentile market capitalization of \$446 million is substantially less than half
of the mean. As demonstrated by the 95th percentile and maximum values of *MktCap*
of more than \$4.1 billion and \$161 billion, respectively, the stocks that comprise our
sample are characterized by a large number of small- to medium-sized stocks along
with a small number of very large stocks. Consistent with these characteristics, the
skewness of the cross-sectional distribution of *MktCap* in the average month of 17.17
is very high. The excess kurtosis of *MktCap* is also extremely large, with an average
monthly value of 459.09. The average cross-sectional standard deviation of *MktCap*
is more than \$5.5 billion. Finally, the table demonstrates that in the average month,
there are 4794 stocks for which a valid value of *MktCap* is calculated.

[4]The data are available at www.bls.gov/cpi/data.htm. We use data for the All Urban Consumer series.

Examining the *Size* variable, we see that taking natural logs of *MktCap* results in a variable whose distribution is substantially less skewed, as the skewness of *Size* in the average month is only 0.38. Furthermore, the largest values of *Size* are not nearly as extreme as those for *MktCap*. To see this, note that the maximum value of *MktCap* is almost 29 standard deviations above the median *MktCap* value $((161,217 - 107)/5568)$, while that of *Size* is only 3.8 standard deviations $((11.48 - 4.16)/1.92)$ from its median. Table 9.1, therefore, indicates that applying the log transformation to market capitalization has the desired effect.

The result of adjusting the values of *MktCap* for inflation is that each of the summary statistics, with the exception of skewness and excess kurtosis, is larger for $MktCap^{CPI}$ than for *MktCap*. The mean (median) $MktCap^{CPI}$ for a stock in the sample is more than \$1.7 billion (\$188 million), compared to \$1.1 billion (\$107 million) for the unadjusted values. By necessity, the skewness and kurtosis of $MktCap^{CPI}$ are identical to the corresponding values for *MktCap*, as $MktCap^{CPI}$ is, in the cross section, simply a linearly transformed version of *MktCap*. The average cross-sectional standard deviation of $MktCap^{CPI}$ is greater than \$8.8 billion. As for the log-transformed inflation-adjusted measure, in the average month, $Size^{CPI}$ has a mean (median) of 5.17 (5.01), standard deviation of 1.92 (by necessity), and the same skewness of 0.38 and excess kurtosis of -0.08 as *Size*.

As for the FF versions of the market capitalization measures ($MktCap^{FF}$, $MktCap^{FF,CPI}$, $Size^{FF}$, and $Size^{FF,CPI}$), the table indicates that these variables have distributions that are very similar to the corresponding versions of the variables that are calculated at the end of each month instead of annually at the end of June. In the average month, there are only 4601 stocks for which valid values of the FF measures are available. The reason for this is that, because the measurement of these variables for any given month t requires data from up to 11 months ago (as is the case when the month t corresponds to a May), calculation of these variables for stocks that have recently entered the CRSP database may not be possible. Apart from this fact, the distributions of the FF variables are similar enough to those of the variables measured monthly to forgo further discussion.

We now further investigate the distribution of market capitalization (*MktCap*) by examining the percentage of total market capitalization that comprised extremely large stocks. Figure 9.1 plots the percentage of total stock market capitalization that is captured by the largest 1%, 5%, 10%, and 25% of stocks for the time period covered by our sample. The figure indicates that the largest 1% of stocks comprise at a minimum 31% and as much as 52% of the total market capitalization of all stocks. This maximum of 52% is achieved in March 1999. To put this number in perspective, there are 6838 stocks in our sample for that month. The result indicates that the combined value of the largest 68 of those stocks is greater than the total value of the remaining 6770 stocks. The total market capitalization of the largest 5% of stocks is equal to between 53% and 79% of total market capitalization. The corresponding values for the largest 10% of stocks are 66% and 88%, and the total value of the largest 25% of stocks is between 84% and 96% of the total stock market capitalization.

We devote substantial attention to examining the skewness of the distribution of market capitalization because it manifests itself in many empirical asset pricing

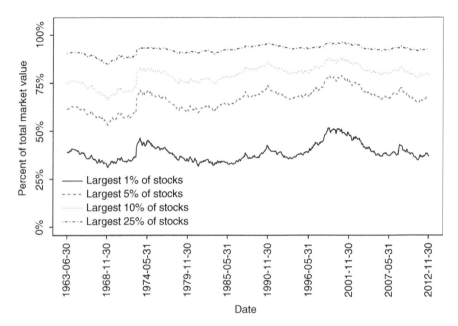

Figure 9.1   Percent of Total Market Value Held by Largest Stocks.
This figure plots the percentage of total market capitalization in the CRSP sample held by the largest 1%, 5%, 10%, and 25% of stocks at the end of each month from June 1963 through November 2011

analyses, especially portfolio analysis. It is therefore important for an empirical asset pricing researcher to understand the effect this may have on the analysis at hand. The effects that the distribution of market capitalization may have on empirical analyses will be exemplified later in this chapter.

9.3   CORRELATIONS

Having analyzed the univariate distributions of the market capitalization variables, we turn our attention now to correlations among these variables as well as the correlations between these variables and market beta (β). Table 9.2 presents the average monthly cross-sectional correlations between pairs of variables. Entries below the diagonal present Pearson product–moment correlations and above-diagonal entries present Spearman rank correlations. Because the inflation-adjusted variables are perfectly linearly related to the unadjusted measures, we examine only the unadjusted measures.

The Pearson correlation between *MktCap* and $MktCap^{FF}$ is 0.99. Similarly, *Size* and $Size^{FF}$ exhibit a Pearson correlation of 0.98. These extremely high correlations are expected because the total market capitalization of a firm will, in most cases, change very little over a period of one year (the maximum lag at which $MktCap^{FF}$ is measured). The results indicate that there is barely any difference between these variables. It is therefore highly unlikely that the results of any statistical analysis using

TABLE 9.2   Correlations
This table presents the time-series averages of the annual cross-sectional Pearson product moment (below-diagonal entries) and Spearman rank (above-diagonal entries) correlations between pairs of variables measuring firm size.

	$MktCap$	$Size$	$MktCap^{FF}$	$Size^{FF}$	β
$MktCap$		1.00	0.98	0.98	0.33
$Size$	0.58		0.98	0.98	0.33
$MktCap^{FF}$	0.99	0.57		1.00	0.34
$Size^{FF}$	0.58	0.98	0.58		0.34
β	0.12	0.31	0.12	0.31	

these measures will differ substantially when using one measure compared to the other. The Spearman rank correlations of 0.98 between these two pairs of variables lead to the same conclusion. The correlation between $MktCap$ and $Size$ is 0.58. In most cases, a correlation of this magnitude would be considered quite high. However, in this case, because $Size$ is the log-transformed version of $MktCap$, meaning that the two are functionally related and thus completely determined by one another, this correlation is better interpreted as indicative of the effect of taking the log transform. The average correlation indicates that, at least for the purposes of linear analyses such as linear regression, the results from using $Size$ may differ somewhat from those generated using $MktCap$. This was probably apparent from the summary statistics presented in Table 9.1. However, the correlation analysis allows us to more precisely quantify how different the two measures are in a linear sense. The correlation between the FF versions of these variables is also 0.58. By necessity, as the natural log function is a strictly monotonically increasing function, the Spearman rank correlation between $MktCap$ and $Size$, as well as between $MktCap^{FF}$ and $Size^{FF}$ is 1.00.

Finally, we look at the correlations between the market capitalization variables and market beta (β). Table 9.2 shows that the Pearson correlation between $MktCap$ and β is 0.12, and the Pearson correlation between $Size$ and β is 0.31. These results indicate that larger stocks tend to have higher market betas. The effect is linearly much stronger when $Size$ is used as the measure of market capitalization instead of $MktCap$. The Spearman correlation of 0.33 between $MktCap$ and β, which is much higher than the Pearson correlation of only 0.12 between these variables, may indicate that the relation between these variables is not linear. The fact that the Spearman correlation of 0.33 between $Size$ and β is very similar to the Pearson correlation of 0.31 indicates that in linear regressions, including both $Size$ and β as independent variables may generate substantially different results than specifications that use only one of the variables. The fact that the Spearman correlation of 0.33 between $MktCap$ and β is identical to the Spearman correlation between $Size$ and β is by necessity, as $Size$ is a strictly increasing function of *MktCap*. The results using the FF versions of the variables are similar and do not warrant further discussion.

9.4 PERSISTENCE

The final analysis of the market capitalization measures we perform before moving to our investigation of the relation between size and future stock returns is a persistence analysis. As with the correlation analysis, we examine only the measures of size that are not adjusted for inflation. The inflation-adjusted measures, by necessity, produce identical results.

Table 9.3 presents the results of the persistence analysis for the different measures of stock size. The results indicate that regardless of how market capitalization is measured, it is highly persistent. Measured at a lag of one month ($\tau = 1$), the persistence of *MktCap* of 0.998 and persistence of *Size* of 0.997 indicate nearly perfect cross-sectional persistence. As would be expected, the persistence decays somewhat over time. But, at lags of one year ($\tau = 12$), the persistence of *MktCap* and persistence of *Size* are 0.980 and 0.967, respectively, still incredibly high. Even at extremely long lags, these measures exhibit very high persistence. Measured five years apart ($\tau = 60$), the persistence of *MktCap* is 0.909 and that of *Size* is 0.888. Even measured 10 years apart ($\tau = 120$), *MktCap* and *Size* have persistence of 0.842 and 0.844, respectively. The results for the FF versions of the variables are very similar. Despite the fact that for lags of less than one year there is a mechanical persistence of the Fama and French variables (because these variables are only updated every June),

TABLE 9.3 Persistence
This table presents the results of persistence analyses of *MktCap*, *Size*, *MktCap^{FF}*, and *Size^{FF}* values. Each month t, the cross-sectional Pearson product–moment correlation between the month t and month $t + \tau$ values of the given variable is calculated. The table presents the time-series averages of the monthly cross-sectional correlations. The column labeled τ indicates the lag at which the persistence is measured.

τ	*MktCap*	*Size*	*MktCap^{FF}*	*Size^{FF}*
1	0.998	0.997	0.998	0.997
3	0.995	0.991	0.995	0.992
6	0.990	0.983	0.990	0.984
12	0.980	0.967	0.980	0.968
24	0.960	0.939	0.960	0.941
36	0.942	0.918	0.942	0.922
48	0.926	0.902	0.926	0.906
60	0.909	0.888	0.910	0.892
120	0.842	0.844	0.842	0.848

empirically this has only very minimal impact, as the persistence of the monthly updated variables (*MktCap* and *Size*) is already extremely high.

9.5 SIZE AND STOCK RETURNS

We turn our attention now to the cross-sectional relation between market capitalization and future stock returns. Several papers (Banz (1981) and Fama and French (1992, 1993)) have investigated the ability of market capitalization to predict future stock returns, and almost all conclude that small stocks, that is, those with lower market capitalization, have higher average future returns. In this section, we present the results of portfolio and regression analyses designed to investigate this relation.

9.5.1 Univariate Portfolio Analysis

Our investigation of the relation between market capitalization and future stock returns begins with a monthly univariate portfolio analysis. There is a small twist in our preliminary portfolio analysis that is different from most of the portfolio analyses performed throughout this book. Instead of calculating the breakpoints using all stocks in our CRSP common stock sample, the breakpoints are calculated using only stocks that trade on the New York Stock Exchange (NYSE).[5] This approach to forming portfolios based on market capitalization, proposed by Fama and French (1992, 1993), is commonly employed in empirical asset pricing research. The reason for this is that, for a large portion of the sample period (1963–2012), NYSE stocks tended to be much larger than stocks listed on the American Stock Exchange (AMEX) or the NASDAQ. This fact was discussed previously in Section 7.1.2 and Figures 9.1 and 9.2. Thus, if the breakpoints were calculated using all stocks in the CRSP sample, the result would be that the breakpoints effectively serve to separate the NYSE stocks from the AMEX and NASDAQ stocks. Calculating the breakpoints using only NYSE stocks ensures that an equal number of NYSE stocks are in each portfolio. It does not ensure equal distribution of the AMEX and NASDAQ stocks among the different portfolios, however. As would be expected and will be seen shortly, regardless of which set of stocks is used to form the breakpoints, a large proportion of AMEX and NASDAQ stocks end up in portfolios comprised of low market capitalization stocks.

In Table 9.4, we present the results of univariate portfolio analyses using breakpoints calculated from only NYSE stocks, with all stocks in our sample sorted into the portfolios. Each month, we form 10 decile portfolios. We perform the analysis using each of *MktCap* and *MktCap^{FF}* as the sort variable. As the log-transformed variables (*Size* and *Size^{FF}*) and inflation-adjusted variables (*MktCap^{CPI}*, *Size^{CPI}*, *MktCap^{FF,CPI}*, and *Size^{FF,CPI}*) are each monotonically increasing functions of either *MktCap* or *MktCap^{FF}*, and portfolio analysis relies only on the ordering of the sort

---

[5]NYSE stocks are identified by a value of 1 in the EXCHCD field in CRSP.

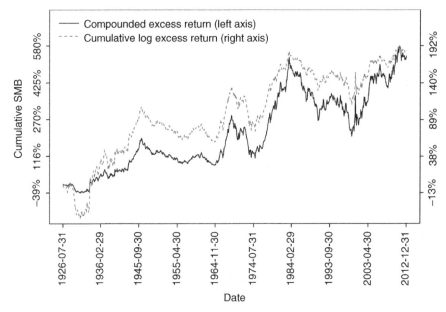

Figure 9.2   Cumulative Returns of *SMB* Portfolio.
This figure plots the cumulate returns of the *SMB* factor for the period from July 1926 through
December 2012. The compounded excess return for month *t* is calculated as 100 times the
cumulative product of one plus the monthly return up to and including the given month. The
cumulate log excess return is calculated as the sum of the monthly log excess returns up to and
including the given month

variables, the results for portfolios formed by sorting on the other variables (not
MktCap or *MktCap^{FF}*) can be perfectly discerned from the table.

Panel A of Table 9.4 presents several characteristics of each of the portfolios.
The first two rows for each section present the average value of the sort variable
as well as the average inflation-adjusted sort variable value for each of the decile
portfolios. We focus on the portfolios formed by sorting on *MktCap*, as results for
the *MktCap^{FF}*-sorted portfolios are very similar. The average market capitalization
(inflation-adjusted market capitalization) of stocks in each of the portfolios increases
from \$32 million (\$57 million) for decile portfolio one to nearly \$20 billion
(\$30 billion) for decile portfolio 10. The third row, labeled % *MktCap*, shows
average percentage of total market capitalization that is held in each of the decile
portfolios. In the average month, portfolio one holds only 1.82% of the total value
of the market portfolio compared to 58.90% for portfolio 10. Thus, the highest
decile portfolio contains, in the average month, more than half of the total market
capitalization. In fact, portfolios one through five hold, on average, less than 11% of
the total market capitalization of all portfolios. The row labeled % NYSE presents
the percentage of stocks in the given portfolio that are listed on the NYSE. The
results indicate that for the small stock portfolio (decile one), 7.46% of such stocks
are NYSE-listed. This percentage monotonically increases to 92.89% for the large

TABLE 9.4   Univariate Portfolio Analysis—NYSE Breakpoints
This table presents the results of univariate portfolio analyses of the relation between each of measures of market capitalization and future stock returns. Monthly portfolios are formed by sorting all stocks in the CRSP sample into portfolios using decile breakpoints calculated based on the given sort variable using the subset of the stocks in the CRSP sample that are listed on the New York Stock Exchange. Panel A shows the average market capitalization (in $millions), CPI-adjusted (2012 dollars) market capitalization, percentage of total market capitalization, percentage of stocks that are listed on the New York Stock Exchange, number of stocks, and β for stocks in each decile portfolio. Panel B (Panel C) shows the average equal-weighted (value-weighted) one-month-ahead excess return and CAPM alpha (in percent per month) for each of the 10 decile portfolios as well as for the long–short zero-cost portfolio that is long the 10th decile portfolio and short the first decile portfolio. Newey and West (1987) t-statistics, adjusted using six lags, testing the null hypothesis that the average portfolio excess return or CAPM alpha is equal to zero, are shown in parentheses.

Panel A: Portfolio Characteristics

Sort Variable	Value	1	2	3	4	5	6	7	8	9	10
MktCap	MktCap	32	126	226	354	538	806	1225	2034	4078	19,987
	$MktCap^{CPI}$	57	211	365	565	854	1278	1953	3239	6288	29,989
	% MktCap	1.82	1.64	1.85	2.32	2.96	3.73	5.18	7.95	13.65	58.90
	% NYSE	7.46	28.75	41.95	50.81	59.61	69.84	77.05	82.38	88.81	92.89
	n	2372	592	383	303	252	211	189	176	162	155
	β	0.60	0.91	0.96	0.97	0.97	0.96	0.97	0.98	0.99	1.03
$MktCap^{FF}$	$MktCap^{FF}$	33	129	227	354	534	799	1212	2019	4040	19,676
	$MktCap^{FF,CPI}$	58	212	364	561	842	1259	1922	3195	6196	29,468
	% MktCap	1.84	1.61	1.84	2.28	2.91	3.71	5.13	8.00	13.67	59.02
	% NYSE	7.69	30.07	43.18	52.46	61.07	70.75	78.25	82.48	89.22	93.17
	n	2275	555	367	289	242	206	183	173	159	152
	β	0.60	0.93	0.96	0.98	0.98	0.96	0.97	0.99	0.99	1.04

Panel B: Equal-Weighted Portfolio Returns

Sort Variable	Coefficient	1	2	3	4	5	6	7	8	9	10	10-1
MktCap	Excess return	0.91	0.63	0.73	0.71	0.71	0.66	0.62	0.61	0.51	0.42	−0.49
		(2.53)	(2.13)	(2.56)	(2.69)	(2.76)	(2.69)	(2.60)	(2.73)	(2.40)	(2.18)	(−1.92)
	CAPM α	0.41	0.07	0.16	0.16	0.17	0.13	0.10	0.11	0.04	−0.03	−0.44
		(1.85)	(0.50)	(1.22)	(1.48)	(1.69)	(1.50)	(1.40)	(1.86)	(0.79)	(−0.82)	(−1.79)
$MktCap^{FF}$	Excess return	0.92	0.62	0.70	0.68	0.69	0.62	0.65	0.59	0.54	0.42	−0.50
		(2.62)	(2.06)	(2.53)	(2.50)	(2.64)	(2.49)	(2.66)	(2.55)	(2.45)	(2.11)	(−2.03)
	CAPM α	0.44	0.05	0.14	0.12	0.15	0.09	0.13	0.08	0.06	−0.04	−0.47
		(1.99)	(0.33)	(1.11)	(1.03)	(1.47)	(0.98)	(1.65)	(1.14)	(0.94)	(−0.92)	(−1.93)
MktCap	Excess return	0.65	0.63	0.73	0.71	0.71	0.65	0.62	0.62	0.51	0.39	−0.27
		(1.94)	(2.13)	(2.57)	(2.68)	(2.76)	(2.67)	(2.63)	(2.77)	(2.39)	(2.09)	(−1.09)
	CAPM α	0.13	0.07	0.16	0.16	0.17	0.13	0.11	0.11	0.04	−0.03	−0.17
		(0.69)	(0.50)	(1.24)	(1.47)	(1.69)	(1.46)	(1.51)	(1.97)	(0.77)	(−0.79)	(−0.73)

(continued)

TABLE 9.4   (*Continued*)

Panel C: Value-Weighted Portfolio Returns												
Sort Variable	Coefficient	1	2	3	4	5	6	7	8	9	10	10-1
$MktCap^{FF}$	Excess	0.74	0.60	0.70	0.68	0.70	0.62	0.66	0.60	0.53	0.40	−0.34
	return	(2.22)	(2.02)	(2.53)	(2.50)	(2.65)	(2.50)	(2.68)	(2.59)	(2.42)	(2.11)	(−1.38)
	CAPM α	0.22	0.04	0.14	0.12	0.15	0.09	0.13	0.09	0.05	−0.03	−0.25
		(1.12)	(0.25)	(1.11)	(1.04)	(1.52)	(1.01)	(1.70)	(1.22)	(0.87)	(−0.64)	(−1.07)

stock portfolio (decile 10). The row labeled *n* shows the average number of stocks in each portfolio. Because the breakpoints are calculated using only NYSE stocks, but then all stocks in the sample are sorted into the portfolios, the number of stocks in each portfolio will not be the same. In fact, the number of stocks in each of the portfolios differs quite dramatically. In the average month, portfolio one holds 2372 stocks. This number decreases monotonically to 155 for portfolio 10. This result exemplifies the skewed distribution of market capitalization among stocks in our sample. Despite holding nearly half of the stocks in the sample, the total market capitalization of stocks in portfolio one comprises only 7.46% of the total market capitalization. On the other end, decile portfolio 10 holds, on average, 155 stocks, or slightly more than 3% of all stocks. These stocks, however, comprise almost 59% of total market capitalization. Finally, the row labeled β presents the average market beta for stocks in each of the decile portfolios. The results indicate that large stocks tend to have higher market betas than small stocks, as the average value of β for stocks in each of the portfolios increases (almost monotonically) from 0.60 for decile portfolio one to 1.04 for decile portfolio 10. It is worth noting that there is a large increase in average beta from portfolio one (average β is 0.60) to portfolio two (average β of 0.91). The average values of β for deciles two through 10 are relatively similar in magnitude.

Panel B of Table 9.4 presents the analysis of the returns of equal-weighted market capitalization-sorted portfolios. Focusing first on the difference portfolio, which is long large stocks (the decile 10 portfolio) and short small stocks (the decile one portfolio), the results indicate that this portfolio generates an economically large average return of −0.49%, which is marginally statistically significant with a Newey and West (1987) *t*-statistic of −1.92. The risk-adjusted abnormal return of this portfolio relative to the CAPM risk model (CAPM α) of −0.44% (*t*-statistic = −1.79) per month is similar in both magnitude and statistical significance to the unadjusted return. The results, therefore, indicate an economically important and marginally statistically significant relation between *MktCap* and future stock returns.

Examining the individual decile portfolio returns, we see that decile portfolio one generates a substantially higher average excess return and CAPM alpha than any of the other decile portfolios. The results indicate a large drop in performance between decile portfolios one and two. For portfolios sorted on *MktCap*, the first decile portfolio generates an average monthly excess return and alpha of 0.91% and 0.41%, respectively, whereas portfolio two generates an excess return of only 0.63% per month and monthly alpha of only 0.07%. The average excess returns and alphas of portfolios two through 10 are relatively similar. The cross-sectional relation between

MktCap and future stock returns, therefore, appears to be driven primarily by the high abnormal returns of the smallest stocks in the sample. Similar patterns hold for portfolios formed by sorting on $MktCap^{FF}$.

Our next analyses employ value-weighted portfolios instead of equal-weighted portfolios. The results of these analyses are presented in Panel C of Table 9.4. It should be noted that, in these analyses, when *MktCap* is used as the sort variable, it is also used as the measure of market capitalization when weighting the portfolios. When $MktCap^{FF}$ is used as the sort variable, we also use $MktCap^{FF}$ to weight the portfolios.

The table indicates that when value-weighted portfolios are used, the negative relation between market capitalization and future stock returns is not detected. The average return and CAPM alpha of the *MktCap*-sorted difference portfolio of −0.27% (*t*-statistic = −1.09) and −0.17% (*t*-statistic = −0.73) per month, respectively, are both statistically insignificant. Furthermore, the magnitudes of the average return and alpha of the value-weighted 10-1 portfolio are substantially smaller than for the equal-weighted portfolios. Examination of portfolios one through 10 indicates that the main difference between the value-weighted and equal-weighted portfolios comes from the first decile portfolio. The average excess return (CAPM alpha) of the first value-weighted decile portfolio is 0.65% (0.13%) per month compared to 0.91% (0.41%) per month for the equal-weighted portfolio. For decile portfolios two through 10, the excess returns and alphas are quite similar for equal-weighted and value-weighted portfolios. The effect of value-weighting on the returns of the first decile portfolio is particularly interesting because the portfolios are formed by sorting on market capitalization. Thus, the first decile portfolio already contains only stocks with low market capitalizations. The result therefore indicates that, even among the stocks with low market capitalizations, stocks with the lowest market capitalizations, meaning stocks with extremely low market capitalizations, are the stocks that generate high returns and are thus driving the equal-weighted portfolio results.

To examine in more depth the driver of the negative relation between market capitalization and future stock returns detected in the equal-weighted portfolio analyses presented in Table 9.4, we now repeat the analyses, this time using all stocks in our sample to calculate the breakpoints instead of using only NYSE stocks. As the CRSP database contains stocks that are listed on the NYSE, AMEX, and NASDAQ, we refer to these breakpoints as NYSE/AMEX/NASDAQ breakpoints.

Table 9.5 presents the results of the univariate portfolio analyses using NYSE/AMEX/NASDAQ breakpoints. We begin our discussion by examining the equal-weighted portfolio returns presented in Panel B and focus on the *MktCap*-sorted portfolios, as the results for the $MktCap^{FF}$-sorted portfolios are very similar. When sorting using NYSE/AMEX/NASDAQ breakpoints, the equal-weighted portfolio analysis detects an extremely strong negative relation between market capitalization and future stock returns. The average return and CAPM alpha of the 10-1 portfolio of −1.59% (*t*-statistic = −4.94) and −1.62% (*t*-statistic = −4.95), respectively, are both economically very large and very highly statistically significant. The results using NYSE/AMEX/NASDAQ breakpoints are much stronger than when using NYSE breakpoints. Similar to the NYSE breakpoint results, however, the result appears to be driven primarily by the first decile portfolio, which generates an

TABLE 9.5   Univariate Portfolio Analysis—NYSE/AMEX/NASDAQ Breakpoints

This table presents the results of univariate portfolio analyses of the relation between each of measures of market capitalization and future stock returns. Monthly portfolios are formed by sorting all stocks in the CRSP sample into portfolios using decile breakpoints calculated based on the given sort variable using all stocks in the CRSP sample. Panel A shows the average market capitalization (in $millions), CPI-adjusted (2012 dollars) market capitalization, percentage of total market capitalization, percentage of stocks that are listed on the New York Stock Exchange, number of stocks, and β for stocks in each decile portfolio. Panel B (Panel C) shows the average equal-weighted (value-weighted) one-month-ahead excess return and CAPM alpha (in percent per month) for each of the 10 decile portfolios as well as for the long–short zero-cost portfolio that is long the 10th decile portfolio and short the first decile portfolio. Newey and West (1987) t-statistics, adjusted using six lags, testing the null hypothesis that the average portfolio excess return or CAPM alpha is equal to zero, are shown in parentheses.

Panel A: Portfolio Characteristics

Sort Variable	Value	1	2	3	4	5	6	7	8	9	10
$MktCap$	$MktCap$	6	16	29	50	84	141	244	458	1049	8923
	$MktCap^{CPI}$	13	31	55	92	149	244	417	771	1759	13,810
	% $MktCap$	0.08	0.19	0.33	0.55	0.88	1.43	2.42	4.51	10.49	79.12
	% NYSE	1.07	3.17	7.46	13.70	21.77	31.28	41.90	54.27	70.45	87.09
	n	480	479	479	479	479	479	479	479	479	480
	β	0.42	0.51	0.60	0.73	0.83	0.90	0.94	0.95	0.94	0.99
$MktCap^{FF}$	$MktCap^{FF}$	7	16	30	51	85	142	247	461	1055	8891
	$MktCap^{FF,CPI}$	14	32	56	93	150	246	420	776	1769	13,767
	% $MktCap$	0.09	0.20	0.34	0.56	0.89	1.45	2.45	4.56	10.60	78.86
	% NYSE	1.00	3.09	7.56	14.38	23.06	32.84	43.71	56.18	71.91	87.72
	n	461	460	460	460	460	460	460	460	460	461
	β	0.40	0.51	0.60	0.73	0.85	0.91	0.95	0.95	0.94	1.00

Panel B: Equal-Weighted Portfolio Returns

Sort Variable	Coefficient	1	2	3	4	5	6	7	8	9	10	10-1
$MktCap$	Excess	2.08	0.64	0.53	0.56	0.59	0.64	0.66	0.67	0.63	0.49	−1.59
	return	(4.75)	(1.70)	(1.55)	(1.68)	(1.89)	(2.23)	(2.38)	(2.60)	(2.68)	(2.38)	(−4.94)
	CAPM α	1.63	0.16	0.04	0.04	0.05	0.09	0.10	0.12	0.12	0.02	−1.62
		(4.95)	(0.65)	(0.19)	(0.19)	(0.30)	(0.64)	(0.83)	(1.29)	(1.57)	(0.47)	(−4.95)
$MktCap^{FF}$	Excess	1.64	0.86	0.73	0.67	0.63	0.65	0.61	0.63	0.63	0.51	−1.13
	return	(3.98)	(2.32)	(2.08)	(2.04)	(2.05)	(2.25)	(2.20)	(2.43)	(2.58)	(2.40)	(−3.89)
	CAPM α	1.23	0.40	0.23	0.15	0.09	0.10	0.06	0.08	0.11	0.03	−1.20
		(4.01)	(1.63)	(1.08)	(0.76)	(0.53)	(0.69)	(0.47)	(0.81)	(1.31)	(0.60)	(−3.92)

TABLE 9.5 *(Continued)*

| | Panel C: Value-Weighted Portfolio Returns | | | | | | | | | | |

Sort Variable	Coefficient	1	2	3	4	5	6	7	8	9	10	10-1
$MktCap$	Excess	1.53	0.63	0.54	0.56	0.59	0.65	0.66	0.67	0.63	0.42	−1.11
	return	(3.69)	(1.67)	(1.57)	(1.70)	(1.88)	(2.25)	(2.41)	(2.59)	(2.68)	(2.20)	(−3.47)
	CAPM α	1.08	0.15	0.05	0.04	0.04	0.10	0.11	0.12	0.12	−0.02	−1.10
		(3.61)	(0.61)	(0.22)	(0.20)	(0.26)	(0.69)	(0.90)	(1.26)	(1.63)	(−0.85)	(−3.47)
$MktCap^{FF}$	Excess	1.41	0.85	0.72	0.66	0.63	0.65	0.62	0.63	0.63	0.43	−0.98
	return	(3.55)	(2.30)	(2.05)	(2.02)	(2.06)	(2.24)	(2.23)	(2.43)	(2.60)	(2.22)	(−3.28)
	CAPM α	1.01	0.39	0.22	0.14	0.09	0.10	0.06	0.08	0.11	−0.01	−1.02
		(3.40)	(1.60)	(1.03)	(0.72)	(0.52)	(0.68)	(0.53)	(0.85)	(1.37)	(−0.41)	(−3.25)

average excess return (CAPM alpha) of 2.08% (1.63%) per month. Also similar to the NYSE breakpoints, the results using NYSE/AMEX/NASDAQ breakpoints indicate that the returns and alphas of portfolios two through 10 are similar. In fact, when using NYSE/AMEX/NASDAQ breakpoints, the decile one portfolio, which is comprised of small stocks, is the only decile portfolio that generates a statistically significant CAPM alpha. The results using value-weighted portfolios, presented in Panel C, indicate that when using NYSE/AMEX/NASDAQ breakpoints, even value-weighted portfolios produce a strong negative difference portfolio return and CAPM alpha, since the value-weighted 10-1 portfolio generates an economically large and highly statistically significant average return (CAPM alpha) of −1.11% (−1.10%) per month.

To understand this in more depth, we refer now to Panel A of Table 9.5, which summarizes each of the decile portfolios. We focus on decile portfolio one because it is this portfolio that appears to drive the negative relation between market capitalization and future stock returns. Panel A indicates that the average market capitalization (*MktCap*) of stocks in the first decile portfolio is only $6 million or $13 million when inflation-adjusted to 2012 dollars. Even though 10% of all stocks are held in portfolio one, these stocks only account for 0.08% of the total stock market capitalization. Thus, the entire size effect (as the negative relation between market capitalization and future stock returns is known) appears to be driven by a subset of stocks that comprise less than one 10th of 1% of the entire stock market. Thus, while some may say that the results in Panels B and C of Table 9.5 indicate that the size effect is quite strong, others may claim that it is economically unimportant as it is driven by an extremely small fraction of the total stock market capitalization. Furthermore, the stocks that drive the phenomenon are likely to be highly illiquid, making implementation of a trading strategy designed to capture the returns of a size-based strategy quite difficult, if not impossible.

In summary, the results of the univariate portfolio analyses presented in this section indicate a negative relation between market capitalization and future stock returns. The result appears to be driven by the smallest stocks in the sample, and the strength of the result varies substantially with different empirical implementations.

The results are quite similar when using either *MktCap*, which is calculated monthly, or *MktCap^{FF}*, which is calculated each June, as the sort variable. For this reason, for the remaining portfolio analyses presented in this chapter, we use only *MktCap* as the measure of market capitalization. In the remaining chapters of this book, *MktCap* and its log-transformed version *Size* will be used as our primary measures of market capitalization.

9.5.2 Bivariate Portfolio Analysis

Having examined the relation between market capitalization and future stock returns using univariate portfolio analysis, we proceed now to use bivariate portfolio analyses to examine this relation. Specifically, we examine the relation between market capitalization and future stock returns after controlling for the effect of market beta (β). We use both dependent-sort and independent-sort portfolios, as well as equal-weighted and value-weighted analyses. In each analysis, we form five groups based on each of the sort variables, with breakpoints calculated as the quintiles of each of the sort variables. Finally, we perform all analyses using both NYSE and NYSE/AMEX/NASDAQ breakpoints.

Theoretically, stocks with high market betas should have high expected returns. Given that stocks with low market capitalization tend to have low betas, there is no theoretical reason to expect that beta would explain the large returns of extremely small stocks. However, in Chapter 8, we demonstrated that some empirical analyses detect a negative relation between β and future stock returns. This result would indicate that it is possible that controlling for β will explain the size effect.

Table 9.6 presents the results of a bivariate dependent-sort portfolio analysis sorting first on β and then, within each β quintile, into *MktCap* quintiles. We use only NYSE stocks to generate the breakpoints. All stocks in the sample are then sorted into portfolios based on the NYSE breakpoints.

We focus first on the results for the average beta portfolio, indicated in the column labeled β Avg. The results for the equal-weighted portfolios, presented in Panel A, indicate that after controlling for β, the average excess return of the *MktCap* 5-1 portfolio, which is long large stocks and short small stocks within each beta group, generates a marginally statistically significant average monthly return of -0.37% with a t-statistic of -1.76. However, subjecting the returns of this portfolio to the CAPM risk model indicates that a substantial portion of the returns are due to sensitivity to the market factor (*MKT*). The CAPM alpha of the *MktCap* difference portfolio of -0.22% is not statistically distinguishable from zero since the associated t-statistic is only -1.08. When value-weighted portfolios are used, Panel B shows that the results are similar. The *MktCap* 5-1 portfolio for the average β quintile generates -0.32% per month with an associated t-statistic of -1.73, but the CAPM alpha of this portfolio of -0.15% has a t-statistic of only -0.86.

Examination of the relation between *MktCap* and future stock returns within each quintile of β indicates that the size effect is actually quite strong among low-β stocks, as the average return and CAPM alpha of the *MktCap* 5-1 portfolio in the first quintile of β is statistically significant. This result holds in both equal-weighted and

TABLE 9.6   Bivariate Dependent-Sort Portfolio Analysis—NYSE Breakpoints

This table presents the results of bivariate dependent-sort portfolio analyses of the relation between *MktCap* and future stock returns after controlling for the effect of β. Each month, all stocks in the CRSP sample are sorted into five groups based on an ascending sort of β. Within each β group, all stocks are sorted into five portfolios based on an ascending sort of *MktCap*. The quintile breakpoints used to create the portfolios are calculated using only stocks that are listed on the New York Stock Exchange. The table presents the average one-month-ahead excess return (in percent per month) for each of the 25 portfolios as well as for the average β quintile portfolio within each quintile of *MktCap*. Also shown are the average return and CAPM alpha of a long–short zero-cost portfolio that is long the fifth *MktCap* quintile portfolio and short the first *MktCap* quintile portfolio in each β quintile. t-statistics (in parentheses), adjusted following Newey and West (1987) using six lags, testing the null hypothesis that the average return or alpha is equal to zero, are shown in parentheses. Panel A presents results for equal-weighted portfolios. Panel B presents results for value-weighted portfolios.

Panel A: Equal-Weighted Portfolio Returns						
	β 1	β 2	β 3	β 4	β 5	β Avg
MktCap 1	1.06	0.98	0.96	0.83	0.45	0.85
MktCap 2	0.75	0.85	0.85	0.83	0.62	0.78
MktCap 3	0.72	0.71	0.79	0.84	0.70	0.75
MktCap 4	0.50	0.66	0.81	0.62	0.63	0.64
MktCap 5	0.41	0.50	0.49	0.53	0.50	0.48
MktCap 5-1	−0.65	−0.48	−0.47	−0.30	0.05	−0.37
	(−3.46)	(−2.32)	(−2.06)	(−1.23)	(0.17)	(−1.76)
MktCap 5-1 CAPM α	−0.56	−0.32	−0.29	−0.12	0.20	−0.22
	(−3.03)	(−1.61)	(−1.34)	(−0.53)	(0.78)	(−1.08)

Panel B: Value-Weighted Portfolio Returns						
	β 1	β 2	β 3	β 4	β 5	β Avg
MktCap 1	0.77	0.83	0.86	0.77	0.40	0.73
MktCap 2	0.76	0.84	0.85	0.83	0.64	0.78
MktCap 3	0.71	0.70	0.79	0.81	0.72	0.74
MktCap 4	0.50	0.65	0.81	0.63	0.59	0.64
MktCap 5	0.34	0.46	0.38	0.47	0.38	0.41
MktCap 5-1	−0.43	−0.37	−0.48	−0.30	−0.02	−0.32
	(−2.74)	(−1.94)	(−2.35)	(−1.37)	(−0.09)	(−1.73)
MktCap 5-1 CAPM α	−0.34	−0.19	−0.30	−0.10	0.17	−0.15
	(−2.20)	(−1.07)	(−1.54)	(−0.48)	(0.74)	(−0.86)

value-weighted portfolios although it is a bit stronger when using equal-weighted portfolios. The CAPM alpha of the *MktCap* 5-1 portfolio in quintiles two through five of β, however, generate abnormal returns relative to the CAPM risk model that are statistically indistinguishable from zero.

The results in Table 9.6 indicate that when portfolios are formed using breakpoints calculated from only NYSE stocks, controlling for β explains the size effect in the average β quintile, but the size effect still exists in stocks with low values of β. We now repeat these analyses using breakpoints calculated from all stocks in the sample.

The results of the bivariate dependent-sort portfolio analyses using NYSE/AMEX/NASDAQ breakpoints are presented in Table 9.7. The results indicate that when breakpoints are calculated using all stocks in the sample, for the average β quintile, the size effect is quite strong. Panel A shows that the equal-weighted *MktCap* 5-1 portfolio for the average β quintile generates an average return of -0.80% per month, with a corresponding t-statistic of -3.07. The *MKT* factor does little to explain this result, as the CAPM alpha of this portfolio is -0.68% (t-statistic $= -2.64$). When value-weighted portfolios are used, however, Panel B

TABLE 9.7 Bivariate Dependent-Sort Portfolio Analysis –NYSE/AMEX/NASDAQ Breakpoints
This table presents the results of bivariate dependent-sort portfolio analyses of the relation between *MktCap* and future stock returns after controlling for the effect of β. Each month, all stocks in the CRSP sample are sorted into five groups based on an ascending sort of β. Within each β group, all stocks are sorted into five portfolios based on an ascending sort of *MktCap*. The quintile breakpoints used to create the portfolios are calculated using all stocks in the CRSP sample. The table presents the average one-month-ahead excess return (in percent per month) for each of the 25 portfolios as well as for the average β quintile portfolio within each quintile of *MktCap*. Also shown are the average return and CAPM alpha of a long–short zero-cost portfolio that is long the fifth *MktCap* quintile portfolio and short the first *MktCap* quintile portfolio in each β quintile. t-statistics (in parentheses), adjusted following Newey and West (1987) using six lags, testing the null hypothesis that the average return or alpha is equal to zero, are shown in parentheses. Panel A presents results for equal-weighted portfolios. Panel B presents results for value-weighted portfolios.

Panel A: Equal-Weighted Portfolio Returns						
	β 1	β 2	β 3	β 4	β 5	β Avg
MktCap 1	2.08	1.48	1.43	0.98	0.70	1.33
MktCap 2	0.70	0.79	0.71	0.51	0.27	0.60
MktCap 3	0.56	0.79	0.84	0.72	0.48	0.68
MktCap 4	0.58	0.79	0.79	0.77	0.58	0.70
MktCap 5	0.56	0.55	0.57	0.58	0.43	0.54
MktCap 5-1	−1.53	−0.93	−0.86	−0.40	−0.27	−0.80
	(−5.95)	(−3.67)	(−2.77)	(−1.34)	(−0.84)	(−3.07)
MktCap 5-1 CAPM α	−1.40	−0.79	−0.78	−0.25	−0.17	−0.68
	(−5.54)	(−3.17)	(−2.51)	(−0.86)	(−0.54)	(−2.64)

Panel B: Value-Weighted Portfolio Returns						
	β 1	β 2	β 3	β 4	β 5	β Avg
MktCap 1	1.53	1.07	0.97	0.63	0.34	0.91
MktCap 2	0.66	0.78	0.70	0.51	0.26	0.58
MktCap 3	0.57	0.79	0.82	0.73	0.48	0.68
MktCap 4	0.59	0.78	0.77	0.76	0.60	0.70
MktCap 5	0.45	0.40	0.47	0.43	0.34	0.42
MktCap 5-1	−1.08	−0.68	−0.50	−0.20	−0.00	−0.49
	(−4.32)	(−2.68)	(−1.83)	(−0.71)	(−0.01)	(−1.96)
MktCap 5-1 CAPM α	−0.95	−0.50	−0.31	−0.01	0.17	−0.32
	(−3.86)	(−2.06)	(−1.16)	(−0.04)	(0.53)	(−1.32)

shows that, while the average return of the *MktCap* 5-1 portfolio for the average β quintile of -0.49% per month remains significant (*t*-statistic $= -1.96$), the CAPM alpha of -0.32% per month is statistically indistinguishable from zero (*t*-statistic of -1.32).

Similar to the results for portfolios formed using NYSE breakpoints, the results using NYSE/AMEX/NASDAQ breakpoints indicate that the size effect is stronger in stocks that have low values of β. Within the lowest NYSE/AMEX/NASDAQ β quintile, Panel A of Table 9.7 shows that the equal-weighted *MktCap* 5-1 portfolio generates an average return and alpha of -1.53% per month (*t*-statistic $= -5.95$) and -1.40% per month (*t*-statistic $= -5.54$), respectively. When using value-weighted portfolios (Panel B), the average return and alpha are -1.08% per month (*t*-statistic $= -4.32$) and -0.95% per month (*t*-statistic $= -3.86$), respectively. The average returns and alphas of the *MktCap* 5-1 portfolios decrease in magnitude monotonically across the quintiles of β. When equal-weighted portfolios are used, quintiles one through three of β produce economically large and statistically significant *MktCap* 5-1 returns and alphas. For value-weighted portfolios, only the lowest two quintiles of β generate an economically important and statistically significant CAPM alpha.

We now repeat the portfolio analyses using independent sorts instead of dependent sorts to calculate the portfolio breakpoints. The independent-sort analyses allow us to examine not only the relation between *MktCap* and expected returns after controlling for β but also the relation between β and expected returns after controlling for *MktCap*.

The results of the independent-sort portfolio analyses using only NYSE stocks to determine the breakpoints are presented in Table 9.8. The results for both the equal-weighted (Panel A) and the value-weighted (Panel B) portfolios are quite similar to those of the dependent-sort analyses presented in Table 9.6. The size effect exists only among stocks in the lowest β quintile. Within quintile one of β, the equal-weighted (value-weighted) *MktCap* 5-1 portfolio generates an average return of -0.71% (-0.48%) per month with a *t*-statistic of -2.92 (-2.36). The equal-weighted (value-weighted) CAPM alpha of -0.60% (-0.38%) produced by this portfolio is also economically large and statistically significant. The CAPM alpha of the *MktCap* 5-1 in each of the other quintiles of β, as well as in the average β quintile, is statistically indistinguishable from zero.

As for the relation between β and future stock returns after controlling for the effect of *MktCap*, Table 9.8 shows that for the average *MktCap* quintile, the β 5-1 portfolio generates economically substantial and statistically significant negative abnormal returns relative to the CAPM risk model. This result holds in each of the lowest three quintiles of *MktCap*, marginally in the fourth quintile of *MktCap*, but disappears among stocks in the highest *MktCap* quintile.

Our final bivariate portfolio analyses use independently sorted portfolios with breakpoints calculated from all stocks in the sample (NYSE/AMEX/NASDAQ breakpoints). The results of these analyses are presented in Table 9.9. As with the dependent-sort analysis using NYSE/AMEX/NASDAQ breakpoints, the independent-sort analysis finds strong evidence of the size effect in equal-weighted (Panel A) portfolios. The *MktCap* 5-1 portfolio for the average β quintile generates an average return −0.84% per month (*t*-statistic = −2.69) and alpha of −0.75% per month. With the exception of β quintile 4, the returns and alphas of the *MktCap* difference portfolio within each of the β quintiles are economically large and highly statistically significant. When value-weighted (Panel B) portfolios are used, however, none of the β quintiles has a *MktCap* 5-1 portfolio that produces a statistically significant alpha.[6] This is true as well of the average β quintile.

TABLE 9.8   Bivariate Independent-Sort Portfolio Analysis—NYSE Breakpoints
This table presents the results of bivariate independent-sort portfolio analyses of the relation between *MktCap* and future stock returns after controlling for the effect of β. Each month, all stocks in the CRSP sample are sorted into five groups based on an ascending sort of β. All stocks are independently sorted into five groups based on an ascending sort of *MktCap*. The quintile breakpoints used to create the groups are calculated using only stocks that are listed on the New York Stock Exchange. The intersections of the β and *MktCap* groups are used to form 25 portfolios. The table presents the average one-month-ahead excess return (in percent per month) for each of the 25 portfolios as well as for the average β quintile portfolio within each quintile of *MktCap* and the average *MktCap* quintile within each β quintile. Also shown are the average return and CAPM alpha of a long–short zero-cost portfolio that is long the fifth *MktCap* (β) quintile portfolio and short the first *MktCap* (β) quintile portfolio in each β (*MktCap*) quintile. *t*-statistics (in parentheses), adjusted following Newey and West (1987) using six lags, testing the null hypothesis that the average return or alpha is equal to zero, are shown in parentheses. Panel A presents results for equal-weighted portfolios. Panel B presents results for value-weighted portfolios.

Panel A: Equal-Weighted Portfolios								
	β 1	β 2	β 3	β 4	β 5	β Avg	β 5-1	β 5-1 CAPM α
MktCap 1	1.02	0.99	0.95	0.82	0.48	0.85	−0.54	−0.98
							(−2.22)	(−4.97)
MktCap 2	0.69	0.87	0.89	0.84	0.60	0.78	−0.09	−0.57
							(−0.33)	(−2.58)
MktCap 3	0.67	0.68	0.84	0.84	0.66	0.74	−0.01	−0.46
							(−0.03)	(−2.08)
MktCap 4	0.52	0.66	0.82	0.60	0.60	0.64	0.08	−0.36
							(0.31)	(−1.78)
MktCap 5	0.31	0.54	0.49	0.53	0.43	0.46	0.11	−0.29
							(0.44)	(−1.43)
MktCap Avg	0.64	0.75	0.80	0.72	0.55		−0.09	−0.53
							(−0.36)	(−2.84)
MktCap 5-1	−0.71	−0.45	−0.45	−0.30	−0.05	−0.39		
	(−2.92)	(−1.64)	(−1.71)	(−1.07)	(−0.20)	(−1.56)		
MktCap 5-1 CAPM α	−0.60	−0.26	−0.27	−0.13	0.08	−0.24		
	(−2.71)	(−1.10)	(−1.16)	(−0.50)	(0.33)	(−1.05)		

[6]The alpha for the *MktCap* 5-1 portfolio in the first quintile of β of −0.43% per month is marginally statistically significant with a *t*-statistic of −1.68.

TABLE 9.8 (*Continued*)

	Panel B: Value-Weighted Portfolios							
	β 1	β 2	β 3	β 4	β 5	β Avg	β 5-1	β 5-1 CAPM α
MktCap 1	0.75	0.83	0.82	0.73	0.34	0.69	−0.41	−0.87
							(−1.51)	(−4.17)
MktCap 2	0.69	0.86	0.85	0.85	0.61	0.77	−0.08	−0.55
							(−0.29)	(−2.54)
MktCap 3	0.65	0.66	0.83	0.83	0.64	0.72	−0.01	−0.46
							(−0.02)	(−2.08)
MktCap 4	0.50	0.64	0.83	0.62	0.59	0.64	0.10	−0.35
							(0.37)	(−1.75)
MktCap 5	0.26	0.49	0.38	0.47	0.35	0.39	0.09	−0.29
							(0.35)	(−1.46)
MktCap Avg	0.57	0.70	0.74	0.70	0.51		−0.06	−0.50
							(−0.25)	(−2.74)
MktCap 5-1	−0.48	−0.34	−0.44	−0.26	0.01	−0.30		
	(−2.36)	(−1.38)	(−1.79)	(−0.99)	(0.05)	(−1.32)		
MktCap 5-1 CAPM α	−0.38	−0.14	−0.24	−0.06	0.20	−0.12		
	(−1.97)	(−0.67)	(−1.10)	(−0.24)	(0.78)	(−0.61)		

Regardless of whether equal-weighted or value-weighted portfolios are used, the independent-sort portfolio analyses using NYSE/AMEX/NASDAQ breakpoints indicate that portfolios consisting of long positions in high-β stocks and short positions in low-β stocks generate negative abnormal returns relative to the CAPM risk model. Within each quintile of *MktCap*, as well as for the average *MktCap* quintile, the CAPM alpha of the β 5-1 portfolio is negative, large in magnitude, and highly statistically significant.[7]

In summary, the results of the bivariate portfolio analyses lead to similar conclusions as those reached using univariate portfolio analysis. The strength of the negative relation between market capitalization and expected stock returns depends highly on the methodology employed. Equal-weighted portfolio analyses indicate a strong relation than value-weighted portfolio analyses. Calculating portfolio breakpoints using only NYSE-listed stocks produces weaker results than when all stocks in the sample are used to determine the breakpoints. In fact, in the bivariate-sort analyses, only equal-weighted portfolios formed from breakpoints calculated using all stocks in the sample provide statistically significant evidence of the size effect in the average quintile of beta. In all other bivariate portfolio analyses, the size effect is not detected. Finally, the use of dependent versus independent sorts when calculating breakpoints has little effect.

[7] In *MktCap* quintile five the alphas of the β 5-1 portfolios are only marginally statistically significant.

9.5.3 Fama–MacBeth Regression Analysis

The portfolio analyses of Sections 9.5.1 and 9.5.2 provide preliminary evidence of a negative relation between market capitalization and stock returns. In this section, we examine that relation using (Fama and MacBeth (1973), FM hereafter) regression analysis. Each month, we run a cross-sectional regression of one-month-ahead excess stock returns on size (*Size*) or size and beta (β). We stress that we use *Size* (the log of market capitalization) instead of *MktCap* in the regression analysis. The reason for this is that, as discussed previously, *MktCap* has a highly skewed distribution. As a

TABLE 9.9   Bivariate Independent-Sort Portfolio Analysis – NYSE/AMEX/NASDAQ Breakpoints

This table presents the results of bivariate independent-sort portfolio analyses of the relation between *MktCap* and future stock returns after controlling for the effect of β. Each month, all stocks in the CRSP sample are sorted into five groups based on an ascending sort of β. All stocks are independently sorted into five groups based on an ascending sort of *MktCap*. The quintile breakpoints used to create the groups are calculated using all stocks in the CRSP sample. The intersections of the β and *MktCap* groups are used to form 25 portfolios. The table presents the average one-month-ahead excess return (in percent per month) for each of the 25 portfolios as well as for the average β quintile portfolio within each quintile of *MktCap* and the average *MktCap* quintile within each β quintile. Also shown are the average return and CAPM alpha of a long–short zero-cost portfolio that is long the fifth *MktCap* (β) quintile portfolio and short the first *MktCap* (β) quintile portfolio in each β (*MktCap*) quintile. t-statistics (in parentheses), adjusted following Newey and West (1987) using six lags, testing the null hypothesis that the average return or alpha is equal to zero, are shown in parentheses. Panel A presents results for equal-weighted portfolios. Panel B presents results for value-weighted portfolios.

	β 1	β 2	β 3	β 4	β 5	β Avg	β 5-1	β 5-1 CAPM α
				Panel A: Equal-Weighted Portfolios				
MktCap 1	1.36	1.40	1.62	1.24	1.19	1.36	−0.17	−0.54
							(−0.56)	(−2.02)
MktCap 2	0.59	0.74	0.72	0.56	0.21	0.56	−0.38	−0.90
							(−1.12)	(−3.35)
MktCap 3	0.59	0.77	0.81	0.62	0.42	0.64	−0.18	−0.69
							(−0.56)	(−2.81)
MktCap 4	0.66	0.74	0.79	0.76	0.50	0.69	−0.16	−0.69
							(−0.53)	(−2.78)
MktCap 5	0.39	0.51	0.60	0.64	0.44	0.52	0.05	−0.42
							(0.17)	(−1.92)
MktCap Avg	0.72	0.83	0.91	0.76	0.55		−0.17	−0.65
							(−0.61)	(−3.07)
MktCap 5-1	−0.97	−0.89	−1.02	−0.60	−0.75	−0.84		
	(−3.34)	(−2.87)	(−2.62)	(−1.54)	(−2.00)	(−2.69)		
MktCap 5-1 CAPM α	−0.85	−0.74	−0.98	−0.46	−0.72	−0.75		
	(−3.20)	(−2.67)	(−2.23)	(−1.27)	(−2.01)	(−2.54)		

TABLE 9.9 (*Continued*)

	$\beta\,1$	$\beta\,2$	$\beta\,3$	$\beta\,4$	$\beta\,5$	β Avg	$\beta\,5\text{-}1$	$\beta\,5\text{-}1$ CAPM α
			Panel B: Value-Weighted Portfolios					
MktCap 1	0.89	1.01	1.15	0.77	0.67	0.90	−0.21	−0.63
							(−0.65)	(−2.20)
MktCap 2	0.61	0.75	0.73	0.58	0.18	0.57	−0.43	−0.95
							(−1.27)	(−3.56)
MktCap 3	0.60	0.76	0.82	0.64	0.42	0.65	−0.18	−0.69
							(−0.58)	(−2.86)
MktCap 4	0.63	0.74	0.78	0.75	0.53	0.68	−0.10	−0.62
							(−0.34)	(−2.49)
MktCap 5	0.35	0.38	0.48	0.44	0.33	0.40	−0.02	−0.41
							(−0.06)	(−1.87)
MktCap Avg	0.62	0.73	0.79	0.64	0.43		−0.19	−0.66
							(−0.70)	(−3.24)
MktCap 5-1	−0.54	−0.63	−0.67	−0.33	−0.34	−0.50		
	(−1.93)	(−1.99)	(−1.81)	(−0.84)	(−0.84)	(−1.57)		
MktCap 5-1 CAPM α	−0.43	−0.46	−0.50	−0.13	−0.22	−0.35		
	(−1.68)	(−1.62)	(−1.44)	(−0.36)	(−0.58)	(−1.22)		

result, if we used *MktCap* as an independent variable, it is possible that a few extreme data points would have an undesirably large effect on the estimated regression coefficients. For this reason, it is standard in the asset pricing literature to use the log of market capitalization (*Size*) in regression analyses. We repeat the analyses using the FF version of size, $Size^{FF}$.

Table 9.10 presents the results of the FM regression analyses. Model (1) shows that when *Size* is the only independent variable in the regression specification, the average slope from the monthly cross-sectional regressions is −0.14 with a corresponding Newey and West (1987)-adjusted t-statistic of −2.93, indicating a statistically significant negative relation between *Size* and future stock returns. Regression model (2) demonstrates that after controlling for the effect of beta, the negative cross-sectional relation between size and future stock returns persists, as the average slope on *Size* is −0.15 with a t-statistic of −2.48. Consistent with the results in Chapter 8, the average coefficient on β remains statistically indistinguishable from zero. Regression models (3) and (4) repeat the regression analyses using $Size^{FF}$ instead of *Size* to measure market capitalization. The results are very similar. Specification (3), which uses on $Size^{FF}$ as the only independent variable, generates an average regression coefficient of −0.12 with a t-statistic of −2.62. When β is included as a control variable, the average slope on *Size* is once again −0.12, this time with a t-statistic of −2.16. Thus, regardless of the measure of market capitalization, the results of the FM regression analyses indicate a statistically strong negative cross-sectional relation between size and future stock returns.

TABLE 9.10   Fama–MacBeth Regression Analysis
This table presents the results of Fama and MacBeth (1973) regression analyses of the relation between expected stock returns and firm size. Each column in the table presents results for a different cross-sectional regression specification. The dependent variable in all specifications is the one-month-ahead excess stock return. The independent variables are indicated in the first column. Independent variables are winsorized at the 0.5% level on a monthly basis. The table presents average slope and intercept coefficients along with t-statistics (in parentheses), adjusted following Newey and West (1987) using six lags, testing the null hypothesis that the average coefficient is equal to zero. The rows labeled Adj. R^2 and n present the average adjusted R-squared and the number of data points, respectively, for the cross-sectional regressions.

	(1)	(2)	(3)	(4)
Size	−0.14	−0.15		
	(−2.93)	(−2.48)		
Size^{FF}			−0.12	−0.12
			(−2.62)	(−2.16)
β		−0.06		−0.11
		(−0.34)		(−0.63)
Intercept	1.31	1.42	1.23	1.35
	(2.81)	(3.33)	(2.70)	(3.23)
Adj. R^2	0.01	0.03	0.01	0.03
n	4781	4426	4578	4420

To examine the economic significance of the relation between size and future stock returns, we take the estimated average slope coefficient on *Size* from the regression specification that includes β as a control (specification (2)) of −0.15 and multiply it by the average cross-sectional standard deviation of *Size* of 1.92 (see Table 9.1) to get −0.29 (−0.15 × 1.92). This indicates that, all else equal, a one-standard-deviation difference in *Size* is associated with a 0.29% per month difference in expected stock returns. Similarly, we calculate the difference in expected returns between stocks whose *Size* falls at the 25th and 75th percentiles. Doing so indicates that the difference in expected returns of two such stocks is 0.40% per month (0.15% × (5.57 − 2.93), see Table 9.1). Finally, we examine the difference in expected returns for very large stocks compared to very small stocks by multiplying the average coefficient on *Size* by the difference between the 95th and fifth percentiles of *Size*, giving an expected return difference of 0.94% per month (0.15% × (7.74 − 1.46)). The results, therefore, indicate that in addition to detecting a statistically significant relation between *Size* and future stock returns, the relation is also highly economically important.

In summary, the results of the portfolio analyses and FM regression analyses presented in this section indicate a negative relation between market capitalization and future stock returns. This phenomenon is commonly referred to as the size effect.

Different variations of portfolio and FM regression analyses produce substantially different results. The size effect appears strongest when using breakpoints calculated using all stocks in the sample, but substantially weaker when only NYSE stocks are used to calculate the portfolio breakpoints. Value-weighted portfolios generate a somewhat weaker size effect than equal-weighted portfolios. Consistent with the findings of Banz (1981) and Fama and French (1992, 1993), we show that the size effect is driven by very large returns on stocks in the smallest decile of market capitalization. The size effect also appears to be concentrated among stocks with low market betas. Consistent with the strongest portfolio results, FM regression analyses indicate an economically and statistically important negative relation between size and future stock returns. The relation persists after controlling for market beta, contradicting the prediction of the (CAPM Sharpe (1964), Lintner (1965), Mossin (1966)) that market beta is the only determinant of cross-sectional variation in expected returns.

Given the existence of a negative relation between market capitalization and abnormal stock returns, an important question that arises is why such a relation exists. As noted by Ball (1978), among others, the portfolio and regression analyses of Section 9.5 do not necessarily indicate market inefficiency. Another plausible explanation is that market capitalization serves as a proxy for exposure to a risk that is not included in the benchmark asset pricing model, in this case the CAPM risk model.

9.6 THE SIZE FACTOR

Taking the point of view that market capitalization proxies for a stock's exposure to a priced but previously undefined risk factor, Fama and French (1993) create a long–short zero-cost portfolio designed to generate returns that approximate the returns associated with taking one unit of risk of this unknown size factor with little sensitivity to other factors. To create the size factor mimicking portfolio, Fama and French (1993) form a portfolio that is long small stocks and short large stocks in equal dollar amounts. They name this portfolio *SMB*, for small minus big.

In June of each year y, Fama and French (1993) divide all U.S.-based common stocks in the CRSP database into two groups. Stocks with market capitalizations that are lower than the median market capitalization among all NYSE stocks comprise the group S (for small). The B (for big) group contains all stocks with market capitalizations above the NYSE median. The entire universe of stocks is also independently sorted into three groups based on the book-to-market ratio (BM). BM is calculated in June of year y as the book value of common equity at the end of the fiscal year ending in the previous calendar year (year $y - 1$) divided by the market capitalization of the stock at the end of December of the previous calendar year (year $y - 1$, see Chapter 10 for more details on calculating BM). The H (for high) group contains all stocks with BM above the 70th percentile of BM for NYSE stocks only. The M (for medium) group holds stocks with BM values between the 30th and 70th NYSE percentiles, and the L (for low) group contains stocks with BM values below the 30th percentile.

The two market capitalization groups and three book-to-market ratio groups are then intersected to create six portfolios labeled $S/H, S/M, S/L, B/H, B/M$, and B/L.

The S/H portfolio contains stocks in the intersection of the small stock (S) group and the high book-to-market ratio (H) group. Holdings in the other portfolios are analogous. The stocks in each of the six portfolios are value-weighted, with the market capitalization as of the end of June of year y, previously defined as $MktCap^{FF}$, used as the weight field. Fama and French (1993) then calculate the monthly returns of each of these six portfolios for the months from July of year y through June of year $y + 1$, at which time the portfolios are reformed. Finally, the return of the size factor mimicking portfolio (SMB) in any month m is taken to be the difference between the simple average of the returns of the three small stock portfolios (S/H, S/M, and S/L) and that of the three large stock portfolios (B/H, B/M, and B/L). The objective of the portfolio design is to create a long–short portfolio whose returns are highly sensitive to return differences between large and small stocks, and relatively insensitive to differences in returns among stocks with high and low book-to-market ratios. The monthly (and daily) returns of the SMB portfolio are available on Kenneth French's website.[8]

During the period from July 1926 through December 2012, the average monthly return (log return) of the SMB portfolio is 0.23% (0.18%), with a sample standard deviation of 3.26% (3.17%) per month. The annualized Sharpe ratio of the monthly SMB returns (log returns) is therefore 0.24 (0.20). The compounded return of the SMB portfolio over this entire period is 537%, and the cumulative log return is therefore 185%. The returns of the SMB portfolio also exhibit a substantial correlation of 0.34 with the market factor (MKT).

Figure 9.2 plots the cumulative returns realized from investing in the SMB portfolio. The solid line shows the compounded return realized by investing in the monthly SMB portfolio. The scale for this line is on the left side of the plot. The dashed line plots the cumulative sum of the monthly log returns of the SMB portfolio, and its scale is on the right side of the plot. The plot shows that, while in the long run the trading strategy underlying the SMB portfolio is profitable, there are some very severe risks involved with this strategy. For example, starting at the beginning of August 1983, the SMB portfolio experiences a prolonged and substantial decline in value. The low point of this drawdown comes at the end of March 1999, at which point the SMB portfolio had lost almost 53% of its previous maximum value. The next time the value of the portfolio reaches the previous high, established at the end of July 1983, is the end of April 2010, more than 26 years after the previous high was achieved. While this drawdown is both the longest and deepest drawdown experienced by the SMB portfolio, it by no means represents the only period of deep or prolonged losses. The second longest drawdown began at the beginning of June 1946, from which point the SMB portfolio had a negative cumulative return until the end of September 1967, more than 21 years later. At its low point during this period, the SMB lost almost 39% of its value as of the end of May 1946. Finally, from the end of December 1968 until the end of December 1974, the SMB portfolio lost more than 46% of its value. The

[8]The URL for Kenneth French's data library is http://mba.tuck.dartmouth.edu/pages/faculty/ken.french/data&uscore;library.html.

previous high was not recaptured until the end of August 1978, almost 10 years after the drawdown began.

In addition to the prolonged periods of poor performance for the *SMB* factor, it is worth noting that if we use the CAPM risk model to assess the abnormal returns of the *SMB* portfolio by regressing the *SMB* monthly return on the monthly excess return of the market (the market factor, *MKT*), we find that the risk-adjusted alpha (the estimated intercept coefficient from the regression), while positive, is statistically insignificant. Specifically, using the period from July 1926 through December 2012, the *SMB* factor generates a CAPM alpha of only 0.10% per month with a Newey and West (1987) t-statistic of only 1.12. Similarly, for the period from July 1963 through December 2012 (the period for which we examine returns throughout this book), the CAPM alpha of the *SMB* portfolio is 0.15% per month with a corresponding t-statistic of 1.25. These results seem to indicate that the excess returns of the *SMB* portfolio can be explained by the sensitivity of the *SMB* portfolio to the market portfolio, as predicted by the CAPM. In fact, even without adjusting the returns of the *SMB* factor to account for sensitivity to the market factor, the average monthly return of the *SMB* factor from July 1963 through December 2012 is an economically small 0.13% per month with a corresponding t-statistic of 1.86, indicating only marginally statistically significant evidence that the *SMB* factor generates positive average returns over this period of nearly 50 years. Despite these facts, Fama and French (1993) show that the *SMB* portfolio has the ability to explain the abnormal returns of portfolios whose returns are not explained by the market factor. For this reason, the *SMB* factor is one of the pillars of empirical asset pricing research, and any study claiming to demonstrate the ability to explain or predict stock returns is expected to demonstrate that this ability persists after controlling for the size effect.

9.7 SUMMARY

In this chapter, we have examined the relation between the market capitalization and expected stock returns. Portfolio and regression analyses detect a strong negative relation between these two variables. The results indicate that small stocks (stocks with low market capitalization) outperform large stocks. Portfolio analyses demonstrate that this result is primarily driven by extremely small stocks that generate very high average returns but comprise a small percentage of total stock market capitalization. The size phenomenon is not explained by cross-sectional variation in market beta, but the magnitude and statistical significance of the effect vary substantially depending on the implementation of the analysis. Value-weighted portfolios tend to produce weaker results than equal-weighted portfolios. Calculation of portfolio breakpoints using only stocks listed on the NYSE substantially diminishes the detected magnitude of the returns associated with size investing compared to portfolios formed using breakpoints calculated using all stocks.

Fama and French (1993) conclude that the difference in expected returns between large and small stocks must be due to exposures to a latent priced risk factor that are cross-sectionally correlated with market capitalization. Based on this, they create the

SMB portfolio consisting of long positions in stocks with low market capitalizations and short positions in stocks with high market capitalizations. This factor-mimicking portfolio is designed to generate returns that would be realized by a portfolio that is long one unit of exposure to the latent risk factor with minimal sensitivity to the other risk factors, and therefore is ideal for use in a multifactor risk model. We show that while the returns of the *SMB* portfolio are on average positive, there are substantial risks associated with this portfolio, and poor performance may persist for extended periods of time.

REFERENCES

Ball, R. 1978. Anomalies in relationships between securities' yields and yield-surrogates. Journal of Financial Economics, 6(2-3), 103–126.

Banz, R. W. 1981. The relationship between return and market value of common stocks. Journal of Financial Economics, 9(1), 3–18.

Fama, E. F. and French, K. R. 1992. The cross-section of expected stock returns. Journal of Finance, 47(2), 427–465.

Fama, E. F. and French, K. R. 1993. Common risk factors in the returns on stocks and bonds. Journal of Financial Economics, 33(1), 3–56.

Fama, E. F. and French, K. R. 2012. Size, value, and momentum in international stock returns. Journal of Financial Economics, 105(3), 457–472.

Fama, E. F. and MacBeth, J. D. 1973. Risk, return, and equilibrium: empirical tests. Journal of Political Economy, 81(3), 607.

Lakonishok, J. and Shapiro, A. 1986. Systematic risk, total risk and size as determinants of stock market returns. Journal of Banking & Finance, 10(1), 115–132.

Lintner, J. 1965. Security prices, risk, and maximal gains from diversification. Journal of Finance, 20(4), 587–615.

Mossin, J. 1966. Equilibrium in a capital asset market. Econometrica, 34(4), 768–783.

Newey, W. K. and West, K. D. 1987. A simple, positive semi-definite, heteroskedasticity and autocorrelation consistent covariance matrix. Econometrica, 55(3), 703–708.

Sharpe, W. F. 1964. Capital asset prices: a theory of market equilibrium under conditions of risk. Journal of Finance, 19(3), 425–442.

10

THE VALUE PREMIUM

Numerous studies document that value stocks, loosely defined as stocks with low prices relative to earnings (Basu (1977), Jaffe, Keim, and Westerfield (1989)), dividends (Lakonishok, Shleifer, and Vishny (1994)), debt (Bhandari (1988)), or the book value of equity (Rosenberg, Reid, and Lanstein (1985), Fama and French (1992, 1993), Chan, Jegadeesh, and Lakonishok (1995)), generate higher long-run returns than growth stocks, or stocks with high prices relative to these measures of fundamental value. Fama and French (1992) show that the relations between each of these variables and future stock returns are subsumed by two variables, market capitalization and the ratio of book value of equity to the market value of equity (book-to-market ratio hereafter). As was shown in Chapter 9, market capitalization has a negative relation with stock returns. The main objective of the present chapter is to empirically investigate the value premium. Specifically, we will demonstrate that the book-to-market ratio has a positive relation with expected stock returns.

The interpretation of the positive relation between book-to-market ratio (or other related measures) and expected stock returns is controversial. Two main explanations have been offered. The first is a risk-based explanation proposed by Fama and French (1993) and Chen and Zhang (1998). These papers argue that the higher (lower) returns of value (growth) stocks are a result of higher (lower) exposure to a priced risk factor. The second explanation, offered by Lakonishok, Shleifer, and Vishny (1994), La Porta (1996), and La Porta, Lakonishok, Shleifer, and Vishny (1997), is behavioral in

Empirical Asset Pricing: The Cross Section of Stock Returns, First Edition.
Turan G. Bali, Robert F. Engle, and Scott Murray.
© 2016 John Wiley & Sons, Inc. Published 2016 by John Wiley & Sons, Inc.

nature. These authors claim that the returns associated with value investing are due to naive investor expectations of future growth that result in mispricing.

Proponents of a risk-based explanation have proposed several possibilities for the exact nature of the risk. Fama and French (1992) suggest that book-to-market ratio (or other variables measuring value) proxy for exposure to a latent fundamental-based risk factor. This hypothesis is supported by Fama and French (1995) and Chen and Zhang (1998), who show that value firms have persistently low earnings, high earnings uncertainty, and high leverage. Fama and French (1993) investigate this hypothesis within the context of a multifactor asset pricing model (Merton (1973); Ross (1976)). They demonstrate that the returns of a portfolio designed to mimic innovations in this factor capture common variation in stock returns. Another possibility proposed by Fama and French (1992) is that the book-to-market ratio may capture the relative distress effect postulated by Chan and Chen (1991). According to this explanation, the low share prices relative to measures of fundamentals reflect the market's judgment that the prospects for the firm are poor. Furthermore, as low market prices result in high market leverage, they claim that this distress can also be interpreted as an involuntary leverage effect.

More recent risk-based studies claim that the value premium can be explained by time-varying risk and risk-premia (Lettau and Ludvigson (2001), Zhang (2005)). Proponents of this explanation argue that the risk of a portfolio, that is, long value stocks and short growth stocks is high (low) when economic conditions are poor (good) and risk premia are high (low). Lettau and Ludvigson (2001) empirically support this claim by showing that during economic downturns, the returns of a portfolio of value stocks are more highly correlated with consumption growth than the returns of a portfolio of growth stocks. Zhang (2005) derives this hypothesis theoretically from a production-based asset pricing model in which value stocks are riskier than growth stocks, especially in states characterized by poor economic conditions and elevated risk premia. Fama and French (1995) find that during such periods, high (low) book-to-market ratios are indicative of persistently low (high) profitability.[1]

Adherents to the behavioral explanation, originally proposed by Lakonishok, Shleifer, and Vishny (1994), claim that the higher returns of value stocks result from mispricing caused by investors' errors in estimating firms' future earnings growth. In particular, Lakonishok, Shleifer, and Vishny (1994) postulate that value strategies work because they are contrary to the strategies followed by naive investors who tend to extrapolate past growth rates too far into the future. Naive investors tend to get overly optimistic about stocks that have performed very well in the past, creating demand for shares that causes these glamor stocks to become overpriced. Similarly, naive investors overreact to stocks that have performed poorly, oversell them, causing these "value" stocks to become underpriced. Accordingly, the predictive power of value-to-price ratios merely reflects the unraveling of past errors made by naive investors. Consistent with this notion, earlier studies on overreaction (De Bondt and

[1] Fama and French (2012) and Asness, Moskowitz, and Pedersen 2013 find evidence of the value premium in many different asset classes and markets and attribute the returns associated with value investing to a common factor.

Thaler (1985, 1987), Chopra, Lakonishok, and Ritter (1992)) show that extreme losers outperform the market over the subsequent several years. Examinations of the ability of these growth forecast errors to explain the superior returns of value stocks by La Porta (1996) and La Porta, Lakonishok, Shleifer, and Vishny (1997) support the mispricing explanation. Griffin and Lemmon (2002) find that firms with high distress risk exhibit the largest return reversals around earnings announcements, thus attributing the distress-risk effect to mispricing. Ali, Hwang, and Trombley (2003) show that the value effect is predominantly driven by stocks whose investors are unsophisticated. Lakonishok, Shleifer, and Vishny (1994) combat risk-based explanation by showing that high value-to-price stocks are no riskier than growth stocks based on conventional notions of systematic risk such as beta and standard deviation. Daniel and Titman (1997) cast doubts on the risk factor interpretation of the superior returns to high book-to-market stocks by demonstrating that expected returns are not significantly higher for stocks whose returns are more highly correlated with the book-to-market factor of Fama and French (1993). In other words, co-movement with the proposed risk factor does not explain expected returns.

To summarize, although many studies provide evidence that helps discriminate between the risk and mispricing explanations, the results remain inconclusive. Whether contrarian strategies generate high returns because stocks are mispriced or because value stocks are fundamentally riskier than growth stocks remains an open question.

In remainder of this chapter, we empirically investigate the value premium by examining the relation between book-to-market ratio and stock returns. We begin by discussing the calculation of the book-to-market ratio. We then investigate the cross-sectional relation between book-to-market ratio and future stock returns using portfolio and Fama and MacBeth (1973) regression analysis. Next, we discuss the *HML* portfolio of Fama and French (1993), designed to capture the returns derived from exposure to the risk associated with the value premium. Finally, we present the Fama and French (1993) three-factor risk model, which has become a widely used standard for measuring risk-adjusted returns.

10.1 CALCULATING BOOK-TO-MARKET RATIO

The book-to-market ratio, which we denote BM, is defined as the book value of a firm's common equity (BE) divided by the market value of the firm's equity (ME), or

$$BM = \frac{BE}{ME} \tag{10.1}$$

where the book value comes from the firm's balance sheet and the market value is identical to the market capitalization of the firm. As will be seen in the summary statistics presented in Section 10.2, the cross-sectional distribution of BM is highly positively skewed. To minimize the effect of extreme values of BM in statistical analyses, we define ln BM as the natural log of BM.

$$\ln BM = \ln (BM). \tag{10.2}$$

It is worth noting that, despite the skewed distribution of *BM*, most empirical research uses the untransformed version of *BM* even in regression and correlation analyses. In this chapter, we will investigate whether applying the log transformation has any qualitative effect on the results of such analyses.

The most commonly implemented calculation of the book-to-market ratio is that of Fama and French (1992, 1993). Calculation of the book value of common equity (*BE*) is done from balance sheet data provided by Compustat. While the files provided by Compustat have changed over time, at the time of this writing (2015), the data necessary for the calculation of *BE* is available in Compustat's North America Fundamentals Annual (funda) file.

The calculation of *BE* begins by taking the book value of stockholder's equity, which is the *SEQ* field in Compustat. We adjust this value for tax effects by adding deferred taxes (*TXDB* field) and investment tax credit (*ITCB* field) to it. Finally, from this, we subtract the book value of preferred stock. The book value of preferred stock is taken to be the redemption value (*PSTKRV* field), the liquidating value (*PSTKL* field), or the par value (*PSTK* field), taken in the given order, as available. If either the stockholders equity (*SEQ*) or the deferred taxes field (*TXDB*) is missing in the Compustat database, the book value of common equity is not calculated and calculation of the book-to-market ratio fails. If investment tax credit (*ITCB*) is missing, it is taken to be zero. Finally, if all of the values for preferred stock are missing, the book value of preferred stock is taken to be zero. We can therefore define the book equity as

$$BE = SEQ + TXDB + ITCB - BVPS \qquad (10.3)$$

where

$$BVPS = \begin{cases} PRTKRV, & \text{if available} \\ PSTKL, & \text{if available and } PSTKRV \text{ not available} \\ PSTK, & \text{if available and } PSTKRV, PSTKL \text{ not available} \\ 0, & \text{otherwise.} \end{cases}$$

All of the fields used in the calculation of *BE* are reported in $millions in the Compustat database. In some cases, the calculation results in a negative value for *BE*. The value of *BE* for these observations is taken to be missing, resulting in a failure to calculate *BM*. This ensures that the book-to-market ratio, when calculated, will be positive. Values of *BM* for observations with negative *BE* are therefore not calculated. It is also worth mentioning that the Compustat database has multiple entries for many firm/date observations, where firm/date observations are identified by unique combinations of the *gvkey* and *datadate* fields in the Compustat database. The correct entry to use in calculation of the book-to-market ratio can be identified by taking the entry where the industry format (*indfmt* field) is set to "INDL" and the data format (*datafmt* field) is set to "STD." In fact, when calculating the book value of equity, only entries with the industry format and data format fields set to the aforementioned values in Compustat's North America Fundamentals Annual file should be used. Thus, it is advised that when using this file to calculate the book value of common equity, all entries with alternative values in either of these fields be removed. The remaining entries will represent unique firm/date observations.[2]

The second step to calculating the book-to-market ratio is to calculate the market equity. The market value of equity used in the calculation of the book-to-market ratio is usually taken to be the market capitalization, defined as the number of shares outstanding times the price of the stock, measured at the end of December of any given year. As discussed in Chapter 9, the number of shares outstanding (*SHROUT* field) and share price (*ALTPRC* or *PRC* field) data used to calculate the market capitalization are taken from the Center for Research in Security Prices (CRSP) daily or monthly files. As CRSP reports the number of shares outstanding in thousands of shares, and the calculation of the book value of common equity was done in $millions, the market equity used in the book-to-market ratio calculation is defined as

$$ME = \frac{|ALTPRC \times SHROUT|}{1000} \qquad (10.4)$$

where *ALTPRC* and *SHROUT* are taken from CRSP monthly stock file on the last trading day in December of the given year. The absolute value in the numerator is because in some situations, CRSP reports the price of a share as a negative number. The reasons for this are discussed in detail in Section 9.1.

The next step to calculating the book-to-market ratio is to properly align the timing of the calculation of the book value of equity (*BE*) with the market value of equity (*ME*). The most standard approach to doing this, proposed by Fama and French (1992, 1993), is to pair the book equity calculated using data for the fiscal year ending in calendar year *y* with the market equity calculated at the end of that same year *y*. Thus, for firms with fiscal year-ends in January, the calculation of book equity will be as of the end of January of the given year, and the calculation of market equity will be as of the end of December of that same year. The timing of the calculation of the book and market values can, therefore, differ by up to 11 months. Fama and French (1992) find that this lag has negligible effect on empirical analyses. The *datadate* field in the Compustat database represents the fiscal year-end date, thus simply taking the year of this date is all that is needed to find the desired year *y*. In some cases, firms change the month in which their fiscal year ends, resulting in two entries in the Compustat database for the same calendar year *y*. In such cases, data from the latest *datadate* in the given calendar year *y* are used.

To ensure that the value of the book-to-market ratio used in empirical research is based on data that would have been publicly available by the time presumed in the analysis, the book-to-market ratio that is calculated using data from calendar year *y* is not assumed to be known until the end of June of year *y* + 1. Thus, the value of $BM_{i,t}$ (the book-to-market ratio for stock *i* in month *t*), for months *t* from June of year *y* + 1 (inclusive) to May of year *y* + 2 (inclusive), is taken to be the book-to-market ratio calculated using data from calendar year *y*. The reason for this approach to the

---

[2]In Compustat's North America Fundamentals Annual file used in writing this book, there is one exception to this claim. There are two entries for *gvkey* 175650 and *datadate* 12/31/2005. We drop both observations for this firm/date combination from our analyses.

timing of the calculation of the book-to-market ratio is that firms have 3 months from the end of their fiscal year-ends to report the required data, but many firms fail to meet this deadline. Thus, Fama and French (1992) assume at least a six-month gap between the end of the fiscal year and the time at which the fiscal year-end data is publicly available. Put succinctly, for the monthly analyses performed in the book, the book-to-market ratio for months t from June of year $y + 1$ through May of year $y + 2$ is taken to be the book value of equity measured at the end of the fiscal year ending in calendar year y divided by the market value of equity at the end of December of calendar year y.

When calculating BM, it is necessary to match entries in the Compustat database to entries in the CRSP database. This task is not trivial as CRSP and Compustat do not have common firm or stock identifiers. Stocks in the CRSP database are identified by the *PERMNO* field. Firms in the Compustat database are identified by *gvkey* field. If access to the CRSP/Compustat merged database, provided by CRSP, is available, then the best way to link the Compustat data used to calculate the book value of common equity to the CRSP data used to calculate the market value of equity is to use the link-used table (CCMXPF_LNKUSED) in the CRSP/Compustat database. The link-used table matches a CRSP *PERMNO* to the Compustat *gvkey* for the same firm and indicates the dates for which the link is valid. There are several types of links in the link-used file, indicated in the ULINKTYPE field. Only links with values of "LU" or "LC" in the ULINKTYPE field should be used.[3] Additionally, only links with values of 1 in the USEDFLAG field in the link-used table should be used.[4] The ULINKDT field in the link-used table indicates the first date for which the link between the CRSP PERMNO and the Compustat gvkey is valid and the ULINK-ENDDT field indicates the last date that the link is valid. If the ULINKENDDT field is not populated it indicates that the link remains valid as of the time that the file was generated. Matches between the Compustat database and the link-used file in the CRSP/Compustat merged database are identified by matching the UGVKEY field in the link-used file to the gvkey field in the Compustat file while requiring that the data-date field in the Compustat file be greater than or equal to the date in the ULINKDT field and less than or equal to the ULINKENDDT field (if the ULINKENDDT field is populated) in the link-used file. The CRSP PERMNO corresponding to the given entry in the Compustat database is taken from the UPERMNO field in the matched entry of the link-used table.

If access to the CRSP/Compustat merged database is not available, then the best approach to merging the CRSP and Compustat databases is to match the cusip (*NCUSIP* field) from CRSP's daily stock names (dsenames) or monthly stock

---

[3] A value of "LU" in the ULINKTYPE field indicates that the link is established by comparing CUSIP values in the Compustat and CRSP databases. A value of "LC" in the ULINKTYPE field indicates that the link has been researched and that the research has verified that the link is correct. For more information on the exact meanings of the different values in the ULINKTYPE field, consult the CRSP/Compustat merged database documentation.

[4] The USEDFLAG field is set to 1 if the *gvkey* represents a direct link to the corresponding PERMNO. For more information on the exact meanings of the different values in the USEDFLAG field, consult the CRSP/Compustat merged database documentation.

names (msenames) file to the first eight characters of the CUSIP (*cusip* field) from Compustat. In CRSP's daily and monthly stock names files, each entry has a start date (*NAMEDT* field) and an end date (*NAMEENDT* field). The matching procedure should require that CRSP's start date be on or prior to the *datadate* from Compustat, and CRSP's end date to be on or after Compustat's *datadate*. In implementing this match, we use CRSP's daily names file.

To maximize the number of CRSP PERMNOs that we can match to the Compustat database, we implement both matching techniques. We first use the links provided by the link-used table in the CRSP/Compustat merged database. For entries in our sample that are not matched using this technique, we attempt to create the link by matching the CUSIPs in the two databases.

10.2 SUMMARY STATISTICS

We begin our empirical investigation by presenting summary statistics for the book-to-market ratio (*BM*) and the natural log of the book-to-market ratio (ln *BM*) using our sample of the U.S.-based common stocks in the CRSP database covering the period from 1963 through 2012. In addition to *BM* and ln *BM*, we present summary statistics for the book value of equity (*BE*) and the market value of equity (*ME*) used to calculate *BM*, both presented in $millions and adjusted to 2012 dollars using the Consumer Price Index (CPI).[5]

Table 10.1 presents the summary statistics for each of these variables. The first row indicates that, in the average month, the mean and median values of *BM* are 0.94 and 0.72, respectively. The standard deviation of *BM* of 1.14 is larger than either the mean or the median. This, combined with the fact that *BM* is bounded below by zero, indicates that a substantial portion of the variation in *BM* is coming from stocks with extremely high *BM* values. Consistent with this, the skewness of the cross-sectional distribution of *BM* in the average month is 10.16, indicating a very positively skewed distribution of *BM*. The distribution of *BM* is also fat-tailed, as the excess kurtosis of *BM* in the average month is nearly 285. The presented percentiles of *BM* indicate that *BM* values range from 0.01 to 32.92 in the average month. The 95th percentile value of 2.32 is only 1.21 standard deviations above the mean, whereas the maximum value of 32.92 is more than 28 standard deviations above the mean.

The summary statistics for ln *BM* indicate that applying the log transformation to the book-to-market ratio has the desired effect of dramatically reducing the skewness of the cross-sectional distribution. The skewness of ln *BM* in the average month of −0.66 is actually negative, in stark contrast to the untransformed variable. The excess kurtosis has also been substantially decreased, although ln *BM* does remain substantially leptokurtic, with an average excess kurtosis of 2.41. The mean and median values of ln *BM* of −0.47 and −0.39, respectively, are reasonably similar. The average cross-sectional standard deviation of ln *BM* is 0.87. Finally, ln *BM* values

---

[5]CPI data are taken from the Bureau of Labor Statistics website. The data are available at www. bls.gov/cpi/data.htm. We use data for the All Urban Consumer series.

TABLE 10.1 Summary Statistics
This table presents summary statistics for variables measuring the ratio of a firm's book value of equity to its market value of equity calculated using the CRSP sample for the months t from June 1963 through November 2012. Each month, the mean (*Mean*), standard deviation (*SD*), skewness (*Skew*), excess kurtosis (*Kurt*), minimum (*Min*), fifth percentile (5%), 25th percentile (25%), median (*Median*), 75th percentile (75%), 95th percentile (95%), and maximum (*Max*) values of the cross-sectional distribution of each variable are calculated. The table presents the time-series means for each cross-sectional value. The column labeled n indicates that average number of stocks for which the given variable is available. *BM* for months t from June of year y through May of year $y + 1$ is calculated as the book value of common equity as of the end of the fiscal year ending in calendar year $y - 1$ to the market value of common equity as of the end of December of year $y - 1$. *ln BM* is the natural log of *BM*. *BE* and *ME* are the book value and market value, respectively, used to calculate *BM*, both adjusted to reflect 2012 dollar using the consumer price index and recorded in millions of dollars. *MktCap* is the share price times the number of shares outstanding.

	Mean	SD	Skew	Kurt	Min	5%	25%	Median	75%	95%	Max	n
BM	0.94	1.14	10.16	284.75	0.01	0.15	0.41	0.72	1.15	2.32	32.92	3409
ln BM	−0.47	0.87	−0.66	2.41	−6.11	−1.98	−0.95	−0.39	0.08	0.77	3.07	3409
BE	1043	4799	16.95	450.54	1	11	50	158	542	3946	129,735	3409
ME	2040	9666	15.50	348.57	2	17	77	269	1021	7220	246,201	3409
MktCap	1234	6035	15.27	338.07	1	7	34	128	530	4574	159,003	3397

range from −6.11, or approximately 6.5 standard deviations below the mean, to 3.07, or about four standard deviations above the mean.

Consistent with the mean of *BM* being below one and the negative mean of ln *BM*, the results in Table 10.1 indicate that values of book equity (*BE*) tend to be smaller in magnitude than values of market equity (*ME*). The CPI-adjusted mean (median) values of *BE* and *ME* are just over \$1 billion and just over \$2 billion (\$158 million and \$269 million), respectively. As expected given the skewness of market capitalization (*MktCap*) observed in Table 9.1, the extreme positive skewness of *BE* and *ME* of greater than 15.00 is expected.

There are only 3409 stocks, on average, for which a valid value of *BM* is available. This compares to 4440 for market beta (β, see Table 8.1) and 4794 for market capitalization (*MktCap*, see Table 9.1). There are three reasons for this. First, the majority of the lost data points are because of a failure to match the Compustat data from which the value of *BE*, and thus *BM*, is calculated, to the CRSP database. Second, a very small number of data points are lost because of a negative calculated value of *BE*, in which case, as discussed earlier, the value of *BE*, and thus *BM*, is taken to be missing. Third, the lag of up to 17 months between the end of a fiscal year and the first month for which balance sheet data from that fiscal year are used to calculate *BM* results, in many cases, in a substantial delay between when a stock enters the CRSP database and when a value of *BM* is first available.

To examine the similarity between the sample of stocks for which values of *BM* are available to the full sample used in our previous analyses, the last line of Table 10.1 presents the distribution of market capitalization (*MktCap*) for stocks with a non-missing *BM* value. Comparing the results here to those for the full market capitalization sample (see Table 9.1) indicates that stocks for which values of *BM* exist are, on average and in median, slightly larger than the stocks in the full sample, as the mean (median) *MktCap* for stocks with a valid *BM* value is $1.2 billion ($128 million), compared to $1.1 billion ($107 million) for the full sample. The decrease in the sample size from 3409 stocks with valid *BM* to 3397 stocks with valid *BM* and *MktCap* indicates that there are a very small number of stocks with valid *BM* but missing *MktCap*.

10.3 CORRELATIONS

We proceed now to examine the cross-sectional correlations between *BM* and ln *BM*, as well as between these variables and the main variables discussed previously in this book, namely market beta (β) and stock size (*Size*, the natural log of market capitalization). Table 10.2 presents correlations between *BM*, ln *BM*, β, and *Size* values. The sample used to calculate these correlations includes only stocks for which a value of *BM* is available. Each of the variables is winsorized at the 0.5% level on a monthly basis. Values below (above) the diagonal present the average cross-sectional Pearson product–moment (Spearman rank) correlation between the given pair of variables.

As would be expected, the Pearson correlation between *BM* and ln *BM* of 0.84 is quite high. This result indicates that taking the log transformation does not have a huge effect on the cross-sectional characteristics of *BM*. By necessity, the Spearman rank correlation between *BM* and ln *BM* is exactly one. The results demonstrate that *BM* is negatively correlated with each of market beta (β) and size (*Size*). *BM* exhibits a Pearson correlation of −0.19 and a Spearman correlation of −0.23 with β. The negative Pearson (Spearman) correlation of −0.27 (−0.26) between *BM* and *Size* is perhaps somewhat mechanical market equity (*ME*), which is calculated in exactly the same manner as market capitalization (of which *Size* is the log), is the denominator in the calculation of *BM*. The Pearson correlations between ln *BM* and each of

TABLE 10.2 Correlations
This table presents the time-series averages of the annual cross-sectional Pearson product–moment (below-diagonal entries) and Spearman rank (above-diagonal entries) correlations between pairs *BM*, ln *BM*, β, and *Size*.

	BM	ln *BM*	β	*Size*
BM		1.00	−0.23	−0.26
ln *BM*	0.84		−0.23	−0.26
β	−0.19	−0.22		0.32
Size	−0.27	−0.24	0.30	

β (correlation = −0.22) and *Size* (correlation = −0.24) are quite similar to the corresponding correlations using *BM* instead of ln *BM*.[6] This, combined with the fact that the Spearman and Pearson correlations are quite similar to each other, indicates either that the skewed distribution of *BM* may not be an important issue empirically or that winsorizing the variables at the 0.5% level is sufficiently effective at adjusting the extreme values of *BM* to ameliorate any negative impact the extreme values may have on the results of statistical analyses.

10.4   PERSISTENCE

In this section, we examine the persistence of both *BM* and ln *BM*. As discussed in the introduction to this chapter, there are two interpretations of the book-to-market ratio that have received particular attention. The first is that book-to-market ratio measures sensitivity to a price risk factor. The second is that book-to-market ratio captures mispricing of some sort. If the factor sensitivity interpretation is correct and this sensitivity is a persistent characteristic of a given stock, it would be expected that book-to-market ratio exhibits strong cross-sectional persistence. On the other hand, if *BM* measures mispricing, it may be expected that book-to-market ratio be a somewhat transient stock characteristic, as its value would tend to change as the mispricing corrects itself.

In Table 10.3, we present the results of persistence analyses of *BM* and ln *BM*. We calculate persistence at lags of between 12 and 120 months. We do not include results for persistence at lags of less than one year because values of *BM* and therefore ln *BM* are only updated once per year, in June. Therefore, persistence measured at shorter lags would be largely mechanical and therefore difficult to interpret.

TABLE 10.3   Persistence
This table presents the results of persistence analyses of *BM* and ln *BM*. Each month *t*, the cross-sectional Pearson product–moment correlation between the month *t* and month $t + \tau$ values of the given variable is calculated. The table presents the time-series averages of the monthly cross-sectional correlations. The column labeled τ indicates the lag at which the persistence is measured.

τ	*BM*	ln *BM*
12	0.799	0.819
24	0.669	0.696
36	0.582	0.611
48	0.521	0.553
60	0.474	0.504
120	0.367	0.393

[6]By necessity, the Spearman correlations using *BM* and ln *BM* are identical.

The results of the persistence analysis indicate that both BM and $\ln BM$ exhibit substantial persistence. At a lag of one year ($\tau = 12$), the results indicate persistence of BM and $\ln BM$ of 0.799 and 0.819, respectively. As would be expected, the persistence decays with longer lags. But, even when measured five years apart ($\tau = 60$), the persistence of BM of 0.474 and persistence of $\ln BM$ of 0.504 remain quite high. After 10 years, however, the persistence of each of these measures drops substantially to 0.367 for BM and 0.393 for $\ln BM$. At all lags, the persistence of $\ln BM$ is slightly higher than that of BM, indicating that if book-to-market ratio does in fact measure a persistent risk factor sensitivity, then $\ln BM$ may be a slightly better measure, especially for use in analyses that assume linearity in the relations between the variables under investigation.

The persistence of BM and $\ln BM$ is substantially higher than that of market beta (β, see Table 8.3), especially for short lags. Given that β measures a factor sensitivity (sensitivity to the market factor), and BM and $\ln BM$ are more persistent than β, the persistence analyses certainly do not dispel and are potentially consistent with the interpretation of BM and $\ln BM$ as factor sensitivities. On the other hand, BM and $\ln BM$ are much less persistent than market capitalization ($MktCap$) and size ($Size$, see Table 9.3).

In summary, book-to-market ratio exhibits high levels of persistence for short lags, but this persistence decays as the length of the lag gets quite long. Even when measured at a lag of 10 years, however, book-to-market ratio still exhibits a substantial persistence, indicating that whatever characteristic is measured by book-to-market ratio, whether it be a factor sensitivity or mispricing, persists for an extended period of time, at least in the average stock.

10.5 BOOK-TO-MARKET RATIO AND STOCK RETURNS

Having sufficiently examined the variables measuring the book-to-market ratio (BM and $\ln BM$), we turn now to investigation of the value premium by examining the cross-sectional relation between book-to-market ratio and expected stock returns. As discussed earlier, the superior long-run returns generated by value stocks is one of the central findings of empirical asset pricing research. In this section, we demonstrate the value premium using portfolio and Fama and MacBeth (1973) regression analyses.

10.5.1 Univariate Portfolio Analysis

We begin our examination of the relation between book-to-market ratio (BM) and future stock returns with univariate portfolio analyses using decile portfolios formed by sorting on BM. As with the portfolio analyses examining the size effect, presented in Chapter 9, we use two sets of breakpoints when examining the relation between BM and future stock returns. The first set of breakpoints uses all stocks in our sample to calculate the breakpoints. We refer to these analyses as using NYSE/AMEX/NASDAQ breakpoints. The second set of breakpoints uses only stocks that trade on the New York Stock Exchange (NYSE) when calculating the

TABLE 10.4 Univariate Portfolio Analysis

This table presents the results of univariate portfolio analyses of the relation between the book-to-market ratio and future stock returns. Monthly portfolios are formed by sorting all stocks in the CRSP sample into portfolios using BM decile breakpoints calculated using all stocks in the CRSP sample (Panel A) or the subset of the stocks in the CRSP sample that are listed on the New York Stock Exchange (Panel B). The Characteristics section of each panel shows the average values of BM, $\ln BM$, $MktCap$, and β, the percentage of stocks that are listed on the New York Stock Exchange, and the number of stocks for each decile portfolio. The EW portfolios (VW portfolios) section in each panel shows the average equal-weighted (value-weighted) one-month-ahead excess return and CAPM alpha (in percent per month) for each of the 10 decile portfolios as well as for the long–short zero-cost portfolio that is long the 10th decile portfolio and short the first decile portfolio. Newey and West (1987) t-statistics, adjusted using six lags, testing the null hypothesis that the average portfolio excess return or CAPM alpha is equal to zero, are shown in parentheses.

Panel A: NYSE/AMEX/NASDAQ Breakpoints

	Value	1	2	3	4	5	6	7	8	9	10	10-1
Characteristics	BM	0.14	0.29	0.41	0.53	0.66	0.79	0.95	1.16	1.49	2.95	
	$\ln BM$	-2.18	-1.32	-0.96	-0.70	-0.49	-0.30	-0.11	0.08	0.33	0.89	
	$MktCap$	2190	2157	1694	1428	1232	1042	899	760	597	334	
	β	1.05	0.98	0.90	0.85	0.81	0.77	0.74	0.70	0.66	0.60	
	% NYSE	28.55	35.40	40.50	43.29	45.78	47.29	45.65	43.94	40.13	32.15	
	n	341	341	341	341	341	341	341	341	341	341	
EW portfolios	Excess return	0.08	0.36	0.50	0.68	0.83	0.85	0.94	1.03	1.18	1.42	1.34
		(0.21)	(1.12)	(1.70)	(2.43)	(2.99)	(3.17)	(3.52)	(3.69)	(4.17)	(4.04)	(6.06)
	CAPM α	-0.57	-0.24	-0.06	0.15	0.35	0.36	0.47	0.57	0.72	0.94	1.51
		(-2.87)	(-1.50)	(-0.44)	(1.11)	(2.00)	(2.69)	(3.38)	(3.75)	(4.48)	(4.33)	(6.57)
VW portfolios	Excess return	0.31	0.33	0.45	0.44	0.46	0.53	0.59	0.67	0.68	0.88	0.57
		(1.17)	(1.54)	(2.25)	(2.08)	(2.24)	(2.78)	(2.88)	(3.15)	(3.37)	(3.60)	(2.40)
	CAPM α	-0.20	-0.15	-0.00	-0.02	0.03	0.12	0.17	0.26	0.26	0.43	0.62
		(-1.52)	(-1.98)	(-0.05)	(-0.32)	(0.28)	(1.50)	(1.77)	(2.15)	(2.10)	(2.93)	(2.55)

Panel B: NYSE Breakpoints

	Value	1	2	3	4	5	6	7	8	9	10	10-1
Characteristics	BM	0.18	0.35	0.47	0.58	0.69	0.81	0.94	1.10	1.37	2.66	
	ln BM	-1.93	-1.11	-0.81	-0.60	-0.42	-0.27	-0.12	0.05	0.26	0.80	
	$MktCap$	2342	1894	1590	1277	1186	1093	908	807	632	360	
	β	1.05	0.94	0.87	0.82	0.80	0.76	0.72	0.70	0.67	0.61	
	% NYSE	31.29	38.94	43.19	44.71	47.00	47.80	47.64	45.44	41.80	33.60	
	n	544	360	318	298	283	276	279	289	323	439	
EW portfolios	Excess return	0.22	0.53	0.64	0.78	0.82	0.86	0.87	0.99	1.16	1.35	1.13
		(0.62)	(1.75)	(2.25)	(2.75)	(2.99)	(3.23)	(3.35)	(3.67)	(4.11)	(3.96)	(5.71)
	CAPM α	-0.41	-0.04	0.09	0.30	0.31	0.38	0.41	0.53	0.69	0.87	1.29
		(-2.31)	(-0.31)	(0.69)	(1.58)	(2.34)	(2.82)	(3.15)	(3.71)	(4.43)	(4.24)	(6.26)
VW portfolios	Excess return	0.35	0.49	0.45	0.46	0.43	0.53	0.61	0.62	0.71	0.77	0.42
		(1.48)	(2.45)	(2.18)	(2.11)	(2.22)	(2.80)	(2.99)	(3.06)	(3.53)	(3.28)	(2.10)
	CAPM α	-0.14	0.03	-0.01	-0.00	0.01	0.13	0.21	0.22	0.29	0.32	0.46
		(-1.42)	(0.48)	(-0.13)	(-0.00)	(0.11)	(1.53)	(1.91)	(1.86)	(2.53)	(2.42)	(2.23)

breakpoints (NYSE breakpoints). While most analyses of the value premium in the empirical asset pricing literature use breakpoints calculated using the full sample of stocks (Fama and French (1992), NYSE/AMEX/NASDAQ breakpoints), we perform the univariate portfolio analyses using both sets of breakpoints to demonstrate the robustness of the effect.[7] In all of the analyses, we sort all stocks in the sample (not just NYSE stocks) into the portfolios. Thus, the only difference is in the calculation of the breakpoints.

The results of the univariate portfolio analyses of the relation between *BM* and future stock returns are presented in Table 10.4. Panel A presents the results for portfolios formed using NYSE/AMEX/NASDAQ breakpoints. The top of the panel presents average characteristics for the stocks in each of the decile portfolios. By construction, the average value of *BM* (ln *BM*) increases monotonically from 0.14 (−2.18) for portfolio 1 to 2.95 (0.89) for portfolio 10. Average market capitalization (*MktCap*) is decreasing monotonically from about $2.2 billion for stocks in the lowest *BM* decile portfolio to $334 million for stocks in the portfolio with high-*BM* stocks. Beta (β) also exhibits a strong negative relation with *BM*, as average β decreases monotonically from 1.05 for stocks in the low-*BM* portfolio to 0.60 for stocks in the high-*BM* portfolio. The negative relations between *BM* and each of *MktCap* and β are consistent with the negative correlations observed in Table 10.2. The row labeled % NYSE indicates the percent of stocks in the given portfolio that are listed on the NYSE. The table indicates that NYSE stocks tend to have relatively moderate values of *BM*, as portfolios consisting of high-*BM* stocks and portfolios consisting of low-*BM* stocks tend to hold a smaller percentage of NYSE-listed stocks. The row labeled *n* indicates that, as necessitated by the use of the same sample for breakpoint calculation and portfolio creation, the average number of stocks in each portfolio is the same (341).

The middle section (EW portfolios) of Panel A presents the average excess returns and risk-adjusted returns relative to the CAPM risk model for the equal-weighted *BM*-sorted portfolio. The results indicate a strong positive relation between *BM* and expected stock returns. The average excess returns of the portfolios increase monotonically from 0.08% per month for decile portfolio 1 to 1.42% per month for the decile portfolio 10. The average return of the difference portfolio of 1.34% per month is highly statistically significant with a Newey and West (1987)-adjusted *t*-statistic of 6.06. Adjusting the returns of the portfolios using the CAPM risk model has very little effect on the results. The CAPM alpha of the decile portfolios increases monotonically from −0.57% per month for the low-*BM* portfolio to 0.94% per month for the high-*BM* portfolio. The alpha of the difference portfolio of 1.51% per month is once again highly statistically significant with a *t*-statistic of 6.57.

---

[7] It is worth noting that when examining the relation between market capitalization and future stock returns, Fama and French (1992) form univariate decile portfolios using only NYSE stocks to calculate the breakpoints. However, when forming univariate decile portfolios based on the book-to-market ratio, Fama and French (1992) use all stocks in their sample to calculate the breakpoints. Additionally, when Fama and French (1992) create their size (*SMB*) and book-to-market (*HML*, to be discussed in Section 10.6) factors, they use only NYSE-listed stocks to calculate the breakpoints.

The average returns and CAPM alphas for value-weighted portfolios are presented at the bottom of Panel A (VW portfolios). The results indicate that, while value-weighting does result in a substantial reduction in the magnitude of the average return and alpha of the difference portfolio, evidence of the value premium remains strong in value-weighted portfolios. The average excess returns of the value-weighted *BM*-sorted decile portfolios increases monotonically from 0.31% per month for decile portfolio 1 to 0.88% per month for decile portfolio 10. The 0.57% per month (*t*-statistic = 2.40) generated by the 10-1 portfolio is once again economically large and highly statistically significant. As with the equal-weighted portfolios, risk-adjusting the returns of the value-weighted portfolios has little effect on the results. The CAPM alpha of the value-weighted difference portfolio of 0.62% per month (*t*-statistic = 2.55) is very similar in magnitude and statistical significance to the average return. Furthermore, the CAPM alphas of the decile portfolios increase nearly monotonically (the exception is decile portfolio 3) from −0.20% per month for decile portfolio one to 0.43% per month for decile portfolio 10.

The results of the portfolio analysis using NYSE breakpoints are presented in Panel B of Table 10.4. The Characteristics portion of Panel B indicates that the average values of *BM*, ln *BM*, *MktCap*, and β in each of the decile portfolios are very similar to the corresponding portfolios created using NYSE/AMEX/NASDAQ breakpoints presented in Panel A. Interestingly, Panel B indicates that the percentage of NYSE stocks in each of the decile portfolios is higher when using NYSE breakpoints than when using NYSE/AMEX/NASDAQ breakpoints. At first, this may not seem logical. The reason for this, however, is that by calculating the breakpoints using only NYSE stocks, there are no longer the same number of stocks in each portfolio. The low-*BM* and high-*BM* portfolios tend to have more stocks than the portfolios containing stocks with moderate levels of *BM*. The reason for this is that a disproportionate number of non-NYSE stocks tend to have values of *BM* that appear extreme (high or low) relative to the subset of NYSE stocks that are used to calculate the breakpoints. For this reason, portfolios containing high-*BM* stocks as well as those containing low-*BM* stocks tend to hold more stocks than the portfolios holding stocks with more moderate *BM* values.

The average excess returns of the equal-weighted and value-weighted portfolios formed using NYSE breakpoints are also very similar to those of the NYSE/AMEX/NASDAQ breakpoint portfolios. The main difference is that the average return and CAPM alpha of the 10-1 portfolio are slightly lower when using NYSE breakpoints than when using NYSE/AMEX/NASDAQ breakpoints. When using NYSE breakpoints, the average return and CAPM alpha of the equal-weighted 10-1 portfolio are 1.13% and 1.29% per month, with *t*-statistics of 5.71 and 6.26, respectively. Value-weighted portfolios generate 10-1 average portfolio returns of 0.42% per month (*t*-statistic = 2.10) and a CAPM alpha of 0.46% per month (*t*-statistic = 2.23). For the equal-weighted portfolios, the returns and alphas are monotonically increasing across the *BM* deciles, while for value-weighted portfolios, monotonicity nearly holds. Thus, while the average returns and alphas of the 10-1 portfolios are slightly lower when using NYSE breakpoints instead of

NYSE/AMEX/NASDAQ breakpoints, the positive relation between *BM* and future stock returns remains strong in all univariate portfolio analyses.

In summary, the univariate portfolio results indicate a strong positive relation between book-to-market ratio and expected stock returns. This phenomenon is known as the value premium, as value stocks (stock with high book-to-market ratios) tend to outperform growth stocks (stocks with low book-to-market ratios). The results are robust when using equal-weighted or value-weighted portfolios although equal-weighted portfolios produce stronger results than value-weighted portfolios. The results are also robust when using NYSE/AMEX/NASDAQ breakpoints or NYSE breakpoints. To be consistent with the prevalent practice in the empirical asset pricing literature, for the remainder of the portfolio analyses presented in this chapter, we use breakpoints constructed using all stocks in the sample (NYSE/AMEX/NASDAQ breakpoints).

10.5.2 Bivariate Portfolio Analysis

The results from the correlation and univariate portfolio analyses indicate that there are strong cross-sectional relations between book-to-market ratio (*BM*) and each of beta (β) and market capitalization (*MktCap*). In this section, we use bivariate portfolio analyses to examine whether the value premium detected in the univariate portfolio analyses can be explained by either of these variables. We use both dependent-sort and independent-sort analyses and sort stocks into five quintile groups based on the control variable (β or *MktCap*) and five quintile groups based on *BM*. The breakpoints are calculated using all stocks in the sample. We perform each analysis using both equal-weighted and value-weighted portfolios.

We begin by presenting the results of dependent-sort portfolio analyses of the relation between *BM* and future stock returns after controlling for the effects of β or *MktCap*. Thus, β or *MktCap* is the first sort variable and *BM* is the second sort variable. Panel A of Table 10.5 presents the average return and CAPM alphas for the difference portfolio that is long high-*BM* stocks and short low-*BM* stocks within each quintile of the given control variable. Focusing first on the results when controlling for β, the table indicates that β cannot explain the value premium. The equal-weighted (Weights = EW) average *BM* difference portfolio (column Control Avg), across all quintiles of β, generates an average monthly return of 0.93% and CAPM alpha of 0.97% with Newey and West (1987) *t*-statistics of 6.51 and 6.74, respectively. When value-weighted (Weights = VW) portfolios are used, the average monthly return and CAPM alpha of the average *BM* difference portfolio are 0.46% (*t*-statistic = 3.37) and 0.47% (*t*-statistic = 3.36). This shows that after controlling for β, the value premium is economically and statistically strong even in value-weighted portfolios.

When using equal-weighted portfolios, the results demonstrate that the value premium is strong not only in the average β quintile but also within each individual β quintile. The average monthly returns (CAPM alphas) of the equal-weighted *BM* difference portfolios range from 0.72% with a *t*-statistic of 4.85 (0.76% with a *t*-statistic of 5.10) for β quintile 3 to 1.21% with a *t*-statistic of 6.56 (1.25% with

TABLE 10.5   Bivariate Dependent-Sort Portfolio Analysis

This table presents the results of bivariate dependent-sort portfolio analyses of the relation between BM and future stock returns after controlling for the effect of each of β and $MktCap$ (control variables). Each month, all stocks in the CRSP sample are sorted into five groups based on an ascending sort of one of the control variables. Within each control variable group, all stocks are sorted into five portfolios based on an ascending sort of BM. The quintile breakpoints used to create the portfolios are calculated using all stocks in the CRSP sample. Panel A presents the average return and CAPM alpha (in percent per month) of the long–short zero-cost portfolios that are long the fifth BM quintile portfolio and short the first BM quintile portfolio in each quintile, as well as for the average quintile, of the control variable. Panel B presents the average return and CAPM alpha for the average control variable quintile portfolio within each BM quintile, as well as for the difference between the fifth and first BM quintiles. Results for equal-weighted (Weights = EW) and value-weighted (Weights = VW) portfolios are shown. t-statistics (in parentheses), adjusted following Newey and West (1987) using six lags, testing the null hypothesis that the average return or alpha is equal to zero, are shown in parentheses.

Panel A: BM Difference Portfolios

Control	Weights	Value	Control 1	Control 2	Control 3	Control 4	Control 5	Control Avg
β	EW	Return	0.97	0.83	0.72	0.94	1.21	0.93
			(5.57)	(5.19)	(4.85)	(5.53)	(6.56)	(6.51)
		CAPM α	1.02	0.87	0.76	0.97	1.25	0.97
			(5.93)	(5.45)	(5.10)	(5.68)	(6.80)	(6.74)
	VW	Return	0.67	0.36	0.40	0.53	0.35	0.46
			(3.46)	(2.18)	(2.51)	(2.79)	(1.50)	(3.37)
		CAPM α	0.65	0.41	0.40	0.54	0.37	0.47
			(3.37)	(2.47)	(2.43)	(2.78)	(1.53)	(3.36)
$MktCap$	EW	Return	0.72	1.17	0.96	0.67	0.30	0.76
			(3.06)	(4.95)	(4.11)	(2.95)	(1.51)	(3.90)
		CAPM α	0.87	1.31	1.14	0.86	0.46	0.93
			(3.79)	(5.54)	(4.99)	(3.76)	(2.25)	(4.77)
	VW	Return	0.87	1.16	0.91	0.67	0.17	0.76
			(3.60)	(4.78)	(3.82)	(3.00)	(0.92)	(3.90)
		CAPM α	1.01	1.30	1.10	0.85	0.25	0.90
			(4.23)	(5.33)	(4.70)	(3.79)	(1.31)	(4.64)

Panel B: Average Control Variable Portfolios

Control	Weights	Value	BM 1	BM 2	BM 3	BM 4	BM 5	BM 5-1
β	EW	Return	0.32	0.65	0.79	0.94	1.25	0.93
			(1.00)	(2.29)	(2.96)	(3.45)	(3.83)	(6.51)
		CAPM α	−0.24	0.12	0.30	0.45	0.73	0.97
			(−1.47)	(0.92)	(2.24)	(3.32)	(4.05)	(6.74)

(*continued*)

TABLE 10.5   (*Continued*)

			Panel B: Average Control Variable Portfolios					
Control	Weights	Value	Control 1	Control 2	Control 3	Control 4	Control 5	Control Avg
	VW	Return	0.34	0.42	0.51	0.59	0.81	0.46
			(1.62)	(2.15)	(2.62)	(3.06)	(3.71)	(3.37)
		CAPM α	−0.10	−0.01	0.10	0.18	0.38	0.47
			(−1.37)	(−0.20)	(1.51)	(2.35)	(3.58)	(3.36)
MktCap	EW	Return	0.33	0.71	0.87	0.93	1.10	0.76
			(0.93)	(2.39)	(3.14)	(3.50)	(3.86)	(3.90)
		CAPM α	−0.30	0.18	0.37	0.47	0.63	0.93
			(−1.52)	(1.15)	(2.71)	(3.42)	(4.02)	(4.77)
	VW	Return	0.23	0.57	0.76	0.83	0.99	0.76
			(0.67)	(2.02)	(2.82)	(3.25)	(3.57)	(3.90)
		CAPM α	−0.38	0.04	0.26	0.37	0.52	0.90
			(−2.08)	(0.33)	(2.08)	(2.97)	(3.45)	(4.64)

a t-statistic of 6.80) for β quintile 5. When value-weighted portfolios are used, the value premium exists in all stocks except those with the highest values of β. In quintiles 1 through 4 of β, the value-weighted average returns and CAPM alphas for the *BM* 5-1 portfolios are each economically large and highly statistically significant. In quintile 5 of β, however, the average return and alpha of the *BM* difference portfolio is statistically indistinguishable from zero.

The results are similar when controlling for market capitalization (*MktCap*). When *MktCap* is used as the first sort variable, the results of the dependent-sort bivariate portfolio analyses show that the average *BM* difference portfolio (column Control Avg) generates an equal-weighted average return of 0.76% per month (t-statistic = 3.90) and a CAPM alpha of 0.93% per month (t-statistic = 4.77). When value-weighted portfolios are used, the average monthly return and CAPM alpha of this portfolio of 0.76% (t-statistic = 3.90) and 0.90% (t-statistic = 4.64), respectively, are very similar to those of the equal-weighted portfolios. It is not surprising, in this case, that the equal-weighted and value-weighted portfolios give very similar results. The reason for this is that, by sorting first on *MktCap*, we have already grouped the stocks by *MktCap*. Since all stocks in each of the portfolios already have similar values of *MktCap*, weighting the portfolios using *MktCap* is unlikely to have a substantial effect on the portfolio's holdings and, therefore, on its returns. The results in Panel A also indicate that, with the exception of the highest *MktCap* quintile, the positive relation between *BM* and future stock returns is robust across all *MktCap* quintiles. Even within quintile 5 of *MktCap*, which contains only the largest stocks in the sample, the equal-weighted 5-1 *BM* portfolio generates an average monthly return of 0.30% and CAPM alpha of 0.46%, with the latter being statistically significant (t-statistic $= 2.25$). When value-weighted portfolios are used, the BM difference portfolio in the fifth $MktCap$ quintile generates a statistically insignificant average return of 0.17% (t-statistic $= 0.92$) and alpha of 0.25% (t-statistic $= 1.31$) per month. These results are consistent with the findings of Loughran (1997), who demonstrates that the value effect is not present in large capitalization stocks.

In Panel B of Table 10.5, we present results for the average portfolios, across all quintiles of the control variable and within each quintile of BM. The results in Panel B allow us to examine the patterns in the returns across the different BM quintiles after controlling for β or $MktCap$. The results indicate that, after controlling for β or $MktCap$, the average returns and CAPM alphas of the BM portfolios are mono- tonically increasing across the quintiles of BM. In most cases, the low-BM portfolio fails to generate a statistically significant average return or alpha. This indicates that the value premium is primarily driven by stocks with high BM values. The exception to this is the value-weighted portfolio for quintile one of BM after controlling for $MktCap$, which generates a statistically significant negative CAPM alpha of -0.38% per month (t-statistic $= -2.08$).

Having examined the relation between BM and future stock returns, after con- trolling for β and $MktCap$, using dependent-sort portfolio analyses, we now perform similar analyses, this time using independently sorted portfolios. Table 10.6 presents the results of the bivariate independent-sort portfolio analysis using β and BM as the sort variables. Results for equal-weighted (value-weighted) portfolios are presented in Panel A (Panel B).

We first look at the returns and alphas of equal-weighted portfolios (Panel A) that are long high-BM stocks and short low-BM stocks in each quintile of β. The row labeled BM 5-1 indicates that within each quintile of β, the BM 5-1 portfolio generates an economically large and statistically significant average return ranging from 0.79% per month to 1.12% per month. For the average β quintile, the BM 5-1 portfolio generates an average return of 0.93% per month with an associated t-statistic of 6.05. Subjecting the returns of the BM 5-1 portfolios to the CAPM risk model does little to explain these results. In fact, the CAPM alphas, in each β quintile as well as for the average β quintile, are higher and more statistically significant than the corresponding average returns. The BM 5-1 portfolio for the average β quintile generates a CAPM alpha of 0.99% per month (t-statistic $= 6.39$).

The independent-sort portfolio analysis also allows us to examine the relation between β and expected stock returns after controlling for BM. The results are quite consistent with what was observed in the univariate portfolio analysis using β as a sort variable shown in Section 8.5.1 and Table 8.4. After controlling for BM, the returns of the β 5-1 portfolios are negative, economically small, and statistically insignificant, with the exception of the β 5-1 portfolio in the lowest BM quintile. This result contra- dicts the main prediction of the Capital Asset Pricing Model (CAPM, Sharpe (1964), Lintner (1965), Mossin (1966)) of a positive relation between β and expected stock returns. The CAPM alphas of the β 5-1 portfolio are all negative, economically large, and highly statistically significant. For the average BM quintile, the β 5-1 portfolio generates a CAPM alpha of -0.56% per month (t-statistic $= -3.10$).

Panel B of Table 10.6 shows that, consistent with the results of the dependent-sort analysis, the value premium is detected by the independent-sort portfolio analysis that controls for β even when value-weighted portfolios are used. The average BM

TABLE 10.6   Bivariate Independent-Sort Portfolio Analysis—Control for β

This table presents the results of bivariate independent-sort portfolio analyses of the relation between BM and future stock returns after controlling for the effect of β. Each month, all stocks in the CRSP sample are sorted into five groups based on an ascending sort of β. All stocks are independently sorted into five groups based on an ascending sort of BM. The quintile breakpoints used to create the groups are calculated using all stocks in the CRSP sample. The intersections of the β and BM groups are used to form 25 portfolios. The table presents the average one-month-ahead excess return (in percent per month) for each of the 25 portfolios as well as for the average β quintile portfolio within each quintile of BM and the average BM quintile portfolio within each β quintile. Also shown are the average return and CAPM alpha of a long–short zero-cost portfolio that is long the fifth BM (β) quintile portfolio and short the first BM (β) quintile portfolio in each β (BM) quintile. t-statistics (in parentheses), adjusted following Newey and West (1987) using six lags, testing the null hypothesis that the average return or alpha is equal to zero, are shown in parentheses. Panel A presents results for equal-weighted portfolios. Panel B presents results for value-weighted portfolios.

	β 1	β 2	β 3	β 4	β 5	β Avg	β 5-1	β 5-1 CAPM α
Panel A: Equal-Weighted Portfolios								
BM 1	0.48	0.42	0.40	0.28	0.05	0.33	−0.42	−0.77
							(−1.93)	(−3.46)
BM 2	0.60	0.67	0.66	0.61	0.59	0.63	−0.01	−0.41
							(−0.06)	(−2.05)
BM 3	0.91	0.77	0.94	0.86	0.75	0.84	−0.16	−0.57
							(−0.75)	(−2.68)
BM 4	0.98	0.98	0.96	0.91	0.97	0.96	−0.01	−0.44
							(−0.05)	(−2.35)
BM 5	1.37	1.32	1.19	1.24	1.17	1.26	−0.20	−0.59
							(−0.82)	(−2.70)
BM Avg	0.87	0.83	0.83	0.78	0.71		−0.16	−0.56
							(−0.83)	(−3.10)
BM 5-1	0.89	0.90	0.79	0.96	1.12	0.93		
	(4.32)	(5.09)	(4.65)	(5.45)	(5.58)	(6.05)		
BM 5-1 CAPM α	0.99	0.94	0.83	1.00	1.17	0.99		
	(5.00)	(5.36)	(4.93)	(5.57)	(5.86)	(6.39)		

TABLE 10.6   *(Continued)*

	Panel B: Value-Weighted Portfolios							
	β 1	β 2	β 3	β 4	β 5	β Avg	β 5-1	β 5-1 CAPM α
BM 1	0.39	0.30	0.40	0.24	0.27	0.32	−0.12	−0.49
							(−0.40)	(−1.81)
BM 2	0.33	0.47	0.38	0.57	0.31	0.41	−0.02	−0.37
							(−0.10)	(−1.69)
BM 3	0.52	0.48	0.48	0.50	0.63	0.52	0.11	−0.25
							(0.44)	(−1.06)
BM 4	0.70	0.61	0.64	0.54	0.63	0.63	−0.07	−0.48
							(−0.29)	(−2.37)
BM 5	0.93	0.77	0.82	0.76	0.70	0.80	−0.23	−0.64
							(−0.90)	(−2.53)
BM Avg	0.57	0.52	0.54	0.53	0.51		−0.07	−0.45
							(−0.30)	(−2.33)
BM 5-1	0.55	0.47	0.42	0.52	0.43	0.48		
	(2.36)	(2.66)	(2.48)	(2.63)	(1.87)	(3.30)		
BM 5-1	0.56	0.51	0.42	0.51	0.40	0.48		
CAPM α	(2.43)	(2.94)	(2.45)	(2.53)	(1.70)	(3.28)		

5-1 portfolio generates an average return and CAPM alpha of 0.48% per month with corresponding *t*-statistics of 3.30 and 3.28, respectively. The positive relation between *BM* and expected returns exists in all but the highest β quintile. Even in the highest β quintile, however, the results remain marginally statistically significant and economically large.

As for the relation between β and future stock returns after controlling for *BM*, the results indicate that within each *BM* quintile, the β 5-1 portfolio generates negative but insignificant average returns and negative and at least marginally significant CAPM alpha. For the average *BM* quintile, the CAPM alpha of the β 5-1 portfolio is an economically important and highly statistically significant −0.45% per month (*t*-statistic = −2.33).

The results of bivariate independent-sort portfolio analyses using *MktCap* and *BM* as the sort variables are presented in Table 10.7. The results for equal-weighted portfolios, presented in Panel A, demonstrate that *MktCap* cannot explain the value premium. Within each quintile of *MktCap*, the *BM* 5-1 portfolio generates economically large and highly statistically significant average returns and CAPM alphas.[8]

---

[8]The average return for the *BM* 5-1 portfolio in *MktCap* quintile 5 is only marginally statistically significant.

TABLE 10.7 Bivariate Independent-Sort Portfolio Analysis—Control for *MktCap*

This table presents the results of bivariate independent-sort portfolio analyses of the relation between *BM* and future stock returns after controlling for the effect of *MktCap*. Each month, all stocks in the CRSP sample are sorted into five groups based on an ascending sort of *MktCap*. All stocks are independently sorted into five groups based on an ascending sort of *BM*. The quintile breakpoints used to create the groups are calculated using all stocks in the CRSP sample. The intersections of the *MktCap* and *BM* groups are used to form 25 portfolios. The table presents the average one-month-ahead excess return (in percent per month) for each of the 25 portfolios as well as for the average *MktCap* quintile portfolio within each quintile of *BM* and the average *BM* quintile within each *MktCap* quintile. Also shown are the average return and CAPM alpha of a long–short zero-cost portfolio that is long the fifth *BM* (*MktCap*) quintile portfolio and short the first *BM* (*MktCap*) quintile portfolio in each *MktCap* (*BM*) quintile. *t*-statistics (in parentheses), adjusted following Newey and West (1987) using six lags, testing the null hypothesis that the average return or alpha is equal to zero, are shown in parentheses. Panel A presents results for equal-weighted portfolios. Panel B presents results for value-weighted portfolios.

Panel A: Equal-Weighted Portfolios								
	MktCap 1	*MktCap* 2	*MktCap* 3	*MktCap* 4	*MktCap* 5	*MktCap* Avg	*MktCap* 5-1	*MktCap* 5-1 CAPM α
BM 1	1.12	−0.09	0.04	0.29	0.37	0.34	−0.75	−0.68
							(−1.96)	(−1.83)
BM 2	1.25	0.38	0.60	0.61	0.50	0.67	−0.75	−0.71
							(−2.41)	(−2.33)
BM 3	1.65	0.76	0.77	0.72	0.60	0.90	−1.05	−1.13
							(−2.99)	(−2.48)
BM 4	1.52	0.84	0.87	0.88	0.65	0.95	−0.87	−0.82
							(−3.48)	(−3.35)
BM 5	1.73	1.06	0.96	0.96	0.70	1.08	−1.03	−1.02
							(−3.94)	(−3.89)
BM Avg	1.46	0.59	0.65	0.69	0.56		−0.89	−0.87
							(−3.24)	(−3.16)
BM 5-1	0.61	1.15	0.92	0.67	0.34	0.74		
	(2.31)	(4.80)	(3.83)	(2.89)	(1.72)	(3.65)		
BM 5-1 CAPM α	0.80	1.31	1.09	0.83	0.46	0.90		
	(3.21)	(5.51)	(4.66)	(3.45)	(2.33)	(4.51)		

TABLE 10.7   *(Continued)*

	Panel B: Value-Weighted Portfolios							
	$MktCap\ 1$	$MktCap\ 2$	$MktCap\ 3$	$MktCap\ 4$	$MktCap\ 5$	$MktCap$ Avg	$MktCap$ 5-1	$MktCap$ 5-1 CAPM α
BM 1	0.48	−0.07	0.08	0.30	0.35	0.23	−0.13	0.02
							(−0.32)	(0.04)
BM 2	0.76	0.37	0.59	0.61	0.43	0.55	−0.34	−0.24
							(−1.06)	(−0.78)
BM 3	1.01	0.75	0.79	0.70	0.45	0.74	−0.56	−0.52
							(−1.89)	(−1.64)
BM 4	1.09	0.87	0.87	0.89	0.53	0.85	−0.57	−0.50
							(−2.15)	(−1.96)
BM 5	1.31	1.05	0.95	0.96	0.55	0.97	−0.76	−0.72
							(−2.96)	(−2.86)
BM Avg	0.93	0.60	0.66	0.69	0.46		−0.47	−0.39
							(−1.66)	(−1.46)
BM 5-1	0.83	1.12	0.87	0.66	0.20	0.74		
	(3.10)	(4.58)	(3.57)	(2.83)	(1.04)	(3.65)		
BM 5-1 CAPM α	1.01	1.28	1.05	0.81	0.27	0.88		
	(3.92)	(5.22)	(4.39)	(3.39)	(1.38)	(4.40)		

Averaged across the *MktCap* quintiles, the *BM* difference portfolio generates an average monthly return of 0.74% (*t*-statistic = 3.65) and CAPM alpha of 0.90% (*t*-statistic = 4.51). The results are very similar to those generated by the dependent-sort portfolio analysis presented in Table 10.5.

When using equal-weighted portfolios (Panel A), Table 10.7 demonstrates that the negative relation between *MktCap* and expected stock returns persists after controlling for the effect of the value premium. Within each quintile of *BM*, the average return and alpha of the *MktCap* difference portfolio are negative, large in magnitude, and statistically significant.[9] For the average *BM* quintile, the *MktCap* difference portfolio produces average returns of −0.89% per month (*t*-statistic = −3.24) and CAPM alpha of −0.87% per month (*t*-statistic = −3.16).

Turning now to the value-weighted portfolio results shown in Panel B, consistent with the previous univariate and dependent-sort bivariate portfolio analyses, the

[9] The *MktCap* 5-1 CAPM alpha for quintile 1 of *BM* of −0.68% per month is only marginally statistically significant with a *t*-statistic of −1.83.

results indicate that the value premium is robust. In the average *MktCap* quintile, the *BM* 5-1 portfolio generates average monthly returns of 0.74% (*t*-statistic = 3.65) and CAPM alpha of 0.88% (*t*-statistic = 4.40). As documented by Loughran (1997) and in the dependent-sort analyses presented earlier in this chapter, the value-weighted portfolio analysis indicates that the value premium does not exist in the highest *MktCap* quintile.

Finally, we turn our attention to the relation between *MktCap* and expected stock returns, after controlling for *BM*, in value-weighted bivariate independent-sort portfolio analysis. The results indicate that the size effect exists only among stocks in quintiles 4 and 5 of *BM*. Stocks with low values of *BM* do not exhibit the size effect in value-weighted portfolios. For the average *BM* quintile, despite being economically quite substantial in magnitude, the average return and CAPM alpha of the *MktCap* 5-1 portfolio of −0.47% and −0.39% per month, respectively, are statistically indistinguishable from zero.

In summary, the results of the dependent-sort and independent-sort bivariate portfolio analyses demonstrate that the value premium cannot be explained by either beta or market capitalization. The negative alpha of portfolios that are long high-beta stocks and short-beta stock persists after controlling for the effect of book-to-market ratio, indicating that the value premium cannot explain the lack of a relation between beta and future stock returns. Similarly, the size effect, which only truly exists in equal-weighted portfolios, is not explained by book-to-market ratio.

10.5.3 Fama–MacBeth Regression Analysis

We continue our examination of the relation between book-to-market ratio (*BM*) and future stock returns using (Fama and MacBeth 1973, FM hereafter) regression analysis. We employ a univariate cross-sectional regression specification using *BM* as the lone independent variable as well as specifications that control for the effects of beta (β) and stock size (*Size*, the log of market capitalization). To account for the possibility that the high skewness of the cross-sectional distribution of *BM* will make the results of FM regressions using *BM* unreliable, we repeat the analyses using the natural log of the book-to-market ratio (ln *BM*) in place of *BM*.

The results of the FM regression analyses, presented in Table 10.8, indicate a strong positive relation between book-to-market ratio and expected stock returns, regardless of whether *BM* or ln *BM* is used as the measure of book-to-market ratio. The univariate regression specification using *BM* as the only independent variable (specification (1)) generates an average slope coefficient on *BM* of 0.41 with a Newey and West (1987) *t*-statistic of 5.30. When β is included as a control (specification (2)), the average coefficient drops to 0.34 with a *t*-statistic of 5.03. When *Size* is the only control variable (specification (3)), the regressions produce an average coefficient of 0.27 (*t*-statistic = 3.32) on *BM*. Finally, when both β and *MktCap* are included as controls, the average coefficient on *BM* of 0.21 remains highly statistically significant, with a *t*-statistic of 3.16. When ln *BM* is used (specifications (5)-(8)) instead of *BM*, the results are similar. All specifications detect a positive and highly statistically

TABLE 10.8   Fama–MacBeth Regression Analysis

This table presents the results of Fama and MacBeth (1973) regression analyses of the relation between expected stock returns and book-to-market ratio. Each column in the table presents results for a different cross-sectional regression specification. The dependent variable in all specifications is the one-month-ahead excess stock return. The independent variables are indicated in the first column. Independent variables are winsorized at the 0.5% level on a monthly basis. The table presents average slope and intercept coefficients along with t-statistics (in parentheses), adjusted following Newey and West (1987) using six lags, testing the null hypothesis that the average coefficient is equal to zero. The rows labeled Adj. R^2 and n present the average adjusted R-squared and the number of data points, respectively, for the cross-sectional regressions.

	(1)	(2)	(3)	(4)	(5)	(6)	(7)	(8)
BM	0.41	0.34	0.27	0.21				
	(5.30)	(5.03)	(3.32)	(3.16)				
ln BM					0.44	0.39	0.31	0.27
					(6.18)	(6.26)	(3.78)	(4.13)
β		−0.17		0.03		−0.12		0.08
		(−1.30)		(0.16)		(−0.97)		(0.49)
Size			−0.15	−0.16			−0.14	−0.16
			(−3.00)	(−2.68)			(−2.81)	(−2.66)
Intercept	0.42	0.62	1.20	1.28	0.98	1.04	1.56	1.56
	(1.44)	(2.55)	(2.37)	(2.88)	(3.48)	(4.18)	(3.35)	(3.68)
Adj. R^2	0.01	0.02	0.02	0.04	0.01	0.02	0.02	0.04
n	3391	3373	3391	3373	3391	3373	3391	3373

significant relation between ln BM and future stock returns, regardless of which set of controls is included in the specification. In fact, the statistical significance of the coefficient on ln BM is even greater than that of the corresponding regression specification using BM. Consistent with the results from previous chapters, regardless of specification, the OLS regressions detect no relation between β and future stock returns and a strong negative relation between $Size$ and future stock returns.

We next examine the economic significance of the average coefficients on BM and ln BM generated by the FM regression analyses. We focus on the specifications that employ the full set of controls (specifications (4) and (8)). Multiplying the coefficient on BM of 0.21 by BM's standard deviation of 1.14 (see Table 10.1) indicates that a one-standard-deviation difference in BM is associated with at 0.24% (0.21 × 1.14) difference in expected monthly return. A similar analysis using ln BM, which has a standard deviation of 0.87, indicates that a one-standard-deviation difference in ln BM is associated with a 0.23% (0.27 × 0.87) difference in expected monthly stock returns. Thus, the results using BM and ln BM appear to be highly similar. To examine the difference in expected returns between stocks with very high and very low levels of BM, we multiply the average regression coefficient of 0.21 by the difference in average BM between the highest and lowest BM quintile portfolios from the univariate portfolio analysis of 2.81 (2.95 − 0.14, see Panel A of Table 10.4). Doing so indicates an average return difference of 0.59% per month between stocks in the top and bottom quintiles of *BM*. This number, while quite high in economic terms, is much smaller than the average return of the equal-weighted *BM* 10-1 portfolio of 1.34% per month. Repeating the analysis using the results for ln *BM* indicates an average return difference of 0.83% (0.27×3.07) between stocks in the highest and lowest quintiles of *BM*. While this result is closer to the 1.34% generated by the *BM* 10-1 portfolio, it remains substantially lower. These results indicate that the value premium may be driven by stocks with very high and very low values of *BM*.

To summarize, the FM regression analyses provide strong evidence of a value premium and no evidence that the value premium is a manifestation of the relations between β or *MktCap* and future stock returns. Furthermore, the results are similar regardless of whether *BM* or ln *BM* is used as the measure of value, indicating that the highly skewed distribution of *BM* does not have a substantial impact on the effectiveness of the FM regression methodology. For this reason, and for consistency with the majority of empirical asset pricing research, throughout the remainder of this book, we will use *BM* as our measure of value.

10.6   THE VALUE FACTOR

Fama and French (1993) claim that the value premium indicates that book-to-market ratio is a proxy for a stock's sensitivity to a distress-risk factor. To approximate the returns associated with taking exposure to this risk factor, Fama and French (1993) create a zero-cost factor mimicking portfolio holding long positions in stocks with high book-to-market ratios and short positions in stocks with low book-to-market ratios. This portfolio is referred to as the *HML* portfolio, for high minus low.

To create the *HML* portfolio, each month, Fama and French (1993) sort all NYSE, American Stock Exchange (AMEX), and NASDAQ stocks into six portfolios based on market capitalization at the end of the most recent June ($MktCap^{FF}$, defined in Chapter 9) and book-to-market ratio (*BM*). The breakpoint dividing stocks into market capitalization groups is the median NYSE market capitalization. All NYSE, AMEX, and NASDAQ stocks are independently divided into three book-to-market ratio groups, with the breakpoints being the 30th and 70th percentiles of book-to-market ratio among NYSE stocks. The six portfolios are then taken to be the intersections of the two market capitalization-based groups and the three book-to-market-based groups. The stocks within each portfolio are value-weighted. These are the same six portfolios that were used to create the *SMB* factor that mimicks the returns associated with the size effect (see Section 9.6). The return of the *HML* portfolio is then taken to be the average return of the two portfolios that contain high book-to-market stocks (S/H and B/H, H refers to high book-to-market ratio, S and B refer to small and big stocks, respectively) minus the average return of the two portfolios holding low book-to-market stocks (S/L and B/L, L refers to low book-to-market ratio). The portfolio is designed to isolate the relation between book-to-market ratio and stock returns while controlling for the effect of market capitalization.

The *HML* portfolio generates an average monthly return (log return) of 0.40% (0.34%) for the period from July 1926 through December 2012. The standard deviation of the portfolio's monthly returns (log returns) is 3.52% (3.42%), resulting in an annualized Sharpe ratio of 0.40 (0.35).[10] The compounded return of the *HML* portfolio over this period is 3431%, giving a cumulative log return of 3.56. The correlation between the monthly returns (log returns) of the *HML* and market factor (*MKT*) is 0.22 (0.19), and that of the *HML* and *SMB* portfolio is 0.13 (0.10). The risk-adjusted alpha of the *HML* portfolio relative to the CAPM model, calculated as the estimated intercept term from a regression of the *HML* return on the excess return of the market portfolio, is 0.32% per month, with *t*-statistic, adjusted following Newey and West (1987) using six lags, of 2.66. The results indicate that the long-run performance of the *HML* portfolio cannot be explained by the market factor. Despite its zero-cost nature, the *HML* portfolio does exhibit moderate exposure to the market factor, as the estimated market sensitivity, or beta, of the *HML* portfolio is 0.14 (*t*-statistic = 1.73). To examine the abnormal returns of the *HML* portfolio after accounting for not only the market factor but also the size factor (*SMB*), we regress the returns of the *HML* portfolio on the *MKT* and *SMB* factors. The estimated alpha from this regression is 0.31% per month (*t*-statistic = 2.60), while the estimated sensitivities to the *MKT* and *SMB* factors are 0.13 (*t*-statistic = 1.66) and 0.07 (*t*-statistic = 0.67), respectively. Thus, the returns of the *HML* portfolio are not driven by sensitivity to the market or size factors.

The cumulative returns earned by investing in the *HML* portfolio from July 1926 through December 2012 are plotted in Figure 10.1. The solid line plots the total compounded return generated by the investment. The scale for this line is presented on the left side of the plot. The dashed line presents the cumulative sum of the monthly log returns for the *HML* portfolio, where the monthly log return is calculated as the natural log of one plus the return. The scale for this line is on the right side of the plot. The returns of the *HML* portfolio are reasonably steady, at least compared to those of the *SMB* portfolio (see Chapter 9, Figure 9.2). The most severe drawdown for the *HML* portfolio began in September 1998. From the beginning of September 1998 to the end of February 2000, the *HML* portfolio realized losses of 45%. The portfolio regained its previous maximum value in July 2001, only two years and 11 months after the previous high water mark had been achieved. The second largest drawdown began in September of 1933 and ended in March 1935, during which time the portfolio lost 42% of its value. This drawdown ended in February 1937, 3 years and six months after it began. Another prolonged drawdown commenced shortly thereafter in April 1937, reached a maximum loss of 37% in May 1940, and ended in February 1943. This drawdown of five years and 11 months was the longest drawdown ever realized by the *HML* portfolio. That being said, the second longest drawdown in the sample began in April 2007 and reached a maximum loss of 25% in February 2009. As of December 2012, five years and nine months after the drawdown began, the *HML* portfolio had not achieved its previous high water mark. Thus, it is likely that

[10]Monthly and daily *HML* portfolio returns are available from Kenneth French's data library at http://mba.tuck.dartmouth.edu/pages/faculty/ken.french/data_library.html.

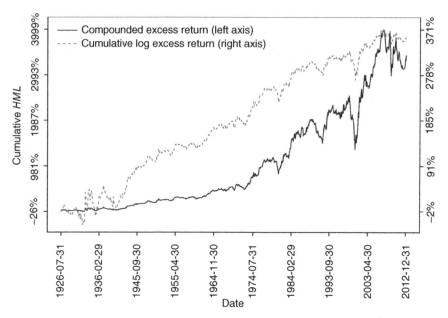

Figure 10.1   Cumulative Returns of *HML* Portfolio.
This figure plots the cumulate returns of the *HML* factor for the period from July 1926 through December 2012. The compounded excess return for month *t* is calculated as 100 times the cumulative product of one plus the monthly return up to and including the given month. The cumulate log excess return is calculated as the sum of the monthly log excess returns up to and including the given month

this drawdown will eclipse the drawdown beginning in 1937 as the most prolonged drawdown for the *HML* portfolio.

10.7   THE FAMA AND FRENCH THREE-FACTOR MODEL

Having completed our discussion of the *HML* portfolio, the final objective of this chapter is to introduce the Fama and French (1993) three-factor (FF) risk model. As with all risk models, the FF risk model is frequently used to assess whether a portfolio (or security) generates an average return that is not due to sensitivity to risk factors. As indicated by its name, the three-factor model includes three risk factors. The first is the market factor (*MKT*, discussed in Chapter 7), the second is the size factor (*SMB*, discussed in Chapter 9), and the third is value factor (*HML*). The returns of each of these portfolios are intended to proxy for the returns associated with taking one unit of the given risk, with minimal exposure to the other risks.

To test whether any given portfolio *p* (or security) generates an average excess return that is not a result of exposure to the market, size, or value factors, we regress the excess return of the portfolio *p* on the excess return of the *MKT*, *SMB*, and *HML* factor mimicking portfolios. The FF factor model can therefore be written as

$$r_{p,t} = \alpha_p + \beta_{MKT,p}MKT_t + \beta_{SMB,p}SMB_t + \beta_{HML,p}HML_t + \epsilon_{p,t} \qquad (10.5)$$

where $r_{p,t}$ is the excess return of the portfolio p during time period t; and MKT_t, SMB_t, and HML_t are the returns of the MKT, SMB, and HML factor mimicking portfolios, respectively. α_p represents the average excess return that is not attributable to the MKT, SMB, or HML portfolio returns. The betas ($\beta_{MKT,p}$, $\beta_{SMB,p}$, and $\beta_{HML,p}$) represent the sensitivities of the portfolio p to the corresponding risk factors. $\epsilon_{p,t}$ is the idiosyncratic portion of portfolio p's return during period t. The parameters α_p, $\beta_{MKT,p}$, $\beta_{SMB,p}$, and $\beta_{HML,p}$ are estimated by executing the time-series regression specified by equation (10.5). An estimated value of α_p that is statistically distinguishable from zero is indicative that the portfolio p generates a nonzero abnormal return (alpha), meaning that a portion of the portfolio's expected excess return is not a result of the portfolio's sensitivity to the market, size, and value risk factors.

10.8 SUMMARY

To summarize, in this chapter, we have examined the value premium by empirically investigating the relation between book-to-market ratio (*BM*) and stock returns. We began by defining the book-to-market ratio as the book value of shareholders' equity divided by its market value and discussed in detail the calculation of the most frequently used measure of this value. The most challenging aspect of the calculation is to make sure that the timings of the book equity and market equity values follow the convention set by Fama and French (1992, 1993).

We then used portfolio and Fama and MacBeth (1973) regression analyses to demonstrate that book-to-market ratio has a strong positive cross-sectional relation with expected stock returns, even after controlling for the effects of beta and size. Next, we introduced the *HML* factor mimicking portfolio that is designed to generate returns associated with exposure to the risk factor that drives the value premium. Finally, we discussed the Fama and French (1993) three-factor risk model, which takes the market factor, the size factor, and the value factor as the set of factors that should explain the returns of all assets.

REFERENCES

Ali, A., Hwang, L.-S., and Trombley, M. A. 2003. Arbitrage risk and the book-to-market anomaly. Journal of Financial Economics, 69(2), 355–373.

Asness, C. S., Moskowitz, T. J., and Pedersen, L. H. 2013. Value and momentum everywhere. Journal of Finance, 68(3), 929–985.

Basu, S. 1977. Investment performance of common stocks in relation to their price-earnings ratios: a test of the efficient market hypothesis. Journal of Finance, 32(3), 663–682.

Bhandari, L. C. 1988. Debt/equity ratio and expected common stock returns: empirical evidence. Journal of Finance, 43(2), 507–528.

Chan, K. C. and Chen, N.-F. 1991. Structural and return characteristics of small and large firms. Journal of Finance, 46(4), 1467–1484.

Chan, L. K. C., Jegadeesh, N., and Lakonishok, J. 1995. Evaluating the performance of values versus glamour stocks: the impact of selection bias. Journal of Financial Economics, 38(3), 269–296.

Chen, N.-F. and Zhang, F. 1998. Risk and return of value stocks. Journal of Business, 71(4), 501–535.

Chopra, N., Lakonishok, J., and Ritter, J. 1992. Measuring abnormal performance: do stocks overreact? Journal of Financial Economics, 31(2), 235–268.

Daniel, K. and Titman, S. 1997. Evidence on the characteristics of cross-sectional variation in stock returns. Journal of Finance, 52(1), 1–33.

De Bondt, W. F. M. and Thaler, R. 1985. Does the stock market overreact? Journal of Finance, 40(3), 793–805.

De Bondt, W. F. M. and Thaler, R. 1987. Further evidence on investor overreaction and stock market seasonality. Journal of Finance, 42(3), 557–581.

Fama, E. F. and French, K. R. 1992. The cross-section of expected stock returns. Journal of Finance, 47(2), 427–465.

Fama, E. F. and French, K. R. 1993. Common risk factors in the returns on stocks and bonds. Journal of Financial Economics, 33(1), 3–56.

Fama, E. F. and French, K. R. 1995. Size and book-to-market factors in earnings and returns. Journal of Finance, 50(1), 131–155.

Fama, E. F. and French, K. R. 2012. Size, value, and momentum in international stock returns. Journal of Financial Economics, 105(3), 457–472.

Fama, E. F. and MacBeth, J. D. 1973. Risk, return, and equilibrium: empirical tests. Journal of Political Economy, 81(3), 607.

Griffin, J. M. and Lemmon, M. 2002. Book-to-market equity, distress risk and stock returns. Journal of Finance, 57(5), 2317–2336.

Jaffe, J., Keim, D. B., and Westerfield, R. 1989. Earnings yields, market values, and stock returns. Journal of Finance, 44(1), 135–148.

Lakonishok, J., Shleifer, A., and Vishny, R. W. 1994. Contrarian investment, extrapolation, and risk. Journal of Finance, 49(5), 1541–1578.

La Porta, R. 1996. Expectations and the cross-section of stock returns. Journal of Finance, 51(5), 1715–1742.

La Porta, R., Lakonishok, J., Shleifer, A., and Vishny, R. W. 1997. Good news for value stocks: further evidence on market efficiency. Journal of Finance, 52(2), 859–874.

Lettau, M. and Ludvigson, S. 2001. Resurrecting the (C)CAPM: a cross-sectional test when risk premia are time-varying. Journal of Political Economy, 109(6), 1238–1287.

Lintner, J. 1965. Security prices, risk, and maximal gains from diversification. Journal of Finance, 20(4), 687–615.

Loughran, T. 1997. Book-to-market across firm size, exchange, and seasonality: is there an effect? Journal of Financial and Quantitative Analysis, 32(3), 249–268.

Merton, R. C. 1973. An intertemporal capital asset pricing model. Econometrica, 41(5), 867–887.

Mossin, J. 1966. Equilibrium in a capital asset market. Econometrica, 34(4), 768–783.

Newey, W. K. and West, K. D. 1987. A simple, positive semi-definite, heteroskedasticity and autocorrelation consistent covariance matrix. Econometrica, 55(3), 703–708.

Rosenberg, B., Reid, K., and Lanstein, R. 1985. Persuasive evidence of market inefficiency. The Journal of Portfolio Management, 11(3), 9–16.

Ross, S. A. 1976. The arbitrage theory of capital asset pricing. Journal of Economic Theory, 13(3), 341–360.

Sharpe, W. F. 1964. Capital asset prices: a theory of market equilibrium under conditions of risk. Journal of Finance, 19(3), 425–442.

Zhang, L. 2005. The value premium. Journal of Finance, 60(1), 67–103.

11

THE MOMENTUM EFFECT

Many studies have shown that previous stock returns have the ability to predict future stock returns in the cross section. One of the most prominent such phenomena, documented by Jegadeesh and Titman (1993) and known as the medium-term momentum effect, is that stocks that have performed well in the medium-term past (six to 12 months) are more likely to outperform in the future. While Jegadeesh and Titman (1993) is the most commonly cited study exemplifying this phenomenon, variations of this effect are examined in previous work. For example, Levy (1967) shows that relative strength, measured as the ratio of the current stock price to the prior 27-week moving-average stock price, is positively related to future stock returns.[1] Several papers, such as Fama and French (2012), Asness, Moskowitz, and Pedersen (2013), and Jostova, Nikolova, and Philipov (2013), find evidence of the momentum phenomenon in international equity markets as well as in different asset classes. The word "medium" in "medium-term momentum effect" is in light of the fact that previous performance over short periods, such as a month or a week, tends to be negatively related to future performance. This phenomenon, documented by Jegadeesh (1990) and Lehmann (1990), is known as the short-term reversal effect and is discussed in detail in Chapter 12. Furthermore, as shown in Jegadeesh and Titman (1993), reversal patterns emerge when using long-term past performance to predict future returns.

The momentum effect is widely considered a behavioral phenomenon, as including controls for risk in statistical analyses fails to change the result. Furthermore,

---

[1] Jensen and Benington (1970) claim that the results in Levy (1967) are a manifestation of selection bias.

Empirical Asset Pricing: The Cross Section of Stock Returns, First Edition.
Turan G. Bali, Robert F. Engle, and Scott Murray.
© 2016 John Wiley & Sons, Inc. Published 2016 by John Wiley & Sons, Inc.

Jegadeesh and Titman (1993) find that while the momentum effect holds for up to 12 months in the future, a long-term reversal effect is present for months 13 through 31. They claim that this result is indicative of a delayed stock-price reaction to firm-specific events. Several subsequent papers (Barberis, Shleifer, and Vishny (1998), Daniel, Hirshleifer, and Subrahmanyam (1998), Hong and Stein (1999)) have developed behavioral models in which the momentum phenomenon arises as a result of investors' delayed reaction and overreaction to information. The predictions of these models are consistent with not only medium-term momentum but also long-term reversal, as in the long run, the inefficient prices generated by investors' behavioral biases are corrected.

Rational explanations for the momentum phenomenon have been offered by Conrad and Kaul (1989) and Lo and MacKinlay (1990a,b). Rational models contend that the momentum phenomenon is a manifestation of cross-sectionally persistent expected stock returns. Stocks that have generated relatively high (low) realized returns in the past have likely done so because of high (low) expected returns. These same stocks have high (low) expected returns and, therefore, have high (low) average realized returns in the future. Such models, however, are difficult to reconcile with the long-term reversal phenomenon. Alternative potential rational explanations have found little empirical support. Lewellen and Nagel (2006) find that the conditional Capital Asset Pricing Model (CAPM) cannot explain the momentum phenomenon and Bali and Engle (2010) demonstrate that the intertemporal CAPM of Merton (1973) fails in this regard as well.

The remainder of this chapter is devoted to an empirical investigation of the momentum effect. We begin by discussing the measurement of momentum. We then proceed to examinations of the relation between momentum and future stock returns. Finally, we discuss the momentum factor of Carhart (1997) and the Fama and French (1993) and Carhart (1997) four-factor risk model.

11.1 MEASURING MOMENTUM

The most commonly used measure of a stock's momentum is the 11-month return of the stock during the period beginning 12 months prior to and ending one month prior to the measurement date. For analyses using monthly samples, such as the analyses presented throughout Part II of this book, the momentum of stock i measured at the end of month t, which we denote $Mom_{i,t}$, is therefore taken to be the return of the stock during the 11-month period covering months $t - 11$ through $t - 1$. Specifically,

$$Mom_{i,t} = 100 \left[\prod_{m \in \{t-11:t-1\}} (R_{i,m} + 1) - 1 \right] \qquad (11.1)$$

where $R_{i,m}$ represents the return of stock i in month m, in decimal form (0.01 is a 1% return). We multiply by 100 so that momentum is represented as a percentage (1.00 is a 1% return). The monthly returns used to calculate Mom are most commonly gathered from the Center for Research in Security Prices' (CRSP) monthly stock file.[2] In calculating momentum for the empirical analyses presented in this chapter, we require a minimum of nine available monthly returns during the 11-month measurement period. Observations with fewer than nine months of available return data are considered missing.

The convention of excluding the stock return during month t from the calculation of momentum is driven by the desire to separate the medium-term momentum effect from the short-term reversal effect, to be discussed in Chapter 12. As the standard measure of the reversal variable is the one-month stock return during month t, excluding this monthly return from the calculation of *Mom* removes the mechanical correlation between the measures of momentum and reversal, thus allaying concerns that such correlation may have undesired ramifications on the results of statistical analyses.

It is worth mentioning that this most commonly used calculation of momentum is slightly different from the measure used in the foundational momentum paper. Jegadeesh and Titman (1993) define momentum for stock i in month t as the stock return during the k months up to and including month t, where $k \in \{3, 6, 9, 12\}$. They account for the reversal effect by demonstrating that their results are robust when excluding the prior one-week return from the calculation of momentum. Furthermore, the original paper uses an overlapping portfolio holding-period methodology, where, while new portfolios are formed on a monthly basis, the portfolios are held for three, six, nine, or 12 months. This approach is not common in empirical asset pricing analyses, and we will therefore not replicate their exact analysis. We will see, however, that methodology can have a substantial effect on the results generated by the analysis. To examine the momentum effect using the measures of momentum in Jegadeesh and Titman (1993), we define R^{12M}, R^{9M}, R^{6M}, and R^{3M} to be the return of the given stock during the 12-, nine-, six-, and three-month periods, respectively, up to and including month t. We require a minimum of 10, 7, 5, and 3 months of available return data, respectively, to calculate these measures.

We also examine two less frequently used measures of momentum. These two measures are the 12-month return during months $t - 12$ through $t - 1$ (denoted $R^{t-12:t-1}$) and the six-month return covering months $t - 6$ through $t - 1$ (denoted $R^{t-6:t-1}$). When calculating $R^{t-12:t-1}$ and $R^{t-6:t-1}$, we require a minimum of 10 and five available monthly return observations, respectively. As will be demonstrated in our empirical analysis, while these measures generate similar results to the most common measure *Mom*, their ability to predict future stock returns is not quite as strong as that of *Mom*.

11.2 SUMMARY STATISTICS

We begin our empirical investigation by presenting summary statistics for our primary momentum variable, *Mom*, as well as the alternative measures of momentum

---

[2]The identical value can be generated by using daily returns over the months $t - 11$ through $t - 1$, taken from the CRSP daily return file. In this case, the summation would be over all days during the 11-month calculation period.

TABLE 11.1 Summary Statistics

This table presents summary statistics for variables measuring momentum using the CRSP sample for the months t from June 1963 through November 2012. Each month, the mean (*Mean*), standard deviation (*SD*), skewness (*Skew*), excess kurtosis (*Kurt*), minimum (*Min*), fifth percentile (5%), 25th percentile (25%), median (*Median*), 75th percentile (75%), 95th percentile (95%), and maximum (*Max*) values of the cross-sectional distribution of each variable are calculated. The table presents the time-series means for each cross-sectional value. The column labeled n indicates the average number of stocks for which the given variable is available. *Mom* in month t is the return of the stock during the 11-month period including months $t - 11$ through $t - 1$. $R^{t-12:t-1}$ is the return of the stock during months $t - 12$ through $t - 1$. $R^{t-6:t-1}$ is the return of the stock during months $t - 6$ through $t - 1$. R^{12M} is the return of the stock during months $t - 11$ through month t. R^{9M} is the return of the stock during months $t - 8$ through month t. R^{6M} is the return of the stock during months $t - 5$ through month t. R^{3M} is the return of the stock during months $t - 3$ through month t.

	Mean	SD	Skew	Kurt	Min	5%	25%	Median	75%	95%	Max	n
Mom	14.12	58.40	4.12	61.62	−89.41	−49.88	−17.11	5.70	31.98	102.73	1064.02	4426
$R^{t-12:t-1}$	15.55	62.23	4.31	66.48	−90.02	−51.34	−17.59	6.29	34.08	109.48	1164.03	4389
$R^{t-6:t-1}$	7.38	39.53	3.63	57.52	−84.36	−39.84	−13.55	2.84	21.00	67.11	689.20	4569
R^{12M}	15.54	62.39	4.30	66.24	−90.40	−51.69	−17.70	6.30	34.19	109.74	1168.12	4423
R^{9M}	11.34	51.02	3.84	55.89	−88.40	−46.79	−15.99	4.55	27.83	88.90	908.54	4533
R^{6M}	7.39	39.69	3.61	57.06	−85.18	−40.13	−13.61	2.85	21.08	67.41	690.85	4603
R^{3M}	3.63	26.69	3.16	48.69	−78.54	−30.25	−10.22	1.18	13.52	43.96	449.21	4667

that have been used throughout the empirical asset pricing literature, for our sample of U.S.-based common stocks in the CRSP database. Table 11.1 presents the time-series averages of the monthly cross-sectional summary statistics for each variable. In analyzing these variables, the reader should remember that each of the measures of momentum is simply the return of the security over a given period.

In the average month, the mean value of *Mom* is 14.12%, the cross-sectional standard deviation is 58.40%, and values range from −89.41% to 1064.02%. There are 4426 valid values of *Mom* in the average month. The skewness of the cross-sectional distribution of *Mom* is 4.12 in the average month and, as would be expected given the strong positive skewness, the median of 5.70% is well below the mean.

The distributions of R^{12M}, R^{9M}, R^{6M}, and R^{3M} are all very similar to that of *Mom*. The main difference is that the magnitude of each of the cross-sectional summary statistics decreases as the length of the measurement period decreases.[3] This is not surprising, as returns would be expected to be larger in magnitude over longer holding periods.[4] Finally, the distributions of $R^{t-12:t-1}$ and $R^{t-6:t-1}$ are, by necessity, nearly identical to those of R_{12M} and R_{6M}, respectively.

[3]The one exception is the excess kurtosis (Kurt), which is higher for R^{6M} than for R^{9M}.
[4]One may argue that this argument is not valid for the skewness (Skew) and excess kurtosis (Kurt) of the cross-sectional distributions of R^{12M}, R^{9M}, R^{6M}, and R^{3M}. This pattern in skewness and excess kurtosis is likely driven by the fact that we are using returns, and not log returns, as the measures of momentum.

11.3 CORRELATIONS

Table 11.2 presents average cross-sectional correlations between the measures of momentum and the variables examined in previous chapters of this book. Specifically, we examine correlations between momentum and each of beta (β), stock size (*Size*, the natural log of market capitalization), and book-to-market ratio (*BM*). We do not present correlations between the different measures of momentum because these measures have a mechanical correlation, making the results difficult to interpret. For this reason, the table presents only a portion of the standard correlation matrix. Pearson product–moment correlations are presented in Panel A and Spearman rank correlations are presented in Panel B.

The results in Table 11.2 show that the correlation between β and momentum is fairly low. The average cross-sectional Pearson correlation between *Mom* and β is only 0.07, and the Spearman correlation of 0.04 is even lower. The other measures of momentum generate Pearson correlations with β between 0.08 for ($R^{t-12:t-1}$) and -0.02 for R^{3M}, and Spearman correlations between 0.05 for $R^{t-12:t-1}$ and -0.02 for R^{3M}. Momentum exhibits a moderate positive correlation with *Size*. The Pearson (Spearman) correlation between *Mom* and *Size* is 0.18 (0.25), while other measures of momentum generate Pearson (Spearman) correlations between 0.19 (0.26) and 0.11 (0.16) with *Size*. Finally, the average cross-sectional Pearson (Spearman) correlation between *Mom* and *BM* is 0.02 (0.04), and other measures of momentum have Pearson (Spearman) correlations between 0.06 (0.08) and 0.01 (0.02) with *BM*. The results therefore indicate very little cross-sectional correlation between momentum and the book-to-market ratio.

TABLE 11.2   Correlations
This table presents the time-series averages of the annual cross-sectional Pearson product–moment (Panel A) and Spearman rank (Panel B) correlations between different measures of momentum and each of β, *Size*, and *BM*.

Panel A: Pearson Correlations							
	Mom	$R^{t-12:t-1}$	$R^{t-6:t-1}$	R^{12M}	R^{9M}	R^{6M}	R^{3M}
β	0.07	0.08	0.01	0.06	0.03	-0.00	-0.02
$Size$	0.18	0.19	0.14	0.19	0.17	0.15	0.11
BM	0.02	0.01	0.06	0.03	0.06	0.06	0.04
Panel B: Spearman Correlations							
	Mom	$R^{t-12:t-1}$	$R^{t-6:t-1}$	R^{12M}	R^{9M}	R^{6M}	R^{3M}
β	0.04	0.05	-0.00	0.03	0.01	-0.01	-0.02
$Size$	0.25	0.26	0.20	0.26	0.24	0.20	0.16
BM	0.04	0.02	0.07	0.05	0.07	0.08	0.05

In the previous chapters in Part II of this book, the correlation analyses have been immediately followed by persistence analyses of the variables under investigation. Because each of the momentum variables is a measure the stock's return, in the case of momentum, persistence analysis would simply be an examination of the relation between past and future stock returns. As this relation is the focus of the subsequent portfolio and Fama and MacBeth (1973) regression analyses presented in the next section, we forgo persistence analysis of the momentum variables in favor of these other methodologies.

11.4 MOMENTUM AND STOCK RETURNS

In this section, we examine the relation between momentum and future stock returns. We demonstrate not only the medium-term momentum effect that is the focal phenomenon of this chapter, but also the long-term reversal effect that is well known but not as frequently analyzed by empirical asset pricing researchers. The results will also provide preliminary indications of a short-term reversal effect that will be examined in depth in Chapter 12.

11.4.1 Univariate Portfolio Analysis

We begin our investigation of the relation between momentum and future stock returns with univariate portfolio analyses. We perform a univariate portfolio analysis using each of the measures of momentum. The portfolio breakpoints in each analysis are calculated as the deciles of the given measure of momentum calculated using all stocks in the sample.

To help understand the characteristics of the stocks comprising each of the *Mom* sorted portfolios, Panel A of Table 11.3 presents the equal-weighted average values of *Mom*, β, *MktCap*, and *BM* for each of the portfolios formed by sorting on *Mom*. We present characteristics for portfolios sorted on *Mom* instead of any of the other momentum variables because *Mom* is the most commonly used measure of momentum in the empirical asset pricing literature.

Panel A demonstrates that average values of *Mom* increase monotonically (by construction) from −52.40% for the first decile of *Mom* to 132.10% for stocks in the 10th *Mom* decile. Average β exhibits a U-shaped pattern across the *Mom*-sorted decile portfolios with the first decile portfolio having an average β of 0.85, the fifth and sixth decile portfolios having average β of 0.71, and the 10th decile portfolio holding stocks with average β of 0.97. The relation between momentum and market capitalization is inverted-U-shaped, as average values of *MktCap* increase from $154 million for stocks in the first decile of *Mom* to more than $1.7 billion for stocks in the seventh *Mom* decile. Stocks in the eight, ninth, and 10th *Mom* deciles, however, exhibit progressively smaller values of average *MktCap* of just under $1.7 billion, about $1.45 billion, and $849 million, respectively. Finally, average values of *BM* are generally increasing across the *Mom* deciles from 0.89 for the *Mom* decile 1 portfolio to 1.00 for the 10th decile portfolio. The average *BM* values for portfolios 2 through 9, however, are all relatively similar, with values between 0.93 and 0.95. Portfolio 1 has a substantially lower average *BM* of 0.89, whereas portfolio 10 has a substantially higher average *BM* of 1.00. Thus, the positive relation between *Mom* and *BM* detected in the correlation analysis appears to be mostly driven by stocks with extreme values of *Mom*.

The average monthly value-weighted excess returns for the decile portfolios created by sorting on each measure of momentum are shown in Panel B of Table 11.3. The final three columns indicate the return (10-1), CAPM alpha (CAPM α), and Fama and French (1993) three-factor alpha (FF α) for the momentum difference portfolio, along with associated *t*-statistics, adjusted following Newey and West (1987) using six lags.

Focusing first on the results for the analysis that uses the standard measure of momentum (*Mom*) as the sort variable, the results in Panel B indicate a strong positive relation between momentum and expected stock returns. The average excess return of the first decile portfolio is −0.76% per month, while that of the 10th decile portfolio is 1.18% per month, resulting in an average difference of 1.95% per month between the return of the high-momentum (decile 10) and low-momentum (decile 1) portfolios. The average return difference of 1.95% per month is highly economically significant, and the associated *t*-statistic of 5.39 indicates that this value is statistically greater than zero. The difference portfolio's abnormal returns of 2.13% per month (*t*-statistic = 6.48) and 2.37% per month (*t*-statistic = 7.54) relative to the CAPM and FF risk models, respectively, are both larger and more statistically significant than the raw return difference. Furthermore, with one exception (decile portfolio 6), the average excess returns of the decile portfolio are increasing across deciles of *Mom*.

Turning our attention now to the other measures of momentum, we notice first that, consistent with the existence of a momentum effect, all measures of momentum generate a positive return difference between the decile portfolio 10 and decile one portfolio. Measures of momentum that use longer calculation periods produce 10-1 return differences and alphas that are both larger and more statistically significant than those with shorter calculation periods. For the six-month (R^{6M}) and three-month measures (R^{3M}) that do not skip a month, the 10-1 return difference is not statistically significant although the risk-adjusted alphas remain significant.

Another important observation from Panel B of Table 11.3 is that holding the length of the measurement period constant, skipping a month between the measurement and portfolio formation periods dramatically increases the predictive power of the momentum measure. The return difference between decile portfolio 10 and decile portfolio one for the 12-month measure that does not skip a month (R^{12M}) is 1.42% per month, with a corresponding *t*-statistic of 3.64. For the 12-month measure that does skip a month ($R^{t-12:t-1}$), the return difference is 1.79% per month with a *t*-statistic of 5.12. The difference is even more substantial when comparing the results using the six-month return measures. Portfolios formed by sorting on $R^{t-6:t-1}$, which skips a month between the end of the measurement period and portfolio formation, generate a 10-1 portfolio return of 1.50% per month (*t*-statistic = 4.11), with CAPM and FF alphas of 1.71% per month (*t*-statistic = 5.14) and 1.86% per month (*t*-statistic = 5.91), respectively. The six-month measure that does not skip a month between

TABLE 11.3 Univariate Portfolio Analysis

This table presents the results of univariate portfolio analyses of the relation between each of the measures of momentum and future stock returns. Monthly portfolios are formed by sorting all stocks in the CRSP sample into portfolios using decile breakpoints calculated based on the given sort variable using all stocks in the CRSP sample. Panel A shows the average values of *Mom*, β, *MktCap*, and *BM* for stocks in each decile portfolio. Panel B (Panel C) shows the average value-weighted (equal-weighted) one-month-ahead excess return (in percent per month) for each of the 10 decile portfolios. The table also shows the average return of the portfolio that is long the 10th decile portfolio and short the first decile portfolio, as well as the CAPM and FF alpha for this portfolio. Newey and West (1987) *t*-statistics, adjusted using six lags, testing the null hypothesis that the average 10-1 portfolio return or alpha is equal to zero, are shown in parentheses.

Panel A: *Mom*-Sorted Portfolio Characteristics									
Value	1	2	3	4	5	6	7	8	9	10
Mom	−52.40	−29.83	−17.21	−7.33	1.44	10.11	19.81	32.24	52.22	132.10
β	0.85	0.80	0.75	0.72	0.71	0.71	0.73	0.76	0.83	0.97
MktCap	154	487	874	1178	1441	1645	1709	1698	1468	849
BM	0.89	0.93	0.93	0.93	0.93	0.94	0.94	0.95	0.95	1.00

Panel B: Value-Weighted Portfolio Returns												
Sort Variable	1	2	3	4	5	6	7	8	9	10	10-1	CAPM α	FF α
Mom	−0.76	−0.12	0.04	0.35	0.39	0.37	0.53	0.67	0.75	1.18	1.95	2.13	2.37
											(5.39)	(6.48)	(7.54)
R^{12M}	−0.36	0.01	0.26	0.39	0.37	0.43	0.54	0.62	0.73	1.05	1.42	1.66	1.93
											(3.64)	(4.81)	(5.82)
R^{9M}	0.02	0.40	0.40	0.40	0.43	0.44	0.44	0.58	0.65	0.97	0.95	1.24	1.45
											(2.51)	(3.67)	(4.48)
R^{6M}	0.21	0.48	0.48	0.50	0.53	0.47	0.51	0.47	0.53	0.78	0.58	0.85	0.98
											(1.71)	(2.76)	(3.30)
R^{3M}	0.33	0.54	0.60	0.60	0.61	0.51	0.46	0.48	0.47	0.63	0.31	0.57	0.69
											(1.07)	(2.08)	(2.40)
$R^{t-12:t-1}$	−0.71	−0.12	0.19	0.31	0.42	0.40	0.48	0.66	0.74	1.08	1.79	1.96	2.23
											(5.12)	(6.21)	(7.33)
$R^{t-6:t-1}$	−0.52	0.22	0.38	0.40	0.51	0.48	0.52	0.51	0.54	0.97	1.50	1.71	1.86
											(4.11)	(5.14)	(5.91)

Panel C: Equal-Weighted Portfolio Returns												
Sort Variable	1	2	3	4	5	6	7	8	9	10	10-1	CAPM α	FF α
Mom	0.29	0.34	0.48	0.64	0.68	0.78	0.92	1.04	1.19	1.37	1.08	1.14	1.36
											(3.42)	(3.85)	(4.62)
R^{12M}	1.10	0.29	0.45	0.52	0.59	0.72	0.84	0.94	1.09	1.20	0.10	0.21	0.45
											(0.28)	(0.64)	(1.36)
R^{9M}	1.27	0.43	0.45	0.50	0.61	0.67	0.75	0.77	0.93	1.18	−0.10	0.05	0.28
											(−0.27)	(0.16)	(0.84)
R^{6M}	1.49	0.53	0.54	0.54	0.55	0.69	0.68	0.72	0.80	0.91	−0.58	−0.43	−0.23
											(−1.75)	(−1.36)	(−0.74)
R^{3M}	1.89	0.68	0.60	0.58	0.66	0.63	0.61	0.64	0.66	0.50	−1.39	−1.23	−1.11
											(−4.72)	(−4.27)	(−3.58)
$R^{t-12:t-1}$	0.39	0.36	0.52	0.63	0.72	0.80	0.91	1.02	1.13	1.28	0.90	0.95	1.20
											(2.84)	(3.23)	(4.04)
$R^{t-6:t-1}$	0.46	0.39	0.56	0.71	0.72	0.78	0.80	0.86	1.00	1.23	0.77	0.87	1.01
											(2.65)	(3.11)	(3.81)

calculation and portfolio formation (R^{6M}) generates an average difference portfolio
return of 0.58% a month with a t-statistic of 1.71. While the CAPM and FF alphas of
0.85% per month (t-statistic = 2.76) and 0.98% per month (t-statistic = 3.30) remain
economically large and highly statistically significant, the returns and alphas for portfolios sorted on R^{6M} are substantially lower than for portfolios sorted on $R^{t-6:t-1}$. The
results indicate that including the most recent month in the measurement of momentum actually reduces the effect. This is consistent with the negative relation between
past one-month returns and future returns, known as the short-term reversal effect,
which will be discussed in Chapter 12.

Having demonstrated the momentum effect using value-weighted portfolios, we
repeat the univariate portfolio analyses using equal-weighted portfolios. The results
of these analyses, shown in Panel C of Table 11.3, indicate that weighting scheme
has a substantial effect on the momentum phenomenon, especially when the measure
of momentum includes the return in the most recent month t.

We first look at equal-weighted portfolios formed by sorting on the primary measure of momentum, Mom. The average excess returns of the Mom-sorted portfolios
increase monotonically from 0.29% per month for decile portfolio 1 to 1.37% per
month for decile portfolio 10. The 10-1 portfolio generates an average monthly return
of 1.08% (t-statistic = 3.42), CAPM alpha of 1.14% (t-statistic = 3.85), and FF alpha
of 1.36% (t-statistic = 4.62). By any objective measure, these results indicate a strong
momentum effect. However, they are not quite as strong, either economically or statistically, as the results for the value-weighted portfolios.

When R^{12M} is used instead of Mom as the sort variable, the results change substantially. The average return of the first R^{12M}-sorted decile portfolio is 1.10% per month,
and that of the 10th decile portfolio is 1.20% per month. The average return of the
R^{12M} 10-1 of 0.10% per month is both economically small and statistically insignificant, with a corresponding t-statistic of 0.28. Adjusting the returns of this portfolio
for risk does not change the conclusions of the analysis. The CAPM alpha of 0.21%
per month and FF alpha of 0.45% per month are both statistically indistinguishable
from zero, with t-statistics of 0.64 and 1.36, respectively. The difference between this
result and the corresponding result using value-weighted portfolios seems to indicate
that the momentum phenomenon is largely a phenomenon among stocks with large
market capitalizations, and that the effect is reduced, if not completely eradicated,
among small stocks.

The difference between the results for equal-weighted portfolios formed by sorting
on Mom and R^{12M} are also quite dramatic, especially given that the only difference
between Mom and R^{12M} is that R^{12M} includes the return of the stock in the most
recent month t, whereas the calculation of Mom excludes this month. The magnitude of the difference in these results indicates that the month t stock return has very
substantially different cross-sectional implications for the one-month-ahead (month
$t + 1$) returns than the returns in months $t - 11$ through $t - 1$. The results of the analyses using R^{9M}, R^{6M}, and R^{3M} as the sort variable indicate that as fewer months
from the more distant past are used in the calculation of momentum, and the impact
of the most recent month's return gains a higher influence on the momentum measure, the returns of the difference portfolio actually become negative, economically

large, and highly statistically significant. When R^{9M} is used as the sort variable, the average return, CAPM alpha, and FF alpha are all statistically indistinguishable from zero. When R^{6M} is used, the average return of -0.58% per month is economically large but only marginally statistically significant, with a t-statistic of -1.75. The CAPM and FF alphas for this portfolio of -0.43% and -0.23% per month, respectively, are statistically insignificant. When R^{3M} is used as the sort variable, the negative returns and alphas of the difference portfolio become economically very large and highly statistically significant since the R^{3M}-sorted 10-1 portfolio generates an average return of -1.39% per month (t-statistic $= -4.72$), CAPM alpha of -1.23% per month (t-statistic $= -4.27$), and FF alpha of -1.11% per month (t-statistic $= -3.58\%$). Examination of the individual decile portfolio returns indicates that the first R^{3M} decile portfolio generates an average excess return of 1.89% per month, much higher than any of the other decile portfolios, whose average excess returns range from 0.50% to 0.68% per month. As with the results for the *Mom*-sorted portfolios, the difference between the value-weighted and equal-weighted portfolio results for portfolios formed by sorting on R^{12M}, R^{9M}, R^{6M}, and R^{3M} indicate that the momentum phenomenon is likely to be driven by high market capitalization stocks.

When a month is skipped between the measurement period and portfolio formation (sort variables $R_{t-12:t-1}$ and $R_{t-6:t-1}$), we once again find a positive, economically large, and highly statistically significant relation between momentum and future stock returns. When using $R^{t-12:t-1}$ as the sort variable, the difference portfolio generates average monthly returns of 0.90% (t-statistic $= 2.84$), CAPM alpha of 0.95% (t-statistic $= 3.23$), and FF alpha of 1.20% (t-statistic $= 4.04$). The results when sorting on $R^{t-6:t-1}$ are similar although the returns, alphas, and corresponding t-statistics for the 10-1 portfolio are slightly lower. The results indicate that skipping a month between the last month used in the calculation of momentum and when the portfolios are formed has a very important effect on the results of the portfolio analysis. When no time is lapsed between calculation of momentum and portfolio formation, equal-weighted portfolios using short measurement periods indicate a reversal effect instead of a momentum effect. When one month is left between measurement of momentum and portfolio formation, the momentum effect appears to be strong.

While these results may initially seem confusing and contradictory, there is a good explanation for them. As will be shown in Chapter 12, there is a strong negative cross-sectional relation between a stock's return in month t and it's return in month $t + 1$. This negative relation is strong in small stocks but quite weak in large stocks. This phenomenon manifests itself in our analyses of momentum in many ways. First, it explains the fact that, when using measures of momentum that do not skip a month between the measurement period and portfolio formation, we observe lower return differences between decile 10 minus decile one of momentum compared to the measures that do skip a month. Second, the fact that the reversal effect is more prevalent in small stocks than in large stocks explains the negative relation between momentum and future returns when using the measures of momentum without a time lapse before portfolio formation in the equal-weighted portfolios. In the equal-weighted analyses, the momentum effect is substantially reduced compared to the value-weighted counterparts. This is true regardless of the measure of momentum. When the return in month t is included in the measure of momentum and equal-weighted portfo-lios are used, both the weighting scheme and the measure of momentum are favor-able to the reversal effect and unfavorable to the momentum effect. Thus, in these equal-weighted analyses using measures of momentum with no time lapse, the rever-sal effect generated by the return in month t dominates the momentum effect from returns in months prior to month t.

Univariate Portfolio Analysis: Predicting k-Month-Ahead Returns

One of the main conclusions that can be drawn from the results of the univariate portfolio analyses presented in Table 11.3 is that the timing of the measurement of momentum plays a substantial role in the nature of the relation between momen-tum and future stock returns. To assess this in more detail and to examine whether momentum has the ability to predict returns further in the future than the next month, we perform univariate portfolio analyses using the k-month-ahead excess return as the outcome variable for values of $k \in \{1, 2, 3, \cdots, 12\}$. Table 11.4 presents the aver-age returns, FF alphas, and associated Newey and West (1987) t-statistics for the 10-1 portfolios from each of these analyses. The first two columns of the table indi-cate the sort variable and the measure of performance. The columns in the table labeled r_{t+k} present results using the k-month-ahead excess stock return as the out-come variable. Panel A presents results for value-weighted portfolios, and the results for equal-weighted portfolios are shown in Panel B.

The value-weighted portfolio results in Panel A of Table 11.4 indicate that using the standard measure of momentum, *Mom*, the momentum phenomenon persists for up to 10 months into the future because the FF alphas for returns up to 10 months in the future (r_{t+10}) are economically large and statistically significant, although the average k-month-ahead returns of these portfolios cease to be statistically distinguish-able from zero when using seven or more month-ahead returns. For returns coming 11 and 12 months after portfolio formation, the FF alphas are statistically indistin-guishable from zero, but the returns of the portfolio actually become negative, large in magnitude, and statistically significant. Consistent with the evidence presented in De Bondt and Thaler (1985) and Jegadeesh and Titman (1993), the results indicate that the medium-term momentum phenomenon may give way to a long-term rever-sal phenomenon. While our analysis differs substantially from that in either of these papers, the general patterns are similar.

When other measures of momentum are used as the sort variable, the results in Panel A of Table 11.4 exhibit patterns consistent with medium-term momentum and provide hints of a long-term reversal effect. The results of the nonlagged 12-month measure of momentum (R^{12M}) are similar to those using *Mom* as the sort variable. The main exception is that the long-term reversal phenomenon does not present itself when forming portfolios sorted on this measure of momentum, even when using 12-month-ahead future excess returns as the outcome variable. Using the nine-month momentum measure (R^{9M}), the portfolio analysis indicates that the momentum phenomenon persists for up to 11 months (r_{t+11}) in the future when examining the FF alphas, but the average return is significant only up to eight months in the future. The six-month (R^{6M}) and three-month (R^{3M}) measures generate the momentum effect using returns as far as 11 months (r_{t+11}) in the future regardless of whether the average return or FF alpha is examined.[5] Interestingly, when using R^{3M} as the sort variable, the strength of the momentum effect does not degrade as the time between the measurement of R^{3M} and portfolio formation increases. In fact, the average 11-month-ahead 10-1 return (r_{t+11}) and the associated FF alpha are

TABLE 11.4   Univariate Portfolio Analysis—k-Month-Ahead Returns
This table presents the results of univariate portfolio analyses of the relation between each of measures of momentum and future stock returns. Monthly portfolios are formed by sorting all stocks in the CRSP sample into portfolios using decile breakpoints calculated based on the given sort variable using all stocks in the CRSP sample. Each panel in the table shows that average k-month-ahead return (as indicated in the column header), in percent per month, along with the associated FF alpha, of the portfolio, that is, long the 10th decile portfolio and short the first decile portfolio. Panel A (Panel B) shows results for value-weighted (equal-weighted) portfolios. Newey and West (1987) t-statistics, adjusted using six lags, testing the null hypothesis that the average portfolio return or alpha is equal to zero are shown in parentheses.

							Panel A: Value-Weighted Portfolios						
Sort Variable	Value	r_{t+1}	r_{t+2}	r_{t+3}	r_{t+4}	r_{t+5}	r_{t+6}	r_{t+7}	r_{t+8}	r_{t+9}	r_{t+10}	r_{t+11}	r_{t+12}
Mom	Return	1.95	1.70	1.25	1.20	0.92	0.71	0.53	0.26	0.04	−0.06	−0.62	−0.63
		(5.39)	(5.00)	(3.47)	(3.25)	(2.85)	(2.50)	(1.62)	(0.82)	(0.15)	(−0.20)	(−1.96)	(−1.95)
	FF α	2.37	2.13	1.61	1.72	1.45	1.23	1.07	0.75	0.54	0.49	−0.05	−0.01
		(7.54)	(7.12)	(4.72)	(5.66)	(5.42)	(5.00)	(4.17)	(2.85)	(2.15)	(1.85)	(−0.20)	(−0.03)
R^{12M}	Return	1.42	1.60	1.37	1.28	1.04	0.93	0.58	0.41	0.08	0.08	−0.30	−0.61
		(3.64)	(4.38)	(3.82)	(3.45)	(2.88)	(2.78)	(1.73)	(1.27)	(0.24)	(0.24)	(−0.96)	(−1.56)
	FF α	1.93	2.06	1.83	1.78	1.60	1.50	1.17	0.95	0.66	0.65	0.23	0.06
		(5.82)	(6.62)	(5.78)	(5.67)	(5.70)	(5.58)	(4.56)	(3.55)	(2.44)	(2.56)	(0.87)	(0.22)
R^{9M}	Return	0.95	1.29	1.54	1.71	1.46	1.33	1.04	0.82	0.39	0.24	0.07	−0.60
		(2.51)	(3.41)	(4.44)	(4.95)	(4.13)	(3.99)	(3.07)	(2.57)	(1.16)	(0.82)	(0.25)	(−1.69)
	FF α	1.45	1.72	1.93	2.08	1.88	1.76	1.59	1.35	0.90	0.71	0.54	−0.01
		(4.48)	(5.27)	(6.24)	(6.94)	(6.33)	(5.89)	(5.74)	(5.24)	(3.40)	(2.86)	(2.26)	(−0.02)
R^{6M}	Return	0.58	1.26	1.21	1.19	1.20	1.35	1.65	1.38	0.94	0.81	0.42	−0.34
		(1.71)	(3.31)	(3.54)	(3.67)	(3.73)	(4.44)	(5.47)	(4.30)	(2.95)	(3.18)	(1.54)	(−1.03)
	FF α	0.98	1.62	1.51	1.43	1.54	1.68	1.99	1.70	1.29	1.17	0.87	0.20
		(3.30)	(5.00)	(4.88)	(4.59)	(5.09)	(5.93)	(7.80)	(6.20)	(4.77)	(5.17)	(3.93)	(0.85)
R^{3M}	Return	0.31	1.04	0.95	0.91	0.71	0.94	0.85	0.97	1.05	1.33	1.09	0.07
		(1.07)	(3.69)	(3.21)	(3.09)	(2.44)	(3.44)	(3.31)	(3.29)	(3.34)	(4.89)	(4.33)	(0.25)
	FF α	0.69	1.32	1.15	1.06	0.94	1.15	1.11	1.25	1.31	1.48	1.24	0.35
		(2.40)	(4.99)	(4.31)	(3.52)	(3.42)	(4.26)	(4.12)	(4.54)	(5.02)	(5.97)	(5.25)	(1.38)
$R^{t-12:t-1}$	Return	1.79	1.42	1.21	1.11	0.87	0.68	0.43	0.07	0.03	−0.26	−0.46	−0.42
		(5.12)	(4.11)	(3.37)	(3.13)	(2.53)	(2.29)	(1.38)	(0.22)	(0.10)	(−0.85)	(−1.41)	(−1.25)
	FF α	2.23	1.87	1.68	1.66	1.41	1.23	0.96	0.61	0.61	0.29	0.15	0.22
		(7.33)	(6.13)	(5.36)	(5.98)	(5.15)	(5.04)	(3.69)	(2.30)	(2.41)	(1.15)	(0.57)	(0.81)
$R^{t-6:t-1}$	Return	1.50	1.29	1.14	1.18	1.24	1.70	1.40	0.97	0.79	0.43	−0.24	−0.80
		(4.11)	(3.90)	(3.59)	(3.58)	(4.13)	(6.08)	(4.54)	(3.18)	(3.01)	(1.60)	(−0.88)	(−2.48)
	FF α	1.86	1.61	1.38	1.51	1.56	2.01	1.73	1.30	1.17	0.91	0.24	−0.29
		(5.91)	(5.43)	(4.44)	(4.96)	(5.56)	(7.85)	(6.46)	(4.97)	(5.08)	(4.03)	(1.08)	(−1.09)

(continued)

[5]The one exception is that the average 11-month-ahead return for the R^{6M} difference portfolio is not statistically significant.

TABLE 11.4 *(Continued)*

Sort Variable	Value	r_{t+1}	r_{t+2}	r_{t+3}	r_{t+4}	r_{t+5}	r_{t+6}	r_{t+7}	r_{t+8}	r_{t+9}	r_{t+10}	r_{t+11}	r_{t+12}
					Panel B: Equal-Weighted Portfolios								
Mom	Return	1.08	0.98	0.73	0.56	0.39	0.12	−0.06	−0.27	−0.34	−0.55	−0.79	−0.99
		(3.42)	(3.23)	(2.41)	(1.84)	(1.31)	(0.43)	(−0.22)	(−0.97)	(−1.44)	(−2.23)	(−3.32)	(−3.89)
	FF α	1.36	1.26	1.05	0.91	0.74	0.48	0.30	0.06	0.02	−0.17	−0.42	−0.58
		(4.62)	(4.49)	(3.81)	(3.44)	(2.85)	(1.93)	(1.21)	(0.24)	(0.07)	(−0.72)	(−1.89)	(−2.55)
R^{12M}	Return	0.10	0.90	0.81	0.60	0.47	0.25	0.04	−0.10	−0.37	−0.45	−0.63	−0.80
		(0.28)	(2.84)	(2.61)	(1.95)	(1.53)	(0.81)	(0.15)	(−0.34)	(−1.31)	(−1.77)	(−2.58)	(−3.23)
	FF α	0.45	1.20	1.11	0.96	0.86	0.63	0.41	0.29	−0.02	−0.06	−0.25	−0.42
		(1.36)	(4.01)	(3.96)	(3.45)	(3.21)	(2.39)	(1.65)	(1.14)	(−0.08)	(−0.23)	(−1.07)	(−1.84)
R^{9M}	Return	−0.10	0.77	0.95	1.08	0.90	0.58	0.34	0.13	−0.15	−0.25	−0.36	−0.61
		(−0.27)	(2.42)	(3.09)	(3.76)	(3.11)	(1.99)	(1.25)	(0.44)	(−0.56)	(−1.01)	(−1.52)	(−2.68)
	FF α	0.28	1.07	1.21	1.32	1.17	0.88	0.66	0.46	0.15	0.07	−0.02	−0.26
		(0.84)	(3.69)	(4.35)	(5.07)	(4.52)	(3.34)	(2.75)	(1.79)	(0.56)	(0.31)	(−0.09)	(−1.21)
R^{6M}	Return	−0.58	0.77	0.93	0.85	0.76	0.72	0.99	0.68	0.24	0.19	0.02	−0.42
		(−1.75)	(2.69)	(3.37)	(3.06)	(2.68)	(2.64)	(3.83)	(2.60)	(0.95)	(0.82)	(0.08)	(−1.88)
	FF α	−0.23	1.01	1.19	1.10	1.03	0.95	1.15	0.88	0.44	0.44	0.30	−0.12
		(−0.74)	(3.83)	(4.99)	(4.53)	(4.12)	(3.90)	(4.85)	(3.65)	(1.69)	(2.01)	(1.40)	(−0.57)
R^{3M}	Return	−1.39	0.47	0.64	0.54	0.61	0.72	0.53	0.37	0.43	0.85	0.59	0.09
		(−4.72)	(2.16)	(2.97)	(2.22)	(2.46)	(3.04)	(2.53)	(1.60)	(1.82)	(4.03)	(3.06)	(0.50)
	FF α	−1.11	0.62	0.80	0.70	0.76	0.93	0.71	0.54	0.53	0.88	0.70	0.27
		(−3.58)	(2.72)	(3.78)	(2.92)	(3.30)	(4.26)	(3.64)	(2.50)	(2.27)	(4.31)	(3.69)	(1.52)
$R^{t-12:t-1}$	Return	0.90	0.82	0.60	0.48	0.25	0.07	−0.10	−0.37	−0.45	−0.63	−0.79	−0.82
		(2.84)	(2.65)	(1.96)	(1.57)	(0.85)	(0.24)	(−0.37)	(−1.30)	(−1.78)	(−2.58)	(−3.18)	(−3.24)
	FF α	1.20	1.13	0.96	0.86	0.64	0.43	0.28	−0.02	−0.05	−0.25	−0.40	−0.42
		(4.04)	(4.02)	(3.48)	(3.25)	(2.42)	(1.76)	(1.12)	(−0.06)	(−0.21)	(−1.08)	(−1.78)	(−1.83)
$R^{t-6:t-1}$	Return	0.77	0.94	0.85	0.77	0.73	0.99	0.67	0.24	0.18	0.02	−0.41	−0.85
		(2.65)	(3.43)	(3.08)	(2.71)	(2.69)	(3.85)	(2.61)	(0.95)	(0.81)	(0.07)	(−1.82)	(−3.59)
	FF α	1.01	1.19	1.10	1.04	0.96	1.15	0.87	0.44	0.44	0.30	−0.10	−0.50
		(3.81)	(5.07)	(4.56)	(4.16)	(3.94)	(4.87)	(3.66)	(1.71)	(2.00)	(1.39)	(−0.50)	(−2.29)

similar in magnitude to and higher in statistical significance than the corresponding values for the 2-month-ahead return difference (r_{t+2}). However, R^{3M} fails to predict 12-month-ahead returns. This result indicates that past returns are positively related to future returns for up to 11 months in the future. Consistent with the observation that including the month t return in the calculation of momentum reduces the strength of the momentum effect, for each of R^{12M}, R^{9M}, R^{6M}, and R^{3M}, the momentum effect is stronger when predicting two-month-ahead returns (r_{t+2}) instead of one-month-ahead returns (r_{t+1}). Finally, examining the persistence of the momentum effect using alternative one-month-lapsed measures of momentum $(R^{t-6:t-1}$ and $R^{t-12:t-1})$, we see that similar patterns exist in these measures as were detected in the nonlapsed measures. The main difference is that, as discussed previously, the predictability of one-month-ahead return is stronger for the lapsed measures, as the lapsed measures are not affected by the reversal effect. Interestingly, when using $R^{t-12:t-1}$ as the sort variable, the long-term reversal phenomenon never becomes statistically significant, whereas when $R^{t-6:t-1}$ is used as the sort variable, the average 12-month ahead return generated by the $R^{t-6:t-1}$ 10-1 portfolio of −0.80% per month is highly statistically significant with a t-statistic of −2.48, but the FF alpha of the 12-month-ahead returns of only −0.29% per month is statistically indistinguishable from zero.

In Panel B of Table 11.4, we present the results of equal-weighted portfolio analyses of the relations between the different measures of momentum and k-month-ahead stock returns, where $k \in \{1, 2, 3, \cdots, 12\}$. When using *Mom* as the sort variable, the results indicate that the *Mom* difference portfolio generates statistically significant average returns for up to three months in the future (r_{t+3}) and statistically significant positive FF alpha for up to six months in the future (r_{t+6}). When using four-month-ahead through nine-month-ahead returns, the analysis detects no relation between *Mom* and future returns. *Mom* exhibits a strong negative relation with 11-month-ahead and 12-month-ahead returns, as the average return and FF alpha of the difference portfolio for each of these analyses are negative, economically large, and statistically significant.

When using equal-weighted portfolios formed by sorting on R^{12M}, R^{9M}, R^{6M}, and R^{3M}, the results indicate a strong momentum effect when examining two-month-ahead (r_{t+2}) returns. Regardless of which of these measures of momentum is used, the momentum phenomenon tends to weaken as the lag until portfolio formation increases. When R^{12M} (R^{9M}) are used as the sort variable, the long-term reversal phenomenon appears in the average return when using 12-month-ahead excess returns as the outcome variable, but the FF alpha remains at best only marginally significant.

Finally, the equal-weighted portfolio analyses using the one-month lagged 12-month return measure of momentum ($R^{t-12:t-1}$) as the sort variable detect a positive FF alpha for the difference portfolio using one-month-ahead (r_{t+1}) through five-month-ahead (r_{t+2}) returns. Beginning with the 10-month-ahead returns (r_{t+10}), the long-term reversal phenomenon appears in the average portfolio returns, with the FF alphas being marginally statistically significant when using the 11-month-ahead and 12-month-ahead returns. When sorting on the one-month lagged 6-month return measure of momentum ($R^{t-6:t-1}$), the medium-term momentum phenomenon is present for up to seven-month-ahead returns (r_{t+7}) and the long-term reversal phenomenon appears when using 12-month-ahead (r_{t+12}) returns as the outcome variable.

A few additional comments regarding the portfolio results presented in Table 11.4 are warranted. When using equal-weighted portfolios (Panel B), the patterns in the results using R^{12M} as the sort variable are very similar to the patterns observed when using $R^{t-12:t-1}$ as the sort variable, except that the patterns in the latter occur one-month earlier. This is not at all a coincidence, as the ability of the 12-month nonlagged measure of momentum (R^{12M}) to predict k-month-ahead return should be the same as the ability of the 12-month lagged measure ($R^{t-12:t-1}$) to predict $k-1$-month-ahead returns. Thus, the empirical differences between these results are completely driven by changes in the sample. As can be seen from the table, these differences are very small and economically unimportant. The same can be said when comparing the results for R^{6M} and $R^{t-6:t-1}$. For example, the two-month-ahead return difference for portfolios sorted on each of R^{12M} and the one-month-ahead return difference for portfolios sorted on $R^{t-12:t-1}$ are both 0.90% per month with a t-statistic of 2.84. Referring back to the corresponding results from the value-weighted analysis in Panel A, we see that the corresponding results fail to exhibit the same similarity. In the value-weighted analysis, the two-month-ahead return difference for the non-lagged 12-month momentum measure (R^{12M}) is 1.60% per month (t-statistic = 4.38) and the one-month-ahead return difference when sorting on the lagged 12-month measure ($R^{t-12:t-1}$) is 1.79% with a t-statistic of 5.12. These two results combined (equal-weighted and value-weighted) indicate that the effect of weighting scheme on persistence analyses is much more substantial, at least in this case, than the effect of a changing sample. If nothing else, this example serves as a caution to researchers that there are potentially many moving parts in even these simple analyses, and they may manifest themselves in unexpected ways. Thus, attention to detail is a necessary component of high-quality empirical asset pricing research.

This completes our examination of the momentum phenomenon using univariate portfolio analysis. The results have actually demonstrated not just the medium-term momentum effect but also the long-term and short-term reversal effects. We discuss the short-term reversal effect in Chapter 12. The long-term reversal effect is a less frequently discussed phenomenon, and thus we will not pay special attention to it in this book. As the primary objective of this chapter is the analysis of the momentum effect, we proceed now to examine whether the momentum effect persists after controlling for other variables known to be related to expected stock returns. In doing so, we focus on the most commonly used measure of momentum, namely, the 11-month return covering months $t - 11$ through $t - 1$, which we have denoted *Mom*. We focus on this measure for two reasons. First, the momentum effect is strongest when using *Mom*, especially when predicting one-month-ahead future returns. Second, this is the most commonly used measure of momentum in the asset pricing literature. This second reason is likely a result of the first.

11.4.2   Bivariate Portfolio Analysis

We now continue our examination of the relation between momentum and expected stock returns by using bivariate portfolio analysis to control for the relations between each of beta, market capitalization, and book-to-market ratio and expected stock returns.

Bivariate Dependent-Sort Portfolio Analysis

Our bivariate portfolio analysis of the momentum effect begins with an analysis of the returns of portfolios formed by sorting first on market capitalization (*MktCap*) and then on momentum (*Mom*). This analysis is motivated by the substantial differences in the value-weighted and equal-weighted univariate portfolio analyses, which detected a much stronger medium-term momentum effect when using value-weighted portfolios than when using equal-weighted portfolios. We begin with dependent-sort portfolio analyses using five *MktCap* groups and five *Mom* groups with breakpoints corresponding to quintiles of each of the sort variables. The outcome variable in these analyses is the one-month-ahead excess stock return.

The results of the analysis using value-weighted portfolios, shown in Panel A of Table 11.5, demonstrate that the momentum phenomenon remains strong after controlling for market capitalization. In the average *MktCap* quintile, the return of the *Mom* 5-1 portfolio is 1.29% per month with a corresponding t-statistic of 5.61. The CAPM and FF risk models fail to explain the returns of this portfolio, since the CAPM alpha of 1.40% per month and FF alpha of 1.55% per month are both economically large and highly statistically significant, with t-statistics of 6.76 and 7.76, respectively. The average returns of the *Mom* quintile portfolios for the *MktCap* Avg portfolio are increasing monotonically from −0.08% per month for the low-momentum (*Mom* 1) portfolio to 1.21% per month for the high-momentum (*Mom* 5) portfolio. The results of the value-weighted portfolio analysis also indicate that the momentum effect is strong for stocks at all market capitalization levels, since the average return, CAPM alpha, and FF alpha of the *Mom* 5-1 portfolio are positive, economically large, and statistically significant within each of the *MktCap* quintiles. Furthermore, within each quintile of *MktCap*, the average portfolio returns are monotonically increasing from quintile one to quintile five of momentum.

We next perform a similar bivariate portfolio analysis using equal-weighted portfolios. The results are presented in Panel B of Table 11.5. Focusing first on the average market capitalization quintile (*MktCap* Avg), the results of the equal-weighted analysis once again provide strong support of the momentum phenomenon, as the average return of the difference portfolio is 1.13% per month with a corresponding t-statistic of 4.97, indicating high levels of both economic and statistical significance. Exposure to the market (*MKT*), size (*SMB*), and value (*HML*) factors does not explain this return, as the risk-adjusted alphas relative to the CAPM and FF models are larger and more statistically significant than the raw return difference. As in the value-weighted analysis, the equal-weighted average returns of the *Mom* quintile portfolios increase monotonically from quintile 1 to 5 of *Mom*. Overall, therefore, the momentum effect is detected by the equal-weighted portfolio analysis.

Examining the individual quintiles of market capitalization uncovers some interesting patterns. Quintiles two through five of market capitalization each exhibit a monotonically increasing average excess return across the quintiles of momentum, with raw return differences and risk-adjusted alphas that are economically large and highly statistically significant. Looking at quintile one of market capitalization, however, we find that using an equal-weighted portfolio analysis, the momentum phenomenon does not exist at all for small stocks. In fact, the *Mom* 5-1 portfolio for the smallest market capitalization quintile generates an economically small and statistically insignificant average monthly return of 0.09% (t-statistic = 0.27). The CAPM and FF alphas of 0.30% per month (t-statistic = 0.97) and 0.36% per month (t-statistic = 1.16) also provide no evidence of a momentum effect among small stocks.

The lack of a medium-term momentum effect among stocks with low market capitalizations is consistent with what was observed in the univariate portfolio analyses, which generated much stronger momentum results when using value-weighted portfolios than when using equal-weighted portfolios. To investigate this phenomenon further, we refine our sorting procedure by breaking the lowest quintile of market capitalization into four separate groups, each holding 5% of all stocks used in the analysis. The first group holds stocks in the lowest 5% of market capitalization. Groups two, three, and four hold percentiles five to 10, 10–15, and 15–20, respectively. Within each of these four groups, we then sort the stocks into five portfolios based on momentum (*Mom*). We perform this analysis using both value-weighted and equal-weighted portfolios.

TABLE 11.5   Bivariate Dependent-Sort Portfolio Analysis—Control for *MktCap*
This table presents the results of bivariate dependent-sort portfolio analyses of the relation
between *Mom* and future stock returns after controlling for the effect of *MktCap*. Each month,
all stocks in the CRSP sample are sorted into five groups based on an ascending sort of *MktCap*.
Within each *MktCap* group, all stocks are sorted into five portfolios based on an ascending sort
of *Mom*. The quintile breakpoints used to create the portfolios are calculated using all stocks
in the CRSP sample. The table presents the average one-month-ahead excess return (in percent
per month) for each of the 25 portfolios as well as for the average *MktCap* quintile portfolio
within each quintile of *Mom*. Also shown are the average return, CAPM alpha, and FF alpha of
a long–short zero-cost portfolio, that is, long the fifth *Mom* quintile portfolio and short the first
Mom quintile portfolio in each *MktCap* quintile. *t*-statistics (in parentheses), adjusted following
Newey and West (1987) using six lags, testing the null hypothesis that the average return or
alpha is equal to zero, are shown in parentheses. Panel A presents results for value-weighted
portfolios. Panel B presents results for equal-weighted portfolios.

Panel A: Value-Weighted Portfolios

	MktCap 1	*MktCap* 2	*MktCap* 3	*MktCap* 4	*MktCap* 5	*MktCap* Avg
Mom 1	0.26	−0.63	−0.31	0.04	0.24	−0.08
Mom 2	0.67	0.35	0.49	0.56	0.36	0.48
Mom 3	0.92	0.72	0.75	0.74	0.33	0.69
Mom 4	1.13	1.01	0.97	0.89	0.54	0.91
Mom 5	1.40	1.38	1.31	1.17	0.81	1.21
Mom 5-1	1.13	2.01	1.62	1.13	0.56	1.29
	(3.55)	(7.56)	(6.12)	(4.78)	(2.41)	(5.61)
Mom 5-1 CAPM α	1.35	2.16	1.72	1.19	0.59	1.40
	(4.74)	(9.11)	(6.95)	(5.42)	(2.57)	(6.76)
Mom 5-1 FF α	1.42	2.30	1.87	1.37	0.79	1.55
	(5.29)	(9.63)	(8.04)	(6.28)	(3.61)	(7.76)

Panel B: Equal-Weighted Portfolios

	MktCap 1	*MktCap* 2	*MktCap* 3	*MktCap* 4	*MktCap* 5	*MktCap* Avg
Mom 1	1.48	−0.61	−0.29	0.02	0.20	0.16
Mom 2	1.29	0.36	0.47	0.58	0.49	0.64
Mom 3	1.24	0.72	0.78	0.75	0.51	0.80
Mom 4	1.38	1.01	0.99	0.92	0.64	0.99
Mom 5	1.57	1.37	1.30	1.18	1.01	1.29
Mom 5-1	0.09	1.99	1.60	1.16	0.80	1.13
	(0.27)	(7.61)	(6.06)	(4.84)	(3.57)	(4.97)
Mom 5-1 CAPM α	0.30	2.14	1.70	1.22	0.83	1.24
	(0.97)	(9.18)	(6.91)	(5.51)	(3.78)	(6.08)
Mom 5-1 FF α	0.36	2.27	1.85	1.39	1.03	1.38
	(1.16)	(9.72)	(8.10)	(6.40)	(4.74)	(6.96)

Panel A of Table 11.6 reports the results of the refined portfolio analysis using value-weighted portfolios. The results indicate that for extremely small stocks, namely those in the bottom 5% of *MktCap*, the momentum phenomenon does not exist. Among such stocks (*MktCap* Pctls 0–5), the average return of the portfolio, that is, long high-*Mom* stocks and short low-*Mom* stocks (*Mom* 5-1) is −0.86% per month, indicating more of a reversal effect than a momentum effect. Despite the large magnitude of the average return, it is statistically indistinguishable from zero as the corresponding t-statistic is −1.67. Adjusting the returns of this portfolio using the CAPM and FF risk models results in large but statistically insignificant alphas of −0.60 (t-statistic = −1.25) and −0.56 (t-statistic = −1.13) per month, respectively. For stocks with market capitalizations between the fifth and 10th, 10th and 15th, and 15th and 20th percentiles of *MktCap*, the medium-term momentum phenomenon is strong, as each of the *Mom* 5-1 portfolios for these *MktCap* groups generates economically large and statistically significant average returns and risk-adjusted alphas.

The results of the equal-weighted portfolio analysis, presented in Panel B of Table 11.6, are even more dramatic than those of the value-weighted portfolios. When equal-weighted portfolios are used, the results show a strong negative relation between *Mom* and future stock returns for stocks in the lowest 5% of *MktCap*. The average monthly return of the equal-weighted *Mom* 5-1 portfolio for these extremely small-cap stocks is an economically large and highly statistically significant −1.60% with a corresponding t-statistic of −2.84. Adjusting the returns of this portfolio for risk does not explain the returns, as the CAPM alpha of −1.34% per month (t-statistic = −2.53) and FF alpha of −1.30% per month (t-statistic = −2.39) are both large in magnitude and statistically significant. The equal-weighted results for stocks in percentiles five through 10, 10 through 15, and 15 through 20 of *MktCap* are very similar to the value-weighted results, as each of the *Mom* 5-1 portfolios for these *MktCap* groups generates positive and statistically significant average monthly returns and alphas.

The results in Table 11.6 demonstrate that for stocks that are not in the smallest 5% of market capitalization, the momentum effect is quite strong. For extremely small stocks, specifically those in the bottom 5% of market capitalization, the effect disappears when using value-weighted portfolios and is reversed (becomes a reversal phenomenon) when using equal-weighted portfolios. The substantial difference between the value-weighted and equal-weighted portfolios, even among only stocks in the bottom 5% of *MktCap*, indicates that even among these very small stocks, it is the smallest of the small stocks that are driving the negative relation between *Mom* and future stock returns among stocks in the bottom 5% of *MktCap*. While we do not investigate the cause of this reversal (instead of momentum) effect in very small stocks, we posit that it may be driven at least in part by microstructure effects such as the bid–ask spread, as well as illiquidity effects, which may cause reversal patterns in the returns of such stocks.[6]

---

[6]The research examining the relation between market imperfections and autocorrelation in stock returns is expansive. A short list of such studies is Fisher (1966), Roll (1984), Atchison, Butler, and Simonds (1987), Lo and MacKinlay (1990a), Campbell, Grossman, and Wang (1993), Boudoukh, Richardson, and Whitelaw (1994), Ahn, Boudoukh, Richardson, and Whitelaw (2002), and Connolly and Stivers (2003).

TABLE 11.6 Bivariate Dependent-Sort Portfolio Analysis—Small Stocks
This table presents the results of bivariate dependent-sort portfolio analyses of the relation between *Mom* and future stock returns after controlling for the effect of *MktCap* using only small stocks. Each month, all stocks with values below the 20th percentile value of *MktCap* in the CRSP sample are sorted into four groups based on an ascending sort of *MktCap*. Within each *MktCap* group, all stocks are sorted into five portfolios based on an ascending sort of *Mom*. The table presents the average one-month-ahead excess return (in percent per month) for each of the 20 portfolios as well as for the average *MktCap* portfolio within each *Mom* group. Also shown are the average return, CAPM alpha, and FF alpha of a long–short zero-cost portfolio, that is, long the fifth *Mom* quintile portfolio and short the first *Mom* quintile portfolio in each *MktCap* group. *t*-statistics (in parentheses), adjusted following Newey and West (1987) using six lags, testing the null hypothesis that the average return or alpha is equal to zero, are shown in parentheses. Panel A presents results for value-weighted portfolios. Panel B presents results for equal-weighted portfolios.

Panel A: Value-Weighted Portfolios			
	MktCap Pctls 0–5	*MktCap* Pctls 5–10	*MktCap* Pctls 10–15	*MktCap* Pctls 15–20
---	---	---	---	---
Mom 1	3.16	0.48	−0.35	−0.44
Mom 2	3.26	1.07	0.41	0.41
Mom 3	2.23	1.00	1.00	0.84
Mom 4	2.20	1.32	1.03	1.09
Mom 5	2.30	1.60	1.33	1.26
Mom 5-1	−0.86	1.12	1.68	1.70
	(−1.67)	(3.17)	(5.20)	(4.83)
Mom 5-1 CAPM α	−0.60	1.36	1.86	1.88
	(−1.25)	(4.23)	(6.20)	(5.80)
Mom 5-1 FF α	−0.56	1.43	1.92	1.94
	(−1.13)	(4.44)	(6.61)	(6.43)

Panel B: Equal-Weighted Portfolios			
	MktCap Pctls 0–5	*MktCap* Pctls 5–10	*MktCap* Pctls 10–15	*MktCap* Pctls 15–20
---	---	---	---	---
Mom 1	4.17	0.52	−0.32	−0.42
Mom 2	3.70	1.13	0.45	0.41
Mom 3	2.70	1.00	1.00	0.84
Mom 4	2.51	1.33	1.02	1.08
Mom 5	2.56	1.59	1.35	1.25
Mom 5-1	−1.60	1.07	1.67	1.68
	(−2.84)	(2.99)	(5.13)	(4.79)
Mom 5-1 CAPM α	−1.34	1.31	1.85	1.86
	(−2.53)	(4.03)	(6.12)	(5.77)
Mom 5-1 FF α	−1.30	1.37	1.92	1.91
	(−2.39)	(4.21)	(6.54)	(6.35)

Having sufficiently examined the effect of controlling for market capitalization on the momentum phenomenon using dependent-sort bivariate portfolio analyses, we proceed now to similar analyses of momentum after controlling for each of beta (β) and book-to-market ratio (BM). The results of bivariate dependent-sort portfolio analyses of the momentum effect using each of beta (β) and book-to-market ratio (BM) as the first, or control, sort variable are presented in Table 11.7. The table presents the average return, CAPM alpha, and FF alpha for the *Mom* 5-1 portfolio within each quintile of the control variable, as well as for the average control variable quintile. Results for value-weighted (Weights = VW) and equal-weighted (Weights = EW) portfolios are tabulated.

The results of the bivariate dependent-sort portfolio analysis using beta (β) as the first sort variable indicate that within each quintile of β, the average return of the *Mom* 5-1 value-weighted portfolio is positive and highly statistically significant, with average returns ranging from 0.75% per month (t-statistic = 2.87) for β quintile three to 1.78% per month (t-statistic = 5.12) for β quintile five. Risk-adjusted alphas relative to the CAPM and FF risk models exhibit similar patterns, with alphas ranging from 0.86% to 2.13% per month. The average *Mom* 5-1 portfolio across all quintiles of β generates an average monthly return of 1.16% per month (t-statistic = 5.01) and FF alpha of 1.43% per month (t-statistic = 6.85). The results using equal-weighed portfolios are qualitatively similar, but perhaps not quite as strong. Each of the *Mom* 5-1 portfolios generates a large and statistically significant average return, CAPM alpha, and FF alpha. The lone exception is the average return of the *Mom* 5-1 portfolio in the smallest β quintile of 0.35% per month, which is statistically insignificant with a t-statistic of 1.36. The *Mom* 5-1 equal-weighted portfolio for the average β quintile generates average monthly returns of 0.94% (t-statistic = 4.12), CAPM alpha of 1.00% per month (t-statistic = 4.82), and FF alpha of 1.17% per month (t-statistic = 5.76). The value-weighted and equal-weighted bivariate dependent-sort portfolio analyses, therefore, indicate that the momentum effect remains highly robust after controlling for the effect of β.

The momentum effect is also robust to controlling for the relation between book-to-market ratio (BM) and expected stock returns. When using value-weighted portfolios, each of the *Mom* 5-1 portfolio produces a large and statistically significant average monthly return, CAPM alpha, and FF alpha, with the only exception being the average return of the *Mom* 5-1 portfolio in the fourth BM quintile of 0.55% per month (t-statistic = 1.58). For the average BM quintile, the average return of 0.88% per month (t-statistic = 3.21), CAPM alpha of 1.01% per month (t-statistic = 4.09), and FF alpha of 1.22% (t-statistic = 5.23) all provide strong evidence that controlling for the relation between BM and future stock returns cannot explain the momentum phenomenon. When using equal-weighted portfolios, the results are similar. The main exception is that in quintile three of BM, the equal-weighted average return and alphas of the *Mom* 5-1 portfolio are statistically indistinguishable from zero. The only other statistically insignificant result in the equal-weighted analysis is the average return of the *Mom* 5-1 portfolio in the fifth quintile of BM. The risk-adjusted returns of this portfolio, however, are highly statistically significant. The average *Mom* 5-1 equal-weighted portfolio across all quintiles of BM produces average

TABLE 11.7 Bivariate Dependent-Sort Portfolio Analysis
This table presents the results of bivariate dependent-sort portfolio analyses of the relation between *Mom* and future stock returns after controlling for the effect of each of β and *BM* (control variables). Each month, all stocks in the CRSP sample are sorted into five groups based on an ascending sort of one of the control variables. Within each control variable group, all stocks are sorted into five portfolios based on an ascending sort of *Mom*. The quintile breakpoints used to create the portfolios are calculated using all stocks in the CRSP sample. The table presents the average return, CAPM alpha, and FF alpha (in percent per month) of the long–short zero-cost portfolios that are long the fifth *Mom* quintile portfolio and short the first *Mom* quintile portfolio in each quintile, as well as for the average quintile, of the control variable. Results for value-weighted (Weights = VW) and equal-weighted (Weights = EW) portfolios are shown. *t*-statistics (in parentheses), adjusted following Newey and West (1987) using six lags, testing the null hypothesis that the average return or alpha is equal to zero, are shown in parentheses.

Control	Weights	Value	Control 1	Control 2	Control 3	Control 4	Control 5	Control Avg
β	VW	Return	1.15	0.96	0.75	1.14	1.78	1.16
			(4.31)	(4.02)	(2.87)	(4.27)	(5.12)	(5.01)
		CAPM α	1.25	1.05	0.86	1.24	1.90	1.26
			(5.08)	(4.60)	(3.38)	(4.77)	(5.86)	(5.92)
		FF α	1.41	1.19	1.02	1.38	2.13	1.43
			(6.09)	(5.35)	(4.13)	(5.26)	(6.53)	(6.85)
	EW	Return	0.35	0.89	0.67	1.31	1.48	0.94
			(1.36)	(3.90)	(2.51)	(5.84)	(4.48)	(4.12)
		CAPM α	0.48	0.97	0.67	1.36	1.53	1.00
			(2.11)	(4.75)	(2.19)	(6.59)	(5.14)	(4.82)
		FF α	0.60	1.11	0.78	1.55	1.83	1.17
			(2.80)	(5.41)	(2.47)	(7.27)	(6.02)	(5.76)
BM	VW	Return	1.75	0.58	0.78	0.55	0.73	0.88
			(5.42)	(1.96)	(2.38)	(1.58)	(2.36)	(3.21)
		CAPM α	1.91	0.71	0.89	0.67	0.85	1.01
			(6.38)	(2.54)	(2.83)	(2.06)	(3.11)	(4.09)
		FF α	2.17	0.88	1.06	0.88	1.12	1.22
			(7.21)	(3.13)	(3.38)	(2.88)	(4.45)	(5.23)
	EW	Return	1.13	0.70	0.44	0.56	0.47	0.66
			(3.96)	(2.60)	(1.39)	(2.22)	(1.63)	(2.64)
		CAPM α	1.23	0.79	0.39	0.63	0.53	0.71
			(4.72)	(3.23)	(1.03)	(2.79)	(2.07)	(3.10)
		FF α	1.46	0.99	0.55	0.81	0.67	0.90
			(5.41)	(3.83)	(1.39)	(3.58)	(2.95)	(3.95)

returns of 0.66% per month (*t*-statistic = 2.64), CAPM alpha of 0.71% per month (*t*-statistic = 3.10), and FF alpha of 0.90% per month (*t*-statistic = 3.95). Once again, consistent with the previous results in this chapter, while the momentum effect is still strong in equal-weighted portfolios, the results using value-weighted portfolios are stronger.

Bivariate Independent-Sort Portfolio Analysis

We now continue our examination of whether the momentum effect is a manifestation of the relation between either beta, market capitalization, or book-to-market ratio and future stock returns using independent-sort instead of dependent-sort bivariate portfolio analysis.

Table 11.8 presents summary results of the bivariate independent-sort portfolio analyses of the relation between momentum (*Mom*) and future stock returns after controlling for each of beta (β), market capitalization (*MktCap*), and book-to-market ratio (*BM*). With the exception of the use of independent-sort portfolios instead of dependent-sort portfolios, the parameters of these portfolio analyses are the same as those used in the dependent-sort analyses presented earlier in this chapter. The table presents only the average returns, CAPM alphas, and FF alphas for the *Mom* 5-1 portfolio within each quintile of the control variable, along with the associated *t*-statistics. Overall, the results of the independent-sort portfolio analyses are very similar to those of the dependent-sort portfolio analyses. Our discussion of these results will therefore be concise.

The top portion of Table 11.8 demonstrates that the momentum phenomenon persists after controlling for β in a bivariate independent-sort portfolio analysis. Both value-weighted and equal-weighted portfolios produce economically and statistically significant average returns, CAPM alphas, and FF alphas for the average β quintile as well as within each individual β quintile.

When controlling for *MktCap*, the results in the middle portion of Table 11.8 show that when using value-weighted independently sorted portfolios, the momentum effect is strong in each *MktCap* quintile, as well as in the average *MktCap* quintile, since all average returns and alphas are positive and statistically significant. When equal-weighted portfolio are used, the momentum effect exists in all but the lowest *MktCap* quintile. This result is very similar to what was observed in the dependent-sort bivariate portfolio analysis.

The positive relation between *Mom* and future stock returns is also robust to controlling for *BM* in independent-sort portfolios. The bottom portion of Table 11.8 shows that when using value-weighted portfolios, the average returns and alphas of the *Mom* 5-1 portfolio are positive, economically large, and statistically significant in all *BM* quintiles. When using equal-weighted portfolios, this result holds for all but quintile three of *BM*. This result is very similar to what was observed in *BM* quintile three when using dependent-sort portfolios. Thus, the results are qualitatively the same regardless of the sorting procedure.

Can Momentum Explain Other Relations

Having found no evidence in our bivariate portfolio analyses that relations between expected returns and beta, market capitalization, or book-to-market ratio can explain the momentum effect, we now use bivariate portfolio analysis to examine whether the momentum effect can explain the negative alpha of portfolios consisting of long positions in high-beta stocks and short positions in low-beta stocks, the size effect, or the value premium.

TABLE 11.8   Bivariate Independent-Sort Portfolio Analysis

This table presents the results of bivariate independent-sort portfolio analyses of the relation between *Mom* and future stock returns after controlling for the effect of each of β, *MktCap*, and *BM* (control variables). Each month, all stocks in the CRSP sample are sorted into five groups based on an ascending sort of the control variable. All stocks are independently sorted into five groups based on an ascending sort of *Mom*. The quintile breakpoints used to create the groups are calculated using all stocks in the CRSP sample. The intersections of the control variable and *Mom* groups are used to form 25 portfolios. The table presents the average return, CAPM alpha, and FF alpha (in percent per month) of the long–short zero-cost portfolios that are long the fifth *Mom* quintile portfolio and short the first *Mom* quintile portfolio in each quintile, as well as for the average quintile, of the control variable. Results for value-weighted (Weights = VW) and equal-weighted (Weights = EW) portfolios are shown. *t*-statistics (in parentheses), adjusted following Newey and West (1987) using six lags, testing the null hypothesis that the average return or alpha is equal to zero, are shown in parentheses.

Control	Weights	Value	Control 1	Control 2	Control 3	Control 4	Control 5	Control Avg
β	VW	Return	1.16	1.20	0.72	0.94	1.39	1.08
			(4.06)	(4.79)	(2.13)	(3.17)	(4.46)	(4.40)
		CAPM α	1.25	1.29	0.85	1.07	1.51	1.19
			(4.74)	(5.29)	(2.68)	(3.87)	(5.19)	(5.33)
		FF α	1.37	1.49	1.02	1.30	1.72	1.38
			(5.29)	(6.36)	(3.19)	(4.90)	(5.82)	(6.40)
	EW	Return	0.47	0.99	0.65	1.28	1.42	0.96
			(1.75)	(3.97)	(2.15)	(5.51)	(4.86)	(4.01)
		CAPM α	0.58	1.08	0.66	1.34	1.46	1.02
			(2.40)	(4.79)	(1.93)	(6.39)	(5.53)	(4.68)
		FF α	0.69	1.21	0.77	1.54	1.77	1.19
			(2.92)	(5.32)	(2.18)	(7.29)	(6.83)	(5.59)
MktCap	VW	Return	0.95	1.90	1.72	1.37	0.97	1.38
			(3.89)	(7.65)	(6.27)	(5.34)	(3.08)	(5.78)
		CAPM α	1.05	2.02	1.84	1.49	1.12	1.50
			(4.70)	(9.00)	(7.26)	(6.39)	(3.85)	(7.03)
		FF α	1.13	2.17	2.00	1.66	1.29	1.65
			(5.30)	(9.52)	(8.39)	(7.52)	(4.72)	(8.22)
	EW	Return	0.26	1.88	1.70	1.40	1.15	1.28
			(1.00)	(7.62)	(6.21)	(5.27)	(4.00)	(5.42)
		CAPM α	0.33	2.00	1.82	1.52	1.28	1.39
			(1.34)	(8.97)	(7.23)	(6.34)	(4.74)	(6.54)
		FF α	0.39	2.14	1.98	1.69	1.43	1.53
			(1.58)	(9.53)	(8.48)	(7.50)	(5.69)	(7.67)
BM	VW	Return	1.49	0.61	0.89	0.72	0.66	0.87
			(5.12)	(2.08)	(2.49)	(1.98)	(2.12)	(3.13)
		CAPM α	1.64	0.75	1.01	0.86	0.78	1.01
			(6.14)	(2.70)	(2.91)	(2.55)	(2.69)	(3.98)
		FF α	1.87	0.91	1.14	1.06	1.01	1.20
			(7.33)	(3.37)	(3.28)	(3.24)	(3.61)	(4.98)
	EW	Return	1.21	0.72	0.48	0.59	0.44	0.69
			(4.52)	(2.64)	(1.42)	(2.22)	(1.71)	(2.77)
		CAPM α	1.30	0.80	0.43	0.66	0.49	0.74
			(5.34)	(3.25)	(1.04)	(2.77)	(2.13)	(3.20)
		FF α	1.51	1.00	0.60	0.84	0.62	0.91
			(6.34)	(3.95)	(1.40)	(3.44)	(2.81)	(4.01)

We begin this investigation by using bivariate dependent-sort portfolio analysis to control for the effect of momentum by using *Mom* as the first sort variable. We then examine the relations between future returns and each of β, *MktCap*, and *BM* within each quintile of *Mom*. The parameters of the portfolio analyses are the same as in the previous dependent-sort analyses. The only difference is that here, the first sort variable is *Mom*, and the second sort variable, which is the variable whose relation with expected returns is the focus of the analysis, is either β, *MktCap*, or *BM*. For the analyses the use *MktCap* as the second sort variable, and thus examine the relation between *MktCap* and future stock returns after controlling for *Mom*, when subjecting the returns of the *MktCap* 5-1 portfolios to the FF risk model, we exclude the size factor (*SMB*) because inclusion of the size factor would amount to examining the size effect after controlling for the size effect. Similarly, the FF alphas of the *BM* difference portfolios are calculated relative to a factor model that excludes the value factor (*SMB*).

The results of these portfolio analyses are presented in Table 11.9. When controlling for *Mom*, the value-weighted β 5-1 portfolios within each *Mom* quintile generate negative but statistically insignificant average returns. The CAPM alphas of each of these portfolios, however, are negative, economically large, and statistically significant. For the average *Mom* quintile, the β 5-1 portfolio generates CAPM alpha of -0.57% per month with a corresponding t-statistic of -3.33. When the FF risk model is used to adjust the returns, the negative alpha of the β 5-1 portfolio is significant only in quintiles two and three of *Mom*, and marginally significant in *Mom* quintile four. However, for the average *Mom* quintile, the β difference portfolio generates statistically significant negative FF alpha of -0.35% per month (t-statistic $= -2.08$). The equal-weighted portfolios produce even stronger empirical evidence of a negative relation between β and future stock returns since, with the exception of the average returns of the β 5-1 portfolio in quintiles three through five of *Mom*, all average returns and alphas are negative and highly statistically significant when equal-weighted portfolios are used. Most importantly, the average returns and alphas of the β 5-1 portfolio for the average *Mom* quintile are all negative, economically large, and highly statistically significant. The analysis therefore fails to find any evidence that controlling for *Mom* explains the negative abnormal returns of portfolios that are long high-β stocks and short low-β stocks.

Similarly, the dependent-sort portfolio analyses examining the relation between *MktCap* and expected returns after controlling for *Mom* find no indication that *Mom* explains the negative relation between *MktCap* and future stock returns. The *MktCap* 5-1 portfolios, within each of the *Mom* quintiles as well as for the average *Mom* quintile, generates a negative and statistically significant average return, CAPM alpha, and FF (after removing the *SMB* factor) alpha, regardless of whether value-weighted or equal-weighted portfolios are used.

The bottom portion of Table 11.9 demonstrates that the positive relation between *BM* and future stock returns cannot be explained by momentum. When using value-weighted portfolios, the average returns and alphas of the *BM* 5-1 portfolios in quintiles one, two, and three of *Mom*, as well as for the average *Mom* quintile, are positive, large, and statistically significant. In *Mom* quintile four, the *BM* 5-1 portfolio generates a positive and marginally statistically significant average return and CAPM

TABLE 11.9   Bivariate Dependent-Sort Portfolio Analysis—Control for *Mom*

This table presents the results of bivariate independent-sort portfolio analyses of the relation between future stock returns and each of β, *MktCap*, and *BM* (second sort variables) after controlling for the effect of *Mom*. Each month, all stocks in the CRSP sample are sorted into five groups based on an ascending sort of *Mom*. All stocks are independently sorted into five groups based on an ascending sort of one of the second sort variables. The quintile breakpoints used to create the groups are calculated using all stocks in the CRSP sample. The intersections of the *Mom* and second sort variable groups are used to form 25 portfolios. The table presents the average return, CAPM alpha, and FF alpha (in percent per month) of the long–short zero-cost portfolios that are long the fifth quintile portfolio and short the first quintile portfolio for the second sort variable in each quintile, as well as for the average quintile, of *Mom*. Results for value-weighted (Weights = VW) and equal-weighted (Weights = EW) portfolios are shown. *t*-statistics (in parentheses), adjusted following Newey and West (1987) using six lags, testing the null hypothesis that the average return or alpha is equal to zero, are shown in parentheses.

Second Sort Variable	Weights	Value	Mom 1	Mom 2	Mom 3	Mom 4	Mom 5	Mom Avg
β	VW	Return	−0.27	−0.33	−0.25	−0.22	−0.20	−0.25
			(−0.88)	(−1.54)	(−1.31)	(−1.13)	(−0.75)	(−1.32)
		CAPM α	−0.62	−0.66	−0.55	−0.51	−0.53	−0.57
			(−2.16)	(−3.38)	(−3.06)	(−2.74)	(−2.13)	(−3.33)
		FF α	−0.35	−0.47	−0.38	−0.32	−0.23	−0.35
			(−1.24)	(−2.29)	(−2.14)	(−1.76)	(−0.85)	(−2.08)
	EW	Return	−1.44	−0.46	−0.28	−0.32	−0.34	−0.57
			(−6.49)	(−2.40)	(−1.41)	(−1.59)	(−1.36)	(−3.04)
		CAPM α	−1.78	−0.83	−0.66	−0.71	−0.73	−0.94
			(−8.00)	(−4.65)	(−3.98)	(−4.08)	(−3.25)	(−5.62)
		FF α	−1.70	−0.74	−0.61	−0.60	−0.47	−0.83
			(−7.78)	(−4.59)	(−3.97)	(−3.80)	(−2.15)	(−5.41)
MktCap	VW	Return	−2.11	−0.63	−0.60	−0.68	−0.58	−0.92
			(−5.58)	(−2.47)	(−2.74)	(−3.00)	(−2.50)	(−4.08)
		CAPM α	−2.30	−0.70	−0.64	−0.71	−0.59	−0.99
			(−5.40)	(−2.64)	(−2.86)	(−3.05)	(−2.48)	(−4.17)
		FF α	−2.33	−0.70	−0.59	−0.66	−0.45	−0.95
			(−5.21)	(−2.63)	(−2.56)	(−2.65)	(−1.86)	(−3.80)
	EW	Return	−2.96	−0.90	−0.73	−0.76	−0.55	−1.18
			(−7.39)	(−3.90)	(−3.49)	(−3.40)	(−2.63)	(−5.52)
		CAPM α	−3.17	−1.01	−0.81	−0.82	−0.60	−1.28
			(−7.01)	(−4.09)	(−3.71)	(−3.52)	(−2.76)	(−5.54)
		FF α	−3.18	−1.01	−0.81	−0.81	−0.46	−1.25
			(−6.76)	(−4.03)	(−3.66)	(−3.27)	(−2.11)	(−5.25)

TABLE 11.9   (*Continued*)

Second Sort Variable	Weights	Value	Mom 1	Mom 2	Mom 3	Mom 4	Mom 5	Mom Avg
BM	VW	Return	0.92	0.67	0.40	0.30	0.20	0.50
			(3.39)	(2.57)	(2.38)	(1.69)	(0.82)	(2.91)
		CAPM α	1.02	0.73	0.45	0.32	0.24	0.55
			(3.60)	(2.58)	(2.55)	(1.77)	(0.96)	(3.05)
		FF α	0.99	0.69	0.42	0.29	0.22	0.52
			(3.47)	(2.45)	(2.39)	(1.59)	(0.92)	(2.93)
	EW	Return	1.41	1.05	1.05	0.88	0.73	1.03
			(6.80)	(5.73)	(6.64)	(4.84)	(3.36)	(6.24)
		CAPM α	1.57	1.19	1.18	1.01	0.84	1.16
			(7.16)	(6.23)	(7.42)	(5.73)	(3.91)	(6.89)
		FF α	1.58	1.17	1.15	0.99	0.85	1.15
			(7.24)	(6.14)	(7.34)	(5.63)	(3.95)	(6.84)

alpha, but statistically insignificant FF (after removing the *HML* factor) alpha. In *Mom* quintile five, the average return and alphas of the *BM* difference portfolio are statistically indistinguishable from zero. Finally, when using equal-weighted portfolios, the average returns and alphas of the *BM* 5-1 portfolios within each *Mom* quintile are positive and highly significant. This is consistent with the results in Chapter 10 that indicated that the value premium is stronger when using equal-weighted portfolios.

We now repeat the analyses of the relations between each of β, *MktCap*, and *BM* after controlling for *Mom* using independent-sort portfolios instead of dependent-sort portfolios. These are exactly the same independent-sort analyses as were used to generate the results in Table 11.8. The only difference here is that we report results pertaining to the relations between future stock returns and each of β, *MktCap*, and *BM* after controlling for *Mom*, instead of examining the relation between returns and *Mom* after controlling for each of the other variables.

The independent-sort analyses lead to very similar conclusions to those stemming from the dependent-sort analyses. The results are presented in Table 11.10. In value weighted independent-sort portfolio analysis, the relation between β and future stock returns is negative but statistically insignificant when examining the average portfolio returns. When risk-adjusted returns are used, consistent with our previous findings that portfolios that are long high-β stocks and short low-β stocks generate negative abnormal returns, the CAPM and FF alphas of the β 5-1 portfolios after controlling for *Mom* are negative and statistically significant.[7] The results are stronger when using equal-weighted portfolios, since with the exception of the average returns of the β 5-1 portfolio in quintiles three through five of *Mom*,

---

[7]The only exception is the FF alpha of the β 5-1 portfolio in quintile five of *Mom*. The FF alpha of the β 5-1 portfolio in quintile two of *Mom* is marginally statistically significant.

TABLE 11.10 Bivariate Independent-Sort Portfolio Analysis—Control for *Mom*

This table presents the results of bivariate independent-sort portfolio analyses of the relation between future stock returns and each of β, *MktCap*, and *BM* (second sort variables) after controlling for the effect of *Mom*. Each month, all stocks in the CRSP sample are sorted into five groups based on an ascending sort of *Mom*. All stocks are independently sorted into five groups based on an ascending sort of one of the second sort variables. The quintile breakpoints used to create the groups are calculated using all stocks in the CRSP sample. The intersections of the *Mom* and second sort variable groups are used to form 25 portfolios. The table presents the average return, CAPM alpha, and FF alpha (in percent per month) of the long–short zero-cost portfolios that are long the fifth quintile portfolio and short the first quintile portfolio for the second sort variable in each quintile, as well as for the average quintile, of *Mom*. Results for value-weighted (Weights = VW) and equal-weighted (Weights = EW) portfolios are shown. *t*-statistics (in parentheses), adjusted following Newey and West (1987) using six lags, testing the null hypothesis that the average return or alpha is equal to zero, are shown in parentheses.

Second Sort Variable	Weights	Value	Mom 1	Mom 2	Mom 3	Mom 4	Mom 5	Mom Avg
β	VW	Return	−0.49	−0.26	−0.31	−0.30	−0.26	−0.32
			(−1.79)	(−1.11)	(−1.24)	(−1.23)	(−0.98)	(−1.51)
		CAPM α	−0.86	−0.62	−0.67	−0.65	−0.60	−0.68
			(−3.26)	(−2.91)	(−2.87)	(−3.00)	(−2.46)	(−3.56)
		FF α	−0.67	−0.40	−0.44	−0.39	−0.33	−0.45
			(−2.66)	(−1.85)	(−1.98)	(−1.96)	(−1.23)	(−2.43)
	EW	Return	−1.31	−0.48	−0.37	−0.35	−0.36	−0.57
			(−6.12)	(−2.24)	(−1.57)	(−1.49)	(−1.51)	(−2.85)
		CAPM α	−1.65	−0.88	−0.79	−0.78	−0.77	−0.98
			(−7.56)	(−4.30)	(−3.87)	(−3.77)	(−3.46)	(−5.23)
		FF α	−1.59	−0.77	−0.68	−0.63	−0.51	−0.83
			(−7.30)	(−4.43)	(−3.86)	(−3.36)	(−2.28)	(−5.08)
MktCap	VW	Return	−0.57	−0.66	−0.78	−0.79	−0.56	−0.67
			(−1.84)	(−2.53)	(−3.39)	(−3.29)	(−2.26)	(−2.89)
		CAPM α	−0.66	−0.71	−0.83	−0.83	−0.59	−0.72
			(−2.07)	(−2.66)	(−3.51)	(−3.38)	(−2.34)	(−3.03)
		FF α	−0.68	−0.71	−0.78	−0.78	−0.45	−0.68
			(−2.04)	(−2.63)	(−3.29)	(−2.97)	(−1.76)	(−2.75)
	EW	Return	−1.49	−0.91	−0.88	−0.86	−0.60	−0.95
			(−4.84)	(−3.86)	(−4.05)	(−3.68)	(−2.67)	(−4.36)
		CAPM α	−1.62	−1.00	−0.97	−0.93	−0.68	−1.04
			(−4.96)	(−4.02)	(−4.26)	(−3.82)	(−2.88)	(−4.48)
		FF α	−1.64	−1.00	−0.98	−0.92	−0.51	−1.01
			(−4.76)	(−3.99)	(−4.26)	(−3.60)	(−2.18)	(−4.25)

TABLE 11.10   (*Continued*)

Second Sort Variable	Weights	Value	Mom 1	Mom 2	Mom 3	Mom 4	Mom 5	Mom Avg
BM	VW	Return	0.91	0.70	0.53	0.34	0.09	0.51
			(3.63)	(2.65)	(3.04)	(1.78)	(0.39)	(3.07)
		CAPM α	1.00	0.76	0.60	0.36	0.14	0.57
			(3.85)	(2.71)	(3.30)	(1.87)	(0.59)	(3.26)
		FF α	0.96	0.73	0.57	0.33	0.12	0.54
			(3.70)	(2.57)	(3.14)	(1.70)	(0.53)	(3.13)
	EW	Return	1.45	1.07	1.15	0.92	0.68	1.05
			(6.95)	(5.66)	(6.23)	(4.77)	(3.31)	(6.24)
		CAPM α	1.61	1.21	1.28	1.06	0.80	1.19
			(7.34)	(6.25)	(7.04)	(5.62)	(3.90)	(6.93)
		FF α	1.61	1.19	1.26	1.04	0.80	1.18
			(7.37)	(6.20)	(6.96)	(5.54)	(3.95)	(6.89)

all average returns and alphas are negative, large in magnitude, and statistically significant. The independent-sort portfolio results provide no evidence that the size effect is explained by the momentum phenomenon, as the average returns and alphas of the *MktCap* 5-1 portfolios are negative, large, and statistically significant. Finally, the results examining the relation between *BM* and future stock returns after controlling for *Mom* using independently sorted portfolios are very similar to the results generated by the dependent-sort portfolio analyses. When using value-weighted portfolios, the positive relation between *BM* and future stock returns is robust in the average *Mom* quintile, but the strength of the effect decreases as *Mom* increases. In the average *Mom* quintile, however, the average return and alphas of the value-weighted *BM* difference portfolio are positive, economically large, and highly statistically significant. All equal-weighted *BM* 5-1 portfolios average returns, CAPM alphas, and FF alphas are positive, large, and highly statistically significant.

In summary, in this section, we have shown that univariate and bivariate portfolio analyses produce strong evidence supporting the existence of a momentum phenomenon. While the results of the analyses are substantially stronger using value-weighted portfolios compared to equal-weighted portfolios, the main conclusion persists regardless of the portfolio weighting scheme. A detailed investigation of the driver of the difference between the value-weighted and equal-weighted analyses finds that while the momentum effect exists for the largest 95% of stocks in our sample, there is actually a negative relation between the standard measure of momentum and one-month-ahead future returns for stocks in the smallest 5% of market capitalization. The bivariate analyses demonstrate that the momentum effect is robust to controlling for each of beta, market capitalization, or book-to-market ratio. Similar analyses fail to find any evidence that the momentum phenomenon is driving the relations between future stock returns and either beta, market capitalization, or book-to-market ratio.

11.4.3 Fama–MacBeth Regression Analysis

We continue our examination of the momentum effect using (Fama and MacBeth 1973, FM hereafter) regression analysis. FM regression analysis allows us to examine the momentum effect after controlling simultaneously for several different variables that have been shown to predict future stock returns. We use several different cross-sectional specifications for our analysis. In all specifications, the dependent variable is the one-month-ahead excess stock return. We begin with a univariate specification using only *Mom* as the independent variable. We also examine specifications that include all possible combinations of β, *Size*, and *BM* as control variables. All independent variables are winsorized at the 0.5% level on a monthly basis.

The time-series averages of the cross-sectional regression coefficients, along with *t*-statistics (in parentheses), adjusted following Newey and West (1987) using six lags, testing the null hypothesis that the average coefficient is equal to zero, are presented in Table 11.11. The results of the FM regressions indicate a strong positive relation between momentum and future stock returns after controlling for the effects of beta (β), size (*Size*), and book-to-market ratio (*BM*) since, regardless of the specification, the average coefficient on *Mom* is positive and statistically significant. When *Mom* is the only independent variable in the regression (specification (1)), the average coefficient is 0.007 with a *t*-statistic of 3.01. In the full specification that includes all control variables (specification (8)), the average coefficient is once again 0.007 with a *t*-statistic of 3.70. For the other specifications that include different combinations of β, *Size*, and *BM* as control variables (specifications (2) through (7)), the average coefficients on *Mom* range from 0.005 to 0.007 with *t*-statistics between 2.51 and 3.77. Thus, controlling for the effects of the other predictors of stock returns appears to have very little effect on the relation between *Mom* and future stock returns.

Consistent with what was observed in Chapter 8, when β is included in the regression specification (specifications (2), (5), (6), and (8)), it carries a negative average coefficient that, in some specifications, is statistically significant. In the specification that includes all control variables, however, the negative average coefficient on β of -0.059 is statistically insignificant with a *t*-statistic of -0.38. All specifications that include *Size* as a control (specifications (3), (5), (7), and (8)) produce negative and statistically significant average coefficients on *Size*, ranging from -0.173 to -0.182 with *t*-statistics between -3.27 and -3.98. The regressions, therefore, indicate that the momentum effect does not explain the size effect. The momentum effect also fails to explain the value premium, as when *BM* is included in as an independent variable (specifications (4), (6)–(8)), the average slope on *BM* is always positive and highly statistically significant.

To assess the economic importance of the relation between *Mom* and future stock returns, we focus on the average coefficient of 0.007 from the regressions that include

TABLE 11.11   Fama–MacBeth Regressions
This table presents the results of Fama and MacBeth (1973) regression analyses of the relation between expected stock returns and momentum. Each column in the table presents results for a different cross-sectional regression specification. The dependent variable in all specifications is the one-month-ahead excess stock return. The independent variables are indicated in the first column. Independent variables are winsorized at the 0.5% level on a monthly basis. The table presents average slope and intercept coefficients along with t-statistics (in parentheses), adjusted following Newey and West (1987) using six lags, testing the null hypothesis that the average coefficient is equal to zero. The rows labeled Adj. R^2 and n present the average adjusted R-squared and the number of data points, respectively, for the cross-sectional regressions.

	(1)	(2)	(3)	(4)	(5)	(6)	(7)	(8)
Mom	0.007	0.006	0.007	0.006	0.007	0.005	0.007	0.007
	(3.01)	(3.06)	(3.77)	(2.51)	(4.28)	(2.52)	(3.33)	(3.70)
β		−0.373			−0.124	−0.285		−0.059
		(−2.91)			(−0.73)	(−2.32)		(−0.38)
Size			−0.182		−0.178		−0.173	−0.177
			(−3.98)		(−3.27)		(−3.69)	(−3.28)
BM				0.405		0.319	0.246	0.183
				(5.41)		(4.93)	(3.09)	(2.84)
Intercept	0.607	0.877	1.356	0.261	1.448	0.544	1.178	1.310
	(2.22)	(3.62)	(3.15)	(0.95)	(3.62)	(2.36)	(2.51)	(3.13)
Adj. R^2	0.01	0.03	0.02	0.02	0.04	0.03	0.03	0.04
n	4410	4410	4410	3370	4409	3370	3370	3370

the full set of control variables (specification (8)). The average coefficient of 0.007 indicates that a difference of 100 in *Mom*, which corresponds to a 100% difference in realized returns during the *Mom* calculation period, results in an expected return difference of 0.70% in the next month. If we multiply the average coefficient of 0.007 by the standard deviation of *Mom* in the average month of 58.40 (see Table 11.1), we find that a one-standard-deviation increase in *Mom* is associated with a 0.41% per month (0.007 × 58.40%) increase in expected returns. Finally, to examine the difference in expected returns between stocks in the highest and lowest deciles of *Mom*, we multiply 0.007 with the difference in average *Mom* between stocks in the highest and lowest *Mom* deciles of 184.50% (132.10 − (−52.40)), see Panel A of Table 11.3) to get a 1.29% difference in expected returns for stocks with extremely high *Mom* compared to stocks with extremely low *Mom*. This value is similar to, although a bit larger than, the average return of 1.08% per month realized by the *Mom* 10-1 portfolio in the equal-weighted univariate portfolio analysis (see Panel C of Table 11.3). Regardless of which approach is used, the results indicate that the average coefficient of 0.007 on *Mom* is very important economically.

In summary, the results of the FM regression analyses strongly support the existence of the momentum effect. Regardless of regression specification, the average coefficient on momentum (*Mom*) is positive, statistically significant, and has a magnitude indicating that the effect is economically important.

11.5 THE MOMENTUM FACTOR

Carhart (1997) investigates the ability of the momentum phenomenon to explain persistence in mutual fund performance documented by several previous studies, and finds that including a momentum-based factor in the risk model substantially decreases the risk-adjusted alpha of momentum-based portfolios of mutual funds.[8] In Carhart (1997), the monthly momentum factor is constructed as the equal-weighted average return of stocks in the top 30% of *Mom* minus that of stocks in the bottom 30% of *Mom*. Since then, researchers have modified the momentum factor by adopting the methodology of Fama and French (1993) to construct a monthly (or daily) return series. In this section, we describe the construction of this factor and examine its properties.

The monthly momentum factor most commonly used in empirical asset pricing is created by sorting all stocks into two groups based on market capitalization calculated at the end of the most recent June and three groups based on momentum. The breakpoint dividing stocks into the two market capitalization groups is the median market capitalization (*MktCap*) of stocks traded on the New York Stock Exchange (NYSE). The breakpoints dividing the stocks into momentum groups are the 30th and 70th percentiles of *Mom* calculated using only NYSE-listed stocks. The market capitalization and momentum breakpoints are calculated independently of one another. The intersections of the market capitalization and momentum groups generate six portfolios, which we term L/U, L/M, L/D, S/U, S/M, and S/D, where L and S stand for "large" and "small" stocks, respectively, and thus represent the market capitalization groups, and U, M, and D stand for "up," "medium," and "down," respectively, indicating the return of the stock during the momentum measurement period. It should be noted that the terms "up" and "down" are misnomers, as it is not necessary that stocks in the U (D) portfolios have positive (negative) values of momentum. The monthly return of the momentum factor is then taken to be the average one-month-ahead return of the two U portfolios minus the average one-month-ahead return of the two D portfolios. As with the *SMB* and *HML* factors, the momentum factor is therefore the return on a zero-cost portfolio designed to be neutral to market capitalization, thereby isolating the effect of momentum on portfolio returns. The momentum factor is commonly referred to as *UMD*, for "up minus down," or by *MOM*, for momentum. We refer to the momentum factor as *MOM* (all capitals) so that it is easily associated with the stock-level momentum variable *Mom* (only first letter capitalized). *MOM* is also the way the momentum factor is denoted in the file containing the monthly factor returns in Kenneth French's data library, which is where we obtain the returns of the *MOM* factor.[9] Because of the requirement of one-year prior data to calculate *Mom*,

---

[8]Studies documenting persistence in mutual fund performance include Grinblatt and Titman (1992), Hendricks, Patel, and Zeckhauser (1993), Elton, Gruber, Das, and Hlavka (1993), Goetzmann and Ibbotson (1994), Grinblatt, Titman, and Wermers (1995), and Elton, Gruber, and Blake (1996).

[9]Monthly and daily momentum factor returns are available from Kenneth French's data library at http://mba.tuck.dartmouth.edu/pages/faculty/ken.french/data_library.html. It is worth noting that while the monthly and annual momentum factor returns from the website are denoted as *MOM*, the daily momentum factor is denoted *UMD*. Additionally, the monthly momentum factor available through the "Fama French & Liquidity Factors" database on Wharton Research Data Services (WRDS) is denoted "UMD."

momentum factor returns are available beginning in January 1927 instead of July 1926, as was the case for the market (*MKT*), size (*SMB*), and value (*HML*) factors.

During the period from January 1927 through December 2012, the *MOM* portfolio produces a mean monthly return (log return) of 0.69% (0.56%), and a monthly (log) return standard deviation of 4.78% (5.31%). The annualized Sharpe ratio of the monthly (log) returns of the *MOM* portfolio is therefore 0.50 (0.36). The cumulative return of the *MOM* portfolio over this period is 31,207%, giving a cumulative log return of 575%. The correlation of the *MOM* factor returns with the *MKT* factor returns, the *SMB* factor returns, and the *HML* factor returns are −0.34, −0.17, and −0.39, respectively. Regressing the *MOM* factor returns on the *MKT*, *SMB*, and *HML* returns indicates that the *MOM* portfolio has a risk-adjusted alpha of 1.02% per month with a Newey and West (1987) adjusted (six lags) t-statistic of 8.24 relative to the FF risk model. The returns of the *MOM* portfolio, therefore, are not explained by exposure to the *MKT*, *SMB*, or *HML* factors. Using the FF model, the *MOM* portfolio's sensitivity to the *MKT* factor is −0.22 with a corresponding t-statistic of −3.13, indicating that the *MOM* portfolio's return has a negative sensitivity to the return of the market portfolio. The sensitivity of *MOM* to the *SMB* portfolio is a statistically insignificant −0.058 (t-statistic = −0.66). Finally, the *MOM* portfolio exhibits a highly statistically significant sensitivity of −0.45 (t-statistic = −3.16) to the *HML* portfolio.

Figure 11.1 plots the cumulative returns (solid line) and cumulative log returns (dashed line) realized by an investor holding the *MOM* portfolio from the end of December 1926 through the end of December of 2012. The chart indicates that from the early 1940s through approximately year 2000, the *MOM* factor mimicking portfolio generated consistently positive returns, with very few and minimally sized drawdowns. Prior to and after this prolonged period of consistent profitability, the portfolio experiences high volatility and extremely large drawdowns. The worst drawdown occurs beginning at the end of June 1932. From this point until the end of September 1939, the *MOM* portfolio loses more than 76% of its value. Starting in October 1939, the portfolio generated generally positive returns, but did not regain its previous maximum value until the end of July 1956, more than 24 years after the drawdown begins. The second largest drawdown occurs toward the end of the financial crisis of 2007 and 2008. Between the end of November 2008 and the end of September 2009 the *MOM* portfolio loses more than 57% of its value. As can be seen in Figure 11.1, as of the end of 2012, the portfolio had yet to regain this lost value, or to even come close. The third largest drawdown also comes on the heels of crisis in the financial markets. Starting at the end of September 2002, approximately the same time that the NASDAQ index hit its post Internet bubble lows, the *MOM* portfolio begins a drawdown that resulted in a cumulative loss of more than 31% by the end of August 2004. The portfolio finally regains its previous high-water mark at the end of June of 2008, only five months before the next severe drawdown begins. It is easily seen by observing the figure that the value of the *MOM* portfolio at the end of December 2012 remains well below its value as of the beginning of this drawdown in September 2002. In fact, the first time the *MOM* portfolio achieved the value it has at the end of the sample period was

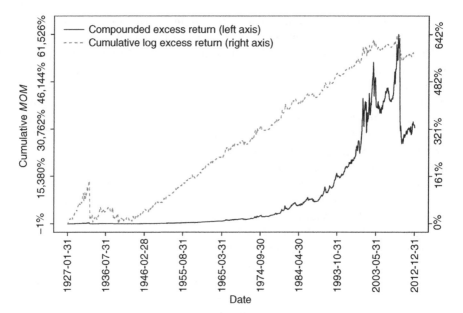

Figure 11.1   Cumulative Returns of *MOM* Portfolio.
This figure plots the cumulate returns of the *MOM* factor for the period from January 1927
through December 2012. The compounded excess return for month *t* is calculated as 100 times
the cumulative product of one plus the monthly return up to and including the given month.
The cumulate log excess return is calculated as the sum of the monthly log excess returns up
to and including the given month

December 1999. From this point forward, while there have been substantial ups and
downs, the *MOM* portfolio has produced a cumulative return of approximately zero.

11.6   THE FAMA, FRENCH, AND CARHART FOUR-FACTOR MODEL

The main objective of Carhart (1997) in generating the momentum factor is to
include it as a factor in risk models. Following Carhart (1997)'s lead, researchers
soon adopted what is now known as the Fama and French (1993) and Carhart (1997)
four-factor, or FFC, model. This model includes the three factors included in the
Fama and French (1993) three-factor model (*MKT*, *SMB*, and *HML*), as well as
the *MOM* factor that captures the returns associated with momentum investing.
The FFC risk model can therefore be written as

$$r_{p,t} = \alpha_p + \beta_{MKT,p}MKT_t + \beta_{SMB,p}SMB_t$$
$$+ \beta_{HML,p}HML_t + \beta_{MOM,p}MOM_t + \epsilon_{p,t} \qquad (11.2)$$

where $r_{p,t}$ is the excess return of portfolio (or security) p during period t, MKT_t, SMB_t,
HML_t, and MOM_t are the month t returns of the market, size, value, and momen-
tum factor mimicking portfolios, respectively. The betas ($\beta_{MKTRF,p}$, $\beta_{SMB,p}$, $\beta_{HML,p}$,

REFERENCES 239

$\beta_{MOM,p}$) in the FFC risk model represent the sensitivity of the return of the portfolio p to the corresponding factors, and $\epsilon_{p,t}$ is the component of the return of portfolio p during period t that is not due to exposure to the factors included in the model. Finally, α_p is the risk-adjusted average return of the portfolio after accounting for the portfolio's sensitivities to the *MKT*, *SMB*, *HML*, and *MOM* factors. A statistically nonzero estimate of α_p is considered evidence that the portfolio p generates nonzero average excess returns that are not related to the factors included in the risk model. Theoretically, if the risk model is correct, the factors included in the model represent all factors priced by investors, and α_p should be equal to zero for all portfolios p. The FFC model has become the most commonly used risk factor model by empirical asset pricing researchers.

11.7 SUMMARY

In this chapter, we have demonstrated that there exists a strong positive cross-sectional relation between momentum (*Mom*), measured as the return of a stock during the period covering months $t - 11$ through $t - 1$, and the return of the stock in month $t + 1$. This phenomenon, documented by Jegadeesh and Titman (1993) and known as the momentum effect, persists after controlling for the relations between expected stock returns and each of beta, market capitalization, and book-to-market ratio. Interestingly, we find that for extremely small stocks, namely those in the bottom 5% of market capitalization, the momentum effect may be reversed. For all other stocks, however, the effect appears strong.

Following Carhart (1997), it has become common for researchers to include the momentum-based factor, *MOM*, in risk models designed to explain asset returns. We therefore introduced the Fama and French (1993) and Carhart (1997) four-factor (FFC) risk model, which uses the excess return of the market portfolio (*MKT*), and returns of the *SMB*, *HML*, and *MOM* portfolios as proxies for factors that are related to security returns. While several different models have been proposed and used throughout the empirical asset pricing literature, the FFC model remains the most commonly accepted and widely used risk model.

REFERENCES

Ahn, D.-H., Boudoukh, J., Richardson, M. P., and Whitelaw, R. F. 2002. Partial adjustment or stale prices? implications from stock index and futures return autocorrelations. Review of Financial Studies, 15(2), 655–689.

Asness, C. S., Moskowitz, T. J., and Pedersen, L. H. 2013. Value and momentum everywhere. Journal of Finance, 68(3), 929–985.

Atchison, M. D., Butler, K. C., and Simonds, R. R. 1987. Nonsynchronous security trading and market index autocorrelation. Journal of Finance, 42(1), 111–118.

Bali, T. G. and Engle, R. F. 2010. The intertemporal capital asset pricing model with dynamic condition correlations. Journal of Monetary Economics, 57(4), 377–390.

Barberis, N., Shleifer, A., and Vishny, R. 1998. A model of investor sentiment. Journal of Financial Economics, 49(3), 307–343.

Boudoukh, J., Richardson, M. P., and Whitelaw, R. F. 1994. A tale of three schools: insights on autocorrelations of short-horizon stock returns. Review of Financial Studies, 7(3), 539–573.

Campbell, J. Y., Grossman, S. J., and Wang, J. 1993. Trading volume and serial correlation in stock returns. Quarterly Journal of Economics, 108(4), 905–939.

Carhart, M. M. 1997. On persistence in mutual fund performance. Journal of Finance, 52(1), 57–82.

Connolly, R. and Stivers, C. 2003. Momentum and reversals in equity-index returns during periods of abnormal turnover and return dispersion. Journal of Finance, 58(4), 1521–1556.

Conrad, J. and Kaul, G. 1989. Mean reversion in short-horizon expected returns. Review of Financial Studies, 2(2), 225–240.

Daniel, K., Hirshleifer, D., and Subrahmanyam, A. 1998. Investor psychology and security market under- and overreactions. Journal of Finance, 53(6), 1839–1885.

De Bondt, W. F. M. and Thaler, R. 1985. Does the stock market overreact? Journal of Finance, 40(3), 793–805.

Elton, E. J., Gruber, M. J., and Blake, C. R. 1996. The persistence of risk-adjusted mutual fund performance. Journal of Business, 69(2), 133–157.

Elton, E. J., Gruber, M. J., Das, S., and Hlavka, M. 1993. Efficiency with costly information: a reinterpretation of evidence from managed portfolios. Review of Financial Studies, 6(1), 1–22.

Fama, E. F. and French, K. R. 1993. Common risk factors in the returns on stocks and bonds. Journal of Financial Economics, 33(1), 3–56.

Fama, E. F. and French, K. R. 2012. Size, value, and momentum in international stock returns. Journal of Financial Economics, 105(3), 457–472.

Fama, E. F. and MacBeth, J. D. 1973. Risk, return, and equilibrium: empirical tests. Journal of Political Economy, 81(3), 607–636.

Fisher, L. 1966. Some new stock-market indexes. Journal of Business, 39(1), 191–225.

Goetzmann, W. N. and Ibbotson, W. N. 1994. Do winners repeat. Journal of Portfolio Management, 20(2), 9–18.

Grinblatt, M. and Titman, S. 1992. The persistence of mutual fund performance. Journal of Finance, 47(5), 1977–1984.

Grinblatt, M., Titman, S., and Wermers, R. 1995. Momentum investment strategies, portfolio performance, and herding: a study of mutual fund behavior. American Economic Review, 85(5), 1088–1105.

Hendricks, D., Patel, J., and Zeckhauser, R. 1993. Hot hands in mutual funds: short-run persistence of relative performance, 1974-1988. Journal of Finance, 48(1), 93–130.

Hong, H. and Stein, J. C. 1999. A unified theory of underreaction, momentum trading, and overreaction in asset markets. Journal of Finance, 54(6), 2143–2184.

Jegadeesh, N. 1990. Evidence of predictable behavior of security returns. Journal of Finance, 45(3), 881–898.

Jegadeesh, N. and Titman, S. 1993. Returns to buying winners and selling losers: implications for stock market efficiency. Journal of Finance, 48(1), 65–91.

Jensen, M. C. and Benington, G. A. 1970. Random walks and technical theories: some additional evidence. Journal of Finance, 25(2), 469–482.

Jostova, G., Nikolova, S., and Philipov, A. 2013. Momentum in corporate bond returns. Review of Financial Studies, 26(7), 1649–1693.

Lehmann, B. N. 1990. Fads, martingales, and market efficiency. Quarterly Journal of Economics, 105(1), 1–28.

Levy, R. A. 1967. Relative strength as a criterion for investment selection. Journal of Finance, 22, 595–610.

Lewellen, J. and Nagel, S. 2006. The conditional CAPM does not explain asset-pricing anomalies. Journal of Financial Economics, 82(2), 289–314.

Lo, A. W. and MacKinlay, A. C. 1990a. An econometric analysis of nonsynchronous trading. Journal of Econometrics, 45(1-2), 181–211.

Lo, A. W. and MacKinlay, A. C. 1990b. When are contrarian profits due to stock market overreaction? Review of Financial Studies, 3(2), 175–205.

Merton, R. C. 1973. An intertemporal capital asset pricing model. Econometrica, 41(5), 867–887.

Newey, W. K. and West, K. D. 1987. A simple, positive semi-definite, heteroskedasticity and autocorrelation consistent covariance matrix. Econometrica, 55(3), 703–708.

Roll, R. 1984. A simple implicit measure of the effective bid-ask spread in an efficient market. Journal of Finance, 39(4), 1127–1139.

12

SHORT-TERM REVERSAL

In this chapter, we examine the short-term reversal effect documented by Jegadeesh (1990) and Lehmann (1990). The short-term reversal effect is both one of the strongest (particularly in equal-weighted analyses) and one of the simplest phenomena documented in the empirical asset pricing literature. As eluded to in the previous chapter, short-term reversal refers to the fact that stock returns over the short-term past, such as one week as in Lehmann (1990) or one month as in Jegadeesh (1990), tend to have a negative cross-sectional relation with returns over the next week or month. Thus, a strategy of buying recent losers and selling recent winners generates positive returns that are not explained by any of the standard risk models.

The reversal phenomenon is most commonly attributed to liquidity and microstructure effects. Several papers have examined the impact of liquidity and microstructure issues on the time-series properties of security and portfolio returns. Roll (1984) generates a model in which the bid–ask spread generates negative serial correlation in time series of stock returns. Many other papers, such as Lo and MacKinlay (1990), Conrad, Gultekin, and Kaul (1997), Keim (1989), Hasbrouck (1991), Admati and Pfleiderer (1989), and Mech (1993), have demonstrated that microstructure issues such as the bid–ask bounce and transaction costs can generate autocorrelation in security returns. Boudoukh, Richardson, and Whitelaw (1994) demonstrate that a large portion of documented serial correlation is attributable to institutional factors such as trading and nontrading periods, market frictions such as the bid–ask spread, or other microstructure effects. Nagel (2012) presents evidence that the returns of short-term reversal strategies can be used as proxies for the returns associated with liquidity provision.

Empirical Asset Pricing: The Cross Section of Stock Returns, First Edition.
Turan G. Bali, Robert F. Engle, and Scott Murray.
© 2016 John Wiley & Sons, Inc. Published 2016 by John Wiley & Sons, Inc.

A common theme among the papers that investigate either the reversal phenomenon or autocorrelation in security returns is that the effect is not reflective of firm fundamentals. Both Jegadeesh (1990) and Lehmann (1990) conclude that their empirical results are inconsistent with the efficient market hypothesis of Fama (1970). Lehmann (1990) goes a step further by proposing that short-term reversal phenomenon is a manifestation of inefficiency in the market for liquidity in stocks that have recently realized large price changes.

In the remainder of this chapter, we empirically examine the short-term reversal phenomenon and discuss the reversal factor, which some researchers have used in augmented risk models.

12.1   MEASURING SHORT-TERM REVERSAL

Short-term reversal is perhaps the easiest variable to calculate in all of empirical asset pricing. In most applications, the short-term reversal of stock i for month t is taken simply to be the return of the stock during the month t. Thus, we have

$$Rev_{i,t} = 100 \times R_{i,t} \qquad (12.1)$$

where $Rev_{i,t}$ denotes short-term reversal and $R_{i,t}$ is the return of stock i in month t. In most cases, the return in month t is taken from the RET field in the monthly stock file from the Center for Research in Security Prices (CRSP). Multiplication by 100 results in Rev being represented as a percentage. In analyses where there may be benefits of using a period shorter than one month for measuring reversal, such as in analyses of future returns where the future return period is less than one month (Lehmann (1990)), some researchers measure reversal using a shorter period. Measurement periods of longer than one month, however, are generally not used.

12.2   SUMMARY STATISTICS

Summary statistics for Rev for our sample of U.S.-based common stocks in the CRSP database from 1963 through 2012 are presented in Table 12.1. The results show that in the average month, the average value of Rev is 1.21% and the median value is 0.06%, indicating that the cross-sectional distribution of reversal has strong positive skewness. Indeed, the skewness of Rev in the average month is 3.11. Values of Rev range from −67.35% to 266.45%, and the cross-sectional standard deviation of Rev is 15.49%. In addition to being highly skewed, the cross-sectional distribution of Rev is highly leptokurtic with an excess kurtosis in the average month of 59.45. There are an average of 4750 stocks with valid values of Rev per month.

12.3   CORRELATIONS

Table 12.2 presents the average cross-sectional Pearson product–moment and Spearman rank correlations between Rev and each of market beta (β), log of market

TABLE 12.1   Summary Statistics

This table presents summary statistics for reversal (*Rev*), measured as the stock return in month *t*, calculated using the CRSP sample for the months *t* from June 1963 through November 2012. Each month, the mean (*Mean*), standard deviation (*SD*), skewness (*Skew*), excess kurtosis (*Kurt*), minimum (*Min*), fifth percentile (5%), 25th percentile (25%), median (*Median*), 75th percentile (75%), 95th percentile (95%), and maximum (*Max*) values of the cross-sectional distribution of each variable is calculated. The table presents the time-series means for each cross-sectional value. The column labeled *n* indicates that average number of stocks for *Rev* is available.

	Mean	SD	Skew	Kurt	Min	5%	25%	Median	75%	95%	Max	n
Rev	1.21	15.49	3.11	59.45	−67.35	−18.93	−6.27	0.06	6.92	24.20	266.45	4750

TABLE 12.2   Correlations

This table presents the time-series averages of the annual cross-sectional Pearson product–moment and Spearman rank correlations between *Rev* and each of β, *Size*, *BM*, and *Mom*.

Correlation	β	Size	BM	Mom
Pearson	−0.02	0.07	0.02	0.02
Spearman	−0.01	0.11	0.03	0.04

capitalization (*Size*), book-to-market ratio(*BM*), and momentum (*Mom*). The results demonstrate that *Rev* is not highly correlated with any of these variables. Reversal is most highly correlated with *Size*, but the average cross-sectional Pearson correlation between these variables is only 0.07, and the corresponding Spearman correlation is only 0.11. The average Pearson (Spearman) correlations between *Rev* and β, *BM*, and *Mom* of −0.02 (−0.01), 0.02 (0.03), and 0.02 (0.04), respectively, are all quite low.

As with the analysis of the momentum variable *Mom*, we forego a persistence analysis of *Rev* because a persistence analysis would simply examine the ability of *Rev* to predict future stock returns, the primary focus of the remainder of this chapter.

12.4   REVERSAL AND STOCK RETURNS

We proceed now to examine the relation between reversal and expected stock returns using portfolio and Fama and MacBeth (1973) regression analysis.

12.4.1   Univariate Portfolio Analysis

We begin our empirical investigation of the short-term reversal phenomenon with univariate decile portfolio analyses. The decile breakpoints are calculated using all stocks in the sample. The results of these analyses are shown in Table 12.3.

TABLE 12.3   Univariate Portfolio Analysis

This table presents the results of univariate portfolio analyses of the relation between reversal and future stock returns. Monthly portfolios are formed by sorting all stocks in the CRSP sample into portfolios using Rev decile breakpoints calculated using all stocks in the CRSP sample. Panel A shows the average values of Rev, β, $MktCap$, BM, and Mom for stocks in each decile portfolio. Panel B (Panel C) shows the average equal-weighted (value-weighted) one-month-ahead excess return (in percent per month), CAPM alpha, FF alpha, and FFC alpha for each of the 10 decile portfolios as well as for the long–short zero-cost portfolio that is long the 10th decile portfolio and short the first decile portfolio. Newey and West (1987) t-statistics, adjusted using six lags, testing the null hypothesis that the average portfolio excess return or CAPM alpha is equal to zero, are shown in parentheses.

Panel A: *Rev*-Sorted Portfolio Characteristics

Value	1	2	3	4	5	6	7	8	9	10
Rev	−21.38	−10.50	−6.29	−3.41	−1.07	1.23	3.75	6.97	12.06	30.80
β	0.89	0.84	0.78	0.73	0.70	0.71	0.73	0.77	0.83	0.84
MktCap	279	716	1048	1316	1435	1547	1524	1485	1110	489
BM	0.93	0.93	0.93	0.94	0.96	0.94	0.94	0.92	0.93	1.02
Mom	11.71	13.72	13.70	13.26	12.80	13.71	14.16	15.03	16.24	14.42

Panel B: Equal-Weighted Portfolio Returns

Value	1	2	3	4	5	6	7	8	9	10	10-1
Excess	2.31	0.99	0.83	0.78	0.76	0.72	0.66	0.50	0.34	−0.38	−2.69
return	(5.56)	(2.93)	(2.74)	(2.71)	(2.73)	(2.73)	(2.52)	(1.78)	(1.12)	(−1.02)	(−9.72)
CAPM α	1.61	0.40	0.30	0.29	0.29	0.30	0.25	0.04	−0.15	−0.91	−2.52
	(5.90)	(2.12)	(1.91)	(1.90)	(2.10)	(2.01)	(1.72)	(0.28)	(−0.98)	(−4.15)	(−9.44)
FF α	1.32	0.12	0.03	0.00	0.01	0.05	0.01	−0.19	−0.37	−1.10	−2.42
	(5.97)	(1.01)	(0.31)	(0.02)	(0.16)	(0.49)	(0.09)	(−2.48)	(−4.39)	(−7.13)	(−8.35)
FFC α	1.86	0.42	0.22	0.14	0.12	0.15	0.10	−0.12	−0.32	−1.07	−2.93
	(6.40)	(2.99)	(2.36)	(1.73)	(1.78)	(1.53)	(0.87)	(−1.42)	(−3.22)	(−6.41)	(−8.31)

Panel C: Value-Weighted Portfolio Returns

Value	1	2	3	4	5	6	7	8	9	10	10-1
Excess	0.72	0.50	0.73	0.68	0.58	0.47	0.48	0.44	0.33	0.12	−0.60
return	(2.07)	(1.79)	(3.22)	(3.16)	(2.84)	(2.46)	(2.41)	(2.08)	(1.52)	(0.45)	(−2.40)
CAPM α	0.01	−0.09	0.20	0.21	0.13	0.04	0.06	0.00	−0.12	−0.40	−0.40
	(0.03)	(−0.72)	(2.34)	(2.98)	(2.21)	(0.78)	(1.08)	(0.00)	(−1.43)	(−2.80)	(−1.69)
FF α	−0.09	−0.15	0.17	0.18	0.10	0.03	0.04	0.01	−0.11	−0.39	−0.31
	(−0.46)	(−1.09)	(1.89)	(2.60)	(1.87)	(0.67)	(0.62)	(0.11)	(−1.25)	(−2.85)	(−1.21)
FFC α	0.28	0.05	0.28	0.24	0.13	0.02	0.03	−0.02	−0.17	−0.48	−0.76
	(1.58)	(0.37)	(2.47)	(2.86)	(2.00)	(0.34)	(0.48)	(−0.28)	(−1.67)	(−3.49)	(−3.21)

In Panel A, we present the equal-weighted average values for each of *Rev*, beta (β), market capitalization (*MktCap*), book-to-market ratio (*BM*), and momentum (*Mom*) for stocks in each of the *Rev*-sorted decile portfolios. By design, the average values of *Rev* increase from −21.38% for decile portfolio 1 to 30.80% for the 10th decile portfolio. β exhibits a U-shaped relation with reversal, as the average values of β decrease from 0.89 in decile portfolio 1 to 0.70 in decile portfolio five, and then increase from there to 0.84 for decile portfolio 10. The relation between *Rev* and market capitalization appears to be inverted U-shaped because average *MktCap* increases from $279 million for stocks in *Rev* decile portfolio 1 to $1.547 billion in portfolio 6, and then decreases to $489 million in portfolio 10. The relation between book-to-market ratio and reversal is quite flat, with the exception of stocks with very high values of *Rev*, which also tend to high values of *BM*. The average values of *BM* for portfolios 1 through 9 range from 0.92 to 0.96, whereas decile portfolio 10 holds stocks with an average *BM* of 1.02. Finally, average values of *Mom* tend to increase, although not monotonically, from 11.71% for portfolio 1 to 16.24% for portfolio 9, before decreasing to 14.42% for decile portfolio 10.

The equal-weighted average excess returns, capital asset pricing model alphas (CAPM α), Fama and French (1993) three-factor alphas (FF α), Fama and French (1993) and Carhart (1997) four-factor alphas (FFC α), and associated Newey and West (1987)-adjusted *t*-statistics (six lags), for the *Rev*-sorted decile portfolios, as well as for the portfolio that is long high-*Rev* stocks and short low-*Rev* stocks (10-1) are shown in Panel B. The excess returns indicate a strong negative relation between *Rev* and future stock returns. The average monthly excess returns of the decile portfolios decrease monotonically from 2.31% per month for the first decile portfolio to −0.38% for the 10th decile portfolio. The resulting −2.69% average monthly return of the 10-1 portfolio is highly statistically significant, with a *t*-statistic of −9.72. The majority of this effect is driven by the extreme decile portfolios. Portfolio 1 generates an extremely high average excess return of 2.31% per month, compared to 0.99% for decile portfolio 2. Similarly, decile portfolio 10 produces an average excess return of −0.38% per month, which is much lower than the 0.34% average monthly excess return generated by portfolio 9. The differences in average excess returns of 1.32% between portfolios 1 and 2, and 0.72% between portfolios 9 and 10, are each higher than the difference in average returns between portfolios 2 and 9 of 0.65% per month.

Adjusting the returns of the equal-weighted portfolios for risk does little to explain the patterns in average excess returns. The CAPM, FF, and FFC alphas of the decile portfolios all decrease, nearly monotonically, from decile portfolio 1 to decile portfolio 10 of *Rev*. The difference portfolio generates CAPM alpha of −2.52% per month (*t*-statistic = −9.44), FF alpha of −2.42% per month (*t*-statistic = −8.35), and FFC alpha of −2.93% per month (*t*-statistic = −8.31), each of which is economically very large and highly statistically significant. In all cases, the positive alphas of decile portfolio 1 and negative alphas of decile portfolio 10 are large and highly statistically significant. This indicates that the reversal phenomenon is driven by stocks with both high and low values of *Rev*.

Panel C of Table 12.3 shows that using value-weighted portfolios instead of equal-weighted portfolios has a very substantial impact on the results of the portfolio analysis, with value-weighted portfolios detecting a much weaker reversal phenomenon than equal-weighted portfolios. The average value-weighted excess returns of the decile portfolios decrease, albeit not monotonically, from 0.72% per month for decile portfolio 1 to 0.12% per month for decile portfolio 10. The average return difference of −0.60% per month remains economically large and statistically significant with a t-statistic of −2.40. However, this return difference of −0.60% per month is much smaller in magnitude and statistical significance than the return difference of −2.69% per month found when using equal-weighted portfolios. When the CAPM and FF models are used to adjust the portfolio returns for risk, the results fail to indicate a statistically significant reversal phenomenon since the Rev 10-1 portfolio produces a CAPM alpha of −0.40% per month (t-statistic = −1.69) and an FF alpha of −0.31% per month (t-statistic = −1.21), neither of which is statistically significant. Interestingly, the FFC alpha of the Rev difference portfolio is −0.76% per month with a corresponding t-statistic of −3.21. Regardless of which risk model is used, the first decile portfolio fails to generate statistically significant abnormal returns. Decile portfolio 10, however, generates large and statistically negative abnormal returns of −0.40% per month (t-statistic = −2.80), −0.39% per month (t-statistic = −2.85), and −0.48% per month (t-statistic = −3.49) relative to the CAPM, FF, and FFC risk models, respectively. The value-weighted portfolio results, therefore, indicate that the reversal phenomenon is driven by stocks with high returns in the previous month.

Predicting k-Month-Ahead Returns

We have thus far demonstrated that Rev, calculated as the month t stock return, has the ability to predict the cross section of month $t + 1$ stock returns. We now examine the ability of more distant previous individual month returns to predict month $t + 1$ returns. To this end, we define $R_{i,t-k}$ for $k \in \{1, 2, 3, \dots, 11\}$ to be the return of stock i in month $t - k$. We then use univariate portfolio analysis to examine the month $t + 1$ returns of portfolios formed at the end of month t when sorting on the returns measured with different lags. Recall that Rev is the return measured at lag zero. The results of the analyses using equal-weighted (Panel A) and value-weighted (Panel B) portfolios are presented in Table 12.4.

The results in Table 12.4 show that when there is a lag introduced between the measurement of reversal and portfolio formation, the reversal phenomenon quickly becomes a momentum phenomenon because the average monthly returns of the 10-1 portfolio sorted on Rev_{t-k} for $k \in \{1, 2, \dots, 11\}$ are all positive and, in most cases, statistically significant. This result holds using both equal-weighted portfolios and value-weighted portfolios. The only exceptions are that the positive average returns of the equal-weighted portfolios formed by sorting on Rev_{t-1}, Rev_{t-7}, Rev_{t-8}, and Rev_{t-9} are all statistically insignificant. The average returns of the value-weighted Rev_{t-3} and Rev_{t-7} 10-1 portfolios are only marginally statistically significant. The results are very similar when the FF risk model is used to adjust the returns. As would be expected, when the FFC model, which includes the momentum (MOM) factor, is used to risk-adjust the portfolio returns, the abnormal returns of the 10-1 portfolios become, for the most part, statistically insignificant. Interestingly, when Rev_{t-10}

TABLE 12.4   Univariate Portfolio Analysis—Lagged Values of Reversal

This table presents the results of univariate portfolio analyses of the relation between previous values of reversal and future stock returns. Monthly portfolios are formed by sorting all stocks in the CRSP sample into portfolios using decile breakpoints calculated based on the given sort variable using all stocks in the CRSP sample. The variables used to form portfolios at the end of month t are the values of reversal (the stock return) measured in month t (Rev) or month $t - k$ (R_{t-k}). Panel A (Panel B) shows the average value-weighted (equal-weighted) month $t + 1$ excess return (in percent per month) for each of the 10 decile portfolios. The table also shows the average month $t + 1$ return of the portfolio that is long the 10th decile portfolio and short the first decile portfolio, as well as the CAPM, FF, and FFC alphas for this portfolio. Newey and West (1987) t-statistics, adjusted using six lags, testing the null hypothesis that the average 10-1 portfolio return or alpha is equal to zero, are shown in parentheses.

Panel A: Equal-Weighted Portfolio Returns

Sort Variable	1	2	3	4	5	6	7	8	9	10	10-1	FF α	FFC α
Rev	2.31	0.99	0.83	0.78	0.76	0.72	0.66	0.50	0.34	−0.38	−2.69	−2.42	−2.93
											(−9.72)	(−8.35)	(−8.31)
R_{t-1}	0.53	0.82	0.87	0.91	0.90	0.82	0.77	0.70	0.68	0.54	0.01	0.18	−0.38
											(0.08)	(0.94)	(−1.66)
R_{t-2}	0.25	0.59	0.71	0.78	0.88	0.83	0.85	0.81	0.90	0.87	0.62	0.70	0.15
											(4.36)	(4.53)	(0.83)
R_{t-3}	0.36	0.57	0.81	0.90	0.96	0.87	0.83	0.75	0.80	0.71	0.35	0.39	−0.09
											(2.29)	(2.62)	(−0.46)
R_{t-4}	0.42	0.63	0.73	0.77	0.85	0.91	0.85	0.84	0.81	0.73	0.31	0.45	−0.03
											(2.06)	(3.45)	(−0.23)
R_{t-5}	0.51	0.57	0.68	0.78	0.85	0.78	0.79	0.83	0.89	0.87	0.36	0.46	−0.06
											(1.83)	(2.31)	(−0.29)
R_{t-6}	0.42	0.56	0.66	0.76	0.81	0.81	0.91	0.86	0.93	0.91	0.49	0.58	0.20
											(3.06)	(4.50)	(1.39)
R_{t-7}	0.63	0.60	0.70	0.78	0.74	0.81	0.84	0.85	0.85	0.85	0.22	0.33	−0.03
											(1.33)	(2.00)	(−0.13)
R_{t-8}	0.65	0.65	0.71	0.76	0.80	0.78	0.77	0.82	0.86	0.91	0.26	0.35	−0.14
											(1.35)	(1.67)	(−0.53)
R_{t-9}	0.66	0.76	0.69	0.76	0.81	0.85	0.93	0.82	0.79	0.79	0.13	0.20	−0.14
											(0.83)	(1.39)	(−1.00)
R_{t-10}	0.46	0.59	0.72	0.75	0.81	0.92	0.91	0.89	0.90	0.96	0.50	0.56	0.32
											(3.34)	(3.94)	(2.29)
R_{t-11}	0.29	0.47	0.55	0.73	0.86	0.85	0.93	0.97	1.10	1.20	0.91	0.89	0.75
											(6.50)	(6.72)	(4.94)
Rev	0.72	0.50	0.73	0.68	0.58	0.47	0.48	0.44	0.33	0.12	−0.60	−0.31	−0.76
											(−2.40)	(−1.21)	(−3.21)

TABLE 12.4   *(Continued)*

| Panel B: Value-Weighted Portfolio Returns |

Sort Variable	1	2	3	4	5	6	7	8	9	10	10-1	FF α	FFC α
R_{t-1}	−0.07	0.50	0.52	0.61	0.58	0.43	0.48	0.40	0.51	0.49	0.57	0.74	0.12
											(2.53)	(3.27)	(0.60)
R_{t-2}	−0.17	0.36	0.37	0.55	0.56	0.54	0.54	0.48	0.51	0.66	0.83	1.02	0.37
											(3.61)	(4.52)	(1.75)
R_{t-3}	0.08	0.32	0.48	0.52	0.50	0.43	0.50	0.54	0.48	0.42	0.34	0.33	−0.24
											(1.71)	(1.58)	(−1.11)
R_{t-4}	0.05	0.31	0.47	0.51	0.50	0.47	0.55	0.54	0.53	0.57	0.51	0.66	0.07
											(2.34)	(3.20)	(0.34)
R_{t-5}	0.09	0.15	0.30	0.44	0.48	0.54	0.43	0.55	0.54	0.66	0.57	0.70	0.15
											(2.19)	(2.68)	(0.62)
R_{t-6}	0.08	0.28	0.40	0.36	0.51	0.42	0.49	0.47	0.52	0.62	0.53	0.60	0.15
											(2.55)	(2.81)	(0.61)
R_{t-7}	0.37	0.32	0.34	0.44	0.39	0.50	0.42	0.52	0.55	0.75	0.38	0.48	0.14
											(1.90)	(2.25)	(0.58)
R_{t-8}	0.21	0.32	0.25	0.36	0.43	0.45	0.41	0.47	0.77	0.85	0.64	0.79	0.28
											(2.69)	(3.35)	(1.28)
R_{t-9}	0.15	0.26	0.25	0.46	0.49	0.50	0.65	0.48	0.61	0.65	0.50	0.59	0.18
											(2.23)	(2.81)	(0.82)
R_{t-10}	−0.09	0.22	0.24	0.36	0.46	0.48	0.59	0.58	0.73	0.79	0.88	1.00	0.58
											(4.95)	(5.58)	(2.79)
R_{t-11}	0.04	0.19	0.27	0.31	0.42	0.47	0.53	0.64	0.77	0.81	0.77	0.80	0.49
											(3.54)	(4.10)	(2.59)

and Rev_{t-11} are used as the sort variable, the FFC alphas of the difference portfolios remain positive and highly statistically significant, indicating that the inclusion of the *MOM* factor in the risk model does not completely capture the momentum effect between returns at extended lags. Thus, while the medium-term momentum effect appears in returns spaced between two and 12 months apart, the reversal phenomenon is a very short-term effect.

12.4.2   Bivariate Portfolio Analyses

The univariate regression analyses provide strong indications of a short-term reversal phenomenon. We now use bivariate portfolio analyses to examine whether this effect can be explained by market beta (β), market capitalization (*MktCap*), book-to-market ratio (*BM*), or momentum (*Mom*). Referring to the correlation analysis in Table 12.2 and the univariate portfolio characteristics in Table 12.3, we see that β has almost no cross-sectional relation with *Rev*, and thus is unlikely to explain the reversal phenomenon. Average *BM* and *Mom* are slightly higher in decile 10 of *Rev* than in decile 1. Since both of these variables are positively related to future returns and the *Rev* decile 10 portfolio generates a lower average return than the *Rev* decile one portfolio, *BM* and *Mom* are unlikely to explain the reversal effect. Average *MktCap* is substantially higher in decile 10 than in decile 1 of *Rev*. Because *MktCap* is negatively related to expected future returns, it is possible that the high (low) average *MktCap* for stocks in the 10th (first) *Rev* decile portfolio is driving the reversal effect.

Dependent-Sort Analysis

We therefore begin our bivariate portfolio analysis of the short-term reversal effect with a dependent-sort analysis using market capitalization (*MktCap*) as the first sort variable and reversal (*Rev*) as the second sort variable. The breakpoints for each sort are the quintiles of the sort variables calculated using all stocks in the sample. Table 12.5 presents the results of this analysis.

When using equal-weighted portfolios, the results in Panel A show that the reversal phenomenon is strong in each quintile of market capitalization although it becomes stronger for smaller capitalization stocks. The *Rev* 5-1 portfolio for the average *MktCap* quintile generates an average monthly return of -1.66% per month with a corresponding t-statistic of -8.74. This result cannot be explained by exposure to any of the factors in the FFC risk model, as the CAPM alpha, FF alpha, and FFC alpha of this portfolio's returns are -1.52% per month (t-statistic $= -8.26$), -1.46% per month (t-statistic $= -7.40$), and -1.77% per month (t-statistic $= -7.99$), respectively. Furthermore, the returns of the *Rev* quintile portfolios for the average *MktCap* quintile decrease monotonically across the quintiles of *Rev*. Examination of the results within each quintile of *MktCap* indicate similar patterns. Within each *MktCap* quintile, the average returns of the *Rev*-sorted portfolios decrease monotonically from quintile one to quintile five of *Rev*. The *Rev* 5-1 portfolios in each of the *MktCap* quintiles all generate economically large and highly statistically significant negative average returns and risk-adjusted alphas. The results are strongest in the lowest *MktCap* quintile and become progressively less strong as the market capitalizations of the stocks in the portfolios increase since the average returns and alphas for the *Rev* 5-1 portfolios decrease monotonically in magnitude from *MktCap* quintile one to *MktCap* quintile five.

The results of the analysis using value-weighted portfolios presented in Panel B of Table 12.5 demonstrate that most of the patterns found in the equal-weighted portfolios also hold when using value-weighted portfolios. However, the magnitudes of the negative average returns and alphas for the *Rev* difference portfolios are somewhat smaller when using value-weighted portfolios instead of equal-weighted portfolios. In fact, when using value-weighted portfolios, the *Rev* 5-1 portfolio in the fifth quintile of *MktCap* generates statistically insignificant CAPM alpha of -0.22% per month (t-statistic $= -1.47$) and FF alpha of -0.16% per month t-statistic $= -0.96$). The FFC alpha for this portfolio of -0.37% per month, however, remains statistically significant with a t-statistic of -2.01. Finally, within the fifth quintile of *MktCap*, the average portfolio excess returns are not quite monotonically decreasing across the

TABLE 12.5   Bivariate Dependent-Sort Portfolio Analysis—Control for *MktCap*

This table presents the results of bivariate dependent-sort portfolio analyses of the relation between *Rev* and future stock returns after controlling for the effect of *MktCap*. Each month, all stocks in the CRSP sample are sorted into five groups based on an ascending sort of *MktCap*. Within each *MktCap* group, all stocks are sorted into five portfolios based on an ascending sort of *Rev*. The quintile breakpoints used to create the portfolios are calculated using all stocks in the CRSP sample. The table presents the average one-month-ahead excess return (in percent per month) for each of the 25 portfolios as well as for the average *MktCap* quintile portfolio within each quintile of *Rev*. Also shown are the average return, CAPM alpha, FF alpha, and FFC alpha of a long–short zero-cost portfolio that is long the fifth *Rev* quintile portfolio and short the first *Rev* quintile portfolio in each *MktCap* quintile. *t*-statistics (in parentheses), adjusted following Newey and West (1987) using six lags, testing the null hypothesis that the average return or alpha is equal to zero, are shown in parentheses. Panel A presents results for equal-weighted portfolios. Panel B presents results for value-weighted portfolios.

Panel A: Equal-Weighted Portfolios						
	MktCap 1	*MktCap 2*	*MktCap 3*	*MktCap 4*	*MktCap 5*	*MktCap Avg*
Rev 1	3.91	1.28	1.00	0.99	0.82	1.60
Rev 2	1.31	0.66	0.71	0.83	0.73	0.85
Rev 3	1.12	0.62	0.66	0.73	0.60	0.75
Rev 4	1.03	0.54	0.60	0.50	0.43	0.62
Rev 5	−0.38	−0.42	0.09	0.20	0.22	−0.06
Rev 5-1	−4.29	−1.70	−0.91	−0.79	−0.61	−1.66
	(−12.38)	(−6.57)	(−4.23)	(−4.47)	(−4.02)	(−8.74)
Rev 5-1 CAPM α	−4.13	−1.55	−0.78	−0.67	−0.49	−1.52
	(−12.10)	(−6.02)	(−3.70)	(−3.95)	(−3.31)	(−8.26)
Rev 5-1 FF α	−4.07	−1.48	−0.69	−0.64	−0.44	−1.46
	(−11.17)	(−5.64)	(−3.11)	(−3.32)	(−2.70)	(−7.40)
Rev 5-1 FFC α	−4.57	−1.84	−0.98	−0.83	−0.65	−1.77
	(−10.51)	(−6.20)	(−4.25)	(−4.22)	(−3.86)	(−7.99)

Panel B: Value-Weighted Portfolios						
	MktCap 1	*MktCap 2*	*MktCap 3*	*MktCap 4*	*MktCap 5*	*MktCap Avg*
Rev 1	2.80	1.26	1.00	0.98	0.57	1.32
Rev 2	1.03	0.67	0.74	0.85	0.58	0.77
Rev 3	0.82	0.63	0.67	0.72	0.47	0.66
Rev 4	0.72	0.56	0.58	0.50	0.35	0.54
Rev 5	−0.54	−0.36	0.12	0.21	0.25	−0.06

(continued)

TABLE 12.5   *(Continued)*

	Panel B: Value-Weighted Portfolios					
	MktCap 1	*MktCap 2*	*MktCap 3*	*MktCap 4*	*MktCap 5*	*MktCap Avg*
Rev 5-1	−3.34	−1.62	−0.89	−0.77	−0.33	−1.39
	(−10.60)	(−6.20)	(−4.10)	(−4.35)	(−2.12)	(−7.48)
Rev 5-1 CAPM α	−3.17	−1.46	−0.75	−0.66	−0.22	−1.25
	(−10.16)	(−5.65)	(−3.59)	(−3.84)	(−1.47)	(−6.93)
Rev 5-1 FF α	−3.09	−1.40	−0.67	−0.62	−0.16	−1.19
	(−9.69)	(−5.27)	(−2.97)	(−3.19)	(−0.96)	(−6.22)
Rev 5-1 FFC α	−3.55	−1.77	−0.95	−0.81	−0.37	−1.49
	(−9.02)	(−5.90)	(−4.15)	(−4.12)	(−2.01)	(−6.82)

quintiles of *Rev* since the *Rev* 1 portfolio generates slightly lower average excess returns (0.57% per month) than the *Rev* 2 portfolio (0.58% per month). With these few exceptions, the results of the value-weighted analysis are qualitatively similar to those of the equal-weighted portfolio analysis. There is little evidence, therefore, that controlling for market capitalization explains the reversal effect. However, the reversal phenomenon is strongest in small stocks.

We proceed now to investigate the effect of controlling for market beta (β), book-to-market ratio (*BM*), and momentum (*Mom*) on the reversal phenomenon, once again using bivariate-sort portfolio analyses. While our preliminary assessments based on the cross-sectional relations between *Rev* and each of β, *BM*, and *Mom* provide no indications that any of these variables may explain the reversal phenomenon, the investigation is worthwhile because even if none of these variables can fully explain the reversal effect, we may observe differences in the strength of the reversal effect among stocks with different values of the given control. We therefore repeat the bivariate-sort portfolio analyses using each of β, *BM*, and *Mom* as the first sort variable. Table 12.6 shows the average return, FF alpha, and FFC alpha for the *Rev* 5-1 portfolio within each quintile, as well as for the average quintile, of each of these control variables. Results using equal-weighted (Weights = EW) and value-weighted (Weights = VW) are presented.

When controlling for β using equal-weighted portfolios, the table indicates that the average return, FF alpha, and FFC alpha for the *Rev* difference portfolio within each quintile of β, as well as for the average β quintile, is negative, economically large, and highly statistically significant. The FFC alpha of the *Rev* 5-1 portfolio in the average β quintile is −1.94% per month with a corresponding *t*-statistic of −8.01. Furthermore, in equal-weighted portfolios, there is no strong indication of differential performance of the *Rev* 5-1 portfolio across the different β quintiles. When using value-weighted portfolios, the reversal effect is strong among stocks in the lowest three β quintiles, as in these β quintiles, the average returns, FF alphas, and FFC alphas of the *Rev* 5-1 portfolios are all negative, large, and statistically significant.

TABLE 12.6 Bivariate Dependent-Sort Portfolio Analysis
This table presents the results of bivariate dependent-sort portfolio analyses of the relation between Rev and future stock returns after controlling for the effect of each of β, BM, and Mom (control variables). Each month, all stocks in the CRSP sample are sorted into five groups based on an ascending sort of one of the control variables. Within each control variable group, all stocks are sorted into five portfolios based on an ascending sort of Rev. The quintile breakpoints used to create the portfolios are calculated using all stocks in the CRSP sample. The table presents the average return, CAPM alpha, FF alpha, and FFC alpha (in percent per month) of the long–short zero-cost portfolios that are long the fifth Rev quintile portfolio and short the first Rev quintile portfolio in each quintile, as well as for the average quintile, of the control variable. Results for equal-weighted (Weights = EW) and value-weighted (Weights = VW) portfolios are shown. t-statistics (in parentheses), adjusted following Newey and West (1987) using six lags, testing the null hypothesis that the average return or alpha is equal to zero, are shown in parentheses.

Control	Weights	Value	Control 1	Control 2	Control 3	Control 4	Control 5	Control Avg
β	EW	Return	−1.81	−1.56	−1.81	−1.75	−1.82	−1.75
			(−8.72)	(−7.81)	(−8.72)	(−7.52)	(−6.80)	(−8.90)
		FF α	−1.61	−1.39	−1.62	−1.48	−1.60	−1.54
			(−7.73)	(−6.73)	(−7.97)	(−6.18)	(−5.73)	(−7.71)
		FFC α	−1.96	−1.69	−1.97	−1.92	−2.17	−1.94
			(−9.02)	(−7.52)	(−8.22)	(−5.76)	(−6.31)	(−8.01)
	VW	Return	−0.72	−0.78	−0.95	−0.19	−0.13	−0.55
			(−3.41)	(−4.21)	(−5.33)	(−1.03)	(−0.54)	(−3.67)
		FF α	−0.53	−0.61	−0.74	0.03	0.10	−0.35
			(−2.39)	(−2.98)	(−4.17)	(0.14)	(0.39)	(−2.21)
		FFC α	−0.74	−0.85	−1.02	−0.28	−0.38	−0.66
			(−3.49)	(−4.00)	(−5.54)	(−1.31)	(−1.62)	(−4.15)
BM	EW	Return	−2.09	−1.78	−1.73	−1.66	−2.20	−1.89
			(−8.78)	(−7.54)	(−8.62)	(−8.06)	(−9.05)	(−9.57)
		FF α	−1.90	−1.59	−1.52	−1.42	−1.99	−1.68
			(−7.27)	(−6.14)	(−6.90)	(−6.96)	(−8.62)	(−8.12)
		FFC α	−2.37	−2.01	−1.86	−1.74	−2.27	−2.05
			(−7.54)	(−6.08)	(−7.18)	(−7.20)	(−9.12)	(−8.09)
	VW	Return	−0.28	−0.64	−0.45	−0.56	−0.54	−0.49
			(−1.21)	(−2.90)	(−2.00)	(−2.71)	(−2.08)	(−2.82)
		FF α	−0.06	−0.42	−0.19	−0.23	−0.24	−0.23
			(−0.25)	(−1.77)	(−0.79)	(−1.08)	(−0.90)	(−1.22)
		FFC α	−0.44	−0.74	−0.49	−0.52	−0.42	−0.52
			(−1.82)	(−2.93)	(−2.07)	(−1.90)	(−1.38)	(−2.62)
Mom	EW	Return	−5.04	−1.74	−1.00	−0.81	−0.62	−1.84
			(−13.19)	(−7.72)	(−5.83)	(−5.14)	(−3.55)	(−10.10)
		FF α	−4.78	−1.55	−0.81	−0.58	−0.38	−1.62
			(−12.11)	(−7.12)	(−4.85)	(−3.64)	(−2.19)	(−8.92)

(*continued*)

TABLE 12.6   *(Continued)*

Control	Weights	Value	Control 1	Control 2	Control 3	Control 4	Control 5	Control Avg
		FFC α	−5.37	−1.92	−1.11	−0.82	−0.63	−1.97
			(−11.97)	(−8.15)	(−6.57)	(−5.07)	(−3.49)	(−9.96)
	VW	Return	−2.17	−0.94	−0.53	−0.39	−0.20	−0.85
			(−6.36)	(−3.80)	(−2.82)	(−2.35)	(−0.99)	(−5.16)
		FF α	−1.90	−0.73	−0.35	−0.25	0.02	−0.64
			(−6.38)	(−2.72)	(−1.88)	(−1.36)	(0.09)	(−3.98)
		FFC α	−2.52	−1.02	−0.57	−0.44	−0.20	−0.95
			(−8.14)	(−3.14)	(−2.87)	(−2.45)	(−1.04)	(−5.63)

In the highest two quintiles of β, however, the average returns and alphas of the *Rev* difference portfolios, while negative, are statistically indistinguishable from zero. For the average β quintile, the value-weighted portfolios indicate a strong reversal phenomenon since the average return, FF alpha, and FFC alpha of −0.55% per month (*t*-statistic = −3.67), −0.35% per month (*t*-statistic = −2.21), and −0.66% per month (*t*-statistic = −4.15) are all economically important and highly statistically significant.

The equal-weighted bivariate dependent-sort portfolio results that use book-to-market ratio (*BM*) as the first sort variable indicate a very strong negative relation between *Rev* and one-month-ahead excess stock returns within each of the *BM* quintiles since, for each *BM* quintile, the average return, FF alpha, and FFC alpha of the *Rev* 5-1 portfolio are negative, large in magnitude, and highly statistically significant. The equal-weighted *Rev* 5-1 portfolio for the average *BM* quintile generates an average return of −1.89% per month (*t*-statistic = −9.57), FF alpha of −1.68% per month (*t*-statistic = −8.12), and FFC alpha of −2.05% per month (*t*-statistic = −8.09). The results change quite substantially when using value-weighted portfolios. In quintile one of *BM*, the average return and FF alpha of the *Rev* difference portfolio are both statistically indistinguishable from zero. The FFC alpha for this portfolio of −0.44% per month, however, is marginally statistically significant with a *t*-statistic of −1.82. None of the *BM* quintiles produce a *Rev* 5-1 portfolio that generates a statistically significant FF alpha (the FF alpha in *BM* quintile two is marginally statistically significant). The FFC alphas for the *Rev* difference portfolios, however, are statistically significant in *BM* quintiles one through four, albeit only marginally in *BM* quintiles one and four. In *BM* quintile five, neither the FF nor FFC alpha of the *Rev* difference portfolio is statistically distinguishable from zero. For the average *BM* quintile, however, the value-weighted *Rev* 5-1 portfolio produces economically large and highly statistically significant average monthly returns of −0.49% per month (*t*-statistic = −2.82) and FFC alpha of −0.52% per month (*t*-statistic = −2.62). The FF alpha for this portfolio of −0.23% per month with a t-statistic of −1.22 is not statistically significant.

Finally, we examine whether controlling for momentum can explain the reversal phenomenon. The results of the equal-weighted portfolio analysis find no evidence that this is the case, as within each *Mom* quintile, as well as for the average *Mom* quintile, the average return, FF alpha, and FFC alpha of the *Rev* 5-1 portfolio are negative and highly statistically significant. There is substantial variation, however, in the strength of the reversal effect among stocks with different levels of momentum. The magnitude of the average monthly returns of the equal-weighted *Rev* 5-1 portfolios in the different *Mom* quintiles drop monotonically from −5.04% in *Mom* quintile 1 to −0.62% in *Mom* quintile five. The patterns in the FF and FFC alphas are similar. The results indicate that the reversal effect is much stronger in low-momentum stocks than in high-momentum stocks. As in the previous analyses, the strength of the reversal effect in the value-weighted portfolio analysis that controls for the effect of *Mom* is substantially weaker than in the equal-weighted analysis. The average return, FF alpha, and FFC alpha of the value-weighted *Rev* 5-1 portfolio for the average *Mom* quintile, however, remain large in magnitude and highly statistically significant. The average return of this portfolio is −0.85% per month with a t-statistic of −5.16 while this portfolio's FFC alpha is −0.95% per month (t-statistic = −5.63). In the fifth quintile of *Mom*, however, the *Rev* 5-1 portfolio fails to generate an average return, FF alpha, or FFC alpha that is economically large or statistically distinguishable from zero. Within quintiles one through four of *Mom*, the *Rev* 5-1 portfolio generates statistically significant negative average returns and FFC alpha. The FF alpha of the *Rev* 5-1 portfolio is statistically significant only in quintiles one and two of *Mom* and is marginally significant in *Mom* quintile three. The value-weighted portfolio results, therefore, demonstrate that while the reversal phenomenon is strong for the average *Mom* quintile, it is much stronger among stocks with low momentum than stocks with high momentum.

Independent-Sort Analysis

The results in Tables 12.5 and 12.6 demonstrate that the reversal phenomenon is detected when using bivariate dependent-sort portfolio analysis to control for the relation between stock returns and beta, market capitalization, book-to-market ratio, or size. The results are strongest in equal-weighted portfolios, but still exist, at least for the average quintile of the control variable, in value-weighted portfolios. We now examine the robustness of these results using bivariate independent-sort, instead of dependent-sort, portfolio analysis.

The results of the independent-sort portfolio analyses of the relation between *Rev* and future stock returns after controlling for each of beta (β), market capitalization (*MktCap*), book-to-market ratio (*BM*), and momentum (*Mom*) are presented in Table 12.7. The analyses demonstrate that when using equal-weighted portfolios, the reversal phenomenon is strong in all quintiles, as well as the average quintile, of each of the control variables. The average returns and FFC alphas of the *Rev* 5-1 portfolios are negative, large, and highly statistically significant for each of these equal-weighted portfolios. Similar to the dependent-sort analyses, the

TABLE 12.7 Bivariate Independent-Sort Portfolio Analysis

This table presents the results of bivariate independent-sort portfolio analyses of the relation between *Rev* and future stock returns after controlling for the effect of each of β, *MktCap*, *BM*, and *Mom* (control variables). Each month, all stocks in the CRSP sample are sorted into five groups based on an ascending sort of the control variable. All stocks are independently sorted into five groups based on an ascending sort of *Rev*. The quintile breakpoints used to create the groups are calculated using all stocks in the CRSP sample. The intersections of the control variable and *Rev* groups are used to form 25 portfolios. The table presents the average return and FFC alpha (in percent per month) of the long–short zero-cost portfolios that are long the fifth *Rev* quintile portfolio and short the first *Rev* quintile portfolio in each quintile, as well as for the average quintile, of the control variable. Results for equal-weighted (Weights = EW) and value-weighted (Weights = VW) portfolios are shown. *t*-statistics (in parentheses), adjusted following Newey and West (1987) using six lags, testing the null hypothesis that the average return or alpha is equal to zero, are shown in parentheses.

Control	Weights	Value	Control 1	Control 2	Control 3	Control 4	Control 5	Control Avg
β	EW	Return	−1.96	−1.68	−1.85	−1.77	−1.75	−1.80
			(−8.71)	(−7.95)	(−8.45)	(−7.91)	(−7.42)	(−9.08)
		FFC α	−2.12	−1.84	−2.03	−1.94	−2.01	−1.99
			(−8.39)	(−7.41)	(−8.05)	(−6.55)	(−7.38)	(−8.25)
	VW	Return	−0.56	−0.92	−0.91	−0.22	−0.23	−0.57
			(−2.37)	(−4.34)	(−4.68)	(−1.18)	(−1.06)	(−3.61)
		FFC α	−0.58	−0.89	−1.02	−0.33	−0.41	−0.65
			(−2.43)	(−3.79)	(−5.32)	(−1.58)	(−2.07)	(−4.13)
MktCap	EW	Return	−3.31	−1.56	−0.90	−0.75	−0.48	−1.40
			(−12.19)	(−6.52)	(−4.21)	(−3.98)	(−2.59)	(−7.59)
		FFC α	−3.51	−1.70	−0.99	−0.84	−0.55	−1.52
			(−10.44)	(−6.33)	(−4.32)	(−4.01)	(−2.74)	(−7.22)
	VW	Return	−2.69	−1.47	−0.87	−0.72	−0.13	−1.18
			(−10.70)	(−6.09)	(−4.05)	(−3.77)	(−0.68)	(−6.53)
		FFC α	−2.86	−1.62	−0.96	−0.80	−0.22	−1.29
			(−8.93)	(−5.99)	(−4.20)	(−3.80)	(−1.03)	(−6.23)
BM	EW	Return	−1.88	−1.74	−1.81	−1.83	−2.18	−1.89
			(−8.69)	(−7.21)	(−8.47)	(−8.47)	(−9.51)	(−9.52)
		FFC α	−2.12	−1.96	−1.97	−1.94	−2.25	−2.05
			(−7.58)	(−6.07)	(−7.09)	(−7.31)	(−9.24)	(−8.04)
	VW	Return	−0.45	−0.57	−0.37	−0.39	−0.53	−0.46
			(−2.12)	(−2.49)	(−1.61)	(−1.72)	(−2.24)	(−2.56)
		FFC α	−0.60	−0.66	−0.45	−0.37	−0.41	−0.50
			(−2.74)	(−2.46)	(−1.84)	(−1.27)	(−1.53)	(−2.47)

TABLE 12.7 *(Continued)*

Control	Weights	Value	Control 1	Control 2	Control 3	Control 4	Control 5	Control Avg
Mom	EW	Return	−3.98	−1.73	−1.03	−0.85	−0.60	−1.64
			(−13.81)	(−7.78)	(−5.25)	(−4.84)	(−3.41)	(−9.11)
		FFC α	−4.23	−1.89	−1.16	−0.88	−0.64	−1.76
			(−12.43)	(−8.21)	(−5.93)	(−4.56)	(−3.12)	(−8.89)
	VW	Return	−1.68	−0.93	−0.37	−0.30	−0.16	−0.69
			(−5.59)	(−3.97)	(−1.68)	(−1.63)	(−0.79)	(−4.10)
		FFC α	−1.93	−1.06	−0.37	−0.42	−0.20	−0.79
			(−6.99)	(−3.74)	(−1.64)	(−2.14)	(−0.95)	(−4.63)

independent-sort analysis indicate that when controlling for each of *MktCap* and *Mom*, the reversal effect is substantially stronger for stocks with low values of the control variable and becomes less strong for stocks with high values of *MktCap* or *Mom*.

As with the equal-weighted portfolios, the value-weighted portfolios generate similar results when using independently sorted portfolios to those generated by the dependently sorted portfolios. The independent-sort value-weighted portfolio analyses indicate that, after controlling separately for each of β, *MktCap*, *BM*, and *Mom*, the average returns and FFC alphas of the *Rev* 5-1 portfolios in the average control variable quintile are negative and statistically significant. Within certain quintiles of each of the control variables, however, the reversal effect is not detected when using value-weighted portfolios. Specifically, the average return of the value-weighted *Rev* difference portfolio is statistically indistinguishable from zero in quintiles four and five of β, and the FFC alpha is insignificant in β quintile four. In quintile five of *MktCap*, the value-weighted *Rev* 5-1 portfolio fails to produce statistically significant average returns or FFC alpha. The average value-weighted return of the *Rev* 5-1 portfolio in quintile three of *BM* is statistically insignificant, while that of *BM* quintile four is only marginally significant. The FFC alphas of the value-weighted *Rev* difference portfolio is insignificant in quintiles four and five of *BM*, and only marginally significant in *BM* quintile three. Finally, when controlling for *Mom*, only quintiles one and two of *Mom* generate statistically significant average value-weighted *Rev* difference portfolio returns, with the average return of the *Rev* 5-1 portfolio in quintile three of *Mom* being marginally statistically significant. The FFC alpha of the value-weighted *Rev* difference portfolios in quintiles three and five of *Mom* are also not statistically significant.

In summary, the results of the bivariate portfolio analyses indicate that the reversal phenomenon is robust to controls for market capitalization, beta, book-to-market ratio, and momentum. The effect is substantially stronger in equal-weighted portfolios than in value-weighted portfolios. The evidence demonstrates that among high-market capitalization and high-momentum stocks, the reversal phenomenon is particularly weak and, when using value-weighted portfolios, nonexistent. The results using independently sorted portfolios are similar to those of dependent-sort portfolio analyses.

Can Reversal Explain Other Relations?

Having shown that the reversal phenomenon is not explained by the relation between beta and stock returns nor by the size, value, or momentum effects, we now explore whether the reversal phenomenon can explain any of these patterns in expected returns that have been documented in previous chapters. To this end, in Table 12.8 we present the results of equal-weighted and value-weighted bivariate dependent-sort portfolio analyses that sort first on Rev and then on either β, $MktCap$, BM, or Mom. The FFC alphas for the analyses examining the relation between $MktCap$ and future stock returns after controlling for Rev are calculated relative to a factor model that includes the market (MKT), value (HML), and momentum (MOM) factors, but excludes the size (SMB) factor. The reason for this is that including the size factor would control for the size effect, which is the exact effect that we are examining. Similarly, for the analyses that use BM as the second sort variable, the FFC alpha is calculated relative to a model that excludes the HML factor. For the same reason, when Mom is the second sort variable, we use the Fama and French (1993) (FF) three-factor risk model, which does not include the momentum factor, instead of the four-factor model.

The results in Table 12.8 show that after controlling for the effect of reversal, the relation between β and future stock returns is negative but statistically insignificant, as the average return of the equal-weighted (value-weighted) β difference portfolio for the average Rev quintile is -0.34% per month (-0.09% per month) with a corresponding t-statistic of -1.62 (-0.38). The FFC alpha of the equal-weighted portfolio of -0.47% per month (t-statistic $= -2.94$) is highly statistically significant, whereas the FFC alpha for the value-weighted portfolio of -0.08% per month (t-statistic $= -0.47$) is not significant. These results lead to slightly different conclusions than the results of the univariate portfolio analyses presented in Tables 8.4 and 8.5 of Chapter 8.[1] The results in Chapter 8 show that in equal-weighted portfolio analysis, both the average returns and CAPM alpha of the β-sorted difference portfolio are significantly negative, whereas the results here indicate that after controlling for Rev, only the alpha, but not the average return, is statistically significant. In value-weighted portfolios, the results in Chapter 8 indicate a statistically insignificant β difference portfolio average return but a significantly negative alpha. Here, the results indicate that while the average monthly return and FFC alpha of the value-weighted β 5-1 portfolio in the average Rev quintile are negative, neither is statistically significant. While there are differences in the methodologies between the analyses presented here and those shown in Chapter 8, including the use of different risk models to assess abnormal returns, this is the first analysis in this book to find a statistically insignificant abnormal return for a portfolio holding long positions in high-β stocks and short

---

[1] In Chapter 8, the variable β is denoted β^{12M}.

TABLE 12.8   Bivariate Dependent-Sort Portfolio Analysis—Control for *Rev*

This table presents the results of bivariate independent-sort portfolio analyses of the relation between future stock returns and each of β, *MktCap*, *BM*, and *Mom* (second sort variables) after controlling for the effect of *Rev*. Each month, all stocks in the CRSP sample are sorted into five groups based on an ascending sort of *Rev*. All stocks are independently sorted into five groups based on an ascending sort of one of the second sort variables. The quintile breakpoints used to create the groups are calculated using all stocks in the CRSP sample. The intersections of the *Rev* and second sort variable groups are used to form 25 portfolios. The table presents the average return and FFC alpha (in percent per month) of the long–short zero-cost portfolios that are long the fifth quintile portfolio and short the first quintile portfolio for the second sort variable in each quintile, as well as for the average quintile, of *Rev*. Results for equal-weighted (Weights = EW) and value-weighted (Weights = VW) portfolios are shown. *t*-statistics (in parentheses), adjusted following Newey and West (1987) using six lags, testing the null hypothesis that the average return or alpha is equal to zero, are shown in parentheses.

Second Sort Variable	Weights	Value	*Rev* 1	*Rev* 2	*Rev* 3	*Rev* 4	*Rev* 5	*Rev* Avg
β	EW	Return	−0.77	0.06	−0.15	−0.43	−0.39	−0.34
			(−3.19)	(0.26)	(−0.70)	(−1.87)	(−1.63)	(−1.62)
		FFC α	−0.77	−0.09	−0.38	−0.64	−0.48	−0.47
			(−3.37)	(−0.53)	(−2.16)	(−3.61)	(−2.33)	(−2.94)
	VW	Return	−0.77	0.09	−0.09	0.20	0.15	−0.09
			(−2.57)	(0.39)	(−0.40)	(0.80)	(0.52)	(−0.38)
		FFC α	−0.66	0.13	−0.18	0.15	0.14	−0.08
			(−2.65)	(0.62)	(−0.86)	(0.73)	(0.60)	(−0.47)
MktCap	EW	Return	−2.75	−0.01	−0.46	−0.55	0.54	−0.65
			(−8.60)	(−0.04)	(−1.68)	(−2.02)	(2.04)	(−2.70)
		FFC α	−3.05	−0.13	−0.74	−0.87	0.47	−0.86
			(−7.51)	(−0.48)	(−2.21)	(−2.41)	(1.75)	(−3.26)
	VW	Return	−2.34	0.09	−0.33	−0.31	0.78	−0.42
			(−7.14)	(0.33)	(−1.19)	(−1.16)	(2.78)	(−1.68)
		FFC α	−2.59	0.05	−0.48	−0.50	0.70	−0.56
			(−6.14)	(0.20)	(−1.68)	(−1.69)	(2.51)	(−2.17)
BM	EW	Return	1.37	0.93	0.85	0.92	1.08	1.03
			(6.36)	(4.96)	(4.90)	(5.07)	(4.40)	(5.75)
		FFC α	1.51	1.10	1.07	1.11	1.30	1.22
			(6.58)	(6.20)	(6.74)	(6.45)	(5.38)	(6.92)
	VW	Return	0.49	0.41	0.51	0.38	0.62	0.48
			(1.99)	(1.88)	(2.36)	(1.84)	(2.56)	(2.66)

(continued)

TABLE 12.8   *(Continued)*

Second Sort Variable	Weights	Value	Rev 1	Rev 2	Rev 3	Rev 4	Rev 5	Rev Avg
		FFC α	0.53	0.56	0.66	0.51	0.75	0.60
			(1.89)	(2.75)	(3.13)	(2.66)	(3.27)	(3.53)
Mom	EW	Return	−0.82	0.83	0.83	1.06	2.96	0.97
			(−2.32)	(3.25)	(3.11)	(3.96)	(11.25)	(3.97)
		FF α	−0.57	1.07	0.99	1.19	3.21	1.18
			(−1.73)	(4.78)	(3.45)	(3.91)	(13.17)	(5.29)
	VW	Return	0.37	0.82	0.83	1.03	2.14	1.04
			(0.86)	(2.53)	(3.04)	(3.78)	(6.92)	(3.69)
		FF α	0.73	1.13	1.02	1.25	2.47	1.32
			(2.17)	(3.90)	(3.86)	(4.83)	(8.35)	(5.44)

positions in low-β stocks. That being said, there are at least two potential reasons for this. The first is that this is the first time that a value-weighted β-sorted portfolio has been subjected to the four-factor risk model, meaning that it is potentially the momentum factor (*MOM*) that is driving this result. Alternatively, it is possible that controlling for *Rev* is driving the difference in results. While the insignificant abnormal return of the value-weighted β 5-1 portfolio for the average *Rev* quintile may indicate that this portfolio does not generate abnormal returns, the portfolio analysis does not give any indications of a positive relation between β and future stock returns, as would be predicted by the CAPM of Sharpe (1964), Lintner (1965), and Mossin (1966). Thus, it appears that the reversal phenomenon cannot completely explain the discrepancy between the theoretical prediction and empirical results.

The bivariate dependent-sort portfolio analyses examining the relation between *MktCap* and future stock returns after controlling for *Rev* generate results that are similar to those of previous analyses. The negative relation between *MktCap* and future stock returns is strong in equal-weighted portfolios, even after controlling for *Rev*, since the average return of −0.65% per month (*t*-statistic = −2.70) and FFC (excluding the *SMB* factor) alpha of −0.86% per month (*t*-statistic = −3.26) for the equal-weighted *MktCap* difference portfolio in the average quintile of *Rev* indicate that *Rev* does not explain the size effect in equal-weighted portfolios. Consistent with what has been seen in previous analyses, the size effect is substantially weaker in value-weighted portfolios. However, the average return and FFC (excluding the *SMB* factor) alpha for the *MktCap* 5-1 value-weighted portfolio in the average *Rev* quintile of −0.42% per month (*t*-statistic = −1.68) and −0.56% per month (*t*-statistic = −2.17), respectively, are both at least marginally statistically significant. Interestingly, the relation between *MktCap* and future stock returns varies very strongly across the quintiles of *Rev*. For stocks in the lowest *Rev* quintile, the previously documented negative relation between *MktCap* and future stock returns is very strong. However, this relation is substantially weaker in quintiles two, three, and four of *Rev*. In *Rev* quintile five, the relation between *MktCap* and future stock returns is actually positive and statistically significant, as the average returns and FFC (excluding the *SMB* factor) alphas of the *MktCap* 5-1 portfolio in *Rev* quintile five are economically large and at least marginally statistically significant in both equal-weighted and value-weighted portfolios.

The relation between *BM* and future stock returns appears to be mostly unchanged after controlling for the effect of *Rev* in the bivariate dependent-sort portfolio analysis. In equal-weighted portfolios, the average returns and FFC alphas (excluding the *HML* factor) of the *BM* 5-1 portfolios in each quintile of *Rev*, including the average *Rev* quintile, are positive and statistically significant. When using value-weighted portfolios, the results are substantially weaker, but the returns and FFC alphas (excluding the *HML* factor) of the *BM* 5-1 portfolios remain at least marginally statistically significant in each quintile, as well as for the average quintile, of *Rev*.

Finally, the results indicate that the reversal phenomenon cannot explain the momentum phenomenon since, in the average *Rev* quintile, the average returns and FF alphas of equal-weighted and value-weighted *Mom* 5-1 portfolios are positive and highly statistically significant. The relation between future stock returns and *Mom* changes dramatically across the quintiles of *Rev*, especially in equal-weighted portfolios. In the lowest *Rev* quintile, when using equal-weighted portfolios, the average return and FFC alpha of the *Mom* 5-1 portfolio are actually negative and at least marginally statistically significant. This result indicates a medium-term reversal phenomenon, not a medium-term momentum phenomenon, among stocks with low values of *Rev*. When using value-weighted portfolios, however, the average return of this portfolio is statistically insignificant but its FF alpha is significantly positive.

We proceed now to examine the relations between expected stock returns and each of beta, market capitalization, book-to-market ratio, and momentum after controlling for reversal, using bivariate portfolio analysis with independently sorted portfolios. These analyses are identical to those whose results are presented in Table 12.7. Here, instead of presenting the results that focus on the relation between *Rev* and future stock returns, we present the results that examine the relations between each of β, *MktCap*, *BM*, and *Mom* and future stock returns after controlling for *Rev*. The results of these independent-sort analyses, which are presented in Table 12.9 are very similar to those of the dependent-sort analyses presented in Table 12.8. Both sets of results can be summarized as indicating that the reversal phenomenon fails to explain the lack of a positive relation between β and expected stock returns as well as the size, value, and momentum effects. While there are interesting patterns in several of these phenomena across the different levels of reversal, for the average stock, each of these effects appears to be a different phenomenon.

TABLE 12.9 Bivariate Independent-Sort Portfolio Analysis—Control for *Rev*

This table presents the results of bivariate independent-sort portfolio analyses of the relation between future stock returns and each of β, *MktCap*, *BM*, and *Mom* (second sort variables) after controlling for the effect of *Rev*. Each month, all stocks in the CRSP sample are sorted into five groups based on an ascending sort of *Rev*. All stocks are independently sorted into five groups based on an ascending sort of one of the second sort variables. The quintile breakpoints used to create the groups are calculated using all stocks in the CRSP sample. The intersections of the *Rev* and second sort variable groups are used to form 25 portfolios. The table presents the average return and FFC alpha (in percent per month) of the long–short zero-cost portfolios that are long the fifth quintile portfolio and short the first quintile portfolio for the second sort variable in each quintile, as well as for the average quintile, of *Rev*. Results for equal-weighted (Weights = EW) and value-weighted (Weights = VW) portfolios are shown. t-statistics (in parentheses), adjusted following Newey and West (1987) using six lags, testing the null hypothesis that the average return or alpha is equal to zero, are shown in parentheses.

Second Sort Variable	Weights	Value	Rev 1	Rev 2	Rev 3	Rev 4	Rev 5	Rev Avg
β	EW	Return	−0.67	0.10	−0.24	−0.60	−0.45	−0.37
			(−2.75)	(0.40)	(−0.95)	(−2.31)	(−1.89)	(−1.65)
		FFC α	−0.66	−0.03	−0.44	−0.76	−0.55	−0.49
			(−2.92)	(−0.14)	(−2.24)	(−3.97)	(−2.75)	(−2.85)
	VW	Return	−0.46	0.19	−0.17	−0.09	−0.13	−0.13
			(−1.75)	(0.79)	(−0.61)	(−0.33)	(−0.45)	(−0.57)
		FFC α	−0.34	0.25	−0.20	−0.15	−0.18	−0.12
			(−1.23)	(1.15)	(−0.83)	(−0.70)	(−0.75)	(−0.65)
MktCap	EW	Return	−2.16	−0.02	−0.48	−0.59	0.66	−0.52
			(−7.05)	(−0.09)	(−1.72)	(−2.12)	(2.38)	(−2.08)
		FFC α	−2.43	−0.16	−0.78	−0.89	0.59	−0.74
			(−6.16)	(−0.59)	(−2.37)	(−2.57)	(2.08)	(−2.72)
	VW	Return	−1.64	0.07	−0.35	−0.40	0.91	−0.28
			(−5.30)	(0.24)	(−1.19)	(−1.41)	(3.13)	(−1.07)
		FFC α	−1.86	0.00	−0.53	−0.58	0.83	−0.43
			(−4.81)	(0.00)	(−1.77)	(−1.93)	(2.83)	(−1.60)
BM	EW	Return	1.36	0.99	0.94	1.05	1.07	1.08
			(6.57)	(5.18)	(4.84)	(5.40)	(4.32)	(5.89)
		FFC α	1.49	1.17	1.18	1.26	1.28	1.28
			(6.84)	(6.48)	(6.60)	(6.65)	(5.29)	(7.07)
	VW	Return	0.69	0.40	0.65	0.47	0.61	0.56
			(2.87)	(1.68)	(2.77)	(2.14)	(2.72)	(2.99)
		FFC α	0.70	0.57	0.79	0.58	0.74	0.68
			(2.78)	(2.46)	(3.36)	(2.76)	(3.38)	(3.74)

TABLE 12.9   *(Continued)*

Second Sort Variable	Weights	Value	Rev 1	Rev 2	Rev 3	Rev 4	Rev 5	Rev Avg
Mom	EW	Return	−0.51	0.85	0.90	1.20	2.86	1.06
			(−1.65)	(2.87)	(2.78)	(4.00)	(11.88)	(4.05)
		FF α	−0.27	1.11	1.05	1.33	3.12	1.27
			(−0.99)	(4.27)	(3.09)	(3.86)	(13.74)	(5.31)
	VW	Return	0.42	0.84	1.02	1.05	1.94	1.05
			(1.10)	(2.40)	(3.12)	(3.36)	(6.38)	(3.59)
		FF α	0.75	1.21	1.29	1.34	2.26	1.37
			(2.59)	(4.12)	(4.26)	(4.68)	(7.71)	(5.57)

12.5   FAMA–MACBETH REGRESSIONS

We continue our analysis of the reversal effect using Fama and MacBeth (1973, FM hereafter) regression analysis. The FM regression methodology allows us to simultaneously control for beta, size, book-to-market ratio, and momentum in examining the reversal phenomenon. We examine a specification that includes only *Rev* as an independent variable, specifications that combine *Rev* with one of β, *MktCap*, *BM*, or *Mom* as independent variables, and a final specification that includes *Rev*, β, *MktCap*, *BM*, and *Mom* as independent variables. All independent variables are winsorized at the 0.5% level on a monthly basis. The dependent variable in all regressions is the one-month-ahead excess stock return.

Table 12.10 presents the results of the FM regression analyses. When only *Rev* is used as an independent variable in the regression (specification (1)), the table shows that the average coefficient on *Rev* is −0.048 with a *t*-statistic of −10.07, indicating a statistically significant negative cross-sectional relation between *Rev* and future stock returns. The models that include β (specification (2)), *Size* (specification (3)), book-to-market ratio (specification (4)), and momentum (specification (5)) generate similar results, with average coefficients of −0.053 (*t*-statistic = −10.78), −0.051 (*t*-statistic = −10.65), −0.055 (*t*-statistic = −10.85), and −0.054 (*t*-statistic = −11.08), respectively, on *Rev*. When all control variables are simultaneously included in the regression model (specification (6)), the average coefficient on *Rev* of −0.063 is slightly larger in magnitude than in any of the other specifications, and remains highly statistically significant with a *t*-statistic of −12.54. The results of the FM regressions, therefore, provide strong evidence that the reversal phenomenon persists after controlling for each of β, *Size*, *BM*, and *Mom*.

The regression results also demonstrate that the previously identified relations between the control variables and future stock returns persist when *Rev* is included in the regression. The average coefficient on β is negative but statistically indistinguishable from zero. The size effect remains strong after controlling for the reversal

TABLE 12.10   Fama–MacBeth Regressions Analysis
This table presents the results of Fama and MacBeth (1973) regression analyses of the relation between expected stock returns and reversal. Each column in the table presents results for a different cross-sectional regression specification. The dependent variable in all specifications is the one-month-ahead excess stock return. The independent variables are indicated in the first column. Independent variables are winsorized at the 0.5% level on a monthly basis. The table presents average slope and intercept coefficients along with t-statistics (in parentheses), adjusted following Newey and West (1987) using six lags, testing the null hypothesis that the average coefficient is equal to zero. The rows labeled Adj. R^2 and n present the average adjusted R-squared and the number of data points, respectively, for the cross-sectional regressions.

	(1)	(2)	(3)	(4)	(5)	(6)
Rev	−0.048	−0.053	−0.051	−0.055	−0.054	−0.063
	(−10.07)	(−10.78)	(−10.65)	(−10.85)	(−11.08)	(−12.54)
β		−0.235				−0.099
		(−1.67)				(−0.61)
Size			−0.106			−0.132
			(−2.13)			(−2.36)
BM				0.415		0.229
				(5.13)		(3.35)
Mom					0.007	0.006
					(2.89)	(3.05)
Intercept	0.760	0.977	1.182	0.439	0.628	1.114
	(2.44)	(3.66)	(2.40)	(1.41)	(2.17)	(2.52)
Adj. R^2	0.01	0.03	0.02	0.02	0.02	0.05
n	4740	4423	4740	3389	4407	3368

effect, since both regression models that include *Size* as an independent variable produce negative and statistically significant average coefficients. The value effect also persists since the average coefficients on *BM* are positive and highly statistically significant. Finally, the results show that the relation between *Mom* and future stock returns remains positive and statistically significant when *Rev* is included in the regression model, indicating that the momentum phenomenon cannot be explained by the reversal phenomenon.

We now examine the economic magnitude of the reversal phenomenon using the average coefficient on *Rev* of −0.063 from the regressions that include all of the control variables (specification (6)). We begin by multiplying the average coefficient on *Rev* by the average cross-sectional standard deviation of reversal, 15.49%, taken from the summary statistics in Table 12.1. The result indicates that a one-standard-deviation difference in reversal results in a highly economically significant 0.98% (0.063 × 15.49%) difference in expected monthly returns. Multiplying the average coefficient by the difference in average reversal of 51.18% (30.80% − (−21.38%), see Table 12.3) between stocks in the top and bottom deciles of *Rev* indicates that the expected monthly return difference between such stocks is 3.28%, which is quite similar to the 2.69% return difference found by the equal-weighted univariate portfolio analysis. Both approaches demonstrate that the magnitude of the reversal phenomenon indicated by the average regression coefficient of −0.063 is economically highly significant.

Decomposing Reversal and Momentum

In Section 12.4.1, we examined the returns of portfolios formed by sorting on the Rev as well as the individual returns in months $t − k$ for $k \in \{1, 2, \ldots, 11\}$, which we denote $R_{t−k}$. Here, we perform a similar investigation using FM regression analysis instead of univariate portfolio analysis. In addition to examining the ability of each of these previous returns to predict future returns individually, the FM regression methodology allows us to examine the conditional predictive power of each of each month's return after controlling for the effects of each of the other month's returns.

The results of these FM regression analyses, presented in Table 12.11, show that when a univariate regression specification is used with only $R_{t−k}$ as the independent variable, there is a positive cross-sectional relation between $R_{t−k}$ and stock returns in month $t + 1$ for each value of $k \in \{2, 3, \ldots, 11\}$ (specifications (3) through (12)). In all cases except that of $R_{t−9}$, this relation is at least marginally statistically significant. The univariate regression analysis detects no relation between $R_{t−1}$ and stock returns in month $t + 1$ (specification (2)). When all of the previous monthly returns are simultaneously included in the regression model (specification (13)), the results show that each of the individual months carries information regarding the return in month $t + 1$ that is orthogonal to the information contained in any other month's return. As documented throughout this chapter, the relation between the return in month t (Rev) and the excess return in month $t + 1$ (the dependent variable) is negative and highly statistically significant. The results of the full-specification regressions indicate a negative and marginally significant relation between $R_{t−1}$ and future stock returns. The relations between $R_{t−k}$ and future stock returns for $k \in \{2, 3, \ldots, 11\}$ are all positive and highly statistically significant. Interestingly, the return during month $t − 11$, which is the return that is exactly 12 months prior to the dependent variable, appears to play a special role, since the coefficient on $R_{t−11}$ is substantially larger and more statistically significant than any of the other coefficients (with the exception of Rev).

We now add β, $Size$, BM, and Mom, both individually and simultaneously, as controls to the specification that includes all previous months' returns and repeat the FM regression analyses. The results of these FM regressions are presented in Table 12.12. Adding β as a control (specification (1)) does little to the coefficients on the other independent variables although the coefficient on $R_{t−1}$ is no longer even marginally significant. Interestingly, in this specification, the coefficient on β becomes negative and highly statistically significant, with an average coefficient of −0.409 and a corresponding t-statistic of −3.66. The results are similar when $Size$ is used as a control (specification (2)), with $Size$ carrying a negative and significant coefficient, as expected. When BM is included as a control (specification (3)), the average coefficients on $R_{t−3}$, $R_{t−4}$, and $R_{t−5}$ are only marginally statistically significant, while the negative average slope on $R_{t−1}$ becomes highly significant. The average coefficient on BM remains positive and significant. When Mom is added to the specification, the coefficients on $R_{t−k}$ for $k \in \{2, 3, \ldots, 10\}$ become statistically indistinguishable

TABLE 12.11   Fama–MacBeth Regression Analysis—Lagged Values of Reversal

This table presents the results of Fama and MacBeth (1973) regression analyses of the relation between expected stock returns and previous values of reversal. Each column in the table presents results for a different cross-sectional regression specification. The dependent variable in all specifications is the one-month-ahead excess stock return. The independent variables are indicated in the first column. R_{t-k} is the stock return in month $t - k$. Independent variables are winsorized at the 0.5% level on a monthly basis. The table presents average slope and intercept coefficients along with t-statistics (in parentheses), adjusted following Newey and West (1987) using six lags, testing the null hypothesis that the average coefficient is equal to zero. The rows labeled Adj. R^2 and n present the average adjusted R-squared and the number of data points, respectively, for the cross-sectional regressions.

	(1)	(2)	(3)	(4)	(5)	(6)	(7)	(8)	(9)	(10)	(11)	(12)	(13)
Rev	−0.048												−0.060
	(−10.07)												(−12.08)
R_{t-1}		−0.000											−0.006
		(−0.09)											(−1.75)
R_{t-2}			0.012										0.010
			(3.84)										(3.32)
R_{t-3}				0.005									0.006
				(1.68)									(2.13)
R_{t-4}					0.007								0.008
					(2.11)								(2.63)
R_{t-5}						0.007							0.009
						(1.73)							(2.48)
R_{t-6}							0.010						0.009
							(3.31)						(3.37)
R_{t-7}								0.007					0.008
								(1.72)					(2.44)
R_{t-8}									0.008				0.010
									(2.27)				(3.00)
R_{t-9}										0.004			0.006
										(1.09)			(2.00)
R_{t-10}											0.010		0.010
											(3.21)		(3.57)
R_{t-11}												0.021	0.019
												(6.64)	(7.65)
Intercept	0.760	0.690	0.726	0.722	0.697	0.729	0.764	0.724	0.792	0.793	0.765	0.780	0.595
	(2.44)	(2.35)	(2.52)	(2.51)	(2.49)	(2.59)	(2.71)	(2.54)	(2.85)	(2.84)	(2.73)	(2.76)	(2.39)
Adj. R^2	0.01	0.00	0.00	0.00	0.00	0.00	0.00	0.00	0.00	0.00	0.00	0.00	0.04
n	4740	4703	4665	4628	4591	4555	4519	4483	4447	4412	4377	4341	4306

from zero. This is not that surprising given that *Mom* is mechanically related to each of these returns. Although it is perhaps surprising that *Mom* captures the effect of each of these months' returns, instead of the individual months' returns explaining the predictive power of *Mom*. The regression results show that the relation between *Mom* and future stock returns persists after controlling for the returns in each of the individual months that comprise the 11-month period covered by *Mom* (months

TABLE 12.12   Fama–MacBeth Regression Analysis—Lagged Values of Reversal with Controls

This table presents the results of Fama and MacBeth (1973) regression analyses of the relation between expected stock returns and previous values of reversal. Each column in the table presents results for a different cross-sectional regression specification. The dependent variable in all specifications is the one-month-ahead excess stock return. The independent variables are indicated in the first column. R_{t-k} is the stock return in month $t - k$. Independent variables are winsorized at the 0.5% level on a monthly basis. The table presents average slope and intercept coefficients along with t-statistics (in parentheses), adjusted following Newey and West (1987) using six lags, testing the null hypothesis that the average coefficient is equal to zero. The rows labeled Adj. R^2 and n present the average adjusted R-squared and the number of data points, respectively, for the cross-sectional regressions.

	(1)	(2)	(3)	(4)	(5)
Rev	−0.061	−0.061	−0.063	−0.061	−0.066
	(−11.97)	(−12.28)	(−12.27)	(−12.07)	(−12.66)
R_{t-1}	−0.005	−0.005	−0.008	−0.013	−0.020
	(−1.52)	(−1.60)	(−2.17)	(−3.14)	(−3.84)
R_{t-2}	0.011	0.012	0.007	0.003	−0.002
	(3.73)	(4.05)	(2.23)	(0.86)	(−0.49)
R_{t-3}	0.006	0.007	0.006	−0.001	−0.005
	(2.24)	(2.61)	(1.85)	(−0.42)	(−1.33)
R_{t-4}	0.008	0.010	0.007	0.001	−0.003
	(2.62)	(3.29)	(1.91)	(0.18)	(−0.67)
R_{t-5}	0.009	0.010	0.006	0.002	−0.002
	(2.88)	(2.99)	(1.79)	(0.38)	(−0.47)
R_{t-6}	0.008	0.010	0.007	0.002	−0.004
	(3.00)	(4.05)	(2.47)	(0.59)	(−1.08)
R_{t-7}	0.009	0.009	0.008	0.001	−0.002
	(2.63)	(2.67)	(2.23)	(0.26)	(−0.49)
R_{t-8}	0.010	0.012	0.009	0.002	−0.001
	(3.26)	(3.93)	(2.63)	(0.66)	(−0.33)
R_{t-9}	0.006	0.007	0.005	−0.002	−0.005
	(2.30)	(2.68)	(1.64)	(−0.53)	(−1.06)
R_{t-10}	0.010	0.010	0.007	0.002	−0.004
	(3.95)	(4.00)	(2.51)	(0.73)	(−1.06)
R_{t-11}	0.019	0.017	0.017	0.012	0.003
	(7.80)	(7.29)	(6.51)	(4.19)	(0.96)
β	−0.409				−0.165
	(−3.66)				(−1.21)
$Size$		−0.162			−0.136
		(−3.85)			(−2.75)
BM			0.372		0.229
			(5.32)		(3.34)
Mom				0.009	0.012
				(4.46)	(4.05)
Intercept	0.791	1.281	0.254	0.583	1.094
	(3.27)	(3.23)	(1.03)	(2.36)	(2.64)
Adj. R^2	0.05	0.05	0.05	0.04	0.06
n	4306	4306	3332	4306	3332

$t - 11$ through $t - 1$). This result seems to indicate that it is stocks whose returns were relatively persistent that are driving the momentum phenomenon. The results once again demonstrate that the relation between R_{t-11} and the return in month $t + 1$ is particularly strong. In this specification, the negative coefficient on R_{t-1} remains highly statistically significant. Finally, when all control variables are included in the regression model (specification (5)), the results show that Rev and R_{t-1} remain negatively and significantly related to future stock returns. The coefficients on R_{t-k} for $k \in \{2, 3, \dots, 10\}$ remain statistically indistinguishable from zero. Here, R_{t-11} also carries an insignificant coefficient, indicating that the predictive power of R_{t-11} that is not captured by β, $Size$, BM, or Mom individually is captured by some linear combination of these variables. Finally, consistent with the results presented throughout this text, the average slope on β is negative but statistically insignificant, the coefficient on $Size$ is negative and highly significant, and the slopes of BM and Mom are positive and highly statistically significant.

In summary, the FM regression results show that the reversal phenomenon is not explained by relations between beta, size, book-to-market ratio, or momentum, and future stock returns. Similarly, neither of these other phenomena is explained by the reversal phenomenon. The returns in each month from $t - 2$ through $t - 11$ are individually positively related to returns in month $t + 1$. However, the effects of each of these individual months' returns are captured by the combination of beta, size, book-to-market ratio, and momentum.

12.6 THE REVERSAL FACTOR

As with the previous variables that have been shown to be related to stock returns, several researchers have included a reversal-based factor in the risk models used to assess the abnormal returns of portfolios or securities. The most commonly used reversal factor is created in exactly the same manner as the value (HML) and momentum (MOM) factors. Each month, all stocks in the CRSP database are sorted into two groups based on market capitalization, with the breakpoint dividing the two groups being the median market capitalization of all NYSE stocks. The same set of stocks is broken into three groups based on reversal (Rev), with the breakpoints being the 30th and 70th percentiles of Rev among NYSE stocks. Six value-weighted portfolios are then formed based on the intersections of the two market capitalization-based and three reversal-based groups of stocks. The monthly reversal factor, which we denote STR for short-term reversal, is taken to be the average one-month-ahead future return of the two low-reversal portfolios minus the average one-month-ahead future return of the two high-reversal portfolios.[2,3]

---

[2]The literature has not adopted a universally recognized acronym for the reversal factor. STR, $STRev$, ST_Rev, and Rev are commonly used.

[3]Daily and monthly returns for the reversal factor are available from Kenneth French's data library at http://mba.tuck.dartmouth.edu/pages/faculty/ken.french/data_library.html.

During the period from July 1926 through December 2012, the *STR* factor generates a mean monthly return (log return) of 0.75% (0.68%) with a monthly standard deviation of 3.50% (3.43%), resulting in an annualized Sharpe ratio of 0.74 (0.69). Over the entire 86-and-a-half year period, the monthly compounded *STR* factor return (log return) is 121,104% (710%), which is substantially higher than the corresponding values for the excess market return (*MKT* factor) or the size (*SMB*), book-to-market (*HML*), or momentum-based (*MOM*) factors. The *STR* factor has a correlation of 0.21 with the *MKT* factor, and its correlations with the *SMB*, *HML*, and *MOM* factors are 0.16, 0.04, and −0.19, respectively. Subjecting the *STR* factor to the FFC four-factor risk model, we find a risk-adjusted alpha of 0.77% per month with a Newey and West (1987) adjusted (six lags) *t*-statistic of 6.37, indicating that the *STR* factor generates economically large and highly statistically significant returns after accounting for the effect of the factors included in the FFC model. The *STR* factor has a sensitivity of 0.09 (*t*-statistic = 2.27) to the *MKT* factor, and statistically insignificant estimated sensitivities of 0.10 (*t*-statistic = 1.49) to the *SMB* factor, −0.06 (*t*-statistic = −0.83) to the *HML* factor, and −0.11 (*t*-statistic = −1.39) to the *MOM* factor.

Figure 12.1 plots the cumulative returns of the *STR* factor from July 1926 through December of 2012. The solid line, whose scale is presented on the left side of the plot,

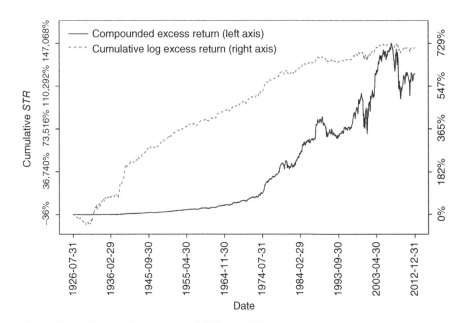

Figure 12.1 Cumulative Returns of *STR* Portfolio.
This figure plots the cumulate returns of the *STR* factor for the period from July 1926 through December 2012. The compounded excess return for month *t* is calculated as 100 times the cumulative product of one plus the monthly return up to and including the given month. The cumulate log excess return is calculated as the sum of the monthly log excess returns up to and including the given month

represents the cumulative compounded return of the factor. The dashed line presents the cumulative sum of monthly log-returns, and its scale is shown on the right side of the chart. As is evident in the chart, the *STR* factor does not exhibit drawdowns that are as extreme as those associated with the other factors. The deepest drawdown for the reversal factor began in January 1927. From this point until the end of November 1929, the reversal factor lost almost 36%. The previous high water mark was regained by the end of October 1931, not quite five years after the drawdown began. While this drawdown is the largest from previous peak to trough, it is only the third most prolonged drawdown experienced by the *STR* factor. The longest, but only the fifth largest, drawdown began at the end of September 1989 and ended in July of 1997. The largest cumulative loss experienced during period drawdown was realized in April 1993, at which point the *STR* factor was down 22% from its previous high. The second largest and fourth longest drawdown for the *STR* factor began at the end of July 1999. From then until December 2000, the *STR* portfolio lost more than 33%. The previous high value was regained by the end of March 2002, a mere 32 months after the drawdown began. Finally, it is worth noting that as of the end of the sample used in this analysis, the *STR* factor was in the midst of a large drawdown that will quite possibly prove to be the longest, and potentially the deepest, drawdown experienced by the portfolio. The all-time high for the *STR* factor was realized at the end of February 2007. By the end of May 2009 the portfolio had lost 32% from this previous high, making this drawdown, as it stands now, the third largest drawdown ever experienced by the reversal factor mimicking portfolio. As can be seen in the graph, as of December 2012, 70 months after the drawdown began, the cumulative compounded return of the *STR* portfolio remains more than 17% below its previous peak.

Despite the strong empirical support for, and wide acceptance of, the reversal phenomenon, the *STR* factor is used substantially less frequently than the *MKT*, *SMB*, *HML*, and *MOM* factors that comprise the Fama and French (1993) and Carhart (1997) four-factor model, which remains the standard in the empirical asset pricing literature. In most cases when the *STR* factor is used, it is appended to the four-factor model and included primarily as a robustness check instead of the main benchmark model.

12.7 SUMMARY

In this chapter, we have discussed and empirically examined the reversal phenomenon documented by Jegadeesh (1990) and Lehmann (1990). The main empirical result is that reversal, measured as the return of a stock in the most recent month, has a strong negative relation with the next month's return. The result is largely driven by small stocks, as the results of value-weighted portfolios are substantially weaker than those of equal-weighted portfolios. While not as frequently used as the previously discussed factors, the reversal factor mimicking portfolio, denoted *STR*, generates larger returns with smaller and less prolonged drawdowns than the portfolios mimicking the market, size, value, and momentum factors.

REFERENCES

Admati, A. R. and Pfleiderer, P. 1989. Divide and conquer: a theory of intraday and day-of-the-week mean effects. Review of Financial Studies, 2(2), 189–223.

Boudoukh, J., Richardson, M. P., and Whitelaw, R. F. 1994. A tale of three schools: insights on autocorrelations of short-horizon stock returns. Review of Financial Studies, 7(3), 539–573.

Carhart, M. M. 1997. On persistence in mutual fund performance. Journal of Finance, 52(1), 57–82.

Conrad, J., Gultekin, M. N., and Kaul, G. 1997. Profitability of short-term contrarian strategies: implications for market efficiency. Journal of Business and Economic Statistics, 15(3), 379–386.

Fama, E. F. 1970. Efficient capital markets: a review of theory and empirical work. Journal of Finance, 25(2), 383–417.

Fama, E. F. and French, K. R. 1993. Common risk factors in the returns on stocks and bonds. Journal of Financial Economics, 33(1), 3–56.

Fama, E. F. and MacBeth, J. D. 1973. Risk, return, and equilibrium: empirical tests. Journal of Political Economy, 81(3), 607.

Hasbrouck, J. 1991. The summary informativeness of stock trades: an economic analysis. Review of Financial Studies, 4(3), 571–595.

Jegadeesh, N. 1990. Evidence of predictable behavior of security returns. Journal of Finance, 45(3), 881–898.

Keim, D. B. 1989. Trading patterns, bid-ask spreads, and estimated security returns: the case of common stocks at calendar turning points. Journal of Financial Economics, 25(1), 75–97.

Lehmann, B. N. 1990. Fads, martingales, and market efficiency. Quarterly Journal of Economics, 105(1), 1–28.

Lintner, J. 1965. Security prices, risk, and maximal gains from diversification. Journal of Finance, 20(4), 687–615.

Lo, A. W. and MacKinlay, A. C. 1990. When are contrarian profits due to stock market overreaction? Review of Financial Studies, 3(2), 175–205.

Mech, T. S. 1993. Portfolio return autocorrelation. Journal of Financial Economics, 34(3), 307–344.

Mossin, J. 1966. Equilibrium in a capital asset market. Econometrica, 34(4), 768–783.

Nagel, S. 2012. Evaporating liquidity. Review of Financial Studies, 25(6), 2005–2039.

Newey, W. K. and West, K. D. 1987. A simple, positive semi-definite, heteroskedasticity and autocorrelation consistent covariance matrix. Econometrica, 55(3), 703–708.

Roll, R. 1984. A simple implicit measure of the effective bid-ask spread in an efficient market. Journal of Finance, 39(4), 1127–1139.

Sharpe, W. F. 1964. Capital asset prices: a theory of market equilibrium under conditions of risk. Journal of Finance, 19(3), 425–442.

13

LIQUIDITY

In this chapter, we examine the effect of liquidity on expected security returns. While it is difficult to provide a precise definition of liquidity, a security's liquidity refers to the ease with which the security can be bought and/or sold. Securities that are difficult or expensive to transact in are considered illiquid, while securities for which the cost of transacting is small or negligible are more liquid.

Examination of the role of liquidity in the pricing of securities can be viewed as an examination of one of the key assumptions of the Capital Asset Pricing Model (CAPM) of Sharpe (1964), Lintner (1965), and Mossin (1966) and the arbitrage pricing theory of Ross (1976), each of which assumes that all securities are perfectly liquid, meaning that transaction costs are zero. Most practitioners and academics, however, acknowledge the shortcomings of this assumption.

Several theoretical and empirical papers have examined the role of liquidity in determining expected stock returns.[1] In a seminal study, Amihud and Mendelson (1986) generate a theoretical model that predicts a positive relation between the bid-ask spread, one of the most commonly used measures of liquidity, and expected security returns.[2] Amihud and Mendelson (1989) empirically test this prediction and find that, consistent with the prediction of a liquidity premium, the bid–ask spread has a positive cross-sectional relation with future stock returns after controlling for other variables related to expected stock returns, such as market beta, market

---

[1] Holden et al. (2014) provide a comprehensive review of empirical analyses of liquidity.
[2] The bid–ask spread is a measure of illiquidity, as securities with higher bid–ask spreads are less liquid.

Empirical Asset Pricing: The Cross Section of Stock Returns, First Edition.
Turan G. Bali, Robert F. Engle, and Scott Murray.
© 2016 John Wiley & Sons, Inc. Published 2016 by John Wiley & Sons, Inc.

capitalization (Banz (1981)), and idiosyncratic volatility (Levy (1978), Merton (1987)).[3] In perhaps the most widely cited article on the relation between liquidity and expected stock returns, Amihud (2002) generates a measure of stock illiquidity that requires only return and volume data to calculate and shows that illiquidity is positively related to expected market returns in both the time series and cross section. Brennan and Subrahmanyam (1996) find similar results using a measure of liquidity generated from intraday data. Acharya and Pedersen (2005) demonstrate theoretically that liquidity shocks should be positively correlated with contemporaneous returns and negatively correlated with future returns.[4,5] Easley, Hvidkjaer, and O'Hara (2002) suggest that some measures of liquidity may be capturing the amount of information-based trading in a stock and show that their measure of information-based trading is positively related to expected stock returns. Bali, Peng, Shen, and Tang (2014) find that shocks to stock-level liquidity are positively related to future stock returns and attribute this predictability to investor underreaction and inattention. Chordia et al. (2001b) document a negative relation between liquidity volatility and expected returns. Pereira and Zhang (2010) provide a theoretical rationale for this relation.

Many other studies have examined the role of aggregate liquidity in the pricing of securities. Chordia, Roll, and Subrahmanyam (2000) document substantial commonality in individual stock liquidity, meaning that individual stock liquidity is highly related to aggregate market liquidity. They find that this effect aggregates to the portfolio level, indicating that shocks to portfolio-level liquidity cannot be diversified away, which supports the claim that an aggregate liquidity factor plays a role in asset pricing. Hasbrouck and Seppi (2001) also find commonality in the liquidity of the stocks that comprise the Dow Jones Industrial Average. Pastor and Stambaugh (2003) demonstrate that an aggregate liquidity factor plays a strong role in determining both cross-sectional variation in individual stock returns and time-series variation in the market risk premium.[6] Kamara, Lou, and Sadka (2008) demonstrate that cross-sectional variation in liquidity commonality has decreased over time and associate this phenomenon with similar patterns in systematic risk and changes in institutional ownership.

Additional work has further characterized the role of liquidity in the financial markets. Chordia, Roll, and Subrahmanyam (2001a) document several properties of aggregate market level liquidity in U.S. equities. They find that liquidity is low during market downturns, periods of high market volatility, and on Fridays; that liquidity

---

[3] Subsequent to the publication of Amihud and Mendelson (1989), additional papers on the relations between expected returns and each of market capitalization and idiosyncratic volatility were published. Fama and French (1992, 1993) demonstrate a strong negative relation between market capitalization and future stock returns. Ang et al. (2006) demonstrate a strong negative relation between idiosyncratic volatility and future stock returns, contrary to the theoretical predictions of Levy (1978) and Merton (1987).

[4] Several other studies such as Eleswarapu (1997), Brennan, Chordia, and Subrahmanyam (1998), Datar, Naik, and Radcliffe (1998) and Hasbrouck (2009) have documented a positive premium associated with illiquidity.

[5] Eleswarapu and Reinganum (1993) demonstrate that this phenomenon has a seasonal component.

[6] Other studies such as Huberman and Halka (2001) document time variation in liquidity.

is high prior to major macroeconomic announcements and on Tuesdays; and that daily aggregate liquidity is negatively serially correlated. Chordia, Roll, and Subrahmanyam (2002) find that imbalances in buy and sell orders result in decreased liquidity and in some cases lead to reversal patterns in the daily returns of individual stocks. Chordia, Roll, and Subrahmanyam (2008) find that increased liquidity leads to increased arbitrage activity and, in turn, enhanced market efficiency.

In this chapter, we discuss the most commonly used measure of stock-level liquidity in empirical asset pricing research. We show that this measure, developed by Amihud (2002), has a strong positive relation with expected stock returns. We then discuss the aggregate liquidity factor generated by Pastor and Stambaugh (2003). This factor is frequently used to augment the Fama and French (1993) and Carhart (1997) four-factor model.

13.1   MEASURING LIQUIDITY

Many different measures of liquidity have been put forth in the finance literature. Roll (1984) proposes that two times the square root of the negative of the covariance between successive prices changes in a given stock measures the effective spread, which is defined as the actual (not quoted) cost investors pay for trading in the given stock, and finds that this measure is negatively related in the cross section to market capitalization, which is known to be positively related to liquidity. Chordia et al. (2001a) define several different measures of illiquidity. They take the quoted spread to be the difference between the bid and the ask price, which they measure both in dollar terms and as a percentage of the security price. The effective spread is taken to be the difference between the midpoint of the best bid and best offer prices and the execution price of a trade. Once again, the effective spread is calculated in dollar terms and as a percentage of price. Market depth is calculated as the average of the number of shares available at the best bid and the best offer. Dollar depth is the average of the best bid price times the number of shares available at that price and the best offer price times the number of shares available at the offer price. Chordia et al. (2001a) also look at volume, dollar volume, and the number of trades as measures of liquidity.

In this chapter, we focus on the Amihud (2002) measure of liquidity. While, by Amihud's own admission, this measure is likely not the most accurate of all measures of liquidity, it has several benefits not offered by many of the other measures. First, calculation of the Amihud measure requires only daily return, volume, and price data, whereas other (potentially more accurate) measures of liquidity such as those of Chordia et al. (2001a) and Brennan and Subrahmanyam (1996) require intraday data. Second, given the minimal data requirements for the Amihud measure, the necessary data are available for a much larger set of assets and generally longer time series than the data required for other measures. This permits much more comprehensive studies of the relation between liquidity and expected security returns. For these reasons, combined with its efficacy, the Amihud (2002) measure of liquidity is the most widely used liquidity variable in the empirical asset pricing literature.

Amihud's measure is actually a measure of *il*liquidity, not liquidity, thus more liquid securities will have lower values and less liquid securities will have higher values. The main idea behind the measure is to calculate the effect of volume on the magnitude of the return of the security. If a security realizes a large absolute return on small volume, this indicates that the stock is quite illiquid, as a small amount of trading had a substantial impact on the price. However, if a security trades at high volume and the price impact is quite small, as reflected in a small magnitude of the return, then the security is considered quite liquid. Accordingly, Amihud calculates illiquidity as the ratio of the absolute value of the daily security return divided by the daily dollar volume traded in the security, averaged over all days in the estimation period. Formulaically, the illiquidity measure is defined as

$$Illiq_i = \frac{1}{D} \sum_{d=1}^{D} \frac{|R_{i,d}|}{VOLD_{i,d}} \tag{13.1}$$

where $R_{i,d}$ is the return of stock i on day d measured as a decimal (0.01 is a 1% return); $VOLD_{i,d}$ is the dollar volume of stock i traded on day d, calculated as the closing price of the stock times the number of shares traded on the given date, measured in millions of dollars; and D is the number of days in the estimation period. When calculating *Illiq*, $R_{i,d}$ is most commonly taken from the RET field in the Center for Research in Security Prices (CRSP) daily stock file. The volume and price used to calculate *VOLD* are taken from the VOL and PRC fields, respectively, in CRSP's daily stock file. Since VOL is recorded in shares and PRC is recorded in dollars, *VOLD* is taken to be the product of these two fields divided by one million. Days where either the PRC field or the VOL field is nonpositive are omitted from the calculation.[7] The summation is taken over all trading days in the calculation period, as described in the next paragraph. The value of *Illiq* can be interpreted as the percentage price impact of trading one million dollars ($10,000), where the percentage impact is measured as a decimal (in percent).

To calculate *Illiq* for stock i in month t, Amihud (2002) uses one year's worth of daily data covering the 12-month period including months $t - 11$ through t, inclusive. Different studies, however, have adopted different measurement periods.[8] We examine four measures of illiquidity in the empirical analyses presented throughout this chapter. Specifically, we calculate the Amihud (2002) measure of illiquidity using one ($Illiq^{1M}$), three ($Illiq^{3M}$), six ($Illiq^{6M}$), and 12 months ($Illiq^{12M}$) worth of data up to and including the month t (the month for which *Illiq* is being calculated). As will be seen in Section 13.2, the distribution of *Illiq* is highly skewed. For this reason, we also use log-transformed versions of the different illiquidity variables. We therefore

---

[7] The reasons for negative values in the PRC field are discussed in Section 9.1.

[8] Amihud (2002) also calculates *Illiq* for each stock during each calendar year and holds the value of *Illiq* for any given stock constant for an entire year. Most subsequent studies that employ this measure calculate *Illiq* at the end of each month t using k months of daily data covering months $t - k + 1$ through t, inclusive, and therefore update their values of *Illiq* on a monthly basis. In Fama and MacBeth (1973) regression analyses, Amihud (2002) also scales *Illiq* by its cross-sectional average in the given month. This approach is not employed in most studies.

define ln $Illiq^{1M}$ to be the natural log of one plus $Illiq^{1M}$. ln $Illiq^{3M}$, ln $Illiq^{6M}$, and ln $Illiq^{12M}$ are defined analogously using $Illiq^{3M}$, $Illiq^{6M}$, and $Illiq^{12M}$, respectively, instead of $Illiq^{1M}$. We require a minimum of 15, 50, 100, and 200 valid daily observations to calculate $Illiq^{1M}$, $Illiq^{3M}$, $Illiq^{6M}$, and $Illiq^{12M}$, respectively. A valid daily observation has a nonmissing return (RET field) as well as positive volume (VOL field) and a nonnegative closing price (PRC field) in CRSP's daily stock file.

13.2   SUMMARY STATISTICS

In Table 13.1, we present summary statistics for the measures of illiquidity using our sample of U.S. stocks during the 1963 through 2012 period. The results show that in the average month, $Illiq^{1M}$ has a cross-sectional mean and median of 3.79 and 0.26, respectively, with a cross-sectional standard deviation of 27.73. In the average month, $Illiq^{1M}$ has cross-sectional skewness of 22.15 and excess kurtosis of 827.12, indicating that the distribution of $Illiq^{1M}$ is highly positively skewed and leptokurtic. This is driven in large part by a small number of stocks that are extremely illiquid. In the average month, the 95th percentile of $Illiq^{1M}$ is 13.39, which is less than 0.35 standard deviations above the mean. The maximum value of $Illiq^{1M}$ in the average month of 1174.73 is more than 42 standard deviations above the mean. The existence of a small number of extremely large values of $Illiq^{1M}$ raise concerns about the reliability of results of statistical analyses that are sensitive to extreme data points, such as correlation and regression analyses. There are 3604 stocks with valid values of $Illiq^{1M}$ in the average month.

TABLE 13.1   Summary Statistics
This table presents summary statistics for variables measuring illiquidity using the CRSP sample for the months t from June 1963 through November 2012. Each month, the mean (*Mean*), standard deviation (*SD*), skewness (*Skew*), excess kurtosis (*Kurt*), minimum (*Min*), fifth percentile (5%), 25th percentile (25%), median (*Median*), 75th percentile (75%), 95th percentile (95%), and maximum (*Max*) values of the cross-sectional distribution of each variable is calculated. The table presents the time-series means for each cross-sectional value. The column labeled n indicates the average number of stocks for which the given variable is available. $Illiq^{1M}$, $Illiq^{3M}$, $Illiq^{6M}$, and $Illiq^{12M}$ are the ratio daily stock return, measured as a decimal, divided by the daily dollar trading volume, measured in millions of dollars, averaged over one, three, six, and 12 months, respectively. ln $Illiq^{1M}$, ln $Illiq^{3M}$, ln $Illiq^{6M}$, and ln $Illiq^{12M}$ are the natural logs of $Illiq^{1M}$, $Illiq^{3M}$, $Illiq^{6M}$, and $Illiq^{12M}$, respectively.

	Mean	SD	Skew	Kurt	Min	5%	25%	Median	75%	95%	Max	n
$Illiq^{1M}$	3.79	27.73	22.15	827.12	0.00	0.01	0.05	0.26	1.35	13.39	1174.73	3604
$Illiq^{3M}$	2.88	18.03	20.09	684.53	0.00	0.01	0.05	0.24	1.17	10.70	687.71	3438
$Illiq^{6M}$	2.76	15.75	18.35	568.03	0.00	0.01	0.05	0.25	1.19	10.65	560.23	3370
$Illiq^{12M}$	2.70	14.01	16.51	451.68	0.00	0.01	0.05	0.26	1.23	10.81	452.60	3247
ln $Illiq^{1M}$	0.57	0.84	2.50	8.08	0.00	0.01	0.05	0.20	0.73	2.39	6.22	3604
ln $Illiq^{3M}$	0.53	0.79	2.50	8.07	0.00	0.01	0.05	0.20	0.68	2.24	5.85	3438
ln $Illiq^{6M}$	0.54	0.79	2.43	7.50	0.00	0.01	0.05	0.20	0.70	2.26	5.72	3370
ln $Illiq^{12M}$	0.55	0.79	2.34	6.81	0.00	0.01	0.05	0.21	0.72	2.29	5.59	3247

The cross-sectional distributions of $Illiq^{3M}$, $Illiq^{6M}$, and $Illiq^{12M}$ exhibit several similar characteristics to the distribution of $Illiq^{1M}$, although the effects of extreme data points become a little bit less severe as the length of the measurement period increases. The maximum values of the illiquidity measures decrease as the measurement period gets longer, since $Illiq^{3M}$, $Illiq^{6M}$, and $Illiq^{12M}$ have average monthly maximum values of 687.71, 560.23, and 452.60, respectively. Similarly, the mean, standard deviation, skewness, and kurtosis of these measures also decrease with extended sample periods. The mean values decrease from 2.88 for $Illiq^{3M}$ to 2.76 for $Illiq^{6M}$ and 2.70 for $Illiq^{12M}$. The standard deviations of $Illiq^{3M}$, $Illiq^{6M}$, and $Illiq^{12M}$ are 18.03, 15.75, and 14.01, respectively. The average cross-sectional skewness of $Illiq^{3M}$ is 20.09. The average skewness decreases to 18.35 for $Illiq^{6M}$ and 16.51 for $Illiq^{12M}$. Finally, $Illiq^{3M}$, $Illiq^{6M}$, and $Illiq^{12M}$ have average cross-sectional excess kurtosis of 684.53, 568.03, and 451.68, respectively.

The summary statistics for the log-transformed measures of illiquidity ($\ln Illiq^{1M}$, $\ln Illiq^{3M}$, $\ln Illiq^{6M}$, and $\ln Illiq^{12M}$) demonstrate that applying the log transformation has very little effect on values in the left tail of the distributions of these variables, but substantially reduces the magnitudes of values in the right tail. The effect is a substantial reduction in the mean, standard deviation, skewness, and excess kurtosis of each of these variables relative to their untransformed counterparts. The mean values of the log-transformed variables of 0.57 for $\ln Illiq^{1M}$, 0.53 for $\ln Illiq^{3M}$, 0.54 for $\ln Illiq^{6M}$, and 0.55 for $\ln Illiq^{12M}$ are all quite similar. The cross-sectional standard deviations of these variables also fall in a narrow range, with $\ln Illiq^{1M}$ having an average standard deviation of 0.84 and $\ln Illiq^{3M}$, $\ln Illiq^{6M}$, and $\ln Illiq^{12M}$ all having standard deviations of 0.79 in the average month. The cross-sectional skewness of the log-transformed measures decreases from 2.50 for $\ln Illiq^{1M}$ and $\ln Illiq^{3M}$ to 2.43 for $\ln Illiq^{6M}$ and 2.34 for $\ln Illiq^{12M}$ Finally, $\ln Illiq^{1M}$ has an average excess kurtosis of 8.08 compared to 8.07 for $\ln Illiq^{3M}$, 7.50 for $\ln Illiq^{6M}$, and 6.81 for $\ln Illiq^{12M}$. Thus, while applying the log transformation certainly reduces the skewness and kurtosis of the distribution of the illiquidity measures, the results indicate that even $\ln Illiq$ remains highly positively skewed and leptokurtic.

13.3 CORRELATIONS

The time-series averages of monthly cross-sectional correlations between the different measures of liquidity, market beta (β), size ($Size$, natural log of market capitalization), book-to-market ratio (BM), momentum (Mom), and reversal (Rev) are shown in Table 13.2. Each of the variables is winsorized at the monthly level before performing the analysis. Pearson product–moment correlations are presented in the below-diagonal entries, and Spearman rank correlations are presented in the above-diagonal entries.

We first examine the correlations between $Illiq$ calculated using different measurement periods. The table indicates that regardless of measurement period, the values of $Illiq$ are highly correlated in the cross section. The Pearson correlations range from 0.81 between $Illiq_{1M}$ and $Illiq_{12M}$ to 0.95 between $Illiq_{6M}$ and $Illiq_{12M}$ as

TABLE 13.2 Correlations

This table presents the time-series averages of the annual cross-sectional Pearson product–moment (below-diagonal entries) and Spearman rank (above-diagonal entries) correlations between pairs of variables measuring illiquidity as well as β, Size, BM, Mom, and Rev.

	$Illiq^{1M}$	$Illiq^{3M}$	$Illiq^{6M}$	$Illiq^{12M}$	$\ln Illiq^{1M}$	$\ln Illiq^{3M}$	$\ln Illiq^{6M}$	$\ln Illiq^{12M}$	β	Size	BM	Mom	Rev
$Illiq^{1M}$		0.98	0.97	0.96	1.00	0.98	0.97	0.96	−0.32	−0.92	0.25	−0.24	−0.08
$Illiq^{3M}$	0.91		0.99	0.98	0.98	1.00	0.99	0.98	−0.30	−0.93	0.24	−0.23	−0.05
$Illiq^{6M}$	0.87	0.95		0.99	0.97	0.99	1.00	0.99	−0.30	−0.93	0.25	−0.20	−0.05
$Illiq^{12M}$	0.81	0.89	0.95		0.96	0.98	0.99	1.00	−0.30	−0.93	0.25	−0.14	−0.04
$\ln Illiq^{1M}$	0.81	0.79	0.78	0.75		0.98	0.97	0.96	−0.32	−0.92	0.25	−0.24	−0.08
$\ln Illiq^{3M}$	0.78	0.83	0.82	0.79	0.96		0.99	0.98	−0.30	−0.93	0.24	−0.23	−0.05
$\ln Illiq^{6M}$	0.75	0.80	0.83	0.82	0.93	0.98		0.99	−0.30	−0.93	0.25	−0.20	−0.05
$\ln Illiq^{12M}$	0.71	0.77	0.80	0.83	0.90	0.94	0.97		−0.30	−0.93	0.25	−0.14	−0.04
β	−0.15	−0.15	−0.15	−0.15	−0.27	−0.25	−0.26	−0.25		0.33	−0.23	0.04	−0.01
Size	−0.42	−0.44	−0.45	−0.46	−0.69	−0.70	−0.71	−0.71	0.31		−0.26	0.25	0.11
BM	0.18	0.18	0.20	0.21	0.26	0.25	0.26	0.27	−0.19	−0.27		0.04	0.03
Mom	−0.16	−0.16	−0.14	−0.09	−0.22	−0.20	−0.17	−0.10	0.07	0.18	0.02		0.04
Rev	−0.04	−0.01	−0.01	−0.00	−0.05	−0.02	−0.01	−0.00	−0.02	0.07	0.02	0.02	

well as between $Illiq^{3M}$ and $Illiq^{6M}$. While there is a mechanical component of these correlations, they are much too high to be driven by this. The Spearman rank correlations are even higher, ranging from 0.96 to 0.99. This indicates that the length of the measurement period used to calculate $Illiq$ has almost no effect on the cross-sectional ordering of stocks by illiquidity. The difference between the Pearson and Spearman correlations indicates that the effect of a few extreme data points may be substantial.

The correlations between the log-transformed measures and the corresponding untransformed measures range from 0.81 between $Illiq^{1M}$ and $\ln Illiq^{1M}$ to 0.83 between each of $Illiq^{3M}$ and $\ln Illiq^{3M}$, $Illiq^{6M}$ and $\ln Illiq^{6M}$, and $Illiq^{12M}$ and $\ln Illiq^{12M}$. Since the transformed and untransformed measures are increasing functions of one another, these correlations capture the effect of the nonlinearity of the log transformation. The correlations between these pairs of variables are low enough to raise concern that the log-transformed variables will generate somewhat different results in linear analyses such as Fama and MacBeth (1973) regressions than the untransformed variables. The Spearman correlations between a given $Illiq$ variable and its log-transformed version $\ln Illiq$ are all, by construction, one.

Examining the Pearson correlations between the log-transformed measures, we see that these correlations are in all cases higher than the correlation between the corresponding pair of untransformed variables. For example, the correlation between $Illiq^{1M}$ and $Illiq^{12M}$ in the average month is 0.81 compared to an average correlation of 0.90 between $\ln Illiq^{1M}$ and $\ln Illiq^{12M}$. The increased correlation when using the log-transformed measures is additional evidence that the influence of extreme data points in the untransformed versions may have an undesired impact on statistical analyses. By necessity, the Spearman correlations between the log-transformed measures are identical to the Spearman correlations for the corresponding pairs of untransformed variables.

Turning now to the correlations between the measures of illiquidity and other stock-level characteristics, the results show that illiquidity is negatively related to beta (β). The Pearson correlations between *Illiq* and β are all -0.15, whereas the correlations between β and ln *Illiq* range from -0.25 to -0.27. The Spearman rank correlations between β and the illiquidity measures range from -0.30 to -0.32. The fact that the correlations between β and the untransformed measures (*Illiq*) are substantially lower in magnitude than the correlations between β and the log-transformed measures (ln *Illiq*) indicates that the controlling for β in linear regression analyses using *Illiq* may not capture the nature of the relation between β and illiquidity, making the control ineffective. The fact that the Spearman rank correlations are reasonably similar to the Pearson product–moment correlations when using ln *Illiq* indicates that the relation between β and ln *Illiq* is probably reasonably linear.

Illiquidity has a strong negative relation with stock size. The Pearson product–moment correlations between *Illiq* and *Size* are between -0.42 and -0.46. The Pearson correlations between ln *Illiq* and *Size* are substantially higher in magnitude, ranging from -0.69 to -0.71. All of these correlations are substantially lower than the Spearman rank correlations between the illiquidity measures and *Size*, which are all between -0.92 and -0.93. The Spearman rank correlations indicate that illiquidity and size have a strong negative and highly monotonic relation. The substantial decrease in the magnitude of these correlations when using the Pearson measure indicates that the relation between stock size and illiquidity may not be linear. The decreases in the magnitude of the correlations when using *Illiq* instead of ln *Illiq* indicate that for linear analyses, ln *Illiq* is likely the better variable. It should be noted that the strong negative correlation between illiquidity and size is somewhat mechanical. *Illiq* is calculated by taking the daily average of absolute stock return divided by dollar trading volume. Dollar trading volume is highly cross-sectionally correlated to stock size, with large stocks having higher dollar trading volume than small stocks. Therefore, the calculation of *Illiq* effectively puts stock size in the denominator, thereby inducing a strong negative serial correlation.

The correlation analyses find a positive relation between illiquidity and book-to-market ratio. The Pearson correlations between *Illiq* and *BM* range from 0.18 to 0.21 depending on the measurement period used to calculate *Illiq*. The Pearson correlations between ln *Illiq* and *BM* are somewhat higher, ranging from 0.25 to 0.27. Finally, the average Spearman correlations between the illiquidity variables and *BM* are all either 0.24 or 0.25, very similar in magnitude to the correlations between ln *Illiq* and *BM*. There is no evidence, therefore, that the effectiveness of controlling for the relation between *BM* and future stock returns in analyses of the relation between illiquidity and future stock returns will be hampered by a nonlinear relation between *BM* and illiquidity, especially if ln *Illiq* is used as the measure of illiquidity.

Illiquidity exhibits a negative relation with *Mom*. This negative relation is stronger when shorter measurement periods are used in the calculation of illiquidity. The magnitudes of the correlations are also slightly stronger when using ln *Illiq* instead of *Illiq*. The Spearman rank correlations are, in all cases, negative and larger in magnitude than the corresponding Pearson correlations. The Spearman correlations range from -0.24 between $Illiq^{1M}$ (or $\ln Illiq^{1M}$) and Mom to -0.14 between $Illiq^{12M}$ (or $\ln Illiq^{12M}$) and Mom, and exhibit the same decreasing pattern as shorter measurement periods are used in the calculation of $Illiq$.

Finally, the results of the correlation analyses indicate a small negative correlation between illiquidity and Rev. This correlation is highest in magnitude when illiquidity is measured using one month of data, with the magnitude decreasing as the measurement period is extended. In all cases, however, the magnitude of the correlations is quite small. The Pearson correlation between $Illiq^{1M}$ and Rev is only -0.04. The Pearson correlation between $\ln Illiq^{1M}$ and Rev of -0.05 is only slightly larger in magnitude. Finally, the Spearman rank correlation between $Illiq^{1M}$ (or $\ln Illiq^{1M}$) and Rev is -0.08. This is the highest (in magnitude) average correlation between any of the measures of illiquidity and Rev, regardless of which measure of correlation is used. Thus, while there may be a slight negative relation between illiquidity and Rev, this relation does not appear to be strong.

In summary, the results indicate that length of the measurement period used to calculate illiquidity is unlikely to have substantial impact on the results of empirical analyses, as measures calculated using different amounts of data are cross-sectionally very similar. The log-transformed measures ($\ln Illiq$) appear to have stronger linear relations with other predictors of future stock returns, indicating the possibility that using $\ln Illiq$, instead of $Illiq$, in regression analyses, will produce more reliable results, especially when examining the relation between illiquidity and future stock returns after controlling for other effects. Finally, the fact that the Spearman correlations tend to be a little bit higher than the Pearson correlations indicates that, even when using the log-transformed measures, the relations between illiquidity and the other predictors of stock returns may be somewhat nonlinear.

13.4 PERSISTENCE

We next examine the persistence of $Illiq$ and $\ln Illiq$. Table 13.3 presents the results of persistence analyses of the $Illiq$ and $\ln Illiq$ variables. Persistence is calculated for each variable at lags of one, three, six, 12, 24, 36, 48, 60, and 120 months. The missing entries in the table represent cases where the measurement period is longer than the lag. These values are omitted because persistence in such cases is likely to be in large part mechanical. The table shows that $Illiq_{1M}$, $Illiq_{3M}$, $Illiq_{6M}$, and $Illiq_{12M}$ have persistence 0.80, 0.84, 0.81, and 0.75 when measured one, three, six, and 12 months apart, respectively, indicating that $Illiq$ is a highly persistent variable. Economically this means that historical illiquidity is a very strong predictor of future illiquidity, making the historical data-based value a useful measure in analyses aimed at discerning the relation between liquidity and expected returns. The persistence of the log-transformed measures of illiquidity ($\ln Illiq^{1M}$, $\ln Illiq^{3M}$, $\ln Illiq^{6M}$, and $\ln Illiq^{12M}$) is even stronger than that of the untransformed variables, as the one-, three-, six-, and 12-month measures produce persistence values of 0.91, 0.92, 0.91, and 0.87 when measured at lags of one, three, six, and 12 months, respectively. This result is quite reassuring since, given the distribution of $Illiq$, it would seem possible

TABLE 13.3 Persistence

This table presents the results of persistence analyses of variables measuring illiquidity. Each month t, the cross-sectional Pearson product–moment correlation between the month t and month $t + \tau$ values of the given variable is calculated. The table presents the time-series averages of the monthly cross-sectional correlations. The column labeled τ indicates the lag at which the persistence is measured.

τ	$Illiq^{1M}$	$Illiq^{3M}$	$Illiq^{6M}$	$Illiq^{12M}$	ln $Illiq^{1M}$	ln $Illiq^{3M}$	ln $Illiq^{6M}$	ln $Illiq^{12M}$
1	0.80				0.91			
3	0.74	0.84			0.87	0.92		
6	0.67	0.76	0.81		0.83	0.88	0.91	
12	0.58	0.64	0.68	0.75	0.76	0.80	0.83	0.87
24	0.45	0.49	0.53	0.57	0.66	0.69	0.71	0.75
36	0.38	0.41	0.43	0.47	0.60	0.62	0.64	0.67
48	0.33	0.36	0.38	0.42	0.56	0.57	0.59	0.62
60	0.31	0.33	0.35	0.38	0.53	0.54	0.56	0.59
120	0.24	0.27	0.28	0.30	0.47	0.47	0.49	0.51

that a very small number of stocks with very large but persistent values of *Illiq* would be driving the apparent persistence of the untransformed measure. The increased persistence of ln *Illiq* compared to *Illiq* indicates that this is not the case.

The results show that at any given lag, measures of illiquidity that are calculated using longer measurement periods are more persistent than measures calculated using shorter measurement periods. The table also shows that the persistence values of the log-transformed (ln *Illiq*) measures are all substantially higher than the corresponding persistence values for the untransformed (*Illiq*) measures. This is potentially an indication that the log-transformed measures are better at capturing a cross-sectionally persistent characteristic and that the untransformed measure may be a somewhat noisy, especially when the measured value of *Illiq* is extreme. Overall, the results of the persistence analyses indicate that the log-transformed measures may be more effective at capturing individual stock-level liquidity.

13.5 LIQUIDITY AND STOCK RETURNS

We now proceed to examine the relation between liquidity and future stock returns. We remind the reader that *Illiq* and ln *Illiq* measure illiquidity and are thus inversely related to liquidity. The finding of a positive relation between *Illiq* (or ln *Illiq*) and future stock returns, therefore, indicates that less liquid stocks command higher expected returns while more liquid stocks command lower expected returns.

13.5.1 Univariate Portfolio Analysis

We begin our investigation of the cross-sectional relation between liquidity and expected returns with univariate sort portfolio analyses. Each month, we sort all stocks in the sample into decile portfolios based on an ascending sort of each of the *Illiq* variables.[9] The results of the portfolio analyses are shown in Table 13.4.

In Panel A, we present equal-weighted average values of $Illiq^{12M}$, β, *MktCap*, *BM*, *Mom*, and *Rev* for each of the $Illiq^{12M}$-sorted decile portfolios. By construction, average $Illiq^{12M}$ increases monotonically from 0.01 for the first decile portfolio to 21.29 for the 10th decile portfolio. Consistent with the correlation analyses that found a negative relation between β and $Illiq^{12M}$, the portfolio analysis indicates that average β decreases monotonically from 1.11 for stocks in the first $Illiq^{12M}$ decile to 0.60 for stocks in $Illiq^{12M}$ decile 10. The portfolio analysis detects a very strong negative relation between illiquidity and market capitalization. Stocks in the first decile of $Illiq^{12M}$ have an average market capitalization of $10.3 billion. In decile two of $Illiq^{12M}$, the average value of *MktCap* decreases by more than 85% to only $1.5 billion. The average *MktCap* of stocks in the third decile portfolio of $690 million is less than half that of the second decile portfolio. The decreasing pattern continues. The average stock in $Illiq^{12M}$ decile seven has a market capitalization of only $102 million, less than 1% of the average *MktCap* for stocks in $Illiq^{12M}$ decile one. Finally, stocks in the 10th decile portfolio have an average market capitalization of only $17 million, less than two-tenths of a percent of the average *MktCap* for stocks in the decile one portfolio. While the strength of the relation between *MktCap* and $Illiq^{12M}$ is striking, perhaps it should not be surprising, as it is well known that small stocks tend to be illiquid and large stocks tend to be liquid.

The results also indicate a positive relation between illiquidity and book-to-market ratio. The average value of *BM* increases monotonically from 0.64 for stocks in the first $Illiq^{12M}$-sorted decile portfolio to 1.47 for stocks in the 10th decile portfolio. The average values of *Mom* increase slightly from 15.80 for the first portfolio to 17.25 for the third portfolio and then decrease monotonically across decile portfolios three through 10. Stocks in the highest illiquidity decile have an average *Mom* of 7.02, substantially lower than any of the other decile portfolios. The portfolio analysis indicates a positive relation between $Illiq^{12M}$ and *Rev*. Average *Rev* increases nearly monotonically from 0.92 in portfolio 1 to 1.79 in portfolio 10. This result is interesting since the correlation analysis detected, if anything, a slight negative relation between *Rev* and $Illiq^{12M}$. The finding of a strong positive relation between *Rev* and $Illiq^{12M}$ in the portfolio analysis likely indicates that portfolios with higher values of $Illiq^{12M}$ are more likely to have stocks with extremely high values of *Rev*. In the correlation analysis, the effect of these values is mollified by winsorizing each variable at the 0.5% level. However, the effect of these values comes through in the portfolio analysis because the values of *Rev* are not winsorized prior to calculating the average values for each portfolio.

The results of the equal-weighted portfolio analysis examining the relation between *Illiq* and one-month-ahead excess stock returns are shown in Panel B of Table 13.4. The table also shows the average returns, Fama and French (1993) and Carhart (1997) four-factor (FFC) alphas, and alphas relative to the FFC model

---

[9]Because ln *Illiq* is a monotonically increasing function of *Illiq*, the results when sorting on ln *Illiq* are identical to those from the analyses that sort on *Illiq*.

TABLE 13.4 Univariate Portfolio Analysis

This table presents the results of univariate portfolio analyses of the relation between illiquidity and future stock returns. Monthly portfolios are formed by sorting all stocks in the CRSP sample into portfolios using decile breakpoints calculated based on the given sort variable using all stocks in the CRSP sample. Panel A shows the average values of $Illiq^{12M}$, ln $Illiq^{12M}$, β, $MktCap$, BM, Mom, and Rev for stocks in each $Illiq^{12M}$ decile portfolio. Panel B (Panel D) shows the average equal-weighted (value-weighted) one-month-ahead excess return (in percent per month) for each of the 10 decile portfolios formed using different measures of illiquidity as the sort variable. Panel C shows the average equal-weighted one-month-ahead non-delisting-adjusted excess return (in percent per month), for each of the 10 decile portfolios formed using different measures of illiquidity as the sort variable. Panels B–D also show the average return of the portfolio that is long the 10th decile portfolio and short the first decile portfolio, as well as the FFC and FFCSTR alphas for this portfolio. Panel E shows the FFCSTR alpha as well as factor sensitivities for decile portfolios formed by sorting on $Illiq^{1M}$. Newey and West (1987) t-statistics, adjusted using six lags, testing the null hypothesis that the average 10-1 portfolio return, alpha, or factor sensitivity is equal to zero, are shown in parentheses.

Panel A: $Illiq^{12M}$-Sorted Portfolio Characteristics

Value	1	2	3	4	5	6	7	8	9	10
$Illiq^{12M}$	0.01	0.02	0.05	0.10	0.19	0.35	0.65	1.27	3.01	21.29
ln $Illiq^{12M}$	0.01	0.02	0.05	0.09	0.16	0.27	0.45	0.73	1.24	2.49
β	1.11	1.06	1.06	1.03	1.00	0.95	0.86	0.76	0.66	0.60
$MktCap$	10,263	1,455	690	392	241	154	102	62	36	17
BM	0.64	0.70	0.70	0.75	0.79	0.87	0.94	1.01	1.15	1.47
Mom	15.80	16.55	17.25	16.94	16.39	15.40	15.39	14.52	11.64	7.02
Rev	0.92	1.06	1.06	1.10	1.04	1.12	1.21	1.27	1.31	1.79

Panel B: Equal-Weighted Portfolio Returns

Sort Variable	1	2	3	4	5	6	7	8	9	10	10-1	FFC α	FFCSTR α
$Illiq^{1M}$	0.53	0.64	0.73	0.76	0.71	0.71	0.79	0.81	0.73	1.11	0.58	0.43	0.35
											(1.93)	(2.09)	(1.74)
$Illiq^{3M}$	0.49	0.62	0.65	0.66	0.67	0.68	0.73	0.83	0.76	1.11	0.62	0.44	0.40
											(1.98)	(2.09)	(1.96)
$Illiq^{6M}$	0.48	0.59	0.62	0.62	0.60	0.63	0.74	0.83	0.79	1.13	0.65	0.42	0.40
											(2.11)	(2.04)	(1.99)
$Illiq^{12M}$	0.46	0.60	0.58	0.61	0.59	0.65	0.77	0.82	0.83	1.23	0.77	0.45	0.44
											(2.49)	(2.11)	(2.14)

Panel C: Equal-Weighted Portfolio Unadjusted Returns

Sort Variable	1	2	3	4	5	6	7	8	9	10	10-1	FFC α	FFCSTR α
$Illiq^{1M}$	0.53	0.63	0.72	0.76	0.72	0.72	0.82	0.85	0.82	1.36	0.83	0.68	0.60
											(2.75)	(3.20)	(2.90)
$Illiq^{3M}$	0.49	0.61	0.65	0.66	0.68	0.70	0.76	0.87	0.85	1.35	0.86	0.68	0.65
											(2.76)	(3.18)	(3.11)
$Illiq^{6M}$	0.47	0.59	0.63	0.63	0.62	0.65	0.77	0.88	0.87	1.37	0.90	0.67	0.65
											(2.88)	(3.13)	(3.12)
$Illiq^{12M}$	0.46	0.60	0.58	0.62	0.61	0.67	0.79	0.87	0.92	1.47	1.01	0.68	0.68
											(3.23)	(3.13)	(3.18)

(continued)

TABLE 13.4   (*Continued*)

					Panel D: Value-Weighted Portfolio Returns								
Sort Variable	1	2	3	4	5	6	7	8	9	10	10-1	FFC α	FFCSTR α
$Illiq^{1M}$	0.42	0.54	0.60	0.62	0.55	0.57	0.64	0.66	0.50	0.24	−0.18	−0.46	−0.52
											(−0.65)	(−3.16)	(−3.48)
$Illiq^{3M}$	0.41	0.57	0.58	0.61	0.61	0.62	0.69	0.78	0.60	0.39	−0.02	−0.34	−0.38
											(−0.07)	(−2.27)	(−2.45)
$Illiq^{6M}$	0.41	0.55	0.58	0.60	0.60	0.62	0.76	0.85	0.67	0.50	0.09	−0.28	−0.28
											(0.32)	(−1.83)	(−1.77)
$Illiq^{12M}$	0.41	0.57	0.58	0.61	0.64	0.70	0.79	0.86	0.80	0.67	0.27	−0.21	−0.19
											(0.89)	(−1.40)	(−1.26)

				Panel E: Value-Weighted $Illiq^{1M}$-Sorted Portfolio FFCSTR Factor Sensitivites							
Value	1	2	3	4	5	6	7	8	9	10	10-1
FFCSTR α	0.03	−0.02	0.01	−0.03	−0.10	−0.10	−0.04	−0.04	−0.23	−0.50	−0.52
	(1.83)	(−0.38)	(0.13)	(−0.60)	(−2.04)	(−1.67)	(−0.62)	(−0.49)	(−2.49)	(−3.34)	(−3.48)
β_{MKT}	0.99	1.06	1.04	1.01	0.99	0.98	0.96	0.93	0.84	0.82	−0.16
	(186.17)	(73.36)	(84.67)	(62.89)	(59.17)	(54.77)	(48.47)	(28.43)	(21.73)	(14.57)	(−2.86)
β_{SMB}	−0.17	0.25	0.45	0.63	0.74	0.82	0.84	0.90	0.98	1.22	1.40
	(−12.04)	(9.91)	(15.23)	(19.02)	(20.36)	(15.81)	(15.18)	(12.54)	(11.04)	(9.85)	(10.39)
β_{HML}	−0.05	0.11	0.11	0.13	0.19	0.27	0.31	0.35	0.39	0.47	0.53
	(−5.10)	(3.65)	(4.34)	(4.79)	(5.60)	(6.49)	(6.56)	(4.81)	(4.67)	(3.87)	(4.16)
β_{MOM}	0.02	−0.05	−0.07	−0.09	−0.14	−0.18	−0.17	−0.19	−0.16	−0.25	−0.27
	(3.40)	(−2.80)	(−3.49)	(−3.91)	(−7.58)	(−6.97)	(−7.00)	(−4.87)	(−3.27)	(−4.43)	(−4.66)
β_{STR}	−0.02	0.01	0.04	0.09	0.08	0.09	0.08	0.09	0.11	0.11	0.13
	(−2.45)	(0.52)	(1.64)	(3.28)	(2.82)	(2.54)	(2.23)	(1.87)	(1.98)	(1.43)	(1.69)

augmented with the short-term reversal factor (FFCSTR) for the *Illiq* 10-1 portfolios, along with Newey and West (1987)-adjusted *t*-statistics testing the null hypothesis that the average return or abnormal return of the given 10-1 portfolio is equal to zero.

For portfolios formed by sorting on $Illiq^{1M}$, the average monthly excess portfolio return increases, although not monotonically, from 0.53% per month for the first decile portfolio to 1.11% per month for the 10th decile portfolio. The average return of the equal-weighted $Illiq^{1M}$ 10-1 portfolio of 0.58% per month is economically large and marginally statistically significant, with a Newey and West (1987)-adjusted *t*-statistic of 1.93. When the returns are adjusted using the FFC risk model, the difference portfolio generates an abnormal return of 0.43% per month with a corresponding *t*-statistic of 2.09. Inclusion of the short-term reversal factor in the risk model, however, seems to explain a small portion of the FFC alpha, since the alpha of the $Illiq^{1M}$ difference portfolio relative to the FFCSTR risk model of 0.35% per month is only marginally statistically significant with a *t*-statistic of 1.74.

When $Illiq^{3M}$ is used as the sort variable, the results of the portfolio analysis are a bit stronger, although very similar to the results of the analysis using $Illiq^{1M}$ as the sort variable. The average return of the equal-weighted $Illiq^{3M}$-sorted 10-1 portfolio is 0.62% per month (*t*-statistic = 1.98). This portfolio generates abnormal returns of

0.44% per month (t-statistic $= 2.09$) relative the FFC model and 0.40% per month (t-statistic $= 1.96$) relative to the FFCSTR risk model.

The results of the portfolio analysis using $Illiq^{6M}$ as the sort variable are very similar to the results generated by the $Illiq^{3M}$-sorted portfolios. The first equal-weighted $Illiq^{6M}$-sorted portfolio generates an average excess return of 0.48% per month. The average excess returns tend to increase, once again not quite monotonically, to 1.13% per month for decile portfolio 10. The $Illiq^{6M}$ 10-1 portfolio produces an average monthly return of 0.65% per month (t-statistic $= 2.11$). The alphas of this portfolio relative to the FFC and FFCSTR risk models of 0.42% per month (t-statistic $= 2.04$) and 0.40% per month (t-statistic $= 1.99$) are both statistically significant and of economically important magnitude.

The relation between illiquidity and expected stock returns appears strongest when $Illiq^{12M}$ is used as the sort variable. The average excess returns of the $Illiq^{12M}$-sorted decile portfolios increase, nearly monotonically, from 0.46% per month for the first decile portfolio to 1.23% per month for the 10th decile portfolio. The average difference in returns of 0.77% per month is highly statistically significant with a t-statistic of 2.49. Adjusting for risk does not explain the returns of this portfolio since the FFC alpha of 0.45% per month (t-statistic $= 2.11$) and FFCSTR alpha of 0.44% per month (t-statistic) are both economically large and statistically significant.

In each of the equal-weighted portfolio analyses, it is the decile 10 portfolio that generates a substantially higher average excess return than any of the other decile portfolios. In fact, regardless of the length of the period used to measure $Illiq$, the difference between the average return of the 10th decile portfolio and the average return of the ninth decile portfolio is larger than the difference in average returns between the decile nine and decile one portfolios. The results therefore indicate that it is highly illiquid stocks, specifically those stocks in the highest illiquidity decile, that are driving the positive relation between illiquidity and average returns. Referring back to Panel A, however, we notice that these stocks tend to have extremely low market capitalizations. The liquidity result, similar to the size effect, is driven primarily by stocks that comprise an extremely small percentage of the total capitalization of the entire stock market.

While the equal-weighted portfolio results presented in Panel B of Table 13.4 indicate a positive relation between $Illiq$ and future stock returns, the strength of this relation is not quite as strong as one might have thought based on the results in previous studies. While every study has its own methodological differences (e.g., Amihud (2002) uses only stocks that are listed on the New York Stock Exchange), one possible reason for this is that stocks that are very illiquid or hardly trade at all are more likely to be delisted. In calculating the excess returns for the stocks in our sample, we followed Shumway (1997) and adjusted for delisting based on the reason the stock was delisted.[10] When a stock is delisted, in a large number of cases, the delisted stocks are assigned a return of -100% for the month during which they delist. It is possible that the weakness of the equal-weighted portfolio results presented in Panel B, therefore,

---

[10] See Section 7.2 for a detailed discussion of how the one-month-ahead excess returns used in our analyses are calculated.

is driven by the fact that a disproportionate number of stocks that are in the highest illiquidity decile tend to delist in the following month. The result of this may be that the return of the decile 10 portfolio is lower than it would be if the unadjusted returns were used instead of the adjusted returns. To examine this possibility, we repeat the equal-weighted univariate portfolio analysis using the unadjusted excess stock return, instead of the delisting-adjusted excess stock return, as the outcome variable.[11]

Panel C of Table 13.4 presents the results of the equal-weighted univariate portfolio analyses using the unadjusted excess stock return as the outcome variable. The results of these analyses indicate a much stronger relation between *Illiq* and future stock returns than the results that used the delisting-adjusted returns as the outcome variable. The average return of the *Illiq*^{1M} 10-1 portfolio of 0.83% per month is highly statistically significant with a *t*-statistic of 2.75. The returns of this portfolio cannot be explained by the factors in the FFCSTR model, as the FFC alpha of 0.68% per month (*t*-statistic = 3.20) and FFCSTR alpha of 0.60% per month (*t*-statistic = 2.90) are both economically large and highly statistically significant. The returns and alphas of this portfolio are each 0.25% per month higher than when the delisting-adjusted returns were used as the outcome variable. In the case of the FFCSTR alpha, this represents more than a 70% increase in the abnormal return generated by the portfolio. When *Illiq*^{3M}, *Illiq*^{6M}, and *Illiq*^{12M} are used as the sort variables, the results are even stronger. When using *Illiq*^{12M} as the sort variable, the difference portfolio generates an average return of 1.01% per month (*t*-statistic = 3.23), FFC alpha of 0.68% per month (*t*-statistic = 3.13) and FFCSTR alpha of 0.68% per month (*t*-statistic = 3.18). Each of these results is economically larger and more statistically significant than the corresponding result from the analyses using the delisting-adjusted excess return as the outcome variable.

While the results using the unadjusted excess returns as the outcome variable presented in Panel C of Table 13.4 are more consistent with the perception among most empirical asset pricing researchers that the illiquidity effect is very strong in equal-weighted portfolios, this does not mean that these results are truly reflective of reality. Our objective in presenting both sets of results is not to make a claim as to which set of results is correct but to demonstrate to the reader that, in this case, the difference between using the delisting-adjusted returns versus the unadjusted returns is actually consequential. In almost all other cases, this difference is empirically unimportant. The differences in the results show that even small methodological changes can have substantial impacts on the results.

We proceed now to repeat the univariate portfolio analyses using value-weighted instead of equal-weighted portfolios. In these analyses, as well as in all subsequent analyses where we do not explicitly state otherwise, we continue to use the delisting-adjusted excess returns that have been used in every other analysis in Part II of this book, as the outcome variable. All aspects of the analyses except for the weighting scheme of the stocks within each portfolio remain the same as the

---

[11]The unadjusted excess return of the stock is simply the return indicated in the RET field of CRSP's monthly stock file minus the return on the risk-free security (see Section 7.2 for more details).

univariate portfolio analyses whose results are shown in Panel A. The results of the value-weighted portfolio analyses are presented in Panel D of Table 13.4.

Consistent with our conjecture that the relation between illiquidity detected in the equal-weighted portfolio analyses is driven by extremely small stocks, the results of the value-weighted portfolio analyses fail to detect a positive relation between $Illiq$ and future stock returns, regardless of the measurement period used to calculate $Illiq$. The average monthly returns of the value-weighted 10-1 portfolios formed by sorting on $Illiq^{1M}$, $Illiq^{3M}$, $Illiq^{6M}$, and $Illiq^{12M}$ of -0.18% (t-statistic $= -0.65$), -0.02% (t-statistic $= -0.07$), 0.09% (t-statistic $= 0.32$), and 0.27% (t-statistic $= 0.89$), respectively, are all statistically indistinguishable from zero. Interestingly, the abnormal returns of these portfolios relative to the FFC and FFCSTR factor models are negative and, with the exception of the $Illiq^{12M}$-sorted portfolios, statistically significant.[12,13]

The insignificance of the average returns and significance of the FFCSTR alphas for value-weighted portfolios formed by sorting on $Illiq^{1M}$, $Illiq^{3M}$, and $Illiq^{6M}$ indicates that the negative alphas must be driven by sensitivities to one or more of the factors in the FFCSTR factor model. We focus on the results for the $Illiq^{1M}$-sorted portfolios. Assuming that the patterns in the value-weighted average characteristics of the $Illiq^{1M}$-sorted decile portfolios are similar to those of the equal-weighted portfolios shown in Panel A of Table 13.4 (unreported analyses indicate that this is the case), the negative relation between $Illiq^{1M}$ and β should result in a negative sensitivity of the $Illiq^{1M}$ 10-1 portfolio to the market factor, meaning that the portfolio would be expected to have negative returns and that the abnormal returns of the portfolio should be higher than the average unadjusted returns. Sensitivity to the MKT factor, therefore, should not be driving the negative abnormal returns of the $Illiq^{1M}$ 10-1 portfolio. Stocks in decile 10 of $Illiq^{1M}$ have lower values of $MktCap$ than stocks in the decile one portfolio. Since the SMB factor is comprised of long positions in low-$MktCap$ stocks and short positions in high-$MktCap$ stocks, we would expect the $Illiq^{1M}$ portfolio to have a positive sensitivity to the SMB factor. This positive sensitivity combined with the failure to generate a positive return may result in a negative abnormal return. Similarly, the high (low) average BM values of stocks in the high (low) $Illiq^{1M}$ deciles indicates that the 10-1 $Illiq^{1M}$ portfolio should have a positive sensitivity to the HML factor, and this sensitivity may result in the negative abnormal returns. Mom is lower in the high-$Illiq^{1M}$ portfolios, which should result in a negative sensitivity of the difference portfolio to the MOM factor, which could not therefore drive the portfolio's negative alpha. Finally, high-$Illiq^{1M}$ stocks tend to be low-Rev stocks. The $Illiq^{1M}$ 10-1 portfolio likely has a positive sensitivity to the STR factor, which could potentially be driving the negative alpha. However, it should be noted that the FFC and FFCSTR alphas of the $Illiq^{1M}$ 10-1 portfolio are very similar,

---

[12] The alphas for the $Illiq^{6M}$-sorted portfolios are only marginally statistically significant.

[13] In unreported results, we repeat the value-weighted portfolio analyses using the unadjusted excess stock returns instead of the delisting-adjusted excess stock returns as the outcome variable. The results of these analyses are qualitatively similar, albeit slightly weaker, than the results presented in Panel D of Table 13.4. The difference between using the adjusted returns and unadjusted returns, therefore, is relatively inconsequential when value-weighted portfolios are used.

indicating it is unlikely that the STR factor sensitivity is driving the portfolio's alpha.

To investigate our hypotheses further, in Panel E of Table 13.4 we present the FFCSTR alpha as well as the factor sensitivities relative to the MKT (β_{MKT}), SMB (β_{SMB}), HML (β_{HML}), MOM (β_{MOM}), and STR (β_{STR}) factors for each of the $Illiq^{1M}$-sorted decile portfolios, as well as for the difference portfolio. t-statistics testing the null hypothesis that the given coefficient is equal to zero are presented in parentheses. Consistent with our predictions, the results show that the 10-1 portfolio has a negative sensitivity to the market factor of -0.16 (t-statistic $= -2.86$) and positive sensitivities of 1.40 (t-statistic $= 10.39$) and 0.53 (t-statistic $= 4.16$) to the SMB and HML factors, respectively. The sensitivity of the $Illiq^{1M}$ 10-1 value-weighted portfolio to the MOM factor of -0.27 (t-statistic $= -4.66$) is negative, as we expected. Finally, the portfolio's sensitivity to the STR factor of 0.13 is, as expected, positive, but statistically insignificant (or at best marginally significant), because the corresponding t-statistic is only 1.69. Furthermore, the factor sensitivities across each of the decile portfolios follow strong patterns consistent with our predictions. As one progresses from decile portfolio one to decile portfolio 10, the values of β_{MKT} decrease (with the exception of portfolio one), the values of β_{SMB} and β_{HML} increase, the values of β_{MOM} decrease (with the exception of portfolios seven and nine), and the values of β_{STR} increase (with the exception of portfolios five and seven). The results indicate strong cross-sectional patterns in the factor sensitivities of the value-weighted $Illiq^{1M}$-sorted portfolios. More importantly, these results indicate that, as discussed previously, based on the high sensitivities of the portfolio to the SMB and HML factors, it would be expected that this portfolio would generate a substantial positive average return. The portfolio's failure to do so results in a negative alpha. Finally, it is worth noting that the vast majority of the negative abnormal return of the 10-1 $Illiq^{1M}$-sorted portfolio is generated by the 10th decile portfolio. The FFCSTR alpha of this portfolio alone is -0.50% per month with a t-statistic of -3.34. The first decile portfolio's alpha of 0.03% per month is economically very small.

13.5.2 Bivariate Portfolio Analysis

We continue our examination of the relation between illiquidity and expected returns by using bivariate-sort portfolio analyses to examine whether the positive relation between illiquidity and future stock returns detected in the univariate portfolio analyses persists when controlling for either beta, market capitalization, book-to-market ratio, momentum, or reversal. In doing so, we use the delisting-adjusted excess return as the outcome variable. This is the same measure of excess return that has been used in almost all other analyses in this book. Furthermore, we choose to use $Illiq^{12M}$ as our measure of illiquidity. We choose to use the 12-month measure of illiquidity because this is the variable that produced the strongest results in the univariate portfolio analysis and this is also the variable used by Amihud (2002).

Before we proceed, a short note regarding analyses that control for market capitalization is warranted. The results of the correlation analyses presented in Table 13.2 show that, in the average month, the Spearman rank correlation between

$Illiq^{12M}$ and *Size* is -0.93.[14] This indicates that, in the average cross section, the ordering of stocks when sorted on $Illiq^{12M}$ is nearly the opposite of that when stocks are sorted on *MktCap*. Thus, using portfolio analysis to disentangle the effects of size and illiquidity on expected returns may be challenging, since sorting on $Illiq^{12M}$ is very similar to sorting (in reverse order) on *MktCap*.

Bivariate Dependent-Sort Portfolio Analysis

Given the anticipated challenges of disentangling the effects of illiquidity and market capitalization on expected stock returns, our first bivariate portfolio analysis is a dependent-sort analysis of the relation between illiquidity and stock returns after controlling for market capitalization. Each month, all stocks in the sample are sorted into five quintiles based on an ascending sort of *MktCap*. Within each *MktCap* quintile, stocks are sorted into quintile portfolios based on an ascending sort of $Illiq_{12M}$. We focus our examination on equal-weighted portfolios since only the equal-weighted univariate $Illiq^{12M}$ 10-1 portfolio generated statistically significant average returns and alphas, whereas the returns and alphas of the value-weighted $Illiq^{12M}$ 10-1 portfolio were small and statistically insignificant.

The results of the equal-weighted portfolio analysis examining the relation between $Illiq^{12M}$ and one-month-ahead excess stock returns after controlling for *MktCap* are presented in Table 13.5. Panel A shows that for the average *MktCap* quintile, the $Illiq^{12M}$ 5-1 portfolio generates an average monthly return of 0.49% that is highly statistically significant with a corresponding t-statistic of 3.75. This result seems to indicate that the positive relation between $Illiq^{12M}$ and future stock returns persists after controlling for *MktCap*. The abnormal monthly return of this portfolio relative to the FFC risk model of 0.12% per month, however, is statistically indistinguishable from zero, with a corresponding t-statistic of only 0.77. Interestingly, when the short-term reversal factor is included in the risk model (FFCSTR), the abnormal return increases to a marginally statistically significant 0.24% per month (t-statistic = 1.78). Examining the returns and alphas of the $Illiq^{12M}$ portfolio within each of the *MktCap* quintiles, we see that the positive relation between $Illiq^{12M}$ and future returns is strongest in *MktCap* quintile one and the strength of this relation decreases as the market capitalization of the stocks in the portfolio gets larger. The FFC and FFCSTR alphas are only statistically significant, however, in *MktCap* quintile one, while the average returns are statistically significant in quintiles one, two, and marginally in quintile three of *MktCap*. While it is tempting to conclude that liquidity matters most among small stocks, the extremely strong negative Spearman correlation between $Illiq^{12M}$ and *MktCap* makes us question even this result, since it is possible that even within a *MktCap* quintile, an ascending sort on $Illiq^{12M}$ is effectively a descending sort on *MktCap*. The results show that the fifth $Illiq^{12M}$ quintile portfolio in the first *MktCap* quintile produces an average return of 1.73%

---

[14]The Spearman rank correlation between $Illiq^{12M}$ and *MktCap* is identical to that between $Illiq^{12M}$ and *Size* because *Size* and *MktCap* are monotonically increasing functions of each other and the Spearman correlation measure relies only on the ordering of the observations based on each of the variables, not on the magnitude of the variables.

TABLE 13.5 Bivariate Dependent-Sort Portfolio Analysis—Control for *MktCap*

This table presents the results of bivariate dependent-sort portfolio analyses of the relation between $Illiq^{12M}$ and future stock returns after controlling for the effect of *MktCap*. Each month, all stocks in the CRSP sample are sorted into five groups based on an ascending sort of *MktCap*. Within each *MktCap* group, all stocks are sorted into five portfolios based on an ascending sort of $Illiq^{12M}$. The quintile breakpoints used to create the portfolios are calculated using all stocks in the CRSP sample. Panel A presents the average one-month-ahead excess return (in percent per month) for each of the 25 equal-weighted portfolios as well as for the average *MktCap* quintile portfolio within each quintile of $Illiq^{12M}$. Also shown are the average return, FFC alpha, and FFCSTR alpha of a long–short zero-cost portfolio that is long the fifth $Illiq^{12M}$ quintile portfolio and short the first $Illiq^{12M}$ quintile portfolio in each *MktCap* quintile. t-statistics (in parentheses), adjusted following Newey and West (1987) using six lags, testing the null hypothesis that the average return or alpha is equal to zero, are shown in parentheses. Panel B presents the average values of *MktCap* for stocks in each of the portfolios.

Panel A: Portfolio Returns

	MktCap 1	MktCap 2	MktCap 3	MktCap 4	MktCap 5	MktCap Avg
$Illiq^{12M}$ 1	0.46	0.25	0.48	0.57	0.40	0.43
$Illiq^{12M}$ 2	0.79	0.76	0.71	0.68	0.51	0.69
$Illiq^{12M}$ 3	0.79	0.76	0.70	0.75	0.57	0.72
$Illiq^{12M}$ 4	1.04	0.89	0.79	0.70	0.63	0.81
$Illiq^{12M}$ 5	1.73	0.85	0.81	0.75	0.49	0.93
$Illiq^{12M}$ 5-1	1.27	0.59	0.34	0.18	0.08	0.49
	(4.85)	(2.67)	(1.94)	(1.37)	(0.87)	(3.75)
$Illiq^{12M}$ 5-1 FFC α	0.76	0.14	−0.07	−0.09	−0.16	0.12
	(2.44)	(0.60)	(−0.44)	(−0.74)	(−1.67)	(0.77)
$Illiq^{12M}$ 5-1 FFCSTR α	0.98	0.26	0.05	0.02	−0.11	0.24
	(3.39)	(1.19)	(0.33)	(0.16)	(−1.33)	(1.78)

Panel B: Average *MktCap*

	MktCap 1	MktCap 2	MktCap 3	MktCap 4	MktCap 5	MktCap Avg
$Illiq^{12M}$ 1	24	73	198	642	19,705	4128
$Illiq^{12M}$ 2	21	66	180	557	4589	1083
$Illiq^{12M}$ 3	18	62	165	488	2494	645
$Illiq^{12M}$ 4	15	57	152	429	1658	462
$Illiq^{12M}$ 5	9	51	141	392	1330	385

per month, much higher than any of the other $Illiq^{12M}$ and $MktCap$-sorted portfolios. The positive average return and alphas of the $Illiq^{12M}$ 5-1 portfolio in the first $MktCap$ quintile, as well as for the average $MktCap$ quintile, are potentially driven by this one portfolio. If this portfolio does in fact contain extremely small stocks, as is likely the case, then this result is consistent with the results of the univariate portfolio analysis of the relation between $MktCap$ and future stock returns (see Table 9.5) in which we found that the size effect appears to be driven by extremely small stocks that in total comprise a very small percentage of total stock market capitalization.

To further examine the possibility that sorting on $Illiq^{12M}$ within each $MktCap$ quintile is effectively the same as performing a descending sort on $MktCap$, in Panel B of Table 13.5 we present the average values of $MktCap$ for stocks in each of the 25 $MktCap$ and $Illiq^{12M}$-sorted portfolios. The results confirm our concerns about the sorting procedure. Within each $MktCap$ quintile, the average $MktCap$ of the stocks in the $Illiq^{12M}$ portfolios decreases monotonically from quintile one to quintile five of $Illiq^{12M}$. Equally as important, the fifth $Illiq^{12M}$ quintile portfolio in the first $MktCap$ quintile, which appears to be driving the results of the bivariate-sort analysis, contains stocks with average $MktCap$ of only \$9 million. This is by far the smallest average $MktCap$ of any of the 25 $MktCap$ and $Illiq^{12M}$-sorted portfolios. The results demonstrate that the Spearman correlation between $MktCap$ and $Illiq^{12M}$ is too high for a bivariate portfolio analysis to distinguish between the effects of illiquidity and size on expected stock returns. The double-sort procedure is not effective at controlling for $MktCap$. In fact, the high correlation potentially indicates that these two effects are indistinguishable. We reserve judgment on this issue until we have seen the results of the remaining analyses in this chapter.

We continue our investigation by examining whether controlling for β, BM, Mom, or Rev can explain the positive relation between $Illiq^{12M}$ and future stock returns. To do so, we use bivariate dependent-sort quintile portfolio analyses sorting first on the control variable (β, BM, Mom, or Rev) and then on $Illiq^{12M}$. The equal-weighted (Weights = EW) and value-weighted (Weights = VW) average returns and FFCSTR alphas for the $Illiq^{12M}$ 5-1 portfolios within each quintile, as well as the average quintile, of the control variable, are presented in Table 13.6.

The results of the bivariate dependent-sort portfolio analyses show that the equal-weighted average return of the $Illiq^{12M}$ 5-1 portfolio in the average β quintile of 0.49% per month is marginally statistically significant with a t-statistic of 1.85. When the returns are adjusted for risk, however, the alphas of 0.27% per month (t-statistic = 1.53) relative to the FFC model and 0.25% per month (t-statistic = 1.46) relative to the FFCSTR model are substantially lower than the unadjusted average return and are no longer statistically significant. This indicates that after controlling for the effect of β, for the average stock, the relation between $Illiq^{12M}$ and future returns is not very strong, and any such relation is potentially driven by sensitivity to the MKT, SMB, HML, MOM, or STR factors. For stocks with low values of β, however, the positive relation between $Illiq^{12M}$ and future stock returns appears strong. In β quintile one, the $Illiq^{12M}$ 5-1 portfolio generates an average monthly return of 1.00% (t-statistic = 3.28) and FFCSTR alpha of 0.79% (t-statistic = 3.77).

TABLE 13.6 Bivariate Dependent-Sort Portfolio Analysis

This table presents the results of bivariate dependent-sort portfolio analyses of the relation between $Illiq^{12M}$ and future stock returns after controlling for the effect of each of β, BM, Mom, and Rev (control variables). Each month, all stocks in the CRSP sample are sorted into five groups based on an ascending sort of one of the control variables. Within each control variable group, all stocks are sorted into five portfolios based on an ascending sort of $Illiq^{12M}$. The quintile breakpoints used to create the portfolios are calculated using all stocks in the CRSP sample. The table presents the average return, FFC alpha, and FFCSTRL alpha (in percent per month) of the long–short zero-cost portfolios that are long the fifth $Illiq^{12M}$ quintile portfolio and short the first $Illiq^{12M}$ quintile portfolio in each quintile, as well as for the average quintile, of the control variable. Results for equal-weighted (Weights = EW) and value-weighted (Weights = VW) portfolios are shown. t-statistics (in parentheses), adjusted following Newey and West (1987) using six lags, testing the null hypothesis that the average return or alpha is equal to zero, are shown in parentheses.

Control	Weights	Value	Control 1	Control 2	Control 3	Control 4	Control 5	Control Avg
β	EW	Return	1.00	0.57	0.36	0.26	0.27	0.49
			(3.28)	(1.99)	(1.28)	(0.91)	(0.99)	(1.85)
		FFC α	0.79	0.39	0.16	0.03	0.00	0.27
			(3.58)	(2.02)	(0.92)	(0.13)	(0.01)	(1.53)
		FFCSTR α	0.79	0.38	0.14	−0.01	−0.06	0.25
			(3.77)	(1.91)	(0.80)	(−0.06)	(−0.23)	(1.46)
	VW	Return	0.51	0.49	0.29	0.33	0.24	0.37
			(1.72)	(1.82)	(1.08)	(1.15)	(0.86)	(1.46)
		FFC α	0.19	0.13	−0.09	−0.18	−0.19	−0.03
			(1.01)	(0.80)	(−0.60)	(−1.14)	(−0.85)	(−0.23)
		FFCSTR α	0.24	0.14	−0.09	−0.17	−0.19	−0.01
			(1.27)	(0.76)	(−0.59)	(−0.95)	(−0.86)	(−0.11)
BM	EW	Return	0.17	0.25	0.27	0.55	0.85	0.42
			(0.62)	(1.04)	(1.25)	(2.33)	(2.95)	(1.80)
		FFC α	−0.08	0.21	0.25	0.51	0.93	0.37
			(−0.37)	(1.05)	(1.45)	(3.17)	(4.00)	(2.16)
		FFCSTR α	−0.12	0.16	0.21	0.51	0.92	0.34
			(−0.59)	(0.88)	(1.34)	(3.30)	(3.93)	(2.14)
	VW	Return	−0.19	0.12	0.20	0.40	0.63	0.23
			(−0.70)	(0.53)	(0.94)	(1.58)	(2.28)	(1.04)
		FFC α	−0.50	−0.03	0.03	0.24	0.52	0.05
			(−2.98)	(−0.22)	(0.27)	(1.64)	(2.73)	(0.46)
		FFCSTR α	−0.53	−0.06	−0.01	0.25	0.50	0.03
			(−3.00)	(−0.39)	(−0.08)	(1.70)	(2.53)	(0.27)
Mom	EW	Return	0.93	0.56	0.80	0.83	0.73	0.77
			(3.30)	(2.51)	(3.80)	(3.81)	(3.52)	(3.86)
		FFC α	0.43	0.07	0.48	0.59	0.57	0.43
			(1.41)	(0.42)	(3.83)	(4.36)	(3.74)	(2.93)

TABLE 13.6 (*Continued*)

Control	Weights	Value	Control 1	Control 2	Control 3	Control 4	Control 5	Control Avg
		FFCSTR α	0.40	0.05	0.45	0.61	0.52	0.41
			(1.32)	(0.28)	(3.51)	(4.35)	(3.40)	(2.83)
	VW	Return	−0.06	0.30	0.64	0.74	0.62	0.45
			(−0.22)	(1.27)	(2.97)	(3.49)	(2.75)	(2.19)
		FFC α	−0.70	−0.30	0.19	0.43	0.35	−0.01
			(−2.95)	(−1.94)	(1.46)	(3.81)	(2.41)	(−0.06)
		FFCSTR α	−0.72	−0.34	0.16	0.46	0.31	−0.03
			(−3.12)	(−2.04)	(1.16)	(3.91)	(2.08)	(−0.24)
Rev	EW	Return	2.10	0.24	0.35	0.17	−0.83	0.41
			(7.38)	(1.02)	(1.41)	(0.70)	(−2.95)	(1.79)
		FFC α	1.85	−0.01	0.07	−0.10	−1.16	0.13
			(6.03)	(−0.06)	(0.40)	(−0.68)	(−5.20)	(0.80)
		FFCSTR α	2.05	0.11	0.09	−0.22	−1.33	0.14
			(7.29)	(0.69)	(0.50)	(−1.42)	(−5.58)	(0.86)
	VW	Return	1.49	0.30	0.46	0.24	−0.55	0.39
			(5.46)	(1.34)	(1.97)	(1.02)	(−2.04)	(1.81)
		FFC α	1.19	−0.09	0.09	−0.14	−0.97	0.02
			(4.53)	(−0.67)	(0.64)	(−1.15)	(−5.04)	(0.14)
		FFCSTR α	1.36	−0.01	0.08	−0.25	−1.11	0.01
			(5.39)	(−0.08)	(0.57)	(−1.94)	(−5.45)	(0.12)

In quintile two of β, the results are not quite as strong, but the average returns of 0.57% (*t*-statistic = 1.99) and FFCSTR alpha of 0.38% (*t*-statistic = 1.91) remain economically important and at least marginally statistically significant. When using value-weighted portfolios, consistent with the univariate portfolio results, there is no evidence of a relation between $Illiq^{12M}$ and future stock returns after controlling for β, since the average returns and alphas of the $Illiq^{12M}$ 5-1 portfolio in each β quintile are statistically indistinguishable from zero.[15]

When sorting first on *BM*, Table 13.6 shows that when using equal-weighted portfolios, for the average *BM* quintile, the positive relation between $Illiq^{12M}$ and future returns persists, since the average return, FFC alpha, and FFCSTR alpha of 0.42% per month (*t*-statistic = 1.80), 0.37% per month (*t*-statistic = 2.16), and 0.34% per month (*t*-statistic = 2.14) are all at least marginally statistically significant. The relation appears to be much stronger among stocks with high values of *BM*. The $Illiq^{12M}$ 5-1 portfolios in quintiles one, two, and three fail to generate statistically significant average returns or alphas. However, in quintiles four and five

---

[15] The two small exceptions are the value-weighted average returns of the $Illiq^{12M}$ 5-1 portfolio in quintiles one and two of β, both of which are marginally statistically significant.

of *BM*, the average returns and alphas of the $Illiq^{12M}$ 5-1 portfolios are large and highly statistically significant. Overall, the results indicate that controlling for *BM* does not explain the positive relation between $Illiq^{12M}$ and future stock returns in equal-weighted portfolios. In value-weighted portfolios, the results show that for the average *BM* quintile, the $Illiq^{12M}$ 5-1 portfolio fails to generate a statistically significant average return or alpha. Once again, however, the relation between $Illiq^{12M}$ and future stock returns appears to vary substantially across different levels of *BM*. The value-weighted $Illiq^{12M}$ 5-1 portfolio in the lowest *BM* quintile actually generates negative and statistically significant alpha of −0.50% per month (*t*-statistic = −2.98) relative to the FFC model and −0.53% (*t*-statistic = −3.00) relative to the FFCSTR model. In quintile five of *BM*, the value-weighted $Illiq^{12M}$ difference portfolio produces large positive average returns of 0.63% per month (*t*-statistic = 2.28) with alphas of 0.52% per month (*t*-statistic = 2.73) and 0.50% per month (*t*-statistic = 2.53) relative to the FFC and FFCSTR risk models, respectively.

The equal-weighted bivariate dependent-sort portfolio analysis indicates that controlling for *Mom* fails to explain the positive relation between $Illiq^{12M}$ and future stock returns. Within each *Mom* quintile, the $Illiq^{12M}$ difference portfolio produces a large and statistically significant average return. With the exception of the first and second *Mom* quintiles, the FFC and FFCSTR alphas of these portfolios are also large and statistically significant. For the average *Mom* quintile, the equal-weighted $Illiq^{12M}$ 5-1 portfolio produces an average monthly return of 0.77% per month (*t*-statistic = 3.86), with corresponding FFC alpha of 0.43% per month (*t*-statistic = 2.93) and FFCSTR alpha of 0.41% per month (*t*-statistic = 2.83). When using value-weighted portfolios, the average return of the $Illiq^{12M}$ 5-1 portfolio for the average *Mom* quintile of 0.45% per month is statistically significant, with a *t*-statistic of 2.19. However, the FFC and FFCSTR alphas of this portfolio are small and statistically insignificant. Once again, a strong pattern appears in the relation between $Illiq^{12M}$ and future returns across the different quintiles of *Mom*. For quintiles one and two of *Mom*, the value-weighted $Illiq^{12M}$ portfolio generates negative and statistically significant abnormal returns, indicating a potential negative relation between illiquidity and stock returns for stocks with low momentum. In quintiles four and five of *Mom*, the value-weighted $Illiq^{12M}$ 5-1 portfolio produces large positive abnormal returns, consistent with the positive relation between illiquidity and expected returns.

When controlling for *Rev*, the results of the equal-weighted bivariate dependent-sort portfolio analysis are quite similar to those for the value-weighted analysis. For the average *Rev* quintile, the $Illiq^{12M}$ 5-1 portfolio produces marginally statistically significant average monthly returns, but the abnormal returns of these portfolios are statistically indistinguishable from zero. However, the positive relation between $Illiq^{12M}$ and future stock returns is very strong among stocks in the lowest *Rev* quintile, since this portfolio generates very high average and abnormal returns regardless of whether equal-weighted or value-weighted portfolios are used. The opposite is true, however, for stocks with high values of *Rev*. The equal-weighted and value-weighted $Illiq^{12M}$ difference portfolio generates large negative average returns and alphas in quintile five of *Rev*.

Bivariate Independent-Sort Portfolio Analysis

We now repeat the bivariate portfolio analyses, this time using independent sorts instead of dependent sorts. The rest of the parameters of the portfolio analyses remain the same. We do not perform an independent-sort portfolio analysis using $MktCap$ and $Illiq^{12M}$ as the sort variables because, as discussed earlier, the cross-sectional Spearman rank correlation between these two variables is extremely high. Thus, sorting in ascending order on $MktCap$ produces almost the opposite ordering as sorting in ascending order on $Illiq^{12M}$. The result of this is that portfolios that would hold stocks with high values of $MktCap$ and high values of $Illiq^{12M}$ frequently do not contain any stocks. The same is true for portfolios that hold stocks with low values of both variables. The results of the bivariate independent-sort analyses of the relation between $Illiq^{12M}$ and one-month-ahead excess stock returns are shown in Table 13.7. The patterns in the returns of the independently sorted portfolios are very similar to those found in the dependently sorted portfolios. We therefore refrain from a detailed discussion of these results, since such a discussion would be repetitive and not provide any new insights. The independent-sort results, therefore, are presented primarily for the reader's reference.

The results of the bivariate-sort portfolio analyses of the relation between $Illiq^{12M}$ can be summarized as follows. First, distinguishing between a size effect and an illiquidity effect using bivariate portfolios sorted on $MktCap$ and $Illiq^{12M}$ is not effective because of the high Spearman rank correlation between these two variables. The results indicate that controlling for β or Rev explains a substantial portion of the positive relation between $Illiq^{12M}$ and future stock returns in equal-weighted portfolios, while BM and Mom have little ability to explain this relation. The relation between $Illiq^{12M}$ and future stock returns varies substantially in the cross section of β, BM, and Rev, with the positive relation being strong in low-β, high-BM, and low-Rev stocks. For high-Rev stocks, the relation between $Illiq^{12M}$ and future stock returns actually becomes strongly negative.

Can Liquidity Explain Other Relations

We next examine the ability of liquidity to explain the failure of beta to exhibit a positive relation with future returns, the positive relations between future returns and each of book-to-market ratio and momentum, or the negative relation between reversal and future returns. To do so, we perform bivariate dependent-sort portfolio analyses using $Illiq^{12M}$ as the first sort variable and each of β, BM, Mom, and Rev as the second sort variable. We do not examine the relation between $MktCap$ and future returns after controlling for $Illiq^{12M}$ because of the extremely high Spearman rank correlation between these variables. As with the previous bivariate portfolio analyses, the breakpoints are taken to be the quintiles of each of the sort variables. The average returns and alphas for the $Illiq^{12M}$ 5-1 portfolios generated by these analyses are presented in Table 13.8. When calculating the FFC and FFCSTR alphas for the portfolios formed using BM as the second sort variable, we exclude the value (HML) factor from the factor model to avoid controlling for the value effect when examining the value effect. Similarly, when examining the momentum phenomenon after controlling for

TABLE 13.7 Bivariate Independent-Sort Portfolio Analysis

This table presents the results of bivariate independent-sort portfolio analyses of the relation between $Illiq^{12M}$ and future stock returns after controlling for the effect of each of β, BM, Mom, and Rev (control variables). Each month, all stocks in the CRSP sample are sorted into five groups based on an ascending sort of the control variable. All stocks are independently sorted into five groups based on an ascending sort of $Illiq^{12M}$. The quintile breakpoints used to create the groups are calculated using all stocks in the CRSP sample. The intersections of the control variable and $Illiq^{12M}$ groups are used to form 25 portfolios. The table presents the average return, FFC alpha, and FFCSTR alpha (in percent per month) of the long–short zero-cost portfolios that are long the fifth $Illiq^{12M}$ quintile portfolio and short the first $Illiq^{12M}$ quintile portfolio in each quintile, as well as for the average quintile, of the control variable. Results for equal-weighted (Weights = EW) and value-weighted (Weights = VW) portfolios are shown. t-statistics (in parentheses), adjusted following Newey and West (1987) using six lags, testing the null hypothesis that the average return or alpha is equal to zero, are shown in parentheses.

Control	Weights	Value	Control 1	Control 2	Control 3	Control 4	Control 5	Control Avg
β	EW	Return	0.66	0.58	0.30	0.18	0.25	0.39
			(2.21)	(1.95)	(0.98)	(0.51)	(0.84)	(1.38)
		FFC α	0.42	0.37	0.12	−0.08	−0.07	0.15
			(2.15)	(1.98)	(0.60)	(−0.31)	(−0.22)	(0.78)
		FFCSTR α	0.41	0.37	0.11	−0.12	−0.15	0.12
			(2.12)	(1.92)	(0.54)	(−0.44)	(−0.52)	(0.65)
	VW	Return	0.38	0.45	0.23	0.23	−0.00	0.26
			(1.50)	(1.65)	(0.80)	(0.71)	(−0.00)	(1.00)
		FFC α	0.07	0.07	−0.18	−0.36	−0.48	−0.18
			(0.44)	(0.44)	(−1.14)	(−1.89)	(−1.81)	(−1.40)
		FFCSTR α	0.08	0.08	−0.20	−0.36	−0.50	−0.18
			(0.51)	(0.44)	(−1.19)	(−1.85)	(−1.97)	(−1.44)
BM	EW	Return	0.38	0.32	0.34	0.55	0.67	0.45
			(1.21)	(1.28)	(1.46)	(2.36)	(2.55)	(1.91)
		FFC α	−0.04	0.19	0.29	0.49	0.66	0.32
			(−0.16)	(0.94)	(1.51)	(3.20)	(3.55)	(1.87)
		FFCSTR α	−0.08	0.16	0.24	0.48	0.62	0.28
			(−0.34)	(0.83)	(1.36)	(3.29)	(3.20)	(1.77)
	VW	Return	−0.02	0.09	0.21	0.43	0.51	0.24
			(−0.05)	(0.35)	(0.89)	(1.72)	(2.12)	(1.06)
		FFC α	−0.47	−0.21	−0.01	0.25	0.38	−0.01
			(−2.28)	(−1.27)	(−0.09)	(1.82)	(2.45)	(−0.12)
		FFCSTR α	−0.49	−0.21	−0.07	0.26	0.33	−0.04
			(−2.32)	(−1.17)	(−0.46)	(1.80)	(2.00)	(−0.32)
Mom	EW	Return	0.48	0.59	0.89	0.92	0.80	0.74
			(1.73)	(2.55)	(3.83)	(4.03)	(3.75)	(3.50)
		FFC α	−0.07	0.09	0.55	0.70	0.66	0.39
			(−0.25)	(0.52)	(3.72)	(4.58)	(4.21)	(2.57)

TABLE 13.7 (*Continued*)

Control	Weights	Value	Control 1	Control 2	Control 3	Control 4	Control 5	Control Avg
		FFCSTR α	−0.12	0.07	0.53	0.72	0.63	0.36
			(−0.45)	(0.36)	(3.49)	(4.49)	(3.93)	(2.53)
	VW	Return	−0.17	0.37	0.71	0.77	0.72	0.48
			(−0.63)	(1.51)	(2.94)	(3.37)	(3.08)	(2.25)
		FFC α	−0.82	−0.25	0.24	0.46	0.47	0.02
			(−3.89)	(−1.56)	(1.59)	(3.61)	(3.04)	(0.18)
		FFCSTR α	−0.84	−0.28	0.23	0.49	0.46	0.01
			(−4.03)	(−1.69)	(1.44)	(3.60)	(2.79)	(0.09)
Rev	EW	Return	2.02	0.35	0.43	0.12	−0.94	0.40
			(7.02)	(1.38)	(1.58)	(0.46)	(−3.30)	(1.66)
		FFC α	1.79	0.07	0.13	−0.16	−1.25	0.12
			(5.96)	(0.40)	(0.67)	(−0.92)	(−5.57)	(0.71)
		FFCSTR α	1.97	0.20	0.16	−0.27	−1.43	0.13
			(7.32)	(1.16)	(0.79)	(−1.53)	(−6.00)	(0.79)
	VW	Return	1.43	0.43	0.47	0.15	−0.60	0.38
			(5.34)	(1.71)	(1.77)	(0.59)	(−2.24)	(1.65)
		FFC α	1.09	−0.02	0.08	−0.24	−0.99	−0.02
			(4.41)	(−0.14)	(0.52)	(−1.60)	(−5.20)	(−0.13)
		FFCSTR α	1.25	0.08	0.09	−0.35	−1.13	−0.01
			(5.32)	(0.56)	(0.57)	(−2.30)	(−5.73)	(−0.09)

liquidity, we exclude the momentum (*MOM*) factor from the factor model, and as a result we use the Fama and French (1993) (FF) three-factor model as well as the FF model augmented with the short-term reversal factor (FFSTR). For the same reason, when we examine the relation between *Rev* and future stock returns after controlling for $Illiq^{12M}$, we do not use the short-term reversal (*STR*) factor in a factor model and, therefore, examine only the raw return and FFC alpha for the *Rev* 5-1 portfolios.

The results show that after controlling for $Illiq^{12M}$, the β 5-1 equal-weighted portfolio for the average $Illiq^{12M}$ quintile generates negative but statistically insignificant average returns of −0.19% per month (*t*-statistic = −0.76). The abnormal returns of this portfolio relative to the FFC and FFCSTR risk models are also negative, similar in magnitude, and statistically insignificant. The same can be said for the equal-weighted β 5-1 portfolio in quintiles one through four of $Illiq^{12M}$. Each of these portfolios generates insignificant average returns and alphas. In quintile five of $Illiq^{12M}$, however, the average return of the β 5-1 portfolio of −0.43% per month is statistically significant with a *t*-statistic of −2.61. This portfolio's abnormal returns of −0.50% per month (*t*-statistic = −3.11) relative to the FFC risk model and −0.56% per month relative to the FFCSTR risk model are also highly statistically significant. The results therefore indicate a negative relation between β and future stock returns

TABLE 13.8 Bivariate Dependent-Sort Portfolio Analysis—Control for *Illiq*^{12M}

This table presents the results of bivariate independent-sort portfolio analyses of the relation between future stock returns and each of β, *BM*, *Mom*, and *Rev* (second sort variables) after controlling for the effect of *Illiq*^{12M}. Each month, all stocks in the CRSP sample are sorted into five groups based on an ascending sort of *Illiq*^{12M}. All stocks are independently sorted into five groups based on an ascending sort of one of the second sort variables. The quintile breakpoints used to create the groups are calculated using all stocks in the CRSP sample. The intersections of the *Illiq*^{12M} and second sort variable groups are used to form 25 portfolios. The table presents the average return, FFC alpha, and FFCSTR alpha (in percent per month) of the long–short zero-cost portfolios that are long the fifth quintile portfolio and short the first quintile portfolio for the second sort variable in each quintile, as well as for the average quintile, of *Illiq*^{12M}. Results for equal-weighted (Weights = EW) and value-weighted (Weights = VW) portfolios are shown. *t*-statistics (in parentheses), adjusted following Newey and West (1987) using six lags, testing the null hypothesis that the average return or alpha is equal to zero, are shown in parentheses.

Second Sort Variable	Weights	Value	$Illiq^{12M}$ 1	$Illiq^{12M}$ 2	$Illiq^{12M}$ 3	$Illiq^{12M}$ 4	$Illiq^{12M}$ 5	$Illiq^{12M}$ Avg
β	EW	Return	−0.11	−0.20	−0.06	−0.16	−0.43	−0.19
			(−0.35)	(−0.64)	(−0.19)	(−0.62)	(−2.61)	(−0.76)
		FFC α	−0.03	−0.16	−0.03	−0.26	−0.50	−0.19
			(−0.17)	(−0.74)	(−0.11)	(−1.02)	(−3.11)	(−1.08)
		FFCSTR α	−0.02	−0.16	−0.06	−0.31	−0.56	−0.22
			(−0.10)	(−0.75)	(−0.26)	(−1.36)	(−3.44)	(−1.26)
	VW	Return	−0.03	−0.06	0.03	−0.25	−0.35	−0.13
			(−0.12)	(−0.20)	(0.09)	(−0.95)	(−1.71)	(−0.52)
		FFC α	−0.07	−0.16	−0.10	−0.52	−0.59	−0.29
			(−0.34)	(−0.82)	(−0.49)	(−2.79)	(−3.58)	(−1.85)
		FFCSTR α	−0.07	−0.12	−0.09	−0.52	−0.62	−0.28
			(−0.28)	(−0.59)	(−0.40)	(−2.74)	(−3.26)	(−1.65)
BM	EW	Return	0.34	0.67	0.88	0.82	0.76	0.70
			(1.68)	(3.11)	(4.01)	(3.57)	(4.46)	(3.90)
		FFC α	0.64	0.88	1.05	0.98	0.82	0.87
			(3.28)	(4.16)	(5.02)	(4.37)	(4.79)	(5.14)
		FFCSTR α	0.66	0.93	1.09	1.01	0.85	0.91
			(3.03)	(3.96)	(4.56)	(3.96)	(4.83)	(4.65)
	VW	Return	0.16	0.60	0.73	0.77	0.73	0.60
			(0.87)	(2.82)	(3.33)	(3.44)	(3.47)	(3.34)
		FFC α	0.37	0.83	0.94	0.98	0.85	0.79
			(2.10)	(3.98)	(4.62)	(4.99)	(4.24)	(4.78)
		FFCSTR α	0.35	0.83	0.88	0.97	0.81	0.77
			(1.84)	(3.63)	(3.86)	(4.12)	(3.88)	(4.09)

TABLE 13.8 (*Continued*)

Second Sort Variable	Weights	Value	$Illiq^{12M}$ 1	$Illiq^{12M}$ 2	$Illiq^{12M}$ 3	$Illiq^{12M}$ 4	$Illiq^{12M}$ 5	$Illiq^{12M}$ Avg
Mom	EW	Return	0.78	1.11	1.50	1.58	1.32	1.26
			(3.24)	(4.44)	(5.24)	(5.43)	(4.89)	(5.19)
		FF α	1.03	1.39	1.78	1.82	1.52	1.51
			(4.50)	(6.17)	(6.95)	(7.33)	(5.65)	(6.97)
		FFSTR α	1.23	1.58	1.97	2.02	1.70	1.70
			(5.00)	(6.85)	(7.48)	(7.83)	(5.99)	(7.49)
	VW	Return	0.61	1.00	1.37	1.64	2.15	1.36
			(2.60)	(4.06)	(4.95)	(6.00)	(8.17)	(5.86)
		FF α	0.86	1.27	1.63	1.89	2.36	1.60
			(3.84)	(5.65)	(6.90)	(8.28)	(9.36)	(7.94)
		FFSTR α	1.05	1.46	1.80	2.08	2.51	1.78
			(4.52)	(6.32)	(6.88)	(8.37)	(9.45)	(8.30)
Rev	EW	Return	−0.35	−0.72	−1.00	−1.47	−3.96	−1.50
			(−2.15)	(−4.09)	(−4.91)	(−5.98)	(−11.55)	(−7.93)
		FFC α	−0.43	−0.85	−1.24	−1.77	−4.19	−1.70
			(−2.39)	(−3.32)	(−4.36)	(−5.72)	(−10.21)	(−6.82)
	VW	Return	−0.18	−0.90	−0.97	−1.14	−2.59	−1.16
			(−1.10)	(−5.41)	(−5.17)	(−5.07)	(−8.56)	(−6.79)
		FFC α	−0.24	−0.95	−1.09	−1.38	−2.82	−1.30
			(−1.27)	(−4.33)	(−4.92)	(−5.37)	(−7.98)	(−6.25)

among highly illiquid stocks. The value-weighted portfolios generate similar results. The main exception is that the FFC alpha of the value-weighted β difference portfolio for the average $Illiq^{12M}$ quintile of −0.29% per month is marginally statistically significant with a t-statistic of −1.85. Furthermore, the FFC and FFCSTR alphas of the value-weighted β 5-1 portfolio in both quintiles four and five of $Illiq^{12M}$ are negative, large in magnitude, and highly statistically significant, whereas in the equal-weighted portfolios this result was only found in quintile five of $Illiq^{12M}$. The results certainly provide no evidence that controlling for illiquidity can explain our failure to empirically detect a positive relation between β and future stock returns, as would be predicted by the CAPM of Sharpe (1964), Lintner (1965), and Mossin (1966).

The table demonstrates that controlling for $Illiq^{12M}$ cannot explain the positive relation between BM and future stock returns, since the average returns and alphas of the BM 5-1 portfolio in the average $Illiq^{12M}$ quintile are all positive and statistically significant. This holds for both equal-weighted and value-weighted portfolios. With the exception of the average return of the value-weighted BM 5-1 portfolio in the first $Illiq^{12M}$ quintile, the average return, FFC alpha, and FFCSTR alpha (the alphas are calculated relative to models that exclude the HML factor) generated by the BM 5-1 portfolio in each quintile, as well as for the average quintile, of $Illiq^{12M}$ is positive and statistically significant.

The momentum phenomenon also remains strong in both equal-weighted and value-weighted portfolios after controlling for illiquidity. The average returns, FF alphas, and FFSTR alphas (the alphas are calculated relative to models that exclude the MOM factor) of the Mom 5-1 portfolios in each quintile of $Illiq^{12M}$, as well as for the average $Illiq^{12M}$ quintile, are positive and highly statistically significant.

The dependent-sort bivariate portfolio analyses using Rev as the second sort variable after controlling for $Illiq^{12M}$ provide no evidence that illiquidity can explain the reversal phenomenon. When using equal-weighted portfolios, the average returns and FFC alphas (we do not calculate FFCSTR alphas because the FFCSTR model includes the short-term reversal factor) of the Rev 5-1 portfolios in each quintile of $Illiq^{12M}$, including the average quintile, are negative and highly statistically significant. The results when using value-weighted portfolios are quite similar. The main differences are that in $Illiq^{12M}$ quintile one, the Rev 5-1 portfolio fails to generate a statistically significant average return or FFC alpha.

The final observation from Table 13.8 that is worth mentioning is that the patterns across the quintiles of $Illiq^{12M}$ exhibited by each of the portfolios are nearly the opposite of the patterns found throughout the previous chapters of this book when $MktCap$ is used as the first sort variable. This, once again, is because in the cross section, ranking stocks in ascending order based on $Illiq^{12M}$ is very similar to ranking stocks in descending order based on $MktCap$.

Table 13.9 presents the average returns, FFC alphas, and FFCSTR alphas for the β, BM, Mom, and Rev difference portfolios from independent-sort portfolio analyses using $Illiq^{12M}$ as one sort variable and one of β, BM, Mom, or Rev as the other sort variable. These are the exact same analyses whose results were shown in Table 13.7. Here, instead of presenting the results for the $Illiq^{12M}$ 5-1 portfolios after controlling for other variables, we present the results for the difference portfolio for each of the other variables after controlling for $Illiq^{12M}$. The results of the independent-sort portfolio analyses are, once again, very similar to those of the dependent-sort analyses and are presented primarily for completeness.

In summary, the results of the bivariate portfolio analyses find no evidence that illiquidity is responsible for the lack of a relation between future stock returns and beta, or for the value effect, the momentum effect, or the reversal effect. While interesting patterns in several of these phenomena are detected across stocks with varying levels of liquidity, for the average stock, none of these patterns in stock returns are explained.

13.5.3 Fama–MacBeth Regression Analysis

We now continue our investigation of the relation between illiquidity and expected stock returns using (Fama and MacBeth 1973, FM hereafter) regression analysis. The FM regressions allow us to control for all of the other effects simultaneously, instead of one at a time, in examining the relation between illiquidity and expected stock returns.

TABLE 13.9   Bivariate Independent-Sort Portfolio Analysis—Control for $Illiq^{12M}$
This table presents the results of bivariate independent-sort portfolio analyses of the relation between future stock returns and each of β, BM, Mom, and Rev (second sort variables) after controlling for the effect of $Illiq^{12M}$. Each month, all stocks in the CRSP sample are sorted into five groups based on an ascending sort of $Illiq^{12M}$. All stocks are independently sorted into five groups based on an ascending sort of one of the second sort variables. The quintile breakpoints used to create the groups are calculated using all stocks in the CRSP sample. The intersections of the $Illiq^{12M}$ and second sort variable groups are used to form 25 portfolios. The table presents the average return, FFC alpha, and FFCSTR alpha (in percent per month) of the long–short zero-cost portfolios that are long the fifth quintile portfolio and short the first quintile portfolio for the second sort variable in each quintile, as well as for the average quintile, of $Illiq^{12M}$. Results for equal-weighted (Weights = EW) and value-weighted (Weights = VW) portfolios are shown. t-statistics (in parentheses), adjusted following Newey and West (1987) using six lags, testing the null hypothesis that the average return or alpha is equal to zero, are shown in parentheses.

Second Sort Variable	Weights	Value	$Illiq^{12M}$ 1	$Illiq^{12M}$ 2	$Illiq^{12M}$ 3	$Illiq^{12M}$ 4	$Illiq^{12M}$ 5	$Illiq^{12M}$ Avg
β	EW	Return	−0.17	−0.03	−0.10	−0.24	−0.57	−0.22
			(−0.57)	(−0.09)	(−0.31)	(−0.84)	(−2.43)	(−0.84)
		FFC α	−0.12	0.00	−0.11	−0.28	−0.61	−0.22
			(−0.58)	(0.01)	(−0.47)	(−0.94)	(−2.69)	(−1.21)
		FFCSTR α	−0.14	−0.02	−0.13	−0.33	−0.70	−0.26
			(−0.60)	(−0.08)	(−0.53)	(−1.27)	(−3.03)	(−1.42)
	VW	Return	−0.15	−0.01	−0.01	−0.36	−0.53	−0.21
			(−0.54)	(−0.02)	(−0.04)	(−1.30)	(−2.04)	(−0.83)
		FFC α	−0.19	−0.13	−0.23	−0.55	−0.74	−0.37
			(−0.83)	(−0.71)	(−1.02)	(−2.20)	(−2.88)	(−2.08)
		FFCSTR α	−0.18	−0.12	−0.23	−0.57	−0.76	−0.37
			(−0.69)	(−0.55)	(−0.94)	(−2.53)	(−2.97)	(−2.04)
BM	EW	Return	0.40	0.70	0.86	0.88	0.69	0.71
			(2.10)	(3.14)	(3.91)	(3.76)	(3.29)	(3.87)
		FFC α	0.65	0.90	1.03	1.06	0.79	0.88
			(3.50)	(4.07)	(4.86)	(4.83)	(4.19)	(5.25)
		FFCSTR α	0.69	0.93	1.08	1.10	0.84	0.93
			(3.38)	(3.71)	(4.41)	(4.45)	(4.34)	(4.73)
	VW	Return	0.20	0.59	0.70	0.91	0.72	0.62
			(1.08)	(2.76)	(3.14)	(4.04)	(2.94)	(3.40)
		FFC α	0.36	0.80	0.92	1.13	0.88	0.82
			(2.00)	(3.70)	(4.44)	(5.71)	(3.95)	(4.79)
		FFCSTR α	0.36	0.79	0.87	1.13	0.85	0.80
			(1.89)	(3.29)	(3.74)	(5.03)	(3.62)	(4.15)

(*continued*)

TABLE 13.9 *(Continued)*

Second Sort Variable	Weights	Value	$Illiq^{12M}$ 1	$Illiq^{12M}$ 2	$Illiq^{12M}$ 3	$Illiq^{12M}$ 4	$Illiq^{12M}$ 5	$Illiq^{12M}$ Avg
Mom	EW	Return	1.02	1.21	1.58	1.55	1.34	1.34
			(3.42)	(4.33)	(5.53)	(5.51)	(6.17)	(5.35)
		FF α	1.34	1.53	1.88	1.77	1.52	1.61
			(5.26)	(6.40)	(7.52)	(6.94)	(6.90)	(7.44)
		FFSTR α	1.56	1.72	2.06	1.96	1.67	1.79
			(5.64)	(6.77)	(7.92)	(7.47)	(7.16)	(7.74)
	VW	Return	1.01	1.14	1.44	1.55	1.90	1.41
			(3.21)	(4.24)	(5.26)	(5.99)	(8.55)	(5.80)
		FF α	1.35	1.46	1.73	1.79	2.06	1.68
			(4.98)	(6.23)	(7.41)	(7.65)	(9.16)	(8.05)
		FFSTR α	1.57	1.65	1.88	1.97	2.19	1.85
			(5.63)	(6.82)	(7.37)	(7.96)	(9.18)	(8.36)
Rev	EW	Return	−0.25	−0.74	−1.01	−1.43	−3.20	−1.33
			(−1.28)	(−3.89)	(−4.97)	(−6.20)	(−11.33)	(−7.20)
		FFC α	−0.35	−0.91	−1.25	−1.71	−3.39	−1.52
			(−1.67)	(−3.25)	(−4.53)	(−6.09)	(−10.13)	(−6.37)
	VW	Return	−0.01	−0.94	−1.00	−1.13	−2.04	−1.02
			(−0.05)	(−5.11)	(−5.35)	(−5.33)	(−8.17)	(−6.17)
		FFC α	−0.10	−1.00	−1.12	−1.33	−2.18	−1.15
			(−0.46)	(−4.17)	(−5.26)	(−5.98)	(−7.90)	(−5.96)

We begin our FM regression analyses using cross-sectional regression specifications that include $Illiq^{12M}$ as the lone independent variable, $Illiq^{12M}$ along with one of β, $Size$, BM, Mom, or Rev as independent variables, and then all of the variables together. Each of the independent variables is winsorized at the 0.5% level on a monthly basis. The dependent variable in all regressions is the delisting-adjusted one-month-ahead excess stock return.

The results of these FM regression analyses are presented in Panel A of Table 13.10. Interestingly, when $Illiq^{12M}$ (specification (1)) is included as the only independent variable in the regression specification, the average coefficient of 0.027 is positive but statistically insignificant, indicating no relation between $Illiq^{12M}$ and future stock returns. This result contrasts with the univariate portfolio analysis presented in Panel B of Table 13.4, which found a significant relation between $Illiq^{12M}$ and future stock returns. This difference indicates the possibility that the linear structure assumed by the regressions does not accurately describe the relation between $Illiq^{12M}$ and future stock returns. When β is added to the regression model (specification (2)), the results are similar since the average coefficient on $Illiq^{12M}$ of 0.022 is statistically insignificant with a t-statistic of 1.03. The negative but

TABLE 13.10 Fama–MacBeth Regression Analysis—$Illiq^{12M}$ and ln $Illiq^{12M}$

This table presents the results of Fama and MacBeth (1973) regression analyses of the relation between expected stock returns and each of $Illiq^{12M}$ (Panel A) and ln $Illiq^{12M}$ (Panel B). Each column in the table presents results for a different cross-sectional regression specification. The dependent variable in all specifications is the one-month-ahead excess stock return. The independent variables are indicated in the first column. Independent variables are winsorized at the 0.5% level on a monthly basis. The table presents average slope and intercept coefficients along with t-statistics (in parentheses), adjusted following Newey and West (1987) using six lags, testing the null hypothesis that the average coefficient is equal to zero. The rows labeled Adj. R^2 and n present the average adjusted R-squared and the number of data points, respectively, for the cross-sectional regressions.

Panel A: $Illiq^{12M}$							
	(1)	(2)	(3)	(4)	(5)	(6)	(7)
$Illiq^{12M}$	0.027	0.022	0.050	0.055	0.037	0.024	0.071
	(1.33)	(1.03)	(2.87)	(2.20)	(1.89)	(1.15)	(3.70)
β		−0.134					−0.151
		(−0.90)					(−0.93)
Size			−0.046				−0.039
			(−0.90)				(−0.74)
BM				0.309			0.192
				(3.63)			(2.54)
Mom					0.010		0.009
					(4.41)		(4.19)
Rev						−0.049	−0.061
						(−9.57)	(−12.18)
Intercept	0.643	0.777	0.835	0.383	0.429	0.692	0.641
	(2.33)	(3.55)	(1.66)	(1.37)	(1.65)	(2.38)	(1.47)
Adj. R^2	0.01	0.03	0.02	0.02	0.03	0.02	0.06
n	3242	3242	3242	2611	3235	3241	2609

Panel B: ln $Illiq^{12M}$							
	(1)	(2)	(3)	(4)	(5)	(6)	(7)
ln $Illiq^{12M}$	0.256	0.238	0.290	0.297	0.335	0.227	0.342
	(2.32)	(1.88)	(3.14)	(2.62)	(3.21)	(1.98)	(3.74)
β		−0.083					−0.132
		(−0.50)					(−0.80)
Size			−0.017				−0.008
			(−0.32)				(−0.16)
BM				0.285			0.200
				(3.32)			(2.66)
Mom					0.010		0.008
					(4.41)		(4.04)
Rev						−0.050	−0.062
						(−9.80)	(−12.27)
Intercept	0.544	0.631	0.618	0.331	0.308	0.612	0.392
	(2.15)	(3.39)	(1.19)	(1.24)	(1.28)	(2.29)	(0.93)
Adj. R^2	0.02	0.04	0.02	0.02	0.03	0.03	0.06
n	3242	3242	3242	2611	3235	3241	2609

statistically insignificant relation between β and future stock returns is consistent with previous analyses presented throughout this book. The specification that includes both $Illiq^{12M}$ and $Size$ (specification (3)) as independent variables finds a highly statistically significant average coefficient of 0.050 on $Illiq^{12M}$ and a statistically insignificant coefficient of −0.046 on $Size$. This indicates that controlling for the effect of illiquidity, the size effect disappears, yet when controlling for size, the illiquidity effect is strong. Thus, it is possible that the size effect is simply a manifestation of the pricing of liquidity. When $Illiq^{12M}$ and BM are the only independent variables in the model (specification (4)), the results indicate that both $Illiq^{12M}$ (coefficient = 0.055, t-statistic = 2.20) and BM (coefficient = 0.309, t-statistic = 3.63) are positively related to future stock returns. When Mom is used as the only control variable (specification (5)), the FM regression analysis detects a marginally statistically significant relation between $Illiq^{12M}$ and future returns, since the average coefficient on $Illiq^{12M}$ of 0.037 carries a t-statistic of 1.89. The positive relation between Mom and future stock returns remains strong (coefficient = 0.010, t-statistic = 4.41). When Rev and $Illiq^{12M}$ are the only independent variables (specification (6)), the analysis detects no relation between $Illiq^{12M}$ and future stock returns since the average coefficient on $Illiq^{12M}$ of 0.024 has a t-statistic of only 1.15. The average coefficient of −0.049 on Rev is highly statistically significant, with a t-statistic of −9.57. Finally, when all variables are included in the regression specification (specification (7)), the analysis finds a strong positive relation between $Illiq^{12M}$ and future stock returns, since the average coefficient of 0.071 has a corresponding t-statistic of 3.70. We find a negative but statistically insignificant relation between β and future stock returns, consistent with previous analyses. The size effect once again appears to have been explained by the inclusion of $Illiq^{12M}$, since the average coefficient of −0.039 on $Size$ is statistically indistinguishable from zero with a t-statistic of −0.74. The positive relation between BM and future stock returns persists after controlling for $Illiq^{12M}$ and the other variables. The momentum effect remains strong since the average coefficient on Mom of 0.009 (t-statistic = 4.19) is highly statistically significant. Finally, the average coefficient of −0.061 (t-statistic = −12.18) on Rev shows that the reversal phenomenon is not explained by any linear combination of the other variables in the regression specification.

We now repeat the FM regression analyses using ln $Illiq^{12M}$ instead of $Illiq^{12M}$ as our measure of illiquidity. All other aspects of the regressions remain unchanged. The results of these analyses presented in Panel B of Table 13.10 indicate that, regardless of the specification, the relation between ln $Illiq^{12M}$ and future stock returns is positive and statistically significant.[16] Once again, regardless of the specification, the average coefficients on β and $Size$ are negative but statistically insignificant, BM and Mom exhibit positive and highly statistically significant relations with future returns, and Rev has a very strong negative relation with future stock returns. Thus, consistent with our conclusions from the correlation and persistence analyses, the results indicate that ln $Illiq^{12M}$ may be a more useful measure of illiquidity than the

---

[16]The relation is only marginally statistically significant when β is the only other independent variable in the regression model (specification (2)).

untransformed version $Illiq^{12M}$, especially in analyses that assume a linear relation between expected returns and the variable under examination. Regardless of which measure is used, however, the specification that includes all of the other variables as controls detects a very strong positive relation between illiquidity and future stock returns.

We proceed now with FM regression analyses examining the relation between illiquidity and expected stock returns using measures of illiquidity calculated from shorter measurement periods. In Panel A of Table 13.11, we present the results of FM regressions that use $Illiq^{1M}$, $Illiq^{3M}$, $Illiq^{6M}$, and for ease of comparison,

TABLE 13.11 Fama–MacBeth Regression Analysis—*Illiq* and ln *Illiq*
This table presents the results of Fama and MacBeth (1973) regression analyses of the relation between expected stock returns and illiquidity. Each column in the table presents results for a different cross-sectional regression specification. The dependent variable in all specifications is the one-month-ahead excess stock return. The independent variables are indicated in the first column. Independent variables are winsorized at the 0.5% level on a monthly basis. The table presents average slope and intercept coefficients along with t-statistics (in parentheses), adjusted following Newey and West (1987) using six lags, testing the null hypothesis that the average coefficient is equal to zero. The rows labeled Adj. R^2 and n present the average adjusted R-squared and the number of data points, respectively, for the cross-sectional regressions.

				Panel A: *Illiq*				
	(1)	(2)	(3)	(4)	(5)	(6)	(7)	(8)
$Illiq^{1M}$	0.050	0.055						
	(1.98)	(3.10)						
$Illiq^{3M}$			0.041	0.082				
			(1.53)	(3.28)				
$Illiq^{6M}$					0.033	0.078		
					(1.31)	(3.30)		
$Illiq^{12M}$							0.027	0.071
							(1.33)	(3.70)
β		−0.182		−0.174		−0.169		−0.151
		(−1.11)		(−1.07)		(−1.04)		(−0.93)
Size		−0.073		−0.047		−0.041		−0.039
		(−1.34)		(−0.87)		(−0.77)		(−0.74)
BM		0.221		0.220		0.200		0.192
		(2.97)		(2.88)		(2.62)		(2.54)
Mom		0.008		0.008		0.009		0.009
		(4.11)		(4.23)		(4.35)		(4.19)
Rev		−0.061		−0.060		−0.061		−0.061
		(−11.83)		(−11.80)		(−12.15)		(−12.18)
Intercept	0.693	0.859	0.661	0.692	0.641	0.658	0.643	0.641
	(2.47)	(1.96)	(2.36)	(1.58)	(2.31)	(1.51)	(2.33)	(1.47)
Adj. R^2	0.01	0.06	0.01	0.06	0.01	0.06	0.01	0.06
n	3600	2723	3433	2640	3365	2628	3242	2609

TABLE 13.11   (*Continued*)

	Panel B: In *Illiq*							
	(1)	(2)	(3)	(4)	(5)	(6)	(7)	(8)
ln $Illiq^{1M}$	0.221	0.113						
	(1.99)	(1.35)						
ln $Illiq^{3M}$			0.220	0.294				
			(1.88)	(3.18)				
ln $Illiq^{6M}$					0.230	0.329		
					(1.98)	(3.47)		
ln $Illiq^{12M}$							0.256	0.342
							(2.32)	(3.74)
β		−0.199		−0.172		−0.157		−0.132
		(−1.19)		(−1.04)		(−0.95)		(−0.80)
Size		−0.101		−0.038		−0.017		−0.008
		(−1.86)		(−0.73)		(−0.33)		(−0.16)
BM		0.233		0.226		0.206		0.200
		(3.15)		(2.97)		(2.72)		(2.66)
Mom		0.008		0.008		0.009		0.008
		(3.81)		(4.05)		(4.21)		(4.04)
Rev		−0.062		−0.060		−0.061		−0.062
		(−11.84)		(−11.82)		(−12.21)		(−12.27)
Intercept	0.645	1.040	0.590	0.607	0.555	0.459	0.544	0.392
	(2.49)	(2.39)	(2.29)	(1.41)	(2.18)	(1.09)	(2.15)	(0.93)
Adj. R^2	0.02	0.06	0.02	0.06	0.02	0.06	0.02	0.06
n	3600	2723	3433	2640	3365	2628	3242	2609

$Illiq^{12M}$ (these results have already been presented in Table 13.10), as the measure of illiquidity. For each measure of illiquidity, we conduct analyses using only *Illiq* as an independent variable and then again with β, *Size*, *BM*, *Mom*, and *Rev* as controls. When using $Illiq^{1M}$ as the measure of illiquidity, both the univariate (specification (1)) and multivariate (specification (2)) specifications generate positive and statistically significant average coefficients on $Illiq^{1M}$. When we take $Illiq^{3M}$ or $Illiq^{6M}$ as the illiquidity variable, the univariate specifications (specifications (3) and (5)) produce insignificant average coefficients of 0.041 (*t*-statistic = 1.53) and 0.033 (*t*-statistic = 1.31), respectively. The corresponding multivariate specifications, however, generate average coefficients that are at least twice as large as those in the corresponding univariate specifications, and highly statistically significant. The results of the analyses using $Illiq^{12M}$ have been previously discussed. Interestingly, regardless of which measure of illiquidity is used, the average coefficient on *Size* is statistically indistinguishable from zero. This result seems to indicate that the size effect is, at least in large part, an illiquidity effect. Consistent with results in previous chapters of this text, in all multivariate specifications, the average coefficient on β is negative but statistically insignificant, the average coefficients on *BM* and *Mom* are both positive and highly statistically significant, and *Rev* exhibits a very strong statistically significant negative relation with future stock returns.

In Panel B of Table 13.11 we present the results of similar FM regressions, this time using the log-transformed illiquidity measures (ln *Illiq*) instead of the untransformed measures. When only ln $Illiq^{1M}$ is included as an independent variable in the regression model (specification (1)), the analysis finds a positive relation between ln $Illiq^{1M}$ and future stock returns since the average coefficient of 0.221 is statistically significant with a t-statistic of 1.99. When the controls are added to the specification (specification (2)), however, the average coefficient on ln $Illiq^{1M}$ of 0.113 is statistically indistinguishable from zero. In this specification, the average coefficient on *Size* of −0.101 is marginally statistically significant with a t-statistic of −1.86. This is the only FM regression analysis that generates a significant (albeit only marginally) average coefficient on *Size*. When ln $Illiq^{3M}$ is used as the measure of illiquidity, the univariate regression analysis (specification (3)) produces a positive and marginally statistically significant coefficient of 0.220 (t-statistic = 1.88) on ln $Illiq^{3M}$. When controls are added, the average coefficient on ln $Illiq^{3M}$ increases to 0.294 and is highly statistically significant with a t-statistic of 3.18. Finally, using ln $Illiq^{6M}$ to measure illiquidity, both the univariate specification (specification (5)) and the multivariate specification (specification (6)) detect positive and statistically significant relations between ln $Illiq^{6M}$ and future stock returns. The univariate specification generates an average coefficient of 0.230 (t-statistic = 1.98) on ln $Illiq^{6M}$, while the average coefficient from the multivariate specification is 0.329 (t-statistic = 3.47). Regardless of the measure of illiquidity, the coefficients on the other variables are qualitatively similar to those of other regressions, with the one exception being the marginally statistically significant negative relation between *Size* and future stock returns when ln $Illiq^{1M}$ is used to measure illiquidity.

Overall, the FM regression analyses provide evidence of a positive relation between illiquidity and future stock returns. The relation is much strong when the full set of control variables is included in the regression specification. Consistent with our previous assessments, the results are strongest when using measures of illiquidity calculated using longer (six-month or 12-month) measurement periods. The statistical significance of the relation between illiquidity and future stock returns in multivariate specifications is approximately the same when using the untransformed measures (*Illiq*) compared to when using the log-transformed measures (ln *Illiq*) calculated using the same measurement period. Thus, despite the extreme skewness of the untransformed measures and the enhanced persistence of the log-transformed measures, the FM regression analyses do not provide much evidence that one measure is better than the other.

To examine the economic magnitude of the relation between illiquidity and future stock returns, we use the average coefficient on $Illiq^{12M}$ of 0.071 from the full regression specification (specification (8) in Panel A of Table 13.11). Multiplying this coefficient by the cross-sectional standard deviation of $Illiq^{12M}$ in the average month of 27.73, we find that a one-standard-deviation difference in $Illiq^{12M}$ is associated with a difference in expected returns of 0.99% (0.071×27.73) per month. To examine the difference in expected returns between stocks in the highest and lowest deciles of

Illiq^{12M}, we multiply the average coefficient of 0.071 by the difference between the average value of *Illiq*^{12M} for stocks in the highest and lowest *Illiq*^{12M} decile portfolios of 21.28 (21.29 − 0.01, see Table 13.4). This indicates that the expected return of the average stock in the 10th decile of *Illiq*^{12M} is 1.51% per month (0.071 × 21.28) higher than that of a stock in the lowest *Illiq*^{12M} decile. Both of these results indicate that illiquidity is very economically important in the pricing of stocks. However, it is possible that both of these estimates overstate the effect of illiquidity on expected stock returns because both the standard deviation of *Illiq*^{12M} and the difference in average *Illiq*^{12M} between stocks in the highest and lowest *Illiq*^{12M} decile portfolios are likely inflated by the fact that the cross-sectional distribution of *Illiq*^{12M} contains a small number of stocks with extremely high values of *Illiq*^{12M}. To examine the effect this may have on our conclusions, we repeat these analyses using the log-transformed version ln *Illiq*^{12M}. The average coefficient on ln *Illiq*^{12M} in the regression that includes the full set of controls is 0.342 (see Table 13.11, Panel B, specification (8)). Multiplying this by the cross-sectional standard deviation of ln *Illiq*^{12M} in the average month, 0.79, indicates that a one-standard-deviation difference in ln *Illiq*^{12M} is associated with a 0.27% (0.342 × 0.79) per month difference in expected stock returns. Multiplying the average coefficient by the difference in average ln *Illiq*^{12M} for stocks in the highest and lowest *Illiq*^{12M} decile portfolios (same as ln *Illiq*^{12M} decile portfolios) of 2.48 (2.49 − 0.01, see Table Panel A of 13.4), we find a difference in expected return between stocks in the highest and lowest ln *Illiq*^{12M} deciles of 0.85% (0.342 × 2.48) per month. This value is very similar to the average return of the equal-weighted *Illiq*^{12M} 10-1 portfolio of 0.77% per month (see Table 13.4). Regardless of which estimates of the premium associated with illiquidity are used, the results indicate that liquidity plays an economically important role in determining expected stock returns.

13.6   LIQUIDITY FACTORS

The previous analyses in this chapter examine whether individual stock-level liquidity plays a role in determining expected stock returns. Standard asset pricing theories, such as the arbitrage pricing theory of Ross (1976), dictate that cross-sectional variation in expected returns is determined only by securities' sensitivities to priced risk factors. According to these theories, it is not the actual liquidity of an individual security that plays a role in determining the security's expected return. What is important is how the security's return is contemporaneously related to aggregate changes in liquidity.

Pastor and Stambaugh (2003, PS hereafter) investigate whether aggregate liquidity is a priced risk factor and find strong empirical evidence that stock-level sensitivity to innovations in an aggregate liquidity factor plays an important role in determining expected stock returns. To accomplish this, PS begin by creating a measure of stock-level liquidity and aggregating this measure across all stocks to generate a measure of market-level liquidity. They then calculate innovations in aggregate stock market liquidity using average changes in stock-level liquidity and take these innovations to be their liquidity factor. This factor is used by PS (and subsequent researchers) to calculate stock-level sensitivities to unexpected changes in aggregate liquidity. Finally, PS use portfolio analysis to demonstrate that stocks with high sensitivities to liquidity innovations generate higher average returns than stocks with low liquidity factor sensitivities.

The returns of the long–short liquidity sensitivity portfolio, commonly referred to as the traded liquidity factor, are widely interpreted as the returns of a factor-mimicking portfolio in the same spirit as the *SMB* and *HML* factors of Fama and French (1993). The traded liquidity factor is, therefore, frequently used by researchers in factor analyses of portfolio returns aimed at calculating the portfolio's alpha after adjusting for aggregate liquidity risk. It is worth noting that the PS liquidity factors have the conceptual advantage that the source of the risk being captured (aggregate liquidity) is known. The innovations series captures unexpected changes in aggregate liquidity while the traded factor captures the returns associated with sensitivity to aggregate liquidity innovations. This contrasts with the *SMB* and *HML* factors that capture returns associated with size and value investing, but the economic risks that the returns of these portfolios are compensating for are not as well understood.

In the remainder of this section, we describe the approach used by PS to generate their measure of aggregate stock market liquidity and examine its time-series properties. We then discuss how they use the aggregate liquidity measure to calculate liquidity innovations. Finally, we examine the time series of returns generated by their portfolio analysis, which is used by many researchers to augment the Fama and French (1993) three-factor model or the Fama and French (1993) and Carhart (1997) four-factor model with a liquidity factor.

13.6.1 Stock-Level Liquidity

The first step toward creating PS's liquidity factor is to generate a measure of stock-level liquidity. Similar to the Amihud (2002) measure of illiquidity, the PS measure of individual stock liquidity is based on the concept that large volume on an illiquid stock will cause the stock to realize a substantial price move. The PS measure differs, however, in that it attempts to capture only the portion of that move that is not related to changes in the fundamental value of the stock. As such, conceptually, what PS capture is whether a given stock tends to realize daily return reversals on days subsequent to days with high trading volume. By PS's own admission, their measure of individual stock liquidity is very noisy and does not exhibit any ability to predict the cross section of future stock returns, or even the cross section of future liquidity. The value of the measure is that it aggregates in a manner that appears to capture the time series of market-level liquidity. This key fact allows them to calculate innovations in aggregate liquidity.

To exemplify the intuition behind their measure, imagine that on certain day, there is a large amount of order flow from investors looking to buy a highly illiquid stock. The result will likely be that the stock will realize high volume on that day combined with a large positive return because the investors' buying pressure pushed the price of the stock up. On the next day, however, the investors' demand for the stock has been satisfied, and the stock is likely to realize a price decrease back toward its fundamental value. The idea behind the PS liquidity measure is to capture this type of behavior in stock returns. A stock that exhibits this phenomenon to a high degree is considered highly illiquid while a stock for which high volume days are not followed by price reversals is considered highly liquid.

Following this intuition, PS measure the illiquidity of stock i in month m to be the estimated coefficient $\gamma_{i,m}$ from regression specification

$$r_{i,d+1} - r_{m,d+1} = \theta_{i,m} + \phi r_{i,d} + \gamma_{i,m}\text{sign}(r_{i,d} - r_{m,d})v_{i,d} + \epsilon_{i,d+1} \qquad (13.2)$$

where $r_{i,d}$ and $r_{m,d}$ are the return of the given stock i and the market portfolio, respectively, on day d and $v_{i,d}$ is the dollar volume traded in stock i on day t, measured in $millions, calculated by multiplying the day d closing price of the stock with the day d number of shares traded and dividing by one million. The regression is run using all days d where both day d and day $d + 1$ are in the given month m. PS require that the regression be fit using at least 15 data points, which is equivalent to requiring that there be 16 valid data points in the month m for the stock i.

As can be seen in equation (13.2), the PS liquidity measure uses the abnormal return of the stock, defined in this context as the difference between the return of stock i and the market return, to capture the reversal effect discussed previously. The term $\phi r_{i,d}$ is used to control for any potential daily reversal effect that is not related to volume or order flow. The key term in equation (13.2), $\text{sign}(r_{i,d} - r_{m,d})v_{i,d}$, is what PS refer to as signed volume. The magnitude of this term is simply the dollar volume in the stock on the given day, and the sign of this term is the same as the sign of the difference between the stock's return and the market return. The idea is that the sign captures the direction of the price pressure or order flow, and the magnitude captures the amount of price pressure. If the coefficient $\gamma_{i,m}$ is negative, this means that the stock tends to underperform (outperform) the market on days subsequent to high buying (selling) pressure days. Thus, high values of $\gamma_{i,m}$ are associated with highly liquid stocks and low values of $\gamma_{i,m}$ indicate illiquid stocks. $\gamma_{i,m}$ can therefore be thought of as the effect on the return of the stock associated with trading one million dollars of stock i. A slightly looser interpretation proposed by PS is that the negative of $\gamma_{i,m}$ is the cost, as a percentage of trade value, associated with trading one million dollars worth of stock.

13.6.2   Aggregate Liquidity

As discussed earlier, PS acknowledge that their measure of individual stock liquidity is very noisy on an individual level. However, when aggregated to the market level, PS demonstrate that the aggregated measure exhibits properties very consistent with what would be expected of a measure of aggregate liquidity. PS define their measure of aggregate liquidity for month m as

$$\widehat{\gamma}_m = \frac{1}{N_m} \sum_{i=1}^{N_m} \widehat{\gamma}_{i,m} \qquad (13.3)$$

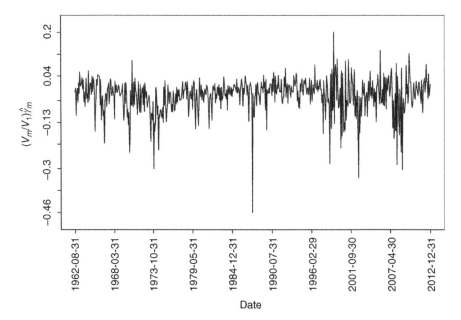

Figure 13.1   Time-Series Plot of $(V_m / V_1)\hat{\gamma}_m$.
This figure plots the values of $(V_m/V_1)\hat{\gamma}_m$, a measure of aggregate stock market liquidity, for the period from August 1962 through December 2012

where $\hat{\gamma}_{i,m}$ is the fitted value of the parameter $\gamma_{i,m}$ from regression (13.2) for stock i in month m and N_m is the number of stocks in the given month m. In addition to requiring that the regression be fitted using at least 15 data points, PS perform the aggregation over only those stocks with share prices between \$5 and \$1000, inclusive, as of the end of the previous month $m - 1$. Similar to their interpretation of the stock-level measure, PS interpret their market-level measure as the cost of trading one million dollars worth of the equal-weighted market portfolio.

In Figure 13.1, we plot the time series of $(V_m/V_1)\hat{\gamma}_m$, where V_m is the total market capitalization of the N_m stocks included in the calculation of $\hat{\gamma}_m$ calculated as of the end of month $m - 1$, and month 1 corresponds to August 1962.[17] PS scale the $\hat{\gamma}_m$ by V_m/V_1 series to account for the fact that trading one million dollars of stock in 1962 is not comparable to trading one million dollars of stock in 2012. PS only calculate their aggregate liquidity measure for months beginning in August 1962. The plotted series, therefore, covers the period from August 1962 through December 2012.

PS point to the fact that several well-documented instances of substantial drops in liquidity are captured by their measure. Specifically, they mention the Mideast oil embargo in November 1973, the Cambodia invasion announcement and shootings at Kent State and Jackson State in May 1980, the October 1987 stock market crash, the Asian financial crisis in October 1997, the Russian debt crisis of August 1998,

---

[17]The $(V_m/V_1)\hat{\gamma}_m$ data were downloaded from Lubos Pastors' website (http://faculty.chicagobooth.edu/lubos.pastor/research/liq_data_1962_2013.txt). This is the series labeled "Levels of aggregate liqidity."

and the collapse of Long Term Capital Management in September 1998. Lending strong support to their measure, subsequent to the publication of the article, the series also detects the bursting of the dot-com bubble in March 2000 and the housing and financial crisis of 2007 and 2008.

13.6.3 Liquidity Innovations

While Figure 13.1 indicates that PS's measure of market liquidity does a reasonable job at capturing overall levels of market liquidity, the series $(V_m/V_1)\widehat{\gamma}_m$ does not capture innovations, or unexpected changes, in liquidity. To capture innovations in liquidity, PS begin by taking the average change in the individual stock-level values of liquidity, averaging across stocks, and adjusting for overall market size

$$\Delta\widehat{\gamma}_m = \left(\frac{V_m}{V_1}\right)\frac{1}{N_m}\sum_{i=1}^{N_m}(\widehat{\gamma}_{i,m} - \widehat{\gamma}_{i,m-1}) \tag{13.4}$$

where this time N_m represents the number of stocks with valid liquidity measures in both months m and $m-1$, and V_m is calculated using only these stocks. To remove the long-run mean and any potential serial correlation in the series $\Delta\widehat{\gamma}_m$, PS run the regression.

$$\Delta\widehat{\gamma}_m = a + b\Delta\widehat{\gamma}_{m-1} + c\left(\frac{V_{m-1}}{V_1}\right)\widehat{\gamma}_{m-1} + u_m. \tag{13.5}$$

Finally, PS define the monthly innovation in aggregate liquidity for month m to be the fitted month m residual from regression 13.5, scaled by 100.

$$L_m = \frac{1}{100}\widehat{u}_m. \tag{13.6}$$

In Figure 13.2, we plot the time series of L_m.[18] The plot looks almost identical to that of the total market-level liquidity measure $\widehat{\gamma}_m$. The two time series exhibit a correlation of 0.81. This is likely in part because of the construction of the measures. However, if we accept each of $\widehat{\gamma}_m$ and L_m as an accurate reflection of what they are attempting to measure, aggregate market-level liquidity and innovations in aggregate market-level liquidity, respectively, this result indicates that the vast majority of time-series variation in aggregate market-level liquidity is unexpected.

13.6.4 Traded Liquidity Factor

As discussed earlier, PS acknowledge that the measure of stock-level liquidity $(\widehat{\gamma}_{i,m})$ is highly noisy, exhibits little cross-sectional persistence, and fails to show any cross-sectional relation to expected or future stock returns. PS show that another stock-level variable, sensitivity of the stock's returns to liquidity innovations, does have a relation with expected stock returns. To demonstrate this, PS calculate the liquidity innovation beta of a stock by using a time-series regression of a stock's

[18]The L_m data were downloaded from Lubos Pastors' website (http://faculty.chicagobooth.edu/lubos .pastor/research/liq_data_1962_2013.txt). This is the series labeled "Innovations in aggregate liquidity."

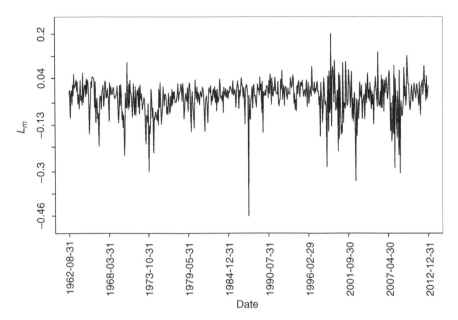

Figure 13.2   Time-Series Plot of L_m.
This figure plots the values of L_m, a measure of aggregate stock market liquidity, for the period from August 1962 through December 2012

excess return on the three factors in the Fama and French (1993) risk model (FF) along with the liquidity innovations L. The estimated coefficient on liquidity innovations is taken to be the stock's liquidity beta. The regression specification is

$$r_{i,t} = \beta_i^0 + \beta_{i,MKT}MKT_t + \beta_{i,SMB}SMB_t + \beta_{i,HML}HML_t + \beta_{i,L}L_t + \epsilon_{i,t} \qquad (13.7)$$

where $r_{i,t}$ is the excess return of stock i during period t and MKT_t, SMB_t, HML_t, and L_t are the market factor, size factor, value factor, and liquidity innovation, respectively, in month t. The regression is estimated using five years worth of historical monthly return data. PS require a minimum of three-years worth of monthly return data to estimate the regression.

There is a slight adjustment to the procedure described earlier that PS make to ensure that their analysis is based on data available at the time of portfolio formation. The liquidity innovations L_m, as described earlier, are calculated as residuals from a regression model that includes the entire time series of $\Delta\hat{\gamma}_m$. This means that the estimated residual for month t is affected by the values of $\Delta\hat{\gamma}_m$ for months m subsequent to month t. To ensure that their asset pricing analyses are based only on data that are available at the time that the portfolios are formed, when calculating liquidity betas for stocks in any given month t, the regression used to calculate liquidity innovations (equation (13.5)) is estimated using only values of $\Delta\hat{\gamma}_m$ for months m where $m \leq t$.[19]

PS estimate liquidity innovation betas at the end of each year and hold them constant for all months during the subsequent year. Thus, the values of $\beta_{i,L}$ calculated at the end of December of year t are used to form portfolios that will be held during all months in calendar year $t + 1$. PS form monthly decile portfolios using all stocks in the CRSP database that trade on the New York Stock Exchange, American Stock Exchange, or NASDAQ. They then calculate the monthly returns of each of these portfolios. The difference in return between the decile 10 portfolio and the decile one portfolio is the return that empirical asset pricing researchers most commonly use as a liquidity factor, which we denote as *PSL*.

PS make *PSL* factor returns for the period from January 1968 through December 2012 available on their websites.[20] During this period, the average monthly return (log return) of the *PSL* portfolio is 0.45% per month (0.39% per month) with a monthly standard deviation of 3.53% (3.50%). The annualized Sharpe ratio of the monthly (log) returns of the *PSL* portfolio is therefore 0.44 (0.38). Over the entire 1968 through 2012 period, the *PSL* factor generated a cumulative return of 701% and a cumulative log return of 208%. The correlations of the *PSL* factor with other factors are quite low. *PSL* has historical monthly return correlations of −0.05 with the *MKT* factor, −0.04 with the *SMB* factor, 0.04 with the *HML* factor, −0.03 with the *MOM* factor, and 0.09 with the *STR* factor. The alpha of the *PSL* factor relative to the Fama and French (1993) three-factor risk model is 0.46% per month with a Newey and West (1987)-adjusted (six lags) t-statistic of 2.93. Relative to the FFC risk model, the *PSL* factor generates alpha of 0.48% per month with a t-statistic of 3.04. When the FFC model is augmented with the reversal factor (*STR*), we find that the *PSL* factor produces FFCSTR alpha of 0.42% per month (t-statistic = 2.58).

In Figure 13.3, we plot the cumulative returns (solid line) and log returns (dashed line) of the *PSL* portfolio. The chart shows that the *PSL* portfolio has produced reasonably consistent returns without any extremely severe single month losses. This does not mean that the *PSL* portfolio is without risk, however. From the end of October 1986 until the end of September 1993, the *PSL* portfolio lost more than 33% of its October 1986 value. This value was not recovered until the end of February 2001, or 14 years and four months after the drawdown began. This represents both the longest and deepest drawdown experienced by the *PSL* portfolio. The later portion of our sample period is the most volatile period for the *PSL* portfolio. Between the end of June 2008 and the end of December 2008, the *PSL* portfolio lost almost 23%. These losses were regained in full two months later, by the end of February 2009, resulting in the

---

[19] While PS take this extra step to ensure the veracity of their results, which set of aggregate liquidity innovations (innovations calculated using the full sample or innovations calculated using backward-looking data only) is used is empirically inconsequential. The time-series correlation between aggregate liquidity innovations calculated using the two different methodologies is greater than 0.99. This result is indicative of the robustness of the aggregate liquidity measures produced by PS.

[20] The *PSL* data were downloaded from Lubos Pastors' website (http://faculty.chicagobooth.edu/lubos .pastor/research/liq_data_1962_2013.txt). This is the series labeled "Traded liquidity factor."

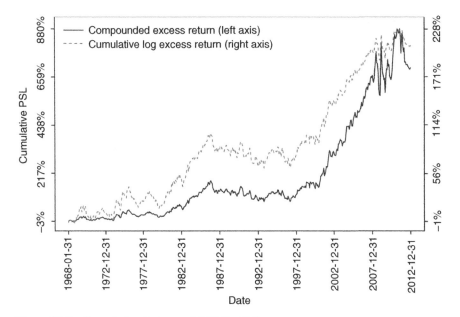

Figure 13.3   Cumulative Returns of *PSL* Portfolio.
This figure plots the cumulate returns of the *PSL* factor for the period from January 1968 through December 2012. The compounded excess return for month *t* is calculated as 100 times the cumulative product of one plus the monthly return up to and including the given month. The cumulate log excess return is calculated as the sum of the monthly log excess returns up to and including the given month

drawdown lasting only eight months. Despite the short duration of this drawdown, it represents the third deepest drawdown in the history of the *PSL* portfolio. The second most extreme drawdown began immediately as this short drawdown ended. From the end of February 2009, the *PSL* portfolio lost more than 24% over the next six months. This drawdown was once again relatively short-lived, since the previous high water mark was regained in October 2010, a mere 20 months after the drawdown began. The second longest and fourth deepest drawdown experienced by the *PSL* portfolio began at the end of January 1976. By the end of December 1979, the portfolio had lost nearly 23% of its value. The previous high was regained by the end of September 1981, five years and eight months after the drawdown began.

As with the short-term reversal factor (*STR*), the Pastor and Stambaugh (2003) liquidity factor is frequently used to augment the Fama and French (1993) and Carhart (1997) four-factor model in analyses of time series of returns. It is most commonly used as a robustness check instead of being included in the benchmark model which, in most cases, remains the four-factor model. Despite this fact, the *PSL* factor remains quite useful, especially for studies documenting a pattern in returns that could potentially be driven by liquidity.

13.7 SUMMARY

In summary, in this chapter we have empirically examined the cross-sectional relation between liquidity and expected stock returns. While numerous different measures of liquidity have been proposed, we focus on the most commonly used measure, that of Amihud (2002). We demonstrate that, consistent with the findings throughout the empirical asset pricing literature, illiquidity has a strong positive cross-sectional relation with future stock returns. This result is consistent with the theoretical prediction that illiquid securities command higher expected returns than more liquid securities. The result exists regardless of whether illiquidity is measured using one, three, six, or 12 months of historical data, but the results are strongest when using variables estimated from long measurement periods. Since most empirical asset pricing researchers calculate illiquidity using one month of daily return data, for the remainder of this text, we will take the one-month measure, denoted $Illiq^{1M}$ throughout this chapter, as our primary measure of illiquidity. Going forward, we will drop the superscript from the variable name and denote this variable $Illiq$.

We then discuss the creation of the traded Pastor and Stambaugh (2003) liquidity factor, PSL, which is designed to capture returns associated with innovations in aggregate liquidity. We demonstrate that the measures of aggregate liquidity as well as aggregate liquidity innovations generated by Pastor and Stambaugh (2003) have the time-series properties that would be expected of such measures. We then show that the PSL factor mimicking portfolio generates substantial long-term average returns.

REFERENCES

Acharya, V. V. and Pedersen, L. H. 2005. Asset pricing with liquidity risk. Journal of Financial Economics, 77(2), 375–410.

Amihud, Y. 2002. Illiquidity and stock returns: cross-section and time-series effects. Journal of Financial Markets, 5(1), 31–56.

Amihud, Y. and Mendelson, H. 1986. Asset pricing and the bid-ask spread. Journal of Financial Economics, 17(2), 223–249.

Amihud, Y. and Mendelson, H. 1989. The effects of beta, bid-ask spread, residual risk, and size on stock returns. Journal of Finance, 44(2), 479–486.

Ang, A., Hodrick, R. J., Xing, Y., and Zhang, X. 2006. The cross-section of volatility and expected returns. Journal of Finance, 61(1), 259–299.

Bali, T. G., Peng, L., Shen, Y., and Tang, Y. 2014. Liquidity shocks and stock market reactions. Review of Financial Studies, 27(5), 1434–1485.

Banz, R. W. 1981. The relationship between return and market value of common stocks. Journal of Financial Economics, 9(1), 3–18.

Brennan, M. J., Chordia, T., and Subrahmanyam, A. 1998. Alternative factor specifications, security characteristics, and the cross-section of expected stock returns. Journal of Financial Economics, 49(3), 345–373.

Brennan, M. J. and Subrahmanyam, A. 1996. Market microstructure and asset pricing: on the compensation for illiquidity in stock returns. Journal of Financial Economics, 41(3), 441–464.

Carhart, M. M. 1997. On persistence in mutual fund performance. Journal of Finance, 52(1), 57–82.

Chordia, T., Roll, R., and Subrahmanyam, A. 2000. Commonality in liquidity. Journal of Financial Economics, 56(1), 3–28.

Chordia, T., Roll, R., and Subrahmanyam, A. 2001a. Market liquidity and trading activity. Journal of Finance, 56(2), 501–530.

Chordia, T., Subrahmanyam, A., and Anshuman, V. R. 2001b. Trading activity and expected stock returns. Journal of Financial Economics, 59(1), 3–32.

Chordia, T., Roll, R., and Subrahmanyam, A. 2002. Order imbalance, liqiudity, and market returns. Journal of Financial Economics, 65(1), 111–130.

Chordia, T., Roll, R., and Subrahmanyam, A. 2008. Liquidity and market efficiency. Journal of Financial Economics, 87(2), 249–268.

Datar, V. T., Naik, N. Y., and Radcliffe, R. 1998. Liquidity and stock returns: an alternative test. Journal of Financial Markets, 1, 203–219.

Easley, D., Hvidkjaer, S., and O'Hara, M. 2002. Is information risk a determinant of asset returns? Journal of Finance, 57(5), 2185–2221.

Eleswarapu, V. R. 1997. Cost of transacting and expected returns in the Nasdaq market. Journal of Finance, 52(5), 2113–2127.

Eleswarapu, V. R. and Reinganum, M. R. 1993. The seasonal behavior of the liquidity premium in asset pricing. Journal of Financial Economics, 34(3), 373–386.

Fama, E. F. and French, K. R. 1992. The cross-section of expected stock returns. Journal of Finance, 47(2), 427–465.

Fama, E. F. and French, K. R. 1993. Common risk factors in the returns on stocks and bonds. Journal of Financial Economics, 33(1), 3–56.

Fama, E. F. and MacBeth, J. D. 1973. Risk, return, and equilibrium: empirical tests. Journal of Political Economy, 81(3), 607.

Hasbrouck, J. 2009. Trading costs and returns for U.S. equities: estimating effective costs from daily data. Journal of Finance, 64(3), 1445–1477.

Hasbrouck, J. and Seppi, D. J. 2001. Common factors in prices, order flows, and liquidity. Journal of Financial Economics, 59(3), 383–411.

Holden, C. W., Jacobsen, S., and Subrahmanyam, A. 2014. The empirical analysis of liquidity. Foundations and Trends in Finance, 8(4), 263–365.

Huberman, G. and Halka, D. 2001. Systematic liquidity. Journal of Financial Research, 24(2), 161–178.

Kamara, A., Lou, X., and Sadka, R. 2008. The divergence of liquidity commonality in the cross-section of stocks. Journal of Financial Economics, 89(3), 444–466.

Levy, H. 1978. Equilibrium in an imperfect market: a constraint on the number of securities in the portfolio. American Economic Review, 68, 643–658.

Lintner, J. 1965. Security prices, risk, and maximal gains from diversification. Journal of Finance, 20(4), 587–615.

Merton, R. C. 1987. A simple model of capital market equilibrium with incomplete information. Journal of Finance, 42, 483–510.

Mossin, J. 1966. Equilibrium in a capital asset market. Econometrica, 34(4), 768–783.

Newey, W. K. and West, K. D. 1987. A simple, positive semi-definite, heteroskedasticity and autocorrelation consistent covariance matrix. Econometrica, 55(3), 703–708.

Pastor, L. and Stambaugh, R. F. 2003. Liquidity risk and expected stock returns. Journal of Political Economy, 111(3), 642–685.

Pereira, J. P. and Zhang, H. H. 2010. Stock returns and the volatility of liquidity. Journal of Financial and Quantitative Analysis, 45(4), 1077–1110.

Roll, R. 1984. A simple implicit measure of the effective bid-ask spread in an efficient market. Journal of Finance, 39(4), 1127–1139.

Ross, S. A. 1976. The arbitrage theory of capital asset pricing. Journal of Economic Theory, 13(3), 341–360.

Sharpe, W. F. 1964. Capital asset prices: a theory of market equilibrium under conditions of risk. Journal of Finance, 19(3), 425–442.

Shumway, T. 1997. The delisting bias in CRSP data. Journal of Finance, 52(1), 327–340.

14

SKEWNESS

According to the mean–variance paradigm introduced by Markowitz (1952), investors make portfolio decisions by optimally trading off expected return (mean) and risk, measured by the variance of a portfolio's return, with high expected return and low risk being desirable portfolio properties. The assumption in the mean–variance paradigm is that all risk relevant to investors' portfolio selection is captured by the second moment, or variance, of the portfolio's return. From the mean–variance paradigm, Sharpe (1964), Lintner (1965), and Mossin (1966) developed the Capital Asset Pricing Model (CAPM). According to the CAPM, the expected return on any security is equal to the risk-free rate of return plus a risk premium, which is equal to the security's market beta times the market risk premium. The empirical failures of the CAPM (Friend and Blume (1970), Fama and MacBeth (1973), Reinganum (1981), Lakonishok and Shapiro (1986), Fama and French (1992, 1993)) prompted researchers to search for other models to describe expected security returns.

The idea that the skewness, or the third moment, of returns is an important consideration to investors when determining optimal investments is introduced by Arditti (1967, 1971), who shows theoretically and empirically that investors demand a higher (lower) rate of return on investments whose return distributions are negatively (positively) skewed. Scott and Horvath (1980) extend this analysis to include not just the third moment, but all higher moments of the distribution of returns, and demonstrate that positive values of even (odd) moments command

Empirical Asset Pricing: The Cross Section of Stock Returns, First Edition.
Turan G. Bali, Robert F. Engle, and Scott Murray.
© 2016 John Wiley & Sons, Inc. Published 2016 by John Wiley & Sons, Inc.

positive (negative) risk premia, and vice versa for negative moment values.[1] Stated alternatively, higher (lower) values of even moments (variance and kurtosis) are associated with higher (lower) expected returns, while higher (lower) values of odd moments (skewness) are associated with lower (higher) expected returns. Kraus and Litzenberger (1976) incorporate this notion into a three-moment capital asset pricing model. According to their model, in equilibrium, expected security returns are determined not only by the amount of systematic (undiversifiable) variance associated with the security but also by the security's systematic skewness. As with the CAPM, according to three-moment model of Kraus and Litzenberger (1976), unsystematic risk (both variance and skewness) is diversifiable and thus does not play a role in determining expected security returns. Harvey and Siddique (2000) introduce systematic skewness into the pricing of securities via a stochastic discount factor that is quadratic in the market return and show that this results in the pricing of conditional co-skewness, defined as the covariance between the excess security return and the squared excess market return, conditional on the market return. Empirically, Harvey and Siddique (2000) find a co-skewness risk premium of 3.60% per year.

Some papers have challenged the notion that idiosyncratic skewness is diversified away and therefore cannot be priced. Kane (1982) shows that the total proportion of wealth that is invested in risky securities is affected by portfolio skewness, and that skewness preference may cause investors to not completely diversify. Simkowitz and Beedles (1978) and Conine and Tamarkin (1981) propose that when investors do not completely diversify, idiosyncratic skewness may be relevant to the pricing of securities. Mitton and Vorkink (2007) develop a model in which heterogeneous skewness preference causes investors to underdiversify and demonstrate that idiosyncratic skewness has an impact on equilibrium prices. These findings are consistent with Barberis and Huang (2008), who show that the cumulative prospect theory of Tversky and Kahneman (1992) predicts a negative relation between individual security skewness and expected return. Boyer, Mitton, and Vorkink (2010) demonstrate that expected idiosyncratic skewness, calculated based on firm-specific characteristics, has a strong negative cross-sectional relation with future stock returns. Bali, Cakici, and Whitelaw (2011) use the maximum daily return over the past month as a proxy for extreme positive skewness and find a strong negative relation with future stock returns.[2]

Given the difficulties in measuring the market's view of the skewness of the distribution of future stock returns from historical data (Boyer et al. (2010), Bali et al. (2011)), recent research has examined the ability of skewness implied from option prices to predict future security returns. The results of such studies are mixed. Consistent with theoretical predictions, Conrad, Dittmar, and Ghysels (2013) find a negative cross-sectional relation between implied skewness and future stock returns, and Bali and Murray (2013) find a negative relation between implied skewness and the returns

---

[1]Dittmar (2002) and Kimball (1993) also conclude that investors are averse to kurtosis.
[2]Bali, Cakici, and Whitelaw (2011) argue that the maximum daily return over the past month measures the attractiveness of the stock to lottery investors, or investors who want to own stocks that have a high probability of a large short-term price increase.

of skewness assets. Boyer and Vorkink (2014) demonstrate that options with high implied skewness generate lower average returns. Amaya, Christoffersen, Jacobs, and Vasquez (2015) demonstrate a negative relation between skewness measures from intraday data and expected returns. On the other hand, Xing, Zhang, and Zhao (2010) and Cremers and Weinbaum (2010) find a positive relation between measures related to implied skewness and future stock returns. The positive relation between implied skewness and future stock returns is potentially explained by demand-based option pricing models of Bollen and Whaley (2004) and Garleanu, Pedersen, and Poteshman (2009). According to demand-based option pricing, investors anticipating positive (negative) returns establish exposure to the stock by buying calls and selling puts (selling calls and buying puts). The price pressure exerted by these trades causes call prices to increase (decrease) relative to put prices resulting in higher (lower) values of option implied skewness for stocks that investors predict will increase (decrease) in value.[3]

In this chapter, we examine the relations between skewness and expected stock returns. We begin by presenting the most commonly used approaches to measuring total skewness, co-skewness (aka systematic skewness), and idiosyncratic skewness. We then proceed to an examination of the ability of these variables to predict future stock returns.

14.1 MEASURING SKEWNESS

In this section, we present the most standard calculations of total skewness, co-skewness, and idiosyncratic skewness. As with several of the other variables discussed throughout this text, measures of skewness can be constructed from historical return data using different data frequencies and estimation periods.

Total skewness is most commonly measured as the sample skewness of historical realized stock returns and is calculated as

$$Skew_i = \frac{\frac{1}{n}\sum_{t=1}^{n}(R_{i,t} - \overline{R_i})^3}{\left(\frac{1}{n}\sum_{t=1}^{n}\left(R_{i,t} - \overline{R_i}\right)^2\right)^{3/2}} \tag{14.1}$$

where $R_{i,t}$ is the return of security i during period t, n is the number of periods used in the calculation, and $\overline{R_i}$ is the average periodic return of stock i over all periods included in the calculation.

Systematic skewness, frequently referred to as co-skewness, is calculated following Harvey and Siddique (2000) as the slope coefficient on the squared excess market return from a regression of excess stock returns on the excess return of the market portfolio and the squared excess market return. Specifically, co-skewness is the estimated slope coefficient $CoSkew_i$ from the regression

$$r_{i,t} = \alpha_i + \beta_{MKT,i}MKT_t + CoSkew_i MKT_t^2 + \epsilon_{i,t} \tag{14.2}$$

---

[3] An, Ang, Bali, and Cakici (2014), Bali and Hovakimian (2009), and DeMiguel, Plyakha, Uppal, and Vilkov (2013) provide empirical evidence consistent with the predictions of demand-based option pricing.

where $r_{i,t}$ is the excess return of stock i during period t and MKT_t is the return of the market factor during period t.

While total skewness and co-skewness are most commonly measured using the simple measures discussed earlier, Boyer, Mitton, and Vorkink (2010) show that measurement of idiosyncratic skewness from historical data can be improved upon, as several firm-specific variables, specifically idiosyncratic volatility, momentum, turnover, size, industry, and whether the firm trades on the NASDAQ exchange increase the accuracy of forecasts of future idiosyncratic skewness. Boyer, Mitton, and Vorkink (2010), therefore, argue that the expectation of future idiosyncratic skewness, which is the theoretically relevant variable for predicting future returns, should be calculated as a function of historical idiosyncratic skewness and these additional firm characteristics. Despite these findings, in this text, we will focus on a measure of idiosyncratic skewness based purely on historical return data. The reasons for this decision are twofold. First, Boyer et al. (2010) demonstrate that there is some persistence in idiosyncratic skewness measured purely from historical data. Measuring idiosyncratic skewness from only historical data allows us to examine this persistence empirically. Second, by using only historical data, we alleviate the possibility that it is the relation between these firm characteristics and future stock returns that is driving the apparent relation between expected idiosyncratic skewness and future stock returns documented by Boyer, Mitton, and Vorkink (2010). We therefore define idiosyncratic skewness as the sample skewness of the residuals from a Fama and French (1993) three-factor model regression. Specifically, we define idiosyncratic skewness as

$$IdioSkew_i = \frac{\frac{1}{n} \sum_{t=1}^{n} \epsilon_{i,t}^3}{\left(\frac{1}{n} \sum_{t=1}^{n} \epsilon_{i,t}^2 \right)^{3/2}} \tag{14.3}$$

where the $\epsilon_{i,t}$ are the residuals from the regression model

$$r_{i,t} = \alpha_i + \beta_{MKT,i} MKT_t + \beta_{SMB,i} SMB_t + \beta_{HML,i} HML_t + \epsilon_{i,t} \tag{14.4}$$

and SMB_t and HML_t are the returns of the size and value factor mimicking portfolios, respectively, during the period t.

In the empirical analyses presented throughout this chapter, we use several different measures of skewness, co-skewness, and idiosyncratic skewness that vary in the length of the measurement period and the frequency of the data used to calculate the variables. Specifically, we calculate each of the variables using one, three, six, and 12 months worth of daily return data. When calculating the daily return-based variables for a given stock i in a given month t, we use daily data during the period covering the months $t - k + 1$ through t, inclusive, where k is the number of months in the measurement period. We require a minimum of 15, 50, 100, and 200 days of valid returns during the measurement period to calculate the one-, three-, six-, and 12-month variables, respectively. We also calculate skewness, co-skewness, and idiosyncratic skewness using one, two, three, and five years worth of monthly return data. We require 10, 20, 24, and 24 months of valid returns during the measurement period to calculate the one-, two-, three-, and five-year variables, respectively.

We denote the measures of total skewness using *Skew*, the co-skewness measures as *CoSkew*, and the idiosyncratic skewness measures with *IdioSkew*. Variables calculated using one, three, six, and 12 months worth of daily data are denoted with superscripts $1M$, $3M$, $6M$, and $12M$, respectively. Variables calculated using one, two , three, and five years of monthly return data are denoted with superscripts $1Y$, $2Y$, $3Y$, and $5Y$, respectively.

Daily and monthly stock return data used to calculate the skewness measures are taken from CRSP's daily and monthly stock files, respectively. Daily and monthly factor and risk-free security returns are gathered from Ken French's data library.[4]

14.2   SUMMARY STATISTICS

Summary statistics for each of the skewness variables are presented in Table 14.1. The values in the table are the time-series averages of monthly cross-sectional distributional statistics calculated using our sample of U.S.-based common stocks in the Center for Research in Security Prices (CRSP) database during the 1963 through 2012 period.

Panel A of Table 14.1 shows summary statistics for the measures of total skewness. The table indicates that the daily returns of individual stocks are, on average and in median, positively skewed. The mean (median) values of daily return skewness range from 0.24 (0.22) for $Skew^{1M}$ to 0.63 (0.46) for the 12-month measure $Skew^{12M}$. The average positivity of the skewness of the daily individual stock returns is interesting when compared to the skewness of the daily returns of the market portfolio, which is consistently found to be negative. During the sample period used to create Table 14.1, the skewness of the daily returns of the market factor is -0.51.[5] The summary statistics show that the measured values of daily return skewness increase as the measurement period gets longer because the mean, as well as each percentile of the cross-sectional distribution (with the exception of the minimum value) increases when the measurement period is extended. For $Skew^{1M}$ and $Skew^{3M}$, more than 25% of stocks exhibit negative daily return skewness, whereas for $Skew^{6M}$ and $Skew^{12M}$, the percentage of stocks exhibiting negative skewness is less than 25%. Some stocks exhibit quite extreme daily return skewness, as the minimum and maximum values are substantially different than the fifth and 95th percentiles, respectively. This phenomenon is more prevalent in the measures that use the longer estimation periods. Consistent with this observation, the table shows that the cross-sectional distribution of *Skew* measured using daily returns becomes more leptokurtic as the length of measurement period increases.

The patterns observed in the summary statistics for the monthly return-based measures of total skewness are similar to those of the daily return measure. The mean

---

[4]The URL for Ken French's data library is http://mba.tuck.dartmouth.edu/pages/faculty/ken.french/data_library.html.

[5]Bakshi and Kapadia (2003) document a similar pattern in option implied skewness and discuss ways in which the positive skewness of individual stocks and negative skewness of the market portfolio can be reconciled.

TABLE 14.1 Summary Statistics

This table presents summary statistics for variables measuring total skewness (Panel A), co-skewness (Panel B), and idiosyncratic skewness (Panel C), using the CRSP sample for the months t from June 1963 through November 2012. Each month, the mean (*Mean*), standard deviation (*SD*), skewness (*Skew*), excess kurtosis (*Kurt*), minimum (*Min*), fifth percentile (5%), 25th percentile (25%), median (*Median*), 75th percentile (75%), 95th percentile (95%), and maximum (*Max*) values of the cross-sectional distribution of each variable is calculated. The table presents the time-series means for each cross-sectional value. The column labeled n indicates the average number of stocks for which the given variable is available. $Skew^{1M}$, $Skew^{3M}$, $Skew^{6M}$, and $Skew^{12M}$ are the skewness of daily stock returns calculated using one, three, six, and 12 months of daily return data. $Skew^{1Y}$, $Skew^{2Y}$, $Skew^{3Y}$, and $Skew^{5Y}$ are the skewness of monthly stock returns calculated using one, two, three, and five years worth of monthly return data. $CoSkew^{1M}$, $CoSkew^{3M}$, $CoSkew^{6M}$, and $CoSkew^{12M}$ are calculated as the slope coefficient on the excess market return squared term from a regression of excess stock returns on the excess market return and the excess market return squared using one, three, six, and 12 months of daily return data. $CoSkew^{1Y}$, $CoSkew^{2Y}$, $CoSkew^{3Y}$, and $CoSkew^{5Y}$ are calculated as the slope coefficient on the excess market return squared term from a regression of excess stock returns on the excess market return and the excess market return squared using one, two, three, and five years of monthly return data. $IdioSkew^{1M}$, $IdioSkew^{3M}$, $IdioSkew^{6M}$, and $IdioSkew^{12M}$ are calculated as the skewness of the residuals from a regression of excess stock returns on the excess market return, the return of the size (*SMB*) factor, and the return of the value (*HML*) factor using one, three, six, and 12 months of daily return data. $IdioSkew^{1Y}$, $IdioSkew^{2Y}$, $IdioSkew^{3Y}$, and $IdioSkew^{5Y}$ are calculated as the skewness of the residuals from a regression of excess stock returns on the excess market return, the return of the size (*SMB*) factor, and the return of the value (*HML*) factor using one, two, three, and five years of monthly return data.

Panel A: *Skew*

	Mean	SD	Skew	Kurt	Min	5%	25%	Median	75%	95%	Max	n
$Skew^{1M}$	0.24	1.02	0.02	2.52	−3.96	−1.38	−0.25	0.22	0.73	1.93	4.14	4704
$Skew^{3M}$	0.43	1.21	0.46	7.03	−6.41	−1.18	−0.09	0.34	0.87	2.35	7.29	4686
$Skew^{6M}$	0.54	1.28	1.05	11.53	−8.26	−0.99	0.01	0.41	0.93	2.53	10.06	4609
$Skew^{12M}$	0.63	1.33	1.90	18.41	−9.53	−0.80	0.09	0.46	0.97	2.63	13.43	4440
$Skew^{1Y}$	0.37	0.74	0.23	0.49	−2.55	−0.78	−0.11	0.33	0.82	1.69	2.92	4422
$Skew^{2Y}$	0.50	0.79	0.71	1.74	−2.78	−0.60	0.00	0.42	0.91	1.93	4.22	4072
$Skew^{3Y}$	0.58	0.82	1.02	2.76	−2.79	−0.52	0.06	0.46	0.97	2.09	5.09	3958
$Skew^{5Y}$	0.67	0.87	1.39	4.44	−2.71	−0.41	0.12	0.52	1.04	2.27	6.33	3992

Panel B: *CoSkew*

	Mean	SD	Skew	Kurt	Min	5%	25%	Median	75%	95%	Max	n
$CoSkew^{1M}$	−6.41	185.52	0.72	37.52	−1885.65	−266.87	−80.93	−5.99	65.65	252.18	2360.93	4742
$CoSkew^{3M}$	−6.46	71.87	0.65	29.61	−666.57	−111.18	−37.39	−5.57	23.84	95.21	861.30	4697
$CoSkew^{6M}$	−6.08	41.98	0.44	20.17	−369.28	−69.24	−24.86	−5.11	12.73	53.89	464.24	4611
$CoSkew^{12M}$	−5.28	24.56	0.26	13.34	−209.73	−43.77	−16.68	−4.40	6.52	30.15	235.67	4440
$CoSkew^{1Y}$	−1.11	38.64	0.91	32.41	−318.36	−57.30	−19.06	−1.25	16.07	55.09	529.65	4423
$CoSkew^{2Y}$	−1.40	18.34	0.67	17.22	−132.93	−29.21	−10.21	−1.33	7.20	25.84	221.45	4072
$CoSkew^{3Y}$	−1.43	12.75	0.69	17.61	−89.72	−20.92	−7.61	−1.34	4.61	17.55	142.32	3958
$CoSkew^{5Y}$	−1.20	9.49	1.86	69.42	−79.85	−14.60	−5.26	−1.11	2.75	11.77	128.72	3992

TABLE 14.1 *(Continued)*

	Mean	SD	Skew	Kurt	Min	5%	25%	Median	75%	95%	Max	n
				Panel C: IdioSkew								
$IdioSkew^{1M}$	0.19	0.91	0.06	2.17	−3.69	−1.27	−0.27	0.17	0.65	1.74	3.88	4742
$IdioSkew^{3M}$	0.41	1.17	0.37	6.45	−6.28	−1.19	−0.09	0.33	0.86	2.30	7.09	4697
$IdioSkew^{6M}$	0.55	1.29	0.90	10.49	−8.22	−1.06	0.01	0.42	0.96	2.57	9.87	4611
$IdioSkew^{12M}$	0.65	1.36	1.70	16.87	−9.61	−0.88	0.09	0.49	1.02	2.72	13.31	4440
$IdioSkew^{1Y}$	0.21	0.66	0.17	0.42	−2.27	−0.82	−0.21	0.19	0.62	1.34	2.59	4423
$IdioSkew^{2Y}$	0.42	0.71	0.65	1.70	−2.63	−0.59	−0.03	0.35	0.79	1.69	3.86	4072
$IdioSkew^{3Y}$	0.53	0.75	0.99	2.81	−2.70	−0.48	0.05	0.43	0.89	1.90	4.75	3958
$IdioSkew^{5Y}$	0.64	0.81	1.42	4.79	−2.64	−0.37	0.14	0.51	0.98	2.13	6.14	3992

(median) values of $Skew^{1Y}$, $Skew^{2Y}$, $Skew^{3Y}$, and $Skew^{5Y}$ of 0.37 (0.33), 0.50 (0.42), 0.58 (0.46), and 0.67 (0.52), respectively, increase as the measurement period is elongated, as do each of the percentiles of the cross-sectional distribution, with the exception of the minimum value. With the exception of $Skew^{1Y}$, each of the monthly return skewness measures indicates that more than 75% of stocks exhibit positive monthly return skewness. The positive values of total skewness once again contrast with negative skewness of the monthly market factor returns of −0.51 for the July 1963 through December 2012 period.[6]

The summary statistics for the measures of co-skewness are presented in Panel B of Table 14.1. The results show that the daily return-based co-skewness measures $CoSkew^{1M}$, $CoSkew^{3M}$, $CoSkew^{6M}$, and $CoSkew^{12M}$ have negative mean (median) values of −6.41 (−5.99), −6.46 (−5.57), −6.08 (−5.11), and −5.28 (−4.40), respectively. Each of these measures has a small number of very extreme observations, as the difference between the minimum and fifth percentile, as well as between the 95th percentile and the maximum, is always more than six standard deviations. The cross-sectional standard deviation of the measures decreases substantially as the measurement period is extended. This indicates that calculation of co-skewness based on short estimation periods may be susceptible to measurement error.

The values of co-skewness measured using monthly return data, $CoSkew^{1Y}$, $CoSkew^{2Y}$, $CoSkew^{3Y}$, and $CoSkew^{5Y}$, also tend to be negative, with mean (median) values of −1.11 (−1.25), −1.40 (−1.33), −1.43 (−1.34), and −1.20 (−1.11), respectively. The dispersion of the measures of co-skewness is substantially higher for measures using shorter estimation periods than longer estimation periods, as the cross-sectional standard deviation decreases from 38.64 for $CoSkew^{1Y}$ to 9.49 for $CoSkew^{5Y}$. These patterns in the summary statistics for $CoSkew$ calculated from monthly data are similar to those found in the daily return-based measures.

Summary statistics for the unsystematic component of skewness, referred to as idiosyncratic skewness, are shown in Panel C of Table 14.1. The results demonstrate

---

[6]It is purely coincidence that the skewness of the daily *MKT* factor returns and the skewness of the monthly *MKT* factor returns are both −0.51.

that idiosyncratic skewness calculated using daily return data is, on average, positive, with mean (median) values of 0.19 (0.17), 0.41 (0.33), 0.55 (0.42), and 0.65 (0.49) for $IdioSkew^{1M}$, $IdioSkew^{3M}$, $IdioSkew^{6M}$, and $IdioSkew^{12M}$, respectively. These values are very similar to the corresponding values of total skewness displayed in Panel A. Furthermore, the patterns in the summary statistics for idiosyncratic skewness are highly consistent with those of total skewness. Specifically, values of $IdioSkew$ based on longer estimation periods exhibit larger cross-sectional standard deviations than values calculated using shorter estimation periods. This phenomenon is largely driven by more extreme values in the very ends of the tails of the cross-sectional distributions, as the magnitudes of the fifth and 95th percentiles are relatively comparable across the measures using different estimation periods, whereas the minimum and maximum values become substantially more extreme as the estimation period is extended. Furthermore, at all reported percentiles of the distribution (with the exception of the minimum value), as well as the mean, the values of idiosyncratic skewness increase as the measurement period is extended.

The last set of variables we analyze are the measures of idiosyncratic skewness calculated from monthly return data. The summary statistics demonstrate that the mean (median) values of $IdioSkew^{1Y}$, $IdioSkew^{2Y}$, $IdioSkew^{3Y}$, and $IdioSkew^{5Y}$ of 0.21 (0.19), 0.42 (0.35), 0.53 (0.43), 0.64 (0.51), respectively, are all positive. The mean, standard deviation, and all reported deciles with the exception of the minimum value are increasing as the estimation period gets longer. Each of these patterns is consistent with what is observed in the measures of total skewness as well as the measures of idiosyncratic skewness measured from daily data. Values of idiosyncratic skewness based on monthly return data are slightly lower than their total skewness counterparts.

14.3 CORRELATIONS

We now examine correlations between the different measures of skewness. We begin by looking at correlations between the different variables that are designed to measure the same aspect of skewness, total skewness ($Skew$), co-skewness ($CoSkew$), and idiosyncratic skewness ($IdioSkew$). We then examine the correlations between total skewness, co-skewness, and idiosyncratic skewness. Finally, we examine the correlations between each of the measures and beta, size, book-to-market ratio, momentum, reversal, and illiquidity.

14.3.1 Total Skewness

In Table 14.2, we present time-series averages of the monthly cross-sectional correlations between the different measures of total skewness. Pearson product–moment correlations are shown in the below-diagonal entries, and Spearman rank correlations are presented in the above-diagonal entries. When calculating the Pearson correlation, each variable is winsorized at the 0.5% level on a monthly basis.

The Pearson correlations between the daily return-based measures of total skewness range from 0.20 between $Skew^{1M}$ and $Skew^{12M}$ to 0.71 between $Skew^{6M}$ and

TABLE 14.2 Correlations—Total Skewness

This table presents the time-series averages of the annual cross-sectional Pearson product–moment (below-diagonal entries) and Spearman rank (above-diagonal entries) correlations between pairs of variables measuring total skewness.

	$Skew^{1M}$	$Skew^{3M}$	$Skew^{6M}$	$Skew^{12M}$	$Skew^{1Y}$	$Skew^{2Y}$	$Skew^{3Y}$	$Skew^{5Y}$
$Skew^{1M}$		0.46	0.30	0.21	0.04	0.05	0.05	0.05
$Skew^{3M}$	0.47		0.65	0.46	0.14	0.13	0.13	0.13
$Skew^{6M}$	0.30	0.67		0.69	0.22	0.21	0.20	0.20
$Skew^{12M}$	0.20	0.46	0.71		0.33	0.31	0.29	0.28
$Skew^{1Y}$	0.05	0.16	0.26	0.37		0.62	0.50	0.41
$Skew^{2Y}$	0.05	0.15	0.23	0.33	0.63		0.79	0.65
$Skew^{3Y}$	0.05	0.14	0.22	0.31	0.50	0.80		0.81
$Skew^{5Y}$	0.05	0.13	0.20	0.28	0.41	0.66	0.82	

$Skew^{12M}$. Two general patterns are present in the correlations. First, the correlations increase as the amount of overlap in the estimation periods increases. For example, $Skew^{1M}$ and $Skew^{3M}$ have one month of overlapping data and a correlation of 0.47, $Skew^{3M}$ and $Skew^{6M}$ have three months of overlapping data and a correlation of 0.67, and $Skew^{6M}$ and $Skew^{12M}$ have six months of overlapping data and a correlation of 0.71. The second pattern is that, for a fixed amount of data overlap, the correlations are decreasing as the amount of nonoverlapping data increases. For example, $Skew^{1M}$ has correlations of 0.47, 0.29, and 0.20 with $Skew^{3M}$, $Skew^{6M}$, and $Skew^{12M}$, which have nonoverlapping data covering two, five, and 11 months, respectively. Both of these patterns are likely to be highly mechanical, making economic conclusions based on these results susceptible to error. It is worth mentioning, however, that the correlation between $Skew^{1M}$ and $Skew^{12M}$ of only 0.20 is quite low given that about 1/12 of the data used in these calculations is overlapping. The important conclusion we can draw from these results is that empirical analyses using $Skew^{1M}$ to measure skewness will quite possibly generate substantially different results than a similar analyses using $Skew^{12M}$, as the correlation between these variables is not high. The Spearman rank correlations between each of the daily return-based total skewness measures are very similar to the Pearson correlations. We are therefore not very concerned about the effect of outliers on linear analyses using these variables.

The Pearson correlations between the measures of total skewness calculated from monthly return data range from 0.41 between $Skew^{1Y}$ and $Skew^{5Y}$ to 0.82 between $Skew^{3Y}$ and $Skew^{5Y}$. The patterns in the correlations are very similar to those found using the daily data, since the correlations increase as the overlap in the estimation period increases and decrease as the length of the nonoverlapping portion of the estimation period increases, consistent with a mechanical effect. While the correlations calculated from the monthly data are on average higher than those from the daily data, so are the lengths of the overlapping estimation period as a percentage of the longer estimation period. Thus, it is possible that the higher correlations are still entirely mechanical. That being said, the results show that there is substantial correlation between all pairs of monthly return-based total skewness measures, indicating that use of monthly skewness measures with different estimation periods in empirical analyses are more likely (compared to the daily return-based measures) to give similar results.

Table 14.2 also shows correlations between the daily and monthly return-based measures of total skewness. For a fixed daily estimation period, the correlation decreases (or stays the same) as the monthly estimation period is extended. This is likely due to the fact that the overlapping time period used to estimate the daily and monthly measures is larger, as a proportion of the total time period used to estimate the monthly measure, for lower monthly estimation period lengths. Thus, this pattern in the correlation is likely mechanical. That being said, when the daily measure's estimation period is six or 12 months, the correlations between $Skew$ measured using daily and monthly data are substantial, ranging from 0.20 between $Skew^{6M}$ and $Skew^{5Y}$ to 0.37 between $Skew^{12M}$ and $Skew^{1Y}$. The results potentially indicate that, at least for daily estimation periods of six months and greater, the daily and monthly return-based versions of $Skew$ are capturing the same characteristic of the stock. At first, this result may seem reassuring, since it indicates that total skewness can be captured using either daily or monthly data. There is one consideration that has not yet been discussed, however, in drawing this conclusion. The formula used to calculate total skewness (equation 14.1) is only correct under the assumption that the periodic returns (regardless of the periodicity of the data) are independent and identically distributed. However, if the daily returns are independent and identically distributed, then if the return of a stock in any given month is approximately the sum of the daily returns of the stock over that month, the central limit theorem indicates that monthly returns should approach a normal distribution, and thus have skewness of zero.[7] There are three reasons why this may not hold. First, the approximation that the daily returns sum to the monthly returns is not quite true and is likely to be substantially less true when the daily returns of the stock are highly skewed (either positively or negatively). Second, when the distribution of daily stock returns is highly skewed, the convergence to normality dictated by the central limit theorem may be too slow for the monthly returns to be approximately normal. Third, the assumption that the returns are independent and identically distributed may not be completely true. Despite these potential issues with the calculation of skewness, the results of the correlation analysis indicate a substantial common component between skewness measured using daily and monthly returns. We raise this issue simply to point out a potential statistical issue that may arise when calculating measures of risk, especially moments of the distribution of returns, from data with differing frequencies.

Once again, the Spearman rank correlations between the daily and monthly measures of total skewness are very similar to the Pearson product–moment correlations.

---

[7]When using log returns, it would hold perfectly that the log of the monthly stock return is equal to the sum of the logs of the daily stock returns. The returns we use when calculating the skewness variables are not log returns. It is therefore only an approximation that the sum of daily returns is equal to the monthly return. For returns of small magnitudes, the log return and return are nearly identical. However, for larger returns, which are likely driving the calculation of skewness, the return and log return may differ substantially.

TABLE 14.3 Correlations—Co-Skewness
This table presents the time-series averages of the annual cross-sectional Pearson product–moment (below-diagonal entries) and Spearman rank (above-diagonal entries) correlations between pairs of variables measuring co-skewness.

	$CoSkew^{1M}$	$CoSkew^{3M}$	$CoSkew^{6M}$	$CoSkew^{12M}$	$CoSkew^{1Y}$	$CoSkew^{2Y}$	$CoSkew^{3Y}$	$CoSkew^{5Y}$
$CoSkew^{1M}$		0.45	0.29	0.19	0.01	0.01	0.01	0.01
$CoSkew^{3M}$	0.48		0.62	0.41	0.02	0.02	0.03	0.03
$CoSkew^{6M}$	0.31	0.65		0.63	0.05	0.05	0.05	0.05
$CoSkew^{12M}$	0.21	0.43	0.66		0.09	0.08	0.08	0.07
$CoSkew^{1Y}$	0.01	0.02	0.04	0.08		0.57	0.42	0.32
$CoSkew^{2Y}$	0.01	0.02	0.04	0.08	0.59		0.73	0.56
$CoSkew^{3Y}$	0.01	0.02	0.04	0.07	0.45	0.76		0.74
$CoSkew^{5Y}$	0.01	0.02	0.04	0.06	0.35	0.60	0.78	

14.3.2 Co-Skewness

Correlations between the different measures of co-skewness are given in Table 14.3. The patterns in correlations between the daily return-based co-skewness measures are very similar to those for total skewness (see Table 14.2). The correlations are higher for pairs of variables with longer overlapping estimation periods and lower for pairs with longer nonoverlapping estimation periods. These results are likely to be largely mechanical. The lowest correlation of 0.21 between $CoSkew^{1M}$ and $CoSkew^{12M}$ indicates that the length of the measurement period may be a significant consideration when calculating $CoSkew$, and that it is reasonably possible that different measurement periods will generate different results in empirical analyses.

The correlations between the measures of co-skewness calculated from monthly return data range from 0.35 between $CoSkew^{1Y}$ and $CoSkew^{5Y}$ to 0.78 between $CoSkew^{3Y}$ and $CoSkew^{5Y}$. As with all previous correlation analyses presented in this chapter, the correlations increase as the length of the overlapping measurement period increases, and decrease as the length of the nonoverlapping portion of the estimation period increases, consistent with a mechanical effect.

The correlations between co-skewness measured using daily and monthly data are quite low. Regardless of the length of the estimation period of the monthly return-based measure, when the daily return-based measure is calculated using less than six-months of daily returns, the Pearson (Spearman) correlations are all 0.04 (0.05) and below, indicating negligible cross-sectional correlation between co-skewness measured at daily and monthly frequencies when the length of the daily estimation period is short. The Pearson (Spearman) correlations between $Skew^{12M}$ and the monthly return-based measures range from 0.06 to 0.08 (0.07 to 0.09) and are decreasing as the length of the monthly estimation period increases. This result indicates that there is likely a mechanical effect involved in these correlations, as the correlation is highest when the period covered by the calculation is identical (i.e., between $CoSkew^{12M}$ and $CoSkew^{1Y}$). The results fail to give a strong indication that measures of co-skewness calculated using daily and monthly return data are capturing the same characteristic of the stock's returns. There are several possible reasons for this. It is possible that one or both of the variables fails to capture the desired characteristic of the stock. We examine this issue in more depth later in this chapter when we employ persistence analyses of skewness variables. It is also possible that daily and monthly return-based co-skewness are capturing different stock-level characteristics. This seems unlikely given that one would expect the sensitivity of a stock's return to any factor, in this case the squared market return, to be the same (or at least similar) regardless of the length of the period for which the sensitivity is being calculated. The low correlations between the daily return-based and monthly return-based measures of co-skewness, therefore, provide preliminary indications that these variables are likely to be very noisy, perhaps to the point of being ineffective at measuring the characteristic of the stock that they are designed to capture, namely co-skewness as defined in Harvey and Siddique (2000).

14.3.3 Idiosyncratic Skewness

The Pearson product–moment (below-diagonal entries) and Spearman rank (above-diagonal entries) correlations between the measures of idiosyncratic skewness are shown in Table 14.4. The correlations between the idiosyncratic skewness measures are highly similar to those of total skewness (see Table 14.2). Looking first at correlations between the daily return-based measures of idiosyncratic skewness, the table demonstrates that the Pearson (Spearman) correlations range from 0.17 (0.18) between $IdioSkew^{1M}$ and $IdioSkew^{12M}$ to 0.71 (0.69) between $IdioSkew^{6M}$

TABLE 14.4 Correlations—Idiosyncratic Skewness
This table presents the time-series averages of the annual cross-sectional Pearson product–moment (below-diagonal entries) and Spearman rank (above-diagonal entries) correlations between pairs of variables measuring idiosyncratic skewness.

	$IdioSkew^{1M}$	$IdioSkew^{3M}$	$IdioSkew^{6M}$	$IdioSkew^{12M}$	$IdioSkew^{1Y}$	$IdioSkew^{2Y}$	$IdioSkew^{3Y}$	$IdioSkew^{5Y}$
$IdioSkew^{1M}$		0.42	0.27	0.18	0.03	0.04	0.04	0.05
$IdioSkew^{3M}$	0.42		0.65	0.45	0.09	0.12	0.12	0.12
$IdioSkew^{6M}$	0.26	0.66		0.69	0.15	0.19	0.19	0.19
$IdioSkew^{12M}$	0.17	0.46	0.71		0.22	0.28	0.28	0.27
$IdioSkew^{1Y}$	0.03	0.12	0.18	0.25		0.47	0.35	0.28
$IdioSkew^{2Y}$	0.05	0.14	0.22	0.31	0.49		0.75	0.59
$IdioSkew^{3Y}$	0.05	0.13	0.21	0.30	0.37	0.77		0.78
$IdioSkew^{5Y}$	0.05	0.12	0.19	0.27	0.28	0.61	0.80	

and $IdioSkew^{12M}$. The correlations are higher for pairs of measures that have longer overlapping measurement periods and lower for pairs of measures that have longer nonoverlapping measurement periods. These results, for reasons discussed earlier, are likely mechanical. The only meaningful conclusion that can be drawn from the correlations, therefore, is that for the purposes of empirical analyses of the relations between idiosyncratic skewness and other variables, the measurement period chosen for estimating idiosyncratic skewness may be important, as different estimation periods result in substantially different cross-sectional properties of idiosyncratic skewness.

Pearson (Spearman) correlations between the monthly data-based measures of idiosyncratic skewness range from 0.28 (0.28) between $IdioSkew^{1Y}$ and $IdioSkew^{5Y}$ to 0.80 (0.78) between $IdioSkew^{3Y}$ and $IdioSkew^{5Y}$. Consistent with a highly mechanical effect, the correlations increase (decrease) as the length of the overlap (nonoverlapping portion) of the estimation period increases.

Finally, the correlations between daily and monthly measures of idiosyncratic skewness are also very similar to those for total skewness (see Table 14.2), especially when the monthly return-based measure is calculated using more than one-year's worth of data. The results show that there is a substantial common component to the daily and monthly measures of idiosyncratic skewness, indicating that the daily and monthly measures are, to some degree, capturing the same characteristic of the stock's return.

14.3.4 Total Skewness, Co-Skewness, and Idiosyncratic Skewness

The above-mentioned correlation analyses have examined each of total skewness, co-skewness, and idiosyncratic skewness in isolation. Here, we examine the cross-sectional correlations between total skewness, co-skewness, and idiosyncratic skewness. The average cross-sectional Pearson product–moment (Panel A) and Spearman rank (Panel B) correlations between $Skew$ and $CoSkew$, $Skew$ and $IdioSkew$, and $CoSkew$ and $IdioSkew$ are presented in Table 14.5. In each analysis, both variables are calculated using the same measurement period and data frequency.

The results show that, regardless of the length of the estimation period, total skewness and co-skewness calculated from daily return data exhibit negligible cross-sectional correlation in the average month, as the average Pearson and Spearman correlations range from −0.01 for the 12-month measures to 0.03 for the one-month measures. While the correlations do appear to be decreasing with the measurement period, the magnitude of the correlations indicates no substantial cross-sectional relation between $Skew$ and $CoSkew$ calculated from daily return data. The correlations between $Skew$ and $CoSkew$ calculated using monthly data are a little bit higher, with Pearson (Spearman) correlations decreasing from 0.09 (0.11) between $Skew^{1Y}$ and $CoSkew^{1Y}$ to 0.07 (0.08) between $Skew^{5Y}$ and $CoSkew^{5Y}$. The correlations indicate a small but not negligible positive relation between total skewness and co-skewness of monthly returns, as would be expected if there is a systematic component of individual stock skewness. However, the low levels of

TABLE 14.5   Correlations—Total, Co-, and Idiosyncratic Skewness

This table presents the time-series averages of the annual cross-sectional Pearson product–moment (Panel A) and Spearman rank (Panel B) correlations between pairs of variables measuring total skewness (*Skew*), co-skewness (*CoSkew*), and idiosyncratic skewness (*IdioSkew*) calculated using different data frequencies and measurement period lengths. Correlations between variables calculated from one, three, six, and 12 months of daily return data are shown in the columns 1*M*, 3*M*, 6*M*, and 12*M*, respectively. Correlations between variables calculated from one, two, three, and five months of monthly return data are shown in the columns 1*Y*, 2*Y*, 3*Y*, and 5*Y*, respectively.

Panel A: Pearson Correlations								
Correlation Between	1*M*	3*M*	6*M*	12*M*	1*Y*	2*Y*	3*Y*	5*Y*
Skew and *CoSkew*	0.03	0.02	0.01	−0.01	0.09	0.09	0.08	0.07
Skew and *IdioSkew*	0.84	0.95	0.97	0.97	0.50	0.73	0.80	0.85
CoSkew and *IdioSkew*	−0.10	−0.05	−0.05	−0.05	−0.15	−0.11	−0.10	−0.08

Panel B: Spearman Correlations								
Correlation Between	1*M*	3*M*	6*M*	12*M*	1*Y*	2*Y*	3*Y*	5*Y*
Skew and *CoSkew*	0.03	0.02	0.01	−0.01	0.11	0.10	0.10	0.08
Skew and *IdioSkew*	0.78	0.91	0.94	0.95	0.46	0.67	0.74	0.79
CoSkew and *IdioSkew*	−0.13	−0.08	−0.07	−0.08	−0.16	−0.12	−0.11	−0.10

this correlation indicate that the systematic component of individual stock return skewness is likely to be small.

The second row of each panel indicates a strong and positive cross-sectional relation between total skewness (*Skew*) and idiosyncratic skewness (*IdioSkew*), with average Pearson (Spearman) correlations among the daily return-based measures ranging from 0.84 (0.78) between $Skew^{1M}$ and $IdioSkew^{1M}$ to 0.97 (0.94) between the $Skew^{12M}$ and $IdioSkew^{12M}$. This indicates that, when calculated from daily return data, *Skew* and *IdioSkew* contain almost identical information in the cross section of stocks. The correlations between the monthly return-based measures of total skewness and idiosyncratic skewness are again positive and large in magnitude and exhibit an increasing pattern as the length of the measurement period gets longer. The average Pearson (Spearman) cross-sectional correlations increase from 0.50 (0.46) between $Skew^{1Y}$ and $IdioSkew^{1Y}$ to 0.85 between $Skew^{5Y}$ and $IdioSkew^{5Y}$. The high correlations between total and idiosyncratic skewness are not surprising given that the summary statistics for *Skew* and *IdioSkew* were highly similar (see Table 14.1) and the correlations between total skewness and co-skewness are very low. The results indicate that total skewness is almost completely driven by the portion of the stock's return that is orthogonal to the return of the market factor or the size and book-to-market factors of Fama and French (1993).

Finally, Table 14.5 shows a weak negative cross-sectional correlation between co-skewness and idiosyncratic skewness. When using daily return-based measures of these variables, the average Pearson (Spearman) correlations range from -0.10 (-0.13) between $CoSkew^{1M}$ and $IdioSkew^{1M}$ to -0.05 (-0.07) between $CoSkew^{12M}$ and $IdioSkew^{12M}$ ($CoSkew^{6M}$ and $IdioSkew^{6M}$). When using the monthly return-based measures of co-skewness and idiosyncratic skewness, the results are similar. The average Pearson (Spearman) cross-sectional correlation decreases as the measurement period gets longer from -0.15 (-0.16) between $CoSkew^{1Y}$ and $IdioSkew^{1Y}$ to -0.08 (-0.10) between $CoSkew^{5Y}$ and $IdioSkew^{5Y}$. Thus, while there appears to be a small negative relation between the measured values of co-skewness and idiosyncratic skewness, this relation is not very strong.

14.3.5   Skewness and Other Variables

Having examined the correlations between the measures of skewness in some detail, we proceed now to examine the correlations between each of our skewness measures and beta (β), size ($Size$, log of market capitalization), book-to-market ratio (BM), momentum (Mom), reversal (Rev), and illiquidity ($Illiq$). Table 14.6 presents the average cross-sectional correlations between each of these variables and the measures of total skewness ($Skew$, Panel A), co-skewness ($CoSkew$, Panel B), and idiosyncratic skewness ($IdioSkew$, Panel C).

The results in Panel A show that the correlation between β and total skewness tends to be negative and small in magnitude, regardless of the length of the measurement period or the frequency of the data. The exceptions to this are the Pearson correlation between β and $Skew^{1M}$ and the Spearman correlations between β and each of $Skew^{1M}$ and $Skew^{3M}$, each of which is positive but small in magnitude. Overall, however, total skewness does not exhibit strong correlation with β.

The correlations between the measures of total skewness and $Size$ are all negative, with the magnitude of these correlations increasing substantially as the measurement period is extended, both for daily and monthly return-based measures of total skewness. If skewness from longer measurement periods does a better job at capturing the true skewness of a stock's returns, then the results indicate that total skewness has a meaningful negative relation with $Size$.

Book-to-market ratio (BM) exhibits a weak positive correlation with total skewness. For the daily return-based measures of total skewness, this correlation is stronger when skewness is calculated using longer measurement periods. The length of the measurement has a negligible effect on the average correlations between BM and total skewness measured from monthly return data.

Most of the measures of total skewness have a small positive correlation with Mom. The exceptions to this are the average Pearson product–moment correlation between $Skew^{1M}$ and Mom of -0.02 and the Spearman rank correlations between Mom and each of $Skew^{1M}$ (average correlation $= -0.04$) and $Skew^{5Y}$ (average correlation $= -0.01$). For the daily return-based measures of total skewness, the correlations increase as the measurement period is extended from one to 12 months. This is not surprising, and is likely largely mechanical, since a few large positive (negative) one-day returns within the past year would likely result in high (low) values of both Mom and $Skew^{12M}$. Likely for the same reason, the correlations between the monthly

TABLE 14.6   Correlations—Skewness and Other Variables

This table presents the time-series averages of the annual cross-sectional Pearson product-moment (below-diagonal entries) and Spearman rank (above-diagonal entries) correlations between pairs of variables measuring idiosyncratic volatility.

Panel A: *Skew*

	Pearson Correlations							Spearman Correlations					
	β	*Size*	*BM*	*Mom*	*Rev*	*Illiq*		β	*Size*	*BM*	*Mom*	*Rev*	*Illiq*
$Skew^{1M}$	0.03	−0.03	0.02	−0.02	0.37	0.03	$Skew^{1M}$	0.04	−0.04	0.01	−0.04	0.37	0.05
$Skew^{3M}$	−0.00	−0.10	0.05	0.06	0.21	0.05	$Skew^{3M}$	0.02	−0.12	0.04	0.04	0.18	0.12
$Skew^{6M}$	−0.04	−0.16	0.09	0.11	0.14	0.07	$Skew^{6M}$	−0.01	−0.20	0.07	0.09	0.10	0.19
$Skew^{12M}$	−0.06	−0.22	0.11	0.18	0.10	0.10	$Skew^{12M}$	−0.04	−0.28	0.10	0.17	0.06	0.25
$Skew^{1Y}$	−0.04	−0.20	0.07	0.10	0.06	0.10	$Skew^{1Y}$	−0.04	−0.20	0.05	0.07	−0.02	0.19
$Skew^{2Y}$	−0.06	−0.30	0.09	0.08	0.04	0.15	$Skew^{2Y}$	−0.06	−0.32	0.06	0.02	−0.02	0.28
$Skew^{3Y}$	−0.05	−0.35	0.09	0.07	0.03	0.17	$Skew^{3Y}$	−0.07	−0.37	0.06	0.00	−0.03	0.32
$Skew^{5Y}$	−0.05	−0.38	0.08	0.05	0.03	0.19	$Skew^{5Y}$	−0.06	−0.41	0.05	−0.01	−0.03	0.36

Panel B: *CoSkew*

	Pearson Correlations							Spearman Correlations					
	β	*Size*	*BM*	*Mom*	*Rev*	*Illiq*		β	*Size*	*BM*	*Mom*	*Rev*	*Illiq*
$CoSkew^{1M}$	0.01	0.02	0.00	−0.01	−0.02	−0.00	$CoSkew^{1M}$	0.01	0.02	0.00	−0.01	−0.03	−0.03
$CoSkew^{3M}$	0.03	0.05	−0.00	−0.03	−0.01	−0.01	$CoSkew^{3M}$	0.02	0.05	−0.00	−0.03	−0.01	−0.05
$CoSkew^{6M}$	0.05	0.07	−0.00	−0.04	−0.01	−0.02	$CoSkew^{6M}$	0.04	0.08	−0.00	−0.04	−0.00	−0.08
$CoSkew^{12M}$	0.07	0.11	−0.01	−0.05	−0.00	−0.03	$CoSkew^{12M}$	0.06	0.12	−0.00	−0.04	0.01	−0.12
$CoSkew^{1Y}$	0.02	0.04	−0.01	−0.04	−0.01	−0.02	$CoSkew^{1Y}$	0.02	0.06	−0.00	−0.03	−0.00	−0.04
$CoSkew^{2Y}$	0.03	0.07	0.00	−0.02	0.00	−0.03	$CoSkew^{2Y}$	0.03	0.09	0.01	−0.01	0.01	−0.09
$CoSkew^{3Y}$	0.04	0.09	0.01	−0.01	0.00	−0.04	$CoSkew^{3Y}$	0.05	0.11	0.02	−0.01	0.01	−0.11
$CoSkew^{5Y}$	0.06	0.11	0.02	−0.00	0.00	−0.04	$CoSkew^{5Y}$	0.08	0.14	0.02	0.00	0.01	−0.13

Panel C: *IdioSkew*

	Pearson Correlations							Spearman Correlations					
	β	*Size*	*BM*	*Mom*	*Rev*	*Illiq*		β	*Size*	*BM*	*Mom*	*Rev*	*Illiq*
$IdioSkew^{1M}$	0.02	−0.03	0.02	−0.01	0.33	0.02	$IdioSkew^{1M}$	0.03	−0.03	0.01	−0.02	0.33	0.05
$IdioSkew^{3M}$	−0.00	−0.09	0.05	0.07	0.21	0.04	$IdioSkew^{3M}$	0.02	−0.10	0.03	0.06	0.18	0.11
$IdioSkew^{6M}$	−0.03	−0.15	0.08	0.13	0.15	0.06	$IdioSkew^{6M}$	0.00	−0.17	0.07	0.12	0.11	0.16
$IdioSkew^{12M}$	−0.05	−0.21	0.11	0.20	0.10	0.09	$IdioSkew^{12M}$	−0.02	−0.25	0.09	0.21	0.06	0.23
$IdioSkew^{1Y}$	−0.03	−0.12	0.04	0.10	0.05	0.05	$IdioSkew^{1Y}$	−0.03	−0.12	0.03	0.08	−0.00	0.11
$IdioSkew^{2Y}$	−0.04	−0.25	0.06	0.10	0.04	0.11	$IdioSkew^{2Y}$	−0.05	−0.25	0.05	0.06	−0.02	0.22
$IdioSkew^{3Y}$	−0.05	−0.30	0.06	0.09	0.04	0.14	$IdioSkew^{3Y}$	−0.06	−0.32	0.04	0.04	−0.02	0.28
$IdioSkew^{5Y}$	−0.04	−0.34	0.06	0.07	0.03	0.16	$IdioSkew^{5Y}$	−0.06	−0.36	0.03	0.02	−0.02	0.32

return-based measure of total skewness and *Mom* decrease as the measurement period is extended. In both the cases of the daily return and monthly return-based measures, higher correlations occur when the period covered by the calculation of total skewness is most similar to the period covered by the calculation of momentum.

Likely for similar reasons, $Skew^{1M}$ exhibits a strong positive cross-sectional correlation with *Rev* of 0.37 (both Pearson and Spearman). This correlation drops substantially as longer measurement periods are used for the measures calculated from daily return data. The monthly return measures of total skewness exhibit low correlation with Rev. Interestingly, the Pearson correlations are all slightly positive, ranging from 0.03 between $Skew^{5M}$ and Rev to 0.06 between $Skew^{1Y}$ and Rev. The Spearman correlations, on the other hand, are all negative, ranging from -0.03 between $Skew^{5Y}$ and Rev to -0.02 between Rev and each of $Skew^{1Y}$, $Skew^{2Y}$, and $Skew^{3Y}$. Despite the fact that the Pearson and Spearman correlations carry the opposite signs, the magnitudes of these correlations are negligible.

The results indicate a positive cross-sectional correlation between total skewness and $Illiq$. The Pearson (Spearman) correlations between the daily return total skewness measures and $Illiq$ increase from 0.03 (0.05) for $Skew^{1M}$ to 0.10 (0.25) for $Skew^{12M}$. When using the monthly return-based measures of total skewness, the Pearson (Spearman) correlations between $Illiq$ and total skewness grow from 0.10 (0.19) for $Skew^{1Y}$ to 0.19 (0.36) for $Skew^{5Y}$. The results indicate that less liquid (higher values of $Illiq$) tend to have returns that are more positively skewed. In this case, the difference between the Pearson and Spearman correlations is quite substantial. This is quite possibly driven by the highly skewed distribution of $Illiq$ (see Table 13.1), but may also indicate a nonlinear relation between $Illiq$ and total skewness. Once again assuming that the measures of total skewness calculated from longer measurement periods provide more accurate values of the true skewness of a stock's returns, the results indicate that total skewness and $Illiq$ have a substantial positive correlation.

Moving to the correlations between co-skewness and the variables discussed in previous chapters of this book, the results in Panel B of Table 14.6 provide no evidence of any meaningful cross-sectional correlation between co-skewness and BM, Mom, or Rev since the Pearson and Spearman correlations between each of these variables and $CoSkew$, regardless of the data frequency or measurement period length used to calculate $CoSkew$, range from -0.05 (Pearson correlation between $CoSkew^{12M}$ and Mom) to 0.02 (Pearson and Spearman correlations between $CoSkew^{5Y}$ and BM).

The correlation analyses indicate a small positive correlation between β and co-skewness. These correlations are negligible for values of $CoSkew$ calculated from shorter measurement periods, but for longer measurement periods, the correlations are slightly larger. The Pearson (Spearman) correlation between $CoSkew^{12M}$ and β is 0.07 (0.06) and the correlation between $CoSkew^{5Y}$ and β is 0.06 (0.08). Even these correlations, however, are quite small in magnitude.

Co-skewness exhibits a slightly stronger positive correlation with $Size$, with Pearson (Spearman) correlations for the daily return-based measures of co-skewness ranging from 0.02 (0.02) for $Skew^{1M}$ to 0.11 (0.12) for $Skew^{12M}$. The monthly return-based measures of co-skewness also exhibit correlations that increase with longer measurement periods since the Pearson (Spearman) correlations between the monthly return-based measures of co-skewness and $Size$ increase from 0.04 (0.06) for $CoSkew^{1Y}$ to 0.11 (0.14) for $CoSkew^{5Y}$. Thus, if the measures of co-skewness calculated using longer measurement periods are more accurate than those calculated from shorter measurement periods, the results indicate a nonnegligible, albeit not very large, positive correlation between co-skewness and $Size$.

The Pearson correlations between *CoSkew* and *Illiq* are all negative, but small in magnitude, regardless of the length of the measurement period or the frequency of the data used to calculate co-skewness. These correlations range from −0.04 between $CoSkew^{5Y}$ and *Illiq* to −0.00 between $CoSkew^{1M}$ and *Illiq*. The Spearman correlations are also negative, but a bit larger in magnitude, ranging from −0.13 between $CoSkew^{5Y}$ and *Illiq* to −0.03 between $CoSkew^{1M}$ and *Illiq*. Once again, the magnitudes of these correlations increase as the measurement period used to calculate *CoSkew* is extended. The substantial difference between the Pearson and Spearman correlations is likely driven by a few extreme values in the distribution of *Illiq*.

Finally, Panel C of Table 14.6 shows the correlations between different measures of idiosyncratic skewness and each of β, *Size*, *BM*, *Mom*, *Rev*, and *Illiq*. The correlations between idiosyncratic skewness and these variables are all very similar to the correlations between total skewness and these variables. This is not surprising given that total *Skew* and *IdioSkew* tend to be highly correlated in the cross section (see Table 14.5). In most cases, the correlations between *IdioSkew* and the other variables are of either the same or slightly smaller magnitude or a little bit lower than the corresponding correlation between *Skew* and the other variables. The one exception to this is *Mom*, which exhibits a higher (or equivalent) correlation with the measures of idiosyncratic skewness (with the exception of $IdioSkew^{1M}$) than with the corresponding total skewness variables. The magnitudes of these correlations, however, are still quite similar.

14.4 PERSISTENCE

We continue our examination of the variables measuring total skewness, co-skewness, and idiosyncratic skewness with persistence analyses. If skewness is a persistent characteristic of individual stock returns and the variables, we use to measure skewness do a reasonable job at capturing this characteristic, we would expect the variables to exhibit substantial cross-sectional persistence when measured using different time periods. Several of the correlation analyses indicated that some of the skewness variables exhibit larger correlations with some of the variables discussed in previous chapters of this book when skewness is measured using longer measurement periods. If the persistence analyses lead to the conclusion that longer measurement periods do in fact more accurately capture a persistent characteristic of individual stock returns, then the results of the correlation analyses using skewness variables calculated using longer measurement periods are likely more reflective of the actual relations between skewness and the other stock characteristics. For each variable, we calculate persistence at lags of one, three, six, 12, 24, 36, 48, 60, and 120 months. To avoid mechanical persistence, we only present results for persistence analyses where the lag between the times at which the given variable is measured is at least as long as the measurement period.

14.4.1 Total Skewness

We begin with persistence analyses of the measures of total skewness. The results indicate that there is very little cross-sectional persistence in the total skewness variables measured using daily stock returns. The average cross-sectional correlation between values of $Skew^{1M}$ measured one, three, six, and 12 months apart are each 0.03, indicating almost no relation between present and future values of $Skew^{1M}$. The persistence is even lower (0.01 or 0.02) when measured at lags of 24, 36, 48, 60, and 120 months. For skewness measured using longer estimation periods, the average cross-sectional correlation between values calculated using nonoverlapping measurement periods range from 0.03 for $Skew^{3M}$ measured 120 months apart to 0.14 for $Skew^{12M}$ measured 12 months apart. While slightly higher than the correlations for $Skew^{1M}$, these values are still quite low. The low persistence of the daily return-based skewness variables has two potential causes. The first is that the skewness of the distribution of daily returns is not a persistent property of the stock. The other is that the calculation of daily return skewness is very noisy, meaning that the variable does a poor job at capturing the desired property of the stock. The former explanation seems less likely than the latter for two reasons. First, the highest persistence value comes from $Skew^{12M}$ measured 12 months apart. If lack of persistence in skewness were driving the low correlations, we would expect this measure to exhibit lower lagged correlation than the values calculated using shorter measurement intervals. Second, the fact that the persistence increases as the measurement period increases is likely an indication that skewness is in fact persistent, but that it takes a long estimation period to get an accurate measure of daily return skewness. The results are, therefore, consistent with the hypothesis that $Skew$, measured from daily return data, is a very noisy measure of the actual skewness of the stock's returns. That being said, there does appear to be some information in the longer estimation period measures, and it is possible that despite the fact that the measure appears to be quite noisy, with a large enough sample, it may be capable of detecting patterns in expected returns that are related to skewness.

The results indicate that the persistence of the monthly return-based measures of total skewness is substantially higher than those of the daily return-based measures. For example, the average cross-sectional correlation between $Skew^{5Y}$ measured five years (60 months) apart is 0.25. This indicates that $Skew^{5Y}$ is more persistent when measured five years apart than any of the daily return-based measures, even when they are measured one-year (or less) apart. The results also demonstrate that the persistence of the measures of total skewness increases substantially as the measurement period gets longer, despite the fact that the lag between the measurements is extended. $Skew^{1Y}$ exhibits a persistence of only 0.08 when measured one year apart. $Skew^{2Y}$ exhibits a persistence of 0.16 when measured two years apart. The persistence of $Skew^{3Y}$ when measured three years apart is 0.21. Furthermore, for any given lag between measurement periods, the persistence of the variables calculated using longer measurement periods is higher than that of the variables calculated using shorter measurement periods. This holds for both the monthly return-based measures of total skewness and the daily return-based measures.

These results lead to a few important conclusions. First, assuming that the true skewness of a given stock's returns is reasonably persistent, which is a generally necessary assumption when using historical data to estimate a stock-level characteristic, calculating total skewness from monthly data provides a substantially better measure than the daily data-based measures. Second, there is in fact a substantial degree of persistence in the actual total skewness of individual stock returns. We conclude this

SKEWNESS

because if skewness were not persistent, then there would not be any persistence in any measure of skewness.[8] Finally, longer estimation periods result in better measures of skewness than shorter estimation periods. We conclude this because the persistence of $Skew^{5Y}$ measured five years apart is higher than that of $Skew_{1Y}$ measured one year apart. If $Skew_{1Y}$ and $Skew_{5Y}$ were equally good measures of total skewness, then we would expect the one-year persistence of $Skew_{1Y}$ to be higher than the five-year persistence of $Skew_{5Y}$. The fact that the opposite is true combined with the strong pattern of increasing persistence as the measurement period (and thus lowest nonoverlapping lag) increases indicates that measures of total skewness based on shorter estimation periods are noisier than measures based on higher estimation periods.

14.4.2 Co-Skewness

The results of the persistence analyses of the variables measuring co-skewness, shown in Table 14.7, provide almost no indication of persistence in co-skewness. The highest persistence value for any of the co-skewness variables calculated at any lag is 0.06 for $CoSkew^{12M}$ measured 12 months apart. The daily return-based measures of co-skewness calculated from less than one year's worth of data ($CoSkew^{1M}$, $CoSkew^{3M}$, and $CoSkew^{6M}$) have persistence values ranging between 0.00 and

TABLE 14.7 Persistence—Co-Skewness
This table presents the results of persistence analyses of variables measuring co-skewness. Each month t, the cross-sectional Pearson product–moment correlation between the month t and month $t + \tau$ values of the given variable measured is calculated. The table presents the time-series averages of the monthly cross-sectional correlations. The column labeled τ indicates the lag at which the persistence is measured

τ	$CoSkew^{1M}$	$CoSkew^{3M}$	$CoSkew^{6M}$	$CoSkew^{12M}$	$CoSkew^{1Y}$	$CoSkew^{2Y}$	$CoSkew^{3Y}$	$CoSkew^{5Y}$
1	0.00							
3	0.00	0.02						
6	0.00	0.01	0.03					
12	0.00	0.02	0.03	0.06	0.01			
24	0.00	0.01	0.02	0.04	−0.00	0.00		
36	0.00	0.01	0.02	0.03	0.00	0.01	0.01	
48	0.00	0.01	0.02	0.04	0.00	0.01	0.02	
60	0.00	0.01	0.02	0.04	0.00	0.01	0.02	0.03
120	0.00	0.00	0.01	0.03	0.00	0.02	0.03	0.05

[8] A possible objection to this conclusion would be that, in attempting to measure skewness, we are actually capturing some other persistent characteristic of the stock's returns. This seems unlikely in this case since the measure of skewness is based on the statistical definition of skewness.

338

0.03, indicating practically no cross-sectional persistence in these values. Similarly, for the measures of co-skewness calculated from less than five years of monthly return data, the persistence values range from −0.00 to 0.03, regardless of lag. The highest persistence value for the monthly return-based measures of 0.05 comes from the five-year measure ($CoSkew^{5Y}$) calculated 10 years apart. Interestingly, for $CoSkew^{2Y}$, $CoSkew^{3Y}$, and $CoSkew^{5Y}$, the persistence actually increases as the lag between measurement gets longer. This is potentially driven by the fact that the analyses at long lags require a stock to be in the sample for an extended period of time. For these stocks, which are likely to be well-established large firms, the measurement of co-skewness may exhibit a small amount of persistence. Even if this is the case, the level of persistence in these variables is negligible.

There are a few potential explanations for the lack of persistence detected in the measures of co-skewness. One possibility is that co-skewness is in fact not a cross-sectionally persistent stock-level characteristic. If this is the case, then the assumption that co-skewness measured from historical data provides a reasonable proxy for the market's view of future co-skewness is not a viable assumption. Since this assumption is necessary when using empirical analyses of relations between historical measures of risk and future stock returns to try to understand the trade-offs between risk and expected returns made by investors, the usefulness of the co-skewness measure for individual stocks is questionable. Another potential explanation is that *CoSkew* does a poor job at measuring the stock's actual co-skewness.[9] Regardless of which of these explanations hold, the results indicate that stock-level co-skewness is unlikely to be an empirically strong variable. Despite these results, *CoSkew* remains a widely used variable in the empirical asset pricing literature.

14.4.3   Idiosyncratic Skewness

Finally, in Table 14.8, we present the results of persistence analyses of the variables measuring idiosyncratic skewness. The results of the persistence analyses of idiosyncratic skewness are very similar to those of total skewness presented in Table 14.9. This is not surprising given the high correlations between these variables. For any fixed lag, the persistence values are higher for the variables calculated using longer measurement periods. The highest persistence values are generated by $IdioSkew^{5Y}$, which exhibits persistence of 0.21 when measured with lag of five years and 0.20 when measured at a lag of 10 years. Among the daily return-based measures, $Skew^{12M}$ exhibits the highest level of persistence, with persistence values decreasing from 0.14 when measured with a lag of one year to 0.08 when measured with a lag of 10 years. The low levels of persistence among the daily return-based measures of idiosyncratic skewness are consistent with Boyer, Mitton, and Vorkink (2010), who propose an

---

[9]It is worth noting that in their seminal study, Harvey and Siddique (2000) examine the co-skewness of 32 equity portfolios based on industry as well as the 25 portfolios formed by sorting on size and book-to-market used by Fama and French (1995), with results for individual securities playing a secondary role. Thus, it is possible that measurement noise associated with individual stock co-skewness can be substantially reduced by using portfolio level measures of co-skewness.

TABLE 14.8   Persistence—Idiosyncratic Skewness

This table presents the results of persistence analyses of variables measuring idiosyncratic skewness. Each month t, the cross-sectional Pearson product–moment correlation between the month t and month $t + \tau$ values of the given variable measured is calculated. The table presents the time-series averages of the monthly cross-sectional correlations. The column labeled τ indicates the lag at which the persistence is measured.

τ	$IdioSkew^{1M}$	$IdioSkew^{3M}$	$IdioSkew^{6M}$	$IdioSkew^{12M}$	$IdioSkew^{1Y}$	$IdioSkew^{2Y}$	$IdioSkew^{3Y}$	$IdioSkew^{5Y}$
1	0.03							
3	0.02	0.06						
6	0.02	0.06	0.09					
12	0.02	0.05	0.09	0.14	0.03			
24	0.02	0.05	0.07	0.12	0.03	0.12		
36	0.01	0.04	0.06	0.10	0.03	0.11	0.17	
48	0.01	0.03	0.06	0.10	0.02	0.10	0.16	
60	0.01	0.03	0.05	0.09	0.02	0.10	0.15	0.21
120	0.01	0.03	0.05	0.08	0.02	0.09	0.14	0.20

TABLE 14.9   Persistence—Total Skewness

This table presents the results of persistence analyses of variables measuring total skewness. Each month t, the cross-sectional Pearson product–moment correlation between the month t and month $t + \tau$ values of the given variable measured is calculated. The table presents the time-series averages of the monthly cross-sectional correlations. The column labeled τ indicates the lag at which the persistence is measured.

τ	$Skew^{1M}$	$Skew^{3M}$	$Skew^{6M}$	$Skew^{12M}$	$Skew^{1Y}$	$Skew^{2Y}$	$Skew^{3Y}$	$Skew^{5Y}$
1	0.03							
3	0.03	0.06						
6	0.03	0.06	0.09					
12	0.03	0.05	0.09	0.14	0.08			
24	0.02	0.05	0.08	0.12	0.08	0.16		
36	0.02	0.04	0.06	0.11	0.07	0.15	0.21	
48	0.01	0.03	0.06	0.10	0.06	0.14	0.20	
60	0.02	0.03	0.06	0.10	0.06	0.14	0.19	0.25
120	0.01	0.03	0.05	0.08	0.05	0.12	0.16	0.21

alternative methodology for calculating the market's expectation of future idiosyncratic skewness. The fact that the persistence of idiosyncratic skewness measured from monthly return data, especially when using long measurement periods, is higher than that of the daily return measures indicates that the monthly return measures are likely more effective at capturing a persistent characteristic of the stock. Even for $Skew^{5Y}$, which is the most persistent of the idiosyncratic skewness variables, the magnitude of the persistence is quite low, indicating that either idiosyncratic skewness is not a highly persistent stock-level characteristic or measurement of this characteristic using $Skew^{5Y}$ is highly noisy.

In summary, in Sections 14.1–14.4, we have analyzed in detail measures of total skewness, co-skewness, and idiosyncratic skewness calculated using daily and monthly stock return data. The main conclusions are the following. First, total skewness and idiosyncratic skewness are highly similar, while co-skewness appears to be largely unrelated to either. Both total skewness and idiosyncratic skewness appear to be best measured using long estimation periods and monthly, instead of daily, returns. When long estimation periods are used, these variables appear to do a reasonable, albeit still noisy job at capturing a persistent characteristic of the given stock's returns. Co-skewness, as measured by $CoSkew$, fails to exhibit any substantial persistence or correlation with total skewness or idiosyncratic skewness, leading us to conclude that the variable $CoSkew$ likely fails to capture the amount of systematic skewness associated with individual stocks. Finally, it is worth noting that while the results of the persistence analyses and the correlations between the daily and monthly return-based measures of total skewness and idiosyncratic skewness indicate that these variables do capture the actual skewness of the stock's returns, the levels of persistence and correlations are not high, indicating that regardless of the estimation period or data frequency, the measurement of total skewness and idiosyncratic skewness with $Skew$ and $IdioSkew$, respectively, is highly noisy.

14.5 SKEWNESS AND STOCK RETURNS

We move now to our examination of the relation between expected stock returns and each of total skewness, co-skewness, and idiosyncratic skewness. Before proceeding, we remind the reader that the theoretical results in Harvey and Siddique (2000) predict a negative relation between co-skewness and future stock returns. Mitton and Vorkink (2007) present theoretical support for a negative relation between idiosyncratic skewness and expected stock return. If both systematic skewness (co-skewness) and idiosyncratic skewness have a theoretically negative relation with expected returns, then total skewness should have a negative relation as well. Thus, asset pricing theory unambiguously predicts a negative relation between skewness (total skewness, co-skewness, or idiosyncratic skewness), and expected stock returns.

14.5.1 Univariate Portfolio Analysis

We begin our empirical investigation of the relation between skewness and expected returns using univariate decile portfolio analyses. Because of the large number of skewness variables we are examining in this chapter, we forgo presentation of portfolio level characteristics and proceed directly to the examination of the ability of these variables to predict future stock returns.

Total Skewness

Our first portfolio analyses examine the relations between future stock excess returns and each of the different measures of total skewness. Table 14.10 presents the average monthly returns for each of the total skewness-sorted decile portfolios, as well as for the portfolio that is long the 10th decile portfolio and short the first decile portfolio (10-1). Abnormal returns relative to the Fama and French (1993) and Carhart (1997) four-factor model (FFC), as well as the FFC model augmented with Pastor and Stambaugh (2003)'s liquidity factor (FFCPS), are also shown.[10] t-statistics testing whether the average return, FFC alpha, and FFCPS alpha are equal to zero, adjusted following Newey and West (1987), are shown in parentheses.

Panel A presents results for equal-weighted portfolios. The results demonstrate that portfolios sorted on total skewness measured using one month of daily return data ($Skew^{1M}$) exhibit a strong and nearly monotonically decreasing (the exception is decile portfolio 1) pattern in average returns across the deciles portfolios, with decile portfolio one generating an average excess return of 0.86% per month compared to 0.39% per month for the decile 10 portfolio. The average 10-1 portfolio return of −0.47% per month is highly statistically significant, with a t-statistic of −4.01. The results do not appear to be driven by exposure to the market (MKT), size (SMB), value (HML), or momentum (MOM) factors, since the FFC alpha of the difference portfolio of −0.45% (t-statistic = −4.35) is very similar to the portfolio's average return. Adding the liquidity (PSL) factor to the risk model has little effect since the FFCPS alpha of −0.45% per month (t-statistic = −3.87) is nearly identical to the FFC alpha. When the portfolios are formed by sorting on $Skew^{3M}$, the average return, FFC alpha, and FFCPS alpha for the difference portfolio of −0.28% per month (t-statistic = −1.79), −0.34% per month (t-statistic = −2.03), and −0.34% per month (t-statistic = −1.88), respectively, are also statistically significant (marginally for the unadjusted return and FFCPS alpha). The average returns and alphas for the difference portfolio formed by sorting on each of $Skew^{6M}$, $Skew^{12M}$, $Skew^{1Y}$, $Skew^{2Y}$, $Skew^{3Y}$, and $Skew^{5Y}$ are all statistically insignificant at conventional levels.

The results of the equal-weighted portfolio analyses are quite interesting, especially given our conclusions from the persistence analyses that longer measurement periods result in more accurate calculation of total skewness, with the monthly return measures being potentially more reliable than the daily return measures. Contrary to our prediction that the variables calculated from longer measurement periods would be more likely to provide evidence of a skewness premium, we find that the measures calculated from one month, and to some degree three months, of daily data, are the

---

[10]Note that the Pastor and Stambaugh (2003) factor data are only available beginning in January 1968. The alphas relative to the FFCPS model, along with associated t-statistics, are therefore calculated using portfolio returns realized during the months from January 1968 through December 2012, instead of July 1963 through December 2012, as is the case for all other analyses.

TABLE 14.10 Univariate Portfolio Analysis—Total Skewness
This table presents the results of univariate portfolio analyses of the relation between total skewness and future stock returns. Monthly portfolios are formed by sorting all stocks in the CRSP sample into portfolios using decile breakpoints calculated based on the given sort variable using all stocks in the CRSP sample. Panel A (Panel B) shows the average equal-weighted (value-weighted) one-month-ahead excess return (in percent per month) for each of the 10 decile portfolios formed using different measures of total skewness as the sort variable. The table also shows the average return of the portfolio that is long the 10th decile portfolio and short the first decile portfolio, as well as the FFC and FFCPS alphas for this portfolio. Newey and West (1987) t-statistics, adjusted using six lags, testing the null hypothesis that the average 10-1 portfolio return or alpha is equal to zero, are shown in parentheses.

					Panel A: Equal-Weighted Portfolios							

Sort Variable	1	2	3	4	5	6	7	8	9	10	10-1	FFC α	FFCPS α
$Skew^{1M}$	0.86	0.96	0.96	0.90	0.86	0.72	0.67	0.62	0.49	0.39	−0.47	−0.45	−0.45
											(−4.01)	(−4.35)	(−3.87)
$Skew^{3M}$	0.75	0.88	0.94	0.89	0.79	0.76	0.74	0.65	0.55	0.47	−0.28	−0.34	−0.34
											(−1.79)	(−2.03)	(−1.88)
$Skew^{6M}$	0.64	0.78	0.92	0.86	0.81	0.79	0.75	0.72	0.62	0.55	−0.08	−0.12	−0.11
											(−0.53)	(−0.87)	(−0.71)
$Skew^{12M}$	0.63	0.74	0.79	0.78	0.82	0.82	0.79	0.82	0.81	0.68	0.04	0.00	0.05
											(0.27)	(0.03)	(0.33)
$Skew^{1Y}$	0.84	0.84	0.82	0.80	0.79	0.79	0.75	0.77	0.71	0.63	−0.21	−0.18	−0.17
											(−1.37)	(−1.01)	(−0.95)
$Skew^{2Y}$	0.86	0.86	0.87	0.81	0.83	0.84	0.81	0.77	0.85	0.69	−0.18	−0.20	−0.22
											(−0.94)	(−0.90)	(−0.93)
$Skew^{3Y}$	0.88	0.87	0.85	0.85	0.87	0.82	0.82	0.87	0.83	0.70	−0.19	−0.21	−0.24
											(−0.93)	(−0.88)	(−0.97)
$Skew^{5Y}$	0.82	0.89	0.87	0.84	0.85	0.84	0.84	0.86	0.91	0.65	−0.18	−0.28	−0.32
											(−0.84)	(−1.52)	(−1.57)

					Panel B: Value-Weighted Portfolios							

Sort Variable	1	2	3	4	5	6	7	8	9	10	10-1	FFC α	FFCPS α
$Skew^{1M}$	0.24	0.47	0.41	0.51	0.42	0.51	0.46	0.53	0.57	0.50	0.26	0.25	0.25
											(2.26)	(2.15)	(2.01)
$Skew^{3M}$	0.39	0.48	0.48	0.51	0.49	0.51	0.44	0.46	0.54	0.60	0.22	0.13	0.17
											(1.78)	(1.04)	(1.25)
$Skew^{6M}$	0.46	0.48	0.51	0.49	0.47	0.53	0.40	0.40	0.50	0.58	0.13	−0.02	0.03
											(0.91)	(−0.16)	(0.22)
$Skew^{12M}$	0.34	0.60	0.48	0.45	0.58	0.47	0.45	0.50	0.51	0.68	0.34	0.21	0.26
											(2.38)	(1.64)	(1.81)
$Skew^{1Y}$	0.52	0.59	0.46	0.60	0.44	0.44	0.43	0.47	0.40	0.18	−0.34	−0.31	−0.29
											(−2.49)	(−2.28)	(−1.90)
$Skew^{2Y}$	0.52	0.63	0.51	0.51	0.46	0.54	0.34	0.33	0.39	0.23	−0.29	−0.38	−0.37
											(−1.91)	(−2.27)	(−2.13)
$Skew^{3Y}$	0.53	0.52	0.53	0.57	0.44	0.42	0.22	0.47	0.45	0.28	−0.25	−0.44	−0.39
											(−1.52)	(−2.67)	(−2.18)
$Skew^{5Y}$	0.50	0.56	0.48	0.44	0.49	0.51	0.47	0.38	0.31	0.22	−0.29	−0.52	−0.49
											(−1.63)	(−3.41)	(−2.95)

only variables for which a relation between total skewness and future stock returns is detected. However, the univariate portfolio analyses do not allow us to control for the effects of other variables. One possibility is that high values of $Skew^{1M}$ result from one or two days of very large returns occurring during the measurement month. These few days may also result in high values of reversal (Rev). We therefore defer any strong conclusion regarding these relations until we have performed multivariate analyses.

Average returns and alphas for value-weighted portfolios formed by sorting on the measures of total skewness are presented in Panel B of Table 14.10. When using value-weighted portfolios, the results indicate a strong positive relation between $Skew^{1M}$ and future stock returns, the exact opposite of what was detected in the equal-weighted portfolios. The average return, FFC alpha, and FFCPS alpha for the value-weighted $Skew^{1M}$ difference portfolio of 0.26% per month (t-statistic = 2.26), 0.25% per month (t-statistic = 2.15), and 0.25% per month (t-statistic = 2.01) are all economically large and highly statistically significant. The results show that the majority of the effect is driven by the first decile portfolio, which generates excess returns of only 0.24% per month, compared to between 0.42% and 0.57% per month for each of the other nine decile portfolios. Furthermore, there is no discernable pattern in the excess returns across the $Skew^{1M}$-sorted decile portfolios, indicating that potentially this result may be spurious. The contradictory findings between the equal-weighted and value-weighted analyses indicate that there may be a substantial interaction between market capitalization and $Skew^{1M}$ that affects the relation between $Skew^{1M}$ and future stock returns. That being said, a similar, although not as strong, result is generated by the value-weighted portfolios sorted on $Skew^{12M}$. The average return generated by the $Skew^{12M}$ difference portfolio of 0.34% per month (t-statistic = 2.38) is highly significant. The FFC alpha of 0.21%, however, is statistically insignificant with a t-statistic of only 1.64. When the PSL factor is added to the factor model, the abnormal return increases to 0.26% per month with a corresponding t-statistic of 1.81. Once again, the result appears to be driven by the first decile portfolio since the average excess return of the first $Skew^{12M}$ decile portfolio of 0.34% per month is substantially below that of any of the other portfolios. Also like the value-weighted portfolios formed by sorting on $Skew^{1M}$, the average excess returns of the $Skew^{12M}$-sorted portfolios fail to exhibit a strong pattern across the $Skew^{12M}$ deciles.

The results for value-weighted portfolios formed by sorting on the monthly return-based measures of total skewness indicate a negative and, in many cases, statistically significant negative relation between total skewness and expected stock returns. When the portfolios are formed by sorting on $Skew^{1Y}$, the value-weighted difference portfolio produces a statistically significant average monthly return of -0.34% (t-statistic = -2.49), FFC alpha of -0.31% (t-statistic = -2.28), and FFCPS alpha of -0.29% per month (t-statistic = -1.90). As the length of the period used to calculate total skewness is lengthened, the abnormal returns of the difference portfolios increase substantially. The $Skew^{5Y}$ 10-1 portfolio generates FFC alpha of -0.52% per month (t-statistic = -3.41) and FFCPS alpha of -0.49% per month (t-statistic = -2.95). This negative relation is consistent with theoretical predictions. Furthermore, the fact that the results get stronger as the length of the measurement period is extended is consistent with our previous conclusions that variables calculated using longer measurement periods more accurately reflect values of total skewness.

Co-Skewness

The results of univariate portfolio analyses of the relation between co-skewness and expected stock returns are presented in Table 14.11. The equal-weighted portfolio analysis using $CoSkew^{1M}$ as the sort variable indicates a positive and statistically significant relation between $CoSkew^{1M}$ and future stock returns. The average return of the $CoSkew^{1M}$ 10-1 portfolio is 0.17% per month (t-statistic = 1.89), and the FFC and FFCPS alphas are 0.23% per month (t-statistic = 2.52) and 0.25% per month (t-statistic = 2.50). Thus, while the average return and alphas of this portfolio are at least marginally statistically significant, the magnitudes of these values are actually quite small. Furthermore, the results indicate a strong inverse-U-shaped pattern in the portfolio excess returns. The average monthly excess return for the $CoSkew^{1M}$ decile one portfolio is 0.53% per month. The excess returns increase to 0.85% per month for the decile three portfolio and then decrease nearly monotonically (the exception is decile portfolio seven) to 0.70% per month for $CoSkew^{1M}$ portfolio 10. In fact, while the first $CoSkew^{1M}$ decile portfolio generates the lowest average return of any of the $CoSkew^{1M}$ decile portfolios, the 10th decile portfolio generates the second lowest average return. Overall, the evidence from this portfolio analysis combined with the fact that a positive relation is contrary to theoretical predictions makes us question whether the statistical significance of the average return and alphas of the $CoSkew^{1M}$ 10-1 portfolio is truly indicative of a cross-sectional pattern related to the pricing of co-skewness. The average returns and alphas of the 10-1 portfolios formed by sorting on $CoSkew^{3M}$, $CoSkew^{6M}$, and $CoSkew^{12M}$ are all statistically indistinguishable from zero.

The equal-weighted portfolio analyses using the measures of co-skewness calculated from monthly return data all indicate a negative, and in some cases statistically significant, relation between co-skewness and expected stock returns. When the portfolios are formed by sorting on $CoSkew^{1Y}$, the average returns and alphas of the difference portfolio, while negative, are not significant. For portfolios sorted on $Skew^{2Y}$, the average return produced by the difference portfolio of −0.23% per month (t-statistic = −1.44) is statistically insignificant, but the FFC alpha of −0.42% per month (t-statistic = −1.98) and FFCPS alpha of −0.48% per month (t-statistic = −2.24), are both substantially larger in magnitude and statistically significant. Furthermore, with the exception of deciles seven and eight, the average portfolio returns are monotonically decreasing across the deciles of $CoSkew^{2Y}$. Similar patterns emerge in the $CoSkew^{3Y}$- and $CoSkew^{5Y}$-sorted portfolios. The average monthly returns and alphas for the $CoSkew^{3Y}$- and $CoSkew^{5Y}$-sorted portfolio are all at least marginally statistically significant. As with the $CoSkew^{2Y}$-sorted portfolios, the alphas are substantially larger in magnitude than the average portfolio returns.

The results of the value-weighted portfolios using the different measures of co-skewness as the sort variable are shown in Panel B of Table 14.11. The results

TABLE 14.11 Univariate Portfolio Analysis—Co-Skewness

This table presents the results of univariate portfolio analyses of the relation between co-skewness and future stock returns. Monthly portfolios are formed by sorting all stocks in the CRSP sample into portfolios using decile breakpoints calculated based on the given sort variable using all stocks in the CRSP sample. Panel A (Panel B) shows the average equal-weighted (value-weighted) one-month-ahead excess return (in percent per month) for each of the 10 decile portfolios formed using different measures of co-skewness as the sort variable. The table also shows the average return of the portfolio that is long the 10th decile portfolio and short the first decile portfolio, as well as the FFC and FFCPS alphas for this portfolio. Newey and West (1987) t-statistics, adjusted using six lags, testing the null hypothesis that the average 10-1 portfolio return or alpha is equal to zero, are shown in parentheses.

Panel A: Equal-Weighted Portfolio

Sort Variable	1	2	3	4	5	6	7	8	9	10	10-1	FFC α	FFCPS α
$CoSkew^{1M}$	0.53	0.73	0.85	0.83	0.82	0.78	0.79	0.74	0.73	0.70	0.17	0.23	0.25
											(1.89)	(2.52)	(2.50)
$CoSkew^{3M}$	0.57	0.79	0.83	0.77	0.74	0.82	0.74	0.74	0.77	0.67	0.10	0.25	0.23
											(0.86)	(1.65)	(1.45)
$CoSkew^{6M}$	0.61	0.77	0.86	0.80	0.82	0.76	0.75	0.76	0.69	0.63	0.01	0.18	0.17
											(0.09)	(0.96)	(0.84)
$CoSkew^{12M}$	0.80	0.87	0.80	0.78	0.79	0.77	0.72	0.74	0.66	0.76	−0.04	0.11	0.14
											(−0.26)	(0.56)	(0.67)
$CoSkew^{1Y}$	0.80	0.81	0.81	0.82	0.78	0.83	0.78	0.80	0.72	0.58	−0.22	−0.30	−0.34
											(−1.31)	(−1.52)	(−1.63)
$CoSkew^{2Y}$	0.96	0.89	0.87	0.87	0.83	0.79	0.80	0.71	0.73	0.73	−0.23	−0.42	−0.48
											(−1.44)	(−1.98)	(−2.24)
$CoSkew^{3Y}$	1.01	0.93	0.86	0.87	0.87	0.81	0.80	0.73	0.76	0.72	−0.29	−0.40	−0.47
											(−1.97)	(−1.90)	(−2.18)
$CoSkew^{5Y}$	1.03	0.95	0.87	0.85	0.82	0.84	0.72	0.73	0.81	0.75	−0.28	−0.40	−0.48
											(−1.90)	(−1.92)	(−2.27)

Panel B: Value-Weighted Portfolios

Sort Variable	1	2	3	4	5	6	7	8	9	10	10-1	FFC α	FFCPS α
$CoSkew^{1M}$	0.31	0.53	0.60	0.51	0.53	0.40	0.47	0.46	0.44	0.24	−0.07	0.03	0.06
											(−0.41)	(0.22)	(0.39)
$CoSkew^{3M}$	0.07	0.58	0.49	0.54	0.51	0.50	0.51	0.45	0.49	0.35	0.28	0.61	0.69
											(1.41)	(2.73)	(2.89)
$CoSkew^{6M}$	0.13	0.50	0.49	0.50	0.49	0.64	0.48	0.52	0.43	0.28	0.15	0.63	0.72
											(0.64)	(2.66)	(2.82)
$CoSkew^{12M}$	0.41	0.65	0.51	0.52	0.55	0.52	0.51	0.51	0.34	0.31	−0.10	0.45	0.47
											(−0.41)	(2.00)	(1.79)
$CoSkew^{1Y}$	0.43	0.54	0.50	0.55	0.54	0.43	0.46	0.51	0.46	0.25	−0.17	−0.04	−0.02
											(−0.71)	(−0.19)	(−0.10)
$CoSkew^{2Y}$	0.63	0.54	0.64	0.66	0.55	0.53	0.58	0.41	0.34	0.50	−0.13	−0.13	−0.09
											(−0.69)	(−0.74)	(−0.44)
$CoSkew^{3Y}$	0.55	0.71	0.70	0.60	0.57	0.50	0.52	0.45	0.44	0.39	−0.16	−0.03	−0.03
											(−0.86)	(−0.16)	(−0.17)
$CoSkew^{5Y}$	0.51	0.63	0.68	0.53	0.58	0.52	0.47	0.48	0.43	0.48	−0.03	0.09	0.05
											(−0.16)	(0.55)	(0.27)

show that none of the co-skewness variables generate an average 10-1 portfolio return that is statistically distinguishable from zero. The FFC and FFCPS alphas for portfolios formed by sorting on $CoSkew^{3M}$, $CoSkew^{6M}$, and $CoSkew^{12M}$, however, are economically large and statistically significant. Examination of the average excess returns of the decile portfolios sorted on $CoSkew^{3M}$ provides no indication of a pattern in the average returns across the $CoSkew^{3M}$ deciles. In fact, once again the results show that while the first decile portfolio for each of these variables generates the lowest average return, the 10th decile portfolio generates the second lowest average return. For portfolios sorted on $CoSkew^{12M}$, the average return of the 10-1 portfolio is actually negative, with the 10th portfolio generating the lowest average return and the first decile portfolio generating the third-lowest average return. The results, therefore, are too weak to reach a theoretically contradictory conclusion of a positive relation between co-skewness and stock returns.

Idiosyncratic Skewness

We now repeat the univariate portfolio analyses using the measures of idiosyncratic skewness as the sort variables. The results, shown in Table 14.12, are very similar to the univariate portfolio analyses that use measures of total skewness as the sort variables (see Table 14.10). This is not surprising given the high levels of correlation between the measures of total skewness and idiosyncratic skewness (see Table 14.5).

The only equal-weighted portfolio analysis that detects a significant relation between idiosyncratic skewness and future stock returns is the analysis using $IdioSkew^{1M}$ as the sort variable. The $IdioSkew^{1M}$ 10-1 portfolio generates an average monthly return of -0.31% with a corresponding t-statistic of -2.44. Adjusting for risk using the FFC model does not explain this average return since the FFC (FFCPS) alpha for this portfolio of -0.39% (-0.37%) per month is once again highly statistically significant with a t-statistic of -2.36 (-2.19). For each of the other measures of idiosyncratic skewness, the average returns and alphas of the 10-1 portfolios are statistically indistinguishable from zero.[11]

The value-weighted portfolios formed by sorting on $IdioSkew^{1M}$ indicate a positive relation between idiosyncratic skewness and future stock returns since the difference portfolio produces an average return of 0.36% per month (t-statistic $= 3.60$), FFC alpha of 0.27% per month (t-statistic $= 2.76$), and FFCPS alpha of 0.30% per month (t-statistic $= 2.90$). This result is similar to what was observed in the portfolios formed by sorting on $Skew^{1M}$ (see Table 14.10). When sorting on $IdioSkew^{3M}$, the average 10-1 portfolio return of 0.32% per month (t-statistic $= 2.88$) is highly statistically significant, but the FFC alpha of 0.16% per month (t-statistic $= 1.40$) is small and insignificant and the FFCPS alpha of 0.20% per month (t-statistic $= 1.65$) is also small, albeit marginally statistically significant. Portfolios sorted on $IdioSkew^{6M}$ and $IdioSkew^{12M}$ also generate at least marginally statistically significant average difference portfolio returns of 0.23% per month (t-statistic $= 1.78$) and 0.29% per

---

[11] The only exceptions are the FFC and FFCPS alphas for the $IdioSkew^{3M}$ difference portfolio of -0.29% and -0.30% per month, which are marginally statistically significant with t-statistics of -1.75 and -1.72, respectively.

TABLE 14.12   Univariate Portfolio Analysis—Idiosyncratic Skewness
This table presents the results of univariate portfolio analyses of the relation between idiosyncratic skewness and future stock returns. Monthly portfolios are formed by sorting all stocks in the CRSP sample into portfolios using decile breakpoints calculated based on the given sort variable using all stocks in the CRSP sample. Panel A (Panel B) shows the average equal-weighted (value-weighted) one-month-ahead excess return (in percent per month) for each of the 10 decile portfolios formed using different measures of idiosyncratic skewness as the sort variable. The table also shows the average return of the portfolio that is long the 10th decile portfolio and short the first decile portfolio, as well as the FFC and FFCPS alphas for this portfolio. Newey and West (1987) t-statistics, adjusted using six lags, testing the null hypothesis that the average 10-1 portfolio return or alpha is equal to zero, are shown in parentheses.

Panel A: Equal-Weighted Portfolio

Sort Variable	1	2	3	4	5	6	7	8	9	10	10-1	FFC α	FFCPS α
$IdioSkew^{1M}$	0.80	0.92	0.86	0.85	0.78	0.78	0.79	0.67	0.53	0.49	−0.31	−0.39	−0.37
											(−2.44)	(−2.36)	(−2.19)
$IdioSkew^{3M}$	0.69	0.80	0.85	0.87	0.83	0.81	0.78	0.68	0.62	0.51	−0.18	−0.29	−0.30
											(−1.18)	(−1.75)	(−1.72)
$IdioSkew^{6M}$	0.58	0.70	0.87	0.83	0.82	0.83	0.82	0.78	0.62	0.59	0.01	−0.06	−0.05
											(0.10)	(−0.50)	(−0.34)
$IdioSkew^{12M}$	0.56	0.68	0.75	0.80	0.83	0.84	0.88	0.79	0.85	0.69	0.13	0.06	0.09
											(0.81)	(0.44)	(0.65)
$IdioSkew^{1Y}$	0.74	0.81	0.79	0.78	0.85	0.70	0.84	0.77	0.80	0.66	−0.09	−0.11	−0.11
											(−0.86)	(−1.30)	(−1.13)
$IdioSkew^{2Y}$	0.76	0.78	0.83	0.88	0.84	0.86	0.88	0.87	0.80	0.68	−0.07	−0.14	−0.18
											(−0.47)	(−0.90)	(−1.09)
$IdioSkew^{3Y}$	0.81	0.80	0.84	0.85	0.89	0.86	0.88	0.86	0.85	0.71	−0.11	−0.17	−0.21
											(−0.65)	(−0.98)	(−1.20)
$IdioSkew^{5Y}$	0.80	0.82	0.81	0.87	0.84	0.88	0.90	0.97	0.76	0.70	−0.10	−0.18	−0.24
											(−0.61)	(−1.14)	(−1.40)

Panel B: Value-Weighted Portfolios

Sort Variable	1	2	3	4	5	6	7	8	9	10	10-1	FFC α	FFCPS α
$IdioSkew^{1M}$	0.22	0.39	0.56	0.36	0.42	0.49	0.53	0.56	0.51	0.59	0.36	0.27	0.30
											(3.60)	(2.76)	(2.90)
$IdioSkew^{3M}$	0.29	0.34	0.48	0.49	0.61	0.49	0.57	0.53	0.51	0.62	0.32	0.16	0.20
											(2.88)	(1.40)	(1.65)
$IdioSkew^{6M}$	0.39	0.45	0.53	0.48	0.59	0.45	0.59	0.50	0.45	0.62	0.23	−0.01	0.00
											(1.78)	(−0.11)	(0.04)
$IdioSkew^{12M}$	0.33	0.49	0.54	0.52	0.51	0.55	0.58	0.56	0.66	0.62	0.29	0.06	0.09
											(2.18)	(0.51)	(0.66)
$IdioSkew^{1Y}$	0.48	0.44	0.49	0.44	0.58	0.45	0.52	0.50	0.42	0.40	−0.08	−0.16	−0.12
											(−0.68)	(−1.42)	(−0.94)
$IdioSkew^{2Y}$	0.53	0.53	0.42	0.48	0.47	0.44	0.45	0.49	0.48	0.38	−0.15	−0.34	−0.30
											(−1.14)	(−2.52)	(−2.09)
$IdioSkew^{3Y}$	0.51	0.46	0.48	0.48	0.53	0.49	0.51	0.54	0.50	0.32	−0.19	−0.53	−0.50
											(−1.22)	(−3.42)	(−3.18)
$IdioSkew^{5Y}$	0.43	0.48	0.55	0.50	0.53	0.43	0.55	0.46	0.39	0.26	−0.16	−0.57	−0.53
											(−0.97)	(−3.63)	(−3.17)

month (t-statistic $= 2.18$), respectively. The alphas of these portfolios relative to both the FFC and FFCPS risk models are small and insignificant, however, indicating that sensitivity to one or more of the four factors in the FFC model explains these returns.

When sorting on the measures of idiosyncratic skewness calculated from monthly return data ($IdioSkew^{1Y}$, $IdioSkew^{2Y}$, $IdioSkew^{3Y}$, and $IdioSkew^{5Y}$), the value-weighted portfolio analyses find that the average monthly returns of the 10-1 portfolios are negative, but small and statistically insignificant, ranging from -0.08% per month for portfolios sorted on $IdioSkew^{1Y}$ to -0.19% per month for $IdioSkew^{3Y}$-sorted portfolio. The abnormal returns of these portfolios, however, are all larger in magnitude than the average returns and, when idiosyncratic skewness is measured using more than one year of monthly return data, the alphas are statistically significant. The magnitudes of the alphas increase as the measurement period used to calculate idiosyncratic skewness is lengthened. The $IdioSkew^{5Y}$ 10-1 portfolio generates FFC alpha of -0.57% per month (t-statistic $= -3.63$) and FFCPS alpha of -0.53% per month (t-statistic $= -3.17$). When sorting on $IdioSkew^{5Y}$, while the 10th value-weighted decile portfolio generates the lowest average excess return of 0.26% per month of any of the $IdioSkew^{5Y}$-sorted decile portfolios, the first decile portfolio's return of 0.43% per month is tied for the third-lowest average excess return. This result raises concern about interpreting the negative alpha of the difference portfolio as being indicative of a skewness risk premium. From this perspective, the value-weighted portfolio results that use monthly return-based measures of idiosyncratic skewness as the sort variables are strongest when sorting on $IdioSkew^{2Y}$ since the first decile portfolio in this analysis generates the highest average excess return and the 10th decile portfolio generates the lowest average excess return. The average portfolio returns, however, are not nearly monotonic across the deciles of $IdioSkew^{2M}$. Overall, the results do not provide a convincing evidence of a strong relation between idiosyncratic skewness and expected stock returns. Further analysis is definitely warranted.

In summary, the results of the univariate portfolio analyses presented in Section 13.5.1 are difficult to interpret. In some cases, the results of the equal-weighted portfolio analyses are qualitatively the opposite of those generated by value-weighted portfolio analysis. Such results indicate that it is highly possible that one or more of the other variables known to be related to expected stock returns has a confounding effect on the relation between our measures of skewness and expected stock returns.

In previous chapters, we have performed bivariate sort analyses to examine the relation between the variable of interest and expected stock returns after controlling, one at a time, for the effects of each of the other variables known to be related to expected stock returns. Given the large number of skewness variables being examined in this chapter, we leave such analyses to the reader and proceed directly to Fama and MacBeth (1973) regression analyses of these relations. The Fama and MacBeth (1973) regression analyses allow us to control for all of the other known predictors of stock returns at once, instead of one at a time.

14.5.2   Fama–MacBeth Regressions

We continue our examination of the cross-sectional relation between skewness and future stock returns using (Fama and MacBeth 1973, FM hereafter) regression analysis. For each variable measuring skewness, we perform two FM regression analyses examining the relation of the given variable with future stock returns. The first analysis uses a univariate cross-sectional regression specification with only the given measure of skewness as an independent variable. The second analysis includes the given measure of skewness as well as β, $Size$, BM, Mom, Rev, and $Illiq$ as independent variables in the monthly cross-sectional regressions. Therefore, the full regression specification is

$$r_{i,t+1} = \delta_{0,t} + \delta_{1,t}X_{i,t} + \delta_{2,t}\beta_{i,t} + \delta_{3,t}Size_{i,t} + \delta_{4,t}BM_{i,t}$$
$$+\delta_{5,t}Mom_{i,t} + \delta_{6,t}Rev_{i,t} + \delta_{7,t}Illiq_{i,t} + \epsilon_{i,t} \qquad (14.5)$$

where $r_{i,t+1}$ is the excess return of stock i in month $t + 1$ and $X_{i,t}$ is one of the measures of skewness. All of the independent variables are winsorized at the 0.5% level on a monthly basis. Tables showing results of the FM regression analyses present the time-series averages of the monthly cross-sectional regression coefficients along with t-statistics, adjusted following Newey and West (1987) using six lags, testing the null hypothesis that the average coefficient is equal to zero.

Total Skewness

The results of the FM regression analyses examining the relation between total skewness and expected stock returns are shown in Table 14.13. Using univariate specifications, Panel A shows that FM regression analysis detects a strong negative relation between $Skew^{1M}$ and future stock returns since the average coefficient of -0.150 is highly statistically significant with a t-statistic of -4.08. When using $Skew^{3M}$ as the measure of total skewness, the average coefficient of -0.077 is also statistically significant with a t-statistic of -2.01. None of the other measures of total stock return skewness exhibit any relation with one-month-ahead excess stock returns since in all other univariate specifications, the average coefficient on the variable measuring total skewness is statistically indistinguishable from zero. These results are very similar to the results of the equal-weighted univariate portfolio analyses (see Panel A of Table 14.10), which found a statistically significant negative relation between each of $Skew^{1M}$ and $Skew^{3M}$ and future stock returns, but no relation between any other measure of total skewness and future stock returns.

Panel B of Table 14.13 shows that the results of the FM regressions of total skewness on future stock returns that include the full set of control variables in the regression specification lead to substantially different conclusions. After controlling for the relations between future stock returns and each β, $Size$, BM, Mom, Rev, and $Illiq$, the negative relation between $Skew^{1M}$ and future stock excess returns is no longer detected since the average coefficient on $Skew^{1M}$ of 0.034 is positive and statistically insignificant. The same can be said about the relation between $Skew^{3M}$.

When controlling for other effects, the average coefficient of -0.015 is much smaller than the coefficient from the univariate specification (-0.077) and statistically insignificant, with a t-statistic of -0.60.

The results using each of the other measures of total return skewness, however, indicate strong negative relations between total skewness and expected stock returns. For the daily return-based measures of total skewness, the results find an average coefficient of -0.061 (t-statistic $= -2.24$) on $Skew^{6M}$ and an average coefficient of -0.104 (t-statistic $= -3.82$) on $Skew^{12M}$. When using the monthly return-based measures of total skewness, the average coefficients of -0.145 (t-statistic $= -4.46$) for $Skew^{1Y}$, -0.162 (t-statistic $= -4.58$) for $Skew^{2Y}$, -0.168 (t-statistic $= -4.66$) for $Skew^{3Y}$, and -0.175 (t-statistic $= -4.93$) for $Skew^{5Y}$ are all negative and very highly statistically significant. Furthermore, in both the cases of the daily and monthly

TABLE 14.13   Fama–MacBeth Regression Analysis—*Skew*
This table presents the results of Fama and MacBeth (1973) regression analyses of the relation between expected stock returns and total skewness. Each column in the table presents results for a different cross-sectional regression specification. The dependent variable in all specifications is the one-month-ahead excess stock return. The independent variables are indicated in the first column. Independent variables are winsorized at the 0.5% level on a monthly basis. The table presents average slope and intercept coefficients along with t-statistics (in parentheses), adjusted following Newey and West (1987) using six lags, testing the null hypothesis that the average coefficient is equal to zero. The rows labeled Adj. R^2 and n present the average adjusted R-squared and the number of data points, respectively, for the cross-sectional regressions. Results from univariate (multivariate) specifications are shown in Panel A (Panel B).

	Panel A: Univariate Regressions							
	(1)	(2)	(3)	(4)	(5)	(6)	(7)	(8)
$Skew^{1M}$	-0.150							
	(-4.08)							
$Skew^{3M}$		-0.077						
		(-2.01)						
$Skew^{6M}$			-0.040					
			(-1.06)					
$Skew^{12M}$				0.002				
				(0.06)				
$Skew^{1Y}$					-0.075			
					(-1.30)			
$Skew^{2Y}$						-0.051		
						(-0.76)		
$Skew^{3Y}$							-0.054	
							(-0.76)	
$Skew^{5Y}$								-0.041
								(-0.58)
Intercept	0.778	0.760	0.748	0.747	0.781	0.821	0.841	0.848
	(2.65)	(2.64)	(2.63)	(2.66)	(2.76)	(3.00)	(3.13)	(3.21)
Adj. R^2	0.00	0.00	0.00	0.00	0.00	0.00	0.00	0.01
n	4694	4675	4597	4426	4409	4058	3935	3948

(continued)

TABLE 14.13 *(Continued)*

				Panel B: Multivariate Regressions				
	(1)	(2)	(3)	(4)	(5)	(6)	(7)	(8)
$Skew^{1M}$	0.034							
	(1.27)							
$Skew^{3M}$		−0.015						
		(−0.60)						
$Skew^{6M}$			−0.061					
			(−2.24)					
$Skew^{12M}$				−0.104				
				(−3.82)				
$Skew^{1Y}$					−0.145			
					(−4.46)			
$Skew^{2Y}$						−0.162		
						(−4.58)		
$Skew^{3Y}$							−0.168	
							(−4.66)	
$Skew^{5Y}$								−0.175
								(−4.93)
β	−0.173	−0.172	−0.173	−0.174	−0.180	−0.148	−0.132	−0.128
	(−1.07)	(−1.06)	(−1.06)	(−1.07)	(−1.11)	(−0.93)	(−0.84)	(−0.81)
Size	−0.073	−0.075	−0.079	−0.087	−0.084	−0.098	−0.102	−0.107
	(−1.34)	(−1.40)	(−1.49)	(−1.63)	(−1.59)	(−1.88)	(−1.97)	(−2.06)
BM	0.219	0.219	0.223	0.225	0.220	0.193	0.188	0.181
	(2.96)	(2.96)	(3.00)	(3.05)	(2.97)	(2.66)	(2.59)	(2.51)
Mom	0.008	0.008	0.008	0.009	0.009	0.008	0.008	0.008
	(4.11)	(4.12)	(4.16)	(4.30)	(4.26)	(4.10)	(4.09)	(4.14)
Rev	−0.062	−0.061	−0.060	−0.060	−0.060	−0.062	−0.062	−0.062
	(−11.87)	(−11.82)	(−11.76)	(−11.64)	(−11.77)	(−11.87)	(−12.05)	(−12.03)
Illiq	0.055	0.055	0.055	0.056	0.055	0.047	0.049	0.050
	(3.11)	(3.07)	(3.08)	(3.12)	(3.13)	(2.56)	(2.68)	(2.72)
Intercept	0.849	0.866	0.907	0.965	0.945	1.067	1.105	1.154
	(1.95)	(2.01)	(2.10)	(2.24)	(2.20)	(2.53)	(2.64)	(2.75)
Adj. R^2	0.06	0.06	0.06	0.06	0.06	0.06	0.06	0.06
n	2723	2723	2723	2723	2723	2618	2559	2561

measures, the average coefficients and t-statistics become more negative as the length of the measurement period used to calculate the total skewness variable gets longer. This is consistent with the results of the correlation and persistence analyses that indicated that longer calculation periods resulted in more accurate measurement of total skewness. Overall, the results provide strong evidence that, after controlling for several other variables that are known to be related to expected stock returns, total skewness has the theoretically predicted negative relation with expected returns. The fact that this relation is evident only after controlling for several other characteristics indicates that the effect of total skewness on expected returns is likely not as strong as that of other variables, which makes univariate analysis of the relation between total skewness and expected stock returns very noisy.

To examine the magnitude of the relation between total skewness and expected stock returns, we take the average coefficients from the full-specification FM regression analyses using each of $Skew^{12M}$ and $Skew^{5Y}$ of -0.104 and -0.175, respectively. Multiplying the average coefficient on $Skew^{12M}$ by the standard deviation of the cross-sectional distribution of $Skew^{12M}$ of 1.33 (see Panel A of Table 14.1), we find that a one-standard-deviation difference in $Skew^{12M}$ is associated with an expected return difference of 0.14% (0.104×1.33) per month. We calculate the difference in expected returns between stocks in the 95th and fifth percentiles of $Skew^{12M}$ by multiplying the average coefficient of -0.104 by the difference between the 95th percentile and fifth percentile values of $Skew^{12M}$ of 2.63 and 0.09, respectively. Doing so, we find that the difference in expected returns between two such stocks is 0.36% per month ($0.104 \times [2.63 - (-0.80)]$). Repeating these exercises using $Skew^{5Y}$, we find that a one-standard-deviation difference in $Skew^{5Y}$ is associated with a difference of 0.15% (0.175×0.87) per month in expected stock returns. The difference in expected returns between stocks at the 95th percentile of $Skew^{5Y}$ ($Skew^{5Y} = 2.27$) and the fifth percentile of $Skew^{5Y}$ ($Skew^{5Y} = -0.41$) is -0.47% ($0.175 \times [2.27 - (-0.41)]$). The results indicate that the economic importance of the effect of skewness on stock returns is, as expected, smaller than other previously documented effects. That being said, this effect is not negligible, especially for stocks with extreme high or low total skewness.

The FM regression analyses also demonstrate that the previously documented relations between other variables and expected stock returns are not manifestations of the relation between total skewness and expected stock returns. Regardless of specification, the average coefficient on β is negative and statistically insignificant. The coefficient on $Size$ is negative and, when using $Skew^{2Y}$, $Skew^{3Y}$, or $Skew^{5Y}$ as the measure of total skewness, at least marginally statistically significant. BM, Mom, and $Illiq$ exhibit a strong positive relations with expected stock after controlling for total skewness. The negative relation between Rev and future stock returns persists when total skewness is included in the regression specification.

Co-Skewness

Table 14.14 presents the results of univariate (Panel A) and multivariate (Panel B) FM regression analyses of the relation between co-skewness and expected stock returns. The univariate regression analyses using daily return-based measures of co-skewness provide no indication of a relation between co-skewness and expected returns. The average slopes of -0.000 (t-statistic $= -0.21$) on $CoSkew^{1M}$, 0.002 (t-statistic $= 0.97$) on $CoSkew^{3M}$, -0.002 (t-statistic $= -0.49$) on $CoSkew^{6M}$, and -0.006 (t-statistic $= -1.02$) on $CoSkew^{12M}$ are all statistically indistinguishable from zero. Similarly, when using the measure of co-skewness calculated from one year of monthly return data ($CoSkew^{1Y}$), the FM regression analysis fails to detect a relation between co-skewness and expected stock returns since the average coefficient on $CoSkew^{1Y}$ of -0.005 is statistically insignificant with a t-statistic of -1.44. When co-skewness is calculated from two, three, or five years worth of monthly return data, however, the results provide some evidence of a negative relation between co-skewness and expected stock returns. The average coefficients of -0.010 (t-statistic $= -1.84$) on $CoSkew^{2Y}$, -0.010 (t-statistic $= -1.71$) on $CoSkew^{3Y}$, and -0.012 (t-statistic $= -1.80$) on $CoSkew^{5Y}$ are all marginally statistically significant.

As would be expected, the results of the univariate FM regression analyses are quite similar to those of the univariate equal-weighted portfolio analyses (see Panel A of Table 14.11). The one exception is the analysis of the relation between $CoSkew^{1M}$ and expected stock returns where the equal-weighted portfolio analysis indicated that the 10-1 portfolio generated a marginally statistically significant average monthly return. As discussed previously, however, the pattern in the average returns across the decile portfolios in this analysis cast some doubt upon the robustness in the portfolio analysis result. Our skepticism is confirmed by the FM regression analysis that detect no relation between $CoSkew^{1M}$ and future stock returns. The negative and marginally statistically significant relations between one-month-ahead excess returns and each of $CoSkew^{3Y}$ and $CoSkew^{5Y}$ detected by the FM regression analyses are highly consistent with the corresponding univariate portfolio analyses.

TABLE 14.14   Fama–MacBeth Regression Analysis—*CoSkew*

This table presents the results of Fama and MacBeth (1973) regression analyses of the relation between expected stock returns and co-skewness. Each column in the table presents results for a different cross-sectional regression specification. The dependent variable in all specifications is the one-month-ahead excess stock return. The independent variables are indicated in the first column. Independent variables are winsorized at the 0.5% level on a monthly basis. The table presents average slope and intercept coefficients along with t-statistics (in parentheses), adjusted following Newey and West (1987) using six lags, testing the null hypothesis that the average coefficient is equal to zero. The rows labeled Adj. R^2 and n present the average adjusted R-squared and the number of data points, respectively, for the cross-sectional regressions. Results from univariate (multivariate) specifications are shown in Panel A (Panel B).

			Panel A: Univariate Regressions					
	(1)	(2)	(3)	(4)	(5)	(6)	(7)	(8)
$CoSkew^{1M}$	−0.000							
	(−0.21)							
$CoSkew^{3M}$		0.002						
		(0.97)						
$CoSkew^{6M}$			−0.002					
			(−0.49)					
$CoSkew^{12M}$				−0.006				
				(−1.02)				
$CoSkew^{1Y}$					−0.005			
					(−1.44)			
$CoSkew^{2Y}$						−0.010		
						(−1.84)		
$CoSkew^{3Y}$							−0.010	
							(−1.71)	
$CoSkew^{5Y}$								−0.012
								(−1.80)
Intercept	0.751	0.747	0.746	0.744	0.753	0.793	0.812	0.821
	(2.54)	(2.54)	(2.57)	(2.62)	(2.61)	(2.79)	(2.87)	(2.90)
Adj. R^2	0.00	0.00	0.00	0.00	0.00	0.00	0.00	0.00
n	4732	4686	4599	4426	4410	4058	3935	3948

TABLE 14.14 (*Continued*)

	(1)	(2)	(3)	(4)	(5)	(6)	(7)	(8)
				Panel B: Multivariate Regressions				
$CoSkew^{1M}$	0.001							
	(1.15)							
$CoSkew^{3M}$		0.002						
		(0.97)						
$CoSkew^{6M}$			0.000					
			(0.09)					
$CoSkew^{12M}$				−0.001				
				(−0.27)				
$CoSkew^{1Y}$					−0.002			
					(−0.88)			
$CoSkew^{2Y}$						0.000		
						(0.01)		
$CoSkew^{3Y}$							0.002	
							(0.41)	
$CoSkew^{5Y}$								0.002
								(0.45)
β	−0.180	−0.176	−0.180	−0.176	−0.183	−0.150	−0.140	−0.139
	(−1.10)	(−1.08)	(−1.09)	(−1.07)	(−1.12)	(−0.93)	(−0.87)	(−0.86)
Size	−0.075	−0.074	−0.076	−0.076	−0.072	−0.078	−0.079	−0.080
	(−1.37)	(−1.37)	(−1.41)	(−1.44)	(−1.33)	(−1.45)	(−1.46)	(−1.48)
BM	0.219	0.219	0.218	0.214	0.219	0.190	0.186	0.183
	(2.94)	(2.96)	(2.95)	(2.91)	(2.96)	(2.65)	(2.57)	(2.51)
Mom	0.008	0.008	0.008	0.008	0.008	0.008	0.008	0.008
	(4.08)	(4.08)	(4.20)	(4.20)	(4.06)	(3.87)	(3.92)	(3.87)
Rev	−0.061	−0.061	−0.061	−0.061	−0.061	−0.062	−0.062	−0.062
	(−11.83)	(−11.82)	(−11.83)	(−11.83)	(−11.16)	(−11.64)	(−11.79)	(−11.83)
Illiq	0.055	0.054	0.054	0.054	0.056	0.048	0.051	0.051
	(3.13)	(3.07)	(3.07)	(3.04)	(3.13)	(2.58)	(2.83)	(2.81)
Intercept	0.875	0.872	0.887	0.885	0.854	0.925	0.942	0.958
	(2.00)	(1.99)	(2.05)	(2.07)	(1.96)	(2.14)	(2.19)	(2.22)
Adj. R^2	0.06	0.06	0.06	0.06	0.06	0.06	0.06	0.06
n	2723	2723	2723	2723	2723	2618	2559	2561

Panel B of Table 14.14 presents the results of the FM regression analyses that control for the effects of other variables. The results demonstrate that after controlling for β, *Size*, *BM*, *Mom*, *Rev*, and *Illiq*, none of the co-skewness variables exhibit a cross-sectional relation with expected stock returns. The average coefficient on co-skewness in each analysis is small and statistically insignificant regardless of which measure of co-skewness is used. The results indicate that the marginally statistically significant relations detected in the univariate portfolio analyses are explained by the other variables since the coefficients on $CoSkew^{2Y}$, $CoSkew^{3Y}$, and $CoSkew^{5Y}$ decrease substantially in both magnitude and statistical significance when using the multivariate specifications. The results of the FM regressions, therefore, fail to provide any indication of a relation between co-skewness and expected stock returns. Furthermore, they demonstrate that the weak results realized in the univariate equal-weighted portfolio analyses and FM regression analyses are driven by cross-sectional relations between co-skewness and other variables known to be related to expected stock returns. Finally, the FM regressions show that, after controlling for co-skewness, the relations between expected stock returns and each of β, *Size*, *BM*, *Mom*, *Rev*, and *Illiq* are similar to those documented in previous chapters of this book.

Idiosyncratic Skewness

The results of the FM regression analyses examining the relation between idiosyncratic skewness and expected stock returns, presented in Table 14.15, are very similar to the results of the FM regressions examining the relation between total skewness and expected stock returns (see Table 14.13). This is to be expected given the high correlations between idiosyncratic skewness and total skewness (see Table 14.5).

TABLE 14.15 Fama–MacBeth Regression Analysis—*IdioSkew*

This table presents the results of Fama and MacBeth (1973) regression analyses of the relation between expected stock returns and idiosyncratic skewness. Each column in the table presents results for a different cross-sectional regression specification. The dependent variable in all specifications is the one-month-ahead excess stock return. The independent variables are indicated in the first column. Independent variables are winsorized at the 0.5% level on a monthly basis. The table presents average slope and intercept coefficients along with *t*-statistics (in parentheses), adjusted following Newey and West (1987) using six lags, testing the null hypothesis that the average coefficient is equal to zero. The rows labeled Adj. R^2 and *n* present the average adjusted R-squared and the number of data points, respectively, for the cross-sectional regressions. Results from univariate (multivariate) specifications are shown in Panel A (Panel B).

	Panel A: Univariate Regressions							
	(1)	(2)	(3)	(4)	(5)	(6)	(7)	(8)
$IdioSkew^{1M}$	−0.117							
	(−3.02)							
$IdioSkew^{3M}$		−0.048						
		(−1.28)						
$IdioSkew^{6M}$			−0.013					
			(−0.36)					
$IdioSkew^{12M}$				0.024				
				(0.62)				
$IdioSkew^{1Y}$					−0.029			
					(−0.69)			
$IdioSkew^{2Y}$						−0.017		
						(−0.29)		
$IdioSkew^{3Y}$							−0.038	
							(−0.61)	
$IdioSkew^{5Y}$								−0.032
								(−0.51)
Intercept	0.766	0.750	0.737	0.738	0.776	0.821	0.847	0.853
	(2.60)	(2.59)	(2.58)	(2.62)	(2.69)	(2.96)	(3.12)	(3.20)
Adj. R^2	0.00	0.00	0.00	0.00	0.00	0.00	0.00	0.00
n	4732	4686	4599	4426	4410	4058	3935	3948

TABLE 14.15   *(Continued)*

	Panel B: Multivariate Regressions							
	(1)	(2)	(3)	(4)	(5)	(6)	(7)	(8)
$IdioSkew^{1M}$	0.076							
	(2.79)							
$IdioSkew^{3M}$		0.023						
		(0.87)						
$IdioSkew^{6M}$			−0.031					
			(−1.16)					
$IdioSkew^{12M}$				−0.080				
				(−3.06)				
$IdioSkew^{1Y}$					−0.095			
					(−3.42)			
$IdioSkew^{2Y}$						−0.145		
						(−4.90)		
$IdioSkew^{3Y}$							−0.167	
							(−5.18)	
$IdioSkew^{5Y}$								−0.163
								(−4.88)
β	−0.184	−0.178	−0.177	−0.175	−0.181	−0.150	−0.137	−0.133
	(−1.13)	(−1.10)	(−1.09)	(−1.08)	(−1.11)	(−0.93)	(−0.86)	(−0.83)
Size	−0.071	−0.072	−0.077	−0.083	−0.078	−0.093	−0.098	−0.101
	(−1.32)	(−1.35)	(−1.45)	(−1.56)	(−1.44)	(−1.75)	(−1.84)	(−1.91)
BM	0.221	0.219	0.222	0.225	0.221	0.193	0.186	0.181
	(2.97)	(2.96)	(2.99)	(3.04)	(2.97)	(2.66)	(2.56)	(2.49)
Mom	0.008	0.008	0.008	0.009	0.008	0.008	0.008	0.008
	(4.11)	(4.08)	(4.12)	(4.25)	(4.17)	(4.06)	(4.04)	(4.06)
Rev	−0.062	−0.061	−0.061	−0.061	−0.061	−0.062	−0.062	−0.062
	(−11.99)	(−11.86)	(−11.75)	(−11.63)	(−11.76)	(−11.80)	(−11.99)	(−11.98)
Illiq	0.054	0.055	0.055	0.056	0.055	0.047	0.050	0.049
	(3.09)	(3.06)	(3.08)	(3.11)	(3.12)	(2.58)	(2.69)	(2.66)
Intercept	0.840	0.850	0.892	0.945	0.897	1.041	1.091	1.125
	(1.92)	(1.97)	(2.06)	(2.18)	(2.06)	(2.43)	(2.55)	(2.64)
Adj. R^2	0.06	0.06	0.06	0.06	0.06	0.06	0.06	0.06
n	2723	2723	2723	2723	2723	2618	2559	2561

When using the univariate specifications (Panel A), the only idiosyncratic skewness variable for which a relation with future returns is detected is the measure calculated from one month of daily return data, $IdioSkew^{1M}$, for which the average coefficient of −0.117 is negative and statistically significant, with a t-statistic of −3.02. These results are similar to those of the univariate FM regression analyses using the total skewness variables, which produced statistically significant average slopes on only $Skew^{1M}$ and $Skew^{3M}$. Unlike the total skewness measures, however, when idiosyncratic skewness is measured using three months of daily returns ($IdioSkew^{3M}$), the average coefficient of −0.048 is statistically indistinguishable from zero with a t-statistic of −1.28.

The results of the FM regressions using the multivariate specifications, presented in Panel B of Table 14.12, are very different than the univariate FM regression results.

When using $IdioSkew^{1M}$ as the measure of idiosyncratic skewness, the results actually indicate a strong positive relation between idiosyncratic skewness and expected stock returns after controlling for the effects of each of the other variables. The average slope on $IdioSkew^{1M}$ of 0.076 is highly statistically significant with a t-statistic of 2.79. This result is actually similar to the result generated by the value-weighted univariate portfolio analysis examining the relation between $IdioSkew^{1M}$ and future stock returns, which found that the $IdioSkew^{1M}$ 10-1 portfolio generated positive and statistically significant average monthly returns. This strong positive coefficient is inconsistent with theoretical predictions.

When using idiosyncratic skewness measures from either three months ($IdioSkew^{3M}$) or six months ($IdioSkew^{6M}$) worth of daily return data, the multivariate FM regression analyses find no relation between idiosyncratic skewness and expected stock returns. The average coefficients of 0.023 (t-statistic = 0.87) on $IdioSkew^{3M}$ and -0.031 (t-statistic = -1.16) on $IdioSkew^{6M}$ are both statistically insignificant. The latter result differs somewhat from the multivariate FM regression results for $Skew^{6M}$, which detected a significantly negative relation between $Skew^{6M}$ and future stock returns (see Panel B of Table 14.13).

When using idiosyncratic skewness measured from 12 months of daily return data ($IdioSkew^{12M}$) or any of the monthly return-based measures of idiosyncratic skewness ($IdioSkew^{1Y}$, $IdioSkew^{2Y}$, $IdioSkew^{3Y}$, and $IdioSkew^{5Y}$), the results indicate a negative and statistically significant relation between idiosyncratic skewness and expected stock returns. The regressions using $IdioSkew^{12M}$ as the measure of idiosyncratic skewness generate an average coefficient of -0.080 with a t-statistic of -3.06. When using the monthly return-based measures of idiosyncratic skewness, the result is strongest when using measures of idiosyncratic skewness calculated from three or five years worth of data. The FM regression analysis using $IdioSkew^{5Y}$ to measure idiosyncratic skewness produces an average slope on $IdioSkew^{5Y}$ of -0.163 with a corresponding t-statistic of -4.88.

As with the previous multivariate regressions presented in this chapter, including idiosyncratic skewness, in the regression specification has little effect on the coefficients on the other variables. The average coefficient on β remains negative and statistically insignificant. $Size$ has a negative and, depending the measure of idiosyncratic volatility, either insignificant or marginally significant average slope. BM, Mom, and $Illiq$ each have positive and highly statistically significant average coefficients, and the average coefficient on Rev is negative and highly statistically significant.

We now examine the economic magnitudes of the relations between the idiosyncratic skewness variables and expected stock returns. We begin this analysis by using $IdioSkew^{1M}$ as the measure of idiosyncratic skewness. This is the only skewness variable for which the multivariate FM regression analysis produced a positive and statistically significant average coefficient. Given that the persistence analyses failed to find any evidence that $IdioSkew^{1M}$ captured a persistent characteristic of the stock's returns, we are somewhat skeptical that this result is truly indicative of a relation between skewness and expected stock returns. Nonetheless, we proceed with the analysis. Multiplying the average coefficient of 0.076 by the average cross-sectional standard deviation of $IdioSkew^{1M}$ of 0.91, we find that the results imply that a one-standard-deviation difference in $IdioSkew^{1M}$ is associated with a difference in expected returns of 0.07% (0.076×0.91) per month. Multiplying the average coefficient by the difference in the average 95th percentile $IdioSkew^{1M}$ value of 1.74 and the fifth percentile value of -1.27, we find that the difference in expected returns between stocks with very high and very low values of $IdioSkew^{1M}$ is 0.23% ($0.076 \times [1.74 - (-1.27)]$) per month, which while not very large, is also not trivial.

Applying similar analyses to $IdioSkew^{12M}$, we multiply the average coefficient of -0.080 on $IdioSkew^{12M}$ with the average standard deviation $IdioSkew^{12M}$ of 1.36. The result indicates that a one-standard-deviation difference in $IdioSkew^{12M}$ corresponds to a 0.11% (0.080×1.33) difference in expected monthly returns. Multiplying the average coefficient by the difference between the 95th percentile (2.72) and fifth percentile (-0.88) values of $IdioSkew^{12M}$ indicates that the difference in expected returns between stocks with very high and very low values of $IdioSkew^{12M}$ is 0.29% ($0.080 \times [2.72 - (-0.88)]$) per month.

Finally, we multiply the average coefficient on $IdioSkew^{5Y}$ of -0.163 by the standard deviation of $IdioSkew^{5Y}$ in the average month of 0.81 and find that a one-standard-deviation difference in $IdioSkew^{5Y}$ results in an expected return difference of 0.13% (0.163×0.81). The difference in expected returns between stocks with high (95th percentile value of 2.13) and low (fifth percentile value of -0.37) values of $IdioSkew^{5Y}$ is -0.41% ($0.163 \times [2.13 - (-0.37)]$). This value, while once again not huge given that it represents the difference in expected returns for stocks with extremely high and low values of $IdioSkew^{5Y}$, is certainly economically important.

14.6 SUMMARY

In this chapter, we have outlined the theoretical predictions regarding the relation between skewness and expected security returns. We then provide an extended empirical analysis of measures of total skewness, co-skewness, and idiosyncratic skewness. The results indicate that skewness is an extremely difficult property of a stock to measure since most of the measures fail to exhibit substantial persistence. The evidence indicates that total and idiosyncratic skewness are more accurately measured using long estimation periods, and that monthly return-based measures tend to capture skewness better than daily return-based measures. Measurement of co-skewness is a challenge regardless of the length of the measurement period or the frequency of the data.

Portfolio and Fama and MacBeth (1973) regression analyses provide mixed results regarding relations between the measures of skewness and future stock returns, with the results being highly dependent on the parameters of the empirical analysis, such as whether equal-weighted or value-weighted portfolios are used, as well as whether univariate or multivariate regression specifications are used. FM regression analyses that control for the other effects documented in previous chapters of this book tend to find a negative relation between expected stock returns and each of total skewness and idiosyncratic skewness. Similar regressions examining the relation between co-skewness and expected stock returns find no evidence of such a relation.

Because both Harvey and Siddique (2000) and Boyer, Mitton, and Vorkink (2010) use measures of co-skewness and idiosyncratic skewness, respectively, calculated from five years worth of monthly return data, for the remainder of this book, we use $CoSkew^{5Y}$ as our primary measure of co-skewness and $IdioSkew^{5Y}$ as our primary measure of idiosyncratic skewness.[12] Going forward, for simplicity, we denote these variables $CoSkew$ and $IdioSkew$, respectively.

REFERENCES

Amaya, D., Christoffersen, P., Jacobs, K., and Vasquez, A. 2015. Does realized skewness predict the cross-section of equity returns? Journal of Financial Economics, forthcoming.

An, B.-J., Ang, A., Bali, T. G., and Cakici, N. 2014. The joint cross section of stocks and options. Journal of Finance, 69(5), 2279–2337.

Arditti, F. D. 1967. Risk and the required return on equity. Journal of Finance, 22(1), 19–36.

Arditti, F. D. 1971. Another look at mutual fund performance. Journal of Financial and Quantitative Analysis, 6(3), 909–912.

Bakshi, G. and Kapadia, N. 2003. Delta-hedged gains and the negative volatility risk premium. Review of Financial Studies, 16(2), 527–566.

Bali, T. G., Cakici, N., and Whitelaw, R. F. 2011. Maxing out: stocks as lotteries and the cross-section of expected returns. Journal of Financial Economics, 99(2), 427–446.

Bali, T. G. and Hovakimian, A. 2009. Volatility spreads and expected stock returns. Management Science, 55(11), 1797–1812.

Bali, T. G. and Murray, S. 2013. Does risk-neutral skewness predict the cross-section of equity option portfolio returns? Journal of Financial and Quantitative Analysis, 48(4), 1145–1171.

Barberis, N. and Huang, M. 2008. Stocks as lotteries: the implications of probability weighting for security prices. American Economic Review, 98(5), 2066–2100.

Bollen, N. P. B. and Whaley, R. E. 2004. Does net buying pressure affect the shape of implied volatility functions. Journal of Finance, 59(2), 711–753.

Boyer, B., Mitton, T., and Vorkink, K. 2010. Expected idiosyncratic skewness. Review of Financial Studies, 23(1), 169–202.

Boyer, B. and Vorkink, K. 2014. Stock options as lotteries. Journal of Finance, 69(4), 1485–1527.

Carhart, M. M. 1997. On persistence in mutual fund performance. Journal of Finance, 52(1), 57–82.

Conine, T. E. and Tamarkin, M. J. 1981. On diversification given asymmetry in returns. Journal of Finance, 36(5), 1143–1155.

Conrad, J. S., Dittmar, R. F., and Ghysels, E. 2013. Ex ante skewness and expected stock returns. Journal of Finance, 68(1), 85–124.

Cremers, M. and Weinbaum, D. 2010. Deviations from put-call parity and stock return predictability. Journal of Financial Quantitative Analysis, 45(2), 335–367.

[12]Harvey and Siddique (2000) is the seminal paper on co-skewness. Boyer, Mitton, and Vorkink (2010) is a foundation paper on idiosyncratic skewness.

DeMiguel, V., Plyakha, Y., Uppal, R., and Vilkov, G. 2013. Improving portfolio selection using option-implied volatility and skewness. Journal of Financial and Quantitative Analysis, forthcoming.

Dittmar, R. F. 2002. Nonlinear pricing kernels, kurtosis preference, and evidence from the cross section of equity returns. Journal of Finance, 57(1), 369–403.

Fama, E. F. and French, K. R. 1992. The cross-section of expected stock returns. Journal of Finance, 47(2), 427–465.

Fama, E. F. and French, K. R. 1993. Common risk factors in the returns on stocks and bonds. Journal of Financial Economics, 33(1), 3–56.

Fama, E. F. and French, K. R. 1995. Size and book-to-market factors in earnings and returns. Journal of Finance, 50(1), 131–155.

Fama, E. F. and MacBeth, J. D. 1973. Risk, return, and equilibrium: empirical tests. Journal of Political Economy, 81(3), 607.

Friend, I. and Blume, M. 1970. Measurement of portfolio performance under uncertainty. American Economic Review, 60(4), 607–636.

Garleanu, N., Pedersen, L. H., and Poteshman, A. M. 2009. Demand-based option pricing. Review of Financial Studies, 22(10), 4259–4299.

Harvey, C. R. and Siddique, A. 2000. Conditional skewness in asset pricing tests. Journal of Finance, 55(3), 1263–1295.

Kane, A. 1982. Skewness preference and portfolio choice. Journal of Financial and Quantitative Analysis, 17(1), 15–25.

Kimball, M. S. 1993. Standard risk aversion. Econometrica, 61(3), 589–611.

Kraus, A. and Litzenberger, R. H. 1976. Skewness preference and the valuation of risk assets. Journal of Finance, 31(4), 1085–1100.

Lakonishok, J. and Shapiro, A. 1986. Systematic risk, total risk and size as determinants of stock market returns. Journal of Banking & Finance, 10(1), 115–132.

Lintner, J. 1965. Security prices, risk, and maximal gains from diversification. Journal of Finance, 20(4), 687–615.

Markowitz, H. 1952. Portfolio selection. Journal of Finance, 7(1), 77–91.

Mitton, T. and Vorkink, K. 2007. Equilibrium underdiversification and the preference for skewness. Review of Financial Studies, 20(4), 1255–1288.

Mossin, J. 1966. Equilibrium in a capital asset market. Econometrica, 34(4), 768–783.

Newey, W. K. and West, K. D. 1987. A simple, positive semi-definite, heteroskedasticity and autocorrelation consistent covariance matrix. Econometrica, 55(3), 703–708.

Pastor, L. and Stambaugh, R. F. 2003. Liquidity risk and expected stock returns. Journal of Political Economy, 111(3), 642–685.

Reinganum, M. R. 1981. A new empirical perspective of the CAPM. Journal of Quantitative and Empirical Finance, 16(4), 439–462.

Scott, R. C. and Horvath, P. A. 1980. On the direction of preference of moments of higher order than the variance. Journal of Finance, 35(4), 915–919.

Sharpe, W. F. 1964. Capital asset prices: a theory of market equilibrium under conditions of risk. Journal of Finance, 19(3), 425–442.

Simkowitz, M. A. and Beedles, W. L. 1978. Diversification in a three-moment world. Journal of Financial and Quantitative Analysis, 13(5), 927–941.

Tversky, A. and Kahneman, D. 1992. Advances in prospect theory: cumulative representation of uncertainty. Journal of Risk and Uncertainty, 5(4), 297–323.

Xing, Y., Zhang, X., and Zhao, R. 2010. What does the individual option volatility smirk tell us about future equity returns? Journal of Financial Quantitative Analysis, 45(3), 641–662.

15

IDIOSYNCRATIC VOLATILITY

According to many asset pricing models, including the Capital Asset Pricing Model (CAPM, Sharpe (1964), Lintner (1965), Mossin (1966)) and arbitrage pricing theory (APT, Ross (1976)), investors can create portfolios that have zero exposure to firm-specific risk by holding a well-diversified portfolio with a large number of securities. Firm-specific risk, therefore, does not command a risk premium. The empirical implication of this is that measures of firm-specific risk, or risk that is not related to a systematic factor, should exhibit no relation with future stock returns. The CAPM and APT are based on the assumption of perfect markets. Specifically, these theories assume that all assets are perfectly liquid (frictionless) and that all investors have complete information.[1,2]

Pointing to evidence that the assumptions underlying the CAPM and APT may be too restrictive to adequately explain investor behavior, Levy (1978) and Merton (1987) develop models of market equilibrium that relax these assumptions.[3] In Levy's model, each investor is constrained to hold at most a certain number of

---

[1]A perfectly liquid or frictionless market refers to a market in which there are no transaction costs, no taxes, and unconstrained borrowing and short-selling.
[2]The complete information assumption is that all investors have instantaneous access to all publicly available information and act on new information immediately upon its acquisition.
[3]Reasons given for the relaxation of these assumptions are the realities of transaction costs, costs of acquiring and processing information, the imperfect and noninstantaneous diffusion of information to all market participants, market segmentation, institutional restrictions, limits on borrowing and short-selling, taxation, and indivisibility of securities.

Empirical Asset Pricing: The Cross Section of Stock Returns, First Edition.
Turan G. Bali, Robert F. Engle, and Scott Murray.
© 2016 John Wiley & Sons, Inc. Published 2016 by John Wiley & Sons, Inc.

risky securities.[4] Merton's model is similar, but the restriction on the number of risky securities is explicitly said to arise from the fact that a given investor only has information about certain securities. The main implication of each of these models is that, in equilibrium, firm-specific risk is priced. Specifically, there is a positive risk premium associated with firm-specific risk.[5]

Empirically, the prediction of a positive relation between firm-specific risk and expected stock returns has received substantial attention. Early empirical studies by Friend, Westerfield, and Granito (1978), Levy (1978), Tinic and West (1986), and Lehmann (1990) find weak evidence of a positive cross-sectional relation between idiosyncratic volatility (the most commonly used measure of firm-specific risk) and stock returns, while the results in Fama and MacBeth (1973) provide no indication of such a relation. The samples and empirical techniques employed by these studies, however, indicate that these results may not be widely generalizable.

The most widely cited study of the cross-sectional relation between firm-specific risk and expected stock returns is Ang, Hodrick, Xing, and Zhang (2006), which finds a strong negative cross-sectional relation between idiosyncratic volatility and future stock returns. This result is highly inconsistent with the predictions of all theoretical models.[6] While Ang et al. demonstrate that a small portion of this relation can be explained by exposure to aggregate volatility risk, which is empirically shown to carry a negative risk premium, this phenomenon does not entirely explain the result. The negative relation between idiosyncratic volatility and future stock returns is therefore widely considered a puzzle.

Several subsequent papers have proposed explanations for the idiosyncratic volatility puzzle. Bali and Cakici (2008) demonstrate that data frequency, portfolio weighting scheme, portfolio breakpoint calculation methodology, and the screens used to create the sample all have a substantial impact on the idiosyncratic volatility puzzle, and that the relation disappears for many choices of these parameters. Fu (2009) uses an exponential GARCH model to estimate expected idiosyncratic volatility, and finds a positive relation between this measure and future stock returns, although Guo, Kassa, and Ferguson (2014) show that this study is potentially afflicted by the in-sample nature of the estimation of expected idiosyncratic volatility. Huang et al. (2010) demonstrate that the negative relation between idiosyncratic volatility and future stock returns is driven by the short-term reversal phenomenon. Han and Lesmond (2011) provide evidence that the idiosyncratic volatility puzzle is a manifestation of liquidity shocks and microstucture effects. Bali, Cakici, and Whitelaw (2011) find that after controlling for demand for lottery-like stocks, the negative relation between idiosyncratic volatility and future stock returns disappears,

---

[4]The constraint on the number of securities may vary from investor to investor. All investors, however, are constrained, and therefore no investor can invest in all available risky assets.

[5]It is worth noting that in both models, when the restriction on the number of risky securities in which each investor can invest is removed, the models simplify to the CAPM. Thus, both models can be viewed as generalized versions of the CAPM.

[6]Ang, Hodrick, Xing, and Zhang (2009) demonstrate that this phenomenon exists in international stock markets, not just the U.S. market.

and in some analyses the relation becomes positive. Baker, Bradley, and Wurgler (2011) show that benchmarking by institutional investors may result in a limit to arbitrage, thus allowing this phenomenon to persist.[7]

The remainder of this chapter is devoted to an empirical examination of idiosyncratic volatility and expected stock returns. As part of our investigation, we also examine measures to total stock return volatility. We do this to demonstrate to the reader that idiosyncratic volatility and total volatility are very similar in the cross section. While total volatility is a function of idiosyncratic volatility and systematic risk (captured by beta in the CAPM model), it is important for a researcher to recognize that these variables are highly similar empirically. We begin by discussing in detail several different approaches to calculating idiosyncratic volatility and total volatility. We then proceed to examine the cross-sectional properties of total and idiosyncratic volatility. Next, we investigate the relation between idiosyncratic volatility and future stock returns.

15.1 MEASURING TOTAL VOLATILITY

There are two frequently used approaches to calculating the total volatility of a stock's returns. The first is to simply calculate the standard deviation of the periodic stock returns. Because volatilities are most easily interpreted when presented as annualized values and expressed in percent, the total volatility of a stock's return can be calculated as

$$Vol_i = 100\sqrt{\frac{\sum_{t=1}^{n}(R_{i,t} - \overline{R_i})^2}{n-1}}\sqrt{m} \qquad (15.1)$$

where $R_{i,t}$ is the return of stock i during period t, $\overline{R_i}$ is the average return of stock i taken over all periods used in the calculation of Vol, n is the number of periods of data used in the calculation, and m is the number of periods in one year. The multiplication by $\sqrt{m}$ converts the standard deviation of the periodic returns to an annualized value, and multiplication by 100 is performed because the values of the periodic returns $(R_{i,t})$ are assumed to be represented in decimal form.

In many cases, an even simpler approach is taken by empirical asset pricing researchers. In this alternative approach, we simply take the sum of the squared periodic returns, $R_{i,t}^2$, instead of the squared demeaned periodic returns, $(R_{i,t} - \overline{R_i})^2$, in the numerator, and divide by n instead of $n-1$. The thinking behind this approach is that in almost all cases, the true expected return of any stock in a given period t is quite small and poorly captured by the average value over all periods in the calculation, $\overline{R_i}$. This method therefore effectively replaces $\overline{R_i}$ in equation (15.1) with zero. The summation in the numerator of the equation, therefore, simply becomes

---

[7]Baker and Wurgler (2014) attribute the idiosyncratic volatility puzzle to mispricing and examine its implications on firms' capital structure decisions.

the sum of the squared periodic stock returns. For this reason, we denote this variable with SS in the superscript and calculate it as

$$Vol_i^{SS} = 100\sqrt{\frac{\sum_{t=1}^n R_{i,t}^2}{n}}\sqrt{m}. \tag{15.2}$$

15.2   MEASURING IDIOSYNCRATIC VOLATILITY

Idiosyncratic volatility is measured as the residual standard error from a time-series regression of periodic excess stock returns on the returns of factor-mimicking portfolios. The model used most frequently to calculate idiosyncratic volatility is the Fama and French (1993) three-factor (FF) model. This model includes the market (*MKT*), size (*SMB*), and value (*HML*) factors as independent variables in the regression. Therefore, the regression specification is

$$r_{i,t} = \alpha_i + \beta_{MKT,i}MKT_t + \beta_{SMB,i}SMB_t + \beta_{HML,i}HML_t + \epsilon_{i,t} \tag{15.3}$$

where $r_{i,t}$ is the excess return of stock i during time period t, and MKT_t, SMB_t, and HML_t are the period t returns of the market, size, and book-to-market factors, respectively.

In some cases, researchers use a simple CAPM regression or a four-factor regression based on the four-factor model of Fama and French (1993) and Carhart (1997) (FFC). In these cases, the regression specification is

$$r_{i,t} = \alpha_i + \beta_{MKT,i}MKT_t + \epsilon_{i,t} \tag{15.4}$$

when using the CAPM model and

$$r_{i,t} = \alpha_i + \beta_{MKT,i}MKT_t + \beta_{SMB,i}SMB_t \\ + \beta_{HML,i}HML_t + \beta_{MOM,i}MOM_t + \epsilon_{i,t} \tag{15.5}$$

when the FFC model is used.

The residual standard error from the regression is then calculated as

$$RSE_i = \sqrt{\frac{\sum_{j=1}^n \epsilon_{i,j}^2}{n-k}} \tag{15.6}$$

where n is the number of data points that are used to fit the regression and k is the number of parameters estimated by the regression.

When the FF model is used there are four parameters estimated by the regression (α_i, $\beta_{MKT,i}$, $\beta_{SMB,i}$, and $\beta_{HML,i}$), and thus in this case $k = 4$.[8] When the CAPM model

---

[8]Frequently, researchers will omit the subtraction of k from the denominator of the calculation, or simply use $k = 1$, which statistically assumes that the parameter estimates are exact, and therefore that *RSE* represents an unbiased estimate of the standard deviation of the residuals.

is used there are two parameters ($k = 2$), and when the FFC model is used, there are five parameters ($k = 5$).

Idiosyncratic volatility is then calculated by multiplying the residual standard error by $\sqrt{m}$ (m is the number of return periods in a year) so that it represents an annualized value. If the periodic excess returns used in the regression are represented in decimal form, the annualized residual standard error is frequently then multiplied by 100 so that idiosyncratic volatility is measured in percent. We therefore define idiosyncratic volatility as

$$IdioVol_i = 100RSE_i \times \sqrt{m}. \tag{15.7}$$

We use several different combinations of measurement period and data frequency to calculate both total volatility (Vol and Vol^{SS}) and idiosyncratic volatility. Specifically, we calculate each of our measures using one, three, six, and 12 months of daily return data and one, two, three, and five years worth of monthly return data. The one-, three-, six-, and 12-month daily return-based variables are denoted with $1M$, $3M$, $6M$, and $12M$ in the superscript, respectively. We require a minimum of 15, 50, 100, and 200 days worth of return data to calculate the one-, three-, six-, and 12-month variables, respectively. The one-, two-, three-, and five-year monthly return-based measures are denoted with $1Y$, $2Y$, $3Y$, and $5Y$ in the superscript and we require, 10, 20, 24, and 24 months of return data to calculate these variables, respectively. The value of each variable for stock i in month t is calculated using return data from months $t - k + 1$ through t, inclusive, where k is the number of months in the measurement period. We denote idiosyncratic volatility variables calculated using the CAPM model with $CAPM$ in the superscript, variables calculated using the FF model with FF in the superscript, and those calculated using the FFC model with FFC in the superscript.

The daily (monthly) return data used in the calculation of each of the volatility variables come from the RET field in the Center for Research in Security Price's daily (monthly) stock file. Risk-free security and factor return data are taken from Ken French's data library.[9]

15.3   SUMMARY STATISTICS

In Table 15.1, we present summary statistics for each of the total and idiosyncratic volatility variables for our 1963–2012 sample of U.S.-based common stocks in the CRSP database. Panel A presents results for the measure of total volatility calculated using the sample standard deviation of periodic returns (Vol). When Vol is calculated using daily return data, the average values increase slightly as the length of the measurement period increases from 50.71% for the one-month measure (Vol^{1M}) to 53.43% for the 12-month measure (Vol^{12M}). This increasing pattern is also found in each of the cross-sectional percentiles, with the exception of the 95th percentile

---

[9]The URL for Ken French's data library is http://mba.tuck.dartmouth.edu/pages/faculty/ken.french/data&uscore;library.html.

TABLE 15.1 Summary Statistics
This table presents summary statistics for variables measuring total and idiosyncratic volatility using the CRSP sample for the months t from June 1963 through November 2012. Each month, the mean (*Mean*), standard deviation (*SD*), skewness (*Skew*), excess kurtosis (*Kurt*), minimum (*Min*), 5th percentile (5%), 25th percentile (25%), median (*Median*), 75th percentile (75%), 95th percentile (95%), and maximum (*Max*) values of the cross-sectional distribution of each variable is calculated. The table presents the time-series means for each cross-sectional value. The column labeled n indicates the average number of stocks for which the given variable is available. *Vol* is the annualized standard deviation of periodic stock returns. Vol^{SS} is the annualized sum of the squared periodic stock returns. $IdioVol^{CAPM}$ is the annualized standard deviation of the residuals from a regression of excess stock returns on the market factor. $IdioVol^{FF}$ is the annualized standard deviation of the residuals from a regression of excess stock returns on the market factor, the size factor (*SMB*), and the value factor (*HML*). $IdioVol^{FFC}$ is the annualized standard deviation of the residuals from a regression of excess stock returns on the market factor, the size factor (*SMB*), the value factor (*HML*), and the momentum factor (*MOM*). Variables denoted $1M$, $3M$, $6M$, and $12M$ are calculated from one, three, six, and 12 months of daily return data, respectively. Variables denoted $1Y$, $2Y$, $3Y$, and $5Y$ are calculated from one, two, three, and five years of monthly return data, respectively.

Panel A: *Vol*

	Mean	SD	Skew	Kurt	Min	5%	25%	Median	75%	95%	Max	n
Vol^{1M}	50.71	40.11	4.22	61.02	1.26	13.55	26.82	41.11	62.71	118.31	743.34	4761
Vol^{3M}	52.63	36.41	3.54	43.40	2.49	17.28	29.80	44.12	64.94	115.67	633.42	4697
Vol^{6M}	53.24	34.37	3.14	33.84	3.53	18.78	31.00	45.31	65.75	113.89	571.08	4611
Vol^{12M}	53.43	32.43	2.81	27.44	5.29	19.92	31.82	46.07	66.14	111.46	513.06	4440
Vol^{1Y}	46.87	31.16	3.92	56.45	2.70	16.17	27.56	39.88	57.61	99.21	579.54	4423
Vol^{2Y}	47.33	28.17	3.14	36.79	5.10	18.11	28.97	41.16	58.27	95.68	472.85	4072
Vol^{3Y}	47.77	27.01	2.84	31.39	6.63	18.98	29.66	41.96	58.98	94.97	433.11	3958
Vol^{5Y}	48.48	26.14	2.64	29.63	7.64	19.75	30.46	43.05	60.16	94.63	410.30	3992

Panel B: Vol^{SS}

	Mean	SD	Skew	Kurt	Min	5%	25%	Median	75%	95%	Max	n
$Vol^{SS,1M}$	50.51	39.79	4.24	61.95	1.26	13.59	26.83	41.02	62.43	117.43	741.62	4761
$Vol^{SS,3M}$	52.56	36.33	3.56	43.93	2.49	17.31	29.80	44.08	64.85	115.37	634.86	4697
$Vol^{SS,6M}$	53.21	34.34	3.15	34.25	3.54	18.80	31.01	45.30	65.71	113.75	573.18	4611
$Vol^{SS,12M}$	53.43	32.43	2.82	27.80	5.30	19.93	31.83	46.07	66.13	111.41	515.21	4440
$Vol^{SS,1Y}$	47.11	30.91	3.90	56.55	2.88	16.58	27.89	40.19	57.91	98.90	574.90	4423
$Vol^{SS,2Y}$	47.50	28.04	3.14	36.95	5.27	18.41	29.19	41.37	58.44	95.60	471.01	4072
$Vol^{SS,3Y}$	47.92	26.89	2.84	31.61	6.84	19.25	29.87	42.14	59.12	94.83	432.08	3958
$Vol^{SS,5Y}$	48.62	26.01	2.65	29.98	7.95	20.01	30.69	43.25	60.27	94.54	409.49	3992

Panel C: $IdioVol^{CAPM}$

	Mean	SD	Skew	Kurt	Min	5%	25%	Median	75%	95%	Max	n
$IdioVol^{CAPM,1M}$	48.66	40.15	4.28	61.28	1.43	12.74	24.73	38.57	60.12	116.84	744.85	4742
$IdioVol^{CAPM,3M}$	50.42	36.53	3.57	42.99	2.46	15.82	27.51	41.50	62.40	114.30	633.88	4697

TABLE 15.1 *(Continued)*

$IdioVol^{CAPM,6M}$	51.02	34.54	3.16	33.18	3.49	17.17	28.67	42.67	63.25	112.56	571.21	4611
$IdioVol^{CAPM,12M}$	51.18	32.64	2.82	26.67	5.17	18.14	29.41	43.40	63.66	110.18	513.06	4440
$IdioVol^{CAPM,1Y}$	42.93	30.89	4.07	56.39	2.61	14.05	23.91	35.47	52.89	95.03	579.50	4423
$IdioVol^{CAPM,2Y}$	43.31	27.77	3.29	37.74	4.90	15.93	25.28	36.75	53.49	91.28	472.56	4072
$IdioVol^{CAPM,3Y}$	43.73	26.60	2.99	32.46	6.34	16.72	25.94	37.54	54.26	90.45	433.33	3958
$IdioVol^{CAPM,5Y}$	44.52	25.72	2.77	30.35	7.35	17.47	26.76	38.72	55.58	90.31	409.48	3992

Panel D: $IdioVol^{FF}$

	Mean	SD	Skew	Kurt	Min	5%	25%	Median	75%	95%	Max	n
$IdioVol^{FF,1M}$	48.07	40.25	4.31	61.51	1.40	12.41	24.15	37.84	59.40	116.48	748.45	4742
$IdioVol^{FF,3M}$	49.88	36.52	3.59	43.25	2.45	15.53	27.02	40.86	61.71	113.83	634.32	4697
$IdioVol^{FF,6M}$	50.48	34.51	3.18	33.25	3.48	16.87	28.19	42.04	62.58	112.07	571.65	4611
$IdioVol^{FF,12M}$	50.65	32.61	2.84	26.68	5.14	17.83	28.94	42.76	62.99	109.71	513.17	4440
$IdioVol^{FF,1Y}$	40.95	30.16	4.08	52.97	2.31	12.92	22.51	33.59	50.44	91.96	554.13	4423
$IdioVol^{FF,2Y}$	41.59	26.94	3.27	33.71	4.73	15.15	24.23	35.18	51.25	88.11	448.38	4072
$IdioVol^{FF,3Y}$	42.03	25.74	2.93	27.65	6.20	15.99	24.92	36.02	51.94	87.24	408.82	3958
$IdioVol^{FF,5Y}$	42.82	24.87	2.71	25.82	7.21	16.78	25.79	37.19	53.27	87.07	386.82	3992

Panel E: $IdioVol^{FFC}$

	Mean	SD	Skew	Kurt	Min	5%	25%	Median	75%	95%	Max	n
$IdioVol^{FFC,1M}$	47.91	40.31	4.32	61.66	1.39	12.27	23.97	37.63	59.19	116.45	751.85	4742
$IdioVol^{FFC,3M}$	49.77	36.53	3.60	43.36	2.45	15.44	26.91	40.73	61.58	113.74	635.46	4697
$IdioVol^{FFC,6M}$	50.37	34.52	3.18	33.32	3.47	16.78	28.10	41.93	62.46	111.99	572.19	4611
$IdioVol^{FFC,12M}$	50.56	32.62	2.84	26.71	5.12	17.75	28.85	42.66	62.89	109.61	513.34	4440
$IdioVol^{FFC,1Y}$	40.34	30.06	4.10	52.82	2.13	12.40	21.97	33.01	49.83	90.99	553.62	4423
$IdioVol^{FFC,2Y}$	41.20	26.77	3.29	34.04	4.68	14.91	23.99	34.85	50.82	87.29	448.03	4072
$IdioVol^{FFC,3Y}$	41.70	25.58	2.94	27.60	6.14	15.79	24.72	35.76	51.58	86.48	408.46	3958
$IdioVol^{FFC,5Y}$	42.54	24.72	2.71	25.93	7.16	16.63	25.62	36.97	52.92	86.50	385.86	3992

and the maximum value, which exhibit a decreasing pattern as the measurement period is elongated. The fact that the average maximum values decrease as the measurement period is extended is likely due to the fact that variables calculated from longer measurement periods are less susceptible to measurement errors driven by one extreme daily return. The distribution of *Vol* is positively skewed, with average cross-sectional skewness of 4.22, 3.54, 3.14, and 2.81 for Vol^{1M}, Vol^{3M}, Vol^{6M}, and Vol^{12M}, respectively. As with many of the variables we have seen previously in this book, the positive skewness is driven by a small number of stocks for which the values of *Vol* are very high. The cross-sectional distributions of the daily return-based total volatility variables are also highly leptokurtic, with average excess kurtosis between 32.43 for Vol^{12M} and 40.11 for Vol^{1M}.

The summary statistics for the monthly return-based *Vol* variables (Vol^{1Y}, Vol^{2Y}, Vol^{3Y}, and Vol^{5Y}) indicate that the monthly return-based measures have many of the same distributional characteristics as the daily return-based measures. The average values of the monthly return-based variables range from 46.87% for Vol^{1Y} to 48.48% for Vol^{5Y}. Once again, the average values exhibit an increasing pattern as the measurement period is extended. The average values of the monthly return-based measures are slightly lower than the daily return-based measures. As with the daily return-based measures, the cross-sectional distributions of the monthly return-based Vol variables are positively skewed, leptokurtic, and characterized by a small number of very large values.

Characteristics of the average cross-sectional distributions of the measures of total volatility calculated using the sum of the squared periodic returns (Vol^{SS}), shown in Panel B of Table 15.1, are extremely similar to those of Vol. In all cases, the differences between the summary statistics for Vol and those for Vol^{SS} are negligible. The greatest takeaway from Panel B, therefore, is that there is almost no impact of using the simpler undemeaned sum-squared-based approach to calculating total volatility, instead of the sample standard deviation-based approach, on the cross-sectional distribution of total volatility.

In Panels C–E of Table 15.1, we present summary statistics for the $IdioVol^{CAPM}$, $IdioVol^{FF}$, and $IdioVol^{FFC}$ variables. As with the measures of total volatility, the different approaches to calculating idiosyncratic volatility all generate variables whose cross-sectional distributions are very similar. We focus our discussion on $IdioVol^{FF}$ (Panel D) because idiosyncratic volatility is most commonly calculated by empirical asset pricing researchers using the FF model. The daily return-based $IdioVol^{FF}$ variables have average values ranging from 48.07% for $IdioVol^{FF,1M}$ to 50.65% for $IdioVol^{FF,12M}$. For the monthly return-based measures, the average values range from 40.95% for $IdioVol^{FF,1Y}$ to 42.82% for $IdioVol^{FF,5Y}$. Thus, on average, the monthly return-based values of idiosyncratic volatility are substantially lower than the daily return-based values. Similar to total volatility, with the exception of the 95th percentile and the maximum value, each of the reported percentiles (as well as the mean) of the cross-sectional distributions of the $IdioVol^{FF}$ variables increases as the length of the measurement period is made longer. Finally, the cross-sectional distributions of the $IdioVol^{FF}$ measures are positively skewed and leptokurtic.

It is perhaps not a surprise that the different measures of total volatility are so similar to each other, nor that the measures of idiosyncratic volatility are so similar to each other. A part of this is largely mechanical since the calculations of each of the different measures are highly similar. What is potentially more interesting is that the cross-sectional distribution of idiosyncratic volatility is very similar to the cross-sectional distribution of total volatility. This indicates either that for the average stock, the vast majority of total volatility is idiosyncratic, or that the regressions used to calculate idiosyncratic volatility fail to effectively capture the systematic effect.

15.4 CORRELATIONS

We now examine the cross-sectional correlations between the different measures of volatility, as well as between volatility and other variables that have been examined in previous chapters of this book. We begin by examining the correlations between variables calculated using the same methodology but with different measurement periods and data frequencies. In all correlation analyses presented throughout this section, each variable is winsorized at the 0.5% level on a monthly basis prior to calculating the correlation.

In Panel A of Table 15.2, we present the time-series averages of the monthly cross-sectional correlations between each of the measures of total volatility calculated using the sample standard deviation of the periodic returns (Vol). Pearson product–moment correlations are presented in the below-diagonal entries, and Spearman rank correlations are shown in the above-diagonal entries. The results show that regardless of measurement period length or data frequency, the different Vol variables have high cross-sectional correlations. A substantial portion of this is mechanical, especially for the correlations between two variables that use the same data frequency, but the correlations are way too high for the entire effect

TABLE 15.2   Correlations—Total Volatility
This table presents the time-series averages of the annual cross-sectional Pearson product–moment (below-diagonal entries) and Spearman rank (above-diagonal entries) correlations between pairs of variables measuring total volatility. Panel A presents correlations between values of Vol calculated using different data frequencies and measurement period lengths. Panel B presents correlations between values of Vol^{SS} calculated using different data frequencies and measurement period lengths.

Panel A: Vol

	Vol^{1M}	Vol^{3M}	Vol^{6M}	Vol^{12M}	Vol^{1Y}	Vol^{2Y}	Vol^{3Y}	Vol^{5Y}
Vol^{1M}		0.87	0.82	0.79	0.64	0.65	0.65	0.64
Vol^{3M}	0.86		0.95	0.90	0.74	0.75	0.74	0.73
Vol^{6M}	0.80	0.94		0.96	0.79	0.80	0.79	0.77
Vol^{12M}	0.76	0.88	0.95		0.82	0.84	0.83	0.82
Vol^{1Y}	0.57	0.67	0.73	0.78		0.90	0.86	0.81
Vol^{2Y}	0.57	0.67	0.72	0.78	0.88		0.96	0.91
Vol^{3Y}	0.56	0.65	0.71	0.76	0.82	0.94		0.96
Vol^{5Y}	0.55	0.64	0.69	0.74	0.77	0.89	0.95	

Panel B: Vol^{SS}

	$Vol^{SS,1M}$	$Vol^{SS,3M}$	$Vol^{SS,6M}$	$Vol^{SS,12M}$	$Vol^{SS,1Y}$	$Vol^{SS,2Y}$	$Vol^{SS,3Y}$	$Vol^{SS,5Y}$
$Vol^{SS,1M}$		0.87	0.82	0.79	0.66	0.66	0.65	0.64
$Vol^{SS,3M}$	0.86		0.95	0.90	0.75	0.75	0.74	0.73
$Vol^{SS,6M}$	0.80	0.94		0.96	0.80	0.80	0.79	0.77
$Vol^{SS,12M}$	0.76	0.88	0.95		0.83	0.84	0.83	0.81
$Vol^{SS,1Y}$	0.58	0.68	0.74	0.78		0.91	0.86	0.82
$Vol^{SS,2Y}$	0.58	0.67	0.72	0.78	0.88		0.96	0.91
$Vol^{SS,3Y}$	0.57	0.65	0.71	0.76	0.82	0.94		0.96
$Vol^{SS,5Y}$	0.55	0.64	0.69	0.74	0.77	0.89	0.95	

to be mechanical. Looking first at the correlations between the daily return-based measures, the table indicates average Pearson cross-sectional correlations ranging from 0.76 between Vol^{1M} and Vol^{12M} to 0.95 between Vol^{6M} and Vol^{12M}. As would be expected given the mechanical effect, the correlations are increasing as the length of the overlapping portion of the measurement period increases and decreasing as the length of the nonoverlapping portion of the estimation period increases. However, Vol^{1M} and Vol^{12M} are calculated from only one month of overlapping data, with Vol^{12M} using 11 months of data not included in Vol^{1M}. The correlation of 0.76 between these measures gives a strong indication that these variables are both effective at capturing the same characteristic of stock returns. The Spearman rank correlations between the daily return-based Vol variables are slightly higher than the Pearson correlations. The correlations between the monthly return-based Vol variables are similarly high, ranging from 0.77 between Vol^{1Y} and Vol^{5Y} to 0.95 between Vol^{3Y} and Vol^{5Y}. Once again, the patterns in the correlations are consistent with a mechanical effect, but the magnitudes of the correlations are much too high for the results to be purely mechanical. As with the daily return-based measures, the monthly return-based measures have slightly higher Spearman rank correlations than Pearson product–moment correlations.

Pearson (Spearman) correlations between the daily and monthly data-based Vol measures range from 0.55 (0.64) between Vol^{1M} and Vol^{5Y} to 0.78 (0.84) between Vol^{12M} and Vol^{2Y}. The results indicate that there is a very strong common component to these variables. This effect is likely not nearly as mechanical as the results for variables calculated using the same data frequency. The results therefore give us a high level of confidence that both the daily return-based measures and the monthly return-based measures are capturing the same stock-level characteristic. Once again, the Spearman correlations are somewhat higher than the Pearson correlations, potentially indicating that, at least for extreme values, the measurement of these variables is quite noisy.

Panel B of Table 15.2 shows that the correlations between the sum-of-squared returns-based total volatility variables (Vol^{SS}) are extremely similar to the corresponding correlations between the Vol variables. The largest difference between corresponding correlations for the Vol^{SS} and Vol variables is the Spearman correlation of 0.66 between the $Vol^{SS,1M}$ and $Vol^{SS,1Y}$, which differs by a negligible 0.02 from the Spearman correlation between Vol^{1M} and Vol^{1Y} of 0.64. All other correlations between the Vol^{SS} variables differ by either 0.01 (rounded to 2 decimal points) or less from the correlation between the corresponding pair of Vol variables. As was the case with the summary statistics, the results indicate that the characteristics of the variables produced using the two different approaches used to calculate total volatility are highly similar.

Table 15.3 shows the average cross-sectional correlations between the $IdioVol^{CAPM}$ variables (Panel A), the $IdioVol^{FF}$ variables (Panel B), and the $IdioVol^{FFC}$ variables (Panel C). Regardless of which model (CAPM, FF, or FFC) is used to calculate idiosyncratic volatility, the results are highly similar. We therefore focus our discussion on the correlations between the measures of idiosyncratic volatility calculated using the FF risk model.

Pearson correlations between the daily return-based measures of idiosyncratic volatility range from 0.77 between $IdioVol^{FF,1M}$ and $IdioVol^{FF,12M}$ to 0.95 between $IdioVol^{FF,6M}$ and $IdioVol^{FF,12M}$. Similarly, the monthly return-based measures have Pearson correlations ranging from 0.75 between $IdioVol^{FF,1Y}$ and $IdioVol^{FF,5Y}$ to 0.95 between $IdioVol^{FF,3Y}$ and $IdioVol^{FF,5Y}$. Pearson correlations between the daily and monthly measures are a bit lower, ranging from 0.55 between $IdioVol^{FF,1M}$

TABLE 15.3 Correlations—Idiosyncratic Volatility
This table presents the time-series averages of the annual cross-sectional Pearson product–moment (below-diagonal entries) and Spearman rank (above-diagonal entries) correlations between pairs of variables measuring idiosyncratic volatility. Panel A presents correlations between values of $IdioVol^{CAPM}$ calculated using different data frequencies and measurement period lengths. Panel B presents correlations between values of $IdioVol^{FF}$ calculated using different data frequencies and measurement period lengths. Panel C presents correlations between values of $IdioVol^{FFC}$ calculated using different data frequencies and measurement period lengths.

Panel A: $IdioVol^{CAPM}$

	$IdioVol^{CAPM,1M}$	$IdioVol^{CAPM,3M}$	$IdioVol^{CAPM,6M}$	$IdioVol^{CAPM,12M}$	$IdioVol^{CAPM,1Y}$	$IdioVol^{CAPM,2Y}$	$IdioVol^{CAPM,3Y}$	$IdioVol^{CAPM,5Y}$
$IdioVol^{CAPM,1M}$		0.87	0.83	0.80	0.64	0.66	0.66	0.65
$IdioVol^{CAPM,3M}$	0.86		0.95	0.91	0.74	0.75	0.75	0.74
$IdioVol^{CAPM,6M}$	0.81	0.94		0.96	0.79	0.80	0.80	0.78
$IdioVol^{CAPM,12M}$	0.77	0.88	0.95		0.82	0.84	0.84	0.82
$IdioVol^{CAPM,1Y}$	0.57	0.67	0.73	0.78		0.90	0.85	0.81
$IdioVol^{CAPM,2Y}$	0.58	0.67	0.72	0.78	0.87		0.96	0.91
$IdioVol^{CAPM,3Y}$	0.57	0.66	0.71	0.76	0.82	0.94		0.96
$IdioVol^{CAPM,5Y}$	0.56	0.64	0.69	0.74	0.77	0.89	0.95	

Panel B: $IdioVol^{FF}$

	$IdioVol^{FF,1M}$	$IdioVol^{FF,3M}$	$IdioVol^{FF,6M}$	$IdioVol^{FF,12M}$	$IdioVol^{FF,1Y}$	$IdioVol^{FF,2Y}$	$IdioVol^{FF,3Y}$	$IdioVol^{FF,5Y}$
$IdioVol^{FF,1M}$		0.87	0.83	0.80	0.62	0.65	0.65	0.64
$IdioVol^{FF,3M}$	0.86		0.95	0.91	0.71	0.74	0.74	0.73
$IdioVol^{FF,6M}$	0.81	0.94		0.96	0.76	0.79	0.79	0.78
$IdioVol^{FF,12M}$	0.77	0.88	0.95		0.79	0.83	0.83	0.82
$IdioVol^{FF,1Y}$	0.55	0.65	0.71	0.75		0.88	0.83	0.79
$IdioVol^{FF,2Y}$	0.56	0.66	0.71	0.76	0.86		0.95	0.91
$IdioVol^{FF,3Y}$	0.56	0.65	0.70	0.75	0.80	0.94		0.96
$IdioVol^{FF,5Y}$	0.55	0.64	0.69	0.74	0.75	0.88	0.95	

(continued)

TABLE 15.3   (*Continued*)

	Panel C: *IdioVol*^{FFC}							
	$IdioVol^{FFC,1M}$	$IdioVol^{FFC,3M}$	$IdioVol^{FFC,6M}$	$IdioVol^{FFC,12M}$	$IdioVol^{FFC,1Y}$	$IdioVol^{FFC,2Y}$	$IdioVol^{FFC,3Y}$	$IdioVol^{FFC,5Y}$
$IdioVol^{FFC,1M}$		0.87	0.82	0.80	0.60	0.64	0.65	0.64
$IdioVol^{FFC,3M}$	0.86		0.95	0.91	0.70	0.74	0.74	0.73
$IdioVol^{FFC,6M}$	0.80	0.94		0.96	0.75	0.79	0.79	0.78
$IdioVol^{FFC,12M}$	0.76	0.88	0.95		0.78	0.83	0.83	0.82
$IdioVol^{FFC,1Y}$	0.54	0.64	0.70	0.74		0.86	0.81	0.77
$IdioVol^{FFC,2Y}$	0.56	0.65	0.71	0.76	0.85		0.95	0.90
$IdioVol^{FFC,3Y}$	0.56	0.65	0.70	0.75	0.79	0.94		0.96
$IdioVol^{FFC,5Y}$	0.55	0.64	0.69	0.74	0.74	0.88	0.95	

and $IdioVol^{FF,5Y}$ to 0.76 between $IdioVol^{FF,12M}$ and $IdioVol^{FF,2Y}$. In all cases, the Spearman correlations are similar to, and slightly higher than, the corresponding Pearson correlations.

The final notable result from Tables 15.2 and 15.3 is that the results for *Vol* and Vol^{SS} (Table 15.2), while similar to each other, are also very similar to the results for each of $IdioVol^{CAPM}$, $IdioVol^{FF}$, and $IdioVol^{FFC}$ (Table 15.3). In all cases, when fixing the measurement period and data frequency for each of the variables for which the correlation is being calculated, the correlations observed using different measures of total and idiosyncratic volatility are very similar.

The summary statistics and correlation results presented thus far show that *Vol*, Vol^{SS}, $IdioVol^{CAPM}$, $IdioVol^{FF}$, and $IdioVol^{FFC}$ all have very similar characteristics. To gain additional insight into this, in Table 15.4 we present correlations between pairs of variables calculated using different methodologies but holding the length of the measurement period and data frequency constant. The results show that the Pearson correlations (Panel A) between each pair of variables are extremely high. The average cross-sectional correlations between *Vol* and Vol^{SS} range from 0.993 when the variables are calculated using one year of monthly return data to 1.000 (rounded to 3 decimal points) when *Vol* and Vol^{SS} are calculated using six or 12 months of daily return data.

The Pearson correlations between *Vol* and idiosyncratic volatility range from 0.912 between Vol^{1Y} and $IdioVol^{FFC,1Y}$ to 0.995 between *Vol* and *IdioVol* calculated using either six or 12 months of daily data. The correlations between the Vol^{SS} and *IdioVol* variables are very similar, although in general slightly lower than those between *Vol* and *IdioVol*. That being said, the lowest correlation between these pairs of variables is 0.908 between $Vol^{SS,1Y}$ and $IdioVol^{FFC,1Y}$.

The results indicate that the three different measures of idiosyncratic volatility are extremely similar in the cross section. The lowest Pearson correlation between any of the pairs of idiosyncratic volatility variables is 0.943 between $IdioVol^{CAPM,1Y}$ and $IdioVol^{FFC,1Y}$. Idiosyncratic volatility measured using the FF and FFC risk models

TABLE 15.4   Correlations—Total and Idiosyncratic Volatility

This table presents the time-series averages of the annual cross-sectional Pearson product–moment (Panel A) and Spearman rank (Panel B) correlations between pairs of variables measuring total volatility (Vol and Vol^{SS}) and idiosyncratic volatility ($IdioVol^{CAPM}$, $IdioVol^{FF}$, and $IdioVol^{FFC}$) calculated using different data frequencies and measurement period lengths. Correlations between variables calculated from one, three, six, and 12 months of daily return data are shown in the columns $1M$, $3M$, $6M$, and $12M$, respectively. Correlations between variables calculated from one, two, three, and five months of monthly return data are shown in the columns $1Y$, $2Y$, $3Y$, and $5Y$, respectively.

Panel A: Pearson Correlations

Correlation Between	$1M$	$3M$	$6M$	$12M$	$1Y$	$2Y$	$3Y$	$5Y$
Vol and Vol^{SS}	0.999	1.000	1.000	1.000	0.993	0.998	0.999	0.999
Vol and $IdioVol^{CAPM}$	0.990	0.994	0.995	0.995	0.968	0.979	0.983	0.986
Vol and $IdioVol^{FF}$	0.983	0.991	0.993	0.994	0.932	0.964	0.971	0.977
Vol and $IdioVol^{FFC}$	0.979	0.990	0.992	0.993	0.912	0.957	0.967	0.974
Vol^{SS} and $IdioVol^{CAPM}$	0.989	0.994	0.995	0.995	0.963	0.977	0.982	0.986
Vol^{SS} and $IdioVol^{FF}$	0.982	0.991	0.993	0.994	0.928	0.962	0.970	0.976
Vol^{SS} and $IdioVol^{FFC}$	0.978	0.990	0.992	0.993	0.908	0.955	0.966	0.973
$IdioVol^{CAPM}$ and $IdioVol^{FF}$	0.994	0.999	0.999	1.000	0.962	0.984	0.989	0.992
$IdioVol^{CAPM}$ and $IdioVol^{FFC}$	0.991	0.998	0.999	0.999	0.943	0.979	0.986	0.990
$IdioVol^{FF}$ and $IdioVol^{FFC}$	0.997	1.000	1.000	1.000	0.981	0.995	0.997	0.998

Panel B: Spearman Correlations

Correlation Between	$1M$	$3M$	$6M$	$12M$	$1Y$	$2Y$	$3Y$	$5Y$
Vol and Vol^{SS}	0.999	1.000	1.000	1.000	0.991	0.997	0.999	0.999
Vol and $IdioVol^{CAPM}$	0.982	0.988	0.990	0.991	0.953	0.970	0.977	0.982
Vol and $IdioVol^{FF}$	0.973	0.985	0.987	0.989	0.914	0.955	0.966	0.974
Vol and $IdioVol^{FFC}$	0.968	0.983	0.986	0.988	0.893	0.949	0.962	0.971
Vol^{SS} and $IdioVol^{CAPM}$	0.981	0.988	0.990	0.991	0.947	0.968	0.975	0.981
Vol^{SS} and $IdioVol^{FF}$	0.972	0.985	0.987	0.989	0.909	0.953	0.964	0.973
Vol^{SS} and $IdioVol^{FFC}$	0.967	0.983	0.986	0.988	0.889	0.947	0.961	0.971
$IdioVol^{CAPM}$ and $IdioVol^{FF}$	0.992	0.998	0.999	0.999	0.958	0.984	0.990	0.993
$IdioVol^{CAPM}$ and $IdioVol^{FFC}$	0.989	0.997	0.998	0.999	0.937	0.979	0.987	0.991
$IdioVol^{FF}$ and $IdioVol^{FFC}$	0.996	0.999	1.000	1.000	0.978	0.995	0.997	0.999

are nearly perfectly correlated in the cross section, with the lowest average correlation between these variables of 0.981 once again being generated by the measures calculated from one year of monthly data. In fact, in all cases, the lowest correlation between each given pair of variables is the correlation generated by the measures calculated from one year of monthly data. For each given measurement period and data frequency, the pairs of variables that generate the lowest correlations are Vol and $IdioVol^{FFC}$, as well as Vol^{SS} and $IdioVol^{FFC}$. These correlations, however, are still very high.

The Spearman rank correlations presented in Panel B of Table 15.4 give a very similar story. The lowest average cross-sectional Spearman correlation that appears in the table is 0.889 between $Vol^{SS,1Y}$ and $IdioVol^{FFC,1Y}$. The only other Spearman correlation that falls below 0.900 is, not surprisingly, the correlation between Vol^{1Y} and $IdioVol^{FFC,1Y}$. The same patterns that emerge in the Pearson correlations are also present in the Spearman correlations.

The conclusion to be drawn from Table 15.4 is clear. The results demonstrate that the methodology used to calculate total volatility or idiosyncratic volatility is inconsequential. Total volatility and idiosyncratic volatility are very highly correlated in the cross section. The correlations are high enough to alleviate any reasonable concern that empirical results will differ substantially when using one approach to measure volatility instead of another. For this reason, for most of the remainder of this chapter, we use only measures of idiosyncratic volatility calculated using the FF risk model ($IdioVol^{FF}$) as our volatility variables. While the correlation analysis presented in Panel B of Table 15.3 indicated that correlations between $IdioVol^{FF}$ calculated using different measurement periods and data frequencies are high, the correlations are not high enough to be confident that empirical results will not be substantially different when the measurement period and data frequency are changed. For this reason, we continue to examine all of the $IdioVol^{FF}$ variables. We choose to use $IdioVol^{FF}$ as our measure of idiosyncratic volatility because this is the measure used by Ang et al. (2006) and is the most commonly used measure of idiosyncratic volatility in empirical asset pricing research.

Having examined the relations between the different measures of idiosyncratic volatility (as well as total volatility), we now examine the cross-sectional relations between idiosyncratic volatility and other variables whose relations with expected stock returns have been examined in previous chapters.

In Table 15.5, we present the Pearson product–moment (Panel A) and Spearman rank (Panel B) correlations between $IdioVol^{FF}$ and each of beta (β), size (Size, log of market capitalization), book-to-market ratio (BM), momentum (Mom), reversal (Rev), illiquidity (Illiq), co-skewness (CoSkew), and idiosyncratic skewness (IdioSkew). The results indicate a weak positive relation between idiosyncratic volatility and β. When using the daily return-based measures of $IdioVol^{FF}$, the average correlations between $IdioVol^{FF}$ and β increase as the measurement period is elongated from 0.08 for $IdioVol^{FF,1M}$ to 0.11 for $IdioVol^{FF,12M}$. For the monthly return-based measures, the same pattern of increasing correlation as the measurement period is lengthened is observed. The correlations between β and the monthly return-based measures of idiosyncratic volatility range from 0.13 for $IdioVol^{FF,1Y}$ to 0.16 for $IdioVol^{FF,3Y}$ and $IdioVol^{FF,5Y}$. Thus, the correlation between idiosyncratic volatility and beta appears to be slightly higher when idiosyncratic volatility is measured using monthly return data. The Spearman rank correlations between β and $IdioVol^{FF}$, which range from 0.16 between β and $IdioVol^{FF,1M}$ to 0.20 between β and each of $IdioVol^{FF,2Y}$, $IdioVol^{FF,3Y}$, and $IdioVol^{FF,5Y}$, are a little higher than the Pearson correlations, but follow the same general patterns.

Idiosyncratic volatility has a strong negative relation with Size, since the Pearson (Spearman) correlations between $IdioVol^{FF}$ and Size range from -0.42 (-0.46)

TABLE 15.5 Correlations—Idiosyncratic Volatility and Other Variables
This table presents the time-series averages of the annual cross-sectional Pearson product–moment (Panel A) and Spearman rank (Panel B) correlations between pairs of variables measuring idiosyncratic volatility and each of β, $Size$, BM, Mom, Rev, $Illiq$, $CoSkew$, and $IdioSkew$.

Panel A: Pearson Correlations

	β	$Size$	BM	Mom	Rev	$Illiq$	$CoSkew$	$IdioSkew$
$IdioVol^{FF,1M}$	0.08	−0.45	0.07	−0.16	0.10	0.48	−0.06	0.25
$IdioVol^{FF,3M}$	0.09	−0.52	0.08	−0.14	0.02	0.49	−0.06	0.29
$IdioVol^{FF,6M}$	0.10	−0.55	0.09	−0.12	0.00	0.50	−0.07	0.32
$IdioVol^{FF,12M}$	0.11	−0.58	0.10	−0.08	−0.01	0.49	−0.07	0.35
$IdioVol^{FF,1Y}$	0.13	−0.42	0.04	0.10	0.04	0.24	−0.08	0.39
$IdioVol^{FF,2Y}$	0.15	−0.48	0.02	0.05	0.01	0.27	−0.08	0.48
$IdioVol^{FF,3Y}$	0.16	−0.50	0.00	0.03	0.00	0.27	−0.09	0.52
$IdioVol^{FF,5Y}$	0.16	−0.51	−0.02	0.01	−0.00	0.28	−0.09	0.56

Panel B: Spearman Correlations

	β	$Size$	BM	Mom	Rev	$Illiq$	$CoSkew$	$IdioSkew$
$IdioVol^{FF,1M}$	0.16	−0.48	−0.01	−0.22	0.00	0.54	−0.07	0.26
$IdioVol^{FF,3M}$	0.17	−0.55	−0.01	−0.22	−0.06	0.57	−0.09	0.30
$IdioVol^{FF,6M}$	0.17	−0.59	−0.01	−0.21	−0.07	0.59	−0.09	0.33
$IdioVol^{FF,12M}$	0.18	−0.62	−0.00	−0.19	−0.08	0.60	−0.10	0.35
$IdioVol^{FF,1Y}$	0.19	−0.46	−0.06	−0.06	−0.05	0.38	−0.09	0.33
$IdioVol^{FF,2Y}$	0.20	−0.52	−0.08	−0.11	−0.06	0.44	−0.10	0.40
$IdioVol^{FF,3Y}$	0.20	−0.54	−0.08	−0.12	−0.07	0.46	−0.11	0.44
$IdioVol^{FF,5Y}$	0.20	−0.55	−0.10	−0.12	−0.07	0.47	−0.12	0.47

between $Size$ and $IdioVol^{FF,1Y}$ to −0.58 (−0.62) between $Size$ and $IdioVol^{FF,12M}$. For each $IdioVol^{FF}$ variable, the Spearman correlation with $Size$ is slightly larger in magnitude than the Pearson correlation.

Table 15.5 provides mixed results regarding the correlation between idiosyncratic volatility and BM. The Pearson correlations between BM and the daily return-based $IdioVol^{FF}$ variables ($IdioVol^{FF,1M}$, $IdioVol^{FF,3M}$, $IdioVol^{FF,6M}$, and $IdioVol^{FF,12M}$) are positive, ranging from 0.07 between BM and $IdioVol^{FF,1M}$ to 0.10 between BM and $IdioVol^{FF,12M}$. While these correlations are not very large, they are not quite low enough to be considered completely negligible. Interestingly, the corresponding average Spearman correlations are all negative, albeit very small in magnitude (−0.01 or less). The correlations between BM and the monthly return-based $IdioVol^{FF}$ variables exhibit the opposite patterns, with the Pearson correlations being negligible (between −0.02 and 0.04) and the Spearman correlations being negative and, while small, not quite negligibly small (between −0.06 and −0.10).

IDIOSYNCRATIC VOLATILITY

The results of the correlation analyses examining the relation between idiosyncratic volatility and momentum are also mixed. $IdioVol^{FF}$ calculated from daily stock returns exhibits a negative relation with Mom, with the magnitude of the Pearson correlation decreasing as the length of the measurement period is extended from -0.16 for $IdioVol^{FF,1M}$ to -0.08 for $IdioVol^{FF,12M}$. The corresponding Spearman correlations exhibit the same pattern, but are substantially higher in magnitude than the Pearson correlations. When the monthly return-based measures of idiosyncratic volatility are used, the Pearson correlations actually become positive, ranging from 0.10 between Mom and $IdioVol^{FF,1Y}$ to 0.01 between Mom and $IdioVol^{FF,5Y}$. These positive correlations may be driven somewhat by the fact that Mom is calculated as the 11-month return during months $t-11$ through $t-1$ and $IdioVol^{FF,1Y}$ is calculated using the 12 monthly returns covering months $t-11$ through t. If a stock experiences a very high return in one of the months $t-11$ through $t-1$, this will cause both Mom and $IdioVol^{FF,1Y}$ to be high. One might reasonably argue that a large negative return should result in a high value of $IdioVol^{FF,1M}$ but a low value of Mom, which would result in a negative correlation. However, in Tables 7.2 and 14.1, we saw evidence that monthly stock returns are positively skewed, a phenomenon that is potentially driven by the fact that the maximum monthly return is infinite while the minimum possible monthly return is -100%. Therefore, it makes sense that this effect would manifest itself in a positive relation between idiosyncratic skewness (which is very similar to total skewness) and momentum. Consistent with a mechanical effect, as the length of the overlapping period of data used in the calculation of momentum and idiosyncratic volatility becomes a smaller percentage of the length of the $IdioVol^{FF}$ measurement period, this effect weakens. Consistent with this explanation, the Spearman correlations between idiosyncratic volatility measured from monthly return data and momentum range from -0.06 between Mom and $IdioVol^{FF,1Y}$ to -0.12 between Mom and $IdioVol^{FF,5Y}$. The fact that these correlations are negative indicates that the positive Pearson correlations are likely driven by a small number of extreme data points.

With the exception of the correlation of 0.10 between Rev and $IdioVol^{FF,1M}$, the average Pearson correlations between idiosyncratic volatility and reversal are negligibly small, with magnitudes that are less than 0.04 in all other cases. The positive correlation between Rev and $IdioVol^{FF,1M}$ is once again likely mechanical because both Rev and $IdioVol^{1M}$ are measured using only return data from the most recent month t. As for the Spearman correlations, each of the $IdioVol^{FF}$ variables exhibits a slightly negative relation with Rev, with the exception of the measure calculated from one month of daily returns ($IdioVol^{FF,1M}$). Once again, this effect is likely mechanical.

Idiosyncratic volatility has a strong negative relation with illiquidity. When using the daily return-based measures of idiosyncratic volatility ($IdioVol^{FF,1M}$, $IdioVol^{FF,3M}$, $IdioVol^{FF,6M}$, and $IdioVol^{FF,12M}$), the average Pearson correlations are between 0.48 and 0.50. The corresponding Spearman correlations are slightly higher, ranging from 0.54 to 0.60. Correlation between $Illiq$ and the monthly return-based measures of idiosyncratic volatility ($IdioVol^{FF,1Y}$, $IdioVol^{FF,2Y}$, $IdioVol^{FF,3Y}$, and $IdioVol^{FF,5Y}$) are substantially lower, ranging from 0.24 to 0.28 when using the Pearson correlation and from 0.38 to 0.47 when using the Spearman correlation.

Despite being lower than the correlations with the daily return-based measures, these correlations still indicate a strong positive relation between illiquidity and idiosyncratic volatility. It is possible that the lower correlation in the monthly return-based measures is because prices of highly illiquid stocks may move up and down substantially on a day-to-day basis to satisfy demand for liquidity, resulting in high idiosyncratic volatility in daily returns. Over the horizon of one month, however, the price effects of daily liquidity demand tend to offset each other, resulting in less idiosyncratic volatility when monthly returns are used in the calculation.

The results in Table 15.5 indicate a weak negative relation between idiosyncratic volatility and co-skewness, with Pearson correlations ranging from -0.06 to -0.09 and Spearman correlations ranging from -0.07 to -0.12. The correlations increase as the length of the $IdioVol^{FF}$ measurement period is increased.

Finally, the correlation analyses indicate a strong positive correlation between idiosyncratic volatility and idiosyncratic skewness. The Pearson correlations between $IdioSkew$ and $IdioVol^{FF}$ are increasing in the length of the $IdioVol^{FF}$ measurement period and are higher when $IdioVol^{FF}$ is measured using monthly return data. Both of these effects are potentially mechanical. Recall that we are calculating $IdioSkew$ using five years of monthly return data. As discussed previously, monthly returns are positively skewed. This, combined with the fact that high volatility stocks are more likely to produce extreme returns, as well as the fact that idiosyncratic volatility and idiosyncratic skewness are very similar to total volatility and total skewness, respectively, is likely the driving force behind the strong positive relation between $IdioVol^{FF}$ and $IdioSkew$. The Spearman rank correlations between the daily return-based measures of $IdioVol^{FF}$ and $IdioSkew$ are similar to the corresponding Pearson correlations. For the monthly return-based measures of $IdioVol^{FF}$, while the Spearman correlations remain large and positive, they are lower than the Pearson product–moment correlations, indicating that the Pearson correlations may be influenced by a small number of extreme data points.

In summary, the results of the correlation analyses indicate that for a fixed measurement period and data frequency, total volatility and idiosyncratic volatility are extremely similar in the cross section, regardless of the methodology used to measure the variables. Correlations between measures calculated using different measurement periods and data frequencies are high, but not so high as to indicate that empirical analysis of variables calculated using different measurement periods and data frequencies will necessarily produce highly similar results. Given these results, for reasons discussed earlier, we choose to proceed by using idiosyncratic volatility calculated relative to the FF risk model ($IdioVol^{FF}$) as our measure of idiosyncratic volatility. We continue to examine this measure calculated using different measurement periods and data frequencies.

We then examine the correlation between idiosyncratic volatility and other variables examined previously in this book. The results demonstrate that idiosyncratic volatility has a strong negative cross-sectional relation with stock size and a strong positive relation with each of illiquidity and idiosyncratic skewness. There is a positive but relatively weak relation between idiosyncratic volatility and beta, and a relatively weak negative relation between idiosyncratic volatility and co-skewness.

15.5 PERSISTENCE

Our last analysis of the idiosyncratic volatility variables before proceeding to our examination of the relation between idiosyncratic volatility and expected stock returns is a persistence analysis. The results of the persistence analysis for each of the $IdioVol^{FF}$ variables using lags of $\tau \in \{1, 3, 6, 12, 24, 36, 48, 60, 120\}$ months are shown in Table 15.6. We omit results for lags where the lag is less than the length of the measurement period to ensure that our analysis is not based on mechanical results. Prior to performing the persistence analysis, each variable is winsorized at the 0.5% level on a monthly basis.

The results indicate that $IdioVol^{FF}$ is highly persistent. When measured using daily return data, the persistence values of 0.65, 0.76, 0.80, and 0.80 for the variables calculated from one month ($IdioVol^{FF,1M}$), three months ($IdioVol^{FF,3M}$), six months ($IdioVol^{FF,6M}$), and 12 months ($IdioVol^{FF,12M}$), respectively, of daily data, measured at a lag equal to the length of the measurement period, are substantially higher than the corresponding values for β (see Table 8.3) or any of the skewness variables (see Tables 14.7–14.9). The same can be said for the idiosyncratic volatility variables calculated from monthly data, since $IdioVol^{FF,1Y}$, $IdioVol^{FF,2Y}$, $IdioVol^{FF,3Y}$, and $IdioVol^{FF,5Y}$ generate persistence values of 0.51, 0.61, 0.64, and 0.66 at lags of one, two, three, and five years, respectively. These levels of persistence are high enough to conclude that $IdioVol^{FF}$ is capturing a cross-sectionally persistent characteristic of stock returns.

Similar to the results for β and the skewness variables, the persistence increases as the length of the measurement period increases, indicating that longer measurement

TABLE 15.6 Persistence

This table presents the results of persistence analyses of variables measuring idiosyncratic volatility. Each month t, the cross-sectional Pearson product–moment correlation between the month t and month $t + \tau$ values of the given variable measured is calculated. The table presents the time-series averages of the monthly cross-sectional correlations. The column labeled τ indicates the lag at which the persistence is measured.

τ	$IdioVol^{FF,1M}$	$IdioVol^{FF,3M}$	$IdioVol^{FF,6M}$	$IdioVol^{FF,12M}$	$IdioVol^{FF,1Y}$	$IdioVol^{FF,2Y}$	$IdioVol^{FF,3Y}$	$IdioVol^{FF,5Y}$
1	0.65							
3	0.60	0.76						
6	0.57	0.71	0.80					
12	0.53	0.66	0.73	0.80	0.51			
24	0.46	0.58	0.65	0.71	0.46	0.61		
36	0.43	0.53	0.60	0.65	0.44	0.57	0.64	
48	0.40	0.50	0.56	0.62	0.42	0.54	0.61	
60	0.39	0.48	0.54	0.59	0.40	0.52	0.58	0.66
120	0.34	0.43	0.47	0.52	0.36	0.47	0.52	0.58

periods generate stronger estimates of the true idiosyncratic volatility of the stock's returns. Fixing the length of the lag (τ) at which the persistence is measured and the frequency of the data used, the persistence is always highest when using the variable calculated from a longer measurement period. Finally, looking only at the variables calculated from 12 months of daily return data ($IdioVol^{FF,12M}$) and five years of monthly return data ($IdioVol^{FF,5Y}$), which are the longest measurement periods for their respective data frequencies, we see that at long lags of 5 years ($\tau = 60$) and 10 years ($\tau = 120$), the persistence of $IdioVol^{FF,5Y}$ is slightly higher than that of $IdioVol^{FF,12M}$. However, because $IdioVol^{FF,5Y}$ requires at least two years of monthly returns (we require a minimum of 24 months of return data to calculate $IdioVol^{FF,5Y}$), for a stock to have a valid value of $IdioVol^{FF,5Y}$ in month t, it must have entered the CRSP database, at the latest, in month $t - 23$. Given that we require a minimum of 200 daily data points to calculate $IdioVol^{FF,12M}$, it is possible for a valid value of $IdioVol^{FF,12M}$ to be calculated in month t if the stock entered the CRSP database in month $t - 9$, only 10 months prior.[10] Thus, researchers may face a trade-off between the benefit of slightly higher measurement accuracy using the variable calculated from five years of monthly data ($IdioVol^{FF,5Y}$) and the ability to include more stocks in the sample when using idiosyncratic volatility calculated from 12 months of daily data ($IdioVol^{FF,12M}$).

One last comment regarding the persistence of idiosyncratic volatility is warranted. Despite the discussion in the previous paragraph indicating that longer estimation periods give more accurate measurement, the persistence of the variable calculated from one month of daily return data ($IdioVol^{FF,1M}$) measured at a lag of one month ($\tau = 1$) of 0.65 is quite high. Thus, even short measurement periods capture a highly persistent characteristic of the stock quite well. In the most widely cited study of the relation between idiosyncratic volatility and expected stock returns, Ang et al. (2006) use $IdioVol^{FF,1M}$ as their primary measure of idiosyncratic volatility. Most subsequent studies follow their lead. $IdioVol^{FF,1M}$, therefore, has become the most frequently used measure of idiosyncratic volatility in empirical asset pricing research.

15.6   IDIOSYNCRATIC VOLATILITY AND STOCK RETURNS

Having completed our analysis of the different measures of idiosyncratic volatility (and total volatility), we proceed now to examine the relation between idiosyncratic volatility and expected stock returns. As discussed in the introduction to this chapter, perfect market-based asset pricing theories such as the CAPM (Sharpe (1964), Lintner (1965), Mossin (1966)) and the APT of Ross (1976) predict that there should be no relation between idiosyncratic volatility and expected stock returns because all idiosyncratic risk can be diversified away. Theoretical models that introduce market frictions, such as those developed by Levy (1978) and Merton (1987), predict a positive relation between idiosyncratic volatility and expected returns. There is no

---

[10]There are at least 200 trading days in every 10-month span during our sample period.

rational theoretical model that predicts a negative relation between idiosyncratic volatility and expected stock returns.

15.6.1 Univariate Portfolio Analysis

Our investigation of the relation between idiosyncratic volatility and expected stock returns begins with univariate portfolio analyses. Each month, we sort all stocks in our sample into decile portfolios based on each of the FF idiosyncratic volatility variables. Table 15.7 presents the one-month-ahead value-weighted (Panel A) and equal-weighted (Panel B) excess returns for each of the portfolios each month, as well as the average return of the portfolio that is long the decile 10 portfolio and short the decile one portfolio, and alphas of this portfolio relative to the FFC risk model, as well as the FFC risk model augmented with the Pastor and Stambaugh (2003) liquidity factor (FFCPS). The numbers in parentheses are t-statistics, adjusted following Newey and West (1987) using six lags, testing the null hypothesis that the 10-1 portfolio average return or alpha is equal to zero.[11]

The results of the value-weighted portfolio analyses, presented in Panel A, provide strong evidence of a negative relation between idiosyncratic volatility measured from daily return data ($IdioVol^{FF,1M}$, $IdioVol^{FF,3M}$, $IdioVol^{FF,6M}$, and $IdioVol^{FF,12M}$) and future stock returns. This result strongly contradicts the theoretical predictions. For portfolios formed by sorting on $IdioVol^{FF,1M}$, the 10-1 value-weighted portfolio generates economically large and highly statistically significant average returns of -1.27% per month with a t-statistic of -3.48. The FFC alpha of -1.43% per month (t-statistic $= -5.25$) and FFCPS alpha of -1.47% per month (t-statistic $= -4.90$) indicate that none of the factors included in either of these risk models explains the returns of the $IdioVol^{FF,1M}$ difference portfolio. Examining the excess returns of the individual decile portfolios, we see that decile portfolios one through six generate similar average excess returns of between 0.48% per month for decile portfolios one and two and 0.62% per month for decile portfolio six. Starting with portfolio seven, the average excess returns of the decile portfolios fall sharply to 0.38% per month for the decile seven portfolio and 0.15%, -0.21%, and -0.79% per month for the $IdioVol^{FF,1M}$ decile eight, nine, and 10 portfolios, respectively. The substantially lower average returns of the high decile portfolios indicate that it is the high idiosyncratic volatility stocks that are driving this theoretically contradictory negative relation.

Examination of the results for value-weighted portfolios formed by sorting stocks on $IdioVol^{FF,3M}$, $IdioVol^{FF,6M}$, and $IdioVol^{FF,12M}$ are similar. The average return and alphas of the difference portfolio formed by sorting on each of these measures of idiosyncratic volatility are negative, large in magnitude, and highly statistically significant. Additionally, the large decrease in average excess returns beginning with

---

[11]Note that the *PSL* factor data are only available beginning in January of 1968. The alphas relative to the FFCPS model, along with associated t-statistics, are therefore calculated using portfolio returns realized during the months from January 1968 through December 2012, instead of July 1963 through December 2012, as is the case for all other analyses.

TABLE 15.7 Univariate Portfolio Analysis

This table presents the results of univariate portfolio analyses of the relation between idiosyncratic volatility and future stock returns. Monthly portfolios are formed by sorting all stocks in the CRSP sample into portfolios decile breakpoints calculated based on the given sort variable using all stocks in the CRSP sample. Panel A (Panel B) shows the average value-weighted (equal-weighted) one-month-ahead excess return (in percent per month) for each of the 10 decile portfolios formed using different measures of idiosyncratic volatility as the sort variable. The table also shows the average return of the portfolio that is long the 10th decile portfolio and short the first decile portfolio, as well as the FFC and FFCPS alphas for this portfolio. Newey and West (1987) t-statistics, adjusted using six lags, testing the null hypothesis that the average 10-1 portfolio return or alpha is equal to zero, are shown in parentheses.

Panel A: Value-Weighted Portfolios

Sort Variable	1	2	3	4	5	6	7	8	9	10	10-1	FFC α	FFCPS α
$IdioVol^{FF,1M}$	0.48	0.48	0.53	0.57	0.60	0.62	0.38	0.15	−0.21	−0.79	−1.27	−1.43	−1.47
											(−3.48)	(−5.25)	(−4.90)
$IdioVol^{FF,3M}$	0.50	0.50	0.52	0.60	0.71	0.58	0.32	0.00	−0.41	−0.87	−1.37	−1.58	−1.59
											(−3.39)	(−5.93)	(−5.70)
$IdioVol^{FF,6M}$	0.48	0.52	0.52	0.61	0.65	0.52	0.36	−0.05	−0.46	−0.85	−1.33	−1.52	−1.54
											(−3.08)	(−4.53)	(−4.22)
$IdioVol^{FF,12M}$	0.48	0.49	0.54	0.61	0.58	0.58	0.30	0.06	−0.18	−0.60	−1.08	−1.39	−1.38
											(−2.50)	(−4.87)	(−4.51)
$IdioVol^{FF,1Y}$	0.54	0.42	0.50	0.53	0.46	0.51	0.54	0.47	0.33	−0.15	−0.69	−1.03	−0.99
											(−1.97)	(−4.19)	(−3.71)
$IdioVol^{FF,2Y}$	0.45	0.53	0.57	0.50	0.63	0.54	0.57	0.40	0.31	−0.14	−0.60	−0.95	−0.94
											(−1.62)	(−3.45)	(−3.15)
$IdioVol^{FF,3Y}$	0.43	0.57	0.50	0.59	0.58	0.65	0.59	0.59	0.19	−0.11	−0.55	−0.88	−0.88
											(−1.52)	(−3.35)	(−3.11)
$IdioVol^{FF,5Y}$	0.45	0.50	0.53	0.63	0.53	0.77	0.56	0.45	0.25	−0.19	−0.64	−0.93	−0.94
											(−1.82)	(−3.69)	(−3.45)

Panel B: Equal-Weighted Portfolios

Sort Variable	1	2	3	4	5	6	7	8	9	10	10-1	FFC α	FFCPS α
$IdioVol^{FF,1M}$	0.69	0.76	0.87	0.94	0.93	0.90	0.85	0.70	0.56	0.28	−0.41	−0.58	−0.60
											(−1.12)	(−2.11)	(−2.09)
$IdioVol^{FF,3M}$	0.66	0.78	0.85	0.93	0.97	0.92	0.83	0.62	0.47	0.40	−0.26	−0.34	−0.38
											(−0.62)	(−1.09)	(−1.16)
$IdioVol^{FF,6M}$	0.67	0.77	0.84	0.94	0.89	0.89	0.76	0.60	0.50	0.58	−0.09	−0.17	−0.20
											(−0.20)	(−0.52)	(−0.59)
$IdioVol^{FF,12M}$	0.66	0.75	0.84	0.89	0.85	0.88	0.71	0.65	0.64	0.82	0.16	0.03	0.01
											(0.34)	(0.08)	(0.03)
$IdioVol^{FF,1Y}$	0.76	0.80	0.82	0.84	0.82	0.79	0.78	0.84	0.74	0.52	−0.24	−0.36	−0.37
											(−0.62)	(−1.23)	(−1.19)
$IdioVol^{FF,2Y}$	0.69	0.80	0.83	0.82	0.88	0.83	0.87	0.89	0.96	0.62	−0.07	−0.16	−0.19
											(−0.17)	(−0.51)	(−0.55)
$IdioVol^{FF,3Y}$	0.68	0.78	0.81	0.82	0.85	0.91	0.90	1.02	0.90	0.69	0.00	−0.07	−0.09
											(0.00)	(−0.20)	(−0.26)
$IdioVol^{FF,5Y}$	0.65	0.75	0.84	0.80	0.86	0.93	0.92	0.98	0.97	0.66	0.01	−0.01	−0.04
											(0.03)	(−0.02)	(−0.13)

the seventh decile portfolio is evident in portfolios formed by sorting on each of these variables. Regardless of the length of the measurement period, therefore, the value-weighted univariate portfolio analyses detect a strong negative cross-sectional relation between idiosyncratic volatility measured from daily return data and future stock returns.

The results from the value-weighted portfolios formed by sorting on the monthly return-based measures of idiosyncratic volatility ($IdioVol^{FF,1Y}$, $IdioVol^{FF,2Y}$, $IdioVol^{FF,3Y}$, and $IdioVol^{FF,5Y}$) are similar, but slightly weaker. When using $IdioVol^{FF,1Y}$ as the sort variable, the 10-1 portfolio generates an average return of −0.69% per month with a t-statistic of −1.97. While the average return of this portfolio is substantially lower than the average returns of the 10-1 portfolios formed by sorting on the daily return-based idiosyncratic volatility variables, it is nonetheless not only economically large in magnitude but also highly statistically significant. Both the FFC alpha of −1.03% per month (t-statistic = −4.19) and the FFCPS alpha of −0.99% per month (t-statistic = −3.71) are very large in magnitude and highly statistically significant. Once again, we observe a substantial drop in the average excess returns for the high-$IdioVol^{FF,1Y}$ portfolios. In this case, the drop appears to begin with decile portfolio nine. Decile portfolios one through eight all generate average excess returns between 0.42% per month and 0.54% per month, whereas $IdioVol^{FF,1Y}$ decile portfolio nine generates an average excess return of only 0.33% per month and the average excess return of the 10th decile portfolio is −0.15% per month.

When sorting on $IdioVol^{FF,2Y}$ or $IdioVol^{FF,3Y}$, Panel A of Table 15.7 shows that the average returns of the value-weighted 10-1 portfolios of −0.60% per month and −0.55% per month are not quite statistically significant, with associated t-statistics of −1.62 and −1.52, respectively. The FFC alphas and FFCPS alphas for these portfolios, however, are substantially larger than the average returns and, in each case, highly statistically significant. As with the portfolios formed by sorting on $IdioVol^{FF,1Y}$, the average portfolio excess returns for the decile nine and 10 portfolios are lower than the excess returns of any of the other decile portfolios.

When sorting on $IdioVol^{FF,5Y}$, the average return of the 10-1 value-weighted portfolio of −0.64% per month is marginally statistically significant with a t-statistic of −1.82. Both the FFC and the FFCPS alpha of this portfolio of 0.93% and 0.94% per month are highly statistically significant, with t-statistics of −3.69 and −3.32, respectively. Similar to the results of the univariate portfolios analyses using the other measures of monthly return-based idiosyncratic volatility, the average excess returns of $IdioVol^{FF,5Y}$ decile portfolios nine and 10 are much lower than the average excess returns of the other eight decile portfolios.

In Panel B of Table 15.7, we present the results of the equal-weighted univariate portfolio analyses of the relation between idiosyncratic volatility and expected stock returns. The results contrast starkly with those of the value-weighted portfolio analyses. When the equal-weighted portfolios are formed by sorting on idiosyncratic volatility calculated from one month of daily return data ($IdioVol^{FF,1M}$), the table shows that the 10-1 portfolio generates an average monthly return of −0.41%, which, while of substantial economic magnitude, is statistically indistinguishable from zero with a t-statistic of -1.12. The FFC and FFCPS alphas for this portfolio of -0.58% (t-statistic $= -2.11$) and -0.60% per month (t-statistic $= -2.09$), respectively, however, are larger in magnitude and highly statistically significant. Examination of the individual decile portfolio returns indicates somewhat of an inverse U-shaped pattern in the average excess portfolio returns across the deciles of $IdioVol^{FF,1M}$. The average excess returns of the portfolios increase from 0.69% per month for decile portfolio one to 0.94% per month for decile portfolio four and then decrease to 0.28% per month for decile portfolio 10. As with the value-weighted portfolios, decile portfolio 10 generates substantially lower average portfolio returns than any of the other decile portfolios.

The equal-weighted univariate portfolio analyses using each of the other measures of idiosyncratic volatility (not $IdioVol^{FF,1M}$) as the sort variable all fail to detect any cross-sectional relation between idiosyncratic volatility and expected stock returns. For each of these analyses, the average return, FFC alpha, and FFCPS alpha of the 10-1 portfolio are statistically indistinguishable from zero. Thus, with the exception of the portfolios formed by sorting on $IdioVol^{FF,1M}$, the puzzling negative relation between idiosyncratic volatility detected in the value-weighted portfolio analyses is not found when using equal-weighted portfolios.

In summary, consistent with the results in Ang et al. (2006), the value-weighted portfolio analyses detect a strong negative relation between idiosyncratic volatility and expected stock returns. With the exception of portfolios sorted on $IdioVol^{FF,1M}$, equal-weighted portfolio analyses fail to provide any indication of such a relation.

The negative relation between $IdioVol^{FF,1M}$ and future stock returns detected in the equal-weighted portfolios, while consistent with the value-weighted portfolio results, is inconsistent with results in Bali and Cakici (2008), who perform a similar analysis and find no relation between $IdioVol^{FF,1M}$ and future stock returns in equal-weighted portfolios. One of the main differences between the analyses in Bali and Cakici (2008) and the analyses whose results are shown in Table 15.7 is that, following Ang et al. (2006), Bali and Cakici (2008) do not adjust their returns for delisting according to Shumway (1997). In unreported analyses, we confirm the results in each of Ang et al. (2006) and Bali and Cakici (2008) by restricting our sample to the sample periods of the given papers, 1963 through 2000 and 1963 through 2004, respectively, and using unadjusted excess returns instead of delisting-adjusted excess returns. Our replications produce extremely similar results to those in the original papers, indicating that the results of analyses examining the relation between idiosyncratic volatility and future stock returns are highly sensitive to both sample period and the details of the empirical methodology. To examine the effect of using delisting-adjusted returns on the results of the univariate portfolio analyses in our sample covering the 1963 through 2012 period, we repeat the univariate portfolio analyses whose results are presented in Table 15.7 using the unadjusted excess returns as the outcome variable instead of the delisting-adjusted excess returns.[12]

Table 15.8 presents the results of the univariate portfolio analyses using unadjusted excess returns as the outcome variable. Panel A shows that when using

---

[12] See Section 7.2 for more details on unadjusted and delisting-adjusted returns.

TABLE 15.8 Univariate Portfolio Analysis—Unadjusted Returns

This table presents the results of univariate portfolio analyses of the relation between idiosyncratic volatility and nondelisting-adjusted future stock returns. Monthly portfolios are formed by sorting all stocks in the CRSP sample into portfolios using decile breakpoints calculated based on the given sort variable using all stocks in the CRSP sample. Panel A (Panel B) shows the average value-weighted (equal-weighted) one-month-ahead nondelisting-adjusted excess return (in percent per month) for each of the 10 decile portfolios formed using different measures of idiosyncratic volatility as the sort variable. The table also shows the average return of the portfolio that is long the 10th decile portfolio and short the first decile portfolio, as well as the FFC and FFCPS alphas for this portfolio. Newey and West (1987) t-statistics, adjusted using six lags, testing the null hypothesis that the average 10-1 portfolio return or alpha is equal to zero, are shown in parentheses.

Panel A: Value-Weighted Portfolios

Sort Variable	1	2	3	4	5	6	7	8	9	10	10-1	FFC α	FFCPS α
$IdioVol^{FF,1M}$	0.48	0.48	0.53	0.57	0.60	0.62	0.38	0.15	−0.20	−0.70	−1.18	−1.33	−1.37
											(−3.20)	(−4.86)	(−4.51)
$IdioVol^{FF,3M}$	0.50	0.49	0.52	0.60	0.71	0.58	0.31	−0.00	−0.41	−0.75	−1.26	−1.48	−1.48
											(−3.07)	(−5.53)	(−5.28)
$IdioVol^{FF,6M}$	0.48	0.52	0.52	0.61	0.66	0.51	0.34	−0.05	−0.46	−0.71	−1.19	−1.39	−1.39
											(−2.71)	(−4.04)	(−3.73)
$IdioVol^{FF,12M}$	0.48	0.49	0.54	0.62	0.56	0.57	0.30	0.06	−0.16	−0.50	−0.97	−1.30	−1.29
											(−2.22)	(−4.56)	(−4.20)
$IdioVol^{FF,1Y}$	0.54	0.42	0.50	0.52	0.46	0.51	0.55	0.46	0.33	−0.15	−0.70	−1.06	−1.01
											(−1.93)	(−4.24)	(−3.75)
$IdioVol^{FF,2Y}$	0.45	0.53	0.57	0.49	0.62	0.53	0.56	0.40	0.31	−0.11	−0.56	−0.93	−0.92
											(−1.51)	(−3.35)	(−3.05)
$IdioVol^{FF,3Y}$	0.43	0.57	0.49	0.59	0.56	0.64	0.60	0.59	0.19	−0.08	−0.52	−0.86	−0.86
											(−1.43)	(−3.28)	(−3.03)
$IdioVol^{FF,5Y}$	0.45	0.50	0.53	0.63	0.53	0.77	0.57	0.45	0.27	−0.16	−0.61	−0.92	−0.93
											(−1.75)	(−3.68)	(−3.43)

Panel B: Equal-Weighted Portfolios

Sort Variable	1	2	3	4	5	6	7	8	9	10	10-1	FFC α	FFCPS α
$IdioVol^{FF,1M}$	0.66	0.76	0.87	0.94	0.94	0.90	0.87	0.73	0.63	0.66	0.01	−0.07	−0.08
											(0.02)	(−0.27)	(−0.27)
$IdioVol^{FF,3M}$	0.66	0.78	0.84	0.93	0.98	0.93	0.84	0.65	0.53	0.77	0.11	−0.03	−0.05
											(0.25)	(−0.10)	(−0.14)
$IdioVol^{FF,6M}$	0.67	0.77	0.84	0.93	0.90	0.89	0.77	0.63	0.57	0.96	0.29	0.15	0.14
											(0.66)	(0.46)	(0.41)
$IdioVol^{FF,12M}$	0.66	0.75	0.84	0.88	0.85	0.88	0.72	0.67	0.72	1.20	0.53	0.34	0.34
											(1.15)	(1.01)	(0.97)
$IdioVol^{FF,1Y}$	0.76	0.81	0.82	0.85	0.82	0.81	0.82	0.90	0.86	0.75	−0.01	−0.20	−0.20
											(−0.03)	(−0.76)	(−0.71)
$IdioVol^{FF,2Y}$	0.69	0.79	0.83	0.82	0.88	0.84	0.89	0.95	1.09	0.84	0.16	−0.02	−0.04
											(0.39)	(−0.09)	(−0.12)
$IdioVol^{FF,3Y}$	0.68	0.78	0.81	0.82	0.85	0.92	0.92	1.09	1.04	0.89	0.21	0.05	0.04
											(0.51)	(0.18)	(0.12)
$IdioVol^{FF,5Y}$	0.65	0.75	0.83	0.81	0.87	0.94	0.96	1.05	1.10	0.85	0.20	0.09	0.06
											(0.49)	(0.31)	(0.20)

value-weighted portfolios, the results of the univariate portfolio analyses are very similar to the results produced using the delisting-adjusted excess returns. Regardless of the measure of idiosyncratic volatility used as the sort variable, the results indicate a strong negative cross-sectional relation between idiosyncratic volatility and future stock returns.

When equal-weighted portfolios are used, however, the results for the portfolios formed by sorting on $IdioVol^{FF,1M}$ change substantially. The average unadjusted return of the $IdioVol^{FF,1M}$ 10-1 portfolio is 0.01% per month, compared to -0.41% per month when using the delisting-adjusted returns. Furthermore, both the FFC and FFCPS alphas calculated from the analysis using the unadjusted returns of -0.07% per month (t-statistic $= -0.27$) and -0.08% per month (t-statistic $= -0.35$) are statistically indistinguishable from zero. These results are very different from the corresponding results when delisting-adjusted returns are used as the dependent variable. When delisting-adjusted returns are used, the FFC and FFCPS alphas are -0.58% per month (t-statistic $= -2.11$) and -0.60% per month (t-statistic $= -2.09$), respectively, both of which are much larger in magnitude than the corresponding results from the analysis using unadjusted returns. Furthermore, when adjusted returns are used, the alphas are highly statistically significant, whereas when unadjusted returns are used, the alphas are not even close to significant.

Further comparison of the results indicates that the equal-weighted delisting-adjusted and unadjusted average excess returns for the first nine $IdioVol^{FF,1M}$ decile portfolios are very similar. However, the equal-weighted average unadjusted excess return of the 10th $IdioVol^{FF,1M}$ decile portfolio is 0.66% per month, compared to an average delisting-adjusted return of only 0.28% per month. This likely indicates that stocks in the highest $IdioVol^{FF,1M}$ decile are substantially more likely to delist, and thus realize a large negative delisting-adjusted return, than stocks in the first decile of $IdioVol^{FF,1M}$.

While the divergence between the results of the equal-weighted univariate portfolio when using unadjusted compared to delisting-adjusted returns is interesting, not well-known by empirical asset pricing researchers, and worthy of further investigation, we do not investigate this issue further. For the remainder of this chapter, we continue to use the delisting-adjusted returns, as we have done in most analyses in this book, as the measure of future stock returns.

In Table 15.9, we present the equal-weighted average values of $IdioVol^{FF,1M}$, beta (β), market capitalization ($MktCap$), book-to-market ratio (BM), momentum (Mom), reversal (Rev), illiquidity ($Illiq$), co-skewness ($CoSkew$), and idiosyncratic skewness ($IdioSkew$) for decile portfolios formed by sorting on $IdioVol^{FF,1M}$. We choose to present average characteristics for portfolio sorted on $IdioVol^{FF,1M}$ instead of some other variable measuring idiosyncratic volatility for two reasons. First, this is the only variable that produced statistically significant results in both the value-weighted and equal-weighted portfolio analyses. Second, this is the most commonly used measure of idiosyncratic volatility in empirical asset pricing research. In addition to understanding the characteristics of the stocks that comprise each of the $IdioVol^{FF,1M}$-sorted portfolios, the average characteristics can be used,

TABLE 15.9   Portfolio Characteristics—$IdioVol^{FF,1M}$

This table presents the average characteristics for stocks in decile portfolios formed by sorting on $IdioVol^{FF,1M}$. Monthly portfolios are formed by sorting all stocks in the CRSP sample into portfolios using $IdioVol^{FF,1M}$ decile breakpoints calculated using all stocks in the CRSP sample. The table shows the average values of $IdioVol^{FF,1M}$, β, MktCap, BM, Mom, Rev, Illiq, CoSkew, and IdioSkew for each of the decile portfolios.

Value	1	2	3	4	5	6	7	8	9	10
$IdioVol^{FF,1M}$	11.51	19.01	24.16	29.26	34.82	41.21	49.03	59.62	76.66	135.40
β	0.48	0.65	0.73	0.79	0.85	0.89	0.92	0.91	0.87	0.76
MktCap	3730	2622	1626	1088	716	498	342	226	139	70
BM	0.95	0.87	0.86	0.86	0.88	0.89	0.93	0.98	1.04	1.20
Mom	14.65	15.46	16.11	17.20	18.08	18.67	18.14	16.26	11.12	−2.91
Rev	0.27	0.39	0.41	0.45	0.47	0.47	0.59	0.81	1.52	6.83
Illiq	0.15	0.24	0.36	0.53	0.77	1.14	1.72	2.83	5.59	28.14
CoSkew	−0.77	−0.66	−0.77	−0.87	−1.01	−1.12	−1.30	−1.53	−1.85	−2.29
IdioSkew	0.46	0.40	0.44	0.49	0.56	0.63	0.71	0.80	0.92	1.08

along with the correlation analyses presented in Table 15.5, to identify variables that may potentially be driving the idiosyncratic volatility puzzle.

The results in Table 15.9 show that, by construction, average $IdioVol^{FF,1M}$ increases monotonically from 11.51% for stocks in decile portfolio one to 135.40% for stocks in the 10th decile portfolio.

Average β exhibits an inverse U-shaped pattern across the $IdioVol^{FF,1M}$ deciles, increasing from 0.48 in decile portfolio one to 0.92 in decile portfolio seven and then decreasing to 0.76 in decile portfolio 10.

Consistent with the results of the correlation analysis, MktCap exhibits a strong negative relation with $IdioVol^{FF,1M}$ since the average market capitalization decreases monotonically from $3.73 billion for stocks in the first $IdioVol^{FF,1M}$ decile portfolio to only $70 million for stocks in the 10th decile portfolio. Since low-MktCap stocks tend to generate high average returns, it is unlikely that market capitalization is driving the negative relation between idiosyncratic volatility and future stock returns.

The table indicates a U-shaped relation between BM and $IdioVol^{FF,1M}$. The average values of BM decrease from 0.95 for the first decile portfolio to 0.86 for the third and fourth decile portfolios and then increase to 1.20 for the 10th decile portfolio.

The relation between Mom and $IdioVol^{FF,1M}$ is inverse U-shaped, with average values of Mom increasing from 14.65 in decile portfolio one to 18.67 in decile portfolio six, and the dropping dramatically to −2.91 in decile portfolio 10. Because stocks with low values of Mom generate low average returns, the extremely low values of momentum in the high $IdioVol^{FF,1M}$ indicate that Mom may play an important role in the low returns of the high-$IdioVol^{FF,1M}$ portfolios.

Rev exhibits a strong positive relation with $IdioVol^{FF,1M}$, with average values of Rev increasing monotonically from 0.27 in decile portfolio one to 6.83 in the 10th decile portfolio. Since Rev is negatively related to future returns, it is also possible that the reversal phenomenon is driving the negative relation between idiosyncratic volatility and future returns. Interestingly, despite the apparent strength of the positive relation between $IdioVol^{FF,1M}$ detected in the average portfolio values of *Rev*, the correlation analyses in Table 15.5 indicates only a weak Pearson correlation of 0.10 between $IdioVol^{FF,1M}$ and *Rev*, and a Spearman correlation between these two variables of 0.00 in the average month.

Consistent with the strong positive relation between *Illiq* and $IdioVol^{FF,1M}$ detected in the correlation analyses, the average values of *Illiq* increase monotonically from 0.15 for stocks in the first $IdioVol^{FF,1M}$ decile portfolio to 28.14 for stocks in the 10th decile portfolio. Stocks with high values of *Illiq*, however, tend to generate high returns; thus, *Illiq* is unlikely to explain the negative relation between idiosyncratic volatility and future stock returns.

Table 15.9 shows a strong negative relation between $IdioVol^{FF,1M}$ and *CoSkew* since average values of *CoSkew* decrease nearly monotonically (the exception is decile portfolio two) from -0.77 for stocks in decile portfolio one to -2.29 for stocks in decile portfolio 10. Given that *CoSkew* failed to exhibit an empirical relation with future stock returns and theoretically low co-skewness is associated with higher average returns, *CoSkew* is unlikely to explain the idiosyncratic volatility puzzle.

Finally, with the exception of decile portfolio one, average values of *IdioSkew* increase monotonically across the deciles of $IdioVol^{FF,1M}$, with stocks in the decile two portfolio having average *IdioSkew* of 0.40 and stocks in the 10th decile portfolio having average *IdioSkew* of 1.08. This result is consistent with the strong positive relation between *IdioSkew* and $IdioVol^{FF,1M}$ detected in the correlation analyses (Table 15.5). The positive relation between $IdioVol^{FF,1M}$ and *IdioSkew* combined with the negative relation between *IdioSkew* and future stock returns (see Chapter 14) indicates that it is possible that idiosyncratic skewness is driving the idiosyncratic volatility puzzle.

15.6.2 Bivariate Portfolio Analysis

We proceed now to examine whether controlling for any of the variables examined previously in this book can explain the idiosyncratic volatility puzzle. The average portfolio characteristics presented in Table 15.9 show that momentum (*Mom*), reversal (*Rev*), and idiosyncratic skewness (*IdioSkew*) have cross-sectional relations with $IdioVol^{FF,1M}$ indicating that these variables may provide an explanation for the idiosyncratic volatility puzzle.

Bivariate Dependent-Sort Portfolio Analysis

Our first analyses investigating potential explanations for the idiosyncratic volatility puzzle are bivariate dependent-sort portfolio analyses using each of β, *MktCap*, *BM*, *Mom*, *Rev*, *Illiq*, *CoSkew*, and *IdioSkew* as the first sort variable and $IdioVol^{FF,1M}$ as the second sort variable. We sort all stocks into five groups based on the first sort variable and then, within each quintile of the first sort variable, we sort stocks into quintile portfolios based on $IdioVol^{FF,1M}$. The portfolio breakpoints are calculated using all stocks in the sample. Table 15.10 shows the value-weighted average returns, FFC alphas, and FFCPS alphas for the zero-cost portfolio that is long high-$IdioVol^{FF,1M}$ stocks and short low-$IdioVol^{FF,1M}$ stocks within each quintile of the given control variable, as well as for the average control variable quintile. Newey and West (1987)-adjusted *t*-statistics are presented in parentheses.

TABLE 15.10   Bivariate Dependent-Sort Portfolio Analysis—Value-Weighted

This table presents the results of bivariate dependent-sort portfolio analyses of the relation between $IdioVol^{FF,1M}$ and future stock returns after controlling for the effect of each of β, $MktCap$, BM, Mom, Rev, $Illiq$, $CoSkew$, and $IdioSkew$ (control variables). Each month, all stocks in the CRSP sample are sorted into five groups based on an ascending sort of one of the control variables. Within each control variable group, all stocks are sorted into five value-weighted portfolios based on an ascending sort of $IdioVol^{FF,1M}$. The quintile breakpoints used to create the portfolios are calculated using all stocks in the CRSP sample. The table presents the average return, FFC alpha, and FFCPS alpha (in percent per month) of the long–short zero-cost portfolios that are long the fifth $IdioVol^{FF,1M}$ quintile portfolio and short the first $IdioVol^{FF,1M}$ quintile portfolio in each quintile, as well as for the average quintile, of the control variable. t-statistics (in parentheses), adjusted following Newey and West (1987) using six lags, testing the null hypothesis that the average return or alpha is equal to zero, are shown in parentheses.

Control	Value	Control 1	Control 2	Control 3	Control 4	Control 5	Control Avg
β	Return	−0.44	−0.17	−0.49	−0.58	−1.08	−0.55
		(−1.44)	(−0.69)	(−1.71)	(−2.21)	(−3.36)	(−2.28)
	FFC α	−0.78	−0.41	−0.69	−0.79	−1.22	−0.78
		(−3.26)	(−2.35)	(−2.90)	(−3.72)	(−4.93)	(−5.00)
	FFCPS α	−0.86	−0.49	−0.79	−0.78	−1.18	−0.82
		(−3.17)	(−2.60)	(−3.22)	(−3.50)	(−4.30)	(−4.80)
$MktCap$	Return	−0.94	−1.63	−1.23	−0.72	−0.19	−0.94
		(−2.73)	(−5.38)	(−4.34)	(−2.62)	(−0.81)	(−3.59)
	FFC α	−1.22	−1.76	−1.28	−0.75	−0.27	−1.06
		(−4.21)	(−7.50)	(−6.44)	(−4.13)	(−1.57)	(−6.40)
	FFCPS α	−1.24	−1.80	−1.28	−0.75	−0.29	−1.07
		(−4.03)	(−7.22)	(−5.96)	(−3.79)	(−1.50)	(−6.01)
BM	Return	−1.31	−0.81	−0.21	−0.07	0.22	−0.44
		(−3.75)	(−2.92)	(−0.69)	(−0.20)	(0.62)	(−1.57)
	FFC α	−1.36	−0.82	−0.27	−0.39	0.04	−0.56
		(−5.09)	(−3.39)	(−1.28)	(−1.60)	(0.15)	(−3.24)
	FFCPS α	−1.46	−0.92	−0.36	−0.54	−0.03	−0.66
		(−4.97)	(−3.50)	(−1.58)	(−2.15)	(−0.08)	(−3.53)
Mom	Return	−2.47	−0.82	−0.41	−0.20	−0.42	−0.87
		(−7.16)	(−2.90)	(−1.55)	(−0.81)	(−1.62)	(−3.72)
	FFC α	−2.98	−1.26	−0.67	−0.34	−0.70	−1.19
		(−10.31)	(−5.70)	(−3.61)	(−2.20)	(−2.90)	(−8.86)
	FFCPS α	−3.00	−1.30	−0.78	−0.27	−0.70	−1.21
		(−8.91)	(−5.35)	(−3.79)	(−1.53)	(−2.63)	(−7.75)

TABLE 15.10   *(Continued)*

Control	Value	Control 1	Control 2	Control 3	Control 4	Control 5	Control Avg
Rev	Return	−1.20	−0.80	−0.71	−0.58	−1.11	−0.88
		(−3.29)	(−2.31)	(−2.26)	(−1.88)	(−3.40)	(−3.06)
	FFC α	−1.32	−1.10	−1.08	−0.79	−1.26	−1.11
		(−4.23)	(−5.03)	(−6.65)	(−3.51)	(−4.25)	(−6.55)
	FFCPS α	−1.28	−1.19	−1.08	−0.81	−1.36	−1.14
		(−3.85)	(−4.87)	(−5.88)	(−3.34)	(−4.24)	(−6.17)
Illiq	Return	−0.22	−0.42	−0.90	−1.36	−2.08	−0.99
		(−0.87)	(−1.43)	(−2.78)	(−4.42)	(−6.91)	(−3.67)
	FFC α	−0.34	−0.44	−0.92	−1.39	−2.14	−1.05
		(−1.91)	(−2.30)	(−4.19)	(−6.14)	(−9.51)	(−6.43)
	FFCPS α	−0.34	−0.45	−0.96	−1.44	−2.21	−1.08
		(−1.75)	(−2.13)	(−3.92)	(−5.95)	(−8.93)	(−6.06)
CoSkew	Return	−1.31	−0.52	−0.36	−0.57	−0.89	−0.73
		(−3.61)	(−1.65)	(−1.26)	(−2.18)	(−2.74)	(−2.75)
	FFC α	−1.11	−0.73	−0.57	−0.69	−1.05	−0.83
		(−3.54)	(−2.73)	(−2.87)	(−3.27)	(−4.49)	(−4.86)
	FFCPS α	−1.06	−0.75	−0.63	−0.77	−1.11	−0.86
		(−2.95)	(−2.49)	(−2.85)	(−3.42)	(−4.25)	(−4.40)
IdioSkew	Return	−0.17	−0.51	−0.38	−0.78	−1.48	−0.66
		(−0.57)	(−1.62)	(−1.29)	(−2.06)	(−4.38)	(−2.38)
	FFC α	−0.25	−0.62	−0.56	−0.96	−1.54	−0.79
		(−1.12)	(−2.87)	(−2.86)	(−3.11)	(−5.75)	(−4.72)
	FFCPS α	−0.19	−0.61	−0.64	−1.08	−1.54	−0.81
		(−0.75)	(−2.49)	(−2.94)	(−3.22)	(−5.03)	(−4.29)

The results in Table 15.10 show that none of the control variables fully explain the idiosyncratic volatility puzzle in value-weighted portfolios since the average return, FFC alpha, and FFCPS alpha of the *IdioVol*^{FF,1M} 5-1 portfolio for the average control variable quintile are economically large and highly statistically significant in all analyses. The one exception is the average return of the *IdioVol*^{FF,1M} difference portfolio for the average *BM* quintile of −0.44% per month, which, while economically large, is statistically insignificant with a *t*-statistic of −1.57.

After controlling for β, while the average returns of the *IdioVol*^{FF,1M} difference portfolio in the first and second quintiles of β are statistically insignificant, and that of the third β quintile is only marginally significant, all of the difference portfolios generate abnormal returns relative to both the FFC and FFCPS risk models that are economically large and highly statistically significant.

When controlling for *MktCap*, the average returns and alphas of the *IdioVol*^{FF,1M} 5-1 portfolios are negative, economically large, and highly statistically significant in all but the fifth quintile of *MktCap*, indicating that the idiosyncratic volatility puzzle exists in all but the largest stocks in our sample. This result is interesting given that the univariate portfolio results are stronger when using value-weighted portfolios instead of equal-weighted portfolios. Based on the univariate portfolio results, one may have expected the negative relation to be strong among large stocks. The results indicate the opposite.

When the portfolios are formed by first sorting on *BM*, the results in Table 15.10 show that the idiosyncratic volatility puzzle only exists in low *BM* stocks. The average returns and alphas of the $IdioVol^{FF,1M}$ 5-1 portfolio in quintiles one and two of *BM* are negative, economically large, and highly statistically significant. In quintiles three, four, and five of *BM*, however, the average returns and alphas of the $IdioVol^{FF,1M}$ difference portfolios are statistically insignificant.[13] The difference portfolio in the fifth *BM* quintile is the only portfolio in any of the value-weighted portfolio analyses that generates a positive average or abnormal return.

Controlling for *Mom*, one of the variables whose cross-sectional relation with $IdioVol^{FF,1M}$ indicated a possible explanation, the results of the value-weighted bivariate dependent-sort portfolio analysis indicate that in all quintiles of *Mom*, the FFC and FFCPS alphas of the $IdioVol^{FF,1M}$ portfolio are negative and statistically significant, with the exception of the FFCPS alpha in the fourth *Mom* quintile. The average returns of the $IdioVol^{FF,1M}$ difference portfolios, while negative in all quintiles of *Mom*, are only significant in the first two *Mom* quintiles.

When controlling for *Rev*, another variable whose relation with $IdioVol^{FF,1M}$ indicated a potential explanation for the idiosyncratic volatility puzzle, the average returns and alphas of the $IdioVol^{FF,1M}$ 5-1 portfolio in each quintile of *Rev* are all negative, economically large, and highly statistically significant, with the exception of the average return of the portfolio in the fourth *Rev* quintile of −0.58% per month, which is only marginally significant with a *t*-statistic of −1.88.

The idiosyncratic volatility puzzle is strong in all but the most liquid stocks, since the average returns and alphas of the $IdioVol^{FF,1M}$ 5-1 portfolio in quintiles two through five of *Illiq* are all negative, large in magnitude, and statistically significant.[14] In quintile one of *Illiq*, which holds the most liquid stocks, while the FFC and FFCPS alphas of −0.34% per month are marginally significant with *t*-statistics of −1.91 and −1.75, respectively, the average return of −0.22% per month (*t*-statistic = −0.87) is statistically indistinguishable from zero. The results demonstrate that the idiosyncratic volatility puzzle becomes stronger for more illiquid stocks since the average returns and alphas of the $IdioVol^{FF,1M}$ difference portfolio increase monotonically in magnitude from quintile one to quintile five of *Illiq*.

The results in Table 15.10 provide no evidence that *CoSkew* can explain the idiosyncratic volatility puzzle in value-weighted portfolios, since, with only two exceptions, within each quintile of *CoSkew*, the average return and alphas of

---

[13]The one exception is the FFCPS alpha of the $IdioVol^{FF,1M}$ 5-1 portfolio in the fourth *BM* quintile of −0.54% per month, which is statistically significant with a *t*-statistic of −2.15.
[14]The only exception is the average return in the $IdioVol^{FF,1M}$ 5-1 portfolio in the second *Illiq* quintile of −0.42% per month, which is statistically insignificant with a *t*-statistic of −1.43.

the $IdioVol^{FF,1M}$ 5-1 portfolio are negative, economically large, and statistically significant. The exceptions are the average returns in *CoSkew* quintiles two and three of -0.52% per month (t-statistic $= -1.65$) and -0.36% per month (t-statistic $= -1.26\%$), respectively, which, while economically meaningful, are not statistically significant.

Finally, the value-weighted bivariate dependent-sort portfolio analyses show that the idiosyncratic volatility puzzle is stronger among stocks with high levels of *IdioSkew*. The $IdioVol^{FF,1M}$ 5-1 portfolio in the first quintile of *IdioSkew* fails to produce significant average or abnormal returns. In quintiles two and three of *IdioSkew*, the average returns of the $IdioVol^{FF,1M}$ difference portfolio are statistically insignificant, but the FFC and FFCPS alphas are significant. In quintiles four and five of *IdioSkew*, the average returns and alphas are all statistically significant. Furthermore, the magnitudes of the average returns and alphas of the $IdioVol^{FF,1M}$ 5-1 portfolio increase monotonically (with the exception of the average return and FFC alpha for the second *IdioSkew* quintile) across the quintiles of *IdioSkew*.

Having found no evidence using value-weighted portfolio that any of the control variables can fully explain the idiosyncratic volatility puzzle, we repeat the analyses using equal-weighted portfolios. Recall that the univariate portfolio analysis results in Table 15.7 demonstrated that the idiosyncratic volatility puzzle is substantially weaker in equal-weighted portfolios than in value-weighted portfolios. In fact, the univariate portfolio analysis indicated a statistically significant idiosyncratic volatility puzzle only when the variable calculated from one month of daily return data ($IdioVol^{FF,1M}$) is used as the sort variable. Even then, the average return of the $IdioVol^{FF,1M}$ difference portfolio was statistically indistinguishable from zero, but the FFC and FFCPS alphas were significant.

Table 15.11 presents the results of the equal-weighted bivariate dependent-sort portfolio analyses of the relation between $IdioVol^{FF,1M}$ and future returns after controlling for each of β, *MktCap*, *BM*, *Rev*, *Illiq*, *CoSkew*, and *IdioSkew*. The results provide evidence that after controlling for the effects of β, *BM*, *CoSkew*, or *IdioSkew*, the idiosyncratic volatility puzzle is no longer present in equal-weighted portfolios, since the average returns and alphas of the $IdioVol^{FF,1M}$ 5-1 portfolio in the average quintile of each of these control variables are statistically indistinguishable from zero. Interestingly, when controlling for *MktCap*, and *Illiq*, the idiosyncratic volatility puzzle appears stronger in the bivariate portfolio analysis than in the univariate portfolio analysis. In these cases, not only are the alphas of the $IdioVol^{FF,1M}$ difference portfolio negative and significant for the average control variable quintile, but the average returns of this portfolio are also significant. Finally, when controlling for *Mom* or *Rev*, the results for the average control variable quintile are similar to the equal-weighted univariate portfolio results, since these analyses find a statistically insignificant average return for the $IdioVol^{FF,1M}$ difference portfolio but statistically significant FFC and FFCPS alphas.

The results of the analysis that uses β as the control variable show that the relation between $IdioVol^{FF,1M}$ changes substantially for stocks with different levels of β in equal-weighted portfolios, with the relation being positive for stocks with low values of β and negative for stocks with high values of β. The average return

TABLE 15.11   Bivariate Dependent-Sort Portfolio Analysis—Equal-Weighted

This table presents the results of bivariate dependent-sort portfolio analyses of the relation between $IdioVol^{FF,1M}$ and future stock returns after controlling for the effect of each of β, $MktCap$, BM, Mom, Rev, $Illiq$, $CoSkew$, and $IdioSkew$ (control variables). Each month, all stocks in the CRSP sample are sorted into five groups based on an ascending sort of one of the control variables. Within each control variable group, all stocks are sorted into five equal-weighted portfolios based on an ascending sort of $IdioVol^{FF,1M}$. The quintile break-points used to create the portfolios are calculated using all stocks in the CRSP sample. The table presents the average return, FFC alpha, and FFCPS alpha (in percent per month) of the long–short zero-cost portfolios that are long the fifth $IdioVol^{FF,1M}$ quintile portfolio and short the first $IdioVol^{FF,1M}$ quintile portfolio in each quintile, as well as for the average quintile, of the control variable. t-statistics (in parentheses), adjusted following Newey and West (1987) using six lags, testing the null hypothesis that the average return or alpha is equal to zero, are shown in parentheses.

Control	Value	Control 1	Control 2	Control 3	Control 4	Control 5	Control Avg
β	Return	0.62	0.10	−0.22	−0.51	−1.00	−0.20
		(1.98)	(0.34)	(−0.64)	(−1.73)	(−3.10)	(−0.71)
	FFC α	0.37	−0.02	−0.46	−0.58	−0.99	−0.34
		(1.57)	(−0.10)	(−1.15)	(−2.34)	(−3.29)	(−1.50)
	FFCPS α	0.36	−0.05	−0.47	−0.61	−0.92	−0.34
		(1.43)	(−0.20)	(−1.16)	(−2.36)	(−2.86)	(−1.42)
$MktCap$	Return	0.19	−1.57	−1.25	−0.74	−0.24	−0.72
		(0.52)	(−5.23)	(−4.41)	(−2.68)	(−0.99)	(−2.71)
	FFC α	−0.11	−1.70	−1.31	−0.77	−0.25	−0.83
		(−0.28)	(−7.23)	(−6.50)	(−4.30)	(−1.63)	(−4.68)
	FFCPS α	−0.00	−1.75	−1.31	−0.77	−0.24	−0.81
		(−0.01)	(−6.98)	(−6.06)	(−3.95)	(−1.41)	(−4.31)
BM	Return	−0.74	−0.12	−0.04	0.30	0.51	−0.02
		(−2.17)	(−0.42)	(−0.12)	(0.99)	(1.80)	(−0.07)
	FFC α	−0.69	−0.09	−0.28	0.15	0.47	−0.09
		(−2.23)	(−0.35)	(−0.60)	(0.73)	(2.13)	(−0.37)
	FFCPS α	−0.78	−0.20	−0.30	0.10	0.46	−0.15
		(−2.41)	(−0.74)	(−0.63)	(0.43)	(1.97)	(−0.60)
Mom	Return	−0.74	−0.03	0.15	0.23	−0.27	−0.13
		(−2.23)	(−0.13)	(0.58)	(0.84)	(−1.08)	(−0.53)
	FFC α	−1.22	−0.32	−0.13	−0.07	−0.55	−0.46
		(−3.00)	(−1.74)	(−0.92)	(−0.46)	(−3.09)	(−2.84)
	FFCPS α	−1.13	−0.34	−0.20	−0.09	−0.51	−0.45
		(−2.71)	(−1.75)	(−1.26)	(−0.51)	(−2.60)	(−2.61)

TABLE 15.11 (*Continued*)

Control	Value		Control 1	Control 2	Control 3	Control 4	Control 5	Control Avg
Rev	Return		1.36	−0.45	−0.45	−0.69	−1.89	−0.42
			(3.94)	(−1.46)	(−1.31)	(−2.05)	(−5.79)	(−1.42)
	FFC α		1.43	−0.57	−0.84	−1.07	−2.08	−0.62
			(4.49)	(−3.06)	(−3.07)	(−3.53)	(−8.49)	(−3.28)
	FFCPS α		1.58	−0.62	−0.86	−1.12	−2.18	−0.64
			(4.67)	(−3.19)	(−3.05)	(−3.63)	(−8.07)	(−3.18)
Illiq	Return		−0.19	−0.46	−0.89	−1.35	−0.71	−0.72
			(−0.75)	(−1.67)	(−2.83)	(−4.12)	(−2.10)	(−2.56)
	FFC α		−0.29	−0.48	−0.85	−1.27	−0.73	−0.72
			(−1.84)	(−2.49)	(−3.54)	(−4.43)	(−2.45)	(−3.62)
	FFCPS α		−0.26	−0.46	−0.84	−1.31	−0.69	−0.71
			(−1.51)	(−2.21)	(−3.24)	(−4.30)	(−2.10)	(−3.31)
CoSkew	Return		−0.55	−0.14	−0.05	−0.03	−0.22	−0.20
			(−1.50)	(−0.48)	(−0.20)	(−0.12)	(−0.70)	(−0.70)
	FFC α		−0.73	−0.33	−0.21	−0.15	−0.19	−0.32
			(−1.56)	(−1.73)	(−1.22)	(−0.77)	(−0.67)	(−1.50)
	FFCPS α		−0.66	−0.36	−0.22	−0.16	−0.23	−0.33
			(−1.38)	(−1.72)	(−1.23)	(−0.79)	(−0.78)	(−1.45)
IdioSkew	Return		0.25	0.07	−0.08	−0.28	−0.72	−0.16
			(0.80)	(0.24)	(−0.27)	(−0.76)	(−2.43)	(−0.53)
	FFC α		0.19	−0.03	−0.18	−0.63	−0.73	−0.28
			(0.95)	(−0.15)	(−0.89)	(−1.39)	(−2.76)	(−1.28)
	FFCPS α		0.23	−0.03	−0.25	−0.63	−0.75	−0.29
			(1.05)	(−0.14)	(−1.16)	(−1.38)	(−2.75)	(−1.28)

of the $IdioVol^{FF,1M}$ difference portfolio in the first β quintile of 0.62% per month is actually not only positive but also statistically significant, with a t-statistic of 1.98. The FFC and FFCPS alphas of this portfolio, however, are statistically indistinguishable from zero. In β quintiles two and three, the average and abnormal returns of the $IdioVol^{FF,1M}$ 5-1 portfolio are economically small and statistically insignificant. The idiosyncratic volatility puzzle is present only among stocks in the highest two β quintiles. In quintiles four and five of β, the $IdioVol^{FF,1M}$ difference portfolios generates negative, economically large, and statistically significant (at least marginally) average returns and alphas.

When controlling for *MktCap*, the equal-weighted portfolio results in Table 15.11 show that the idiosyncratic volatility puzzle does not exist for stocks in the first or fifth quintiles of *MktCap*, but is very strong in quintiles two, three, and four of *MktCap*, indicating that it is likely moderately sized stocks that are driving the phenomenon.

The idiosyncratic volatility puzzle is strong among stocks with low values of BM, since the average return and alphas of the $IdioVol^{FF,1M}$ portfolio in quintile one of BM are negative, large in magnitude, and statistically significant. However, in quintile two, three, and four of BM, the effect does not exist since the average returns and alphas are all insignificant. In quintile five of BM, the results actually indicate a positive and marginally significant relation between $IdioVol^{FF,1M}$ and average stock returns.

The results of the analysis that use Mom as the control variable indicate that the negative relation between idiosyncratic volatility and future stock returns is strongest in stocks with low and high momentum, but does not exist among stocks with moderate levels of momentum. In quintiles one, two, and five of Mom, the alphas (and average return for quintile one) of the $IdioVol^{FF,1M}$ 5-1 portfolio are at least marginally statistically significant, whereas no significant relation between $IdioVol^{FF,1M}$ and future returns is detected in quintiles three and four of Mom.

The relation between $IdioVol^{FF,1M}$ and future stock returns varies very strongly across the quintile of Rev. In the first Rev quintile, the equal-weighted portfolio analysis detects a strong positive relation between $IdioVol^{FF,1M}$ and future stock returns, since the average return of the $IdioVol^{FF,1M}$ 5-1 portfolio of 1.36% per month (t-statistic = 3.94), and corresponding FFC alpha of 1.43% per month (t-statistic = 4.49) and FFCPS alpha of 1.58% per month (t-statistic = 4.67) are very large and highly statistically significant. In quintiles two through five of Rev, however, the relation between $IdioVol^{FF,1M}$ and future stock returns is negative. In each of these quintiles, the FFC and FFCPS alphas of the $IdioVol^{FF,1M}$ difference portfolio are negative, large in magnitude, and highly significant. The average returns of these portfolios are negative, economically large, but in the cases of Rev quintiles two and three, not statistically significant.

Using $Illiq$ as the first sort variable in the equal-weighted bivariate portfolio analysis, we find that the negative relation between $IdioVol^{FF,1M}$ and future stock returns is detected in all but the first $Illiq$ quintile, which holds the most liquid stocks. The results of this analysis are very similar to those of the corresponding value-weighted analysis. Perhaps the main difference is that in the value-weighted portfolio results, the idiosyncratic volatility puzzle became much stronger as illiquidity increased, whereas in the equal-weighted analysis, this is not the case.

Controlling for co-skewness has a very substantial impact on the idiosyncratic volatility puzzle in equal-weighted portfolios. None of the $CoSkew$ quintiles have $IdioVol^{FF,1M}$ difference portfolios that generate statistically significant average or abnormal returns. The lone exception is the FFC alpha of the $IdioVol^{FF,1M}$ 5-1 portfolio in the second $CoSkew$ quintile of -0.33%, which is marginally statistically significant with a t-statistic of -1.73.

Finally, Table 15.11 shows that when controlling for $IdioSkew$, the negative relation between $IdioVol^{FF,1M}$ and future stock returns exists only for stocks in the fifth $IdioSkew$ quintile. In quintiles one through four of $IdioSkew$, the average returns and alphas of the equal-weighted $IdioVol^{FF,1M}$ 5-1 portfolios are all statistically indistinguishable from zero.

In summary, the results of the bivariate dependent-sort portfolio analyses indicate that, in value-weighted portfolios, none of the variables previously examined in this book explain the idiosyncratic volatility puzzle. In equal-weighted portfolios, the idiosyncratic volatility puzzle is not present after controlling for β, BM, $CoSkew$, or $IdioSkew$.

Bivariate Independent-Sort Portfolio Analysis

To examine the robustness of these results, we repeat the bivariate-sort portfolio analyses, this time using independently sorted portfolios. With the exception of the change in the sorting procedure, all other aspects of the analyses are the same as in the previous bivariate portfolio analyses. Since the results of these analyses are, in most cases, highly similar to those of the dependent-sort analyses presented in Tables 15.10 and 15.11, we focus our discussion of the independent-sort portfolio analysis results on the outcomes that are different from the dependent-sort results.

Table 15.12 presents the average returns and alphas for the $IdioVol^{FF,1M}$ 5-1 portfolios generated by the value-weighted bivariate independent-sort portfolio analyses. Similar to the dependent-sort results, there is no indication that the negative relation between idiosyncratic volatility and future stock returns is explained by β, $MktCap$, BM, Mom, Rev, $Illiq$, $CoSkew$, or $IdioSkew$. The main differences between these results and those of the dependently sorted portfolios come from the analyses that use $MktCap$, $Illiq$, and $IdioSkew$ as the control variable. When $MktCap$ is used as the control variable, in the dependent-sort value-weighted portfolio analysis, the negative relation between $IdioVol^{FF,1M}$ was present among stocks in the lowest $MktCap$ quintile, but not in the highest $MktCap$ quintile (see Table 15.10). When independent-sort portfolio analysis is used, the results indicate that the negative relation between $IdioVol^{FF,1M}$ exists among large stocks, but not among the stocks in the lowest quintile of $MktCap$. In the value-weighted analysis that sorts on $Illiq$ and $IdioVol^{FF,1M}$, the dependent-sort analysis indicated that the idiosyncratic volatility puzzle was weak among stocks in the lowest two quintiles of $Illiq$. We do not find this result when using independently sorted portfolios. The results of the independent-sort portfolio analysis indicate that the negative relation between $IdioVol^{FF,1M}$ and future stock returns is strong in all $Illiq$ quintiles. Lastly, when using dependently sorted portfolios, we found that the $IdioVol^{FF,1M}$ 5-1 portfolio in the first quintile of $IdioSkew$ failed to generate statistically significant average and abnormal returns. When independent-sort portfolio analysis is used, the average return and alphas of $IdioVol^{FF,1M}$ difference portfolio in the first $IdioSkew$ quintile are negative, economically large, and highly statistically significant. Apart from these relatively minor differences, the results of the dependent- and independent-sort value-weighted portfolio analyses are qualitatively similar.

The results of the equal-weighted bivariate independent-sort portfolio analyses, shown in Table 15.13, are perhaps even more similar to their dependent-sort counterparts. The main conclusions from the equal-weighted portfolio analyses remain the same when independently sorted portfolios are used. Specifically, the idiosyncratic volatility puzzle is not present in the average quintile of the control variable

TABLE 15.12   Bivariate Independent-Sort Portfolio Analysis—Value-Weighted

This table presents the results of bivariate independent-sort portfolio analyses of the relation between $IdioVol^{FF,1M}$ and future stock returns after controlling for the effect of each of β, $MktCap$, BM, Mom, Rev, $Illiq$, $CoSkew$, and $IdioSkew$ (control variables). Each month, all stocks in the CRSP sample are sorted into five groups based on an ascending sort of the control variable. All stocks are independently sorted into five groups based on an ascending sort of $IdioVol^{FF,1M}$. The quintile breakpoints used to create the groups are calculated using all stocks in the CRSP sample. The intersections of the control variable and $IdioVol^{FF,1M}$ groups are used to form 25 value-weighted portfolios. The table presents the average return, FFC alpha, and FFCPS alpha (in percent per month) of the long–short zero-cost portfolios that are long the fifth $IdioVol^{FF,1M}$ quintile portfolio and short the first $IdioVol^{FF,1M}$ quintile portfolio in each quintile, as well as for the average quintile, of the control variable. t-statistics (in parentheses), adjusted following Newey and West (1987) using six lags, testing the null hypothesis that the average return or alpha is equal to zero, are shown in parentheses.

Control	Value	Control 1	Control 2	Control 3	Control 4	Control 5	Control Avg
β	Return	−0.53	−0.45	−0.55	−0.67	−0.89	−0.61
		(−1.80)	(−1.69)	(−1.79)	(−2.49)	(−2.60)	(−2.41)
	FFC α	−0.79	−0.63	−0.79	−0.89	−1.02	−0.82
		(−3.32)	(−3.15)	(−3.00)	(−4.31)	(−3.88)	(−5.15)
	FFCPS α	−0.82	−0.71	−0.85	−0.88	−1.03	−0.85
		(−3.04)	(−3.43)	(−3.08)	(−3.89)	(−3.62)	(−4.81)
$MktCap$	Return	−0.10	−1.17	−1.35	−1.37	−1.06	−1.00
		(−0.30)	(−3.68)	(−4.35)	(−4.14)	(−2.73)	(−3.38)
	FFC α	−0.35	−1.37	−1.43	−1.30	−1.10	−1.11
		(−1.23)	(−6.14)	(−6.45)	(−5.07)	(−3.19)	(−5.70)
	FFCPS α	−0.33	−1.38	−1.41	−1.27	−1.31	−1.14
		(−1.10)	(−5.83)	(−5.93)	(−4.52)	(−3.50)	(−5.30)
BM	Return	−1.28	−0.75	−0.32	−0.22	0.22	−0.47
		(−3.57)	(−2.45)	(−0.98)	(−0.61)	(0.66)	(−1.60)
	FFC α	−1.30	−0.74	−0.38	−0.59	−0.01	−0.61
		(−4.99)	(−2.75)	(−1.51)	(−2.31)	(−0.03)	(−3.22)
	FFCPS α	−1.33	−0.91	−0.51	−0.80	−0.08	−0.73
		(−4.52)	(−3.20)	(−1.94)	(−2.94)	(−0.26)	(−3.56)
Mom	Return	−1.68	−0.85	−0.49	−0.21	−0.47	−0.74
		(−3.51)	(−2.71)	(−1.61)	(−0.70)	(−1.63)	(−2.67)
	FFC α	−2.10	−1.19	−0.77	−0.37	−0.63	−1.01
		(−4.38)	(−5.44)	(−3.53)	(−1.53)	(−2.47)	(−5.80)
	FFCPS α	−2.03	−1.20	−0.92	−0.31	−0.61	−1.02
		(−3.99)	(−4.76)	(−3.70)	(−1.16)	(−2.26)	(−5.18)

TABLE 15.12 (*Continued*)

Control	Value	Control 1	Control 2	Control 3	Control 4	Control 5	Control Avg
Rev	Return	−1.12	−1.27	−1.35	−1.04	−0.62	−1.08
		(−3.11)	(−3.07)	(−3.20)	(−2.71)	(−1.86)	(−3.27)
	FFC α	−1.49	−1.48	−1.67	−1.09	−0.74	−1.30
		(−3.98)	(−5.54)	(−6.67)	(−3.69)	(−2.65)	(−6.47)
	FFCPS α	−1.45	−1.57	−1.73	−1.13	−0.80	−1.34
		(−3.69)	(−5.30)	(−6.25)	(−3.53)	(−2.64)	(−5.99)
Illiq	Return	−0.80	−0.91	−1.18	−1.23	−0.99	−1.03
		(−2.17)	(−2.74)	(−3.29)	(−3.83)	(−3.09)	(−3.42)
	FFC α	−0.91	−0.92	−1.18	−1.31	−1.14	−1.10
		(−3.08)	(−3.72)	(−4.61)	(−5.92)	(−4.55)	(−5.76)
	FFCPS α	−0.99	−0.94	−1.19	−1.34	−1.27	−1.15
		(−3.00)	(−3.45)	(−4.20)	(−5.79)	(−4.72)	(−5.43)
CoSkew	Return	−1.26	−0.65	−0.76	−0.70	−0.84	−0.84
		(−3.93)	(−1.95)	(−2.41)	(−2.26)	(−2.64)	(−2.99)
	FFC α	−1.22	−0.84	−0.87	−0.91	−0.98	−0.96
		(−5.28)	(−2.77)	(−3.55)	(−3.61)	(−4.56)	(−5.17)
	FFCPS α	−1.26	−0.87	−0.90	−1.00	−1.03	−1.01
		(−4.95)	(−2.58)	(−3.42)	(−3.62)	(−4.30)	(−4.81)
IdioSkew	Return	−0.82	−0.57	−0.48	−0.76	−1.09	−0.74
		(−2.42)	(−1.48)	(−1.54)	(−2.12)	(−3.41)	(−2.47)
	FFC α	−0.95	−0.64	−0.56	−0.99	−1.27	−0.88
		(−3.92)	(−2.06)	(−2.61)	(−3.55)	(−5.23)	(−4.66)
	FFCPS α	−0.98	−0.72	−0.61	−1.11	−1.29	−0.94
		(−3.73)	(−2.07)	(−2.65)	(−3.71)	(−4.74)	(−4.48)

when the control variable is β, *BM*, *CoSkew*, or *IdioSkew*, but persists when the control variable is *MktCap*, *Mom*, *Rev*, or *Illiq*. The only qualitative differences between the dependent- and independent-sort analyses come from the portfolios formed by sorting on either *MktCap* or *Illiq*, and *IdioVol*. When *MktCap* is the control variable, the equal-weighted dependent-sort portfolio analysis fails to detect a negative relation between $IdioVol^{FF,1M}$ in the highest *MktCap* quintile (see Table 15.11), whereas in the independent-sort analysis, the $IdioVol^{FF,1M}$ 5-1 portfolio in the fifth *MktCap* quintile generates large, negative, and statistically significant average and abnormal returns. When *Illiq* is used as the control variable, the equal-weighted dependent-sort analyses found that the idiosyncratic volatility puzzle does not exist among stocks in the lowest *Illiq* quintile, but does exist among stocks in the highest *Illiq* quintile. The opposite is found in the independently sorted portfolios. The results in Table 15.13 show that when equal-weighted independently sorted portfolios are used, the $IdioVol^{FF,1M}$

TABLE 15.13 Bivariate Independent-Sort Portfolio Analysis—Equal-Weighted

This table presents the results of bivariate independent-sort portfolio analyses of the relation between $IdioVol^{FF,1M}$ and future stock returns after controlling for the effect of each of β, $MktCap$, BM, Mom, Rev, $Illiq$, $CoSkew$, and $IdioSkew$ (control variables). Each month, all stocks in the CRSP sample are sorted into five groups based on an ascending sort of the control variable. All stocks are independently sorted into five groups based on an ascending sort of $IdioVol^{FF,1M}$. The quintile breakpoints used to create the groups are calculated using all stocks in the CRSP sample. The intersections of the control variable and $IdioVol^{FF,1M}$ groups are used to form 25 equal-weighted portfolios. The table presents the average return, FFC alpha, and FFCPS alpha (in percent per month) of the long–short zero-cost portfolios that are long the fifth $IdioVol^{FF,1M}$ quintile portfolio and short the first $IdioVol^{FF,1M}$ quintile portfolio in each quintile, as well as for the average quintile, of the control variable. t-statistics (in parentheses), adjusted following Newey and West (1987) using six lags, testing the null hypothesis that the average return or alpha is equal to zero, are shown in parentheses.

Control	Value	Control 1	Control 2	Control 3	Control 4	Control 5	Control Avg
β	Return	0.54	−0.02	−0.21	−0.48	−0.79	−0.19
		(1.74)	(−0.08)	(−0.57)	(−1.51)	(−2.26)	(−0.61)
	FFC α	0.32	−0.09	−0.41	−0.56	−0.75	−0.30
		(1.30)	(−0.39)	(−1.02)	(−2.24)	(−2.72)	(−1.31)
	FFCPS α	0.32	−0.13	−0.40	−0.57	−0.69	−0.30
		(1.23)	(−0.54)	(−0.97)	(−2.18)	(−2.33)	(−1.22)
$MktCap$	Return	0.56	−1.12	−1.36	−1.41	−1.22	−0.90
		(1.62)	(−3.56)	(−4.40)	(−4.29)	(−3.23)	(−3.05)
	FFC α	0.28	−1.32	−1.44	−1.35	−1.14	−0.99
		(0.71)	(−5.92)	(−6.34)	(−5.29)	(−3.50)	(−4.92)
	FFCPS α	0.33	−1.34	−1.43	−1.31	−1.30	−1.01
		(0.84)	(−5.64)	(−5.90)	(−4.65)	(−3.59)	(−4.55)
BM	Return	−0.65	−0.07	−0.08	0.24	0.48	−0.02
		(−1.84)	(−0.21)	(−0.21)	(0.79)	(1.68)	(−0.05)
	FFC α	−0.59	−0.05	−0.33	0.09	0.38	−0.10
		(−1.94)	(−0.16)	(−0.64)	(0.38)	(1.75)	(−0.41)
	FFCPS α	−0.66	−0.19	−0.38	−0.01	0.35	−0.18
		(−2.06)	(−0.64)	(−0.71)	(−0.05)	(1.50)	(−0.70)
Mom	Return	−0.93	0.03	0.08	0.07	−0.37	−0.23
		(−2.10)	(0.11)	(0.28)	(0.20)	(−1.31)	(−0.81)
	FFC α	−1.49	−0.23	−0.19	−0.24	−0.69	−0.57
		(−2.07)	(−1.17)	(−1.09)	(−1.17)	(−3.38)	(−2.76)
	FFCPS α	−1.45	−0.23	−0.26	−0.30	−0.67	−0.58
		(−2.01)	(−1.12)	(−1.41)	(−1.31)	(−3.00)	(−2.70)

TABLE 15.13   (*Continued*)

Control	Value		Control 1	Control 2	Control 3	Control 4	Control 5	Control Avg
Rev	Return	1.28	−0.54	−0.72	−1.03	−1.33	−0.47
		(3.71)	(−1.52)	(−1.84)	(−2.75)	(−3.54)	(−1.40)
	FFC α	1.34	−0.68	−1.02	−1.26	−1.54	−0.64
		(4.40)	(−2.95)	(−3.95)	(−4.66)	(−5.83)	(−3.09)
	FFCPS α	1.42	−0.71	−1.06	−1.34	−1.61	−0.67
		(4.49)	(−2.95)	(−3.89)	(−4.65)	(−5.48)	(−3.02)
Illiq	Return	−0.93	−0.97	−1.16	−1.16	−0.11	−0.88
		(−2.78)	(−3.00)	(−3.36)	(−3.33)	(−0.30)	(−2.83)
	FFC α	−0.91	−0.94	−1.11	−1.14	−0.23	−0.88
		(−3.76)	(−3.68)	(−4.00)	(−4.13)	(−0.73)	(−3.96)
	FFCPS α	−0.88	−0.91	−1.09	−1.17	−0.30	−0.88
		(−3.22)	(−3.25)	(−3.62)	(−4.01)	(−0.92)	(−3.61)
CoSkew	Return	−0.48	−0.20	−0.13	−0.14	−0.14	−0.22
		(−1.19)	(−0.67)	(−0.43)	(−0.43)	(−0.45)	(−0.72)
	FFC α	−0.83	−0.38	−0.25	−0.25	−0.15	−0.37
		(−1.39)	(−1.85)	(−1.16)	(−1.07)	(−0.55)	(−1.56)
	FFCPS α	−0.82	−0.39	−0.25	−0.27	−0.18	−0.38
		(−1.35)	(−1.81)	(−1.11)	(−1.08)	(−0.64)	(−1.54)
IdioSkew	Return	0.12	−0.00	−0.04	−0.39	−0.43	−0.15
		(0.34)	(−0.01)	(−0.13)	(−0.98)	(−1.45)	(−0.49)
	FFC α	0.04	−0.07	−0.10	−0.82	−0.52	−0.30
		(0.16)	(−0.31)	(−0.44)	(−1.50)	(−2.19)	(−1.26)
	FFCPS α	0.08	−0.06	−0.16	−0.82	−0.53	−0.30
		(0.30)	(−0.24)	(−0.69)	(−1.49)	(−2.14)	(−1.23)

5-1 portfolio in the first *Illiq* quintile generates large negative average and abnormal returns, but the average return and alphas of the $IdioVol^{FF,1M}$ difference portfolio in the fifth *Illiq* quintile are insignificant. Apart from these small differences, the results of the equal-weighted independent-sort portfolio analyses of the relation between $IdioVol^{FF,1M}$ and future stock returns are qualitatively the same as those of the equal-weighted dependent-sort portfolio results.

In summary, the bivariate sort portfolio analyses indicate that, consistent with the univariate sort portfolio analysis results, when using value-weighted portfolios, the idiosyncratic volatility puzzle is robust after controlling for beta, size, book-to-market ratio, momentum, reversal, illiquidity, co-skewness, or idiosyncratic skewness. When using equal-weighted portfolios, the idiosyncratic volatility puzzle is substantially weaker and, in some cases, does not persist in bivariate portfolio analyses.

15.6.3 Fama–MacBeth Regression Analysis

We continue our investigation of the idiosyncratic volatility puzzle using (Fama and MacBeth 1973, FM hereafter) regression analysis. FM regression analysis allows us to control for the relations between all of the control variables and future stock returns at once. We execute FM regression analyses using several different regression specifications. We begin with a specification that uses $IdioVol^{FF,1M}$ as the only independent variable. We also use specifications that include $IdioVol^{FF,1M}$ along with one control variable as independent variables. Finally, we examine a specification that includes $IdioVol^{FF,1M}$ and all of the other variables together. This specification allows us to examine the relation between $IdioVol^{FF,1M}$ and future stock returns after controlling for all other effects simultaneously. It also allows us to examine whether other effects documented previously in this book can be explained by the relation between idiosyncratic volatility and future stock returns. The dependent variable in each of the FM regression analyses is the one-month-ahead excess stock return. All independent variables in the regressions are winsorized at the 0.5% level on a monthly basis.

In Table 15.14, we present the time-series averages of the monthly cross-sectional regression coefficients along with Newey and West (1987) t-statistics, adjusted using six lags, testing the null hypothesis that the average coefficient is equal to zero (in parentheses). The specification including only $IdioVol^{FF,1M}$ as an independent variable (specification (1)) detects a negative and statistically significant relation between idiosyncratic volatility and future stock returns, since the average coefficient on $IdioVol^{FF,1M}$ of -0.008 has an associated t-statistic of -2.52. The results are similar when beta (β, specification (2)), size ($Size$, specification (3)), momentum (Mom, specification (5)), illiquidity ($Illiq$, specification (7)), co-skewness ($CoSkew$, specification (8)), or idiosyncratic skewness ($IdioSkew$, specification (9)) is included as the lone control variable. In each of these analyses, the average coefficient on $IdioVol^{FF,1M}$ remains negative and statistically significant. In fact, when $Size$ or $Illiq$ is used as the control variable, the magnitude of the average coefficient becomes substantially larger than in other specifications. This is not surprising. High $IdioVol^{FF,1M}$ stocks tend to generate low average returns. The correlation (Table 15.5) and portfolio characteristics (Table 15.9) show that high $IdioVol^{FF,1M}$ stocks also tend to be small stocks, which were shown in Chapter 9 to generate high average returns. Thus, after controlling for the size effect, the negative relation between $IdioVol^{FF,1M}$ should be even stronger. Similarly, high $IdioVol^{FF,1M}$ stocks tend to be high $Illiq$ stocks, which were shown in Chapter 13 to generate higher average returns. Thus, when controlling for this effect, the negative relation between $IdioVol^{FF,1M}$ would be expected to become even stronger. This is exactly what the regression results demonstrate. When either BM (specification (4)) or Rev (specification (6)) is included as the control variable, the FM regression analysis fails to detect a negative relation between $IdioVol^{FF,1M}$ and future stock returns since, in each of these cases, the average coefficient on Rev is statistically indistinguishable from zero, albeit still negative.

When all control variables are simultaneously included in the regression specification (specification (10)), the results indicate a strong negative relation between

TABLE 15.14   Fama–MacBeth Regression Analysis
This table presents the results of Fama and MacBeth (1973) regression analyses of the relation between expected stock returns and $IdioVol^{FF,1M}$. Each column in the table presents results for a different cross-sectional regression specification. The dependent variable in all specifications is the one-month-ahead excess stock return. The independent variables are indicated in the first column. Independent variables are winsorized at the 0.5% level on a monthly basis. The table presents average slope and intercept coefficients along with t-statistics (in parentheses), adjusted following Newey and West (1987) using six lags, testing the null hypothesis that the average coefficient is equal to zero. The rows labeled Adj. R^2 and n present the average adjusted r-squared and the number of data points, respectively, for the cross-sectional regressions.

	(1)	(2)	(3)	(4)	(5)	(6)	(7)	(8)	(9)	(10)
$IdioVol^{FF,1M}$	−0.008	−0.007	−0.014	−0.005	−0.007	−0.006	−0.018	−0.008	−0.008	−0.013
	(−2.52)	(−2.35)	(−5.25)	(−1.44)	(−2.38)	(−1.61)	(−5.39)	(−2.37)	(−2.47)	(−5.85)
β		−0.211								0.004
		(−1.71)								(0.03)
Size			−0.228							−0.179
			(−5.96)							(−4.15)
BM				0.345						0.141
				(4.71)						(1.99)
Mom					0.006					0.007
					(2.94)					(3.85)
Rev						−0.056				−0.059
						(−11.49)				(−11.32)
Illiq							0.096			0.067
							(4.10)			(3.74)
CoSkew								−0.016		0.001
								(−2.46)		(0.13)
IdioSkew									0.003	−0.123
									(0.07)	(−3.85)
Intercept	1.040	1.153	2.296	0.644	0.849	0.994	1.352	1.047	1.061	1.915
	(5.01)	(5.92)	(6.50)	(2.99)	(4.17)	(4.56)	(6.64)	(5.23)	(5.26)	(5.46)
Adj. R^2	0.02	0.03	0.02	0.02	0.03	0.03	0.03	0.02	0.02	0.07
n	4732	4408	4732	3379	4392	4720	3600	3932	3932	2561

$IdioVol^{FF,1M}$ and future stock returns, with the average coefficient of −0.013 having an associated t-statistic of −5.85. Thus, the results show that the idiosyncratic volatility puzzle is quite strong when all of the effects discussed in previous chapters of this book are simultaneously controlled for. Interestingly, in this specification, the average coefficient on β becomes slightly positive. All previous FM regression analyses in this text have generated a theoretically contradictory negative (but insignificant) average coefficient on β. In the full specification that includes $IdioVol^{FF,1M}$, while the coefficient remains statistically insignificant, it has the theoretically predicted sign. The results also indicate that the negative relations between each of Size, Rev, and IdioSkew and future stock returns are robust to the inclusion of $IdioVol^{FF,1M}$, as are the positive relations between each of BM, Mom, and Illiq, and future stock returns. Consistent with the results in Chapter 14, when the full specification is used, the FM regression analysis detects no relation between co-skewness (CoSkew) and future stock returns.

To examine the economic magnitude of the negative relation between $IdioVol^{FF,1M}$ and expected stock returns, we use the average coefficient of -0.013 from the full-specification FM regression analysis in Table 15.14. To find the effect of a one-standard-deviation difference in $IdioVol^{FF,1M}$ on expected returns, we multiply the average coefficient by 40.25, the average cross-sectional standard deviation of $IdioVol^{FF,1M}$ (see Panel D of Table 15.1). Doing so, we find that a one-standard-deviation difference in $IdioVol^{FF,1M}$ is associated with an economically large 0.52% (0.013×40.25) per month difference in expected return. If we multiply the average coefficient by the difference between the average 95th and 5th $IdioVol^{FF,1M}$ percentiles of 104.07 ($116.48 - 12.41$), we find that an expected return difference of 1.35% (0.13×104.07) per month between stocks with very high and very low values of $IdioVol^{FF,1M}$. Both analyses indicate that the average coefficient of -0.013 is of substantial economic magnitude.

The results in Table 15.14 demonstrate that the idiosyncratic volatility puzzle is not a manifestation of one of the other stock return phenomena examined in previous chapters of this book. However, we have only examined in depth the relation between idiosyncratic volatility measured from one month of daily return data ($IdioVol^{FF,1M}$) and future stock returns. While the correlation analyses presented in Section 15.4 demonstrated that, holding the length of the measurement period and data frequency constant, measures of idiosyncratic volatility calculated relative to different risk models (CAPM, FF, or FFC) are extremely similar, the results indicated nontrivial differences between measures calculated using different measurement periods and data frequencies. To examine whether the idiosyncratic volatility puzzle is robust to the use of different measurement periods and data frequencies in calculating idiosyncratic volatility, we perform FM regression analyses on the measures of idiosyncratic volatility calculated using each of the different measurement period lengths and data frequencies examined earlier in this chapter. In this analysis, we continue to use measures of idiosyncratic volatility calculated from the FF risk model. For each measure of idiosyncratic volatility, we perform an FM regression analysis using the specification that includes all other variables as controls.

The results of the FM regression analyses using the $IdioVol^{FF}$ variables calculated from different measurement period lengths and data frequencies are shown in Table 15.15. The measurement period length is indicated in the first row of the table. 1M, 3M, 6M, and 12M indicate that $IdioVol^{FF}$ is calculated using one, three, six, and 12 months of daily data, respectively. The columns labeled 1Y, 2Y, 3Y, and 5Y use $IdioVol^{FF}$ calculated from one, two, three, and five years of monthly data, respectively, as the measure of idiosyncratic volatility. It is worth recalling that in the equal-weighted portfolio analyses (Panel B of Table 15.7), the idiosyncratic volatility puzzle was only evident when using $IdioVol^{FF,1M}$ as the sort variable. $IdioVol^{FF}$ calculated using other measurement periods and data frequencies failed to generate the phenomenon.

The FM regression analysis results show that, after controlling for β, Size, BM, Mom, Rev, Illiq, CoSkew, and IdioSkew, regardless of the measurement period or data frequency used to calculate $IdioVol^{FF}$, there is a negative and statistically significant

TABLE 15.15   Fama–MacBeth Regression Analysis—$IdioVol^{FF}$

This table presents the results of Fama and MacBeth (1973) regression analyses of the relation between expected stock returns and $IdioVol^{FF}$. Each column in the table presents results for a different cross-sectional regression specification. The columns labeled 1M, 3M, 6M, 12M, 1Y, 2Y, 3Y, 5Y present results for specifications using $IdioVol^{FF,1M}$, $IdioVol^{FF,3M}$, $IdioVol^{FF,6M}$, $IdioVol^{FF,12M}$, $IdioVol^{FF,1Y}$, $IdioVol^{FF,2Y}$, $IdioVol^{FF,3Y}$, and $IdioVol^{FF,5Y}$ as the measure of idiosyncratic volatility. The dependent variable in all specifications is the one-month-ahead excess stock return. The independent variables are indicated in the first column. The row labeled $IdioVol^{FF}$ shows results for the given measure of idiosyncratic volatility. Independent variables are winsorized at the 0.5% level on a monthly basis. The table presents average slope and intercept coefficients along with t-statistics (in parentheses), adjusted following Newey and West (1987) using six lags, testing the null hypothesis that the average coefficient is equal to zero. The rows labeled Adj. R^2 and n present the average adjusted r-squared and the number of data points, respectively, for the cross-sectional regressions.

	1M	3M	6M	12M	1Y	2Y	3Y	5Y
$IdioVol^{FF}$	−0.013	−0.016	−0.015	−0.011	−0.015	−0.012	−0.011	−0.009
	(−5.85)	(−5.11)	(−4.11)	(−2.61)	(−5.55)	(−3.34)	(−2.70)	(−1.97)
β	0.004	0.038	0.023	−0.017	−0.005	−0.006	−0.008	−0.027
	(0.03)	(0.28)	(0.18)	(−0.14)	(−0.04)	(−0.05)	(−0.06)	(−0.22)
Size	−0.179	−0.198	−0.190	−0.166	−0.170	−0.166	−0.163	−0.154
	(−4.15)	(−5.12)	(−5.16)	(−4.75)	(−3.89)	(−4.02)	(−4.15)	(−4.06)
BM	0.141	0.141	0.149	0.153	0.147	0.136	0.125	0.122
	(1.99)	(2.00)	(2.11)	(2.12)	(2.08)	(1.94)	(1.80)	(1.79)
Mom	0.007	0.008	0.008	0.008	0.009	0.009	0.008	0.008
	(3.85)	(4.03)	(4.37)	(4.46)	(4.68)	(4.43)	(4.30)	(4.17)
Rev	−0.059	−0.061	−0.062	−0.062	−0.061	−0.062	−0.062	−0.063
	(−11.32)	(−11.77)	(−11.97)	(−12.12)	(−11.66)	(−11.84)	(−12.02)	(−12.11)
Illiq	0.067	0.072	0.069	0.063	0.055	0.054	0.053	0.052
	(3.74)	(4.11)	(3.99)	(3.70)	(3.02)	(3.04)	(2.95)	(2.89)
CoSkew	0.001	−0.000	−0.001	−0.001	−0.001	−0.000	−0.000	−0.000
	(0.13)	(−0.06)	(−0.17)	(−0.25)	(−0.12)	(−0.10)	(−0.05)	(−0.01)
IdioSkew	−0.123	−0.107	−0.104	−0.119	−0.088	−0.066	−0.050	−0.041
	(−3.85)	(−3.45)	(−3.32)	(−3.73)	(−2.73)	(−1.83)	(−1.26)	(−0.87)
Intercept	1.915	2.126	2.039	1.802	1.835	1.800	1.794	1.721
	(5.46)	(6.51)	(6.41)	(5.79)	(5.28)	(5.52)	(5.80)	(5.75)
Adj. R^2	0.07	0.07	0.07	0.07	0.07	0.07	0.07	0.07
n	2561	2561	2561	2561	2561	2559	2559	2561

relation between $IdioVol^{FF}$ and future stock returns. The idiosyncratic volatility puzzle therefore appears to exist regardless of how idiosyncratic volatility is calculated. The previously documented relations between future stock returns and other variables are also robust. The one exception is that, when $IdioVol^{FF,3Y}$ or $IdioVol^{FF,5Y}$ is used as the measure of idiosyncratic volatility, the negative relation between $IdioSkew$ and future stock returns becomes statistically insignificant.

As discussed previously, the different measures of total and idiosyncratic volatility are all highly correlated with each other when calculated using the same measurement period and data frequency. For this reason, to this point, we have only used $IdioVol^{FF}$ to measure idiosyncratic volatility. To verify our claim that changing the approach to calculating total or idiosyncratic volatility will have negligible effects on the results of empirical analyses, we repeat the full-specification FM regression analyses with total volatility (Vol) measured using each of the different measurement periods and data frequencies employed throughout this chapter, as our variable of interest. It is worth noting that Vol measures total volatility, not idiosyncratic volatility. Thus, in performing these analyses, we are also examining whether the idiosyncratic volatility puzzle holds for total volatility as well.

TABLE 15.16 Fama–MacBeth Regression Analysis—Total Volatility
This table presents the results of Fama and MacBeth (1973) regression analyses of the relation between expected stock returns and total volatility. Each column in the table presents results for a different cross-sectional regression specification. The columns labeled 1M, 3M, 6M, 12M, 1Y, 2Y, 3Y, 5Y present results for specifications using Vol^{1M}, Vol^{3M}, Vol^{6M}, Vol^{12M}, Vol^{1Y}, Vol^{2Y}, Vol^{3Y}, and Vol^{5Y} as the measure of idiosyncratic volatility. The dependent variable in all specifications is the one-month-ahead excess stock return. The independent variables are indicated in the first column. The row labeled Vol shows results for the given measure of volatility. Independent variables are winsorized at the 0.5% level on a monthly basis. The table presents average slope and intercept coefficients along with t-statistics (in parentheses), adjusted following Newey and West (1987) using six lags, testing the null hypothesis that the average coefficient is equal to zero. The rows labeled Adj. R^2 and n present the average adjusted r-squared and the number of data points, respectively, for the cross-sectional regressions.

	1M	3M	6M	12M	1Y	2Y	3Y	5Y
Vol	−0.013	−0.017	−0.016	−0.011	−0.013	−0.009	−0.008	−0.006
	(−5.89)	(−5.14)	(−4.12)	(−2.58)	(−4.45)	(−2.27)	(−1.76)	(−1.18)
β	0.080	0.121	0.091	0.033	0.026	−0.004	−0.018	−0.049
	(0.58)	(0.94)	(0.75)	(0.28)	(0.20)	(−0.04)	(−0.15)	(−0.44)
Size	−0.177	−0.194	−0.188	−0.165	−0.166	−0.155	−0.149	−0.137
	(−4.07)	(−4.95)	(−5.05)	(−4.68)	(−3.94)	(−3.94)	(−4.03)	(−3.88)
BM	0.141	0.141	0.150	0.153	0.143	0.133	0.128	0.132
	(1.99)	(2.00)	(2.11)	(2.12)	(2.02)	(1.91)	(1.86)	(1.96)
Mom	0.007	0.008	0.008	0.008	0.009	0.008	0.008	0.008
	(3.87)	(4.04)	(4.37)	(4.46)	(4.83)	(4.52)	(4.40)	(4.24)
Rev	−0.059	−0.061	−0.062	−0.063	−0.063	−0.063	−0.064	−0.064
	(−11.30)	(−11.76)	(−11.97)	(−12.11)	(−11.82)	(−11.97)	(−12.13)	(−12.20)
Illiq	0.068	0.073	0.070	0.063	0.056	0.053	0.052	0.050
	(3.79)	(4.18)	(4.01)	(3.68)	(3.12)	(3.05)	(2.93)	(2.84)
CoSkew	0.001	−0.000	−0.001	−0.001	−0.001	0.000	0.000	−0.000
	(0.11)	(−0.05)	(−0.20)	(−0.26)	(−0.16)	(0.05)	(0.00)	(−0.09)
IdioSkew	−0.124	−0.109	−0.105	−0.120	−0.098	−0.087	−0.081	−0.078
	(−3.92)	(−3.51)	(−3.37)	(−3.76)	(−2.95)	(−2.37)	(−1.98)	(−1.66)
Intercept	1.903	2.098	2.026	1.794	1.799	1.704	1.658	1.556
	(5.41)	(6.39)	(6.34)	(5.74)	(5.42)	(5.53)	(5.83)	(5.69)
Adj. R^2	0.07	0.07	0.07	0.07	0.07	0.07	0.07	0.07
n	2561	2561	2561	2561	2561	2559	2559	2561

The results of these analyses, presented in Table 15.16, show that in most cases, the relation between total volatility, measured using *Vol*, and future stock returns, is very similar to the measure between the corresponding $IdioVol^{FF}$ variable and future returns. The exceptions are when *Vol* is calculated using three years (3Y) or five years (5Y) of monthly return data. When Vol^{3Y} is used as the measure of total volatility, the FM regressions detect only a marginally significant negative relation between total volatility and future stock returns. When Vol^{5Y} is used, the relation becomes statistically insignificant. Regardless of the length of the measurement period, when monthly returns are used, the results using *Vol* as the measure of volatility are slightly weaker than the corresponding FM regression results that use $IdioVol^{FF}$ as the measure of idiosyncratic volatility.

In summary, the results of the empirical analyses examining the relation between idiosyncratic volatility and future stock returns indicate a negative relation between idiosyncratic volatility and future stock returns. The relation is robust in value-weighted portfolios and, depending on which measure of idiosyncratic volatility is used, disappears when equal-weighted portfolios are used. Fama and MacBeth (1973) regression analyses indicate that the statistical significance of the negative relation between idiosyncratic volatility and future stock returns is somewhat dependent on specification. However, after controlling simultaneously for all other effects discussed in the previous chapters of this book, the negative relation is both statistically significant and economically important.

15.6.4   Cumulative Returns of $IdioVol^{FF,1M}$ Portfolio

For many of the variables known to be related to future stock returns, researchers have created a risk factor mimicking portfolio associated with the given variable and claimed that the returns of that portfolio proxy for the returns associated with taking a unit risk in whatever latent factor is captured by the given predictive variable. This is not the case with idiosyncratic volatility. The reason for this is that it is not possible to tell a risk story for the negative relation between idiosyncratic volatility and future returns. As discussed earlier, all risk-based explanations for such a relation predict a positive, not negative relation.

To assess the time series of returns associated with an investment strategy based on idiosyncratic volatility, we therefore use the excess returns of a portfolio that is long stocks with low idiosyncratic volatility and short stocks with high idiosyncratic volatility. Specifically, we analyze the negative of the monthly returns of the value-weighted 10-1 $IdioVol^{FF,1M}$ portfolio from Panel A of Table 15.7. Thus, the portfolio we investigate is a zero-cost portfolio that takes long positions in all stocks in the lowest decile of $IdioVol^{FF,1M}$ and short positions in all stocks in the highest decile of $IdioVol^{FF,1M}$, where the long positions and short positions are independently value-weighted. We refer to this portfolio as the Low–High $IdioVol^{FF,1M}$ portfolio. We diverge from our standard approach of taking a long (short) position in high idiosyncratic volatility (low idiosyncratic volatility) stocks so that the portfolio we examine in this section has positive average returns.

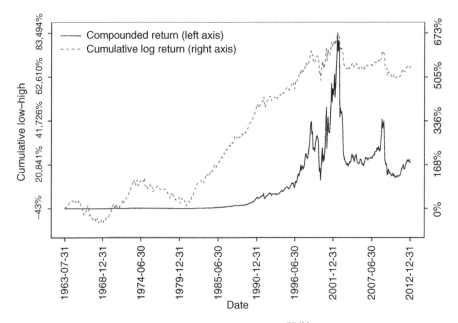

Figure 15.1   Cumulative Returns of Low–High $IdioVol^{FF,1M}$ Portfolio.
This figure plots the cumulate returns of the decile one minus decile 10 $IdioVol^{FF,1M}$
value-weighted portfolio for the period from July 1963 through December 2012. The compounded excess return for month t is calculated as 100 times the cumulative product of one
plus the monthly return up to and including the given month. The cumulate log excess return
is calculated as the sum of monthly log excess returns up to and including the given month.

As seen in Table 15.7, during the period from July 1963 through December of
2012, the Low–High $IdioVol^{FF,1M}$ portfolio generates an average monthly return of
1.27% with a monthly standard deviation of 8.22%, giving an annualized Sharpe ratio
of 0.53. Using log returns instead of returns, we find a mean monthly log return of
0.91%, a standard deviation of 8.55%, and thus an annualized Sharpe ratio of 0.37.
Over the entire sample period, the monthly compounded return that would have been
realized by this investment strategy is 21,897%, meaning that an initial investment of
$1 at the end of June 1963 would have turned into $219.97 by the end of December
2012. Taken on the log scale, this corresponds to a cumulative sum of log monthly
returns equal to 539%.

The cumulative returns of the Low–High $IdioVol^{FF,1M}$ portfolio are plotted in
Figure 15.1 for the period from July 1963 through December 2012. The solid line
represents the cumulative monthly compounded return and has its scale on the left
side of the plot. The cumulative sum of monthly log returns is shown by the dashed
line, the scale for which is on the right side of the plot. The plot shows that while, in
the long-run, the Low–High $IdioVol^{FF,1M}$ portfolio has generated substantial returns,
the ride has been quite bumpy, and as of the end of 2012, the portfolio value remains
well below its previous high. As can be seen in Figure 15.1, the investment strategy

experienced a dramatic loss starting in August 2002. In August 2002, the Low–High $IdioVol^{FF,1M}$ portfolio experienced a loss of 10.31%. It rebounded slightly in September with a 6.66% gain, only to lose 6.44% in October. In November 2002, a huge loss of 41.74% was realized, the largest single-month loss realized by the strategy during the entire sample period. A few months later, in June 2003, the portfolio realized another devastating loss of 28.89%. The subsequent low point for the portfolio came at the end of November 2010, at which point the portfolio had lost more than 82% of its previous maximum value. The portfolio has not even come close to regaining its previous high water mark. As of the end of 2012, the cumulative return of the investment strategy remains almost 74% lower than its previous high value. The drawdown realized beginning in August 2002 is both the largest and most prolonged drawdown experienced by the idiosyncratic volatility investment strategy.

While the losses realized in the period subsequent to the end of July 2002 are severe, the investment strategy based on idiosyncratic volatility produces several additional large and prolonged drawdowns. The second largest drawdown began in November of 1998. Between then and the end of February 2000, the portfolio lost almost 67%. In this case, the recovery was quite quick. By the end of November 2000, the portfolio had achieved a new high water mark. The third largest and second longest drawdown began in January 1975. The portfolio lost almost 66% of its value between then and November 1980. It finally recovered its previous high value in August 1983. Finally, the fourth largest and third most prolonged drawdown began in January 1965, from which point the portfolio lost more than 58% of its value by the end of January 1969, with a complete recovery realized in November 1971. In summary, while the long-run returns of the Low–High $IdioVol^{FF,1M}$ portfolio have been substantial, this investment strategy involves a very high level of risk. As of the end of 2012, the portfolio remains well below its previous high, which was achieved in 2002, more than 10 years earlier.

15.7 SUMMARY

In this chapter, we have examined the relation between idiosyncratic volatility and expected stock returns. We begin by calculating and examining several different measures of total and idiosyncratic volatility. Comparison of the different measures of idiosyncratic volatility indicates that the decision of whether to use the one-factor market model (CAPM), Fama and French (1993) three-factor model (FF), or the Fama and French (1993) and Carhart (1997) four-factor model (FFC) to calculate idiosyncratic volatility is largely inconsequential, as the measures are extremely highly correlated and very similar in magnitude in the cross section. Additionally, idiosyncratic volatility and total volatility are extremely similar in the cross section. Following the empirical asset pricing literature, we focus on the measure of idiosyncratic volatility that is calculated using the FF risk model and one month of daily return data.

The main result of the chapter is what is known as the idiosyncratic volatility puzzle. Specifically, the results of our empirical analyses detect a negative cross-sectional relation between idiosyncratic volatility and future stock returns. This relation is very strong when using value-weighted portfolio analysis but substantially weaker and, depending on the measure of idiosyncratic volatility used, nonexistent, in equal-weighted portfolios. Fama and MacBeth (1973) regression analyses produce results similar to the equal-weighted portfolio analyses. The strength of the negative relation between idiosyncratic volatility and future stock returns detected by the regression analyses depends on the regression specification. However, when a full set of controls is employed, the results indicate a negative cross-sectional relation between idiosyncratic volatility and expected stock returns.

For the remaining chapters of this book, we will continue to use idiosyncratic volatility calculated relative to the FF risk model from one month of daily return data as our measure of idiosyncratic volatility. In this chapter, we have denoted this variable $IdioVol^{FF,1M}$. Moving forward, this variable will be denoted $IdioVol$.

REFERENCES

Ang, A., Hodrick, R. J., Xing, Y., and Zhang, X. 2006. The cross-section of volatility and expected returns. Journal of Finance, 61(1), 259–299.

Ang, A., Hodrick, R. J., Xing, Y., and Zhang, X. 2009. High idiosyncratic volatility and low returns: international and further U.S. evidence. Journal of Financial Economics, 91(1), 1–23.

Baker, M., Bradley, B., and Wurgler, J. 2011. Benchmarks as limits to arbitrage: understanding the low-volatility anomaly. Financial Analysts Journal, 67(1), 40–54.

Baker, M. and Wurgler, J. 2014. The Risk Anomaly Tradeoff of Leverage. SSRN eLibrary.

Bali, T. and Cakici, N. 2008. Idiosyncratic volatility and the cross-section of expected returns. Journal of Financial and Quantitative Analysis, 43, 29–58.

Bali, T. G., Cakici, N., and Whitelaw, R. F. 2011. Maxing out: stocks as lotteries and the cross-section of expected returns. Journal of Financial Economics, 99(2), 427–446.

Carhart, M. M. 1997. On persistence in mutual fund performance. Journal of Finance, 52(1), 57–82.

Fama, E. F. and French, K. R. 1993. Common risk factors in the returns on stocks and bonds. Journal of Financial Economics, 33(1), 3–56.

Fama, E. F. and MacBeth, J. D. 1973. Risk, return, and equilibrium: empirical tests. Journal of Political Economy, 81(3), 607.

Friend, I., Westerfield, R., and Granito, M. 1978. New evidence on the capital asset pricing model. Journal of Finance, 33(3), 903–917.

Fu, F. 2009. Idiosyncratic risk and the cross-section of expected stock returns. Journal of Financial Economics, 91(1), 24–37.

Guo, H., Kassa, H., and Ferguson, M. F. 2014. On the relation between EGARCH idiosyncratic volatility and expected stock returns. Journal of Financial and Quantitative Analysis, 49(1), 271–296.

Han, Y. and Lesmond, D. 2011. Liquidity biases and the pricing of cross-sectional idiosyncratic volatility. Review of Financial Studies, 24(5), 1590–1629.

Huang, W., Liu, Q., Rhee, S. G., and Zhang, L. 2010. Return reversals, idiosyncratic risk, and expected returns. Review of Financial Studies, 23(1), 147–168.

Lehmann, B. N. 1990. Residual risk revisited. Journal of Econometrics, 45(1-2), 71–97.

Levy, H. 1978. Equilibrium in an imperfect market: a constraint on the number of securities in the portfolio. American Economic Review, 68, 643–658.

Lintner, J. 1965. Security prices, risk, and maximal gains from diversification. Journal of Finance, 20(4), 687–615.

Merton, R. C. 1987. A simple model of capital market equilibrium with incomplete information. Journal of Finance, 42, 483–510.

Mossin, J. 1966. Equilibrium in a capital asset market. Econometrica, 34(4), 768–783.

Newey, W. K. and West, K. D. 1987. A simple, positive semi-definite, heteroskedasticity and autocorrelation consistent covariance matrix. Econometrica, 55(3), 703–708.

Pastor, L. and Stambaugh, R. F. 2003. Liquidity risk and expected stock returns. Journal of Political Economy, 111(3), 642–685.

Ross, S. A. 1976. The arbitrage theory of capital asset pricing. Journal of Economic Theory, 13(3), 341–360.

Sharpe, W. F. 1964. Capital asset prices: a theory of market equilibrium under conditions of risk. Journal of Finance, 19(3), 425–442.

Shumway, T. 1997. The delisting bias in CRSP data. Journal of Finance, 52(1), 327–340.

Tinic, S. M. and West, R. R. 1986. Risk, return, and equilibrium: a revisit. Journal of Political Economy, 94(1), 126–147.

16

LIQUID SAMPLES

In the previous chapters of Part II of this book, we have examined several different phenomena observed in historical stock returns. In doing so, we have used a sample of stocks consisting of all U.S.-based common stocks in the Center for Research in Security Prices (CRSP) database, which we have referred to as the CRSP sample. The construction of this sample was discussed in detail in Section 7.1.1.

As discussed in Chapter 9, the CRSP sample is characterized by a small number of extremely large stocks and a large number of very small stocks. Many researchers prefer to exclude some of the smallest and most illiquid stocks from the sample used in empirical analyses. There are several reasons for this. First, the pricing of small stocks, especially stocks with low share prices, tends to be less efficient and informative than the pricing of large and liquid stocks. For stocks that are not heavily traded, the price at which the last trade was executed may not be indicative of the value of the stock at the end of the day. Price changes for such stocks are also more susceptible to microstructure issues such as the bid–ask bounce. McLean and Pontiff (2015) show that the strength of many anomalies documented in the empirical asset pricing literature, especially those concentrated among low-liquidity stocks, lose strength in out-of-sample tests. Second, even though these stocks may be large in number, as shown in Chapter 9, they are very small in total market value. Thus, excluding such stocks from the sample still allows the researcher to draw conclusions that pertain to the vast majority of stock market wealth. Many researchers believe that excluding small and illiquid stocks from the sample substantially reduces the measurement error

Empirical Asset Pricing: The Cross Section of Stock Returns, First Edition.
Turan G. Bali, Robert F. Engle, and Scott Murray.
© 2016 John Wiley & Sons, Inc. Published 2016 by John Wiley & Sons, Inc.

in variables whose calculation relies on historical returns, such as beta, momentum, reversal, co-skewness, idiosyncratic skewness, and idiosyncratic volatility. If this is the case, then removing such stocks from the sample can alleviate the possibility that measurement error in these variables is driving the empirical results. Furthermore, in many cases, the results of analyses that exclude such stocks may be more indicative of realistic investment opportunities because the cost of transacting in small and illiquid stocks can negate any profits that may be realized.

In this chapter, we introduce some commonly used screens that researchers use to remove small and illiquid stocks from the sample. We then repeat several of the analyses presented throughout the text using samples restricted according to these criteria. In addition to presenting the results from analyses using the restricted samples, we also show the corresponding CRSP sample results that have been presented throughout the previous chapters of this book. The results in this chapter can, therefore, be thought of as both examining the phenomena documented in previous chapters of this book using different samples of stocks and summarizing the results generated throughout the previous chapters.

16.1 SAMPLES

In addition to the CRSP sample, in this chapter we examine two commonly used subsamples of the CRSP sample. The first subsample includes all stocks that have a share price between \$5 and \$1000, inclusive, at the end of month t. The idea behind using this sample is that the excluded stocks (stocks with share prices less than \$5 or more than \$1000) are likely illiquid and expensive to trade. We refer to this sample as the Price sample. To generate the Price sample, for each month t, we begin with the CRSP sample, and then remove all stocks with a price at the end of month t, as indicated in the ALTPRC field in CRSP's monthly stock file, that is less than \$5 or more than \$1000.[1]

The second new sample we use is the subset of stocks in the Price sample that have a market capitalization that is equal to or greater than the 10th percentile market capitalization of stocks listed on the New York Stock Exchange (NYSE). We refer to this sample as the Size sample. To generate the Size sample in any given month t, we calculate the 10th percentile of month t $MktCap$ (defined in Section 9.1), across all stocks in the CRSP database that are listed on the NYSE at the end of month t.[2] The Size sample is then generated by removing all stocks from the Price sample with $MktCap$ values less than the 10th percentile of $MktCap$ among NYSE stocks. The Size sample can, therefore, be described as the set of stocks that have a share price between \$5 and \$1000 (inclusive) with market capitalizations greater than or equal to the 10th percentile market capitalization of NYSE-listed stocks.

---

[1]For reasons discussed in Section 7.1.2, in some cases the ALTPRC field may be negative. In such cases, the stock price is taken to be the absolute value of the value in the ALTPRC field.
[2]The set of stocks that are NYSE-listed at the end of month t is taken to be the set of stocks in the CRSP sample with a value of 1 in the EXCHCD field in CRSP's monthly stock names file.

16.2 SUMMARY STATISTICS

Table 16.1 presents summary statistics for each of the main variables examined throughout the previous chapters of Part II of this book. Specifically, we present summary statistics for each of β, *MktCap*, *Size*, *BM*, *Mom*, *Rev*, *Illiq*, *CoSkew*, *IdioSkew*, and *IdioVol*. Summary statistics for the CRSP sample are presented in Panel A, Price sample summary statistics are shown in Panel B, and Size sample

TABLE 16.1 Summary Statistics
This table presents summary statistics for variables defined in the previous chapters of Part II or this book. Panel A presents results for the CRSP sample. Panel B presents results for the Price sample, which includes stocks in the CRSP sample with month-end share price of $5 or more. Panel C presents results for the Size sample, which includes stocks in the Price sample that have market capitalization above the 10th percentile of market capitalization calculated among stocks listed on the New York Stock Exchange. Each sample covers the months t from June 1963 through November 2012. Each month, the mean (*Mean*), standard deviation (*SD*), skewness (*Skew*), excess kurtosis (*Kurt*), minimum (*Min*), 5th percentile (5%), 25th percentile (25%), median (*Median*), 75th percentile (75%), 95th percentile (95%), and maximum (*Max*) values of the cross-sectional distribution of each variable is calculated. The table presents the time-series means for each cross-sectional value. The column labeled n indicates that average number of stocks for which the given variable is available.

Panel A: CRSP Sample											
	Mean	SD	Skew	Kurt	Min	5%	25%	Median	75%	95%	Max	n
β	0.78	0.61	0.49	1.46	−2.16	−0.05	0.35	0.71	1.15	1.89	3.90	4440
MktCap	1101	5568	18	459	0	6	29	107	446	4108	161,217	4794
Size	4.33	1.92	0.38	−0.08	−1.18	1.46	2.93	4.16	5.57	7.74	11.48	4794
BM	0.94	1.14	10.16	284.75	0.01	0.15	0.41	0.72	1.15	2.32	32.92	3409
Mom	14.12	58.40	4.12	61.62	−89.41	−49.88	−17.11	5.70	31.98	102.73	1064.02	4426
Rev	1.21	15.49	3.11	59.45	−67.35	−18.93	−6.27	0.06	6.92	24.20	266.45	4750
Illiq	3.79	27.73	22.15	827.12	0.00	0.01	0.05	0.26	1.35	13.39	1174.73	3604
CoSkew	−1.20	9.49	1.86	69.42	−79.85	−14.60	−5.26	−1.11	2.75	11.77	128.72	3992
IdioSkew	0.64	0.81	1.42	4.79	−2.64	−0.37	0.14	0.51	0.98	2.13	6.14	3992
IdioVol	48.07	40.25	4.31	61.51	1.40	12.41	24.15	37.84	59.40	116.48	748.45	4742

Panel B: Price Sample											
	Mean	SD	Skew	Kurt	Min	5%	25%	Median	75%	95%	Max	n
β	0.83	0.58	0.63	0.62	−1.05	0.04	0.41	0.76	1.17	1.90	3.32	3277
MktCap	1449	6376	16	350	3	17	66	200	704	5495	161,217	3529
Size	4.97	1.69	0.49	0.02	0.71	2.50	3.73	4.78	6.04	8.01	11.48	3529
BM	0.84	0.85	7.65	152.16	0.01	0.16	0.41	0.69	1.06	1.94	19.04	2481
Mom	20.93	55.22	4.48	64.16	−76.48	−34.50	−7.83	11.24	35.80	104.97	972.76	3267
Rev	1.85	12.23	2.45	40.33	−48.91	−14.29	−4.71	0.73	6.89	21.21	168.31	3499
Illiq	0.73	1.88	8.53	165.18	0.00	0.01	0.04	0.16	0.62	3.39	37.70	2885
CoSkew	−0.87	7.64	0.52	16.50	−59.00	−11.89	−4.43	−0.85	2.57	10.04	76.17	2961
IdioSkew	0.52	0.71	1.39	5.47	−2.38	−0.39	0.09	0.42	0.83	1.78	5.60	2961
IdioVol	36.90	23.37	3.29	46.47	1.49	11.98	21.60	31.89	46.38	77.63	362.70	3502

TABLE 16.1   (*Continued*)

	Mean	SD	Skew	Kurt	Min	5%	25%	Median	75%	95%	Max	n
					Panel C: Size Sample							
β	0.95	0.55	0.71	0.65	−0.63	0.21	0.54	0.86	1.26	1.99	3.26	2215
MktCap	2083	7589	13	233	88	102	187	417	1218	7818	161,217	2339
Size	5.84	1.33	0.92	0.52	4.07	4.21	4.78	5.57	6.65	8.37	11.48	2339
BM	0.75	0.69	6.96	132.10	0.01	0.16	0.38	0.63	0.95	1.65	13.40	1752
Mom	21.83	52.72	4.21	53.72	−72.70	−31.36	−5.76	12.54	36.13	102.51	823.92	2210
Rev	1.85	11.14	1.72	21.43	−44.15	−13.41	−4.34	0.97	6.85	19.68	119.28	2325
Illiq	0.24	0.53	12.04	291.81	0.00	0.00	0.02	0.08	0.25	0.97	9.62	2130
CoSkew	−0.51	6.88	0.24	13.30	−51.78	−10.45	−3.76	−0.50	2.66	9.41	55.56	2045
IdioSkew	0.41	0.65	1.42	6.36	−2.23	−0.43	0.03	0.34	0.70	1.52	5.14	2045
IdioVol	33.31	19.48	2.87	31.56	2.01	12.14	20.41	29.13	41.44	67.65	259.93	2329

summary statistics are shown in Panel C. Since the summary statistics for the CRSP sample have been discussed in previous chapters of this book, our discussion of the summary statistics focuses on comparisons of the different samples.

The summary statistics for β are quite similar in the CRSP and Price samples. Perhaps the most prevalent difference is in the average excess kurtosis of the cross-sectional distribution of β, which is 1.46 in the CRSP sample and only 0.62 in the Price sample. The decrease in kurtosis is a manifestation of the removal of stocks with extreme values of β when the Price sample restrictions are imposed. In the average month, the minimum value of β for stocks in the Price sample is −1.05 compared to −2.16 for the CRSP sample. Similarly, the maximum value of β for stocks in the Price sample is 3.32 compared to 3.90 in the CRSP sample. The other shown percentiles of β are similar in the CRSP and Price samples. It is also interesting that, despite the removal of stocks with extreme values of β, the standard deviation of β in the Price sample of 0.58 is very similar to the corresponding CRSP sample standard deviation of 0.61, indicating that the kurtosis of β in the CRSP sample is driven by a very small number of stocks with stock prices below \$5 or above \$1000. In the average month, there are 3277 stocks in the Price sample with valid values of β compared to 4440 in the CRSP sample. The distribution of β in the Size sample is similar to the distribution of β in the Price sample, except that values at all percentiles (except for the maximum value) of β, as well as the mean, are slightly higher in the Size sample than in the Price sample. This is driven by the fact that the NYSE 10th percentile size screen results in the removal of stocks that have low values of β. In the average month, the minimum β for Size sample stocks is −0.63, compared to −1.05 for stocks in the Price sample. The additional restriction reduces the average number of stocks with a valid value of β in the Size sample to 2215 from 3277 in the Price sample.

The summary statistics for *MktCap* show that, in the average month, all percentiles as well as the mean of *MktCap* are higher among stocks in the Price sample than in the CRSP sample, with the Price sample having a mean (median) *MktCap* of \$1.45 billion (\$200 million) compared to \$1.10 billion (\$107 million) for the CRSP sample.

This is expected since the removal of stocks with prices less than $5 is likely to result in the exclusion of stocks with low values of *MktCap* from the Price sample. There are relatively few stocks with a price greater than $1000, so this condition is not nearly as restrictive. In the average month, the Price sample has only 3529 stocks with valid values of *MktCap* compared to 4794 in the CRSP sample. The increase in *MktCap* values in the Size sample is even more dramatic. This is not surprising since the NYSE 10th percentile size screen is explicitly a screen that removes stocks with low values of *MktCap*. The mean (median) *MktCap* for stocks in the Size sample is just over $2 billion ($417 million). The additional screen results in only 2339 stocks in the Size sample, in the average month, with valid values of *MktCap*. The summary statistics for *Size*, which is the natural log of *MktCap*, are reflective of the summary statistics for *MktCap* and thus do not warrant further discussion.

The average and median values of *BM* are lower in the Price sample than in the CRSP sample and lower in the Size sample than in the Price sample. The mean value of *BM* in the Price (Size) sample is 0.84 (0.75) compared to 0.94 in the CRSP sample. The summary statistics indicate that the price screen, and then in turn the NYSE 10th percentile size screen, result primarily in the removal of stocks with high values of *BM* because the minimum, 5th percentile, and 25th percentile values of *BM* are all similar across the different samples. However, the median, 75th percentile, 95th percentile, and maximum values are substantially lower in the Size sample that in the Price sample, and lower in the Price sample than in the CRSP sample. In the average month, the Price (Size) sample has 2481 (1752) stocks with valid values of *BM* compared to 3409 in the CRSP sample.

Mom is, on average, highest among stocks in the Size sample and higher in the Price sample than in the CRSP sample. At first glance, this result may seem contradictory given that *Mom* is simply a measure of return and small stocks, which have been targeted for removal by the different screens have been shown to generate relatively high returns. The likely explanation for this pattern is that, since *Mom* in month t measures returns during the months $t - 11$ through $t - 1$, stocks with low values of *Mom* have realized very large negative returns in the medium-term past resulting in low share prices and market capitalizations, resulting in the removal of low-*Mom* stocks from the restricted samples. Both the Price sample and Size sample average *Mom* values of 21.83 and 20.93, respectively, are substantially higher than the average *Mom* value of 14.12 in the CRSP sample. The minimum, fifth percentile, 25th percentile, and median values of *Mom* in the Price sample are similar to the corresponding values for the Size sample. These percentiles from the Price and Size samples are substantially higher than the corresponding values from the CRSP sample. 75th and 95th percentile values are more similar across all three samples. The summary statistics, therefore, indicate that it is indeed stocks with low values of *Mom* (loser stocks) that tend to be removed by the price and size screens. The Price (Size) sample has 2210 (3267) stocks with valid values of *Mom* in the average month compared to 4426 for the CRSP sample.

The patterns in *Rev* across the different samples are very similar to those of *Mom*. Stocks with low values of *Rev* are more likely to be removed from the sample than stocks with high values of *Rev*. The likely reason for this is once again that stocks with high values of *Rev* are more likely to have share prices and market capitalizations that satisfy the price and size screens since *Rev* is simply the return of the stock in the given month t. The distribution of *Rev* is very similar in both the Price and Size samples. In both restricted samples, the average *Rev* value is 1.85 and all percentiles are reasonably similar. The minimum, fifth percentile, 25th percentile, and median values of *Rev* in the Price and Size samples are substantially higher than the corresponding values for the CRSP sample, while the 75th percentile and 95th percentile values are relatively similar across all three samples. In the average month, the Price (Size) sample has 3499 (2325) stocks with valid *Rev* values, while the CRSP sample has 4750 such stocks.

The summary statistics presented in Table 16.1 demonstrate that the screens are very effective at removing illiquid stocks from the sample. The average value of *Illiq* for stocks in the Price (Size) sample is 0.73 (0.24) compared to 3.79 for stocks in the CRSP sample. In the average month, the maximum and 95th percentile values of *Illiq* for stocks in the Price (Size) sample are 37.70 (9.62) and 3.39 (0.97) compared to 1174.73 and 13.39, respectively, for the CRSP sample. Thus, the price screen succeeds at removing the most illiquid stocks from the CRSP sample, and the size screen succeeds at removing the most illiquid stocks from the Price sample. In the average month, the Price sample has 2885 stocks with a valid value of *Illiq*, and the Size sample has 2130 such stocks. The CRSP sample has 3604 stocks, on average, with a valid value of *Illiq*.

Average values of *CoSkew* in the Price and Size samples of −0.87 and −0.51, respectively, are slightly higher than the average in the CRSP sample of −1.20, but this difference is relatively minor. The main difference between the distribution of *CoSkew* among stocks in the different samples is that price and size screens tend to remove stocks with extreme (high and low) values of *CoSkew*. For this reason, the standard deviation and excess kurtosis of the cross-sectional distribution of *CoSkew* are lowest in the Size sample, second lowest in the Price sample, and highest in the CRSP sample. There are, in the average month, 2961 stocks in the Price sample and 2045 stocks in the Size sample with valid values of *CoSkew* compared to an average of 3992 stocks in the CRSP sample.

The cross-sectional distribution of *IdioSkew* is similar in all three samples. At all presented percentiles (with the exception of the minimum value), as well as at the mean, the values of *IdioSkew* are lowest in the Size sample, second lowest in the Price sample, and highest in the CRSP sample. Since *IdioSkew* is calculated using the exact same set of returns as *CoSkew* and the data requirements for these two variables are the same, the number of stocks with valid values of *IdioSkew* in each sample is the same as number of stocks with valid *CoSkew* values.

Finally, values of *IdioVol* are, on average and in median, substantially lower in the Price and Size samples than in the CRSP sample. For stocks in the Price sample, the average (median) value of *IdioVol* is 36.90 (31.89), and for stocks in the Size sample the average (median) *IdioVol* is 33.31 (29.13). The CRSP sample, for comparison, is comprised of stocks with an average (median) *IdioVol* value of 48.07 (37.84). With the exception of the minimum and fifth percentile values, each of the presented cross-sectional percentiles of *IdioVol* is highest in the CRSP sample, substantially lower in the Price sample, and lower still in the Size sample. The results indicate that the price and size screens tend to remove stocks with high values of *IdioVol*. The Price (Size) sample has 3502 (2329) stocks with valid values of *IdioVol* compared to 4742 such stocks in the CRSP sample.

16.3 CORRELATIONS

The average cross-sectional Pearson product–moment and Spearman rank correlations between each of the pairs of variables for the CRSP (Panel A), Price (Panel B), and Size (Panel C) samples are shown in Table 16.2. Pearson correlations are presented in the below-diagonal entries and Spearman correlations are shown in the above-diagonal entries. In most cases, the correlation between any given pair of variables is similar across each of the three samples. We therefore discuss only the correlations that differ substantially between the different samples.

16.3.1 CRSP Sample and Price Sample

We begin by comparing correlations in the Price sample to the corresponding correlations in the CRSP sample.

The negative Pearson correlation between β and *Illiq* is much larger in magnitude in the Price sample than in the CRSP sample. In the Price sample, β and *Illiq* have an average cross-sectional correlation of −0.25 compared to −0.15 in the CRSP sample. Interestingly, the Spearman correlations between these variables of −0.33 in the Price sample and −0.32 in the CRSP sample are very similar. This indicates that the relatively low correlation between β and *Illiq* in the CRSP sample is driven by nonlinearity in the relation between *Illiq* and β that largely disappears when the price screen is applied.

The positive Pearson (Spearman) correlation between β and *IdioVol* in the Price sample of 0.22 (0.28) is much higher than the corresponding correlation in the CRSP sample of 0.08 (0.16). This likely indicates that the true relation between β and *IdioVol* is stronger than indicated by the CRSP sample results. Noisy measurement of both β and *IdioVol* for illiquid and low-priced stocks in the CRSP sample likely results in the relatively low CRSP sample correlations. Restricting the sample to more liquid stocks that do not have low share prices increases the accuracy of the measurement of both β and *IdioVol* for the average stock in the Price sample, resulting in more accurate measurement of the correlation between these variables.

The correlation between *Size* and *Mom* is much smaller in the Price sample than in the CRSP sample. In the Price sample, the Pearson (Spearman) correlation between these variables is 0.03 (0.08) compared to 0.18 (0.25) in the CRSP sample. The CRSP sample correlation is likely driven by the fact that stocks with very low values of *Mom*, which captures medium-term past returns, are, as a result of this poor performance, likely to have low market capitalization, thus generating the positive correlation between *Size* and *Mom* in the CRSP sample. These low *Mom* stocks, however, are also likely to be removed by the price screen, resulting in a decreased correlation between *Size* and *Mom* in the Price sample.

TABLE 16.2 Correlations

This table presents the time-series averages of the annual cross-sectional Pearson product–moment (below-diagonal entries) and Spearman rank (above-diagonal entries) correlations between pairs of β, *Size*, *BM*, *Mom*, *Rev*, *Illiq*, *CoSkew*, *IdioSkew*, and *IdioVol*. Panel A presents results of the CRSP sample. Panel B presents results for the Price sample. Panel C presents results for the Size sample.

Panel A: CRSP Sample

	β	Size	BM	Mom	Rev	Illiq	CoSkew	IdioSkew	IdioVol
β		0.33	−0.23	0.04	−0.01	−0.32	0.08	−0.06	0.16
Size	0.31		−0.26	0.25	0.11	−0.92	0.14	−0.36	−0.48
BM	−0.19	−0.27		0.04	0.03	0.25	0.02	0.03	−0.01
Mom	0.07	0.18	0.02		0.04	−0.24	0.00	0.02	−0.22
Rev	−0.02	0.07	0.02	0.02		−0.08	0.01	−0.02	0.00
Illiq	−0.15	−0.42	0.18	−0.16	−0.04		−0.13	0.32	0.54
CoSkew	0.06	0.11	0.02	−0.00	0.00	−0.04		−0.10	−0.07
IdioSkew	−0.04	−0.34	0.06	0.07	0.03	0.16	−0.08		0.26
IdioVol	0.08	−0.45	0.07	−0.16	0.10	0.48	−0.06	0.25	

Panel B: Price Sample

	β	Size	BM	Mom	Rev	Illiq	CoSkew	IdioSkew	IdioVol
β		0.32	−0.25	0.01	−0.02	−0.33	0.08	−0.03	0.28
Size	0.30		−0.26	0.08	0.04	−0.90	0.14	−0.30	−0.34
BM	−0.21	−0.25		0.04	0.03	0.24	0.02	0.04	−0.08
Mom	0.06	0.03	0.04		0.00	−0.11	−0.03	0.09	−0.06
Rev	−0.02	0.00	0.03	0.01		−0.03	−0.00	0.01	0.08
Illiq	−0.25	−0.50	0.19	−0.08	0.00		−0.13	0.26	0.39
CoSkew	0.07	0.12	0.02	−0.03	−0.00	−0.06		−0.09	−0.05
IdioSkew	−0.02	−0.28	0.05	0.14	0.05	0.15	−0.07		0.18
IdioVol	0.22	−0.33	−0.01	0.02	0.18	0.29	−0.04	0.19	

Panel C: Size Sample

	β	Size	BM	Mom	Rev	Illiq	CoSkew	IdioSkew	IdioVol
β		0.09	−0.20	0.02	−0.02	−0.22	0.06	0.05	0.40
Size	0.07		−0.13	0.04	0.02	−0.85	0.11	−0.23	−0.34
BM	−0.16	−0.14		0.03	0.02	0.15	0.05	−0.01	−0.14
Mom	0.07	−0.01	0.02		0.01	−0.08	−0.04	0.10	−0.03
Rev	−0.01	−0.01	0.03	0.02		−0.02	−0.00	0.01	0.08
Illiq	−0.18	−0.42	0.12	−0.06	−0.00		−0.11	0.19	0.30
CoSkew	0.06	0.09	0.05	−0.03	−0.01	−0.05		−0.07	−0.04
IdioSkew	0.07	−0.21	0.01	0.15	0.05	0.11	−0.05		0.15
IdioVol	0.36	−0.32	−0.08	0.05	0.16	0.17	−0.03	0.17	

Size is also less negatively correlated with *IdioVol* in the Price sample compared to the CRSP sample. The Pearson (Spearman) correlation between *Size* and *IdioVol* in the Price sample is −0.33 (−0.34), whereas this correlation is −0.45 (−0.48) in the CRSP sample. The summary statistics presented in Table 16.1 indicate that a substantial number of stocks with low values of *Size* and high values of *IdioVol* are removed by the price screen. The decrease in the magnitude of the correlation, therefore, indicates that the relatively strong correlation in the CRSP sample is driven by a strong propensity of such very small stocks to have very high idiosyncratic volatility.

The correlation between *Mom* and *Illiq* in the Price sample is much smaller in magnitude than in the CRSP sample. In the Price sample, both the Pearson correlation of −0.16 and the Spearman correlation of −0.24 are substantially negative. This indicates that in the CRSP sample, stocks that have had large negative returns in the medium-term past, as captured by *Mom*, tend to be highly illiquid. In the Price sample, the diminished Pearson (Spearman) correlation of −0.08 (−0.11) indicates that the stocks driving this relation have been removed by the price screen. However, even after removing stocks with extremely low or high share prices, a nonnegligible negative correlation between *Mom* and *Illiq* still exists.

In the Price sample, the Pearson (Spearman) correlation between *Mom* and *IdioVol* of 0.02 (−0.06) is quite small. In the CRSP sample, however, the correlation between these variables of −0.16 (−0.22) is much stronger. The substantial negative correlation between *Mom* and *IdioVol* in the CRSP sample indicates that high *IdioVol* stocks are likely to have experienced substantial losses (low values of *Mom*) in the medium-term past. These losses tend to drop the stock price below \$5, causing them to be excluded from the Price sample. The exclusion of such stocks from the Price sample results in a lower correlation between *Mom* and *IdioVol*.

The Pearson (Spearman) correlation of 0.29 (0.39) between *Illiq* and *IdioVol* in the Price sample is much lower than the corresponding correlation in the CRSP sample of 0.48 (0.54). The likely reason for this is that stocks with low or high share prices are likely to be highly illiquid and also to experience high levels of idiosyncratic volatility due to either illiquidity or microstructure issues. The removal of these stocks from the Price sample, therefore, results in a reduced correlation between *Illiq* and *IdioVol* among the remaining stocks.

16.3.2   Price Sample and Size Sample

We proceed now to compare the pairwise correlations for the Size sample to those of the Price sample.

Panel C on Table 16.2 shows that the Pearson (Spearman) correlation between β and *Size* is only 0.07 (0.09) compared to 0.30 (0.32) in the Price sample. The strong decrease in the correlation between β and *Size* when small stocks are removed indicates that the positive correlation between β and *Size* in the Price sample is largely driven by very small stocks that tend to have very low betas.

The Pearson (Spearman) correlation of −0.18 (−0.22) between β and *Illiq* is substantially reduced in magnitude from the correlation between these variables of −0.25 (−0.33) in the Price sample. A decrease in this correlation of similar magnitude was detected when moving from the CRSP sample to the Price sample. The reason for this decrease in both cases is likely the same. Less liquid stocks tend to have extremely low values of β. The removal of highly illiquid stocks, therefore, results in a weakening of the cross-sectional relation between β and *Illiq*.

β is more strongly positively correlated with *IdioVol* in the Size sample than in the Price sample. The Pearson (Spearman) correlation between these two variables is 0.36 (0.40) in the Size sample compared to 0.22 (0.28) in the Price sample. As discussed in our analysis of the increased correlation between these variables when moving from the CRSP sample to the Price sample, this result is likely a manifestation of increased measurement error in β and *IdioVol* among small stocks. The result indicates that beta and idiosyncratic volatility have a strong cross-sectional relation.

The magnitude of the negative correlation between *Size* and *BM* in the Size sample is lower than in the Price sample. In the Size sample, the Pearson (Spearman) correlation between *Size* and *BM* is -0.14 (-0.13) compared to -0.25 (-0.26) in the Price sample. The drop in the magnitude of this correlation indicates that the stronger negative correlation found in the Price sample is largely driven by small stocks that tend to have high values of *BM*.

Finally, the results in Panel C of Table 16.2 indicate a substantially lower correlation between *Illiq* and *IdioVol* in the Size sample than in the Price sample. In the Size sample, the Pearson (Spearman) correlation between *Illiq* and *IdioVol* is 0.22 (0.31) compared to 0.33 (0.40) in the Price sample. Recall that a similar decrease in the correlation between *Illiq* and *IdioVol* was observed in the Price sample compared to the full CRSP sample. The reason for the reduction in this correlation in the Size sample compared to the Price sample is likely similar to the reason for the reduction in correlation in the Price sample relative to the CRSP sample. Small and illiquid stocks tend to have higher firm-specific risk. Therefore, when such stocks are removed from the sample, the strength of the relation between illiquidity and firm-specific risk decreases.

16.4 PERSISTENCE

Our final analyses before proceeding to examination of the relations between the main asset pricing variables examined throughout this book and future stock returns are persistence analyses of each of these variables. The results of the persistence analyses for each of β, *MktCap*, *Size*, *BM*, *Mom*, *Rev*, *Illiq*, *CoSkew*, *IdioSkew*, and *IdioVol* are presented in Table 16.3. Results for the CRSP sample, the Price sample, and the Size sample are shown in Panels A, B, and C, respectively. Because results for the CRSP sample have already been discussed throughout the previous chapters of Part II of this book, our discussion examines only the differences in the results of the persistence analyses between the samples. Furthermore, quick examination of the results of the persistence analyses for the Price sample (Panel B) and Size sample (Panel C) indicates that the results are very similar for both of these restricted samples. None of the differences in the results of the persistence analyses between these two samples are large enough to warrant discussion. We therefore only discuss

TABLE 16.3 Persistence

This table presents the results of persistence analyses of β, *MktCap*, *Size*, *BM*, *Mom*, *Rev*, *Illiq*, *CoSkew*, *IdioSkew*, and *IdioVol* using the CRSP (Panel A), Price (Panel B), and Size (Panel C) samples. Each month t, the cross-sectional Pearson product–moment correlation between the month t and month $t + \tau$ values of the given variable is calculated. The table presents the time-series averages of the monthly cross-sectional correlations. The column labeled τ indicates the lag at which the persistence is measured.

Panel A: CRSP Sample

τ	β	MktCap	Size	BM	Mom	Rev	Illiq	CoSkew	IdioSkew	IdioVol
1		1.00	1.00	0.98		−0.04	0.80			0.65
3		0.99	0.99	0.95		0.01	0.74			0.60
6		0.99	0.98	0.90		0.01	0.67			0.57
12	0.63	0.98	0.97	0.80	0.02	0.02	0.58			0.53
24	0.55	0.96	0.94	0.67	−0.04	0.01	0.45			0.46
36	0.50	0.94	0.92	0.58	−0.02	0.01	0.38			0.43
48	0.47	0.93	0.90	0.52	−0.02	0.01	0.33			0.40
60	0.44	0.91	0.89	0.47	−0.04	0.01	0.31	0.03	0.21	0.39
120	0.35	0.84	0.84	0.37	0.01	0.01	0.24	0.05	0.20	0.34

Panel B: Price Sample

τ	β	MktCap	Size	BM	Mom	Rev	Illiq	CoSkew	IdioSkew	IdioVol
1		1.00	1.00	0.99		−0.03	0.79			0.57
3		0.99	0.99	0.96		0.01	0.74			0.53
6		0.99	0.99	0.92		0.01	0.69			0.50
12	0.73	0.98	0.98	0.85	0.02	0.01	0.63			0.46
24	0.65	0.96	0.96	0.75	−0.04	0.01	0.55			0.41
36	0.60	0.94	0.94	0.68	−0.03	0.01	0.50			0.38
48	0.56	0.93	0.92	0.63	−0.02	0.01	0.47			0.35
60	0.53	0.91	0.91	0.58	−0.04	0.00	0.44	0.05	0.15	0.34
120	0.42	0.84	0.86	0.46	0.01	0.01	0.38	0.06	0.14	0.27

the differences between the Price and CRSP samples. Similar interpretation applies to the differences between the Size and CRSP samples.

The results in Table 16.3 demonstrate that β is more persistent in the Price and Size samples than in the CRSP sample. In the Price sample, the persistence values of β measured at a lags of one year ($\tau = 12$), two years ($\tau = 24$), and three years ($\tau = 36$) of 0.73, 0.65, and 0.60, respectively, are 0.10 higher than the corresponding persistence values in the CRSP sample. At lags of four years ($\tau = 48$), five years ($\tau = 60$), and 10 years ($\tau = 120$), β has persistence of 0.56, 0.53, and 0.42 in the

TABLE 16.3   (*Continued*)

<table>
<tr><th colspan="11">Panel C: Size Sample</th></tr>
<tr><th>τ</th><th>β</th><th>MktCap</th><th>Size</th><th>BM</th><th>Mom</th><th>Rev</th><th>Illiq</th><th>CoSkew</th><th>IdioSkew</th><th>IdioVol</th></tr>
<tr><td>1</td><td></td><td>1.00</td><td>1.00</td><td>0.99</td><td></td><td>−0.03</td><td>0.82</td><td></td><td></td><td>0.56</td></tr>
<tr><td>3</td><td></td><td>0.99</td><td>0.99</td><td>0.96</td><td></td><td>0.01</td><td>0.76</td><td></td><td></td><td>0.53</td></tr>
<tr><td>6</td><td></td><td>0.99</td><td>0.98</td><td>0.92</td><td></td><td>0.01</td><td>0.72</td><td></td><td></td><td>0.50</td></tr>
<tr><td>12</td><td>0.73</td><td>0.98</td><td>0.97</td><td>0.85</td><td>0.04</td><td>0.01</td><td>0.66</td><td></td><td></td><td>0.47</td></tr>
<tr><td>24</td><td>0.65</td><td>0.96</td><td>0.94</td><td>0.74</td><td>−0.04</td><td>0.01</td><td>0.58</td><td></td><td></td><td>0.42</td></tr>
<tr><td>36</td><td>0.59</td><td>0.94</td><td>0.91</td><td>0.67</td><td>−0.02</td><td>0.01</td><td>0.53</td><td></td><td></td><td>0.39</td></tr>
<tr><td>48</td><td>0.55</td><td>0.92</td><td>0.89</td><td>0.62</td><td>−0.01</td><td>0.01</td><td>0.49</td><td></td><td></td><td>0.37</td></tr>
<tr><td>60</td><td>0.52</td><td>0.90</td><td>0.88</td><td>0.57</td><td>−0.03</td><td>0.01</td><td>0.46</td><td>0.05</td><td>0.10</td><td>0.35</td></tr>
<tr><td>120</td><td>0.40</td><td>0.83</td><td>0.81</td><td>0.45</td><td>0.00</td><td>0.01</td><td>0.38</td><td>0.05</td><td>0.10</td><td>0.28</td></tr>
</table>

Price sample compared to 0.47, 0.44, and 0.35, respectively, in the CRSP sample. One likely driver of the increased persistence of β in the restricted samples is that measurement of β is more accurate for more liquid stocks. Thus, when illiquid stocks, for which β is likely to be measured with substantial error, are removed from the sample, the persistence increases.

The persistence of *MktCap* and *Size* is not only extremely high, but very similar across each of the different samples. The results indicate that the cross-sectional correlation between *MktCap* (*Size*) measured at two times separated by a period of 10 years is, on average, 0.84 (0.86) for stocks in the Price sample. *MktCap* and *Size* are by far the most persistent of the variables examined in this book.

BM is more persistent in the Price sample than in the CRSP sample, especially when the persistence is measured at longer lags. The increased persistence of *BM* in the restricted samples indicates that, if in fact *BM* does capture a persistent sensitivity to a priced risk factor, this sensitivity is measured with more accuracy for stocks that survive the price and size screens than for stocks that are removed by these screens.

The persistence of both *Mom* and *Rev* in all three samples is negligibly low. This is not surprising because both *Mom* and *Rev* are measures of historical returns. If *Mom* or *Rev* exhibited strong persistence, it would indicate that the cross section of stock returns is highly predictable from past performance.

The results in Table 16.3 show that *Illiq* is more persistent in the restricted samples than in the CRSP sample. This result is interesting because it indicates that, even after removing the most illiquid stocks from the sample, not only are there still persistent cross-sectional differences in liquidity between the stocks that remain, but that the cross section of historical liquidity is more indicative of future liquidity for the more liquid stocks that remain in the Price and Size samples than for the stocks that are removed from the sample. One might have thought that it is the highly illiquid stocks that remain highly illiquid, and that this would drive the persistence of *Illiq* in the CRSP sample. The results actually indicate that it is cross-sectional persistence of

Illiq among the more liquid stocks that remain after the price and size screens are implemented that is driving the persistence of *Illiq*.

CoSkew exhibits extremely low persistence in all samples. With the exception of *Mom* and *Rev*, for which substantial persistence would indicate a strong ability to predict future returns, *CoSkew* exhibits the lowest persistence of any of the variables used throughout this book.

The persistence of *IdioSkew* is also low, but not as low as that of *CoSkew*. Interestingly, the persistence of *IdioSkew* in the Price and Size samples is lower than the persistence of *IdioSkew* in the CRSP sample. Given that the Price and Size samples contain more liquid stocks for which the measurement of *IdioSkew* is likely more accurate, it would be expected that if *IdioSkew* does in fact measure a persistent characteristic of the stock's returns, then *IdioSkew* would be more persistent among stocks for which this measurement error is low. This is not the case. A potential explanation for this finding is that the returns of the more liquid stocks in the Price and Size sample exhibit relatively similar levels of idiosyncratic skewness, and that the stocks for which idiosyncratic skewness differs substantially are those stocks that have been removed from the restricted samples. The summary statistics presented in Table 16.1 provide some evidence that this may be the case since the standard deviation of the cross-sectional distribution of *IdioSkew* is lower in the more restricted samples.

Finally, Table 16.3 shows that *IdioVol* is also slightly less persistent in the Price and Size samples than in the CRSP sample. Once again, one might have predicted the opposite given that idiosyncratic volatility may be hard to accurately estimate for illiquid stocks. However, it may in fact be the illiquid nature of some stocks that causes the values of *IdioVol* for these stocks to be high. Consistent with this conjecture, the summary statistics in Table 16.1 demonstrate that high *IdioVol* tend to be removed from the sample when the price and size screens are implemented.

16.5 EXPECTED STOCK RETURNS

Having examined the summary statistics, correlations, and persistence of our variables using each of the CRSP, Price, and Size samples, we proceed now to examine the relations between each of these variables and expected stock returns using each of the samples. While most of the results for the CRSP sample have been presented in previous chapters, we repeat them here for several reasons. First, there are a few results that were not presented in previous chapters. Specifically, in some cases, we did not show the alphas of some portfolios using factor models that had not yet been introduced when the results of the portfolio analysis were presented. For example, when we presented the results of the univariate portfolio analysis using β as the sort variable in Section 8.5.1, we had not yet introduced the size (*SMB*), value (*HML*), or momentum (*MOM*) factors; thus, we did not subject the returns of the β-sorted portfolio to the Fama and French (1993) and Carhart (1997) four-factor (FFC) model. Second, these results are not only the main results presented in this book, but they are the foundational findings of empirical asset pricing research. They therefore warrant repeating. Third, presenting the results all in one place provides an easy-to-use summary of the main results of empirical asset pricing research. Finally, having the results of the analyses generated by each of the samples in the same place facilitates comparisons across the samples.

16.5.1   Univariate Portfolio Analysis

We begin our examination of the relations between each of the variables of interest and expected stock returns with univariate decile portfolio analyses. For each analysis, the table presenting the results shows the average monthly excess return for each of the decile portfolios. We also show the average difference in return between the decile 10 portfolio and the decile one portfolio, as well as this portfolio's FFC alpha and the alpha of this portfolio relative to the FFC model augmented by the Pastor and Stambaugh (2003) liquidity factor (PSL), which we refer to as the FFCPS alpha. When the sort variable is $MktCap$, the values reported in the tables in the columns labeled FFC α and FFCPS α are alphas relative to a model that excludes the size (SMB) factor. The reason for this is that to examine the effect of $MktCap$ on expected stock returns, it does not make sense to remove the component of the portfolio's return that is due to the size effect, which is captured by the SMB factor. Similarly, when examining portfolios formed by sorting on BM, the value factor (HML) is excluded from the risk models, and for portfolios formed by sorting on Mom, the momentum factor (MOM) is excluded from the factor models.

CRSP Sample

Table 16.4 shows the results of univariate decile portfolio analyses of the relations between each of the variables and expected stock returns using the CRSP sample. When value-weighted portfolios are used, the analysis detects no relation between β and future stock returns. This result is surprising given that the Capital Asset Pricing Model (CAPM, Sharpe (1964), Lintner (1965), Mossin (1966)), the foundational asset pricing theory, predicts a positive relative between beta and expected stock returns. The FFC and FFCPS alphas for this portfolio are also very small and statistically indistinguishable from zero. When equal-weighted portfolios are used, however, the β 10-1 portfolio generates a negative and statistically significant average return of -0.53% per month with a t-statistic of -2.04. This portfolio's alphas relative to the FFC and FFCPS risk models of -0.61% per month and -0.59% per month, respectively, are even more negative.[3] This is to be expected since the β 10-1 portfolio should have a positive exposure to the market factor and the market factor carries a positive risk premium. The results are similar to those of Reinganum (1981), Lakonishok and Shapiro (1986), Fama and French (1992), Frazzini and Pedersen (2014), and Bali, Brown, Murray, and Tang (2014).

The value-weighted and equal-weighted portfolio analyses detect a strong negative relation between $MktCap$ and future stock returns. This result was

---

[3]This result, first documented by Black et al. (1972), suggests that high-beta stocks generate lower risk-adjusted returns than low-beta stocks, indicating that the security market line is flatter than predicted by the CAPM. Black (1972, 1993) propose that this phenomenon is explained by restricted borrowing.

TABLE 16.4   Univariate Portfolio Analysis—CRSP Sample

This table presents the results of univariate portfolio analyses of the relation between each of the variables discussed in previous chapters of Part II of this book and future stock returns. Monthly portfolios are formed by sorting all stocks in the CRSP sample into portfolios using decile breakpoints calculated based on the given sort variable using all stocks in the CRSP sample. Panel A (Panel B) shows the average value-weighted (equal-weighted) one-month-ahead excess return (in percent per month) for each of the 10 decile portfolios formed using different variables as the sort variable. The table also shows the average return of the portfolio that is long the 10th decile portfolio and short the first decile portfolio, as well as the FFC and FFCPS alphas for this portfolio. Newey and West (1987) t-statistics, adjusted using six lags, testing the null hypothesis that the average 10-1 portfolio return or alpha is equal to zero, are shown in parentheses.

Panel A: Value-Weighted Portfolios

Sort Variable	1	2	3	4	5	6	7	8	9	10	10-1	FFC α	FFCPS α
β	0.39	0.53	0.54	0.43	0.56	0.48	0.51	0.43	0.39	0.34	−0.05	−0.01	−0.02
											(−0.18)	(−0.03)	(−0.08)
MktCap	1.53	0.63	0.54	0.56	0.59	0.65	0.66	0.67	0.63	0.42	−1.11	−1.40	−1.34
											(−3.47)	(−3.97)	(−3.76)
BM	0.31	0.33	0.45	0.44	0.46	0.53	0.59	0.67	0.68	0.88	0.57	0.73	0.83
											(2.40)	(3.13)	(3.51)
Mom	−0.76	−0.12	0.04	0.35	0.39	0.37	0.53	0.67	0.75	1.18	1.95	2.37	2.36
											(5.39)	(7.54)	(6.76)
Rev	0.72	0.50	0.73	0.68	0.58	0.47	0.48	0.44	0.33	0.12	−0.60	−0.76	−0.69
											(−2.40)	(−3.21)	(−2.77)
Illiq	0.42	0.54	0.60	0.62	0.55	0.57	0.64	0.66	0.50	0.24	−0.18	−0.46	−0.51
											(−0.65)	(−3.16)	(−3.30)
CoSkew	0.51	0.63	0.68	0.53	0.58	0.52	0.47	0.48	0.43	0.48	−0.03	0.09	0.05
											(−0.16)	(0.55)	(0.27)
IdioSkew	0.43	0.48	0.55	0.50	0.53	0.43	0.55	0.46	0.39	0.26	−0.16	−0.57	−0.53
											(−0.97)	(−3.63)	(−3.17)
IdioVol	0.48	0.48	0.53	0.57	0.60	0.62	0.38	0.15	−0.21	−0.79	−1.27	−1.43	−1.47
											(−3.48)	(−5.25)	(−4.90)

Panel B: Equal-Weighted Portfolios

Sort Variable	1	2	3	4	5	6	7	8	9	10	10-1	FFC α	FFCPS α
β	0.92	0.87	0.91	0.85	0.86	0.87	0.77	0.65	0.60	0.38	−0.53	−0.61	−0.59
											(−2.04)	(−2.78)	(−2.56)
MktCap	2.08	0.64	0.53	0.56	0.59	0.64	0.66	0.67	0.63	0.49	−1.59	−1.96	−1.96
											(−4.94)	(−5.23)	(−5.11)
BM	0.08	0.36	0.50	0.68	0.83	0.85	0.94	1.03	1.18	1.42	1.34	1.58	1.63
											(6.06)	(6.95)	(6.66)
Mom	0.29	0.34	0.48	0.64	0.68	0.78	0.92	1.04	1.19	1.37	1.08	1.36	1.33
											(3.42)	(4.62)	(4.16)
Rev	2.31	0.99	0.83	0.78	0.76	0.72	0.66	0.50	0.34	−0.38	−2.69	−2.93	−2.95
											(−9.72)	(−8.31)	(−8.24)
Illiq	0.53	0.64	0.73	0.76	0.71	0.71	0.79	0.81	0.73	1.11	0.58	0.43	0.43
											(1.93)	(2.09)	(1.97)
CoSkew	1.03	0.95	0.87	0.85	0.82	0.84	0.72	0.73	0.81	0.75	−0.28	−0.40	−0.48
											(−1.90)	(−1.92)	(−2.27)
IdioSkew	0.80	0.82	0.81	0.87	0.84	0.88	0.90	0.97	0.76	0.70	−0.10	−0.18	−0.24
											(−0.61)	(−1.14)	(−1.40)
IdioVol	0.69	0.76	0.87	0.94	0.93	0.90	0.85	0.70	0.56	0.28	−0.41	−0.58	−0.60
											(−1.12)	(−2.11)	(−2.09)

first documented by Banz (1981) and Fama and French (1992). When using value-weighted and equal-weighted portfolios, the average returns produced by the *MktCap* 10-1 portfolios of -1.11% per month (t-statistic $= -3.47$) and -1.59% per month (t-statistic $= -4.94$), respectively, are both economically very large and highly statistically significant. The alphas of these portfolios are even larger and remain highly statistically significant, indicating that the *MKT*, *HML*, *MOM*, and *PSL* factors fail to explain the returns of the *MktCap* 10-1 portfolios.

Consistent with Fama and French (1992, 1993), the results in Table 16.4 indicate a strong positive relation between *BM* and future stock returns. The value-weighted *BM* 10-1 portfolio generates an average return of 0.57% per month (t-statistic $= 2.40$) and the equal-weighted *BM* 10-1 portfolio produces an average return of 1.34% per month (t-statistic $= 6.06$). Once again, the alphas are even larger and of higher statistical significance than the average returns, indicating that the *MKT*, *SMB*, *MOM*, and *PSL* factors fail to explain the returns of the *BM* difference portfolios.

The momentum effect of Jegadeesh and Titman (1993) exists in both value-weighted and equal-weighted portfolios since the average return of the value-weighted (equal-weighted) *Mom* 10-1 portfolio is 1.95% per month (1.08% per month) with a t-statistic of 5.39 (3.42). The alphas of the *Mom* difference portfolio relative to each of the risk models, which as discussed earlier, exclude the momentum factor (*MOM*), remain very economically large and highly statistically significant.

Table 16.4 shows that the reversal effect exists in both value-weighted and equal-weighted portfolios but is much stronger in equal-weighted portfolios. The average return of the value-weighted *Rev* 10-1 portfolio is -0.60% with a t-statistic of -2.40. When using equal-weighted portfolios, the *Rev* 10-1 portfolio generates -2.69% per month with a corresponding t-statistic of -9.72. In both value-weighted and equal-weighted portfolios, the FFC and FFCPS risk models fail to explain the returns of the *Rev* 10-1 portfolio.

When value-weighted portfolios are used, the results of the univariate decile portfolio analysis indicates that the *Illiq* 10-1 portfolio generates a statistically insignificant average return of -0.18% per month. However, adjusting the returns of this portfolio for risk using the FFC and FFCPS models, the results indicate that high *Illiq* stocks underperform low *Illiq* stocks since the alphas of -0.76% per month (t-statistic $= -3.21$) and -0.69% per month (t-statistic $= -2.77$) when using the FFC and FFCPS models, respectively, are negative, large in magnitude, and highly statistically significant. When equal-weighted portfolios are used, consistent with Amihud (2002) and Pastor and Stambaugh (2003), the results indicate a strong positive relation between illiquidity and future stock returns. The average return of the equal-weighted *Illiq* 10-1 portfolio of 0.58% (t-statistic $= 1.93$) is marginally statistically significant. The FFC and FFCPS alphas of 0.43% per month (t-statistic $= 2.09$) and 0.43% per month (t-statistic $= 1.97$), respectively, are also statistically significant.

The value-weighted portfolio analysis detects no relation between co-skewness, calculated following Harvey and Siddique (2000), and future stock returns since the average return and alphas of the *CoSkew* 10-1 portfolio are all small and statistically insignificant. When equal-weighted portfolios are used, the univariate portfolio analysis detects a negative and statistically significant relation between *CoSkew* and future returns, consistent with the theoretical predictions (Kraus and Litzenberger (1976), Kane (1982), Harvey and Siddique (2000)). The average return, FFC alpha, and FFCPS alpha of the equal-weighted *CoSkew* 10-1 portfolio are −0.28% per month (*t*-statistic = −1.90), −0.40% per month (*t*-statistic = −1.92), and −0.48% per month (*t*-statistic = −2.27), respectively.

When portfolios are formed by sorting on idiosyncratic skewness, the average returns of the *IdioSkew* 10-1 value-weighted and equal-weighted portfolios of −0.16% per month (*t*-statistic = −0.97) and −0.10% per month (*t*-statistic = −0.61) are both small and statistically indistinguishable from zero. The FFC alpha of −0.57% per month (*t*-statistic = −3.63) and FFCPS alpha of −0.53% per month (*t*-statistic = −3.17) generated by the value-weighted *IdioSkew* 10-1 portfolio, however, are negative, large in magnitude, and highly statistically significant. The results indicate that after controlling for risk, *IdioSkew* exhibits a negative relation with future stock returns, consistent with Boyer, Mitton, and Vorkink (2010).

Consistent with the empirical evidence presented by Ang, Hodrick, Xing, and Zhang (2006), but contradictory to theoretical predictions of Levy (1978) and Merton (1987), the portfolio analyses detect a negative relation between idiosyncratic volatility and future stock returns. When value-weighted portfolios are used, the *IdioVol* 10-1 portfolio generates an average monthly return of −1.27% (*t*-statistic = −3.48), FFC alpha of −1.43% (*t*-statistic = −5.25), and FFCPS alpha of −1.47% (*t*-statistic = −4.90). Consistent with Bali and Cakici (2008), the results indicate that the idiosyncratic volatility puzzle is weaker in equal-weighted portfolios since the equal-weighted *IdioVol* 10-1 portfolio generates an insignificant average return −0.41% per month (*t*-statistic = −1.12). The FFC alpha of −0.58% per month (*t*-statistic = −2.11) and FFCPS alpha of −0.60% per month (*t*-statistic = −2.09), however, are both large and statistically significant.

Price Sample

Having presented and briefly discussed the results of the univariate portfolio analyses using the full CRSP sample, in Table 16.5 we show the results of similar analyses using the Price sample, which is the subset of the stocks in the CRSP sample that have month-end share prices between $5 and $1000, inclusive. Results using value-weighted (equal-weighted) portfolios are shown in Panel A (Panel B). We focus our discussion here on the differences between the results generated using the CRSP sample and the results generated using the Price sample.

When sorting Price sample stocks into β-based decile portfolios, the value-weighted portfolio analysis finds no evidence of a relation between β and expected stock returns since the average return and the FFC and FFCPS alphas are all small and statistically insignificant. This is consistent with the value-weighted results generated by the CRSP sample. When equal-weighted portfolios are used, the Price sample results show that the average return of the β 10-1 portfolio of −0.35% per month is statistically insignificant with a *t*-statistic of −1.14. This is slightly different from the results generated using the CRSP sample, which indicated a statistically significant negative average return of the equal-weighted

TABLE 16.5   Univariate Portfolio Analysis—Price Sample
This table presents the results of univariate portfolio analyses of the relation between each of the variables discussed in previous chapters of Part II of this book and future stock returns. Monthly portfolios are formed by sorting all stocks in the Price sample into portfolios using decile breakpoints calculated based on the given sort variable using all stocks in the Price sample. Panel A (Panel B) shows the average value-weighted (equal-weighted) one-month-ahead excess return (in percent per month) for each of the 10 decile portfolios formed using different variables as the sort variable. The table also shows the average return of the portfolio that is long the 10th decile portfolio and short the first decile portfolio, as well as the FFC and FFCPS alphas for this portfolio. Newey and West (1987) t-statistics, adjusted using six lags, testing the null hypothesis that the average 10-1 portfolio return or alpha is equal to zero, are shown in parentheses.

						Panel A: Value-Weighted Portfolios							
Sort Variable	1	2	3	4	5	6	7	8	9	10	10-1	FFC α	FFCPS α
β	0.47	0.56	0.45	0.50	0.54	0.49	0.48	0.45	0.37	0.36	−0.12	−0.12	−0.14
											(−0.40)	(−0.51)	(−0.55)
MktCap	0.75	0.73	0.73	0.69	0.64	0.66	0.68	0.63	0.60	0.40	−0.35	−0.34	−0.28
											(−1.60)	(−1.60)	(−1.31)
BM	0.36	0.33	0.49	0.39	0.47	0.51	0.52	0.62	0.68	0.74	0.38	0.55	0.65
											(1.67)	(2.42)	(2.81)
Mom	−0.40	0.15	0.31	0.38	0.33	0.42	0.57	0.64	0.80	1.24	1.64	1.97	1.99
											(5.74)	(7.24)	(6.87)
Rev	0.48	0.61	0.71	0.56	0.52	0.48	0.43	0.46	0.26	0.18	−0.30	−0.41	−0.32
											(−1.41)	(−1.84)	(−1.32)
Illiq	0.41	0.53	0.50	0.65	0.56	0.54	0.60	0.62	0.68	0.41	0.00	−0.27	−0.27
											(0.01)	(−2.36)	(−2.28)
CoSkew	0.56	0.60	0.63	0.56	0.56	0.51	0.49	0.47	0.41	0.42	−0.14	0.01	0.01
											(−0.86)	(0.09)	(0.03)
IdioSkew	0.45	0.45	0.50	0.59	0.42	0.59	0.41	0.54	0.41	0.34	−0.11	−0.55	−0.49
											(−0.79)	(−4.47)	(−3.82)
IdioVol	0.46	0.50	0.49	0.54	0.55	0.58	0.57	0.35	0.19	−0.49	−0.96	−1.10	−1.12
											(−3.04)	(−5.46)	(−5.06)

						Panel B: Equal-Weighted Portfolios							
Sort Variable	1	2	3	4	5	6	7	8	9	10	10-1	FFC α	FFCPS α
β	0.69	0.78	0.78	0.76	0.80	0.74	0.72	0.63	0.52	0.35	−0.35	−0.51	−0.48
											(−1.14)	(−2.43)	(−2.16)
MktCap	0.79	0.73	0.72	0.69	0.65	0.66	0.69	0.64	0.60	0.45	−0.34	−0.37	−0.31
											(−1.65)	(−1.82)	(−1.53)
BM	0.12	0.33	0.52	0.58	0.66	0.73	0.77	0.87	0.96	1.00	0.88	1.16	1.17
											(3.77)	(5.19)	(5.18)
Mom	−0.42	0.28	0.47	0.59	0.68	0.77	0.89	0.98	1.18	1.38	1.80	2.03	2.08
											(7.52)	(9.03)	(8.33)
Rev	1.11	0.94	0.82	0.78	0.72	0.72	0.60	0.52	0.34	0.03	−1.11	−1.04	−1.04
											(−5.93)	(−5.88)	(−4.95)
Illiq	0.51	0.62	0.61	0.75	0.70	0.70	0.71	0.75	0.78	0.58	0.07	−0.13	−0.14
											(0.36)	(−1.03)	(−1.08)
CoSkew	0.68	0.83	0.79	0.76	0.77	0.74	0.68	0.65	0.70	0.61	−0.07	−0.04	−0.07
											(−0.66)	(−0.42)	(−0.56)
IdioSkew	0.70	0.68	0.75	0.75	0.77	0.79	0.74	0.77	0.68	0.59	−0.11	−0.31	−0.33
											(−0.87)	(−3.27)	(−3.22)
IdioVol	0.61	0.78	0.82	0.91	0.92	0.95	0.81	0.74	0.43	−0.35	−0.96	−1.17	−1.16
											(−3.56)	(−8.12)	(−7.50)

β 10-1 portfolio. However, as discussed previously, the CAPM predicts that the average return of a portfolio that is long high-β stocks and short low-β stocks should be positive. Not surprisingly, therefore, after adjusting for risk using the FFC and FFCPS risk models, the results indicate that the β 10-1 portfolio significantly underperforms. The FFC and FFCPS alphas for this portfolio are −0.51% per month (*t*-statistic = −2.43) and −0.48% per month (*t*-statistic = −2.16), respectively, both of which are economically important and highly statistically significant.

The results using the Price sample fail to indicate a strong relation between stock size and future stock returns. Regardless of whether value-weighted or equal-weighted portfolios are used, the average return and alphas of the *MktCap* 10-1 portfolio are all small and statistically indistinguishable from zero. The one exception is the alpha generated by the equal-weighted *MktCap* 10-1 portfolio of −0.37% per month (*t*-statistic = −1.82) relative to a risk model that includes the market (*MKT*), value (*HML*), and momentum (*MOM*) factors.[4] This differs substantially from the CRSP sample, in which a strong negative relation between *MktCap* and future stock returns was detected. The result is not that surprising, however, since the objective in creating the Price sample is to remove small and illiquid stocks from the sample. As was shown in Chapter 9, the size effect is largely driven by very small stocks. The summary statistics presented in Table 16.1 demonstrate that many such small stocks have been removed by the price screen used to create the Price sample.

The value effect in the Price sample is slightly weaker than in the CRSP sample, but it is still present. When using value-weighted portfolios, the average return of the *BM* 10-1 portfolio using the Price sample is a marginally significant 0.38% per month (*t*-statistic = 1.67). The alpha of this portfolio relative to a model that includes the market (*MKT*), size (*SMB*), and momentum (*MOM*) factors of 0.55% per month (*t*-statistic = 2.42) is larger than the average return and highly statistically significant. The alpha is higher once again when the liquidity (*PSL*) factor is included in the model. The results are stronger when equal-weighted portfolios are used. The equal-weighted *BM* 10-1 portfolio's average return of 0.88% per month (*t*-statistic = 3.77) is much higher than the average return of the value-weighted portfolio. The same can be said of the alphas.

The results in Table 16.5 indicate that the momentum phenomenon is extremely strong in the Price sample. The value-weighted *Mom* 10-1 portfolio generates an average return of 1.64% per month (*t*-statistic = 5.74) and alphas of 1.97% per month (*t*-statistic = 7.24) and 1.99% per month (*t*-statistic = 6.87) relative to the FFC and FFCPS risk models with the *MOM* factor removed. When using equal-weighted portfolios, the average return, FFC (*MOM* factor removed) alpha, and FFCPS (*MOM* factor removed) alpha of the *Mom* 10-1 portfolio are 1.80% per month (*t*-statistic = 7.52), 2.03% per month (*t*-statistic = 9.03), and 2.08% per month (*t*-statistic = 8.33), respectively. These results are even stronger than the CRSP sample equal-weighted portfolio results.

---

[4]Recall that we exclude the size (*SMB*) factor when risk-adjusting the returns of portfolios formed by sorting on *MktCap*.

The average return of the value-weighted *Rev* 10-1 portfolio using the Price sample is a statistically insignificant −0.30% per month (*t*-statistic = −1.41). However, when adjusting for risk using the FFC model, this portfolio's alpha of −0.41% per month (*t*-statistic = −1.84) is marginally statistically significant. This pattern is consistent with what was observed in the CRSP sample, except that in the CRSP sample the magnitudes of the average return and alpha were substantially larger and highly statistically significant. When the *PSL* factor is added to the risk model, the Price sample alpha of −0.32% per month (*t*-statistic = −1.32) once again becomes insignificant. When using equal-weighted portfolios, the average return and alphas of the *Rev* 10-1 portfolio are all negative and highly statistically significant, indicating that none of the factors can explain the negative average return of the equal-weighted *Rev* 10-1 portfolio. These Price sample results are similar to the corresponding results from the CRSP sample, although the reversal phenomenon appears to be stronger in the CRSP sample. Overall, the reversal phenomenon is weaker in the Price sample than in the CRSP sample.

The Price sample results provide only scant evidence of a relation between illiquidity and expected returns. This is not surprising because the Price sample was designed to exclude highly illiquid stocks, which were shown in Chapter 16 to be the drivers of the positive relation between *Illiq* and future stock returns detected in the CRSP sample. In the Price sample, neither the value-weighted nor equal-weighted *Illiq* 10-1 portfolios generates a statistically significant average return. However, consistent with the results from the CRSP sample, when value-weighted portfolios are formed using the Price sample, the FFC alpha of −0.27% per month (*t*-statistic = −2.36) and FFCPS alpha of −0.27% per month (*t*-statistic = −2.28) generated by the *Illiq* 10-1 portfolio are not only negative, but highly statistically significant. When using equal-weighted portfolios however, the alphas of the *Illiq* 10-1 portfolio are statistically indistinguishable from zero. This contrasts with the positive and significant alphas of the equal-weighted *Illiq* difference portfolio formed using the CRSP sample.

The univariate portfolio analyses using the Price sample fail to detect any relation between co-skewness and future stock returns. The average return and alphas of the *CoSkew* 10-1 portfolio are small and statistically indistinguishable from zero regardless of whether value-weighted or equal-weighted portfolios are used. This contrasts somewhat with the results of the CRSP sample. Using the CRSP sample, the average return and alphas of the equal-weighted *CoSkew* 10-1 portfolio were negative and at least marginally statistically significant.

Similar to the results generated by the CRSP sample, when using the Price sample, the value-weighted *IdioSkew* 10-1 portfolio generates a negative but statistically insignificant average return, but the FFC alpha of −0.55% per month (*t*-statistic = −4.47) and FFCPS alpha of −0.49% per month (*t*-statistic = −3.82) are both large in magnitude and highly significant. These results indicate a negative relation between idiosyncratic skewness and future stock returns after controlling for risk captured by the factors included in the risk models. The equal-weighted Price sample results are similar to the Price sample value-weighted results in that the average equal-weighted *IdioSkew* 10-1 portfolio generates insignificant abnormal returns but large, negative, and significant risk-adjusted returns. The equal-weighted results in the Price sample are stronger than the equal-weighted results in the CRSP sample. In the CRSP sample, the average return and alphas of the equal-weighted *IdioSkew* 10-1 portfolio are not significant.

The idiosyncratic volatility puzzle is strong in the Price sample. Regardless of weighting scheme, the average return and alphas of the *IdioVol* 10-1 portfolio are negative, large in magnitude, and highly statistically significant. When using equal-weighted portfolios, the results are stronger in the Price sample than in the CRSP sample. In the CRSP sample, the equal-weighted average return of the *IdioVol* 10-1 portfolio was insignificant. In the Price sample, not only is the average return generated by the *IdioVol* 10-1 portfolio of −0.93% per month (*t*-statistic = −3.62) statistically significant, it is substantially larger in magnitude than the average return of the corresponding portfolio from the CRSP sample. The same is true of the alphas, which, when using equal-weighted portfolios, are much larger in magnitude using the Price sample than the CRSP sample.

Size Sample

We now turn to the results of the univariate decile portfolio analyses using the Size sample. The Size sample is created by restricting the Price sample to those stocks that have market capitalizations at least as large as the 10th percentile market capitalization among all NYSE-listed stocks in the given month. The results of the univariate portfolio analyses using the Size sample are shown in Table 16.6. Since the Size sample is a subset of the Price sample, our discussion of the Size sample results focuses on the differences between the Size and Price samples.

The Size sample univariate portfolio analyses detect no relation between β and future stock returns. The average return and alphas of the β 10-1 portfolio, regardless of how the portfolios are weighted, are statistically indistinguishable from zero. The Size sample and Price sample value-weighed portfolio results are quite similar. When using equal-weighted portfolios, however, the alphas of the β 10-1 portfolio in the Price sample are negative and significant, whereas this result is not found in the Size sample.

When sorting Size sample stocks into *MktCap*-based portfolios, the average return of the *MktCap* 10-1 portfolio, while negative, is statistically insignificant, regardless of weighting scheme. The same can be said for the alphas relative to risk models that include the market (*MKT*), value (*HML*), momentum (*MOM*), and liquidity (*PSL*) factors. These results are similar to the results from the Price sample. The only exception is that in the Price sample, the alpha of the equal-weighted *MktCap* 10-1 portfolio relative to a risk model that includes the *MKT*, *HML*, and *MOM* factors is marginally statistically significant. We do not find this result in the Size sample.

The univariate portfolio analysis using the Size sample and sorting on *BM* detects a positive and marginally significant value-weighted *BM* 10-1 portfolio average return of 0.38% per month (*t*-statistic = 1.66). The alphas of this portfolio relative to the FFC and FFCPS risk models that exclude the value (*HML*) factor are larger than the average return and highly statistically significant. The average return and alphas of the *BM* 10-1 equal-weighted portfolio are all economically large and highly

TABLE 16.6   Univariate Portfolios—Size Sample
This table presents the results of univariate portfolio analyses of the relation between each of the variables discussed in previous chapters of Part II of this book and future stock returns. Monthly portfolios are formed by sorting all stocks in the Size sample into portfolios using decile breakpoints calculated based on the given sort variable using all stocks in the Size sample. Panel A (Panel B) shows the average value-weighted (equal-weighted) one-month-ahead excess return (in percent per month) for each of the 10 decile portfolios formed using different variables as the sort variable. The table also shows the average return of the portfolio that is long the 10th decile portfolio and short the first decile portfolio, as well as the FFC and FFCPS alphas for this portfolio. Newey and West (1987) t-statistics, adjusted using six lags, testing the null hypothesis that the average 10-1 portfolio return or alpha is equal to zero, are shown in parentheses.

Panel A: Value-Weighted Portfolios												
Sort Variable	1	2	3	4	5	6	7	8	9	10	10-1	FFC α	FFCPS α
β	0.45	0.41	0.48	0.48	0.58	0.49	0.48	0.38	0.38	0.36	−0.09	−0.17	−0.21
											(−0.28)	(−0.73)	(−0.88)
MktCap	0.66	0.65	0.68	0.68	0.72	0.68	0.62	0.63	0.55	0.39	−0.27	−0.16	−0.12
											(−1.50)	(−0.96)	(−0.69)
BM	0.32	0.33	0.47	0.45	0.42	0.48	0.51	0.56	0.64	0.70	0.38	0.60	0.68
											(1.66)	(2.69)	(3.03)
Mom	−0.26	0.24	0.39	0.39	0.37	0.42	0.52	0.65	0.79	1.19	1.45	1.77	1.78
											(4.99)	(6.39)	(6.05)
Rev	0.42	0.66	0.66	0.50	0.50	0.48	0.41	0.42	0.31	0.24	−0.18	−0.29	−0.20
											(−0.83)	(−1.30)	(−0.81)
Illiq	0.41	0.55	0.51	0.54	0.63	0.60	0.56	0.57	0.55	0.52	0.12	−0.16	−0.17
											(0.74)	(−1.91)	(−1.78)
CoSkew	0.64	0.63	0.53	0.55	0.55	0.49	0.45	0.49	0.37	0.45	−0.19	−0.03	−0.02
											(−1.19)	(−0.23)	(−0.10)
IdioSkew	0.44	0.42	0.54	0.53	0.51	0.48	0.55	0.45	0.50	0.35	−0.09	−0.48	−0.45
											(−0.70)	(−3.83)	(−3.36)
IdioVol	0.45	0.54	0.49	0.47	0.59	0.53	0.62	0.52	0.27	−0.27	−0.72	−0.83	−0.86
											(−2.34)	(−4.22)	(−3.89)

Panel B: Equal-Weighted Portfolios												
Sort Variable	1	2	3	4	5	6	7	8	9	10	10-1	FFC α	FFCPS α
β	0.63	0.64	0.70	0.73	0.72	0.75	0.70	0.62	0.52	0.37	−0.26	−0.35	−0.34
											(−0.79)	(−1.65)	(−1.48)
MktCap	0.66	0.64	0.67	0.68	0.72	0.68	0.63	0.62	0.56	0.43	−0.23	−0.15	−0.11
											(−1.42)	(−0.98)	(−0.70)
BM	0.17	0.32	0.49	0.62	0.62	0.72	0.73	0.79	0.85	0.91	0.74	1.01	1.03
											(3.07)	(4.39)	(4.54)
Mom	−0.25	0.29	0.49	0.57	0.62	0.67	0.78	0.87	1.06	1.29	1.54	1.80	1.83
											(5.97)	(7.40)	(6.92)
Rev	0.90	0.94	0.82	0.74	0.71	0.64	0.52	0.50	0.30	0.17	−0.74	−0.80	−0.73
											(−3.76)	(−3.94)	(−3.23)
Illiq	0.51	0.62	0.61	0.66	0.76	0.74	0.70	0.69	0.65	0.54	0.04	−0.19	−0.19
											(0.23)	(−2.04)	(−1.88)
CoSkew	0.68	0.72	0.73	0.73	0.74	0.67	0.65	0.61	0.65	0.54	−0.14	−0.08	−0.08
											(−1.28)	(−0.67)	(−0.60)
IdioSkew	0.65	0.63	0.72	0.69	0.73	0.73	0.72	0.73	0.63	0.49	−0.17	−0.38	−0.40
											(−1.28)	(−3.66)	(−3.44)
IdioVol	0.57	0.71	0.77	0.78	0.88	0.82	0.81	0.69	0.49	−0.25	−0.82	−0.98	−0.96
											(−2.83)	(−5.84)	(−5.27)

statistically significant. All of the Size sample results for *BM*-sorted portfolios are very similar to the corresponding results produced by the Price sample.

The momentum phenomenon is very strong in the Size sample. The average return and alphas of the *Mom* 10-1 portfolio, regardless of portfolio weighting scheme, are positive and highly statistically significant. While the average return and alphas are somewhat smaller in the Size sample than in the corresponding Price sample portfolios, they remain very economically important in the Size sample.

The results for *Rev*-sorted portfolios using the Size sample are similar to, but slightly weaker than, those found using the Price sample. When using value-weighted portfolios, the Size sample *Rev* 10-1 portfolio generates statistically insignificant average return and alphas. When using equal-weighted portfolios, consistent with the results from the Price sample, the Size sample *Rev* 10-1 portfolio generates a negative and significant average return, FFC alpha, and FFCPS alpha. The results of the Size sample univariate decile portfolio analyses using *Illiq* as the sort variable are quite interesting. Regardless of weighting scheme, the average return of the *Illiq* 10-1 portfolio is positive but economically small and statistically insignificant. The FFC and FFCPS alphas of this portfolio, however, are negative and at least marginally statistically significant. Thus, we not only fail to detect a positive relation between illiquidity and future stock returns in the Size sample, but the results indicate that stock with high values of *Illiq* tend to underperform, on a risk-adjusted basis, stocks with low values of *Illiq*. In the Price sample, this effect only existed in value-weighted portfolios. In the Size sample, the *Illiq* difference portfolio generates negative abnormal returns regardless of weighting scheme.

Similar to the Price sample, the Size sample produces no evidence of a relation between co-skewness and expected stock returns. The average return, FFC alpha, and FFCPS alpha of the Size sample *CoSkew* 10-1 portfolio, regardless of weighting scheme, are economically small and statistically insignificant.

The results of the portfolio analysis of the relation between idiosyncratic skewness and future stock returns using the Size sample are, once again, highly similar to the corresponding results from the Price sample. Regardless of weighting scheme, the *IdioSkew* 10-1 portfolio generates a negative but insignificant average return. The FFC and FFCPS alphas of this portfolio, however, are negative, economically important, and highly statistically significant.

Finally, as was the case in the Price sample, the idiosyncratic volatility puzzle is strong in the Size sample. Regardless of weighting scheme, the average return, FFC alpha, and FFCPS alpha of the *IdioVol* 10-1 portfolio are negative, large, and highly statistically significant. The results are very similar to the corresponding Price sample results.

This completes our portfolio analysis of the relations between each of the variables examined in this book and future stock returns using the CRSP, Price, and Size samples. Due to the large number of pairs of variables that could be used to perform bivariate portfolio analyses, and the impracticality of presenting all such results for each of the samples, we proceed directly to (Fama and MacBeth (1973), FM hereafter) regression analyses of the relations between these variables and future stock returns.

16.5.2   Fama–MacBeth Regression Analysis

For each sample, we perform FM regression analyses using several different cross-sectional regression specifications. For each variable, we use a univariate specification with only the given variable as an independent variable in the regression. We then employ a specification that includes all of the variables as independent variables simultaneously. We refer to this specification as the full specification.

The results of the FM regression analyses are presented in Table 16.7. Results using the CRSP, Price, and Size samples are presented in Panels A, B, and C, respectively. The table shows the time-series averages of the monthly cross-sectional regression coefficients, along with Newey and West (1987)-adjusted (six lags) t-statistics testing the null hypothesis that the average coefficient is equal to zero. To facilitate comparison of the results across the different sample, Table 16.7 is laid out in a different manner than the previous tables reporting FM regression results. In the portion of each panel labeled Univariate Specifications, each column corresponds to a different specification, with the lone independent variable used in the specification displayed at the top of each column. The rows labeled Slope and Intercept present the average slope and intercept coefficients, respectively, from the given FM regression. In the section of each panel labeled Multivariate Specification, we present results for the multivariate specification that includes all of the variables as independent variables. Each column shows the average coefficient on the variable indicated at the top of the column.

Consistent with the equal-weighted univariate portfolio results, the univariate regression specifications using β as the only independent variable detect a negative and significant relation between β and future stock returns in the CRSP sample, but no such relation is detected in the Price or Size samples, since the restricted sample regressions generate average coefficients on β that, while negative, are statistically indistinguishable from zero. When the multivariate specification is employed, regardless of which sample is used, the FM regressions detect no relation between β and future stock returns. This result is a contradiction of the CAPM's main prediction of a positive cross-sectional relation between beta and expected stock returns.

The univariate FM regression analysis using $Size$ as the only independent variable in the regression specification detect a negative relation between $Size$ and future stock returns in the CRSP sample, but no such relation in the Price or Size samples. This is once again consistent with the equal-weighted portfolio analyses. When using the full specification, however, regardless of which sample is used, the FM regression analysis detects a strong negative relation between $Size$ and future stock returns after controlling for the effects of all of the other variables. The results, therefore, indicate that the size effect is present, even in the restricted samples.

As was the case in the equal-weighted portfolio analyses, the univariate FM regression analyses detect a strong positive relation between BM and future stock returns in all samples. In the full-specification analysis, however, while the value effect is robust in the CRSP and Price samples, the coefficient on BM in the Size sample is positive but statistically insignificant. Among stocks that pass the price and size screens, therefore, the value effect appears to be explained by the other variables examined in this book.

TABLE 16.7 Fama–MacBeth Regression Analysis

This table presents the results of Fama and MacBeth (1973) regression analyses of the relation between expected stock returns and the variables examined throughout this book. Panels A, B, and C show results for the CRSP sample, the Price sample, and the Size sample, respectively. Each panel presents results for univariate regression specifications and a multivariate regression specification that includes all of the independent variables. Each column presenting univariate specification results corresponds to an analysis using a different independent variable, indicated in the column header. When presenting the results of the multivariate specification, the average coefficient for each independent variable is presented in a different column, indicated in the column header. The dependent variable in all specifications is the one-month-ahead excess stock return. Independent variables are winsorized at the 0.5% level on a monthly basis. t-statistics, adjusted following Newey and West (1987) using six lags, testing the null hypothesis that the average coefficient is equal to zero, are shown in parenthesis. The table also presents the average adjusted R-squared (Adj. R^2) and the number of data points (n) for the cross-sectional regressions.

Panel A: CRSP Sample

Univariate Specifications

	β	Size	BM	Mom	Rev	Illiq	CoSkew	IdioSkew	IdioVol
Slope	−0.265	−0.142	0.415	0.007	−0.048	0.050	−0.012	−0.032	−0.008
	(−1.96)	(−2.93)	(5.30)	(3.01)	(−10.07)	(1.98)	(−1.80)	(−0.51)	(−2.52)
Intercept	0.971	1.314	0.423	0.607	0.760	0.693	0.821	0.853	1.040
	(3.85)	(2.81)	(1.44)	(2.22)	(2.44)	(2.47)	(2.90)	(3.20)	(5.01)
Adj. R^2	0.02	0.01	0.01	0.01	0.01	0.01	0.00	0.00	0.02
n	4426	4781	3391	4410	4740	3600	3948	3948	4732

Multivariate Specification

Intercept	β	Size	BM	Mom	Rev	Illiq	CoSkew	IdioSkew	IdioVol
1.915	0.004	−0.179	0.141	0.007	−0.059	0.067	0.001	−0.123	−0.013
(5.46)	(0.03)	(−4.15)	(1.99)	(3.85)	(−11.32)	(3.74)	(0.13)	(−3.85)	(−5.85)

Adj. R^2: 0.07, n: 2561.

Panel B: Price Sample

Univariate Specifications

	β	Size	BM	Mom	Rev	Illiq	CoSkew	IdioSkew	IdioVol
Slope	−0.175	−0.053	0.346	0.010	−0.026	−0.015	−0.005	−0.044	−0.016
	(−1.08)	(−1.39)	(3.69)	(6.08)	(−6.16)	(−0.39)	(−0.98)	(−0.87)	(−4.60)
Intercept	0.817	0.883	0.373	0.480	0.686	0.689	0.719	0.742	1.230
	(4.03)	(2.36)	(1.34)	(2.00)	(2.61)	(2.74)	(2.93)	(3.11)	(6.36)
Adj. R^2	0.03	0.01	0.01	0.02	0.01	0.01	0.00	0.00	0.02
n	3273	3524	2478	3262	3495	2883	2957	2957	3498

Multivariate Specification

Intercept	β	Size	BM	Mom	Rev	Illiq	CoSkew	IdioSkew	IdioVol
1.951	−0.033	−0.170	0.156	0.008	−0.040	−0.042	0.004	−0.105	−0.016
(5.90)	(−0.22)	(−4.25)	(2.10)	(4.98)	(−8.49)	(−1.38)	(0.73)	(−3.20)	(−7.93)

Adj. R^2: 0.07, n: 2033.

TABLE 16.7 (*Continued*)

				Panel C: Size Sample					

				Univariate Specifications					
	β	Size	BM	Mom	Rev	Illiq	CoSkew	IdioSkew	IdioVol
Slope	−0.115	−0.047	0.312	0.009	−0.021	−0.861	−0.008	−0.063	−0.016
	(−0.64)	(−1.16)	(2.56)	(4.89)	(−4.52)	(−1.45)	(−1.24)	(−1.22)	(−3.96)
Intercept	0.751	0.864	0.390	0.434	0.667	0.665	0.672	0.701	1.139
	(4.17)	(2.07)	(1.42)	(1.88)	(2.69)	(2.74)	(2.85)	(3.04)	(6.15)
Adj. R^2	0.04	0.01	0.01	0.02	0.01	0.00	0.00	0.00	0.02
n	2213	2337	1751	2208	2323	2128	2043	2043	2327

				Multivariate Specification					
Intercept	β	Size	BM	Mom	Rev	Illiq	CoSkew	IdioSkew	IdioVol
1.800	−0.013	−0.156	0.125	0.008	−0.037	−0.221	0.002	−0.096	−0.012
(5.24)	(−0.09)	(−3.81)	(1.40)	(4.43)	(−7.55)	(−0.27)	(0.28)	(−2.88)	(−5.65)
				Adj. R^2: 0.08, n: 1563.					

The FM regression analyses detect a strong momentum effect in all samples. The average coefficients of 0.007 (t-statistic = 3.01), 0.010 (t-statistic = 6.08), and 0.009 (t-statistic = 4.89) in the univariate specifications using the CRSP sample, Price sample, and Size sample, respectively, are all positive and highly statistically significant. Consistent with the univariate portfolio analyses, the results indicate that the momentum phenomenon is stronger in the restricted samples than in the unrestricted CRSP sample. The same is true when using the multivariate regression specification. The CRSP sample multivariate FM regression analysis produces an average coefficient on *Mom* of 0.007 (t-statistic = 3.85). The corresponding analyses for the Price and Size sample generate average coefficients of 0.008 (t-statistic = 4.98) and 0.008 (t-statistic = 4.43), respectively.

The reversal phenomenon is also strong in all samples. Both the univariate and multivariate specifications produce average coefficients on *Rev* that are negative and highly statistically significant. In each sample, the average coefficient on *Rev* is larger in magnitude when using the full specification than in the univariate specification, indicating that not only is the reversal phenomenon not explained by the other variables, but that when the other variables are controlled for, the magnitude of the effect is actually larger than indicated by the univariate analyses.

Table 16.7 indicates that the positive relation between illiquidity and expected stock returns is present only in the full CRSP sample. In the CRSP sample, the average coefficient on *Illiq* of 0.050 (t-statistic = 1.98) in the univariate specification and 0.067 (t-statistic = 3.74) in the multivariate specification are both positive and statistically significant. However, in the Price sample and the Size sample, both the univariate and multivariate specifications generate statistically insignificant average coefficients on *Illiq*. These results are consistent with the results of the equal-weighted univariate portfolio analyses that failed to indicate a positive relation between *Illiq* and future stock returns in the Price and Size samples. In fact, in the Size sample, when adjusting the returns of the *Illiq* 10-1 portfolio for risk using the FFC or FFCPS models, the results indicate a negative and at least marginally significant alpha. The results of the full-specification FM regression analysis using the Size sample, however, fail to detect any relation between *Illiq* and future stock returns. The average coefficient on *Illiq* in the Size sample univariate specification of −0.861, while insignificant, is much larger in magnitude than the coefficient on *Illiq* in the full specification of −0.221. This indicates that the negative alphas of the *Illiq* 10-1 portfolio are likely explained by other variables included in the full FM regression specification.

Consistent with the negative and marginally statistically significant average return produced by the equal-weighted CRSP sample *CoSkew* 10-1 portfolio, the CRSP sample univariate FM regression analysis using *CoSkew* as the only independent variable produces a marginally statistically significant average coefficient of −0.012 (*t*-statistic = −1.80) on *CoSkew*. The results of the full-specification analysis, however, find an insignificant average coefficient of 0.001 (*t*-statistic = 0.13) on *CoSkew*, indicating that any relation between *CoSkew* and future stock returns is explained by the other variables. In the Price and Size samples, the FM regression analyses provide no indication of a relation between co-skewness and expected stock returns since the average coefficient on *CoSkew* in both the univariate and multivariate analyses is statistically indistinguishable from zero.

Regardless of which sample is used, the univariate FM regression analyses generate a negative but statistically insignificant average coefficient on *IdioSkew*. However, the full-specification FM regression analyses detect a strong negative relation between idiosyncratic skewness and future stock returns. The average full-specification coefficients on *IdioSkew* in the CRSP, Price, and Size samples are −0.123 (*t*-statistic = −3.85), −0.105 (*t*-statistic = −3.20), and −0.096 (*t*-statistic = −2.88), respectively. For the Price and Size samples, these results are similar to the univariate portfolio analyses, which indicated that the *IdioSkew* 10-1 portfolios generated insignificant average returns but negative and significant alphas. Both analyses indicate that to isolate the effect of idiosyncratic skewness, it is necessary to control for other effects first.

Finally, the FM regression results indicate a strong negative relation between idiosyncratic volatility and future stock returns. In all three samples, both the univariate and multivariate regression specifications generate a negative and highly statistically significant average coefficient on *IdioVol*. The results indicate that the idiosyncratic volatility puzzle is present even among the larger and more liquid stocks that comprise the Price and Size samples.

16.6 SUMMARY

In this chapter, we have examined the main results of empirical asset pricing research, documented throughout this book, using three samples. The CRSP sample, which is used in all previous chapters of Part II of this book, contains all U.S.-based common stocks that are listed on the New York Stock Exchange, the American Stock

Exchange, and the NASDAQ. The Price sample is the subset of stocks in the CRSP sample that have a share price between $5 and $1000, inclusive. The Size sample further restricts the set of stocks to include only those with market capitalizations above the 10th percentile market capitalization among NYSE-listed stocks.

Portfolio and Fama and MacBeth (1973) regression analyses fail to indicate a robust relation between beta and expected stock returns in any of the samples. A negative relation between stock size and expected stock returns is detected in all samples, but is substantially weaker in the restricted samples. Portfolio analyses fail to detect a size effect in the Price and Size sample. The regression analyses detect a negative relation between stock size and expected returns in the restricted samples only when other effects are controlled for. A positive relation between book-to-market ratio and expected stock returns, known as the value effect, is present in all samples, although in the Size sample, regression results indicate that this phenomenon is explained by other variables. The momentum effect is very strong in all samples regardless of empirical methodology. A negative relation between reversal, measured as the stock return in the most recent months, is detected in most of the empirical analyses. However, value-weighted portfolio analyses fail to detect the reversal phenomenon in the Price and Size samples, indicating that reversal is primarily a small stock effect. The portfolio and regression analyses fail to detect a consistent relation between illiquidity and future stock returns. Equal-weighted portfolio analysis and regression analysis using the full CRSP sample indicate that less liquid stocks command higher expected returns. Other analyses fail to detect a strong relation between illiquidity and expected stock returns. The results of the analyses provide very little indication of a relation between co-skewness and expected stock returns. There is evidence, however, that idiosyncratic skewness is related to expected stock returns, though this result is only found when other effects are controlled for. Finally, the results indicate that idiosyncratic volatility has a strong negative relation with future stock returns. This result is commonly referred to as the idiosyncratic volatility puzzle.

REFERENCES

Amihud, Y. 2002. Illiquidity and stock returns: cross-section and time-series effects. Journal of Financial Markets, 5(1), 31–56.

Ang, A., Hodrick, R. J., Xing, Y., and Zhang, X. 2006. The cross-section of volatility and expected returns. Journal of Finance, 61(1), 259–299.

Bali, T. G., Brown, S. J., Murray, S., and Tang, Y. 2014. A Lottery Demand-Based Explanation of the Beta Anomaly. SSRN eLibrary.

Bali, T. and Cakici, N. 2008. Idiosyncratic volatility and the cross-section of expected returns. Journal of Financial and Quantitative Analysis, 43, 29–58.

Banz, R. W. 1981. The relationship between return and market value of common stocks. Journal of Financial Economics, 9(1), 3–18.

Black, F. 1972. Capital market equilibrium with restricted borrowing. The Journal of Business, 45(3), 444–455.

Black, F. 1993. Beta and return. Journal of Portfolio Management, 20(1), 8–18.

Black, F., Jensen, M. C., and Scholes, M. S. The capital asset pricing model: some empirical tests. *Studies in the Theory of Capital Markets*. Praeger, New York, 1972.

Boyer, B., Mitton, T., and Vorkink, K. 2010. Expected idiosyncratic skewness. Review of Financial Studies, 23(1), 169–202.

Carhart, M. M. 1997. On persistence in mutual fund performance. Journal of Finance, 52(1), 57–82.

Fama, E. F. and French, K. R. 1992. The cross-section of expected stock returns. Journal of Finance, 47(2), 427–465.

Fama, E. F. and French, K. R. 1993. Common risk factors in the returns on stocks and bonds. Journal of Financial Economics, 33(1), 3–56.

Fama, E. F. and MacBeth, J. D. 1973. Risk, return, and equilibrium: empirical tests. Journal of Political Economy, 81(3), 607.

Frazzini, A. and Pedersen, L. H. 2014. Betting against beta. Journal of Financial Economics, 111(1), 1–25.

Harvey, C. R. and Siddique, A. 2000. Conditional skewness in asset pricing tests. Journal of Finance, 55(3), 1263–1295.

Jegadeesh, N. and Titman, S. 1993. Returns to buying winners and selling losers: implications for stock market efficiency. Journal of Finance, 48(1), 65–91.

Kane, A. 1982. Skewness preference and portfolio choice. Journal of Financial and Quantitative Analysis, 17(1), 15–25.

Kraus, A. and Litzenberger, R. H. 1976. Skewness preference and the valuation of risk assets. Journal of Finance, 31(4), 1085–1100.

Lakonishok, J. and Shapiro, A. 1986. Systematic risk, total risk and size as determinants of stock market returns. Journal of Banking & Finance, 10(1), 115–132.

Levy, H. 1978. Equilibrium in an imperfect market: a constraint on the number of securities in the portfolio. American Economic Review, 68, 643–658.

Lintner, J. 1965. Security prices, risk, and maximal gains from diversification. Journal of Finance, 20(4), 687–615.

McLean, R. D. and Pontiff, J. 2015. Does academic research destroy stock return predictability? Journal of Finance, forthcoming.

Merton, R. C. 1987. A simple model of capital market equilibrium with incomplete information. Journal of Finance, 42, 483–510.

Mossin, J. 1966. Equilibrium in a capital asset market. Econometrica, 34(4), 768–783.

Newey, W. K. and West, K. D. 1987. A simple, positive semi-definite, heteroskedasticity and autocorrelation consistent covariance matrix. Econometrica, 55(3), 703–708.

Pastor, L. and Stambaugh, R. F. 2003. Liquidity risk and expected stock returns. Journal of Political Economy, 111(3), 642–685.

Reinganum, M. R. 1981. A new empirical perspective of the CAPM. Journal of Quantitative and Empirical Finance, 16(4), 439–462.

Sharpe, W. F. 1964. Capital asset prices: a theory of market equilibrium under conditions of risk. Journal of Finance, 19(3), 425–442.

17

OPTION-IMPLIED VOLATILITY

In this, the final empirical chapter of this book, we investigate the ability of variables calculated from option prices to predict future stock returns and future option returns. The empirical asset pricing literature has identified several cross-sectional relations between option-based variables and future stock and option returns. Here, we provide a brief overview of several of the main results in this area of research.

Bali and Hovakimian (2009) find that the difference between the implied volatility of at-the-money (ATM) call options and ATM put options, a measure commonly referred to as the call minus put implied volatility spread, has a strong positive relation with future stock returns. Cremers and Weinbaum (2010) document a similar phenomenon using implied volatilities of options across a wider range of strikes. The explanations for the ability of the call minus put implied volatility spread to predict future stock returns vary between the two papers. Bali and Hovakimian (2009) find that the call minus put implied volatility spread is strongly positively related, in the cross section, to jump risk and conclude that the high average returns of stocks with high call minus put implied volatility spreads represents a jump risk premium. Bali and Hovakimian (2009) also find evidence of informed trading in the option markets that may be an additional driver of this phenomenon. Cremers and Weinbaum (2010) note that the ability of the call minus put implied volatility spread to predict future stock returns is strongest among stocks that have highly liquid options and relatively illiquid stocks, and that the ability of this measure to predict future stock returns deteriorates over time. Based on these results, Cremers and Weinbaum (2010) attribute this effect to stock mispricing.

Empirical Asset Pricing: The Cross Section of Stock Returns, First Edition.
Turan G. Bali, Robert F. Engle, and Scott Murray.
© 2016 John Wiley & Sons, Inc. Published 2016 by John Wiley & Sons, Inc.

A second phenomenon documented by Bali and Hovakimian (2009) is the strong negative relation between future stock returns and the realized minus implied volatility spread, which is defined as the difference between volatility calculated from historical stock returns and option-implied volatility calculated from option prices. They claim that the realized minus implied volatility spread can be interpreted as a measure of volatility risk and the returns, therefore, capture the premium associated with volatility risk. This finding is consistent with several other papers that document a negative volatility risk premium. Jackwerth and Rubinstein (1996) demonstrate that the implied volatilities of options written on the S&P 500 index are higher than historical realized volatility. Bakshi and Kapadia (2003a) find that delta-hedged option portfolios that constitute long volatility positions generate negative average returns. Bakshi and Kapadia (2003b) demonstrate that implied volatilities of individual equities are also, on average, higher than volatility measured from historical returns. Ang, Hodrick, Xing, and Zhang (2006) show that stocks with high sensitivities to innovations in aggregate volatility generate low average returns. Carr and Wu (2009) find strong evidence of a negative variance risk premium by comparing variance swap rates implied from option prices to realized variances.

Xing, Zhang, and Zhao (2010) show that the slope of the implied volatility smirk, which measures risk-neutral skewness, has a strong cross-sectional relation with future stock returns. Specifically, Xing et al. (2010) find that the implied volatility of an out-of-the-money (OTM) put option minus the implied volatility of an ATM call option, which is negatively related to risk-neutral skewness (high values of this measure indicate a more negatively skewed risk-neutral distribution), is negatively related to future stock returns. Their results, therefore, indicate a positive relation between risk-neutral skewness and expected stock returns. Several other papers such as Rehman and Vilkov (2012) and DeMiguel, Plyakha, Uppal, and Vilkov (2013) document a similar positive relation between implied risk-neutral skewness (or related measures) and future stock returns. This positive relation is consistent with the predictions generated by demand-based option pricing models of Bollen and Whaley (2004) and Garleanu, Pedersen, and Poteshman (2009). According to demand-based option pricing, when informed investors predict positive returns on a stock, they express this view in the market by buying calls and selling puts. This price pressure increases the prices of OTM calls and decreases the prices of OTM puts. The option-implied distribution of future stock returns, therefore, has fatter right tails and thinner left tails for stocks expected by market participants to appreciate in value. The opposite is true for stocks forecast to lose value.

It should be noted that the positive relation between skewness and expected returns is contrary to the predictions of equilibrium asset pricing models. Models produced by Arditti (1967, 1971), Kraus and Litzenberger (1976), Simkowitz and Beedles (1978), Scott and Horvath (1980), Conine and Tamarkin (1981), Kane (1982), Harvey and Siddique (2000), and Mitton and Vorkink (2007) all show that investors have preference for, and thus command lower expected returns from, assets with more positively skewed return distributions. Consistent with these theories, Conrad, Dittmar, and Ghysels (2013) find evidence of a negative relation between risk-neutral skewness and expected stock returns, and Chang, Christoffersen, and

Jacobs (2013) demonstrate that stocks whose returns exhibit higher exposures to innovations in the option-implied skewness of the S&P 500 index returns generate lower average returns.

An, Ang, Bali, and Cakici (2014) further the research on informed trading in option markets by examining whether changes in call implied volatility and changes in put implied volatility predict future stock returns. Their results demonstrate that month-to-month changes in the implied volatility of ATM call options are positively related to future stock returns and, after controlling for this effect, changes in the implied volatility of ATM put options are negatively related to future stock returns.

In addition to the growing literature that examines cross-sectional relations between option price-based variables and stock returns, there is a smaller line or research that examines the returns of options. Goyal and Saretto (2009) demonstrate that the realized minus implied volatility spread, discussed earlier, has a very strong positive cross-sectional relation with the future returns of straddles, delta-hedged calls, and delta-hedged puts. They attribute this phenomenon to mispricing in the option market. According to Goyal and Saretto (2009), high (low) implied volatilities relative to historical volatility are indications of overpriced (underpriced) options. Large negative (positive) values of historical minus implied volatility, therefore, coincide with overpriced (underpriced) options and thus lower (higher) future returns for strategies designed to capture volatility. Cao and Han (2013) demonstrate that delta-hedged option returns are negatively related, in the cross section, to idiosyncratic volatility. Finally, Bali and Murray (2013) demonstrate a negative relation between risk-neutral skewness and the returns of positions consisting of options and shares in a manner such that the effect skewness is isolated.

In the remainder of this chapter, we examine several of the above-mentioned phenomena. Doing so requires us to introduce a new database, OptionMetrics (OM hereafter), which is the most commonly used source of option price and Greek data. We also discuss the construction of a new sample, generated from the OM database, that contains only the subset of stocks upon which options are traded.

17.1   OPTIONS SAMPLE

The set of stocks upon which options trade is substantially smaller than the full set of U.S.-based common stocks that comprise the CRSP sample used throughout the majority of this book. The source most commonly used by empirical asset pricing researchers for options data is the OM database. The OM database provides price, implied volatility, and Greeks for all U.S.-listed index and equity options. The data began in January of 1996 and, for the version of the database used for the analyses whose results are presented in this text, end in January 2013. OM also provides data on interest rates, individual stocks, and equity indices. These data, however, are intended only to complement the options data and do not represent complete data sets.

Our sample of optionable stocks for any month t, which we refer to as the Options sample, consists of all common stocks in the OM database for which there is a valid price in OM's security price (secprd) table on the last trading day of the given month.

The security price table gives price, volume, return, and shares outstanding data for securities underlying the options in the OM database. We remove entries where the closing price (close field) in the security price table is less than or equal to $0.01.[1] Common stocks are identified as those securities with a value of 0 in the issue_type field in OM's security (securd) table.

The CRSP database is merged to the OM database using CUSIPs. The OM database identifies each underlying security using a security identifier (secid), which is stored in the secid field in many different OM tables. To match OM secids to CRSP PERMNOs, we match the cusip field in OM's security (securd) file to the NCUSIP field in CRSP's daily stock names (dsenames) file. The security file in the OM database contains only one entry for each secid. The daily stock names file in the CRSP database, however, often contains many different entries for the same PERMNO, with each entry being valid for a nonoverlapping date range indicated by the NAMEDT (beginning of date range) and NAMEENDT (end of date range) fields in the daily stock names file. When matching a CRSP PERMNO to a given month, secid combination in our options sample, we require that this date range in the CRSP database include the last calendar day of the given month t. Finally, for consistency with the CRSP sample used throughout most of this text, the last month t we include in our options sample is November 2012, meaning that our analyses of returns will examine returns in months $t + 1$ from February 1996 through December 2012.

17.2   OPTION-BASED VARIABLES

In this section, we define several variables whose relations with expected stock returns will be examined. We also define several variables that are used to measure the returns associated with option positions.

17.2.1   Predictive Variables

Before proceeding to the definition of the focal variables of the analyses to be performed in this chapter, it is useful to define a few intermediate variables that will be used to construct several of the option-based variables of interest.

We begin by defining the ATM call implied volatility, ATM put implied volatility, and OTM put implied volatility for stock i in month t. The ATM implied volatilities come from OM's standardized option price (stdopd) file. This file contains prices, implied volatilities, and Greeks for at-the-forward-money call and put options with fixed days until expiration. Specifically, data are provided for options with 30, 60, 91, 182, 273, 365, 547, and 730 days until expiration. The strike prices of all options in this file are set to be equal to the forward price of the underlying stock with the forward delivery date equal to the expiration date of the options. Since options with the exact expirations and strikes indicated in the file are not available in the market,

---

[1] A negative value in the close field in OM's security price database indicates that the value given in this field is the average of the closing bid and ask values. We exclude stocks with negative values in the close field from our sample.

values in this table are generated from an implied volatility surface that is calculated by OM for each stock on each day using values interpolated from available option price data. Specifically, the implied volatility of each option is calculated from OM's implied volatility surface, which is discussed in more detail below. The option price and Greeks are then calculated from the implied volatility using the Cox, Ross, and Rubinstein (1979) binomial tree model. OM uses the Cox et al. (1979) model to generate equity option prices (and implied volatilities from prices) instead of the Black and Scholes (1973) model because the Cox et al. (1979) model can account for possibility of early exercise that arises due to the fact that exchange-traded options are American in nature. In addition to providing option data, OM's standardized option price file gives a forward price for each stock for each given expiration. We take ATM call and put implied volatilities, which we denote $IVolC_{i,t}^{ATM}$ and $IVolP_{i,t}^{ATM}$, for a given stock i in a given month t to be the implied volatilities, taken from the standardized option price file on the month's last trading day, of the 30-day ATM call and put options, respectively. We require that the recorded implied volatility, forward price, and option price indicated in the OM database be greater than zero.[2] We also define the ATM volatility, denoted $IVol$, to be the average of the ATM call implied volatility and the ATM put implied volatility. Specifically, we have $IVol_{i,t} = (IVolC_{i,t}^{ATM} + IVolP_{i,t}^{ATM})/2$.

Calculation of the implied volatility skew of Xing et al. (2010) requires the implied volatility of an OTM put option. The OTM put implied volatility, which we denote $IVolP^{OTM}$, is taken from OM's volatility surface (vsurfd) file. The volatility surface file contains option prices and implied volatilities for options with fixed days until expiration and fixed deltas. The days to expiration are the same as in the standardized option price file. The volatility surface file includes data for call and put options with absolute deltas from 0.20 to 0.80 in increments of 0.05. We define $IVolP_{i,t}^{OTM}$ to be the implied volatility of the 30-day put option written on stock i with delta of -0.20, taken on the last trading day of the given month t.

Having described the necessary components of the OM database and the preliminary variables, we can now define the option-based variables of interest.

Call Minus Put Implied Volatility Spread

We define the call minus put implied volatility spread, $IVolSpread$, shown by Bali and Hovakimian (2009) and Cremers and Weinbaum (2010) to be positively related to future stock returns, as the difference between the ATM call implied volatility and the ATM call implied volatility. Specifically, we have

$$IVolSpread_{i,t} = IVolC_{i,t}^{ATM} - IVolP_{i,t}^{ATM}. \qquad (17.1)$$

Realized Minus Implied Volatility Spread

We define two versions of the realized minus implied volatility spread. The first follows Bali and Hovakimian (2009), who find that the difference between realized

---

[2] When an implied volatility or Greek cannot be calculated for an option, OM puts a value of -99.00 in the given field.

and implied volatility has a strong negative relation with future stock returns. Bali and Hovakimian (2009) calculate realized volatility using one month of daily return data. We therefore take $Vol^{1M}_{i,t} - IVol_{i,t}$ to be one measure of the difference between realized and implied volatility. Vol^{1M} is the sample standard deviation of the daily returns of the given stock i in the given month t, as defined in Chapter 15.

Goyal and Saretto (2009) demonstrate that the realized minus implied volatility spread, where realized volatility is measured as the standard deviation of daily stock returns over the past year, has a strong positive relation with future straddle, delta-hedged call, and delta-hedged put returns. We therefore let $Vol^{12M} - IVol$ be the difference between the 12-month realized volatility and the ATM implied volatility, where Vol^{12M} is once again defined in Chapter 15. While the main results of Goyal and Saretto (2009) hold when realized volatility is calculated using one month of daily return data, we use $Vol^{12M} - IVol$ to more accurately replicate their results.

Implied Volatility Skew

The implied volatility skew measures the steepness of the implied volatility smirk. Following Xing et al. (2010), we define the volatility skew, denoted $IVolSkew$, as the difference between the implied volatility of the OTM put and the implied volatility of the ATM call, giving

$$IVolSkew = IVolP^{OTM}_{i,t} - IVolC^{ATM}_{i,t}. \tag{17.2}$$

Holding the ATM call implied volatility constant, $IVolSkew$ is higher for higher values of OTM put implied volatility. Since a high OTM put implied volatility is a symptom of a fat left tail of the risk-neutral distribution of future stock returns, high values of $IVolSkew$ are actually indicative of large negative skewness of the risk-neutral distribution. $IVolSkew$ therefore measures negative skewness. The negative relation between $IVolSkew$ and future stock returns documented by Xing et al. (2010), therefore, reflects a positive relation between risk-neutral skewness and future stock returns.

Implied Volatility Changes

The volatility spread and skew variables defined above all measure volatility at the end of month t. An et al. (2014) show that changes in implied volatility over time predict the cross section of future stock returns. We therefore define the change in ATM call implied volatility as the difference between the ATM call implied volatility measured at the end of month t and the ATM call implied volatility measured at the end of month $t - 1$.

$$\Delta IVolC_{i,t} = IVolC^{ATM}_{i,t} - IVolC^{ATM}_{i,t-1}. \tag{17.3}$$

We define the change in ATM put implied volatility analogously.

$$\Delta IVolP_{i,t} = IVolP^{ATM}_{i,t} - IVolP^{ATM}_{i,t-1}. \tag{17.4}$$

17.2.2 Option Returns

In addition to examining the ability of option-based variables to predict future stock returns, some studies examine the returns associated with option positions. The option positions whose returns are most frequently examined are straddles, delta-hedged calls, and delta-hedged puts.

Straddle Returns

A straddle position consists of a call and a put with the same strike and same expiration. Straddle returns are calculated assuming that the straddle is created from the same options used to determine the ATM call implied volatility ($IVol^{C,ATM}$) and the ATM put implied volatility ($IVol^{P,ATM}$). In addition to providing implied volatility data, OM's standardized options table provides the price (premium field) and the strike price (strike_price field), which is the same as the forward price, for all options in the table. The price of the straddle position is, therefore, the sum of the price of the 30-day at-the-forward-money call and put options on the last trading day of the month t.

The payoff of the straddle position is the absolute value of the difference between the spot price of the stock at expiration and the strike price of the options used to create the straddle. The spot price of the stock at expiration is taken from OM's security price file on the last trading day on or prior to 30 days after the formation of the straddle position.[3] As mentioned earlier, the straddle position is formed on the last trading day of month t.

The return of the straddle in month $t + 1$ is then calculated as the payoff of the straddle divided by the price of the straddle minus one. To calculate the excess straddle return, we then subtract the return of the risk-free security during the period from the time at which the straddle was created until the time at which the return of the straddle is calculated. Since the holding period for the straddle is not necessarily the entire calendar month $t + 1$, the return on the risk-free security is calculated as the compounded daily risk-free security returns over all days during the holding period. Daily risk-free security return data are taken from Ken French's data library.[4]

Delta-Hedged Call Returns

Delta-hedged call returns are calculated assuming that a long position in the 30-day ATM call option is taken on the last trading day of the month t and delta-hedged at that time using a position in the 30-day forward contract. The number of forward contracts shorted is the delta of the call option, as reported in the delta field in OM's standard option file. Both the call and forward positions are held unchanged until expiration. Since the cost of entering a forward contract is zero, the price of the delta-hedged call position is simply the price of the call option.

The payoff of the delta-hedged call position at expiration is simply the sum of the payoffs of the call position and the forward position. The payoff of the call position

---

[3]The expiration stock price is adjusted for splits using the adjustment factor (cfadj) field in OM's security price table.
[4]The URL for Ken French's data library is http://mba.tuck.dartmouth.edu/pages/faculty/ken.french/data_library.html.

is the maximum of the spot price at expiration minus the strike price of the call, and zero. The payoff of the forward position is the position in the forward contract (the negative of the call's delta at the time the delta-hedged call is constructed) times the difference between the spot price at expiration and the initial forward price. The payoff of the delta-hedged call is simply the sum of the payoffs of the call position and the forward position.

The delta-hedged call's return in month $t + 1$ is found by dividing the payoff by the initial price. The excess return is then calculated by taking the return and subtracting the return of the risk-free security during the period for which the call and forward positions are held.

Delta-Hedged Put Returns

The returns of delta-hedged put positions are calculated analogously to returns of the delta-hedged calls. On the last day of month t, a long position in a 30-day at-the-forward-money put is taken. A long forward position is also taken, with the number of forward contracts being equal to the negative of the put's delta (the delta of a put is negative). The price of the position is the price of the put option. The delta-hedged put's payoff is the payoff of the put option (the maximum of the strike price minus the spot price at expiration, and zero) plus the payoff of the forward contract times the size of the position in the forward contract. The month $t + 1$ return of the delta-hedged put is the payoff divided by the price, and the excess return is the return minus the return of the risk-free security during the holding period.

17.2.3 Additional Notes

Before proceeding to our empirical investigations, a few additional notes on the calculation of the option-based variables are warranted. Many of the variables used in our analyses are not calculated in exactly the same way as in the original studies documenting the results. One reason for this is that we have chosen to use data from OM's implied volatility surface. There are a few advantages to this approach. First, OM's implied volatility surface gives data for options with standardized expirations and moneyness. Thus, there is no need to further address potential differences in the time to expiration or moneyness of the options used for different stocks in the sample. Second, because the implied volatility surface is calculated by interpolating all available option price data on the given day, using the implied volatility surface provides a larger sample than would be permitted by other approaches.[5]

Despite these benefits, many studies choose to use data pertaining to actual traded options. OM provides this data in its option price (opprcd) file. The data include the closing best bid and offer prices, Greeks, and an implied volatility for each available option on each day. While on any given day, options for a given stock and expiration combination may not be traded or quoted, some researchers prefer to use the actual option price data instead of data taken from OM's implied volatility surface.

---

[5]OM only provides volatility surface data for a stock if there exists enough option price data on the given date to accurately calibrate the volatility surface.

17.3 SUMMARY STATISTICS

Table 17.1 presents summary statistics for the Options sample. In addition to showing summary statistics for the option-based variables, we show summary statistics for other variables used throughout this book. The reason for this is that the Options

TABLE 17.1 Summary Statistics
This table presents summary statistics for option-based variables (Panel A), excess stock and option returns (Panel B), and other variables (Panel C) calculated using the Options sample for the months t from January 1996 through November 2012. Each month, the mean (*Mean*), standard deviation (*SD*), skewness (*Skew*), excess kurtosis (*Kurt*), minimum (*Min*), fifth percentile (5%), 25th percentile (25%), median (*Median*), 75th percentile (75%), 95th percentile (95%), and maximum (*Max*) values of the cross-sectional distribution of each variable is calculated. The table presents the time-series means for each cross-sectional value. The column labeled n indicates that average number of stocks for which the given variable is available. *IVolSpread* is the difference between the implied volatilities of at-the-money call and put options. $Vol^{1M} - IVol$ (Vol^{12M}) is the difference between historical volatility calculated from one month (12 months) of daily return data and the average of the implied volatilities of the at-the-money call and put options. *IVolSkew* is the difference between the implied volatilities of an out-of-the-money put option and an at-the-money call option. $\Delta IVolC$ and $\Delta IVolP$ are the changes in the implied volatilities of at-the-money call and put options, respectively, from the previous month end. *IVol* is the average of the at-the-money call and put implied volatilities. Vol^{1M} (Vol^{12M}) is historical volatility calculated from one month (12 months) of daily return data. $IVolC^{ATM}$ and $IVolP^{ATM}$ are the implied volatilities of at-the-money call and put options. $IVolP^{OTM}$ is the implied volatility of an out-of-the-money put option. Panel B presents summary statistics for excess stock returns, straddle returns, delta-hedged call returns, and delta-hedged put returns. The options used to calculate each of these variables have expiration in 30 days.

Panel A: Option Variables											
	Mean	SD	Skew	Kurt	Min	5%	25%	Median	75%	95%	Max	n
IVolSpread	−0.84	9.66	−0.78	106.79	−131.03	−11.34	−2.83	−0.54	1.49	8.74	124.79	2110
$Vol^{1M} - IVol$	−3.03	19.74	1.98	51.32	−140.09	−28.77	−11.09	−3.43	4.16	23.60	236.12	1617
IVolSkew	5.88	11.65	0.83	51.65	−120.29	−6.31	1.61	4.70	8.95	22.25	140.87	2110
$\Delta IVolC$	−0.06	12.97	0.02	54.61	−143.82	−15.52	−4.52	−0.17	4.23	15.87	144.97	2072
$\Delta IVolP$	−0.06	12.76	0.22	55.73	−141.36	−14.83	−4.29	−0.20	3.97	15.20	144.96	2072
$Vol^{12M} - IVol$	0.39	14.38	0.02	44.18	−134.36	−18.57	−4.63	0.64	6.01	18.25	155.26	1587
IVol	50.25	22.89	1.66	6.91	8.86	23.35	33.66	45.46	61.97	92.32	225.75	2110
Vol^{1M}	46.46	25.74	3.27	40.13	6.07	19.11	29.42	40.76	57.24	91.09	332.91	1617
Vol^{12M}	49.68	21.68	1.92	13.77	14.81	23.71	33.84	45.43	61.60	87.96	246.22	1587
$IVolC^{ATM}$	49.83	23.28	1.86	9.43	7.47	22.72	33.19	45.00	61.52	92.08	242.76	2110
$IVolP^{ATM}$	50.67	23.63	1.86	8.98	8.66	23.47	33.82	45.66	62.30	93.59	246.22	2110
$IVolP^{OTM}$	55.71	23.88	1.83	8.91	13.06	27.60	38.79	51.05	67.51	98.54	253.95	2110

Panel B: Excess Returns											
	Mean	SD	Skew	Kurt	Min	5%	25%	Median	75%	95%	Max	n
Stock	0.70	13.27	0.73	9.66	−66.08	−18.78	−6.41	0.21	7.12	21.60	101.38	1617
Straddle	−8.87	75.62	2.08	14.40	−100.14	−93.11	−64.16	−25.07	27.29	128.92	697.49	2105
ΔHedged call	−7.78	76.82	2.16	16.40	−100.14	−93.06	−63.87	−24.25	28.75	131.73	739.56	2105
ΔHedged put	−9.41	74.95	2.06	13.58	−100.14	−93.17	−64.43	−25.33	26.70	126.90	692.00	2105

(continued)

TABLE 17.1 (*Continued*)

					Panel C: Firm Characteristics						
	Mean	*SD*	*Skew*	*Kurt*	*Min*	*5%*	*25%*	*Median*	*75%*	*95%*	*Max*	*n*
β	1.13	0.51	0.70	0.66	−0.27	0.44	0.76	1.04	1.43	2.09	3.32	1587
MktCap	6140	20,809	9	117	32	149	477	1249	3798	23,410	368,429	1618
BM	0.54	0.55	7.26	119.73	0.00	0.10	0.24	0.42	0.69	1.30	10.47	1394
Mom	18.52	65.10	4.05	45.12	−85.63	−47.02	−14.89	7.51	34.97	117.08	871.05	1584
Rev	1.14	13.60	1.38	21.92	−58.01	−18.32	−6.13	0.50	7.48	22.29	123.68	1616
Illiq	0.01	0.05	12.69	261.35	0.00	0.00	0.00	0.00	0.01	0.06	1.21	1617
CoSkew	0.16	10.00	1.05	18.80	−59.92	−13.41	−4.45	−0.09	4.19	14.58	86.66	1512
IdioSkew	0.38	0.73	1.53	7.00	−2.53	−0.54	−0.05	0.28	0.67	1.64	5.48	1512
IdioVol	39.09	24.79	3.58	43.90	5.06	14.42	23.04	33.22	48.37	82.15	326.72	1617

sample differs substantially from the CRSP sample used in the majority of Part II and also from the subsets of the CRSP sample used in Chapter 16.

Summary statistics for the variables calculated from option-implied volatilities are presented in Panel A. All volatilities are annualized values measured in percent. The average value of *IVolSpread* is −0.84 indicating that, on average, put implied volatilities are slightly higher than call implied volatilities. This can also be seen in the summary statistics for $IVolC^{ATM}$ and $IVolP^{ATM}$, which have means of 49.83 and 50.67, respectively. Values of *IVolSpread* range from −131.03 to 124.79 with a median *IVolSpread* value of −0.54, only slightly higher than the mean. While the cross-sectional distribution of *IVolSpread* is relatively symmetric with an average skewness of −0.78, it is highly leptokurtic with an excess kurtosis of 106.79.

Values of $Vol^{1M} - IVol$ range from −140.09 to 236.12 in the average month, with mean and median values of −3.03 and −3.43, respectively. Consistent with previous work (Jackwerth and Rubinstein (1996), Bakshi and Kapadia (2003a,b) and Carr and Wu (2009)), the negative mean and median values of $Vol^{1M} - IVol$ indicate that implied volatility tends to be, on average, a little bit higher than recent realized volatility.

The mean (median) *IVolSkew* value of 5.88 (4.70) shows that, consistent with a volatility smirk, the implied volatility of an OTM put option tends to be higher than the implied volatility of the ATM call. In the average month, even the 25th percentile *IVolSkew* value of 1.61 is positive, indicating that the vast majority of stocks exhibit a volatility smirk.

As would be expected, average values of $\Delta IVolC$ and $\Delta IVolP$ are very close to zero. However, there is substantial variation in each of these variables, as indicated by the average cross-sectional standard deviations of 12.97 and 12.76 for $\Delta IVolC$ and $\Delta IVolP$, respectively.

Interestingly, the mean and median values of $Vol^{12M} - IVol$ are slightly positive, indicating that, on average, realized volatility calculated from 12 months of daily return data is higher than option-implied volatility. The cross-sectional distribution of $Vol^{12M} - IVol$ is quite symmetric with an average skewness of only 0.02, and highly leptokurtic with an excess kurtosis of 44.18. The range of values of $Vol^{12M} - IVol$ is similar to that of $Vol^{1M} - IVol$.

Panel B of Table 17.1 presents summary statistics for the excess returns of the stocks, straddles, delta-hedged calls, and delta-hedged puts that will be examined throughout this chapter. The mean (median) stock in the Options sample generates an average monthly excess return of 0.70% (0.21%). Straddles generate mean (median) monthly excess returns of −8.87% (−25.07%). Similar results are seen for the delta-hedged calls (average excess return of −7.78% per month, median excess return of −24.25% per month), and the delta-hedged puts (average excess return of −9.41% per month, median excess return of −25.33% per month). The large negative average returns of the straddle, delta-hedged call, and delta-hedged put positions are consistent with previous findings of a negative price of volatility risk (Bakshi and Kapadia (2003a) and Carr and Wu (2009)).

Summary statistics for the variables used in the previous chapters of Part II, calculated using the Options sample, are shown in Panel C of Table 17.1. The most salient difference between the options sample and the stock-based samples examined throughout this book is that the market capitalization of the stocks in the options sample is much larger than that of the stocks in the previously examined samples. This holds even for the Size sample, the most restrictive sample used in Chapter 16. The average stock in the Options sample has a market capitalization of more than $6 billion. While some small stocks are included in the Options sample, the stocks in the options sample are generally much larger than those included in the other samples examined in this book.

Comparing the values of the other variables for stocks in the options sample to those in the CRSP sample used throughout this book, the results indicate that β, *Mom*, and *CoSkew* are all higher, in mean and in median, in the Options sample than in the CRSP sample. *BM*, *Illiq*, *IdioSkew*, and *IdioVol* all tend to be lower in the Options sample than in the CRSP sample. Finally, the mean and median values of *Rev* are approximately the same in both samples. In most cases, these results hold when comparing the Options sample to the Price and Size samples examined in Chapter 16, with a few exceptions. The Price and Size samples both have lower mean and median values of *IdioVol* than the Options sample and higher average values of *Mom* than the Options sample. Perhaps the Options sample can best be characterized as containing the largest and most liquid stocks.

The last noteworthy result in Table 17.1 is that there are, in the average month, 2110 stocks in the Options sample in the average month. Of these, we are only able to match 1618, on average, to stocks in the CRSP database. Thus, analyses that use variables calculated from the CRSP database will have, at most, 1618 stocks in the average month. This is substantially smaller than the 4794 stocks available in the average month in the CRSP sample.

17.4 CORRELATIONS

Average cross-sectional correlations between the variables used to predict future returns are shown in Table 17.2. Below-diagonal entries present the Pearson product-moment correlations, and above-diagonal entries show Spearman correlations.

TABLE 17.2   Correlations

This table presents the time-series averages of the annual cross-sectional Pearson product–moment (below-diagonal entries) and Spearman rank (above-diagonal entries) correlations between pairs of $IVolSpread$, $Vol^{12M} - IVol$, $IVolSkew$, $\Delta IVolC$, $\Delta IVolP$, $Vol^{12M} - IVol$, β, $Size$, BM, Rev, $Illiq$, $CoSkew$, $IdioSkew$, $IdioVol$ using the Options sample.

	$IVolSpread$	$Vol^{1M}-IVol$	$IVolSkew$	$\Delta IVolC$	$\Delta IVolP$	$Vol^{12M}-IVol$	β	$Size$	BM	Mom	Rev	$Illiq$	$CoSkew$	$IdioSkew$	$IdioVol$
$IVolSpread$		−0.00	−0.59	0.29	−0.21	−0.03	−0.00	0.01	0.01	−0.01	−0.07	−0.01	−0.00	−0.02	−0.02
$Vol^{1M}-IVol$	0.01		0.05	−0.13	−0.12	0.32	0.08	0.19	−0.01	0.05	0.13	−0.16	0.02	−0.06	0.31
$IVolSkew$	−0.66	0.03		−0.25	0.06	0.08	−0.01	−0.01	0.02	0.01	0.08	0.02	0.00	−0.00	−0.02
$\Delta IVolC$	0.32	−0.17	−0.27		0.53	−0.33	−0.02	0.01	0.00	0.05	−0.25	−0.01	−0.00	−0.01	0.01
$\Delta IVolP$	−0.26	−0.16	0.11	0.54		−0.33	−0.02	0.01	0.00	0.03	−0.18	−0.01	−0.00	−0.02	0.01
$Vol^{12M}-IVol$	−0.01	0.39	0.05	−0.37	−0.38		0.26	0.08	−0.06	0.06	0.16	−0.10	0.05	0.02	0.05
β	−0.00	0.09	−0.03	−0.01	−0.02	0.24		−0.14	−0.12	−0.04	−0.02	0.09	0.08	0.15	0.41
$Size$	0.02	0.15	−0.02	−0.00	0.00	0.10	−0.12		−0.11	0.23	0.09	−0.93	0.07	−0.23	−0.51
BM	0.01	−0.02	0.03	0.00	0.00	−0.03	−0.09	−0.13		0.00	0.01	0.15	−0.01	−0.02	−0.11
Mom	−0.00	0.03	0.00	0.03	0.02	0.11	0.00	0.13	0.01		0.01	−0.23	0.02	0.04	−0.12
Rev	−0.07	0.13	0.07	−0.24	−0.17	0.16	−0.01	0.07	0.01	−0.00		−0.05	0.02	−0.01	−0.01
$Illiq$	−0.00	−0.12	−0.04	0.01	0.01	−0.14	−0.06	−0.49	0.09	−0.17	−0.03		−0.08	0.20	0.44
$CoSkew$	−0.00	0.02	−0.00	−0.01	−0.01	0.06	0.10	0.05	0.00	0.04	0.03	−0.04		0.02	−0.00
$IdioSkew$	−0.02	−0.06	−0.01	−0.02	−0.02	0.04	0.15	−0.22	0.01	0.09	0.02	0.13	0.05		0.20
$IdioVol$	−0.04	0.46	−0.03	0.03	0.03	0.02	0.35	−0.45	−0.05	−0.03	0.02	0.28	0.01	0.19	

We first examine the correlations between the option-based variables. The table shows that $IVolSpread$ is strongly negatively correlated with $IVolSkew$, positively correlated with $\Delta IVolC$, and negatively correlated with $\Delta IVolP$. None of these correlations are surprising and many of them are potentially mechanical. The calculation of $IVolSpread$ has a positive sign on ATM call implied volatility and a negative sign on ATM put implied volatility. Since the calculation of $IVolSkew$ assigns a negative sign to ATM call implied volatility, the calculation of $\Delta IVolC$ has a positive sign on contemporaneous ATM call implied volatility, and the calculation of $\Delta IVolP$ has a positive sign on the contemporaneous ATM put implied volatility, the observed correlations are consistent with a mechanical effect.

The realized minus implied volatility spread, calculated using one-month realized volatility ($Vol^{1M} - IVol$), is negatively correlated with both $\Delta IVolC$ and $\Delta IVolP$ and positively correlated with the realized minus implied volatility spread calculated using 12-month realized volatility ($Vol^{12M} - IVol$). Once again, these correlations are probably at least partially mechanical. ATM call and put implied volatility enter positively into the calculation of $\Delta IVolC$ and $\Delta IVolP$, respectively, and negatively into the calculation of $Vol^{1M} - IVol$, potentially driving the negative correlation. Obviously, $IVol$, which is the average of the ATM call and put implied volatilities, carries a negative sign in the calculation of both $Vol^{1M} - IVol$ and $Vol^{12M} - IVol$, creating a positive correlation.

$IVSkew$ has a negative correlation with $\Delta IVolC$, as would be expected given that $IVolSkew$ is calculated with a positive sign on ATM call implied volatility while $\Delta IVolC$ incorporates ATM call implied volatility with a positive sign. $IVSkew$ also exhibits a relatively small, but not negligible, positive Pearson correlation of 0.11 with $\Delta IVolP$.

Both $\Delta IVolC$ and $\Delta IVolP$ have a negative correlation with $Vol^{12M} - IVol$, which is once again probably a mechanical effect since $\Delta IVolC$ and $\Delta IVolP$ have a positive sign on contemporaneous call and put implied volatility, respectively, and $Vol^{12M} - IVol$ carries a negative sign on contemporaneous ATM call and put implied volatility. Finally, $\Delta IVolC$ and $\Delta IVolP$ have an average cross-sectional Pearson correlation of 0.54, indicating that stocks whose ATM call implied volatility increases are also likely to experience increases in ATM put implied volatility. One may actually think that this correlation is lower than expected. For European options, the put–call parity relation necessitates that the implied volatility of a call and put option with the same strike and expiration be the same. If this holds at the end of both month $t - 1$ and month t, the result would be a perfect correlation between $\Delta IVolC$ and $\Delta IVolP$. The options under consideration, however, are American options, meaning that the call and put implied volatilities may differ from each other without indicating an arbitrage opportunity.

We next examine the correlations between the option variables and the variables discussed in previous chapters of this book. Neither $IVolSpread$ nor $IVolSkew$ exhibit substantial correlation with any of the previously examined variables. $Vol^{1M} - IVol$ exhibits moderate positive correlations with β, $Size$, and Rev, a moderate negative correlation with $Illiq$, and a strong positive correlation with $IdioVol$. This last correlation is expected because Vol^{1M} measures total volatility over the last month and $IdioVol$ measures idiosyncratic volatility over the last month. $Vol^{12M} - IVol$ has similar correlations to β, $Size$, Rev, and $Illiq$ as $Vol^{1M} - IVol$, and a nonnegligible positive correlation with Mom. Interestingly, the correlation between $Vol^{12M} - IVol$ and $IdioVol$ is quite small. Both $\Delta IVolC$ and $\Delta IVolP$ are negatively correlated with Rev and exhibit very little correlation with any of the other previously examined variables.

Finally, the correlations between the variables examined in previous chapters of this book, calculated from the stocks in the Options sample, are similar to those found in the samples examined in Chapter 16. Perhaps the most notable difference is that the average Pearson correlation between β and $Size$ in the option sample of -0.12 is negative and substantial, whereas in the CRSP sample used throughout Part II of this book and the Price and Size samples used in Chapter 16, the correlation between β and $Size$ is substantially positive. Also, the average Pearson correlation of -0.06 between β and $Illiq$ in the options sample is substantially smaller than the corresponding correlation in the previously examined samples.

17.5 PERSISTENCE

We now proceed to persistence analyses of the option variables. The results of these analyses, shown in Panel A of Table 17.3, show that many of the option variables exhibit some persistence at relatively short lags, but none of them exhibit substantial persistence when measured at lags of more than one year.

The persistence of $IVolSpread$ measured at lags of one and three months are 0.16 and 0.11, respectively, indicating a nonnegligible but economically small persistence.

TABLE 17.3 Persistence

This table presents the results of persistence analyses of *IVolSpread*, *Vol*^{1M} − *IVol*, *IVolSkew*, Δ*IVolC*, Δ*IVolP*, *Vol*^{12M} − *IVol* in Panel A, and β, *MktCap*, *Size*, *BM*, *Mom*, *Rev*, *Illiq*, *CoSkew*, *IdioSkew*, and *IdioVol* in Panel B, using the Options sample. Each month *t*, the cross-sectional Pearson product–moment correlation between the month *t* and month *t* + τ values of the given variable is calculated. The table presents the time-series averages of the monthly cross-sectional correlations. The column labeled τ indicates the lag at which the persistence is measured.

Panel A: Option Variables

τ	*IVolSpread*	*Vol*^{1M} − *IVol*	*IVolSkew*	Δ*IVolC*	Δ*IVolP*	*Vol*^{12M} − *IVol*
1	0.16	0.15	0.26	−0.34	−0.33	
3	0.11	0.17	0.19	0.01	0.02	
6	0.08	0.14	0.14	0.02	0.02	
12	0.06	0.13	0.10	0.04	0.04	0.12
24	0.04	0.09	0.06	0.03	0.03	0.09
36	0.02	0.09	0.04	0.03	0.03	0.08
48	0.01	0.07	0.04	0.02	0.03	0.05
60	0.01	0.07	0.04	0.03	0.03	0.06
120	0.00	0.04	0.02	0.02	0.03	0.00

Panel B: Stock Characteristics

τ	β	*MktCap*	*Size*	*BM*	*Mom*	*Rev*	*Illiq*	*CoSkew*	*IdioSkew*	*IdioVol*
1		1.00	1.00			−0.02	0.90			0.54
3		0.99	0.99			0.00	0.84			0.54
6		0.99	0.98			0.01	0.78			0.51
12	0.68	0.97	0.96	0.75	−0.06	0.00	0.66			0.48
24	0.57	0.95	0.92	0.63	−0.05	0.01	0.51			0.43
36	0.51	0.93	0.90	0.56	−0.02	0.01	0.42			0.40
48	0.46	0.91	0.88	0.53	−0.00	0.00	0.36			0.37
60	0.41	0.90	0.87	0.50	−0.03	0.00	0.32	0.05	0.12	0.35
120	0.16	0.86	0.80	0.41	0.02	−0.00	0.29	0.01	0.10	0.27

For lags of six months and greater, however, all persistence values are 0.08 and lower, indicating very little, if any, longer-term persistence in *IVolSpread*.

The results examining the persistence of *Vol*^{1M} − *IVol* are interesting since the persistence appears to increase slightly from 0.15 when measured at a lag of one month to 0.17 when measured at a lag of three months. Since there is no economic reason to think that the persistence of *Vol*^{1M} − *IVol* should increase at longer lags, it seems likely that this result is simply an empirical artifact. At lags of six and 12 months, the persistence values of 0.14 and 0.13 remain nonnegligible, but still quite small. At lags longer than 12 months, however, the persistence decays even further.

IVolSkew exhibits somewhat stronger short-term persistence than *IVolSpread* and *Vol^{1M}* − *IVol*. However, even when measured at a lag of only one month, *IVolSkew*'s persistence of 0.26 is not very high, and this persistence decays quite rapidly as the lag is increased. At a lag of 12 months, the persistence is only 0.10, and at 24 months and longer lags, the persistence values are all 0.06 and lower.

Both Δ*IVolC* and Δ*IVolP* exhibit strong negative cross-sectional correlation when measured at lags of one month. This indicates that large increases in call or put implied volatility tend to indicate pricing errors that are reversed in the following month. At lags of more than one month, neither Δ*IVolC* nor Δ*IVolP* exhibits any notable persistence.

Finally, the persistence of *Vol^{12M}* − *IVol*, which we calculate only at lags of 12 months and longer due to the use of 12 months of data in the calculation of *Vol^{12M}*, is 0.12 at a 12-month lag and decays to zero at a lag of five years.

The general lack of strong persistence exhibited by the option-based variables indicates that any ability of these variables to predict future stock or option returns is likely due to a short-lived effect such as mispricing that informed investors attempt to discretely profit from by trading in the options market. It is unlikely that any of these variables measure a risk that is priced by the market.

Panel B of Table 17.3 shows the results of persistence analyses of all of the previously examined variables using only stocks in the Options sample. The results of these analyses are similar to those of the analyses shown in previous chapters of this book, and thus can be summarized very quickly. The size variables (*MktCap* and *Size*) exhibit extremely high persistence at all lags. β, *BM*, *Illiq*, and *IdioVol* are all strongly persistent. *Mom* and *Rev* exhibit very little persistence, but this is not surprising because these variables simply measure stock returns, and persistence in these variables would amount to a strong ability to predict the cross section of future stock returns. Finally, *CoSkew* exhibits almost no persistence and the persistence of *IdioSkew*, while much smaller than that of other variables, is a little too large to be considered negligible.

Having examined the summary statistics, correlations, and persistence of all of our variables using the options sample, we proceed now to investigate the ability of the option-based variables to predict future stock and option returns. Given the large number of relations being examined in this chapter, we do not dig deep into any single phenomenon. The objective of the remainder of this chapter is to provide the reader with a preliminary overview of the main results pertaining to the option markets.

17.6 STOCK RETURNS

Our investigation of the ability of the option-based variables to predict future stock returns proceeds in two steps. First, we examine the relations between the variables calculated from contemporaneous volatility levels. Specifically, we begin by examining the cross-sectional relations between future stock returns and each of *IVolSpread*, *Vol*^{1M} − *IVol*, and *IVolSkew*. As has been done throughout this book, we use univariate portfolio analysis and (Fama and MacBeth 1973, FM hereafter) regression analysis to investigate these relations.

We then examine the relations between future stock returns and each of Δ*IVolC* and Δ*IVolP*, which capture changes in implied volatility over time. We separate these analyses from the analyses using *IVolSpread*, *IVolSkew*, and *Vol*^{1M} − *IVol* because, as documented by An et al. (2014), the negative relation between Δ*IVolP* and future stock returns is strongest after controlling for Δ*IVolC*. Our investigations of the relations between future stock returns and each of Δ*IVolC* and Δ*IVolP*, therefore, use bivariate (instead of univariate) portfolio analyses and FM regression analyses.

17.6.1   *IVolSpread*, *IVolSkew*, and *Vol*^{1M} − *IVol*

Table 17.4 presents the results of univariate portfolio analyses of the relations between expected stock returns and each of *IVolSpread*, *IVolSkew*, and *Vol*^{1M} − *IVol*. Results for equal-weighted portfolios are shown in Panel A and value-weighted portfolio results are shown in Panel B.

TABLE 17.4   Univariate Portfolio Analysis—Stock Returns
This table presents the results of univariate portfolio analyses of the relation between future stock returns and each of *IVolSpread*, *Vol*^{1M} − *IVol*, and *IVolSkew*. Monthly portfolios are formed by sorting all stocks in the Options sample into portfolios using decile breakpoints calculated based on the given sort variable using all stocks in the Options sample. Panel A (Panel B) shows the average equal-weighted (value-weighted) one-month-ahead excess return (in percent per month) for each of the 10 decile portfolios formed using different variables as the sort variable. The table also shows the average return of the portfolio that is long the 10th decile portfolio and short the first decile portfolio, as well as the FFC and FFCPS alphas for this portfolio. Newey and West (1987) *t*-statistics, adjusted using six lags, testing the null hypothesis that the average 10-1 portfolio return or alpha is equal to zero, are shown in parentheses.

Panel A: Equal-Weighted Portfolio Returns												
Sort Variable	1	2	3	4	5	6	7	8	9	10	10-1	FFC α	FFCPS α
IVolSpread	−0.33	0.36	0.44	0.52	0.65	0.73	0.90	0.83	1.22	1.68	2.02	2.16	2.10
											(8.23)	(7.96)	(8.39)
Vol^{1M} − *IVol*	0.89	0.91	0.80	0.83	0.71	0.71	0.58	0.60	0.52	0.48	−0.41	−0.48	−0.38
											(−2.05)	(−2.23)	(−1.66)
IVolSkew	1.57	1.25	1.00	0.75	0.59	0.57	0.50	0.48	0.42	−0.08	−1.66	−1.74	−1.65
											(−6.65)	(−6.01)	(−6.62)

Panel B: Value-Weighted Portfolio Returns												
Sort Variable	1	2	3	4	5	6	7	8	9	10	10-1	FFC α	FFCPS α
IVolSpread	−0.19	0.08	0.15	0.37	0.55	0.62	0.76	0.77	1.06	1.61	1.80	2.08	2.10
											(4.90)	(5.07)	(4.94)
Vol^{1M} − *IVol*	0.86	0.86	0.96	0.92	0.63	0.57	0.44	0.44	0.30	0.21	−0.65	−0.58	−0.49
											(−1.84)	(−1.64)	(−1.47)
IVolSkew	1.47	1.22	0.93	0.63	0.42	0.45	0.48	0.29	0.25	−0.09	−1.56	−1.70	−1.61
											(−3.53)	(−3.81)	(−3.73)

Consistent with the results of Bali and Hovakimian (2009) and Cremers and Weinbaum (2010), the results in Table 17.4 demonstrate a strong positive relation between *IVolSpread* and future stock returns. When using equal-weighted portfolios, the average monthly excess returns of the decile portfolios increase monotonically from −0.33% for the first decile portfolio to 1.68% per month for the 10th decile portfolio. The average return of the *IVolSpread* 10-1 portfolio of 2.02% per month is not only economically very large but also highly statistically significant with a Newey and West (1987)-adjusted (six lags) *t*-statistic of 8.23. The alphas of this portfolio relative to the Fama and French (1993) and Carhart (1997) four-factor model (FFC) and the FFC model augmented with the Pastor and Stambaugh (2003) liquidity factor (FFCPS) of 2.16% per month (*t*-statistic = 7.96) and 2.10% per month (*t*-statistic = 8.39), respectively, indicate that the large average return of this portfolio is not driven by large factor sensitivities. The results for value-weighted portfolios, shown in Panel B, are nearly as strong. The average excess returns of the decile portfolios increase from −0.19% per month for decile portfolio one to 1.61 for decile portfolio 10. The difference portfolio's average return of 1.80% per month is highly statistically significant with a *t*-statistic of 4.90. Once again, the FFC and FFCPS models fail to explain the returns of this portfolio since the alphas of 2.08% per month (*t*-statistic = 5.07) and 2.10% per month (*t*-statistic = 4.94), respectively, remain economically very large and highly statistically significant.

The results of the univariate portfolio analyses using $Vol^{1M} - IVol$ as the sort variable indicate, as demonstrated by Bali and Hovakimian (2009), a negative relation between $Vol^{1M} - IVol$ and future stock returns. This relation, however, is not quite as strong as some of the other relations examined in this chapter. When using equal-weighted portfolios, the average return of the $Vol^{1M} - IVol$ 10-1 portfolio of 0.41% per month (*t*-statistic = −2.05) is economically meaningful and highly statistically significant. The FFC alpha of −0.48% per month (*t*-statistic = −2.23) generated by this portfolio is slightly larger in magnitude and higher in statistical significance than the average return. Interestingly, however, the FFCPS alpha decreases in magnitude to a marginally statistically significant −0.38% per month (*t*-statistic = −1.66), indicating that a portion of this portfolio's average return is driven by aggregate liquidity sensitivity. The average return of the value-weighted $Vol^{1M} - IVol$ 10-1 of −0.65% per month (*t*-statistic = −1.84) is larger in magnitude than that of the equal-weighted portfolio, albeit slightly lower in statistical significance. Similarly, both the FFC and FFCPS alphas of −0.58% per month (*t*-statistic = −1.64) and −0.49% per month (*t*-statistic = −1.47), respectively, of the value-weighted difference portfolio are larger in magnitude, but carry lower *t*-statistics, than their equal-weighted counterparts. Thus, while the economic significance of these results is quite substantial, the statistical significance is relatively low. It should be noted, however, that these analyses only cover returns in the months from February 1996 through December 2012, a relatively short sample period. It is possible, therefore, that the low *t*-statistics are a manifestation of the short sample period causing a lack of power in the statistical tests.

The last set of portfolio analyses whose results are presented in Table 17.4 examine the relation between *IVolSkew* and future stock returns. Consistent with

Xing et al. (2010), the results demonstrate a strong negative relation between *IVolSkew* and future stock returns. The average excess returns of the equal-weighted decile portfolios decrease monotonically from 1.57% per month for the first decile portfolio to −0.08% per month for the 10th decile portfolio. The *IVolSkew* difference portfolio therefore generates an average return of −1.66% per month with a corresponding *t*-statistic of −6.65. The FFC alpha of −1.74% per month (*t*-statistic = −6.01) and FFCPS alpha of −1.65% per month (*t*-statistic = −6.62) are similar in magnitude and statistical significance. The excess returns of value-weighted *IVolSkew*-sorted decile portfolios decrease monotonically from 1.47% per month for decile portfolio one to −0.09% per month for decile portfolio 10. The average return, FFC alpha, and FFCPS alpha generated by the value-weighted difference portfolio of −1.56% per month (*t*-statistic = −3.53), −1.70% per month (*t*-statistic = −3.81) and −1.61% per month (*t*-statistic = −3.73) are all economically large in magnitude, highly statistically significant, and very similar to their equal-weighted counterparts.

The results of the univariate portfolio analyses presented in Table 17.4 demonstrate a strong positive univariate relation between *IVolSpread* and future stock returns and negative univariate relations between future stock returns and each of $Vol^{1M} - IVol$ and *IVolSkew*. We now use FM regression analyses to examine whether these relations can be explained by any of the phenomena documented in previous chapters of this book. We employ several different specifications for the monthly cross-sectional regressions. We begin with univariate specifications using each *IVolSpread*, $Vol^{1M} - IVol$, and *IVolSkew* as the only independent variable. We then include these three measures as independent variables in the same specification. Finally, we repeat each of these analyses while also controlling for β, *Size*, *BM*, *Mom*, *Rev*, *Illiq*, *CoSkew*, *IdioSkew*, and *IdioVol*. Given the strong and highly mechanical relation between $Vol^{1M} - IVol$ and *IdioVol*, following An et al. (2014) we exclude *IdioVol* from specifications that include $Vol^{1M} - IVol$. The independent variables in all specifications are winsorized at the 0.5% level on a monthly basis.

The results of the FM regression analyses are presented in Table 17.5. Specification (1) shows that the positive relation between *IVolSpread* and future stock returns is strongly detected using FM regression analysis since the average coefficient of 0.077 on *IVolSpread* is highly statistically significant with a *t*-statistic of 9.28. Similarly, the negative relations between one-month-ahead excess stock returns and each of $Vol^{1M} - IVol$ and *IVolSkew* are also found using FM regression analysis since both the average coefficient of −0.006 (*t*-statistic = −1.89, specification (2)) on $Vol^{1M} - IVol$ and the average coefficient of −0.050 (*t*-statistic = −7.77, specification (3)) on *IVolSkew* are statistically significant. When all three option-based variables are included simultaneously as independent variables (specification (4)), the results are very similar. The average coefficients on *IVolSpread*, $Vol^{1M} - IVol$, and *IVolSkew* of 0.053 (*t*-statistic = 4.51), −0.005 (*t*-statistic = −1.81), and −0.025 (*t*-statistic = −2.90) are all statistically significant and of similar (albeit slightly smaller) magnitude than the corresponding coefficients from the univariate specifications.

The specifications that include the control variables demonstrate that none of these cross-sectional relations are driven by previously documented patterns in stock returns. When the univariate specifications are augmented with the control variables,

TABLE 17.5 Fama–MacBeth Regression Analysis—Stock Returns

This table presents the results of Fama and MacBeth (1973) regression analyses of the relations between expected stock returns and each of *IVolSpread*, *Vol*^{1M} − *IVol*, and *IVolSkew*. Each column in the table presents results for a different cross-sectional regression specification. The dependent variable in all specifications is the one-month-ahead excess stock return. The independent variables are indicated in the first column. Independent variables are winsorized at the 0.5% level on a monthly basis. The table presents average slope and intercept coefficients along with *t*-statistics (in parentheses), adjusted following Newey and West (1987) using six lags, testing the null hypothesis that the average coefficient is equal to zero. The rows labeled Adj. R^2 and *n* present the average adjusted R-squared and the number of data points, respectively, for the cross-sectional regressions.

	Option Variables							
	(1)	(2)	(3)	(4)	(5)	(6)	(7)	(8)
IVolSpread	0.077			0.053	0.071			0.052
	(9.28)			(4.51)	(8.91)			(5.35)
Vol^{1M} − *IVol*		−0.006		−0.005		−0.008		−0.008
		(−1.89)		(−1.81)		(−2.80)		(−2.78)
IVolSkew			−0.050	−0.025			−0.047	−0.022
			(−7.77)	(−2.90)			(−7.78)	(−3.19)
β					0.140	0.139	0.142	0.147
					(0.38)	(0.36)	(0.39)	(0.39)
Size					−0.170	−0.125	−0.174	−0.133
					(−2.24)	(−1.43)	(−2.32)	(−1.52)
BM					−0.049	−0.007	−0.017	0.007
					(−0.26)	(−0.03)	(−0.09)	(0.04)
Mom					−0.002	−0.002	−0.002	−0.002
					(−0.37)	(−0.50)	(−0.36)	(−0.47)
Rev					−0.014	−0.016	−0.014	−0.013
					(−1.87)	(−2.10)	(−1.84)	(−1.69)
Illiq					−0.064	−1.116	−0.653	−1.688
					(−0.02)	(−0.37)	(−0.21)	(−0.56)
CoSkew					0.014	0.015	0.014	0.015
					(1.77)	(1.84)	(1.77)	(1.82)
IdioSkew					−0.091	−0.116	−0.104	−0.114
					(−1.35)	(−1.68)	(−1.54)	(−1.65)
IdioVol					−0.007		−0.008	
					(−1.87)		(−2.09)	
Intercept	0.771	0.722	0.971	0.898	2.061	1.453	2.304	1.661
	(1.69)	(1.61)	(2.09)	(1.95)	(3.05)	(1.85)	(3.43)	(2.09)
Adj. R^2	0.00	0.00	0.00	0.01	0.09	0.08	0.09	0.09
n	1617	1616	1617	1616	1338	1338	1338	1338

specifications (5)–(7) demonstrate that the positive relation between *IVolSpread* and future stock returns, and the negative relations between future stock returns and each of *Vol*^{1M} − *IVol* and *IVolSkew*, all persist. The same is true when all variables are included in the regression specification (specification (8)). In fact, the magnitude and statistical strength of the negative relation between *Vol*^{1M} − *IVol* and future stock returns are substantially enhanced when the control variables are included. Specification (8) produces an average coefficient of 0.052 (t-statistic = 5.35) on *IVolSpread*, an average coefficient of -0.008 (t-statistic = -2.78) on $Vol^{1M} - IVol$, and an average coefficient of -0.022 (t-statistic = -3.19) on *IVolSkew*.

We examine the economic importance of these relations by multiplying the average coefficients from specification (8) by the average standard deviation, as well as the difference between the 95th and fifth percentiles, of the cross-sectional distributions of each of *IVolSpread*, $Vol^{1M} - IVol$, and *IVolSkew*. Multiplying the average coefficient on *IVolSpread* of 0.052 by the standard deviation of *IVolSpread*, we find that a one-standard-deviation difference in *IVolSpread* is associated with a 0.50% (0.052 × 9.66, see Table 17.1) per month difference in expected returns. The difference in expected returns between a stock at the fifth and 95th percentiles of *IVolSpread* is 1.04% (0.052 × [8.74 − (−11.34)]) per month. A similar analysis shows that while a one-standard-deviation difference in $Vol^{1M} - IVol$ results in only a 0.16% (0.008 × 19.74) per month difference in expected returns, the difference in expected returns between stocks with high (95th percentile) and low (fifth percentile) $Vol^{1M} - IVol$ values of 0.42% (0.008 × [23.60 − (−28.77)]) per month is economically important. Finally, a one-standard-deviation difference in *IVolSkew* generates an expected return difference of 0.26% (0.022 × 11.65) per month, while the difference in expected returns for stocks at the 95th and fifth percentiles of *IVolSkew* is 0.63% (0.022 × [22.25 − (−6.31)]) per month.

Finally, it is worth mentioning that when using the specification with the full set of control variables (specification (8)), the average coefficient on several of the variables previously shown to predict future stock returns are statistically indistinguishable from zero. Specifically, the average coefficients on *Size*, *BM*, *Mom*, and *Illiq* are all statistically insignificant. The reversal effect is substantially weaker than in previous analyses, with an average coefficient on *Rev* of -0.013 (t-statistic = -1.69). Interestingly, the average coefficient on *CoSkew* of 0.015 is marginally statistically significant with a t-statistic of 1.82. Finally, the average coefficient on *IdioSkew* of -0.114 (t-statistic = -1.65) is negative and marginally statistically significant. The failure of this analysis to detect relations between future stock returns and each of *Size*, *BM*, *Mom*, and *Illiq* is consistent with previous empirical work. These relations do not appear to be present when the sample is restricted to stocks with traded options.

In summary, consistent with the results of the univariate portfolio analyses, the results of the FM regression analyses indicate that *IVolSpread* is positively related, in the cross section, to future stock returns while both $Vol^{1M} - IVol$ and *IVolSkew* are negatively related to future stock returns. Each of these relations is highly statistically significant and economically important.

17.6.2 ΔIVolC and ΔIVolP

We proceed now to examine the ability of each of ΔIVolC and ΔIVolP to predict future stock returns. An et al. (2014) find a positive relation between ΔIVolC and future stock returns and a negative relation between ΔIVolP and stock returns after controlling for the effect of ΔIVolC. As discussed in An et al. (2014), because ΔIVolC and $\Delta IVolP$ are strongly positively correlated in the cross section, it is important to control for $\Delta IVolC$ when examining the relation between $\Delta IVolP$ and future stock returns. For this reason, we forego univariate portfolio analyses in favor of bivariate portfolio analyses in our examination of the relations between these variables and future stock returns.

In Table 17.6, we present the results of dependent-sort bivariate portfolio analyses examining the relation between $\Delta IVolC$ and future stock returns after controlling for $\Delta IVolP$. Each month, we sort all stocks in the options sample into $\Delta IVolP$ quintiles. Within each $\Delta IVolP$ quintile, we sort stocks into quintile portfolios based on $\Delta IVolC$. The table presents the average excess returns for each of the resulting 25 portfolios, as well as average returns and alphas for the portfolios that are long the $\Delta IVolC$ quintile five portfolio and short the $\Delta IVolC$ quintile one portfolio within each quintile of $\Delta IVolP$. Results for the average $\Delta IVolP$ portfolio within each $\Delta IVolC$ quintile are also presented.

The results of the equal-weighted bivariate dependent-sort analysis, shown in Panel A, demonstrate that within each quintile of $\Delta IVolP$, the average monthly return of the $\Delta IVolC$ 5-1 portfolio is positive, economically large, and highly statistically significant. The same is true of the FFC and FFCPS alphas. In the average $\Delta IVolP$ quintile, the $\Delta IVolC$ 5-1 portfolio generates an average monthly return of 0.88% (t-statistic = 5.47), FFC alpha of 0.87% per month (t-statistic = 5.31), and FFCPS alpha of 0.86% per month (t-statistic = 5.14). In each $\Delta IVolP$ quintile, the first $\Delta IVolC$ quintile portfolio generates the lowest average return and, with the exception of $\Delta IVolP$ quintile five, the fifth $\Delta IVolC$ quintile portfolio generates the highest average return.

Panel B of Table 17.6 presents the average excess returns of value-weighted portfolios created using the same sorting procedure. The results indicate that the positive relation between $\Delta IVolC$ and future stock returns persists, although it is not quite as strong, when using value-weighted portfolios. In quintiles one through four of $\Delta IVolP$, the average return and alphas of the $\Delta IVolC$ difference portfolio are positive and statistically significant (at least marginally). The exception is the FFCPS alpha of the $\Delta IVolC$ 5-1 portfolio in the first $\Delta IVolP$ quintile. In quintile five of $\Delta IVolP$, however, the average return and alphas of the $\Delta IVolC$ 5-1 portfolio, while positive and of substantial economic magnitude, are all statistically indistinguishable from zero. In the average $\Delta IVolP$ quintile, the $\Delta IVolC$ 5-1 portfolio produces a positive and highly statistically significant average return of 0.76% per month with a corresponding t-statistic of 3.67. Adjusting for risk using the FFC and FFCPS factor models does little to explain the returns of this portfolio since the FFC alpha of 0.70% (t-statistic = 3.32) and FFCPS alpha of 0.68% per month (t-statistic = 3.21) are very similar in magnitude to the average return, and highly statistically significant.

We next examine the relation between $\Delta IVolP$ and future stock returns after controlling for $\Delta IVolC$ using bivariate dependent-sort portfolio analyses. To do so, we sort stocks first into $\Delta IVolC$ quintiles and then, within each $\Delta IVolC$ quintile, into $\Delta IVolP$ quintiles. Table 17.7 presents the results of these analyses using equal-weighted (Panel A) and value-weighted (Panel B) portfolios.

TABLE 17.6   Bivariate Dependent-Sort Portfolio Analysis—Δ*IVolC*

This table presents the results of bivariate dependent-sort portfolio analyses of the relation between Δ*IVolC* and future stock returns after controlling for the effect of Δ*IVolP*. Each month, all stocks in the Options sample are sorted into five groups based on an ascending sort of Δ*IVolP*. Within each Δ*IVolP* group all stocks are sorted into five portfolios based on an ascending sort of Δ*IVolC*. The quintile breakpoints used to create the portfolios are calculated using all stocks in the CRSP sample. The table presents the average one-month-ahead excess return (in percent per month) for each of the 25 portfolios as well as for the average Δ*IVolP* quintile portfolio within each quintile of Δ*IVolC*. Also shown are the average return, FFC alpha, and FFCPS alpha of a long–short zero-cost portfolio that is long the fifth Δ*IVolC* quintile portfolio and short the first Δ*IVolC* quintile portfolio in each Δ*IVolP* quintile. *t*-statistics (in parentheses), adjusted following Newey and West (1987) using six lags, testing the null hypothesis that the average return or alpha is equal to zero, are shown in parentheses. Panel A presents results for equal-weighted portfolios. Panel B presents results for value-weighted portfolios.

Panel A: Equal-Weighted Portfolio Returns						
	Δ*IVolP* 1	Δ*IVolP* 2	Δ*IVolP* 3	Δ*IVolP* 4	Δ*IVolP* 5	Δ*IVolP* Avg
Δ*IVolC* 1	0.04	0.31	0.33	0.39	−0.20	0.17
Δ*IVolC* 2	0.57	0.58	0.65	0.82	0.62	0.65
Δ*IVolC* 3	0.50	0.55	0.74	0.93	0.68	0.68
Δ*IVolC* 4	0.79	0.78	0.87	0.85	1.16	0.89
Δ*IVolC* 5	1.30	1.27	1.10	1.03	0.58	1.06
Δ*IVolC* 5-1	1.26	0.96	0.76	0.64	0.78	0.88
	(3.96)	(4.13)	(3.57)	(2.72)	(2.45)	(5.47)
Δ*IVolC* 5-1 FFC α	1.22	0.99	0.78	0.65	0.71	0.87
	(4.10)	(4.17)	(3.54)	(2.71)	(2.40)	(5.31)
Δ*IVolC* 5-1 FFCPS α	1.16	0.96	0.75	0.67	0.74	0.86
	(3.85)	(4.01)	(3.35)	(2.74)	(2.46)	(5.14)
Panel B: Value-Weighted Portfolio Returns						
	Δ*IVolP* 1	Δ*IVolP* 2	Δ*IVolP* 3	Δ*IVolP* 4	Δ*IVolP* 5	Δ*IVolP* Avg
Δ*IVolC* 1	0.10	0.04	0.44	0.19	−0.45	0.07
Δ*IVolC* 2	0.24	0.33	0.71	0.38	0.24	0.38
Δ*IVolC* 3	0.43	0.56	0.32	0.58	0.77	0.54
Δ*IVolC* 4	0.41	0.83	0.57	1.10	1.44	0.87
Δ*IVolC* 5	0.95	1.05	0.94	0.94	0.25	0.83
Δ*IVolC* 5-1	0.85	1.00	0.50	0.75	0.71	0.76
	(2.04)	(2.75)	(1.71)	(2.11)	(1.28)	(3.67)
Δ*IVolC* 5-1 FFC α	0.74	1.17	0.52	0.61	0.43	0.70
	(1.79)	(3.14)	(1.77)	(1.72)	(0.82)	(3.32)
Δ*IVolC* 5-1 FFCPS α	0.57	1.11	0.46	0.66	0.60	0.68
	(1.38)	(2.96)	(1.56)	(1.82)	(1.15)	(3.21)

TABLE 17.7   Bivariate Dependent-Sort Portfolio Analysis—$\Delta IVolP$
This table presents the results of bivariate dependent-sort portfolio analyses of the relation between $\Delta IVolP$ and future stock returns after controlling for the effect of $\Delta IVolC$. Each month, all stocks in the Options sample are sorted into five groups based on an ascending sort of $\Delta IVolC$. Within each $\Delta IVolC$ group all stocks are sorted into five portfolios based on an ascending sort of $\Delta IVolP$. The quintile breakpoints used to create the portfolios are calculated using all stocks in the CRSP sample. The table presents the average one-month-ahead excess return (in percent per month) for each of the 25 portfolios as well as for the average $\Delta IVolC$ quintile portfolio within each quintile of $\Delta IVolP$. Also shown are the average return, FFC alpha, and FFCPS alpha of a long–short zero-cost portfolio that is long the fifth $\Delta IVolP$ quintile portfolio and short the first $\Delta IVolP$ quintile portfolio in each $\Delta IVolC$ quintile. t-statistics (in parentheses), adjusted following Newey and West (1987) using six lags, testing the null hypothesis that the average return or alpha is equal to zero, are shown in parentheses. Panel A presents results for equal-weighted portfolios. Panel B presents results for value-weighted portfolios.

Panel A: Equal-Weighted Portfolio Returns						
	$\Delta IVolC$ 1	$\Delta IVolC$ 2	$\Delta IVolC$ 3	$\Delta IVolC$ 4	$\Delta IVolC$ 5	$\Delta IVolC$ Avg
$\Delta IVolP$ 1	0.34	0.78	0.97	1.02	1.60	0.94
$\Delta IVolP$ 2	0.32	0.53	0.80	1.04	1.08	0.75
$\Delta IVolP$ 3	0.13	0.55	0.60	0.96	1.04	0.66
$\Delta IVolP$ 4	0.20	0.49	0.78	0.71	1.34	0.70
$\Delta IVolP$ 5	0.02	0.42	0.71	0.59	0.25	0.40
$\Delta IVolP$ 5-1	−0.32	−0.36	−0.25	−0.43	−1.35	−0.54
	(−1.04)	(−1.75)	(−1.34)	(−2.11)	(−4.61)	(−4.02)
$\Delta IVolP$ 5-1 FFC α	−0.33	−0.47	−0.30	−0.49	−1.38	−0.59
	(−1.13)	(−2.31)	(−1.54)	(−2.43)	(−5.05)	(−4.35)
$\Delta IVolP$ 5-1 FFCPS α	−0.46	−0.49	−0.39	−0.54	−1.36	−0.65
	(−1.60)	(−2.41)	(−2.02)	(−2.64)	(−4.90)	(−4.77)

Panel B: Value-Weighted Portfolio Returns						
	$\Delta IVolC$ 1	$\Delta IVolC$ 2	$\Delta IVolC$ 3	$\Delta IVolC$ 4	$\Delta IVolC$ 5	$\Delta IVolC$ Avg
$\Delta IVolP$ 1	0.35	0.21	1.11	1.24	1.23	0.83
$\Delta IVolP$ 2	0.27	0.19	0.51	0.70	0.81	0.49
$\Delta IVolP$ 3	0.21	0.60	0.30	0.81	1.01	0.59
$\Delta IVolP$ 4	−0.01	0.46	0.51	0.73	1.36	0.61
$\Delta IVolP$ 5	0.11	0.13	0.38	0.67	−0.04	0.25
$\Delta IVolP$ 5-1	−0.24	−0.08	−0.73	−0.57	−1.26	−0.58
	(−0.45)	(−0.25)	(−2.48)	(−1.78)	(−2.65)	(−2.83)
$\Delta IVolP$ 5-1 FFC α	−0.39	−0.22	−0.78	−0.65	−1.47	−0.70
	(−0.75)	(−0.67)	(−2.58)	(−2.08)	(−3.16)	(−3.41)
$\Delta IVolP$ 5-1 FFCPS α	−0.65	−0.30	−0.88	−0.71	−1.33	−0.77
	(−1.26)	(−0.91)	(−2.91)	(−2.23)	(−2.86)	(−3.76)

When using equal-weighted portfolios, the average returns and alphas of the $\Delta IVolP$ 5-1 portfolios are all negative and, in most cases, statistically significant. The results are strongest for stocks with high values of $\Delta IVolC$. In quintiles four and five of $\Delta IVolC$, the $\Delta IVolP$ difference portfolio generates an average return -0.43% per month (t-statistic $= -2.11$) and -1.35% per month (t-statistic $= -4.61$), respectively. Adjusting for risk does not explain the returns of these portfolios since the FFC and FFCPS alphas are similar in magnitude and statistical significance to the average returns. In $\Delta IVolC$ quintile three, the average return and FFC alpha of the $\Delta IVolP$ 5-1 portfolio are statistically indistinguishable from zero, but the FFCPS alpha of -0.39% per month (t-statistic $= -2.02$) is statistically negative. In quintile two of $\Delta IVolC$, the $\Delta IVolP$ difference portfolio generates a negative and statistically significant average return, FFC alpha, and FFCPS alpha, but in the first $\Delta IVolC$ quintile, the average return and alphas of the $\Delta IVolP$ 5-1 portfolio are statistically indistinguishable from zero. Most importantly, the average return, FFC alpha, and FFCPS alpha generated by the $\Delta IVolP$ 5-1 portfolio in the average $\Delta IVolC$ quintile of -0.54% per month (t-statistic $= -4.02$), -0.59% per month (t-statistic $= -4.35$), and -0.65% per month (t-statistic $= -4.77$), respectively, are all negative, of economically important magnitude, and highly statistically significant.

The results of the value-weighted portfolio analysis, shown in Panel B of Table 17.7, are similar. As in the equal-weighted portfolio analysis, the negative relation between $\Delta IVolP$ and future stock returns is strongest among stocks with high values of $\Delta IVolC$. In the first two $\Delta IVolC$ quintiles, the average return and alphas of the $\Delta IVolP$ 5-1 portfolio are negative but statistically indistinguishable from zero. In $\Delta IVolC$ quintiles three, four, and five, however, the $\Delta IVolP$ 5-1 portfolio generates large negative average and abnormal returns that are highly statistically significant. In the average $\Delta IVolC$ quintile, the $\Delta IVolP$ difference portfolio produces an average return of -0.58% per month (t-statistic $= -2.83$), FFC alpha of -0.70% per month (t-statistic $= -3.41$), and FFCPS alpha of -0.77% per month (t-statistic $= -3.76$), indicating a strong negative relation between $\Delta IVolP$ and one-month-ahead stock returns.

To further examine the ability of each of $\Delta IVolC$ and $\Delta IVolP$ to predict future stock returns, we perform equal-weighted and value-weighted bivariate independent-sort portfolio analyses of these relations. The results of these analyses, presented in Table 17.8, are similar to those of the dependent-sort analyses.

When using equal-weighted portfolios (Panel A), the $\Delta IVolC$ 5-1 portfolio in the average $\Delta IVolP$ quintile generates an average monthly return of 1.26% (t-statistic $= 6.38$), FFC alpha of 1.22% (t-statistic $= 6.04$), and FFCPS alpha of 1.20% (t-statistic $= 5.88$). Furthermore, within each $\Delta IVolP$ quintile, the $\Delta IVolC$ difference portfolio generates large, positive, and highly statistically significant raw and abnormal returns.

The negative relation between $\Delta IVolP$ and future stock returns is also strong in the equal-weighted portfolio analysis. The $\Delta IVolP$ 5-1 portfolio in the average $\Delta IVolC$ quintile generates a raw return of -0.69% per month with a corresponding t-statistic of -3.43. The FFC alpha of -0.73% per month (t-statistic $= -3.52$) and FFCPS alpha of -0.82% per month (t-statistic $= -3.97$) once again indicate that the average return is not driven by sensitivity to the factors included in these

TABLE 17.8   Bivariate Independent-Sort Portfolio Analysis—$\Delta IVolC$ and $\Delta IVolP$

This table presents the results of bivariate independent-sort portfolio analyses of the relation between future stock returns and each of $\Delta IVolC$ and $\Delta IVolP$ after controlling for the other. Each month, all stocks in the Options sample are sorted into five groups based on an ascending sort of $\Delta IVolC$. All stocks are independently sorted into five groups based on an ascending sort of $\Delta IVolP$. The quintile breakpoints used to create the groups are calculated using all stocks in the Options sample. The intersections of the $\Delta IVolC$ and $\Delta IVolP$ groups are used to form 25 portfolios. The table presents the average one-month-ahead excess return (in percent per month) for each of the 25 portfolios as well as for the average $\Delta IVolC$ quintile portfolio within each quintile of $\Delta IVolP$ and the average $\Delta IVolP$ quintile within each $\Delta IVolC$ quintile. Also shown are the average return, FFC alpha, and FFCPS alpha of a long–short zero-cost portfolio that is long the fifth $\Delta IVolC$ ($\Delta IVolP$) quintile portfolio and short the first $\Delta IVolC$ ($\Delta IVolP$) quintile portfolio in each $\Delta IVolP$ ($\Delta IVolC$) quintile. t-statistics (in parentheses), adjusted following Newey and West (1987) using six lags, testing the null hypothesis that the average return or alpha is equal to zero, are shown in parentheses. Panel A presents results for equal-weighted portfolios. Panel B presents results for value-weighted portfolios.

	Panel A: Equal-Weighted Portfolio Returns								
	$\Delta IVolP$ 1	$\Delta IVolP$ 2	$\Delta IVolP$ 3	$\Delta IVolP$ 4	$\Delta IVolP$ 5	$\Delta IVolP$ Avg	$\Delta IVolP$ 5-1	$\Delta IVolP$ 5-1 FFC α	$\Delta IVolP$ 5-1 FFCPS α
$\Delta IVolC$ 1	0.31	0.36	0.27	0.27	−0.51	0.14	−0.82	−0.83	−0.93
							(−2.60)	(−2.71)	(−3.05)
$\Delta IVolC$ 2	0.80	0.52	0.49	0.61	−0.01	0.48	−0.81	−0.93	−1.00
							(−2.16)	(−2.42)	(−2.57)
$\Delta IVolC$ 3	1.16	0.71	0.71	0.82	0.69	0.82	−0.47	−0.52	−0.67
							(−1.28)	(−1.38)	(−1.76)
$\Delta IVolC$ 4	0.86	1.16	0.94	0.90	0.42	0.86	−0.44	−0.42	−0.52
							(−1.22)	(−1.16)	(−1.42)
$\Delta IVolC$ 5	1.78	1.81	1.47	1.09	0.86	1.40	−0.92	−0.94	−0.98
							(−2.61)	(−2.68)	(−2.74)
$\Delta IVolC$ Avg	0.98	0.91	0.78	0.74	0.29		−0.69	−0.73	−0.82
							(−3.43)	(−3.52)	(−3.97)
$\Delta IVolC$ 5-1	1.48	1.44	1.20	0.81	1.37	1.26			
	(3.90)	(3.86)	(3.28)	(2.28)	(4.80)	(6.38)			
$\Delta IVolC$ 5-1 FFC α	1.39	1.46	1.10	0.86	1.27	1.22			
	(3.74)	(3.85)	(2.95)	(2.36)	(4.53)	(6.04)			
$\Delta IVolC$ 5-1 FFCPS α	1.33	1.39	1.11	0.90	1.28	1.20			
	(3.52)	(3.63)	(2.93)	(2.44)	(4.48)	(5.88)			

(continued)

models. Interestingly, in the independent-sort analysis, the negative relation between $\Delta IVolP$ and future stock returns appears strongest for stocks with high or low values of $\Delta IVolC$, and relatively weak for stocks with more moderate $\Delta IVolC$ values. In quintiles one, two, and five of $\Delta IVolC$, the average return and alphas of the $\Delta IVolP$

TABLE 17.8 *(Continued)*

	Panel B: Value-Weighted Portfolio Returns								
	$\Delta IVolP$ 1	$\Delta IVolP$ 2	$\Delta IVolP$ 3	$\Delta IVolP$ 4	$\Delta IVolP$ 5	$\Delta IVolP$ Avg	$\Delta IVolP$ 5-1	$\Delta IVolP$ 5-1 FFC α	$\Delta IVolP$ 5-1 FFCPS α
$\Delta IVolC$ 1	0.30	0.18	0.50	0.26	−0.01	0.25	−0.31	−0.43	−0.63
							(−0.64)	(−0.89)	(−1.33)
$\Delta IVolC$ 2	0.12	0.44	0.65	0.05	−0.04	0.24	−0.16	−0.21	−0.28
							(−0.35)	(−0.44)	(−0.59)
$\Delta IVolC$ 3	1.02	0.75	0.30	0.55	0.32	0.59	−0.70	−0.94	−1.07
							(−1.33)	(−1.78)	(−2.01)
$\Delta IVolC$ 4	0.78	1.15	0.75	0.90	0.45	0.81	−0.33	−0.46	−0.47
							(−0.72)	(−1.01)	(−1.04)
$\Delta IVolC$ 5	1.75	1.73	1.01	0.88	0.80	1.23	−0.95	−0.89	−0.93
							(−2.02)	(−1.92)	(−1.98)
$\Delta IVolC$ Avg	0.79	0.85	0.64	0.53	0.30		−0.49	−0.58	−0.68
							(−2.02)	(−2.38)	(−2.76)
$\Delta IVolC$ 5-1	1.45	1.55	0.50	0.62	0.81	0.99			
	(3.14)	(3.62)	(1.45)	(1.37)	(1.58)	(4.69)			
$\Delta IVolC$ 5-1 FFC α	1.12	1.57	0.49	0.56	0.65	0.88			
	(2.48)	(3.63)	(1.38)	(1.25)	(1.31)	(4.22)			
$\Delta IVolC$ 5-1 FFCPS α	1.07	1.52	0.51	0.72	0.77	0.92			
	(2.33)	(3.46)	(1.42)	(1.58)	(1.54)	(4.34)			

difference portfolios are negative and highly statistically significant. In quintiles three and four of $\Delta IVolC$, however, the $\Delta IVolP$ 5-1 portfolio generates negative, economically large, but statistically insignificant (with the exception of the FFCPS alpha in $\Delta IVolC$ quintile three) average returns and alphas.

The results of the independent-sort value-weighted portfolio analysis, shown in Panel B of Table 17.8, show that both the positive relation between $\Delta IVolC$ and future stock returns, and the negative relation between $\Delta IVolP$ and future stock returns, are robust to the use of value-weighted portfolios. In the average $\Delta IVolP$ quintile, the value-weighted $\Delta IVolC$ 5-1 portfolio generates an average monthly return of 0.99% (*t*-statistic = 4.69), FFC alpha of 0.88% (*t*-statistic = 4.22), and FFCPS alpha of 0.92% (*t*-statistic = 4.34). Looking at the individual $\Delta IVolP$ quintiles, however, the results indicate that the positive relation between $\Delta IVolC$ and future stock returns is driven by stocks with low values of $\Delta IVolP$. In the lowest two $\Delta IVolP$ quintiles, the average raw and abnormal returns of the $\Delta IVolC$ 5-1 portfolios are positive, large, and highly statistically significant. In quintiles three, four, and five of $\Delta IVolP$, however, while the $\Delta IVolC$ difference portfolio generates positive and economically large average returns and alphas, none of these values are statistically distinguishable from zero.

The $\Delta IVolP$ 5-1 portfolio for the average $\Delta IVolC$ quintile in the independent-sort value-weighted portfolio analysis generates an average return of −0.49% per month (*t*-statistic = −2.02), FFC alpha of −0.58% per month (*t*-statistic = −2.38), and FFCPS alpha of −0.68% per month (*t*-statistic = −2.76), each of which is economically important and highly statistically significant. Interestingly, while the raw returns and alphas of the Δ*IVolP* 5-1 portfolios in each Δ*IVolC* quintile are all negative, they are statistically significant only in the fifth Δ*IVolC* quintile.

The final set of analyses we perform to examine the ability of Δ*IVolC* and Δ*IVolP* to predict the cross section of future stock returns are FM regression analyses. The results of these analyses are shown in Table 17.9.

Specification (1) includes only Δ*IVolC* and Δ*IVolP* as independent variables in the cross-sectional regressions. Consistent with the results of the portfolio analyses, the FM regression analysis produces an average coefficient of 0.039 on Δ*IVolC* with a corresponding *t*-statistic of 5.26, indicating a strong positive relation between Δ*IVolC* and future stock returns. The negative average coefficient of −0.030 (*t*-statistic = −4.98) indicates a strong negative relation between Δ*IVolP* and future stock returns.

In specification (2), we include $Vol^{1M} - IVol$ and *IVolSkew* as control variables. We do not include *IVolSpread* as a control because of mechanical multicolinearity between Δ*IVolC*, Δ*IVolP*, and *IVolSpread*. The results indicate that $Vol^{1M} - IVol$ and *IVolSkew* fail to explain the relations between future stock returns and each of Δ*IVolC* and Δ*IVolP* since the average coefficient of 0.022 (*t*-statistic = 2.81) on Δ*IVolC* remains positive and statistically significant, and the average coefficient of −0.017 (*t*-statistic = −2.54) on Δ*IVolP* remains negative and statistically significant. Furthermore, the results indicate that the negative relations between future stock returns and each of $Vol^{1M} - IVol$ and *IVolSkew* are not driven by changes in call or put implied volatility since the average coefficients on both $Vol^{1M} - IVol$ and *IVolSkew* are negative and statistically significant.

We next examine a specification that controls for the variables used in previous chapters of this book. The results of specification (3) in Table 17.9 show that the positive relation between Δ*IVolC* and future stock returns, as well as the negative relation between Δ*IVolP* and future stock returns, remain highly statistically significant after controlling for β, *Size*, *BM*, *Mom*, *Rev*, *Illiq*, *CoSkew*, *IdioSkew*, and *IdioVol*.

The last specification we examine includes all of the variables as independent variables in the cross-sectional regressions. As discussed earlier, due to the mechanical relation between $Vol^{1M} - IVol$ and *IdioVol*, we exclude *IdioVol* from this analysis. The average coefficient of 0.015 (*t*-statistic = 2.65) on Δ*IVolC* indicates that none of the other variables can explain the strong positive relation between Δ*IVolC* and future stock returns. Similarly, the average coefficient of −0.022 (*t*-statistic = −3.05) on Δ*IVolP* shows that the negative relation between Δ*IVolP* and future stock returns is robust to controls for all other phenomena documented in this book. Additionally, the negative coefficients on each of $Vol^{1M} - IVol$ and *IVolSkew* are negative and highly statistically significant, indicating that the negative relations between these variables and future stock returns are robust to the inclusion of the full set of control variables.

We examine the economic magnitude of the Δ*IVolC* and Δ*IVolP* effects by multiplying the average coefficient from specification (4) by the average standard deviation of the cross-sectional distribution of the given variable (shown in Table 17.1). The results indicate that a one-standard-deviation difference in Δ*IVolC*

TABLE 17.9   Fama–MacBeth Regression Analysis—Implied Volatility Changes
This table presents the results of Fama and MacBeth (1973) regression analyses of the relations between expected stock returns and each of $\Delta IVolC$ and $\Delta IVolP$. Each column in the table presents results for a different cross-sectional regression specification. The dependent variable in all specifications is the one-month-ahead excess stock return. The independent variables are indicated in the first column. Independent variables are winsorized at the 0.5% level on a monthly basis. The table presents average slope and intercept coefficients along with t-statistics (in parentheses), adjusted following Newey and West (1987) using six lags, testing the null hypothesis that the average coefficient is equal to zero. The rows labeled Adj. R^2 and n present the average adjusted R-squared and the number of data points, respectively, for the cross-sectional regressions.

Panel A: Option Variables			
	(1)	(2)	(3)	(4)
---	---	---	---	---
$\Delta IVolC$	0.039	0.022	0.032	0.015
	(5.26)	(2.81)	(5.73)	(2.65)
$\Delta IVolP$	−0.030	−0.017	−0.033	−0.022
	(−4.98)	(−2.54)	(−5.00)	(−3.05)
$Vol^{1M} - IVol$		−0.006		−0.009
		(−1.90)		(−3.35)
$IVolSkew$		−0.038		−0.037
		(−5.96)		(−6.03)
β			0.170	0.160
			(0.46)	(0.43)
$Size$			−0.158	−0.118
			(−2.07)	(−1.36)
BM			−0.061	0.014
			(−0.33)	(0.08)
Mom			−0.002	−0.002
			(−0.45)	(−0.50)
Rev			−0.018	−0.017
			(−2.25)	(−2.11)
$Illiq$			−0.057	−2.198
			(−0.02)	(−0.70)
$CoSkew$			0.015	0.016
			(1.80)	(1.83)
$IdioSkew$			−0.086	−0.113
			(−1.25)	(−1.60)
$IdioVol$			−0.008	
			(−2.08)	
Intercept	0.710	0.932	1.924	1.580
	(1.56)	(2.13)	(2.85)	(2.01)
Adj. R^2	0.01	0.01	0.09	0.09
n	1599	1599	1328	1328

corresponds to a difference of 0.19% (0.015 × 12.97) in expected monthly return. A one-standard-deviation difference in $\Delta IVolP$ corresponds to an expected return difference of 0.28% (0.022 × 12.76) per month. To examine the difference in expected returns between stocks with extremely high and low changes in call and put implied volatility, we multiply the average coefficient by the difference between the 95th percentile and fifth percentile of the cross-sectional distribution of the given variable in the average month. Doing so, we find that the difference in expected return between stocks with 95th percentile and fifth percentile values of $\Delta IVolC$ is 0.47% (0.015 × [15.87 − (−15.52)]) per month. For $\Delta IVolP$, this difference is 0.66% (0.022 × [15.20 − (−14.83)]) per month. The results therefore indicate that, after controlling for all of the other effects documented in this book, the relations between future stock returns and each of $\Delta IVolC$ and $\Delta IVolP$ are not only highly statistically significant but also economically important.

In summary, the results presented in this section indicate that, consistent with Bali and Hovakimian (2009) and Cremers and Weinbaum (2010), there is a strong positive relation between $IVolSpread$ and future stock returns. We also demonstrate a strong negative relation between $Vol^{1M} − IVol$ and future stock returns, as in Bali and Hovakimian (2009) and a strong negative relation between $IVolSkew$ and future stock returns, as in Xing et al. (2010). Finally, our analyses detect a positive relation between $\Delta IVolC$ and future stock returns and a negative relation between $\Delta IVolP$ and future stock returns, as documented by An et al. (2014).

17.7   OPTION RETURNS

In the final set of analyses we undertake in this book, we examine the ability of the realized minus implied volatility spread to predict future straddle, delta-hedged call, and delta-hedge put returns. Each of these positions is designed to effectively take a long volatility position while having little exposure to moves in the underlying stock. Goyal and Saretto (2009) show that the returns of each of these option positions is positively related to the realized minus implied volatility spread. Following Goyal and Saretto (2009), when calculating the realized minus implied volatility spread, we use 12 months of daily return data to calculate realized volatility. The predictive variable of interest in this section, therefore, is $Vol^{12M} − IVol$. However, in unreported analyses, we have verified that the relations are robust to the use of $Vol^{1M} − IVol$ as the measure of realized minus implied volatility spread.

We begin with univariate portfolio analyses examining the ability of $Vol^{12M} − IVol$ to predict future straddle, delta-hedged call, and delta-hedged put returns. The results of these analyses are presented in Table 17.10. When performing the factor analyses of the returns of the difference portfolios, it is necessary to calculate the returns of the factors for the period during which the option positions are held, which does not, in most cases, correspond perfectly to a calendar month. Factor returns corresponding to the holding periods are therefore calculated by compounding the daily returns of the market (MKT), size (SMB), value (HML), and momentum (MOM) factors over all

TABLE 17.10   Univariate Portfolio Analysis—Option Returns

This table presents the results of univariate portfolio analyses of the relation between $Vol^{12M} - IVol$ and future option returns. Monthly portfolios are formed by sorting all stocks in the Options sample into portfolios using $Vol^{12M} - IVol$ decile breakpoints calculated using all stocks in the Options sample. Panel A (Panel B) shows the average equal-weighted (value-weighted) one-month-ahead excess return (in percent per month) for portfolios of straddles, delta-hedged calls, and delta-hedged puts for each of the 10 decile portfolios. The table also shows the average return and FFC alpha of the portfolio that is long the 10th decile portfolio and short the first decile portfolio. Newey and West (1987) t-statistics, adjusted using six lags, testing the null hypothesis that the average 10-1 portfolio return or alpha is equal to zero, are shown in parentheses.

Panel A: Equal-Weighted Portfolios Returns

Position	1	2	3	4	5	6	7	8	9	10	10-1	FFC α
Straddle	−23.85	−15.50	−12.57	−10.64	−8.44	−7.35	−6.50	−5.70	−1.89	−0.05	23.81	23.83
											(12.48)	(12.79)
ΔHedged call	−22.31	−14.92	−12.07	−10.07	−7.84	−6.69	−5.70	−4.78	−0.69	1.77	24.08	24.20
											(12.38)	(12.78)
ΔHedged put	−23.58	−15.96	−13.07	−11.26	−9.03	−8.06	−7.23	−6.46	−2.64	−1.09	22.49	22.54
											(12.22)	(12.38)

Panel B: Value-Weighted Portfolios Returns

Position	1	2	3	4	5	6	7	8	9	10	10-1	FFC α
Straddle	−22.51	−16.61	−12.29	−12.16	−10.58	−11.70	−9.00	−7.51	−4.32	−2.48	20.02	19.53
											(6.50)	(6.92)
ΔHedged call	−21.27	−16.15	−12.08	−11.88	−10.54	−11.26	−8.40	−6.82	−3.38	−1.03	20.24	19.67
											(6.73)	(7.07)
ΔHedged put	−22.42	−17.16	−12.61	−12.69	−11.12	−12.43	−9.70	−8.09	−4.97	−3.37	19.04	18.46
											(6.29)	(6.63)

days during the holding period. Daily factor return data are taken from Ken French's data library. Since daily return data for the Pastor and Stambaugh (2003) liquidity factor are not available, we use only the FFC model when risk-adjusting the returns of the option portfolios.

Panel A of Table 17.10 demonstrates that when using equal-weighted portfolios, the average excess returns of the straddle portfolios increase monotonically from −23.85% per month for straddles on stocks in decile one of $Vol^{12M} - IVol$ to −0.05% per month straddles on for stocks in $Vol^{12M} - IVol$ decile 10. The $Vol^{12M} - IVol$ 10-1 straddle portfolio generates an average monthly return of 23.81% (t-statistic = 12.48), indicating a strong positive relation between $Vol^{12M} - IVol$ and future straddle returns. Risk-adjusting the returns of this portfolio has very little effect. The FFC alpha of 23.81% per month (t-statistic = 12.79) is very similar to the average return.

It should be noted that while the return of the difference portfolio is extremely large in magnitude, it is potentially not reflective of the actual returns that could be realized by a long–short straddle portfolio. The main reason for this is that to enter into short straddle positions, it is necessary to satisfy margin requirements in excess of the price of the straddle.[6] Furthermore, options, by their nature, are highly levered securities. Thus, instead of interpreting this result as the return of a long–short straddle portfolio, it may be more accurate to interpret it as the difference in average returns between straddles on stocks in the 10th decile of $Vol^{12M} - IVol$ and those in the first decile of $Vol^{12M} - IVol$. A similar commentary holds for the remaining portfolio analyses discussed in this section.

Table 17.10 shows that the returns of delta-hedged calls and delta-hedged puts exhibit similar cross-sectional patterns. The average excess returns of the equal-weighted delta-hedged call portfolios increase from -22.31% per month for stocks in $Vol^{12M} - IVol$ decile one to 1.77% per month for stocks in the 10th $Vol^{12M} - IVol$ decile portfolio. The 10-1 portfolio generates an average return of 24.08% per month (t-statistic = 12.38) and FFC alpha of 24.20% per month (t-statistic = 12.78). For portfolios of delta-hedged puts, the average excess returns increase monotonically from -23.58% for decile portfolio one to -1.09% per month for decile portfolio 10. The difference of 22.49% per month (t-statistic = 12.22), as well as the associated FFC alpha of 22.54% per month (t-statistic = 12.38), are all positive, economically large, and highly statistically significant.

The results of value-weighted univariate portfolio analyses, presented in Panel B of Table 17.10, are very similar to those of the equal-weighted portfolio analyses. We therefore refrain from a prolonged evaluation of these results. However, there is one issue pertaining to value-weighted analyses that warrants a short discussion. In the analyses whose results are presented in Panel B, we have used *MktCap* as the weighting variable, consistent with all other value-weighted portfolio analyses performed in this book. However, one may argue that because the positions held in the portfolios are not stocks, but option positions (and in the case of the delta-hedged calls and puts, forward positions) it may be more appropriate to weight the portfolios using some other weighting variable, such as option open interest, that is more indicative of the importance of a given stock's options in the overall option market. We leave this exercise to the reader.

Our final set of analyses examines the relation between $Vol^{12M} - IVol$ and future option returns using FM regression analyses. For each option position (straddle, delta-hedged call, and delta-hedged put), we employ a specification that includes only $Vol^{12M} - IVol$ as an independent variable, $Vol^{12M} - IVol$ along with *IVolSpread*, *IVolSkew*, $\Delta IVolC$, and $\Delta IVolP$ as controls, and then all of these option variables along with all of the variables examined in the previous chapters as independent variables. None of our specifications include $Vol^{1M} - IVol$ as an independent variable due to its mechanical relation with the focal variable $Vol^{12M} - IVol$. The dependent variable in the regressions is the one-month-ahead straddle, delta-hedged call, or delta-hedged put excess return.

The results of the FM regression analyses are presented in Table 17.11. The results show that, regardless of specification, $Vol^{12M} - IVol$ has a strong positive

---

[6]Goyal and Saretto (2009) indicate that margin requirements and execution costs may substantially decrease the profitability of a trading strategy based on the results in Table 17.10. Murray (2013) examines the effects of margin requirements on the returns of short option positions.

TABLE 17.11   Fama–MacBeth Regression Analysis—Option Returns

This table presents the results of Fama and MacBeth (1973) regression analyses of the relations between $Vol^{12M} - IVol$ and the expected returns of straddles, delta-hedged calls, and delta-hedged puts. Each column in the table presents results for a different cross-sectional regression specification. The option position whose excess return is used as the independent variable is indicated in the column headers. The independent variables are indicated in the first column. Independent variables are winsorized at the 0.5% level on a monthly basis. The table presents average slope and intercept coefficients along with t-statistics (in parentheses), adjusted following Newey and West (1987) using six lags, testing the null hypothesis that the average coefficient is equal to zero. The rows labeled Adj. R^2 and n present the average adjusted R-squared and the number of data points, respectively, for the cross-sectional regressions.

	Straddle	Straddle	Straddle	Δ Hedged Call	Δ Hedged Call	Δ Hedged Call	Δ Hedged Put	Δ Hedged Put	Δ Hedged Put
$Vol^{12M} - IVol$	0.560	0.541	0.542	0.566	0.543	0.544	0.530	0.520	0.523
	(11.50)	(10.50)	(10.56)	(11.10)	(10.59)	(10.53)	(11.15)	(9.99)	(9.88)
IVolSpread		0.186	0.181		-0.640	-0.647		0.901	0.915
		(3.40)	(3.02)		(-12.71)	(-11.75)		(12.46)	(11.74)
IVolSkew		0.133	0.150		0.141	0.158		0.160	0.179
		(3.25)	(3.27)		(3.49)	(3.46)		(3.80)	(3.72)
ΔIVolC		-0.010	-0.068		-0.058	-0.116		0.027	-0.026
		(-0.36)	(-2.46)		(-2.11)	(-3.78)		(1.06)	(-1.00)
ΔIVolP		-0.009	-0.029		0.037	0.027		-0.046	-0.064
		(-0.26)	(-0.89)		(1.11)	(0.79)		(-1.43)	(-2.08)
β			1.118			0.763			1.073
			(0.93)			(0.64)			(0.89)
Size			-0.986			-0.999			-0.986
			(-3.07)			(-3.22)			(-3.15)
BM			-0.209			-0.123			0.035
			(-0.22)			(-0.13)			(0.04)
Mom			-0.028			-0.026			-0.028
			(-1.77)			(-1.83)			(-1.87)
Rev			-0.183			-0.167			-0.175
			(-4.96)			(-4.64)			(-4.98)
Illiq			-59.571			-57.661			-56.609
			(-4.27)			(-3.94)			(-4.18)
CoSkew			0.080			0.072			0.069
			(3.12)			(3.03)			(2.78)
IdioSkew			-0.648			-0.623			-0.633
			(-1.67)			(-1.54)			(-1.65)
IdioVol			-0.058			-0.058			-0.053
			(-3.60)			(-3.55)			(-3.47)
Intercept	-8.871	-9.301	-1.719	-7.950	-9.037	-1.002	-9.478	-9.632	-2.239
	(-5.21)	(-5.49)	(-0.52)	(-4.19)	(-4.90)	(-0.30)	(-5.42)	(-5.48)	(-0.70)
Adj. R^2	0.01	0.01	0.04	0.01	0.02	0.04	0.01	0.02	0.04
n	1582	1569	1325	1582	1569	1325	1582	1569	1325

cross-sectional relation with future option returns. When straddle excess return is the dependent variable, the average coefficient on $Vol^{12M} - IVol$ of 0.560 in the univariate specification is highly statistically significant with a t-statistic of 11.50. When the other option variables are included as controls, the average coefficient 0.541 (t-statistic = 10.50) is very similar. Finally, including the variables discussed in previous chapters of this book has almost no effect. In the full-specification regression, the average coefficient on $Vol^{12M} - IVol$ is 0.542 with a t-statistic of 10.56.

The results are very similar when the future delta-hedged call or put excess returns are used as the dependent variable. In the univariate regressions using delta-hedged call (delta-hedged put) excess return as the dependent variable, the average coefficient on $Vol^{12M} - IVol$ of 0.566 (0.530) is highly statistically significant with a t-statistic of 11.10 (11.15). When the option-based variables are included as controls, the average coefficient on $Vol^{12M} - IVol$ of 0.543 (0.520) remains highly statistically significant with a t-statistic of 10.59 (9.99). When the full set of controls is included in the specification, the average coefficient on $Vol^{12M} - IVol$ when the dependent variable is the delta-hedged call excess return of 0.544 (t-statistic = 10.53) remains positive and highly statistically significant. When delta-hedged put excess returns are used as the dependent variable, the average coefficient of 0.523 is once again highly statistically significant with a t-statistic of 9.88.

As in previous analyses, we examine the economic importance of the average coefficients on $Vol^{12M} - IVol$ by multiplying them by the standard deviation of 14.38 as well as the difference between the 95th and fifth percentile of 36.82 ($18.25 - (-18.57)$) of $Vol^{12M} - IVol$ in the average month (see Table 17.1). In all cases, we use the coefficient from the regression that includes the full set of controls. A one-standard-deviation difference in $Vol^{12M} - IVol$ is associated with 7.79% (0.542×14.38) difference in expected monthly straddle returns, a difference of 7.82% (0.544×14.38) in expected monthly delta-hedged call returns, and a difference of 7.52% (0.523×14.38) per month in expected delta-hedged put returns. The difference in expected option position returns for stocks with 95th and fifth percentile values of $Vol^{12M} - IVol$ is 19.96% (0.542×36.82) per month for straddles, 20.03% (0.544×36.82) per month for delta-hedged calls, and 19.26% (0.523×36.82) per month for delta-hedged puts. The magnitudes of these return differences are similar to those found in the portfolio analyses and indicate that not only are the relations between $Vol^{12M} - IVol$ and future option returns statistically significant, but they are also very economically large.

Finally, it is worth noting that the results in Table 17.11 indicate significant relations between several other variables and future option returns. The regressions indicate a positive relation between *IVolSpread* and each of future straddle and delta-hedged put returns, and a negative relation between *IVolSpread* and future delta-hedged call positions. *IVolSkew* is positively related to the future returns of all three option positions. $\Delta IVolC$ is negatively related to future delta-hedged call returns while $\Delta IVolP$ is negative related to future delta-hedged put returns. Additionally, *Size*, *Mom*, *Rev*, *Illiq*, and *IdioVol* all exhibit statistically significant negative relations with future option returns while *CoSkew* appears to be positively related to future option returns. These relations have not received a lot of attention in the empirical asset pricing literature and may warrant further investigation.

17.8 SUMMARY

In summary, in this chapter we investigate relations between variables generated from option data and future stock and option returns. Consistent with Bali and Hovakimian (2009) and Cremers and Weinbaum (2010), we demonstrate that the difference between put and call implied volatility is positively related to future stock returns. The difference between realized and implied volatility is, as documented by Bali and Hovakimian (2009), negatively related to future stock returns, as is the difference between OTM put implied volatility and ATM call implied volatility (Xing et al. (2010)). We also show that changes in call implied volatility are positively related to future stock returns and changes in put implied volatility are negatively related to future stock returns, a finding first put forth by An et al. (2014). The results for option returns indicate that, as demonstrated by Goyal and Saretto (2009), the realized minus implied volatility spread is strongly positively related to the returns of straddle positions, delta-hedged call positions, and delta-hedged put positions.

REFERENCES

An, B.-J., Ang, A., Bali, T. G., and Cakici, N. 2014. The joint cross section of stocks and options. Journal of Finance, 69(5), 2279–2337.

Ang, A., Hodrick, R. J., Xing, Y., and Zhang, X. 2006. The cross-section of volatility and expected returns. Journal of Finance, 61(1), 259–299.

Arditti, F. D. 1967. Risk and the required return on equity. Journal of Finance, 22(1), 19–36.

Arditti, F. D. 1971. Another look at mutual fund performance. Journal of Financial and Quantitative Analysis, 6(3), 909–912.

Bakshi, G. and Kapadia, N. 2003a. Delta-hedged gains and the negative volatility risk premium. Review of Financial Studies, 16(2), 527–566.

Bakshi, G. and Kapadia, N. 2003b. Volatility risk premium embedded in individual equity options: some new insights. Journal of Derivatives, 11(1), 45–54.

Bali, T. G. and Hovakimian, A. 2009. Volatility spreads and expected stock returns. Management Science, 55(11), 1797–1812.

Bali, T. G. and Murray, S. 2013. Does risk-neutral skewness predict the cross-section of equity option portfolio returns? Journal of Financial and Quantitative Analysis, 48(4), 1145–1171.

Black, F. and Scholes, M. S. 1973. The pricing of options and corporate liabilities. Journal of Political Economy, 81(3), 637–654.

Bollen, N. P. B. and Whaley, R. E. 2004. Does net buying pressure affect the shape of implied volatility functions. Journal of Finance, 59(2), 711–753.

Cao, J. and Han, B. 2013. Cross-section of option returns and idiosyncratic stock volatility. Journal of Financial Economics, 108(1), 231–249.

Carhart, M. M. 1997. On persistence in mutual fund performance. Journal of Finance, 52(1), 57–82.

Carr, P. and Wu, L. 2009. Variance risk premiums. Review of Financial Studies, 22(3), 1311–1341.

Chang, B. Y., Christoffersen, P., and Jacobs, K. 2013. Market skewness risk and the cross section of stock returns. Journal of Financial Economics, 107(1), 46–68.

Conine, T. E. and Tamarkin, M. J. 1981. On diversification given asymmetry in returns. Journal of Finance, 36(5), 1143–1155.

Conrad, J. S., Dittmar, R. F., and Ghysels, E. 2013. Ex ante skewness and expected stock returns. Journal of Finance, 68(1), 85–124.

Cox, J. C., Ross, S. A., and Rubinstein, M. 1979. Option pricing: a simplified approach. Journal of Financial Economics, 7(3), 229–263.

Cremers, M. and Weinbaum, D. 2010. Deviations from put-call parity and stock return predictability. Journal of Financial Quantitative Analysis, 45(2), 335–367.

DeMiguel, V., Plyakha, Y., Uppal, R., and Vilkov, G. 2013. Improving portfolio selection using option-implied volatility and skewness. Journal of Financial and Quantitative Analysis, 48(6), 1813–1845.

Fama, E. F. and French, K. R. 1993. Common risk factors in the returns on stocks and bonds. Journal of Financial Economics, 33(1), 3–56.

Fama, E. F. and MacBeth, J. D. 1973. Risk, return, and equilibrium: empirical tests. Journal of Political Economy, 81(3), 607.

Garleanu, N., Pedersen, L. H., and Poteshman, A. M. 2009. Demand-based option pricing. Review of Financial Studies, 22(10), 4259–4299.

Goyal, A. and Saretto, A. 2009. Cross-section of option returns and volatility. Journal of Financial Economics, 94(2), 310–326.

Harvey, C. R. and Siddique, A. 2000. Conditional skewness in asset pricing tests. Journal of Finance, 55(3), 1263–1295.

Jackwerth, J. C. and Rubinstein, M. 1996. Recovering probability distributions from option prices. Journal of Finance, 51(5), 1611–1631.

Kane, A. 1982. Skewness preference and portfolio choice. Journal of Financial and Quantitative Analysis, 17(1), 15–25.

Kraus, A. and Litzenberger, R. H. 1976. Skewness preference and the valuation of risk assets. Journal of Finance, 31(4), 1085–1100.

Mitton, T. and Vorkink, K. 2007. Equilibrium underdiversification and the preference for skewness. Review of Financial Studies, 20(4), 1255–1288.

Murray, S. 2013. A margin requirement based return calculation for portfolios of short option positions. Managerial Finance, 39(6), 550–568.

Newey, W. K. and West, K. D. 1987. A simple, positive semi-definite, heteroskedasticity and autocorrelation consistent covariance matrix. Econometrica, 55(3), 703–708.

Pastor, L. and Stambaugh, R. F. 2003. Liquidity risk and expected stock returns. Journal of Political Economy, 111(3), 642–685.

Rehman, Z. and Vilkov, G. 2012. Risk-Neutral Skewness: Return Predictability and its Sources. SSRN eLibrary.

Scott, R. C. and Horvath, P. A. 1980. On the direction of preference of moments of higher order than the variance. Journal of Finance, 35(4), 915–919.

Simkowitz, M. A. and Beedles, W. L. 1978. Diversification in a three-moment world. Journal of Financial and Quantitative Analysis, 13(5), 927–941.

Xing, Y., Zhang, X., and Zhao, R. 2010. What does the individual option volatility smirk tell us about future equity returns? Journal of Financial Quantitative Analysis, 45(3), 641–662.

18

OTHER STOCK RETURN PREDICTORS

In this chapter, we conclude this book by briefly discussing several additional stock return phenomena documented throughout the empirical asset pricing literature. While the effects documented in the previous chapters of Part II are the most widely recognized, controlled for, and cited effects, several of the variables discussed in this chapter are just as strong, if not stronger, predictors of future stock returns than the variables discussed in previous chapters. Many of the results discussed in this chapter are considered to be behavioral in nature and/or have their roots in accounting and financial statement data. While our intention in writing this chapter is to provide the reader with as wide-ranging an overview as is reasonable of empirical asset pricing research not discussed in previous chapters, the set of phenomena documented in this and previous chapters is by no means complete. In fact, Harvey, Liu, and Zhu (2015) catalog 316 documented factors related to cross-sectional pricing effects. Green, Hand, and Zhang (2013) examine 330 different signals proposed by previous work.[1] Additional surveys of the cross-sectional predictors of stock returns are provided by Haugen and Baker (1996), Barberis and Thaler (2003), Schwert (2003), and McLean and Pontiff (2015).[2] Hirshleifer (2015) provides an introduction to the

---

[1]Both Harvey, Liu, and Zhu (2015) and Green, Hand, and Zhang (2013) find that many of the documented predictors of stock returns capture the same underlying economic phenomena. Thus, the number of orthogonal drivers of expected stock returns is likely to be substantially lower.

[2]McLean and Pontiff (2015) provide evidence that some of the return patterns documented by academic research may be exaggerated in magnitude and fail to persist after publication of articles identifying the given phenomenon.

Empirical Asset Pricing: The Cross Section of Stock Returns, First Edition.
Turan G. Bali, Robert F. Engle, and Scott Murray.
© 2016 John Wiley & Sons, Inc. Published 2016 by John Wiley & Sons, Inc.

foundations of behavioral phenomena in the stock market along with a survey of previous empirical results.

We present no empirical results in this chapter. Instead, we very briefly describe the main results and conclusions and provide citations to the most important papers in each line of research. For researchers looking for a more in-depth understanding of any given topic, the references herein should serve as a good starting point.

18.1 ASSET GROWTH

There is a long line of research that has demonstrated a negative relation between changes in firm-level assets and future stock returns. Specifically, several studies have shown that firms tend to experience negative abnormal returns in periods following actions that increase assets (equity offerings and acquisitions), whereas firms that decrease assets (share repurchases and spinoffs) tend to realize positive abnormal returns in subsequent periods.

Several papers have documented that measures of firm growth are negatively related, in the cross section, to future stock returns. Lakonishok, Shleifer, and Vishny (1994) demonstrate a negative relation between growth in sales and future stock returns and La Porta (1996) finds a similar negative relation between expected earnings growth, calculated from analyst forecasts, and future stock returns.

The objective of both Lakonishok, Shleifer, and Vishny (1994) and La Porta (1996) is to examine whether the value premium (the positive relation between book-to-market ratio and future stock returns, see Chapter 10) is a manifestation of risk or of a behavioral phenomenon. Lakonishok, Shleifer, and Vishny (1994) hypothesize that investors extrapolate past performance into the future, thereby expecting firms that have exhibited high (low) past performance, as measured by growth in sales, to continue this strong (weak) performance. When pricing stocks, therefore, investors tend to overprice (underprice) stocks with previous strong (weak) performance, resulting in the positive relation between book-to-market ratio and future stock returns. Both Lakonishok, Shleifer, and Vishny (1994) and La Porta (1996) investigate and reject the possibility of a risk-based explanation for this result and conclude that the phenomenon is behavioral in nature.

Sloan (1996) expands on this work by investigating which components of earnings are responsible for the overpricing (underpricing) of high-growth (low-growth) stocks and finds that firms with large accruals exhibit lower earnings persistence and that it is the accruals component of earnings that is negatively related to future stock returns. Hirshleifer, Hou, Teoh, and Zhang (2004) examine whether investors focus their attention on accounting profitability instead of cash profitability and show that the difference (accounting profitability minus cash profitability), measured by net operating assets, is negatively related to future stock returns. Titman, Wei, and Xie (2004) find that increases in capital investments are negatively related to future stock returns and attribute this result to investors' failure to incorporate the effects of managers' empire-building incentives when valuing capital investments.

Other papers have investigated the performance of stocks subsequent to capital raising events and found that firms that raise (disperse) capital exhibit low (high) long-term abnormal returns. Ritter (1991) and Loughran (1993) demonstrate that stocks experience negative abnormal returns in the years after an initial public offering with Ritter (1991) finding evidence that this result is driven by firms' tendency to go public when investors are irrationally optimistic about future prospects. Loughran and Ritter (1995) document a similar pattern in returns following seasoned public equity offerings. Lakonishok and Vermaelen (1990) and Ikenberry, Lakonishok, and Vermaelen (1995) look at share repurchases and find that repurchasing stocks exhibit subsequent outperformance, with the effect being concentrated among small stocks and value stocks. Fama and French (2008a,b) demonstrate that net share issuance is negatively related to future stock returns.[3] Rau and Vermaelen (1998) find a similar result for firms issuing tender offers.

Another strand of this literature investigates corporate actions such as acquisitions and spinoffs. Agrawal, Jaffe, and Mandelker (1992), Loughran and Vijh (1997), and Rau and Vermaelen (1998) find that acquiring firms realize very low returns subsequent to the acquisition. Rau and Vermaelen (1998) demonstrate that this phenomenon is concentrated among stocks with low book-to-market ratios. On the other hand, Cusatis, Miles, and Woolridge (1993) and McConnell and Ovtchinnikov (2004) find that firms that execute spinoffs realize positive abnormal returns subsequent to the spinoff event.

Recent work has examined whether the results listed above are generated by the same underlying economic phenomenon. Pontiff and Woodgate (2008) find evidence that the negative abnormal returns subsequent to equity issuances and acquisitions, as well as the positive abnormal returns subsequent to stock repurchases, are all driven by a common share-issuance effect. Fairfield, Whisenant, and Yohn (2003) provide evidence that the accrual effect (Sloan 1996) is a manifestation of a larger growth effect. Cooper, Gulen, and Schill (2008) find that growth in total assets captures a component that is common to many of these anomalies.

18.2   INVESTOR SENTIMENT

Investor sentiment can roughly be thought of as the deviation between investors' view of the prospects for a stock and a purely rational assessment of the stock's prospects. In a perfectly rational world, the two would be the same. However, many researchers believe that, even in the aggregate, investors are not perfectly rational. In a world that is not perfectly rational, therefore, investor sentiment can influence stock prices and, thus, future stock returns.

---

[3]The empirical evidence in Hovakimian, Opler, and Titman (2001) indicates that firms tend to repurchase (issue) shares when their stock prices perform poorly (well) relative to changes in their cash flows. Baker and Wurgler (2002) point out that this tendency reflects the fact that managers time the equity markets. Daniel and Titman (2006) provide evidence that if managers issue equity when stocks are overvalued, then stock issuance will negatively predict returns.

The impetus for the investor sentiment literature comes from several phenomena empirically observed in stock returns. First, many papers find evidence that investors underreact to news in the short run. Cutler, Poterba, and Summers (1991) find that stock returns exhibit positive serial correlation over periods of less than one year. Ball and Brown (1968), Foster, Olsen, and Shevlin (1984), and Bernard and Thomas (1989, 1990) demonstrate a phenomenon known as post earnings announcement drift, which refers to the empirical finding that firms realizing positive (negative) earnings surprises experience, on average, positive (negative) abnormal returns for many months subsequent to the earnings announcement, indicating that investors underreact to the earnings news. As discussed in Chapter 11, Jegadeesh and Titman (1993) show that there is a very strong momentum effect in the cross section of stock returns. Chan, Jegadeesh, and Lakonishok (1996) conclude that both the post earnings announcement drift and momentum phenomena result from sluggish reaction by the market to new information.

Second, several researchers find that over periods of many years, investors tend to overreact to new information. Cutler et al. (1991) demonstrate that over periods of three to five years, returns tend to exhibit negative autocorrelation. This is consistent with the long-term reversal phenomenon discussed briefly in Chapter 11. De Bondt and Thaler (1985) and Chopra, Lakonishok, and Ritter (1992) find similar evidence and attribute the phenomenon to overreaction, not compensation for risk.

A seminal theoretical article, Barberis, Shleifer, and Vishny (1998) develop a model of investor belief formation that generates predictions consistent with not only the observed underreaction and overreaction phenomena discussed in the previous paragraphs but also the representativeness (Tverskey and Kahneman (1974)) and conservatism (Edwards (1968)) phenomena documented by cognitive psychologists. Daniel, Hirshleifer, and Subrahmanyam (1998) generate a model based on different psychological phenomena, overconfidence (Griffin and Tversky (1992)) and attribution (Bem (1965)), that produces similar predictions.

Since then, numerous papers have been written examining the relation between investor sentiment and future security returns. Neal and Wheatley (1998) find evidence that investor sentiment partially explains the size effect discussed in Chapter 9. Baker and Stein (2004) develop a model relating investor sentiment to liquidity and showing that high investor sentiment can result in overvaluation. Baker and Wurgler (2006) show that young, risky firms underperform significantly after periods of high sentiment. Once again, the notion here is that periods of high sentiment reflect overvaluation, especially for hard to value firms (i.e., young firms with high return volatility). Grinblatt and Han (2005) demonstrate that a tendency of some investors to hold on to losing trades generates the momentum phenomenon. Han (2008) finds that for S&P 500 index options, the implied volatility smile is more pronounced and the implied risk-neutral skewness is more negative when investor sentiment is low. Stambaugh, Yu, and Yuan (2012, 2014) demonstrate that several empirical anomalies detected in stock returns are stronger following periods of high investor sentiment, and that this result is driven by the short positions in long–short portfolios.

18.3 INVESTOR ATTENTION

The literature on investor attention is related to the research on investor sentiment in that its main objective is to explain the underreaction of stock prices to relevant news documented by many papers discussed earlier (Ball and Brown (1968), Cutler, Poterba, and Summers (1991), Foster, Olsen, and Shevlin (1984), Bernard and Thomas (1990) and Jegadeesh and Titman (1993)). However, the work on investor attention posits another driver of these phenomena, specifically investors' limited attention capacity. As with the models describing investor sentiment, models of investor attention have the roots in cognitive psychology. Kahneman (1973)'s theory of attention indicates that attention is a scarce cognitive resource. The implication of attention theory in financial markets is that limited availability of time and cognitive resources imposes constraints on how fast investors can process information.

Recent theoretical models have shown that limited investor attention can lead to underreaction to information and thus slow price adjustments. Hirshleifer and Teoh (2003) examine the effects of information presentation and clarity on the speed and accuracy of stock price reactions and valuations. Peng (2005) derives an equilibrium model in which investors optimally allocate their attention. Peng and Xiong (2006) find that limited attention capacity leads investors to focus on market-level and sector-level information and to ignore firm-specific information. When combined with investor overconfidence, this focus on market-level and sector-level information explains many empirically observed stock price dynamics that are difficult to rationalize in standard asset pricing models that assume instantaneous and complete information processing. The main implication of each of these models is that limited attention capacity results in delayed stock price reactions to value-relevant public information.

This central prediction derived from models of investor inattention has been confirmed by several recent empirical studies. Hirshleifer, Lim, and Teoh (2009) find that stock price reaction to earnings announcements is slower, and post earnings announcement drift (Ball and Brown (1968), Foster, Olsen, and Shevlin (1984), Bernard and Thomas (1989, 1990)) is much stronger, for earnings announced on days with a large number of earnings announcements, when investor attention is a highly scarce resource. DellaVigna and Pollet (2009) demonstrate that investors react much more slowly to earnings news released on Fridays, when investor attention is likely to be low.[4] Li and Yu (2012) show that the Dow Jones Industrial Average exhibits a positive trend when it is near the 52-week high and a negative trend when it is near its historical high and attribute these effects to investor attention. Da, Gurun, and Warachka (2014) find that investors' tendency to underreact is attenuated when information is released gradually instead of in a single announcement. Bali, Peng, Shen, and Tang (2014b) provide evidence that the theory of investor inattention is important in understanding stock market underreactions to liquidity shocks.

---

[4]DellaVigna and Pollet (2007) find that investors fail to fully account for demographic information when forecasting future sales, leading to stock return predictability. They offer investor inattention as one possible explanation for this phenomenon.

18.4 DIFFERENCES OF OPINION

Miller (1977) hypothesizes that stock prices reflect an upward bias as long as there exists divergence of opinion among investors about stock value and pessimistic investors are constrained with respect to the size of the short position they can take. In Miller's model, overvaluation arises because potential short-sellers are restricted to hold zero shares. The result is that the determination of market prices for securities is driven primarily by the beliefs of more optimistic investors. Since divergence of opinion is likely to be higher for riskier stocks, Miller (1977) conjectures that divergence of opinion plays a role in the historically low (high) abnormal returns generated by stocks with high (low) levels of firm-specific risk (see Chapter 15 and Ang, Hodrick, Xing, and Zhang (2006)).[5] Hong and Stein (2003) produce a model of market crashes in which the negative opinions held by potential short-sellers only influence stock prices when previously bullish investors sell their positions, resulting in large drops in market prices.

The role of differences of opinion in the cross section of stock returns has been empirically examined in several papers. Diether, Malloy, and Scherbina (2002) use dispersion in analysts earnings forecasts as a proxy for divergence of opinion and find that stocks with higher analyst forecast dispersion generate significantly lower future returns than those with lower dispersion. Chen, Hong, and Stein (2002) find that breadth of ownership, defined as the number of different investors that own a stock, influences stock returns. The idea is that when only a small number of investors have a long position in the stock, this indicates that short-sale constraints are likely binding, and as a result, the stock is overpriced. The main empirical finding in Chen, Hong, and Stein (2002) is that stocks with recent increases in breadth of ownership significantly outperform those with breadth decreases. Boehme, Danielsen, and Sorescu (2006) demonstrate that both dispersion in investor opinion and short-sale constraints are necessary conditions for overvaluation. Stocks for which either of these conditions fails to hold, therefore, do not exhibit a tendency to be overvalued. Berkman, Dimitrov, Jain, Koch, and Tice (2009) assume that earnings announcements reduce differences of opinion and find that stocks with previously high differences of opinions earn lower returns around earnings announcements than stocks with previously low differences of opinions.

18.5 PROFITABILITY AND INVESTMENT

There is a long line of research that investigates the relation between accounting ratios and expected stock returns. This research has produced two main results.

---

[5]Harris and Raviv (1993) model the effect of differences of opinion in speculative markets. Their model predicts that, in the time series, the magnitude of price changes and trading volume are contemporaneously positively correlated, consecutive price changes are negatively serially correlated, and volume is positively auto-correlated. Bessembinder, Chan, and Seguin (1996) find corroborating empirical evidence using data on S&P 500 index futures.

The first of these results is that there is a strong positive relation between profitability and expected stock returns. Haugen and Baker (1996) and Cohen, Gompers, and Vuolteenaho (2002) find a strong positive relation between return on equity and future stock returns. Bali, Demirtas, and Tehranian (2008) provide evidence that expected stock returns are positively related to the ratio of earnings to total assets. Novy-Marx (2013) finds similar results using the ratio of profits (revenues minus cost of goods sold) to assets as the predictive variable.

The second result is that there exists a negative relation between investment and future stock returns. Fairfield, Whisenant, and Yohn (2003) find that both accruals and net operating assets are negatively related, in the cross section, to future stock returns. Titman, Wei, and Xie (2004) detect a negative relation between growth in capital investment, measured as the ratio of recent capital expenditures to historical capital expenditures, and future stock returns. Cooper, Gulen, and Schill (2008) demonstrate a very strong negative relation between growth in total assets and future stock returns. Aharoni, Grundy, and Zeng (2013) find a negative relation between expected investment and expected stock returns.

Fama and French (2006, 2015) theoretically model these results using a simple dividend discount model and find that, consistent with many of the previous empirical results, holding all else equal, the expected return of a stock is positively related to the book-to-market ratio, positively related to profitability, and negatively related to investment. Based on this, Fama and French (2015) develop a five-factor risk model that includes the market (MKT), size (SMB), and value (HML) factors included in the Fama and French (1993) three-factor model along with new profitability and investment factors. They find that the five-factor model does a better job at capturing cross-sectional variation in stock returns than the three-factor model.

Hou, Xue, and Zhang (2015) develop a similar model based on the q-theory of investment. The Hou et al. (2015) model includes the market factor (MKT), a size factor, a profitability factor, and an investment factor.[6] Notably missing from the Hou et al. (2015) model is a value factor. Hou, Xue, and Zhang (2015) claim that the value factor is both theoretically and empirically captures by the investment factor. Additionally, Hou, Xue, and Zhang (2015) find that the profitability factor captures the momentum effect.

18.6 LOTTERY DEMAND

The final topic we discuss in this chapter is the effect of lottery demand on stock prices. The main premise of the lottery demand literature is that some investors demand lottery-like stocks, or stocks that are more likely to experience large short-term increases in value. While lottery demand is a well-documented phenomenon in the gambling arena (Thaler and Ziemba (1988)), the prevalence and

---

[6]The precise definitions of the size, profitability, and investment factors used by Hou, Xue, and Zhang (2015) are different from those used by Fama and French (1993, 2015).

effect of lottery demand in financial markets has, until recently, received little attention.

Recent work, however, has uncovered strong evidence that lottery demand plays an important role in financial markets. Kumar (2009) uses demographic data to demonstrate that investors who are more likely to play the lottery are also more likely to invest in lottery-like stocks, where lottery-like stocks are defined as stocks with low prices (below $5) whose returns exhibit high idiosyncratic volatility and high idiosyncratic skewness. Han and Kumar (2013) show that retail investors, particularly retail investors with high gambling propensity, invest disproportionately in such stocks.

Bali, Cakici, and Whitelaw (2011) examine the effect of lottery demand on stock pricing. Measuring lottery demand using *MAX*, defined as the highest daily return in the given month, Bali et al. (2011) find a strong negative relation between lottery demand and future U.S. stock returns. Several subsequent papers find similar results in other markets. Annaert, De Ceuster, and Verstegen (2013) and Walkshäusl (2014) show that the lottery demand phenomenon is strong in European markets. Carpenter, Lu, and Whitelaw (2014) find evidence of a negative relation between lottery demand and future stock returns in the Chinese stock market. Consistent with investor preference for lottery-like stocks, Conrad, Kapadia, and Xing (2014) show that stocks with high predicted probabilities for extremely large positive returns earn abnormally low average returns.[7]

While the negative relation between lottery demand and future stock returns is interesting in its own right, there is substantial evidence that this relation may be a driving factor in some of the most persistent and confusing phenomena documented in the empirical asset pricing literature. Specifically, Bali et al. (2011) present evidence that the idiosyncratic volatility puzzle of Ang, Hodrick, Xing, and Zhang (2006) (see Chapter 15) is explained by lottery demand and that, after controlling for lottery demand, the relation between idiosyncratic volatility and future stock returns is positive. Bali, Brown, Murray, and Tang (2014a) show that the empirical failure of the Capital Asset Pricing Model (Sharpe (1964), Lintner (1965) and Mossin (1966)) documented in Chapter 8 is, in part, explained by lottery demand. Specifically, after controlling for lottery demand and other characteristics known to predict future stock returns, the empirical analyses in Bali, Brown, Murray, and Tang (2014a) find a positive relation between beta and future stock returns.

REFERENCES

Agrawal, A., Jaffe, J. F., and Mandelker, G. N. 1992. The post-merger performance of acquiring firms: a re-examination of an anomaly. Journal of Finance, 47(4), 1605–1621.

Aharoni, G., Grundy, B., and Zeng, Q. 2013. Stock returns and the Miller Modigliani valuation formula: revisiting the Fama French analysis. Journal of Financial Economics, 110(2), 347–357.

[7]Campbell, Hilscher, and Szilagyi (2008) show that firms with a high probability of default (distress risk) have low average and risk-adjusted future returns. Conrad, Kapadia, and Xing (2014) show that firms with high distress risk also tend to have a relatively high probability of extremely large positive returns.

Ang, A., Hodrick, R. J., Xing, Y., and Zhang, X. 2006. The cross-section of volatility and expected returns. Journal of Finance, 61(1), 259–299.

Annaert, J., De Ceuster, M., and Verstegen, K. 2013. Are extreme returns price in the stock market? European evidence. Journal of Banking and Finance, 37(9), 3401–3411.

Baker, M. and Stein, J. C. 2004. Market liquidity as a sentiment indicator. Journal of Financial Markets, 7(3), 271–299.

Baker, M. and Wurgler, J. 2002. Market timing and capital structure. Journal of Finance, 57(1), 1–32.

Baker, M. and Wurgler, J. 2006. Investor sentiment and the cross-section of stock returns. Journal of Finance, 61(4), 1645–1680.

Bali, T. G., Brown, S. J., Murray, S., and Tang, Y. 2014a. A Lottery Demand-Based Explanation of the Beta Anomaly. SSRN eLibrary.

Bali, T. G., Cakici, N., and Whitelaw, R. F. 2011. Maxing out: stocks as lotteries and the cross-section of expected returns. Journal of Financial Economics, 99(2), 427–446.

Bali, T. G., Demirtas, K. O., and Tehranian, H. 2008. Aggregate earnings, firm-level earnings, and expected stock returns. Journal of Financial and Quantitative Analysis, 43(3), 657–684.

Bali, T. G., Peng, L., Shen, Y., and Tang, Y. 2014b. Liquidity shocks and stock market reactions. Review of Financial Studies, 27(5), 1434–1485.

Ball, R. and Brown, P. 1968. An empirical evaluation of accounting income numbers. Journal of Accounting Research, 6(2), 159–178.

Barberis, N., Shleifer, A., and Bishny, R. 1998. A model of investor sentiment. Journal of Financial Economics, 49(3), 307–343.

Barberis, N. and Thaler, R. Chapter 18: A survey of behavioral finance. Handbook of the Economics of Finance, pages 1051–1121. Constantinides et al. (2003), 2003, http://www.sciencedirect.com/science/handbooks/15740102.

Bem, D. J. 1965. An experimental analysis of self-persuasion. Journal of Experimental Psychology, 1(3), 199–218.

Berkman, H., Dimitrov, V., Jain, P. C., Koch, P. D., and Tice, S. 2009. Sell on the news: differences of opinion, short-sales constraints, and returns around earnings announcements. Journal of Financial Economics, 92(3), 376–399.

Bernard, V. L. and Thomas, J. K. 1989. Post-earnings-announcement drift: delayed price response of risk premium. Journal of Accounting Research, 27(3), 1–36.

Bernard, V. L. and Thomas, J. K. 1990. Evidence that stock prices do not fully reflect the implications of current earnings for future earnings. Journal of Accounting and Economics, 13(4), 305–340.

Bessembinder, H., Chan, K., and Seguin, P. J. 1996. An empirical examination of information, differences of opinion, and trading activity. Journal of Financial Economics, 40(1), 105–134.

Boehme, R. D., Danielsen, B. R., and Sorescu, S. M. 2006. Short-sale constraints, differences of opinion, and overvaluation. Journal of Financial and Quantitative Analysis, 41(2), 455–487.

Campbell, J. Y., Hilscher, J., and Szilagyi, J. 2008. In search of distress risk. Journal of Finance, 63(6), 2899–2939.

Carpenter, J. N., Lu, F., and Whitelaw, R. F. 2014. Prospect Theory and Stock Returns: An Empirical Test. SSRN eLibrary.

Chan, L. K. C., Jegadeesh, N., and Lakonishok, J. 1996. Momentum strategies. Journal of Finance, 51(5), 1681–1713.

Chen, J., Hong, H., and Stein, J. C. 2002. Breadth of ownership and stock returns. Journal of Financial Economics, 66(2-3), 171–205.

Chopra, N., Lakonishok, J., and Ritter, J. 1992. Measuring abnormal performance: do stocks overreact? Journal of Financial Economics, 31(2), 235–268.

Cohen, R. B., Gompers, P. A., and Vuolteenaho, T. 2002. Who underreacts to cash-flow news? Evidence from trading between individuals and investors. Journal of Financial Economics, 66(2-3), 409–462.

Conrad, J., Kapadia, N., and Xing, Y. 2014. Death and jackpot: Why do individual investors hold overpriced stocks? Journal of Financial Economics, 113(3), 455–475.

Constantinides, G., Harris, M., and Stulz, R. M., editors. Handbook of the Economics of Finance. Elsevier Science, B.V., The Netherlands, 2003.

Cooper, M. J., Gulen, H., and Schill, M. J. 2008. Asset growth and the cross-section of stock returns. Journal of Finance, 63(4), 1609–1651.

Cusatis, P. J., Miles, J. A., and Woolridge, J. R. 1993. Resturcturing through spinoffs: the stock market evidence. Journal of Financial Economics, 33(3), 293–311.

Cutler, D. M., Poterba, J. M., and Summers, L. H. 1991. Speculative dynamics. Review of Economic Studies, 58(3), 529–546.

Da, Z., Gurun, U. G., and Warachka, M. 2014. Frog in the pan: continuous information and momentum. Review of Financial Studies, 27(7), 2171–2218.

Daniel, K., Hirshleifer, D., and Subrahmanyam, A. 1998. Investor psychology and security market under- and overreactions. Journal of Finance, 53(6), 1839–1885.

Daniel, K. and Titman, S. 2006. Market reactions to tangible and intangible information. Journal of Finance, 61(4), 1605–1643.

De Bondt, W. F. M. and Thaler, R. 1985. Does the stock market overreact? Journal of Finance, 40(3), 793–805.

DellaVigna, S. and Pollet, J. M. 2007. Demographics and industry returns. American Economic Review, 97(5), 1666–1702.

DellaVigna, S. and Pollet, J. M. 2009. Investor inattention and Friday earnings announcements. Journal of Finance, 64(2), 709–749.

Diether, K. B., Malloy, C. J., and Scherbina, A. 2002. Differences of opinion and the cross section of stock returns. Journal of Finance, 57(5), 2113–2141.

Edwards, W. Conservatism in human information processing. Formal Representation of Human Judgment, pages 17–52. John Wiley & Sons, New York, 1968.

Fairfield, P. M., Whisenant, J. S., and Yohn, T. L. 2003. Accrued earnings and growth: implications for future profitability and market mispricing. Accounting Review, 78(1), 353–371.

Fama, E. F. and French, K. R. 1993. Common risk factors in the returns on stocks and bonds. Journal of Financial Economics, 33(1), 3–56.

Fama, E. F. and French, K. R. 2006. Profitability, investment and average returns. Journal of Financial Economics, 82(3), 491–518.

Fama, E. F. and French, K. R. 2008a. Average returns, B/M, and share issues. Journal of Finance, 63(6), 2971–2995.

Fama, E. F. and French, K. R. 2008b. Dissecting anomalies. Journal of Finance, 63(4), 1653–1678.

Fama, E. F. and French, K. R. 2015. A five-factor asset pricing model. Journal of Financial Economics, 116(1), 1–22.

Foster, G., Olsen, C., and Shevlin, T. 1984. Earnings releases, anomalies, and the behavior of security returns. Accounting Review, 59(4), 574–603.

Green, H., Hand, J. R. M., and Zhang, X. F. 2013. The supraview of return predictive signals. Review of Accounting Studies, 18(3), 692–730.

Griffin, D. and Tversky, A. 1992. The weighing of evidence and the determinants of confidence. Cognitive Psychology, 24(3), 411–435.

Grinblatt, M. and Han, B. 2005. Prospect theory, mental accounting, and momentum. Journal of Financial Economics, 78(2), 311–339.

Han, B. 2008. Investor sentiment and option prices. Review of Financial Studies, 21(1), 387–414.

Han, B. and Kumar, A. 2013. Speculative retail trading and asset prices. Journal of Financial and Quantitative Analysis, 48(2), 377–404.

Harris, M. and Raviv, A. 1993. Differences of opinion make a horse race. Review of Financial Studies, 6(3), 473–506.

Harvey, C. R., Liu, Y., and Zhu, H. 2015. … and the cross-section of expected returns. Review of Financial Studies, forthcoming.

Haugen, R. A. and Baker, N. L. 1996. Commonality in the determinants of expected stock returns. Journal of Financial Economics, 41(3), 401–439.

Hirshleifer, D. 2015. Behavioral finance. Annual Review of Financial Economics, 7(1).

Hirshleifer, D., Hou, K., Teoh, S. H., and Zhang, Y. 2004. Do investors overvalue firms with bloated balance sheets? Journal of Accounting and Economics, 38(1-3), 297–331.

Hirshleifer, D., Lim, S. S., and Teoh, S. H. 2009. Driven to distraction: extraneous events and underreaction to earnings news. Journal of Finance, 64(5), 2289–2325.

Hirshleifer, D. and Teoh, S. H. 2003. Limited attention, information disclosure, and financial reporting. Journal of Accounting and Economics, 36(1-3), 337–386.

Hong, H. and Stein, J. C. 2003. Differences of opinion, short-sales constraints, and market crashes. Review of Financial Studies, 16(2), 487–525.

Hou, K., Xue, C., and Zhang, L. 2015. Digesting anomalies: an investment approach. Review of Financial Studies, 28(3), 650–705.

Hovakimian, A., Opler, T., and Titman, S. 2001. The debt-equity choice. Journal of Financial and Quantitative Analysis, 36(1), 1–24.

Ikenberry, D., Lakonishok, J., and Vermaelen, T. 1995. Market underreaction to open market share repurchases. Journal of Financial Economics, 39(2-3), 181–208.

Jegadeesh, N. and Titman, S. 1993. Returns to buying winners and selling losers: implications for stock market efficiency. Journal of Finance, 48(1), 65–91.

Kahneman, D. Attention and Effort. Prentice Hall, Englewood Cliffs, NJ, 1973.

Kumar, A. 2009. Who gambles in the stock market? Journal of Finance, 64(4), 1889–1933.

Lakonishok, J., Shleifer, A., and Vishny, R. W. 1994. Contrarian investment, extrapolation, and risk. Journal of Finance, 49(5), 1541–1578.

Lakonishok, J. and Vermaelen, T. 1990. Anomalous price behavior around repurchase tender offers. Journal of Finance, 45(2), 455–477.

La Porta, R. 1996. Expectations and the cross-section of stock returns. Journal of Finance, 51(5), 1715–1742.

Li, J. and Yu, J. 2012. Investor attention, psychological anchors, and stock return predictability. Journal of Financial Economics, 104(2), 401–419.

Lintner, J. 1965. Security prices, risk, and maximal gains from diversification. Journal of Finance, 20(4), 687–615.

Loughran, T. 1993. NYSE vs NASDAQ returns: market microstructure or the poor performance of initial public offerings? Journal of Financial Economics, 33(2), 241–260.

Loughran, T. and Ritter, J. R. 1995. The new issues puzzle. Journal of Finance, 50(1), 23–51.

Loughran, T. and Vijh, A. M. 1997. Do long-term shareholders benefit from corporate acquisitions? Journal of Finance, 52(5), 1765–1790.

McConnell, J. J. and Ovtchinnikov, A. V. 2004. Predictability of long-term spinoff returns. Journal of Investment Management, 2(3), 35–44.

McLean, R. D. and Pontiff, J. 2015. Does academic research destroy stock return predictability? Journal of Finance, forthcoming.

Miller, E. M. 1977. Risk, uncertainty, and divergence of opinion. Journal of Finance, 32(4), 1151–1168.

Mossin, J. 1966. Equilibrium in a capital asset market. Econometrica, 34(4), 768–783.

Neal, R. and Wheatley, S. M. 1998. Do measures of investor sentiment predict returns? Journal of Financial and Quantitative Analysis, 33(4), 523–547.

Novy-Marx, R. 2013. The other side of value: the gross profitability premium. Journal of Financial Economics, 108(1), 1–28.

Peng, L. 2005. Learning with information capacity constraints. Journal of Financial and Quantitative Analysis, 40(2), 307–329.

Peng, L. and Xiong, W. 2006. Investor attention, overconfidence and category learning. Journal of Financial Economics, 80(3), 563–602.

Pontiff, J. and Woodgate, A. 2008. Share issuance and cross-sectional returns. Journal of Finance, 63(2), 921–945.

Rau, P. R. and Vermaelen, T. 1998. Glamour, value and the post-acquisition performance of acquiring firms. Journal of Financial Economics, 49(2), 223–253.

Ritter, J. R. 1991. The long-run performance of initial public offerings. Journal of Finance, 46(1), 3–27.

Schwert, G. W. Chapter 15: Anomalies and market efficiency. Handbook of the Economics of Finance, pages 939–974. In Constantinides et al. (2003), 2003, http://www.sciencedirect.com/science/handbooks/15740102.

Sharpe, W. F. 1964. Capital asset prices: a theory of market equilibrium under conditions of risk. Journal of Finance, 19(3), 425–442.

Sloan, R. G. 1996. Do stock prices fully reflect information in accruals and cash flows about future earnings? The Accounting Review, 71(3), 389–315.

Stambaugh, R. F., Yu, J., and Yuan, Y. 2012. The short of it: investor sentiment and anomalies. Journal of Financial Economics, 104(2), 288–302.

Stambaugh, R. F., Yu, J., and Yuan, Y. 2014. The long of it: odds that investor sentiment spuriously predicts anomaly returns. Journal of Financial Economics, 114(3), 613–619.

Thaler, R. H. and Ziemba, W. T. 1988. Paramutuel betting markets: racetracks and lotteries. Journal of Economic Perspectives, 2(2), 161–174.

Titman, S., Wei, K. C. J., and Xie, F. 2004. Capital investment and stock returns. Journal of Financial and Quantitative Analysis, 39(4), 677–700.

Tversky, A. and Kahneman, D. 1974. Judgment under uncertainty: Heuristics and biases. Science, 185, 1124–1131.

Walkshäusl, C. 2014. The max effect: European evidence. Journal of Banking and Finance, 42, 1–10.

INDEX

Notes: Page numbers in *italics* refer to figures and page numbers in **bold** refer to tables

Empirical Asset Pricing: The Cross Section of Stock Returns, First Edition.
Turan G. Bali, Robert F. Engle, and Scott Murray.
© 2016 John Wiley & Sons, Inc. Published 2016 by John Wiley & Sons, Inc.

Printed and bound by CPI Group (UK) Ltd, Croydon, CR0 4YY

23/04/2025

14660911-0002